FBO Management

Operating, Marketing, and Managing as a Fixed-Base Operator

C. Daniel Prather, PhD, DBA, AAE, CAM

AVIATION SUPPLIES & ACADEMICS, INC.
NEWCASTLE, WASHINGTON

FBO Management: Operating, Marketing, and Managing as a Fixed-Base Operator
by C. Daniel Prather

Aviation Supplies & Academics, Inc.
7005 132nd Place SE
Newcastle, Washington 98059
asa@asa2fly.com | 425-235-1500 | asa2fly.com

See the ASA website at **asa2fly.com/fbomgt** for reader and instructor resources and additional information and updates relating to this book.

ASA-FBO-MGT
ISBN 978-1-64425-229-1

Additional formats available:
eBook EPUB ISBN 978-1-64425-231-4
eBook PDF ISBN 978-1-64425-232-1
eBundle ISBN 978-1-64425-230-7 (print + eBook PDF download code)

Printed in Malaysia
2027 2026 2025 2024 2023 9 8 7 6 5 4 3 2 1

Cover photos: Courtesy of Narrows Aviation, Tacoma Narrows Airport (KTIW).

Chapter start photos: Page 1—Bill Larkins, flickr.com/photos/34076827@N00/5202931667/, CC BY-SA 2.0, creativecommons.org/licenses/by-sa/2.0/. Page 35—Harbucks/Shutterstock.com. Page 59—BoJack/Shutterstock.com. Page 79—Svitlana Hulko/Shutterstock.com. Page 107—Hurst Photo/Shutterstock.com. Page 125—monkeybusiness/Envato. Page 141—narokzaad/stock.adobe.com. Page 161—svitlanah/Envato. Page 181—DC_Studio/Envato. Page 193—Photo by Chris Leipelt on Unsplash. Page 217—Gino Santa Maria/Shutterstock.com. Page 251—monkeybusiness/Envato. Page 271—iStock.com/Ziviani. Page 285—voronaman111/Envato. Page 311—iStock.com/SDI Productions. Page 323—Scharfsinn/Shutterstock.com.

Library of Congress Cataloging-in-Publication Data

Names: Prather, C. Daniel, 1971- author.
Title: FBO management : operating, marketing, and managing as a fixed-base operator / C. Daniel Prather.
Other titles: Fixed-base operator management : operating, marketing, and managing as a fixed-base operator
Description: Newcastle, Washington : Aviation Supplies & Academics, Inc. | "ASA-FBO-MGT"—Title page verso. | Includes bibliographical references and index.
Identifiers: LCCN 2022051581 (print) | LCCN 2022051582 (ebook) | ISBN 9781644252291 (hardback) | ISBN 9781644252314 (epub) | ISBN 9781644252321 (pdf) | ISBN 9781644252307 (eBundle)
Subjects: LCSH: Fixed base operators industry—Management—Textbooks. | Airplanes—Marketing—Textbooks. | Aircraft industry—Management—Textbooks. | Aviation ground crews—Management—Textbooks. | LCGFT: Textbooks.
Classification: LCC HD9711.A2 P74 2022 (print) | LCC HD9711.A2 (ebook) | DDC 338.4/762913334—dc23/eng/20230417
LC record available at https://lccn.loc.gov/2022051581
LC ebook record available at https://lccn.loc.gov/2022051582

Contents

CHAPTER 16

Foreword

It was August 5, 2000, at approximately 3:00 pm, and I was at 1,500 feet in a Cessna 172 on a beautiful sunny day over Long Beach Harbor off the coast of Southern California. We were flying from Catalina Island back to our home airport, Fullerton Municipal, my fellow CFI was flying, and I was watching a sailboat unfurl its sails when everything went black. The next thing I remember, someone was removing my headset as I was laid on a stretcher and put into an ambulance.

I had experienced a seizure and blacked out for about 20 minutes. It was my first seizure, and as of this writing in the year 2023, it has been the only seizure I have ever had. But the seizure was God's way of changing my career trajectory from being a commercial pilot to a business aviation executive.

My father and grandfather were both commercial pilots with American Airlines, and yet shockingly I had never thought about being a pilot. However, upon graduation from Biola University with a business degree in 1998, I was less than excited about my job prospects in the business world, so I took a job working as a customer service representative at an FBO at Orange County's John Wayne Airport (KSNA) in the mornings and worked on my private pilot training in the afternoons. Flying grabbed me, and I loved seeing the Earth from the air. By August 2000, I had earned my CFI, CFII, and MEI and was two months into my first CFI job.

But that Saturday afternoon flight changed my life in a way that I could have never imagined, and for which I am forever grateful, because it launched my career in business aviation, a segment of the global aviation industry that I wasn't aware of prior to my first job at the FBO. After my seizure, I circulated my resume around the FBO and was quickly hired as an aircraft dispatcher by an aircraft management and charter company with five small jets. That job grew to selling private jet charter, eventually managing a charter team and marketing activities, and then on to managing operational, maintenance, and financial aspects for an expanding aircraft management, charter, and maintenance organization. Over the next 14 years, my responsibilities grew with the company, increasing my exposure to many different facets of business aviation, with the company eventually coming to manage 65 jets across cities in the United States and Asia.

In 2013, I joined Clay Lacy Aviation as their vice president of marketing. In 2021, Clay Lacy Aviation was awarded a 35-year lease to build and operate a full-service FBO at John Wayne Airport. For the past few years, I have had the privilege of leading our SNA FBO team in establishing an FBO operation in a temporary facility as we move toward groundbreaking on our new FBO facility later this year. Now, in addition to leading Clay Lacy's marketing activities, I lead our new location development team, sustainability program, and student scholarship initiatives.

You may be asking why I am sharing my story, and how does this relate to a book about FBO management? Well, it's quite simple. Business, as well as life, is about people and relationships. Over the last 23 years in business aviation, I have worked alongside and gotten to know so many wonderful and genuine professionals in business aviation, each with their own story of how they got to where they are in their careers. This is how I came to meet Dr. Prather and learn about the aviation program at California Baptist University, and I have gone on to hire several of his graduates from that fine program who I work alongside today. No two stories are the same, but one thing about these professionals is constant: they love working in business aviation and jump at the opportunity to share their passion with the next generation. My hope is that one day I get to meet you and hear your story. Perhaps this book will spark your interest in joining this awesome industry.

In the following text, Dr. Prather simply and eloquently lays out the foundational principles of FBO management as well as a brief but very well written history of aviation and overview of general aviation. You may be reading this forward-thinking, I am going to be a pilot or technician, or perhaps a flight attendant or airport manager, so what does FBO management have to do with those careers? The information covered in this book, while focused on FBO management, also provides great insight into many careers and functions of businesses around an airport, and the principles and topics covered herein are widely applicable and would be valuable for any aviation professional to be proficient with.

The COVID pandemic reinforced the value and importance of the business aviation industry. Business aviation could not function without FBOs, which serve as the gateway between airside and landside for general aviation aircraft at most airports around the world. Business aviation and its reliance on professional, efficient, and well-run FBOs serve as economic engines for local economies, contribute to enhanced productivity, provide humanitarian support, are a lifeline for communities not served by the airlines, and provide millions of high-paying careers.

Studies published by No Plane No Gain, a joint undertaking of the National Business Aviation Association and General Aviation Manufacturers Association, outline the benefits business aviation plays in our economy and in the quality of life of individuals—benefits which would not be possible without well-run FBOs. Here are just a few highlights.

98% of Fortune magazine's Top 50 "World's Most Admired Companies" use business aviation.

S&P 500 companies using business aviation outperform those that don't by 70%.

95% of Fortune magazine's "Change the World Top 20" companies use business aviation.

Whether you have your sights set on a career in airport management or as a commercial pilot, or perhaps I have opened your mind to a future in business aviation, this book will provide a solid foundation from which to build your career, no matter the twists and turns it may take. See you around the airport one day.

Scott Cutshall
Senior Vice President, Business Development & Sustainability
Clay Lacy Aviation
Connect with me on LinkedIn and share your story: linkedin.com/in/cutsh

Acknowledgments

An author learns quickly during the writing and publication process that bringing an idea to a published book takes time and energy for sure, but it also requires a team of professionals.

This *FBO Management* text would not have been possible were it not for Mr. Alexander Wells' trust in me more than 15 years ago to revise his *General Aviation Marketing and Management* text for the third edition. That book is no longer in print, but it served as a foundation for this much-improved FBO-focused text.

Ms. Jackie Spanitz, general manager of ASA, is a true supporter of me and my efforts. She continues to lead ASA with determination to bring the best aviation products to market, and I thank her for choosing me to participate in that powerful endeavor.

Ms. Laura Fisher, editor at ASA, is a true gem in this industry. Her constructive feedback and ideas for improvement made this text what it is today.

I certainly would not be as knowledgeable of the FBO business if the Hillsborough County Aviation Authority and the City of Riverside (CA) had not believed in me enough to provide me the opportunity to serve as an airport professional for their respective organizations. Thank you Jim Johnson, Ed Cooley, Robert Burr, Grant Young, and all my former colleagues at Tampa International Airport. Thank you Mike Futrell, Edward Enriquez, Kris Martinez, Rafael Guzman, Carl Carey, Shari Call, and my amazing team at Riverside Municipal Airport—Cris Avila, Mike Dean, Eric Jorgensen, Rodger Kane, Benny Lange, and Maria Russey.

My beautiful wife and two children have always supported me and believed in me. Their ability to carry on, even when I am preoccupied with the laptop at times, has been the wind that keeps me moving forward. I love you guys!

My mom has always been my most vocal cheerleader. Her ever-present camera documented much of my life long before smartphones, and even though I was embarrassed at the time, thanks for doing that, Mom.

My dad showed me the value of hard work by his example. He succeeded at everything he set his mind to, and I can mostly say the same thing. Thanks, Dad.

My brother and sister, although both older than me, have always believed in me and supported my efforts. Thank you.

My Nanny was always so impressed with my talents, and even though she went to be with the Lord on August 1, 2021, her spirit is with me and I continue to make her proud, I'm sure.

Most importantly, I am who I am today because of my Lord and Savior Jesus Christ. He provides me wisdom, strength, and energy on a daily basis to glorify Him in all that I do. "Every good and perfect gift is from above, coming down from the Father of the heavenly lights, who does not change like shifting shadows" (James 1:17).

May God bless you, reader. Thank you for choosing this text to learn more about the FBO business.

About the Author

(City of Riverside)

Dr. C. Daniel Prather, PhD, DBA, AAE, CAM, currently serves as airport manager of Riverside Municipal Airport. This general aviation reliever airport, located in Southern California, has more than 200 based aircraft, with 116,000 annual operations as of 2022. Dr. Prather served as assistant director of operations at Tampa International Airport (TPA) from 1998 to 2006, and associate professor of aerospace at Middle Tennessee State University (MTSU) from 2006 to 2012. Dr. Prather was Founding Chair of Aviation Science at California Baptist University (CBU), where he established a new collegiate aviation program in 2012. In this role, he was responsible for developing curriculum and recruiting students and faculty to the nation's newest collegiate aviation program. He continues to serve as professor of aviation science at CBU.

As a former president of the University Aviation Association (UAA), Dr. Prather is active in the American Association of Airport Executives (AAAE), Helicopter Association International (HAI), and the National Business Aviation Association (NBAA). Dr. Prather is an Accredited Airport Executive through AAAE, a Certified Aviation Manager through the NBAA, and an instrument-rated private pilot. He is also an active aviation industry consultant, often busy on projects with the Airport Cooperative Research Program (ACRP) of the Transportation Research Board (TRB), having authored 12 ACRP Synthesis projects since 2009. He holds a doctor of philosophy degree from the University of Nebraska at Lincoln, a doctor of business administration degree from California Southern University, a master of public administration degree from Southern Illinois University at Carbondale, a master of business administration degree from the University of North Alabama, and a bachelor of commercial aviation degree from Delta State University.

In addition to this textbook, Dr. Prather is author of *Airport Management,* which is designed to be a practical guidebook to all aspects of managing today's complex commercial-service airport.

Not counting his one year as a flight coordinator intern at FedEx Express while in college, or flight training he undertook while in high school, Dr. Prather entered the aviation industry in 1996 and has never looked back. Visit Dr. Prather at dprather.com or pdpcredit.com

1

General Aviation: A Historical Perspective

In Chapter 1

Objectives

At the end of this chapter, you should be able to:

1. Discuss some of the major developments in aviation that took place up to the outbreak of World War I.
2. Describe the role of the barnstormers in the development of general aviation.
3. Explain how Wichita became the home for many general aviation (GA) aircraft manufacturers.
4. Describe how Beech, Cessna, Mooney, and Piper got started in GA aircraft manufacturing.
5. Explain aviation highlights of the 1940s.
6. Explain aviation highlights of the 1950s.
7. Explain aviation highlights of the 1960s.
8. Explain aviation highlights of the 1970s.
9. Explain aviation highlights of the 1980s.
10. Explain aviation highlights of the 1990s.
11. Explain aviation highlights of the 2000–2010 time period.
12. Explain aviation highlights of the 2011–2020 time period.
13. Explain the effects of COVID on the GA industry.

The Early Days of General Aviation

It can be said that general aviation (GA) was born on December 17, 1903, when Orville Wright completed the first sustained powered flight in a heavier-than-air aircraft (Figure 1-1). However, it was not until 1908 that the U.S. Army purchased its first Wright Flyer and not until 1911 that it received five more. Consequently, most of the early Wright models were used to instruct new pilots and for pleasure flying. Others became attractions for special events such as fairs, and some were used to take paying passengers into the air for the first time.

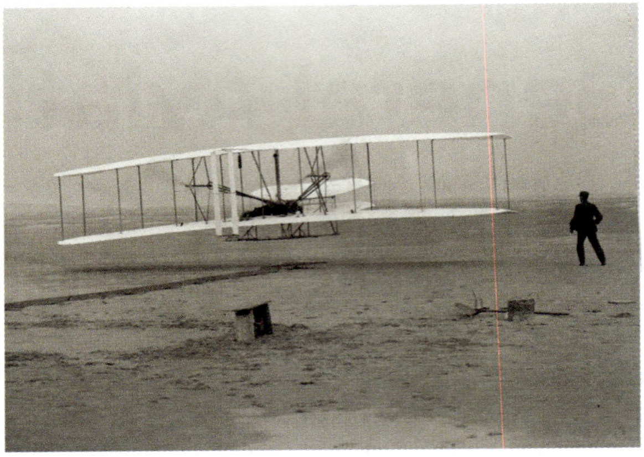

Figure 1-1. *Wright Flyer* first flight. *(John T. Daniels, public domain)*

As early as 1909, the **Wright brothers** encountered their first competition from the Curtiss Aeroplane and Motor Corporation as well as from several foreign models shipped to the United States to take part in flying contests and exhibitions. On June 26, 1909, the first commercial sale of an airplane took place. An improved version of the 1908 Curtiss *June Bug* was sold to the Aeronautic Society of New York for $7,500.

Figure 1-2. Glenn Curtiss winning the Scientific American trophy on July 4, 1908. *(Library of Congress, LCCN 2001705775, public domain)*

Like the Wright brothers, **Glenn Curtiss** was a bicycle maker. By 1902 he had graduated to motorcycles, both building and racing them, and by 1908 his company had grown to more than 100 employees working around the clock to meet demand. Part of the demand came from budding aviators who were charged a premium for Curtiss's coveted air-cooled engines. In 1905, the famed Alexander Graham Bell, inventor of the telephone, hired Curtiss to head up a group of aviation experimenters known as the Aerial Experiment Association. On July 4, 1908, Curtiss's *June Bug* won the Scientific American prize of a silver trophy for the first officially observed flight in the United States exceeding one kilometer (Figure 1-2).

Federation Aeronautique Internationale

AERO CLUB OF AMERICA

No. 1

The above-named Club, recognized by the Federation Aeronautique Internationale, as the governing authority for the United States of America, certifies that

Glenn H. Curtiss

born 21st day of May 1878

having fulfilled all the conditions required by the Federation Aeronautique Internationale, is hereby licensed as Aviator.

Dated June 8th, 1911.

President.

Secretary.

[SEAL]

Signature of Licensee: Glenn H. Curtiss

Figure 1-3. First pilot license issued by the Aero Club of America. *(National Air and Space Museum, public domain)*

In August 1909, Curtiss traveled to Reims, France, to enter the first Gordon Bennett Aviation Trophy race. He won the $10,000 prize money with an average speed of 47.4 miles per hour, which captured the public's imagination on both sides of the Atlantic. Aviation activity experienced a sharp increase between 1909 and 1911 partly as a result of fierce competition among newspapers for aviation news. Another reason was the public's sudden interest in flying. In October 1910, the first international air meet was held in the United States at Belmont Park, New York. Britisher Claude Grahame-White won the second Gordon Bennett Speed Trophy with a speed of 60 miles per hour.

More and more people were entering the general aviation picture, and by 1911 several manufacturers were building airplanes as "professional" devices. Many amateur airplane builders were also involved with aviation projects; some were killed or injured trying to fly their home-built machines. At the close of 1911, there were 82 pilots in the United States licensed to fly in air meets and exhibitions. In addition to the licensed pilots, approximately 50 more individuals had flown solo. The licensing authority at that time was the **Aero Club of America**.

When war broke out in Europe in 1914, the United States had as many as 12 aircraft manufacturers, including some companies that were producing only three or four airplanes per year. Fewer than 200 flying machines had been commercially produced since 1903, and about one-half had gone to the U.S. Army and Navy. The Curtiss Aeroplane and Motor Company, successor to the Aerial Experiment Association, was the largest company in America producing airplanes.

During **World War I**, Curtiss produced about 6,000 JN-4 Jenny trainers for the army (along with the navy version of the Jenny, the N-9). The Jenny was first built in 1914 to meet U.S. Army requirements for a training aircraft. Over 95 percent of the 10,000 American pilots trained during the war years flew this aircraft. Thousands of Curtiss OX-5, water-cooled, 90-horsepower V-8 engines were built. So durable were Jennys that they stayed around for many years after the war, becoming the standard barnstorming plane during the 1920s and continuing in use by the Air Corps until 1927. These aircraft—which had cost the government about $17,000 new depending upon how they were equipped—became surplus after the war and were sold for as high as $750 new and as low as $50 used.

THE BARNSTORMERS

Many of the early **barnstormers** were ex-World War I pilots who could not get aviation out of their systems. Flying war surplus aircraft such as the Curtiss Jenny, they toured the country, putting on aerial shows and giving rides to curious townspeople. Teams of pilots working together as a "flying circus" put on thrilling exhibitions, including wing walking and plane changes, in which a stunt man would transfer between planes in the air.

The largest and best known of the circuses was developed by an ex-automobile racer and salesman, Ivan R. Gates. The **Gates Flying Circus** attracted some of the best stunters and wing-walkers ever to thrill a crowd. Pilots like Clyde Pangborn and Ormer Locklear would fly inverted over a field and perform loops to an astonished audience. These two individuals were as popular as movie stars of the day. The barnstormers kept aviation alive during the early 1920s when most people looked upon the airplane as good for only two things: war and exhibitions.

Figure 1-4. Tennis match, barnstormer style. *(INTERFOTO/Alamy)*

Figure 1-5. Gates Flying Circus flyer. *(Florida Memory, State Library and Archives of Florida, CC PDM 1.0)*

Figure 1-6. Early airmail. *(Bill Whittaker, commons.wikimedia.org/wiki/File:Airmail_1930s_Detroit_Smykowski.jpg, CC BY-SA 3.0, creativecommons.org/licenses/by-sa/3.0/)*

By 1925, crashes and neglect had diminished the surplus warplanes and the barnstormers needed new and better-performing airplanes. Federal legislation also had its effect in shaping the industry. The **Air Mail Act of 1925**, also known as the Kelly Act for Congressman Clyde Kelly who championed the legislation, turned the transport of mail over to private carriers. The newly formed airlines and airmail service lured the barnstormers into more settled work. The **Air Commerce Act of 1926** created the first Aeronautics Branch in the U.S. Department of Commerce and provided the establishment of airports, airways, and NAVAIDs, as well as the first licensing of planes and pilots. It also made stunting difficult, if not illegal in many instances.

The gypsy pilots, as they were called, became more of an oddity, and the flying circuses came to be viewed as bad for aviation. More and more bad days curtailed their barnstorming seasons. In December 1928, the Gates Flying Circus broke up. In its career, it had appeared in 2,500 towns and cities and carried more than 1.5 million passengers.

Commercial and general aviation truly began to go their separate ways around this time. The government asked the budding manufacturers to build aircraft for airmail service, and companies like Boeing, Ryan, Douglas, and Lockheed chose to develop mail and passenger planes. Others, including Wright, Laird, Bellanca, and Aeronca concentrated on smaller planes for racing and sport flying.

Another significant civil market, the corporate user, was also developing. In 1927, 34 non-aviation companies were operating business aircraft; by 1930 that number had grown to 300, and manufacturers such as Stinson, Travel Air, Waco, and Fokker were actively cultivating the market. Even private flying, largely the province of the wealthy, was being eyed as a possible market.

WICHITA: HOME OF GENERAL AVIATION

Jake Moellendick was a wealthy oilman who resided in **Wichita, Kansas**. He was also a gambler. The gamble of aviation appealed to him, and in 1919 he agreed to put up $15,000 to back several barnstormers who needed three new planes to replace their worn-out Curtiss Jennys. Billy Burke was sent to the 1919 Chicago Air Show to find the new aircraft. He approached an aircraft builder by the name of Matty Laird who had recently formed the **E. M. Laird Company** and was developing plans for a new, three-place biplane. Burke realized that Laird's aircraft could easily become the country's first successful commercially sold private plane. Burke wired Jake about the new plane and suggested that, instead of forming the flying circus, they get into the airplane building business. The idea appealed to Jake with the one stipulation that the company be moved from Chicago to Wichita.

The Burke-Moellendick-Laird partnership began work, and in April 1920, the first Laird Swallow rolled out of the hangar. It was everything Billy Burke had hoped for in a barnstorming aircraft: a sturdy, well-built and easy-to-fly craft that set the standard for all subsequent private biplanes of the 1920s. Production went from two planes a month to four, and Jake Moellendick went on a hiring spree to keep the plant meeting its orders. He assembled a group of unknowns, mostly ex-barnstormers like Buck Weaver, who later organized the **Weaver Aircraft Company** (subsequently shortened to WACO). Others included Lloyd Stearman and his brother, Waverly, and Walter Beech. The company should have prospered, but Jake was impossible to work for, and one by one his fine team quit. After 43 Laird Swallows had been sold, Matty Laird went back to his own company in Chicago, which built high-quality private aircraft until World War II. Jake renamed his plant the **Swallow Airplane Manufacturing Company**, but the next year, 1924, the Stearman brothers and

Beech also left Moellendick. In partnership with another barnstormer named Clyde V. Cessna, they formed the **Travel Air Manufacturing Company** in Wichita. Beech, Cessna, and Stearman eventually went their separate ways, each establishing his own company. By now, Wichita had come to house the greatest concentration of aircraft-building talent in the country and to this day remains the heart of the American general aviation industry.

BEECH AIRCRAFT CORPORATION

In 1905 at the age of 14, Walter H. Beech made his first flight in a homemade glider in Pulaski, Tennessee. He later went on the barnstorming circuit, where he developed the experience and piloting skill that helped Travel Air Manufacturing Company become the country's number one plane maker by 1928.

In 1929, Travel Air merged with Curtiss-Wright, and Beech went to New York as vice president of sales and chief pilot. He quit in 1930 and headed back to Wichita. In the depth of the depression in April 1932, he established the **Beech Aircraft Corporation**, with his wife Olive Ann as director and secretary/treasurer, and he rented part of an inactive factory. With chief engineer T. A. Wells, he got the first Model 17—a luxurious, five-place, 200-mile-per-hour cabin biplane called the Staggerwing—into the air on November 4, 1932. It could fly almost 1,000 miles, and in January 1933 it won the Texaco Trophy at the Miami races. The prototype was bought by the Ethyl Corporation, and the money helped the young company to keep producing. By 1934, the already famous Model 17 had begun to sell, and by the end of 1935, a total of 54 units had been sold. The company moved into a new plant to rival those (also in Wichita) of Stearman and Cessna. The Staggerwing Beech continued to sell (up to 781 in 1948) and its distinctive shape had no rival (Figure 1-7).

Figure 1-7. Beech C17 Staggerwing. *(Courtesy of the San Diego Air & Space Museum)*

In 1937, the Model 18 Twin Beech was born. An eight-place monoplane, it was as fast as the Model 17; but instead of being priced at $12,000 to $24,000, it sold for $35,000 with two Jacobs engines, or $38,000 with more powerful 350-horsepower Wright radials.

Employment peaked during **World War II** when the U.S. Army and Navy needed transports and trainers for bombardiers and gunners. The Twin Beech remained in production until November 1969, a 32-year history during which 7,091 were built, almost all with neither of the original engines but with the 450-horsepower Pratt & Whitney Wasp Junior instead.

In 1946, Beech again hit the market exactly right with the V-tail Bonanza. It featured seating for four people (including the pilot), full flight and navigation instruments necessary for day or night VFR cross-country flights, and even a two-way radio as standard equipment. It had fully retractable tricycle landing gear and a 165-horsepower Continental engine. The price tag was set at $7,500, and Beech had more than 500 orders from eager customers before publicity was released about performance. By 1950, the Bonanza represented 53 percent of the aviation industry's deliveries of high-performance, single-engine airplanes. It was Walter Beech's last classic. He died of a heart attack in 1950, and Mrs. Beech was elected president and chairman of the board.

The number of production models tripled, and three additional plants were established. The company supplied the popular T-34 Mentor military trainer and, in conjunction with other major firms, produced transports, fighters, and helicopters. Eventually, Beech had contracts for the Gemini, Apollo, and lunar-module projects.

CESSNA AIRCRAFT COMPANY

Clyde V. Cessna was one of the original barnstorming pioneers. He bought a French-built Bleriot monoplane in 1911, and until the war years, Cessna improved and refined the basic design. Barnstorming was profitable and more fun than building aircraft at that time. On July 5, 1917, Cessna set a notable speed record of 125 miles per hour on a cross-country flight from Blackwell, Oklahoma, to Wichita, Kansas—an event prophetic of many more racing and competition triumphs to be scored by Cessna airplanes.

In 1924, with a total of six successful airplane designs to his credit, which he personally built and flew, Cessna joined Walter Beech and Lloyd Stearman in establishing the Travel Air Manufacturing Company in Wichita and became its president. He sold out his interest in Travel Air to Beech in 1927. Part of the trouble at Travel Air had been Cessna's lack of interest in biplanes. If anything, he was ahead of his time, for he believed the monoplane did not have to be covered with wires and struts in order to be strong and efficient.

Cessna Aircraft Company's first independent production-model airplane, built in 1927, was the four-place, full cantilever high-wing Comet monoplane. His 1928 Model A, an expensive four seater, won the New York–Los Angeles Air Derby and also flew to Siberia and back. Developments followed, but the depression almost brought business to a stop. Despite a $398 glider and a $975 powered version, the new plant closed in 1931. Not until January 1934 did the directors agree to restart the business. Cessna installed his nephew, Dwayne Wallace, as plant manager. A recent aeronautical engineering graduate from Wichita University, Wallace went to work with no salary but with the opportunity to design, build, test, sell, and even race new Cessnas.

Figure 1-8. Cessna Model A. *(Wisconsin Historical Society, WHI-121475)*

Wallace's first creation was the C-34, a high-wing, four-place cabin monoplane with a 145-horsepower Warner Super Scarab engine. The airplane refined the fully cantilevered wing of earlier Cessnas but with added flaps. In 1935, the C-34 won the *Detroit News* trophy race, part of the prestigious National Air Races which put Cessna in the first rank of aircraft builders. The company's reputation as a builder of fast, efficient aircraft was assured, and Cessna retired the following year. The C-34 was developed into various Airmaster models, but Wallace was looking for a light twin-engine aircraft that would be easy to fly and not too sophisticated to build. By 1939, the T-50 was flying, and by 1940 it was in production and ready for buyers. War came and the military bought 5,401 as the AT-17 Bobcat (RCAF Crane) advanced trainer and UC-78 light transport.

After the war, Cessna built the 120/140 series followed by the 190/195 series. These airplanes were strong and simple single-engine aircraft that helped Cessna survive the postwar shakeout and launched it into the 1950s. Modern twins began with the 310, flown in January 1953, and the 318 in 1954, which led to the T-37 twin-jet trainer. The Fanjet 500 (later renamed Citation) began a family of business jets in 1968. Cessna produced a family of light agricultural aircraft, such as the AGwagon, AGpickup, AGtruck, and AGhusky, from 1966 to 1983. The first turboprop was the highly efficient Conquest announced in 1974. Wallace retired in 1975 and was succeeded by Russ Meyer. By 1979, the Pawnee factory making single-engine aircraft in Wichita had topped 120,000 units of production, and Cessna had become the number one builder of general aviation aircraft.

MOONEY AIRCRAFT CORPORATION

In 1929, brothers Albert and Arthur Mooney started **Mooney Aircraft Corporation** in Colorado. With financing supplied by Bridgeport Machine Company, the brothers moved their fledgling manufacturing company to Wichita. The first years were very challenging for the Mooney Brothers. Their first aircraft design, the M-5, failed on an attempted nonstop flight from California to New York due to a bad engine weld. The Great Depression soon hit, forcing Mooney to shut down and liquidate assets.

To provide some income, the brothers went to work for the competition. Albert worked as the chief engineer at Bellanca Aircraft Company, which was still strong thanks to a Navy contract. After developing aircraft designs in his spare time and with funding from Charles Yankey of Culver Aircraft, the Mooney Aircraft Corporation was re-established in 1948. The first aircraft produced by the newly established company was the very popular Mooney Mite M-18, a $1,000 single-place aircraft (Figure 1-9). This aircraft was designed to appeal to the thousands of fighter pilots returning from military service. A total 283 Mites were produced between 1948 and 1955. The Mooney headquarters moved to Kerrville, Texas, in 1953, where it still resides today. Over the years, the company has filed numerous bankruptcies and had a number of different owners. Production was officially halted in November 2019. As of 2021, the company had once again been resurrected, although it is mostly focused on supplying parts for the roughly 7,000 Mooney aircraft that are in service. The future of Mooney Aircraft Corporation remains uncertain.

Figure 1-9. Mooney Mite. *(Bill Larkins, flickr.com/photos/34076827@N00/5202931667/, CC BY-SA 2.0, creativecommons.org/licenses/by-sa/2.0/)*

PIPER AIRCRAFT CORPORATION

William T. Piper entered aviation at a relatively older age than most of the pioneers. When he was 48 years old and a successful oilman in Bradford, Pennsylvania, Piper invested in a local company, the Taylor Brothers Aircraft Corporation, which had designed several light planes. Serving as treasurer, he ended up acquiring the company for $761 when it fell into bankruptcy in 1931. Piper reorganized the assets into **Taylor Aircraft Company**, giving C. Gilbert Taylor half interest in the new enterprise as an inducement to stay with the company. The new company's formula was simple: build easy-to-fly machines and price them low enough to attract buyers.

Figure 1-10. Taylor E-2 Cub. *(Daniel L. Berek, commons.wikimedia.org/wiki/File:Taylor_E-2_Cub_NC13146_DLB.jpg, CC BY-SA 3.0, creativecommons.org/licenses/by-sa/3.0/)*

After an unsuccessful attempt to design a glider, the Taylor Aircraft Company developed the E-2 Cub, an excellent example of Piper's idea of the simple airplane (Figure 1-10). By 1934, the Taylor Cub was making money for the company; it was priced at $1,425 with a 38-horsepower Continental engine. Throughout many years of refining the design, Piper resisted changing the Cub's airfoil or flight characteristics, even though to do so would have increased its speed. He also resisted building fancier, more costly aircraft.

In 1936, Taylor resigned and set up his own company, which eventually went bankrupt in 1946. Piper hired a new chief engineer by the name of Walter Jamouneau and changed the name to the **Piper Aircraft Corporation**.

Following Piper's penchant for simple aircraft, the company did well. In recognition of Jamouneau's contribution to enhancing the E-2, subsequent models were called the J-2 and J-3. The PA-II followed next in the Cub line and finally the PA-18 Super Cub. From its first flight in September

1930, through widespread wartime service and with various improvements and derivations thereafter, the Cub formula provided business for Piper up to the 1950s with a total of more than 40,000 aircraft. Eighty percent of U.S. World War II pilots received their initial training in the Cub.

Piper Aircraft Corporation boomed and then nearly busted during the difficult period that hit general aviation following World War II. The company rebounded to produce the popular Pacer and Tri-Pacer series and to introduce light twin-engine aircraft to buyers who previously had considered nothing but single-engine planes. The model line expanded, as did the Piper facilities, when a major development center was built in Vero Beach, Florida. Piper is actively producing aircraft today.

The 1940s—World War II and Immediate Postwar Period

Even during the darkest days of World War II, the general aviation aircraft manufacturers were aware of the ordinary citizen's desire to fly and were preparing for the postwar period. In 1943, Cessna advertised in *Flying* magazine that "Texas won't be much bigger than Rhode Island when you're driving a Cessna Car-of-the-air . . . the airplane that everyone can fly" (Cessna 1943). Piper called for "Wings for all America." Other advertisements featured pretty girls in bathing suits, fishermen in remote trout streams, and flying couples basking under the Florida sun while their nonflying friends faced winter winds up north.

Surveys, polls, questionnaires, and other marketing studies conducted for and by the industry and the government were the basis for highly optimistic predictions of a staggering potential need for light aircraft after the war. The Department of Commerce, which administered civil aviation at that time, informed the Congress that there would be a demand for as many as 200,000 light aircraft a year for the civilian market. With an eye on the 12 million veterans who would be taking advantage of the educational benefits under the newly legislated **GI Bill**, industry experts concurred that there would be at least 1.3 million private pilots within five years after the war and as many as 400,000 privately owned aircraft by 1950.

Many leading magazines in 1943 and 1944, including journals with such diverse audiences as *Business Week* and *Better Homes and Gardens*, regularly carried major articles featuring postwar airplanes for the common man and woman. *Time* reported that there were 5,750,000 people "conditioned to flying." These included army and navy pilots (numbering 350,000 at the time); 150,000 civilian pilots and students; 2,500,000 skilled aviation men in the war (other than pilots); 250,000 students taking aviation courses; and 2,500,000 men and women employees who worked during the war in aircraft factories. A *Woman's Home Companion* survey showed that 39 percent of the women interviewed were interested in flying themselves and 88 percent had no objection to anyone in their family owning a plane.

The aviation industry acted as quickly as it could to meet the anticipated avalanche of new student pilots and returning veterans who would be the first buyers of postwar civilian aircraft. Surveys indicated that prices should be about $2,000 for a two-place aircraft and $4,000 for a four-place plane. All the wartime light aircraft manufacturers wanted to be in on the market with new models within a few months.

Piper, which had delivered 5,000 Cubs to the armed services, announced that it would soon come out with a two-place, low-wing, tricycle-gear, all-metal plane to be called the Skycycle. Beech and Cessna reorganized their production lines to roll out all-metal planes. Some of the manufacturers of combat aircraft entered the market. Republic Aircraft, which had produced thousands of P-47 fighters, geared up to offer a four-place, single-engine amphibian called the Seabee for sportsman pilots at an announced price of $3,995. North American Aviation, developer of the P-51 fighters and B-25 bombers, designed a bulky, four-place retractable-gear "family car of the air" called the Navion for a price of $5,000.

Despite all the design activity, the first airplanes to appear on the civilian market were the prewar models: the Aeronca Champion, Piper Cub, Taylor Taylorcraft, Stinson Voyager, and Luscombe

Silvaire. Cessna came out with the 120/140 series, and Globe produced the Swift. Production increased, and by the end of 1945 when the war was over, there were 37,789 aircraft of all categories (including airline equipment) in the U.S. civil aircraft fleet.

During 1946, hundreds of civilian flight training schools blossomed all over the country as recently discharged veterans took advantage of the new Veterans Affairs (VA) flight training legislation. It was apparent that the ordinary citizen did want to fly; the dream of a mass market was coming true. In 1946, the first full year of peace, 33,254 light aircraft were built and sold.

No one was concerned that the demand for 200,000 airplanes did not materialize in the first year; everything with wings that was made was sold. It would be better to have the market develop slowly to the 200,000 level. More important, the sales volume was 455 percent higher than it had ever been before the war.

Airline services expanded rapidly after the war, and it was not long before the airlines were demanding that the government regulate small airplanes out of "their" airspace and keep them out of "their" airports. The government refused, and the light aircraft manufacturers seemed to be receiving good news on all fronts. The year 1946 was a record-setting period: Piper produced 7,780 aircraft; Aeronca produced 7,555; Cessna produced 3,959; and Taylorcraft produced 3,151. The non-spinnable Ercoupe sold a surprising 2,503, and Globe and Stinson both went over the 1,000 mark.

Beech introduced the Bonanza for $7,435, and a small aerobatic biplane called the Pitts Special came on the market. Twenty manufacturers were engaged in making planes for the general aviation community. However, there were clouds on the horizon. The all-around utility of the automobile far surpassed that of the light airplane for the simple reason that there were not enough ground-support facilities where people could land that were close to resort and vacation areas. The airplanes also cost a lot more than people had been led to believe they would, particularly when compared with automobiles. The $3,995 Seabee of 1945 had been more realistically priced at $6,000 by the end of 1946. The Bonanza was up to $8,945, Navion to $4,750, the Swift to $3,750, and the Cessna 170 to $5,475—all a long way from the $2,000 price tag advertised during the war.

As for the less expensive models, there were complaints that most were basically prewar models and not very good for cross-country transportation. They were noisy, drafty, cramped, uncomfortable, and not at all reliable for taking carefully planned vacation trips to the mountains or the beach.

The industry also experienced a high percentage of VA students dropping out of flying soon after receiving their private pilot certificate and an increasing number quitting immediately after soloing. Once airport circling had lost its charm, many ex-GIs began to take a hard look at the practicalities versus expenses of flying, particularly when they learned how easily low ceilings or fog could ground them (if not instrument-rated).

Army and Navy veterans who had been flying high-performance airplanes were simply not satisfied to poke along at 95 or 100 miles an hour, especially after a long cross-country flight against a headwind when they could see automobiles making better time on the highways below.

Another problem faced by the light aircraft manufacturers was the availability of war surplus aircraft at bargain prices. In 1946, the **Reconstruction Finance Corporation** sold more than 31,000 aircraft ranging from Cessna T-50 "Bamboo Bombers" to P-51s. Many ex-military C-47s and Twin Beeches, as well as bombers, went into the corporate market to be modified as executive transports.

The manufacturers began to realize that the general public might have been oversold on light-plane flying and that they could not hope to have a mass-production industry comparable to the automobile industry. In 1947, a year before Cessna introduced its 170—which would eventually be developed into the 172, the world's most successful light plane—the industry was beginning to flounder.

Manufacturing companies with delivery ramps clogged with unsold airplanes began to feel the pinch. Globe was in bankruptcy. Republic had discontinued the Seabee. North American Aviation had sold the Navion design to Ryan. Stinson was in deep financial trouble. Taylorcraft was looking for new capital. By the end of 1947, the severity of the problem was evident. Sales were down 44 percent from the previous year, to 15,617 units. The situation worsened in 1948; Sales again dropped by more than 40 percent when only 7,302 airplanes were manufactured.

The public's reluctance to spend money on private flying was understandable. A cold war had developed with the Russians, culminating in the blockade of Berlin in the summer of 1948. The United States countered by mounting the Berlin Airlift, and the possibility of another major conflict was on the horizon. GI flight training was restricted to vocational pursuits, and tougher regulations were enacted to restrict private flying.

The downward trend followed the deteriorating international situation, resulting in an even more dismal year in 1949 when 3,545 aircraft were built. New aircraft designs appeared on the scene, only to disappear from sight forever as light aircraft manufacturers ran out of operating capital.

The 1950s—A Period of Introspection

The 1950s began a period of introspection and review by the general aviation aircraft manufacturers. Executives began to look at the future from a different angle. Mass-producing airplanes for everyone at low prices was not the answer to growth. The future lay in developing a fleet of airplanes that would provide solid, comfortable, reliable business transportation. Aircraft that could operate in instrument conditions with speed and range would be the wave of the future. A certain number of training airplanes would need to be produced to support flight training, but a utility airplane that businessmen could afford was the target design for the future. Some such airplanes were already available, but the business community doubted their utility. The Twin Bonanza and Twin Beech were well thought of, but there was a lingering doubt in the public's mind about single-engine aircraft. One event that helped to change that attitude was a flight by William P. Odom in January 1949 from Hawaii to Oakland, California, in a Beech Bonanza. Three months later he flew the same Bonanza 5,273 miles nonstop from Hawaii to Teterboro, New Jersey.

Cross-country navigation was being made simpler and more efficient by the new very high frequency omni-directional radio ranges—the **VORs**. Spotted around the country, the pilot merely had to follow a needle on the instrument panel. No longer did pilots have to keep sectional charts on their legs hour after hour to check their position or to keep working with their calculators to dead reckon their way under instrument conditions.

In June 1950, the **Korean War** broke out and once again the public's attention was focused on the international scene. General aviation continued to limp along, although the ranks of the manufacturers were thinning. Beech, Bellanca, Cessna, Piper, and Ryan were still producing airplanes, but not all of these companies were sure that they could hang on much longer. Production in 1950 was only 3,520 units.

On the positive side, more and more VORs were commissioned; VHF radios—static free and easy to navigate by—became factory options on more and more airplanes. In 1950, general aviation airplanes were awarded their own frequency, 122.8, called UNICOM. **William "Bill" Lear** developed the first light plane three-axis autopilot in 1950, which made cross-country flying easier and more relaxing. Toward the end of the year, Ryan stopped production of the Navion, but a new company, Aero Design and Engineering, was ready with its five-place Aero Commander. Piper put a nosewheel on its little Pacer, renamed it the Tri-Pacer, and created a new surge of interest in light aircraft for pleasure as well as for business.

Figure 1-11. Bill Lear. *(National Aviation Hall of Fame)*

Aircraft production hit bottom in 1951 with only 2,477 units produced all year, just half the number produced in the month of August 1946. The situation began to look brighter in

1952. Max Conrad flew a Piper Tri-Pacer to Europe and back, which again demonstrated the capability and reliability of light aircraft. In 1952, 3,509 airplanes were delivered, an increase of 1,032 over the previous year. Things were beginning to move. Cessna discontinued the 195 in 1953 and produced the four-place 180, a more powerful aircraft than the 170. Piper stayed with the Tri-Pacer and the Super Cub; Beech was backlogged with orders for the Bonanza, the Twin Bonanza, and the Super-18. Total production hit 3,788 units in 1953, up 279 from the previous year. Growth was solid as the industry emerged from a period of readjustment.

In 1954, Cessna and Piper introduced their four-place light twins—the 310 and the Apache, which would start a long line of descendants. Max Conrad ferried an Apache to Europe and started the transatlantic ferry business. No longer would general aviation aircraft be crated and shipped to Europe for reassembly.

By the mid-1950s, aircraft production hovered around the 4,500 per year mark and the need for instrument flight rules (IFR) capability increased. Companies like ARC, Bendix, Collins, Lear, Mitchell, and Wilcox entered the avionics business. By the end of the decade, Cessna introduced the Skylane as a package airplane—one with basic avionics already installed.

The 1960s—Soaring into the Future

As the 1950s turned into the 1960s, general aviation was developing an unmistakable stability and purpose. Though pleasure flying was far from extinct, it was clear that the general aviation airplane was developing into a viable means of business transportation. In 10 years, the general aviation fleet had more than doubled to 60,000 aircraft, more than half of which were equipped for instrument flying. General aviation had become a major part of the nation's transportation system, with an inventory of light aircraft that were fully capable of flying people in comfort 1,500 miles in one day to thousands of places not served by the commercial air carriers. Expansion, modernization, and increasing complexity characterized the aviation world of the 1960s. A decade that began with radial-engine transports ended with the Concorde and landing a man on the moon.

Beech brought out the Travel Air, to be followed by the Baron, the Queen Air, and the King Air. Cessna put tricycle landing gear on their 170s and 180s in developing the 172 and 182 series, which became the best-selling airplanes in history. Piper terminated the Tri-Pacer and entered the Cherokee, Comanche, and Twin Comanche in the market. Many of the old names such as Bellanca, Mooney, Navion, and North American would come back.

By 1965, the general aviation aircraft fleet had grown to 95,000 airplanes, and production totaled 11,852 new aircraft. The following year, 1966, saw a record 15,768 units produced. General aviation growth during the late 1960s paralleled growth in the economy and all segments of aviation at that time.

Three airplanes in particular that were introduced in the 1960s—the Piper Cherokee, the Beech King Air 90, and the Lear 23—proved to be bellwether designs for years to come.

The Cherokee was the first Piper model to be produced at the company's new Vero Beach, Florida, manufacturing plant. Vero Beach and the Cherokee were Piper's solutions to the high cost of building airplanes in Lock Haven, Pennsylvania. The production line was designed for speed and volume.

Figure 1-12. Piper Cherokee. *(iStock.com/IgorSPb)*

Piper dedicated the Vero Beach plant, rolled out the first Cherokee, and celebrated William Piper's eightieth birthday, all on January 8, 1960. The Cherokee was certified in 1961. Two versions were offered. The PA-28-150 sold for $9,795. An additional $200 bought 10 more horsepower.

The Cherokee marked Piper's break from its traditional tube-and-fabric, high-wing design approach to light singles. It became the template for all of the piston-powered models Piper would develop over the next 20 years, with the exception of the Tomahawk and Navajo.

Beech entered the 1960s with a pair of piston-powered, cabin-class executive transports in the Model 18 and the Queen Air. But the company had been studying turboprops for several years. Beech had a technical agreement with a French firm, Societe Francaise d'Entretien et du Reparation de Materiel Aeronautique, to test Turbomeca turboprop engines on a Travel Air, the new Baron, and a Beech 18.

In December 1962, Beech unveiled a mock-up of a turboprop-powered, pressurized Model 120, an all-new design. The goal was to test the marketing waters before committing to an expensive development program. At the same time, Beech was working on a new pressurized version of the Queen Air 80.

As the potential costs and time to develop a new top-of-the-line turboprop began to mount, Beech executives opted to take a less risky road and adapt turbine power to the Queen Air. Details of the forthcoming King Air were revealed in August 1963. Two 500-shaft horsepower Pratt & Whitney turboprop engines would provide the power to cruise at 270 miles per hour at 16,500 feet, with the cabin pressurized to an altitude of 8,000 feet. The price was projected at about $300,000. In a press release announcing rollout of the first production prototype in November 1963, Beech said it had received $11 million in orders for King Airs. The potential market was estimated to be at least 200 airplanes over the next few years.

The King Air 90 was certified in May 1964, five months after its first flight. Contrary to Beech's modest expectations, the King Air 90 proved to be the tip of the iceberg for the product line. A through F Model 90s would be introduced, along with larger and more powerful King Air 100s, 200s, and the 300.

Beech has dominated the turboprop market from the beginning. Other designs have a considerable performance edge, but the King Air's combination of roomy cabin, docile handling, and commanding presence have made it the passenger-carrying choice for thousands of companies, government agencies, and individuals. Over 4,000 have been built, including 500 for the U.S. Army, Air Force, Navy, and Marines. No other airplane is in service with all four branches of the military.

Just as the King Air 90 started Beech on a new product line that was to define the executive turboprop, Lear Jet Corporation's Lear 23 launched corporate aviation into the jet age (Figure 1-13).

The Learjet has its roots in a European private-venture military jet that never went into full production. The P-16 was a ground-attack warrior that a Swiss firm hoped to sell to the Swiss Air Force. Four were built, but two crashed during test flights. The accidents saddled the airplane with a suspect reputation, and as a consequence, the military could not be sold on it.

One person who was sold on the aircraft was William P. Lear. The prolific inventor, showman, marketer, and chairman of Lear, Incorporated, flew in it several times and was very impressed.

It was to be the first jet designed specifically for general aviation. The Lockheed JetStar and North American Sabreliner already were in service, but they were originally designed to ferry military VIPs and were much larger, heavier, and costlier than the airplane Lear envisioned.

Speed and style were a large part of that vision. The Model 23, with its two small but powerful military-derivative General Electric CJ610 turbojet engines, would cruise at 458 knots and look every bit as fast. Today the Learjet still is regarded by many as the finest example of what a civilian jet should be: fast and easy to handle.

Figure 1-13. Lear 23. *(Gift of Gates Learjet Corporation, Smithsonian National Air and Space Museum)*

Learjet passengers would ride comfortably above the weather in a cocoon-like office. Bill Lear professed disdain for walk-around airplane cabins with lavatories—at least until he designed the Learstar, which eventually became the widebody Canadair Challenger.

The prototype Lear 23 was built in seven months by the new Lear Jet Corporation in Wichita. It flew for the first time on October 7, 1963. Eight months later, the second prototype was flown to the Reading Air Show for a dramatic first public appearance (the first prototype had been destroyed a few days earlier in a nonfatal off-airport landing). Certification took just 10 months, a remarkable achievement considering that the Model 23 was the first jet under 12,500 pounds that the FAA had been asked to certify. It went on the market for $595,000.

The Lear 23 and Lear Jet Corporation would suffer a series of unexplained accidents and a financial recession soon after deliveries began. The airplane survived; the company did not. Bill Lear, who had been forced to sell his shares in Lear, Incorporated, in order to finance development and certification of the Model 23 and its immediate successor, the 24, had to sell Lear Jet Corporation to avoid financial collapse. Gates Rubber bought it in 1967 and, before the decade ended, certified the Model 25, a longer version of the 23/24. Later, the turbofan-powered Lear 35 and 55, an enlarged, stand-up cabin version, would be certified.

The 1970s—Inflation, Regulation, and Record Sales

The 1970s can be briefly summarized as the decade of the Terminal Control Area (TCA), the Airport and Airways Development Act, and fuel crises.

In 1970, the manufacturers of light aircraft established a strong and effective lobbying and public relations organization in Washington, the **General Aviation Manufacturers Association (GAMA)**. The **National Business Aircraft Association** (**NBAA**, later renamed the National Business Aviation Association), blossomed into a highly professional Washington-based service organization for business users. The **Aircraft Owners and Pilots Association (AOPA)** and other special-aircraft-use organizations developed into effective lobbying groups. The **Federal Aviation Administration (FAA)**, under administrator Jack Shaffer, appointed a deputy administrator for general aviation.

Despite an economic recession during the first two years of the 1970s and an oil embargo in 1973, general aviation continued to grow, reaching a high point in 1978 with 17,808 units produced. Personal aviation's production heyday came at a most unusual time. While the post-World War II airplane manufacturing spree held production records for decades (the sales crash that followed in 1947 also set records), the record sales days came, surprisingly, in a decade of sky-rocketing inflation, fuel shortages, and increasingly more restrictive airspace. Despite those factors, more aircraft were sold in the 1970s than before or since.

Figure 1-14. Lines of cars waiting to refuel during the gas shortage in the 1970s. *(National Archives, public domain)*

While the number of aircraft sold was a departure, the aircraft themselves largely were not. Aircraft based on existing models—some dating back to the 1940s and 1950s—formed the bread-and-butter models of this decade of record sales.

In the meantime, the industry saw upstarts like the fast Grumman-American singles mature, and the Rockwell Commanders reached full bloom in the 1970s, even though their production numbers could not touch those of the recycled Cessnas and Pipers. Beech also worked to refine the Aero Club airplanes—the Sierra and Sundowner singles, to name two—but continuing reluctance on the part of the sales staff and buying public ultimately was cited for the closing of that line.

Mooney saw its fortunes change in the 1970s. Finally with stable financial ground under it, the company performed a thorough remake of the M20-series airplanes. The short- and long-fuselage M20 line, which for a time included both 180- and 200-horsepower powerplant options, was condensed into the quick and far more refined 201.

Cessna gambled on improving its product and market image for the 1970s. Although the venerable Skyhawk was selling in unprecedented numbers, Cessna felt the competition from the newer Cherokee line and wanted to respond with something new, bold, and exciting. Their answer was the Cardinal, but it was never a complete success. Sales of the popular 172 continued to grow.

Cessna tried another tack in 1978 by adding new features to a well-known airframe and, in the process, brought pressurization to the piston single. The idea was not new—Mooney tried it with the Mustang, but fewer than 30 were sold before it was terminated in 1970. Cessna introduced the pressurized 210 with weather radar, known-icing equipment, and more radios at a base price of $40,000. A total of 874 were built before the line was shut down in 1986.

While Cessna gambled that the market was there for the P210, Piper took no such risks with its new trainer. Although the Cherokee 140 had been the maker's primary trainer, it was more expensive to buy, maintain, and refuel than the Cessna 150 it competed against. Piper wanted a model to once and for all capture the trainer market from Cessna's 150. Piper queried thousands of flight instructors and fixed-base operators. Respondents indicated the need for an airplane with low maintenance requirements, an engine that would tolerate 100LL fuel, good visibility, and flight characteristics that would make the student respect what a real stall could do, unlike those of the nearly stall-proof Cherokees.

Piper went to work and produced the PA-38 Tomahawk, which, when it debuted in 1978, appeared to be the answer to every instructor's dream. In nine months, Piper churned out nearly 1,000 of the PA-38s, about eight per day, according to the company. With that substantial production rate came quality problems, which severely hurt sales in its second year. Also, some feel that Piper went too far in giving the Tomahawk very noticeable stall characteristics. For instance, many felt the Cessna 150 and 152 were much easier to handle than the Piper Tomahawk.

Nearly 1,500 of the Piper trainers had been made by production's end in 1982. Interestingly, Beech's nearly identical Skipper suffered an equally truncated life: Only 312 were made from 1979 to 1981.

A new market segment opened up in the late 1970s that Piper turned to its advantage. With the price of fuel higher than it had been since the 1973–74 fuel crunch, the manufacturers perceived a demand for relatively inexpensive, efficient twins—aircraft that could provide low-cost, multi-engine training; the light-light twin was born. Piper stepped up with the Seminole, Beech with the Duchess, and Grumman-American with the Cougar.

Of the three, the Seminole sold the best. Piper sold three quarters as many Seminoles the first year, 1979, as the number of Duchesses made by Beech in that airplane's entire five-year life span. When the bottom fell out of the light-light twin market, the Seminole fell too, and the total run of PA-44 Seminoles, ending in 1982, numbered just 468 units (including 86 turbocharged models produced in the last two years), a handful more than the quantity of Duchesses produced.

While not as noteworthy for being a technological hotbed of activity as the 1940s and 1950s, the 1970s was a decade of immense production, providing harsh lessons for the marketing departments of both Cessna and Piper—lessons learned that ultimately helped shape the kinds of airplanes kept alive (or brought back to life) during the lean times of the 1980s.

By the late 1970s, both manufacturer and user began to experience a confidence that general aviation had seldom enjoyed before. Perhaps for the first time, the general aviation community perceived that its potential problems of government controls, charges, fees, and taxes, as well as restrictive legislation, were manageable. Unfortunately, the 1980s brought on a new round of challenges for the industry.

Soaring interest rates and a depressed economy during the early 1980s affected sales. Aircraft shipments dropped from 11,877 in 1980 to 9,457 in 1981 and 4,266 in 1982. By 1985, the number had reached a record low of 2,032 units.

The 1980s—A Decade of Retrenchment

Historically, the general aviation industry has paralleled the economic cycles of the national economy. In the early 1980s, general aviation followed the rest of the economy into recession. Interest rates were at an all-time high when President Reagan took office in January 1981. Everything from housing starts to durable goods sales, including autos and general aviation aircraft sales, plummeted. The economy began to recover in 1983, but unfortunately and uncharacteristically, general aviation did not. In fact, the number of general aviation aircraft delivered fell from a high of 17,811 in 1978 to 928 in 1994.

A number of factors have been cited for this decline:

1. *Costs.* The high interest rates of the late 1970s and early 1980s certainly had an effect at the beginning of the downturn. Acquisition costs, including avionics equipment, rose sharply during the early to mid-1980s despite very little change in design of features in the typical single-engine aircraft. Used aircraft were available, and prospective buyers were reluctant to purchase new equipment at considerably higher prices. Total operating expenses—including fuel, maintenance, hangaring charges, and insurance—all steadily increased during the 1980s, making it more expensive to operate aircraft, especially for the infrequent operator.
2. *Airline Deregulation.* Deregulation of the U.S. commercial airline industry in 1978 affected general aviation. Increased service combined with better connections and lower fares by the air carriers (including regional/commuter carriers) reduced the desirability of using general aviation aircraft when planning business or pleasure trips. As a result, business aircraft proved more difficult to justify.

Figure 1-15. President Jimmy Carter signing the Airline Deregulation Act, 1978. *(National Archives, ID 182032)*

3. *product liability claims.* Product liability claims, which caused the light aircraft manufacturers to concentrate on their higher-priced line of turbine equipment, also impacted GA aircraft production and sales. During the 1980s, annual claims paid by the manufacturers increased from $24 million to over $210 million despite an improved safety record. In 1985, the annual premiums for the manufacturers totaled about $135 million, and based on unit shipments of 2,029 that year, the price approached almost $70,000 per aircraft. This was more than the selling price of many basic two- and four-place aircraft. Dropping its piston aircraft production in 1986, Cessna self-insured up to $100 million. Piper decided to operate without the benefit of product liability coverage, and Beech insured the first $50 million annual aggregate exposure with their own captive insurance company.
4. *Taxes.* Passage of the Tax Reform Act in 1986 eliminated the 10 percent investment tax credit on aircraft purchases. This was followed by a luxury tax on boats and aircraft, which only exacerbated the problem of declining new aircraft sales.
5. *Foreign Aircraft Manufacturers.* In 1980, there were 29 U.S. and 15 foreign manufacturers of piston aircraft. By 1994, there were 29 foreign and only 9 U.S. manufacturers. In 1980, 100 percent of the single-engine pistons sold in the United States were manufactured in the United States. In 1994, less than 70 percent were manufactured in the United States. Many foreign governments have supported their fledgling aviation industries by subsidizing research, development, production, and financing. Foreign manufacturers continue to gain an ever-increasing foothold in the U.S. market. By the late 1980s and early 1990s, more than 50 percent of the aircraft delivered to U.S. customers were made abroad. Even in the

high-end market, sales of foreign-manufactured business jets were close to 40 percent of all business jets sold here in the late 1980s and early 1990s. Foreign-manufactured aircraft continue to trouble U.S. manufacturers.

6. *Other Factors.* Other factors have affected general aviation, especially the personal and business use of aircraft. In 1979, Congress repealed the GI Bill of Rights, which provided dollars for thousands of ex-service personnel to take flying lessons. Changes in redundant, discretionary income; increases in air space; restrictions applied to VFR aircraft; reductions in leisure time; and shifts in personal preferences as to how free time is spent all had their effect on the decline in the 1980s. The traditional aircraft customer's interest in sports and boats, which require less training and recurrence, seemed to have peaked during the 1980s.

In addition to the significant impact on aircraft deliveries, the 1980s also had a dramatic impact on the number of pilots. Specifically, from the late 1970s through the early 1990s, student starts were in a virtual free fall. In 1978, there were 137,032 new student pilot certificates issued. By 1996, this number was only 56,653, almost a 60 percent decline throughout the 1980s and mid-1990s. Similarly, newly rated private pilots went from 58,064 in 1978 to 24,714 in 1996, with the total number of private pilots declining from 357,479 to 247,604 during the same time period (FAA 1970s–1990s).

This decline in the number of pilots and student pilots coincided with the end of the chain of great economic programs and the beginning of a natural life cycle. Beginning in 1939, the United States government provided virtually free flight training for approximately the next 40 years, until the late 1970s. The **Civil Pilot Training Program**, the war training service after Pearl Harbor, trained an amazing 435,165 pilots between 1939 and 1944. The World War II GI Bill (officially the Servicemen's Readjustment Act of 1944) and its subsequent extension, the Korean War GI Bill, continued this trend of providing government-subsidized flight instruction and flight training for those who were interested in flying as "career development." The government subsidies in the form of the GI Bill ended in the late 1970s. In 1984, Mississippi Representative Sonny Montgomery proposed making the GI Bill permanent. The Montgomery GI Bill still exists today. In 2008, the Post-9/11 GI Bill was introduced to provide veterans on active duty on September 11, 2001 (and their dependents) educational benefits. In 2017, the Forever GI Bill was introduced, which eliminates the 15-year limitation for benefits, among other benefits.

The effect of the civil pilot training, the GI Bill, and other training programs was enormous. They were responsible for the majority of flight training students for many years, as well as a larger general aviation infrastructure than would have existed without these programs. Further, these programs stimulated the sale of more aircraft, particularly trainers to support this flight training, than ever before.

Military pilots and others who had received their training during the war and immediate postwar periods, when they were in their twenties and early thirties, were reaching their sixties in the 1980s. They were beginning to retire from flying. Fundamentally, in the 1980s, the GA industry was seeking its natural level, shrinking back to the size it might have been had there never been civil pilot training, war training service, and the GI Bill.

There were other elements at work in the 1980s as well. By the time prospective new pilots were typically over 40 years old and were established in their careers and could meet their financial obligations, time and attitudes had changed dramatically. This generation were in their twenties in the 1960s, the era of the Cold War, the race to the moon, The Beatles, the Great Society, the Vietnam War, hippies, and the antiwar protests. For them, flying was no longer the highest aspiration a young person could have, as it had been in the 1930s. There was no patriotic memory of World War II and the dramatic air battles that were trumpeted every evening on the radio news.

Having come of age in an era when the very foundations of our political and social systems were challenged, they were far less tolerant than previous generations of the hassle factor imposed through militaristic regulation and enforcement by government agencies like the FAA. Economically, they had higher expectations for ownership of consumer goods and services. At a time when their real income, adjusted for inflation, was decreasing, so was competition for their disposable income.

General aviation, which to some degree was characteristic of the attitudes and technology of the 1940s, was simply not able to compete in the marketplace of the 1980s and beyond. By the end of the 1980s, the top sellers in the personal airplane field were no longer the decades-old designs offered by the few light aircraft manufacturers still in the business but, rather, sleek homebuilts that were more attuned to the times.

There were a number of additional challenges that occurred during the 1980s. The nation's air traffic controllers went on strike in August 1981 and were subsequently fired by President Reagan. As a result, the **General Aviation Reservation (GAR) Program** was put into effect for two years. This program put quotas on the number of IFR general aviation flights in each of the nation's ATC centers.

Additionally, changes in ownership occurred at each of the three leading airframe manufacturers. As the calendar turned to 1980, only Piper Aircraft was owned by a conglomerate. All that had changed by the end of 1985. Ironically, at the end of the decade, Piper was the only independently owned company of the big four. Beech and Raytheon Corporation signed a merger deal in 1980. Cessna was acquired by General Dynamics in 1985. France's Euralair—an air charter, executive jet, and cargo operator—bought Mooney in 1984. Piper's owner, Bangor Punta Corporation, was bought by Lear Siegler, which was bought by Forstmann Little & Company. Finally, in 1987 a businessman by the name of M. Stuart Millar purchased the company.

In the mid-1980s, the problems posed by growing costs of insuring newly manufactured aircraft against product liability claims threatened to choke off the nation's supply of new airplanes. The general aviation fleet at large was—and still is—rapidly aging. With $1-million-plus accident settlements now commonplace, each new airplane had to bear the insurance premium burden for all other airplanes. Cessna Aircraft Company's chairman, Russell W. Meyer, Jr., reported in 1985 that 20 to 30 percent of the cost of a new airplane reflected the cost of escalating product liability insurance.

Other financial pressures working against aircraft ownership were also taking place at the same time. The Internal Revenue Service announced a proposal to do away with the 10 percent investment tax credit (ITC) on December 31, 1985, denying prospective owners of aircraft used in business a considerable tax incentive. In a later congressional action (the Tax Reform Act of 1986), the ITC was extended for one year, as long as aircraft purchased by the end of 1986 were put in service before July 1987.

During the 1980s, the manufacturers focused their efforts on turboprops and jets. Among the variety of twin turboprops offered was the Cessna 425 Corsair, later to become the Conquest 1. The 425 is a turboprop version of the 421 Golden Eagle. For operators seeking piston engines, Cessna offered a lower cost version of the pressurized 340A in the Model 335. Cessna also offered its line of Citation business jets. The Citation III was certified in 1982 with a new airframe and supercritical swept wing, becoming Cessna's only medium-sized jet. Cessna also announced a further fuselage stretch to the Citation V.

The booming small-package delivery industry in the 1980s was a benefit to Cessna and the Caravan I, the single-engine turboprop it designed to replace and supplement the workhorse Otters, Beavers, and even smaller Cessna 180s and 206s of earlier decades. Certification was granted in 1984 and a stretched model was certified in 1986.

While production of the larger business aircraft had remained steady for Cessna, sales of single-engine piston aircraft and even the twin turboprops continued to decline in the first half of the decade. In 1986, Cessna announced that it was stopping production of all but the Caravan and Citation models.

Similarly, because of the product liability situation, Beech stopped producing its Sundowner and Sierra light aircraft in the mid-1980s. One single-engine piston aircraft that withstood the test of time is the F33 Bonanza. For a number of years, the Bonanza has been the best-selling single-engine aircraft, though the 1980s saw the last new V-tail V35 Bonanzas. The twin-engine Baron also remained a steady seller.

Like Cessna, Beech felt it needed a machine for its turboprop operators to step up to. In late 1985, it acquired the Mitsubishi Diamond II business jet design from its Japanese builder. While Diamond sales did not live up to expectations for Mitsubishi, Beech turned the Beechjet 400 into a success.

Early in 1988, Beech certified the 1300, a 13-seat commuter airliner version of the King Air B200. Another big hit in the airline industry has been the Beech 1900, a 19-seat commuter aircraft certified in 1983. The Super King Air 300, also a derivative of the B200, was certified in January 1984.

In 1983, Beech contracted with Rutan's Scaled Composites, Incorporated, to build an 85-percent scale model of the airplane called Starship 1. The aviation community watched intently as Beech moved from scaled model to prototype to certification and finally, in June 1988, the first aircraft was delivered at the Paris Air Show.

The Starship not only looked different from other aircraft—with no tail, giant winglets called tip-sails, a movable canard, and pusher engines—but it is also built differently of different material. The airframe was mostly composite. In innovative fashion, manufacturing involved baking the airframe in a high-pressure autoclave.

Mooney Aircraft was also innovative. Most notable is the Mooney PFM. The PFM stands for Porsche Flugmotor, a 217-horsepower derivative of the engine in the Porsche 911 automobile. The engine is housed in a stretched version of the Mooney 252 fuselage with interior appointments given the Porsche touch of class. The panel, too, with many electronic instruments, is different from those of all other Mooneys. The PFM was certified in May 1988, joining the 201, 205, and 252, also introduced in the 1980s. In 1987, Mooney joined French builder Aérospatiale to develop the TBM 700, a single-engine, pressurized turboprop. The first delivery was made in 1990.

The TBM 700 competed for customers in the same class as Piper's most innovative 1980s airplane—the Malibu. Of the general aviation manufacturers, none was the subject of more industry gossip during the 1980s than Piper Aircraft. The rumors of its demise were rampant in the 1980s when it abandoned its Lock Haven, Pennsylvania, plant, which had become synonymous with Piper, and production slowed to a trickle. But within months of Millar's purchase of the company in 1987, he announced that he was putting the venerable Super Cub back into production and that he would also offer the airplane for sale in kit form. At the same time, he announced the Piper Cadet, a stripped-down training version of the Warrior. By the end of 1989, Piper was producing a full line of aircraft from the Cub to the Cheyenne 400 twin turboprop, with the Cheyenne IIIA rapidly becoming the trainer of choice for foreign airlines.

The six-seat Malibu, claimed to be the first cabin-class, pressurized, single-engine aircraft, was certified in 1983 with a 310-horsepower turbocharged Continental engine. The marriage between engine and fuselage was a difficult one, and in 1988 the Continental was replaced with a 350-horsepower Lycoming engine resulting in the Malibu Mirage (Figure 1-16).

While the builders of small aircraft had to seek new niches and markets in order to survive the 1980s, others simply made their big and fast aircraft even bigger and faster. An example is Gulfstream Aerospace. While it too was acquired by a conglomerate (Chrysler Corporation) in the 1980s, it steadily continued to produce and sell large business jets. The Gulfstream IV, a bigger and faster version of the G-III, was certified in 1987.

Figure 1-16. Piper Malibu Mirage. *(Alan Lebeda, commons.wikimedia.org/wiki/File:Piper_PA-46-500TP_Malibu_Meridian_AN1805813.jpg, GFDL 1.2, gnu.org/licenses/old-licenses/fdl-1.2.html)*

Learjet, too, took the same basic fuselage it developed in the 1960s and continued refining it to produce airplanes that appealed to the 1980s buyer. The Learjet 60 was the latest larger variant, while the Learjet 31A has been called an "entry-level jet." The 31, certified in 1988, combines the usual Lear good looks and speed with good handling characteristics.

In sum, the 1980s was a challenging decade, but GA survived and began looking forward to a revitalization in the 1990s. Only time would tell whether the last decade of the twentieth century would be kind to GA.

The 1990s—Revitalization of an Industry

Unfortunately, the anticipated revitalization of the GA industry did not immediately materialize. In fact, GA continued its downward slide into the mid-1990s, reaching a low of 928 aircraft shipments in 1994. However, there were a number of reasons for guarded optimism in the industry. Several ongoing events suggested that general aviation might experience a renaissance. There was a growing realization in the aviation community that general aviation must reinvent itself and create a new demand growth curve, much as it did in the 1950s.

The main reason for this optimism at the time was the industry perception that product liability legislation would hopefully soon be enacted by Congress. The industry felt that passage of this legislation would not only lower its insurance costs but would enable manufacturers to begin to design and produce new technology and more affordable general aviation aircraft.

Fortunately, the amateur-built aircraft market showed steady growth during the early 1990s. Almost 1,000 new amateur-built experimental aircraft received airworthiness certificates, and 2,000 kits were sold by 14 major kit manufacturers in 1992. By 1995, an estimated 23,000 experimental aircraft were included in the general aviation fleet. This represented an increase of roughly 20,900 over the estimated 2,100 in 1970.

The popularity of amateur-built aircraft resulted from several factors, including:

- *Affordability.* Amateur-built aircraft are substantially less expensive than new production aircraft (aircraft produced under a type and production certificate) because of the large amount of labor that the builder provides.
- *Performance.* Many amateur-built aircraft have superior speed, maneuverability, fuel economy, and/or handling characteristics compared to light production aircraft. In many cases, the performance benefits are due to features and technologies not available on used or even most new production aircraft. These benefits include (1) new technology engines, (2) low-drag, natural laminar flow wings and carefully contoured fuselage aerodynamics, and (3) very smooth surfaces held to high tolerances and crafted from advanced composite technologies.

These aircraft represented the test bed for new technologies, which eventually are introduced in the development and manufacture of the next generation of light general aviation production aircraft.

Some kit builders became production companies at the entry level. For instance, **Cirrus Design** began in 1984 as a kit airplane design and manufacturing company in Baraboo, Wisconsin. The company's first airplane, the VK-30, became an inspiration for developing technologically advanced production aircraft. The SR20, with composite construction and advanced aerodynamics, was awarded FAA type certification in 1998. It incorporated flat-panel, multi-function display technology and state-of-the-art safety innovations, including a final level of protection known as the Cirrus Airframe Parachute System (CAPS) (Figure 1-17).

The used aircraft market also remained strong during the early 1990s with almost 36,000 aircraft changing hands in 1992. Additionally, prices for piston aircraft also remained strong, thus reflecting some pent-up demand for these aircraft. The success of the kits and the strength of the used aircraft market showed the creativity and resilience that still existed in the market.

Figure 1-17. Cirrus SR-20 with parachute deployed.
(NASA, public domain)

The international use of general aviation aircraft increased. Based on sample flight-strip data obtained from the North Atlantic oceanic centers, weekly operations of general aviation aircraft increased from 119 in 1983 to 338 in 1991, 293 in 1992, and 396 in 1993. Some of this increase resulted from concerns of business for the safety and security of its traveling employees. However, a large part of it was the result of business adapting to meet expanding global markets and opportunities. The corporate flying market anticipated the new Gulfstream V, capable of flying 7,500 miles nonstop.

Passage of the **General Aviation Revitalization Act (GARA)** of 1994 ushered in a new wave of optimism in the general aviation industry. With some exceptions, GARA imposed an 18-year statute of repose, limiting product liability suits for aircraft having fewer than 20 passenger seats not engaged in scheduled passenger-carrying operations. Cessna immediately announced that it would resume production of single-engine aircraft in 1996. The New Piper Aircraft Corporation was formed, and, in 1995, general aviation aircraft shipments finally increased after a 17-year decline.

In 1997, the optimism so prevalent in the industry since the passage of GARA was evidenced by the release of new products and services, expansion of production facilities, increased student starts, increased aircraft shipments, and record-setting gains in aircraft billings. These conditions suggested continued improvement in the general aviation industry in 1998 and beyond. According to a poll of Aircraft Owners and Pilots Association (AOPA) members conducted in March 1992, only 41 percent said that they were optimistic about the future of general aviation. In response to a similar poll in January 1997, 61 percent responded optimistically, and, by April 1998, the poll of certificated pilots reported that 74.5 percent of its members thought the state of aviation was the same or better than it had been (AOPA 1992–1998). This renewed optimism among the pilot community, aircraft manufacturers, and the industry as a whole could be directly attributed to the strong economy and the passage of GARA in 1994.

In January 1997, Cessna delivered its first new single-engine piston aircraft since 1986. In addition, Lancair International, Diamond Aircraft, and Mooney also produced new piston models. Galaxy Aerospace rolled out its new business jet in the fall of 1996. Aerospatiale and Renault announced plans to join forces to produce light aircraft piston engines for certification in 1999. Piper announced plans to manufacture the Meridian, a single-engine turboprop scheduled for its first flight in 1999 with delivery in 2000.

New manufacturing facilities opened to support expanded production. Cirrus broke ground on two facilities to support production of the SR20. Also, Sabreliner started a large expansion program at their Missouri facility.

In 1999, Cessna announced plans and orders for new Citation models, including the CJ2, Sovereign, and Ultra Encore. Raytheon announced that it would begin deliveries of its Premier I, an entry-level jet that features a composite fuselage with metal wings, in 2000. Mooney delivered its first Eagle in 1999.

Boeing Business Jets announced its plan to build a larger version of its long-range corporate jet, the BBJ-2. Boeing Business Jets, a joint enterprise of Boeing and General Electric, entered the market in 1998 with the long-range BBJ based on a hybrid of the 737-700/800 aircraft. Twenty-eight aircraft were delivered in 1999. Airbus and Fairchild are also marketing business jets that are based on aircraft originally designed for commercial operations.

During the 1990s, **fractional ownership** programs offered by NetJets, Bombardier's Flexjet, Raytheon's Travel Air, Flight Options, and TAG Aviation grew at a rapid pace. From 1993 through the end of 1999, these five major fractional ownership providers increased their fleet size and shareholders at average annual rates above 65 percent. According to AvData, Inc., by the end of 1999, the fractional

Figure 1-18. NetJets website. *(NetJets)*

ownership fleet numbered 329 and shareholders totaled 1,567. Despite this record growth, it is believed that only a small percentage of this market has been developed.

The business aviation community was initially concerned that the success of fractional ownership programs would result in a shutdown of corporate flight departments. These concerns were unfounded. Fractional ownership providers have generally found their business base to be first-time users of corporate aircraft services, users that traditionally utilized commercial air transportation. Once introduced to the benefits of corporate flying, some users of fractional programs found it more cost effective to start their own flight departments instead of incurring the costs of a larger share in a fractional ownership program. As a result, the fractional ownership community may be partially responsible for the increase in traditional flight departments since 1993.

Total aircraft billings in 1999 soared 35.1 percent over 1998, reaching $7.9 billion, and units shipped increased from 2,200 to 2,504, or 12.6 percent. Comparatively, GA aircraft sales in 1999 were quadruple those of 1991. The last year of the decade also marked the first time in GAMA's history that both billings and shipments increased for five consecutive years. It marked the first full year of deliveries of the Cessna 206H Stationair and T206H Turbo Stationair. Deliveries of the composite-construction Cirrus Design SR20 began, and Mooney Aircraft Corporation began production of the Ovation 2, a faster and more fuel-efficient version of the firm's best-selling model, the Ovation.

The biggest jump in 1999 sales revenue, similar to 1998, was in the turbofan aircraft segment. Sales rose 23.9 percent, in large part due to strong incremental growth and fractional ownership programs. Gulfstream Aerospace, for example, experienced almost $2.4 billion in sales, with 70 aircraft deliveries. Cessna's revenues topped $1.8 billion, most of which were Citation sales. Bombardier delivered the first 34 Global Express aircraft into completion. Sales of the 4,000 NM range Challenger 604 remained strong, with 40 deliveries in 1999. The Learjet division also delivered 43 Learjet 45 aircraft. At the end of Bombardier's January 31 fiscal year, its order backlog had climbed to $18.9 million.

According to AvData, the number of corporate flight departments in the United States grew by 6.6 percent in 1999, from 8,236 to 8,778. The National Air Transportation Association reported that charter activity was up by over 20 percent in 1999. The decade closed with across-the-board growth in general aviation activity, corporate flight departments, fractional programs, and charter flights. Revitalization had occurred as hoped for.

This revitalization was partly due to efforts by government, manufacturers, and industry. During the 1990s, there was a growing climate of partnership between the FAA and the general aviation community. The FAA streamlined its certification process for new entry-level aircraft (primary category rule), for example, which should lead to increased production of new light, affordable aircraft.

The **General Aviation Action Plan Coalition** was formed by eleven general aviation organizations to support implementation of the FAA's General Aviation Action Plan. This plan was based on four principles associated with President Clinton's "reinventing government" program. These principles included cutting red tape, putting the customer first, empowering employees, and getting back to basics. Within this framework, the plan set forth several goals relating to general aviation safety and provision of FAA services to general aviation, general aviation product innovation and competitiveness, system access and capacity, and affordability. The goals were:

- Regulatory relief and reduced user costs achieved through reduced rules and processes and implementation of a general aviation parts policy that was consistent with maintaining or increasing safety.
- Improved delivery of FAA services achieved by reducing excess layers of management, decentralization of the decision-making process, and giving the general aviation customers a voice in the development of FAA programs and how services are delivered.
- Elimination of unneeded programs and processes, and investment of FAA resources in those programs that provide the greatest government productivity and responsiveness to its customers' needs.

The FAA continued its efforts to develop common aviation standards. The FAA and the European Joint Aviation Authorities (JAA) established a program in 1991 with the goal of making FAA Federal Aviation Regulations (FARs) and the JAA's Joint Aviation Requirements compatible for smaller aircraft (under 12,500 pounds) seeking type certification. In February 1996, the two organizations developed a new set of "common harmonization patterns" for both U.S. and European small aircraft. These standards apply to new types of aircraft. They are intended to expedite certification and increase safety standards. Under these rules, U.S. manufacturers can use the same standard aircraft design to comply with U.S. regulations as well as those in each JAA member country.

In addition, the FAA continued to expend considerable effort cooperating with aviation authorities in Russia, China, and elsewhere to develop common aviation standards. It was felt that these initiatives, combined with efforts by industry, could tap vast new markets for general aviation products in places where general aviation does not currently exist.

There was also a growing effort to unlock general aviation's transportation potential through product innovation. The FAA and the **National Aeronautics and Space Administration (NASA)** collaborated with the general aviation community to implement a research program aimed at fostering new technologies in general aviation. This program, the **Advanced General Aviation Transport Experiments (AGATE)** consortium, provided a unique partnership between government, industry, and academia that was established to help revive the general aviation industry. The goal of AGATE was to utilize new technology to produce aircraft that are safer, easier to operate, and affordable to today's pilot. The purpose is to make learning to fly less time consuming and less costly. This goal was to be accomplished through employing improved avionics and more crashworthy airframes.

NASA and the FAA also started sponsoring a General Aviation Design Competition for students at U.S. aeronautical and engineering universities in 1994. This competition allowed students to participate in the monumental rebuilding effort of this country's general aviation aircraft sector by attempting to design their own general aviation aircraft in a manner that focuses on current design challenges.

Another example of the programs involving new technology are two contracts signed in September 1996 between NASA and several industry leaders to develop technologies for new intermittent and turbine engines. Under the support of NASA's **General Aviation Propulsion (GAP)** program, two companies were selected to begin three-year design projects for new, smoother, quieter, and more affordable engines. The hope was for NASA, aircraft manufacturers, and supplier industries to work together and share their technical expertise, financial resources, and facilities to demonstrate new general aviation propulsion systems.

Teledyne Continental Motors (TCM) was selected to work with NASA to design a revolutionary intermittent combustion aircraft engine, the CSD 283. One of the goals specified in NASA's General Aviation Propulsion research program was to reduce the complexity of future aircraft engines. CAD (computer-assisted design) and CAM (computer-assisted manufacturing), along with special software, have provided manufacturing processes that have never been used before on piston-powered aircraft engines. TCM's CSD 283 engine is being manufactured using a monoblock process. This means that the case, cylinder walls, and cylinder heads for one-half of the engine are all one piece. The two halves are bolted together after installing the reciprocating parts and actuating gears, and the assembly is finished.

The Aviation Weather Information (AWIN) program was an effort started in the 1990s to put real-time weather information in the cockpit. The FAA Safer Skies Initiative was another effort to improve weather, airspace, and other critical information in graphic and text form for pilots while also reducing the number of fatal air carrier accidents.

The FAA is committed to improving navigation through satellite-based systems such as **Global Positioning System (GPS)** for airport precision approaches. This includes the use of **Wide Area Augmentation System (WAAS)** and **Local Area Augmentation System (LAAS)**. WAAS is designed to provide corrections to GPS signals on a regional or national basis. It consists of a network of ground reference stations, master stations, and a geosynchronous communications satellite, which broadcasts corrections to the GPS signal to aircraft (Figure 1-19). WAAS can support CAT I approaches. The initial 25 WAAS stations were installed in 1998. LAAS consists of a reference station at or near

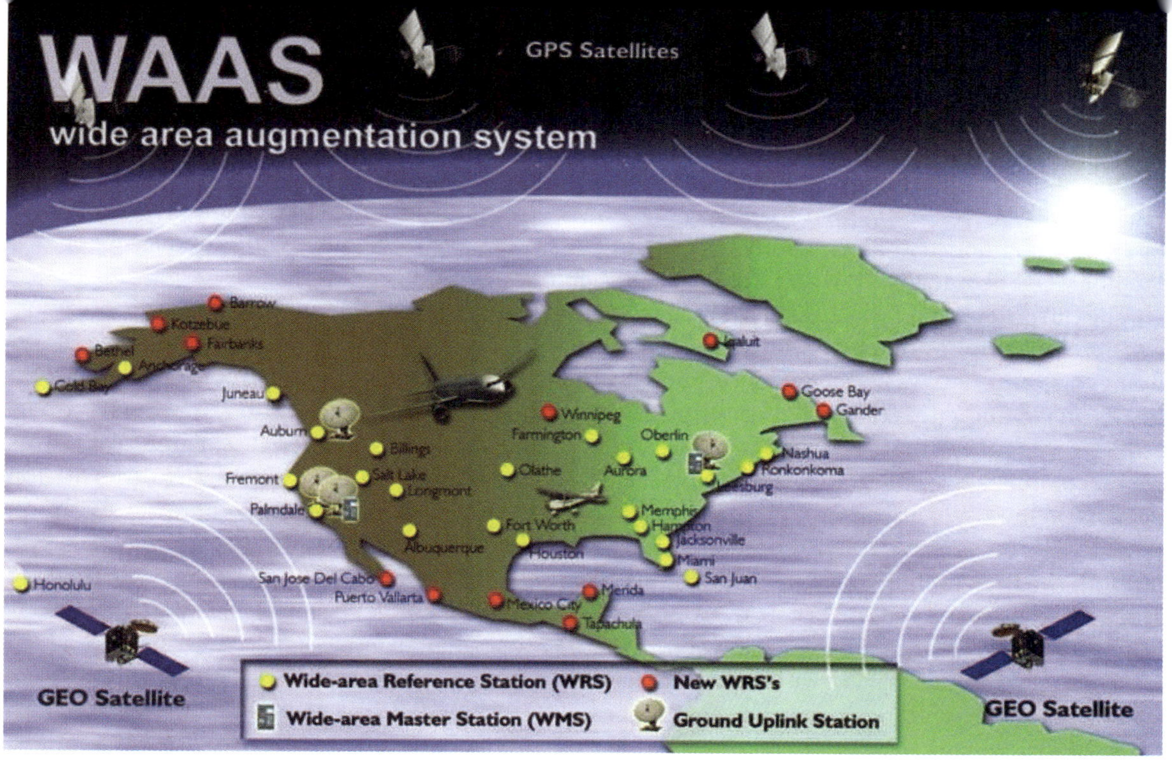

Figure 1-19. Wide Area Augmentation System. *(FAA, public domain)*

an airport and a monitor station that make it possible to measure any GPS errors at that airport. LAAS can support CAT I, II, and III GPS approaches. The FAA began prototype testing of LAAS in 1998. With LAAS and WAAS, advantages are comparable to ILS and the older MLS, yet the signal does not decline as distance from the runway increases.

More recent governmental initiatives include NextGen and SATS. The **Next Generation Air Transportation System (NextGen)** is the FAA's plan to modernize the National Airspace System (NAS) through 2025. Through NextGen, the FAA is addressing the impact of air traffic growth by increasing NAS capacity and efficiency while simultaneously improving safety, environmental impacts, and user access to the NAS.

The **Small Aircraft Transportation System (SATS)** is conceived by the National Aeronautics and Space Administration (NASA) as a safe travel alternative, freeing people and products from existing transportation system delays, by creating access to more communities in less time. The SATS concept of operations uses small aircraft for business and personal transportation for on-demand, point-to-point travel between smaller regional, reliever, general aviation, and other landing facilities, including heliports. The SATS architecture contemplates near-all-weather access to any landing facilities in the U.S.

The general aviation industry launched a series of programs and initiatives during the early 1990s to promote growth. These included the "No Plane, No Gain" campaign sponsored jointly by GAMA and the National Business Aviation Association (NBAA); "Project Pilot" sponsored by AOPA; and the "Learn to Fly" campaign sponsored by the National Air Transportation Association (NATA).

The "No Plane, No Gain" program was directed at the business community and designed to promote the use of general aviation aircraft as an essential tool of business. The thrust of the effort was to show that companies that use GA aircraft in the performance of their day-to-day business are well managed, more efficient, and more profitable than those that do not. The program uses videos, speaker's kits, slide shows, and advocacy materials for distribution among the business community to highlight the benefits of general aviation to business and to the bottom line of a company's balance sheet.

AOPA's Project Pilot encouraged its members to identify individuals who would benefit from special encouragement and assistance in the pursuit of becoming a private pilot. The sponsoring AOPA member then served as a mentor to the student, offering support and assistance to the student during his or her training. AOPA members/mentors were provided with materials designed to help them identify students who would benefit from the program. The participating students were also introduced to the program through a special program kit that included such items as a video on the joy of flying, decals, a special issue of *Pilot* magazine, and AOPA membership information. By year-end 1999, AOPA claimed that, over the course of the program, more than 22,910 members had identified and mentored nearly 33,240 students. Today, AOPA encourages its nearly 400,000 members to become involved as a Project Pilot mentor.

The purpose of NATA's "Learn to Fly" campaign was to increase the number of active GA pilots by increasing the number of student starts and by motivating inactive pilots to return to active flying. The program was designed to promote the benefits of learning to fly. It stimulated the interest of a targeted audience through advertising and promotional efforts. In addition, it provided interested prospects with fast and easy access to information on how to go about learning to fly. This was accomplished through the use of a toll-free telephone number: 1-800-I-CAN-FLY. Information packets were provided through direct mail responses resulting from telephone inquiries, with follow-up calls by participating flight schools in the interested caller's ZIP code area.

Both the Project Pilot and Learn to Fly programs were interested in rekindling the desire to fly of students who had abandoned their training by encouraging them to complete their certification, as well as to convince licensed pilots who stopped flying to return to active status.

Another program started in the mid-1990s to stimulate new interest in learning to fly was the Young Eagles program sponsored by the Experimental Aircraft Association (EAA). This program takes young people ages 12 to 14 on their first flight in a small aircraft, possibly sparking their interest in learning to fly.

Cessna also played a role in these efforts. On July 3, 1996, Cessna dedicated its new 500,000-square-foot final assembly plant in Independence, Kansas. Cessna committed to resume production of selected single-engine piston aircraft models—the 172, the 182, and the 206. It would be the first new single-engine piston Cessna produced since 1986.

Another important industry program known as the Piston Engine Aircraft Revitalization Committee (PEARC) completed its work in 1996. The committee included senior managers and directors from GAMA member companies, aviation organizations, academic institutions, and the FAA. The committee's goal was to find new methods of expansion and growth for the general aviation industry and to review the efforts already undertaken by the industry in order to adopt the best practices. The committee estimated that there were approximately 1.2 million individuals—900,000 men and 300,000 women—interested in flying. According to the committee's findings, 57 percent of the potential pilots were between the ages of 25 and 40. In addition, committee findings indicated that many potential pilots generally overestimate both the time and the cost of learning to fly.

Thus, GA Team 2000 was initiated. This program, started in 1996, was sponsored jointly by AOPA and GAMA and supported by more than 100 industry organizations. The goals of GA Team 2000 were multifaceted:

- To revitalize the influx of new pilots
- To generate flight training leads
- To encourage improvement in flight school marketing and training infrastructure
- To secure additional funding to expand the GA Team 2000 effort

The program encouraged people of all ages to "Stop Dreaming and Start Flying." Renamed the "Be A Pilot" program, it began issuing introductory flight certificates to interested respondents in May 1997. The certificates could be redeemed for a first flight lesson at a cost of $35.

In the first four years of the program, more than 110,000 certificates had been requested. In 2000, there were more than 35,000 requests for certificates. The program had attracted over 3,500 participating flight schools and attracts new market entrants via the internet and cable television advertising.

During the 1990s, the light aircraft manufacturers launched programs to make aircraft ownership easier. The New Piper Aircraft Company created Piper Financial Services (PFS), which offered competitive interest rates for the purchase and/or leasing of Piper aircraft. Cessna accepted refundable deposits for nontransferable position reservations for its new aircraft. The Experimental Aircraft

Association entered into an agreement with TFC Textron (formerly Green Tree Financial Servicing Corporation) to finance kit-built planes. The general aviation industry also sought to increase the number of lending institutions that offered special low, competitive rates for aircraft financing.

The number of fractional ownership programs for general aviation aircraft continued to grow. NetJets (formerly Executive Jet) became the dominant name in fractional ownership. However, manufacturers also joined the movement. They formed their own programs or allied themselves with ongoing programs. Boeing Business Jets and Gulfstream started working relationships with NetJets. Raytheon established Raytheon Travel Air (now Flight Options). Bombardier Aerospace (Flexjet) also entered the competition, along with Dassault Falcon Jets. Fractional ownership also arrived in the rotorcraft market with the entry of the Lynton Group. These programs have greatly increased the accessibility of aircraft ownership for many who could not otherwise afford it (refer to Chapter 11 for more on fractional ownership).

Finally, several industry organizations are also targeting young people through the internet to pique their interest in the world of aviation. The NBAA sponsors "AvKids," a program designed to educate elementary school students about the benefits of business aviation to the community and career opportunities available to them in business aviation. The National Agricultural Aviation Association developed a webpage with information on careers in aerial application. GAMA offers publications, awards, and scholarships to bring education into the nation's classrooms. AOPA created the Apple Program to bring aviation into the classroom, targeting middle and high school students.

2000–2010—The New Security Mindset

As the year 2000 approached, the future of general aviation looked bright as evidenced by the industry's actions to stimulate the development and production of new general aviation products and services. New manufacturing facilities were being built and old facilities were being expanded. Sales of general aviation aircraft were setting new records for value of aircraft shipped. Much of this record sales value was for aircraft at the higher priced end of the general aviation fleet—turbine powered aircraft—and was likely due in part to the increase in fractional ownership. More than 900 turbine aircraft were delivered in 2000 as production capacity soared to keep up with record backlogs in manufacturers' order books. Cessna, for example, doubled the number of Excels it delivered and increased Bravo production by 50 percent. Dassault Falcon Jet deliveries reached 73, five more than in 1999, while its backlog of orders increased. Learjet 45 deliveries were up from 43 in 1999 to 71 in 2000. Even deliveries of the venerable Raytheon Hawker 800 XP increased by 22 percent.

Piston aircraft shipments grew by almost 11 percent, buoyed by an infusion of new technology from Lancair and Cirrus Design as well as increased piston deliveries from Cessna's plant in Independence, Kansas. The year 2000 saw the first deliveries of Lancair's Columbia 300. Cirrus delivered 95 new four-seat SR20 models. Cessna piston singles deliveries increased to 912 units.

In 1996, Williams International began working with NASA to design an ultra-quiet, more efficient turbofan engine with low exhaust emissions, the FJX-2. The Williams FJX-2 is a high-bypass-ratio turbofan engine that produces 700 pounds of thrust yet weighs only 85–100 pounds. Burt Rutan and Scaled Composites built the V-JET II, an all-composite turbofan-powered aircraft, utilizing two of the FJX-2 engines (Minijets, n.d.; Williams International 1997).

In 2001, Cirrus Design's 310-horsepower SR22, capable of flying faster than a Raytheon Bonanza A36 at less than half the price, joined the piston-engine singles market. Cessna's Turbo Skylane went back into production, this time with a fuel-injected Lycoming 540 engine.

The business jet section, though, is where major changes were occurring. The Sino Swearingen SBO-2, having made its first test flight in production configuration in 2000, made its debut as an entry-level fanjet. While having the smallest cabin cross section of any business jet in production, the SBO-2 offered mid-size jet speed and range.

Embraer's Legacy, a derivative of its best-selling EMB-145 regional jet fitted with winglets, made its introduction in two forms: a 19-passenger corporate shuttle and a 12-passenger executive transport. The Legacy Executive, fitted with auxiliary fuel tanks, has extended range and the most cabin volume of any mid-size business jet.

Boeing Business Jets offered its BBJ2 in 2001, a $60 million version of its next generation 737-800 fitted with auxiliary fuel tanks, winglets, and upgraded engines, enabling it to fly 22 passengers from Los Angeles to London.

Everything changed, however, on September 11, 2001, also known as **9/11**. On that day, terrorists used aviation to attack the United States. Two aircraft were flown into the World Trade Center towers in New York City, one aircraft was flown into the Pentagon, and another, possibly en route to the White House, crashed in a field in Shanksville, Pennsylvania, after passengers attempted to thwart the hijackers' plan. In total, 2,996 lives were lost in the attacks.

The aviation industry was severely impacted. All aircraft were initially grounded by the FAA at 9:25 a.m. EDT on September 11, 2001, in an attempt to prevent further attacks. After this pause, the FAA allowed commercial flights to resume again on September 13, 2001. 14 CFR Part 91 IFR operations were once again allowed on September 14, 2001. Agricultural and aerial photo flights were allowed again beginning on September 18, 2001; limited VFR Part 91 operations on September 19, 2001; and most flight training activities on September 22, 2001.

These events, including the prohibition of certain flights for extended periods, created an economy-wide economic slowdown within the aviation industry, with GA specifically bearing the brunt of this impact. Although GA activity was severely curtailed, it did begin a slow recovery.

Meanwhile, two of the most substantial enhancements to GA during the 2000–2010 time period occurred—LSAs and VLJs. **Light-sport aircraft (LSA)** were a new breed of aircraft having a maximum gross weight of 1,320 pounds (1,430 for seaplanes), an unpressurized cabin, a fixed or ground-adjustable propeller, a single, reciprocating engine, fixed landing gear (retractable landing gear for seaplanes), one- or two-person occupancy, maximum stall speed of 45 knots, and maximum speed in level flight with maximum continuous power of 120 knots (Figure 1-20). These aircraft were developed in response to the long-awaited Sport Pilot and Light Sport Aircraft rule, which was implemented in July 2004. GA industry organizations, such as AOPA, lobbied for this new rule for nine years, mainly to provide a means for pilots without current medicals to be able to fly again. As expected, a sport pilot must accrue 20 hours of flight instruction, be at least 17 years of age, have a valid state driver's license, be proficient in the English language, and be able to affirm general good health without use of substances or medications that impede judgment, cognition, or motor skills.

Figure 1-20. Light-sport aircraft. *(B H Conway, commons.wikimedia.org/wiki/File:Skyleader_'GP_One'_light_sport_aircraft.jpg, CC BY-SA 4.0, creativecommons.org/licenses/by-sa/4.0/)*

Very light jets (VLJs) were another new breed of aircraft that may also be known as personal jets or microjets, because they are designed as small jet aircraft that hold few passengers and can fly into smaller airports that are typically closer to the passenger's intended destination (Figure 1-21). These aircraft weigh 10,000 pounds or less maximum certificated takeoff weight, are certificated for single pilot operations, have slower approach speeds than a typical jet, are capable of flight level (FL) 380–450, have a range of 1,000–1,400 miles, and contain advanced flight automation systems (such as moving map GPS and multifunction

Figure 1-21. Very light jet. *(Josh Hallett, DayJet Air Taxi Service, Eclipse 500 VLJ, flickr.com/photos/12734746@N00/545248173/, CC BY-SA 2.0, creativecommons.org/licenses/by-sa/2.0/)*

displays). Current manufacturers include Cessna, Diamond, Eclipse, Embraer, Honda, Spectrum, and Piper. These new jets are expected to change the face of business and personal aviation. They typically cost one-fourth the initial purchase price of a standard corporate jet and have one-third the operating cost. Specifically, VLJ prices range from $1–3 million, with operating costs around $1,700 per flight hour.

These jets have also been adopted by fractional ownership companies and air taxi operators. For instance, DayJet was established in January 2002 and began providing point-to-point, on-demand service utilizing Eclipse 500 VLJs. Although operations ceased in September 2008, DayJet had proven the point-to-point model using VLJs. Although insurance companies were initially concerned about the safety of this new type of aircraft, those concerns no longer exist. Mentor pilot programs were industry's response to this initial concern. With a focus on safety, the mentor pilot allows an experienced pilot to coach less experienced pilots as they transition into VLJs.

Unfortunately, this decade was marred by the Great Recession. Between December 2007 and June 2009, household net worth fell 17.3 percent, unemployment increased to 10 percent, and business across the economy struggled with this economic downturn. Spending on flight training, fuel sales, new GA aircraft, and more were greatly reduced, impacting the fixed-based operator (FBO) business. Fuel prices increased dramatically as crude approached $150 barrel, thus impacting demand for aviation fuel as prices rose accordingly. FBOs certainly did not escape the impacts of the Great Recession.

2011–2020—A Period of Transformation

The second decade of the twenty-first century was characterized by significant transformation. During this decade, numerous advances were made for the industry, possibly none more exciting than electric and urban air mobility, with **eVTOL** (electric vertical take-off and landing) development seen as a game-changer for this segment.

In 2011, the **National Transportation Safety Board (NTSB)** added "general aviation safety" to the agency's "Most Wanted List." This was seen as a significant statement by the NTSB to enhance GA safety, which challenged manufacturers, operators, and regulators. Further reducing GA accident rates and enhancing GA safety should be on the most wanted list of all GA-interested parties.

In 2015, the General Aviation Manufacturers Association (GAMA) established a new associate member category for electric and hybrid propulsion aircraft. This new member category was designed to "better enable the worldwide development, growth, and airworthiness certification of electric and hybrid propulsion technology to benefit the future of general aviation" (GAMA 2015, para. 1). Although this may seem insignificant, it was a recognition by the premier aviation manufacturer's association that electric and hybrid propulsion had entered the mainstream.

In 2016, the **International Civil Aviation Organization (ICAO)** developed the first-ever standard to limit the emission of carbon dioxide (CO_2) from aircraft. The new CO_2 emissions standard would not only be applicable to new aircraft type designs as of 2020 but also to new deliveries of current in-production aircraft types from 2023. The standard acknowledges that CO_2 reductions are achieved through a range of possible technology innovations, whether structural, aerodynamic, or propulsion-based. This renewed interest in sustainable aviation solutions is a positive step forward for the industry.

Normal category aircraft certification rules (14 CFR Part 23) were revised in 2018, allowing aircraft manufacturers to quickly implement new and cost-saving technologies (including improving the capabilities of high-speed, single-pilot airplanes in icing conditions) and more efficient production methods. The revised Part 23 also accelerated the development of electric propulsion and VTOL aircraft (Namowitz 2018). The willingness of the FAA to revise regulations to better meet the needs of industry has been well-received by numerous industry stakeholders.

In 2017, Honeywell issued a forecast for business aircraft that may be termed "slow but steady." The 26th annual Global Business Aviation Outlook indicated a variety of external factors are expected to drive low single-digit growth over the next 10 years, with up to 8,300 new business jet deliveries worth $249 billion from 2017 to 2027 (Honeywell 2017).

Industry continues to be focused on generating interest in aviation among the next generation. In 2019, GAMA released a video highlighting the top ten reasons to work in general aviation. These reasons are:

- It's fun.
- There is no typical day on the job.
- Great pay and benefits.
- It feels like family.
- The cool factor.
- There is room for career growth.
- It is a dynamic, growing industry.
- You can be proud of what you do.
- General aviation needs you!
- Did we mention the pay?

During late 2019 and 2020, the coronavirus **(COVID-19)** pandemic spread around the world and wreaked havoc on the worldwide economy, with the GA industry also suffering. Air travel declined precipitously, with social distancing, facial coverings, and various stay-at-home orders in effect worldwide. Although this downturn in travel did provide opportunity to upgrade and perform maintenance on aircraft, it also provided an opportunity to upgrade facilities and equipment at FBOs. That being said, it was a difficult time to spend money, as revenues were reduced, thus making strict control of budgets a necessity. Further, staffing was challenged as employees who were exposed to COVID were required to quarantine at home for 10–14 days, thus reducing the staff available to perform essential tasks in the workplace. Performing the tasks of several co-workers became the norm for many. Many businesses transitioned to remote work, sending employees home rather than risk employee exposure to COVID. However, some functions of the FBO (fueling, aircraft maintenance, etc.) simply could not be performed from home. Thus, strict protocols had to be adopted by FBOs to enable some essential employees to return to work. Chapter 13 presents greater insight into the COVID effects on FBOs as well as FBO practices during this pandemic.

Effective January 1, 2020, aircraft operating in airspace defined in 14 CFR §91.225 were required to have an Automatic Dependent Surveillance–Broadcast (**ADS-B**) system that includes a certified position source capable of meeting requirements defined in §91.227. ADS-B is part of NextGen and allows aircraft to be tracked using satellite signals, thus improving accuracy, integrity, and reliability for air traffic controllers. This has allowed controllers to reduce the minimum separation distance between aircraft, which has increased capacity in the National Airspace System (NAS).

In 2020, Textron Aviation began production of a new Beechcraft King Air 360 model. The new King Air 360 features a reduced workload for pilots and a more comfortable cabin environment for passengers.

In 2020, Honeywell gained FAA approval for 3D printing of a flight-critical engine part. This is rather innovative, allowing Honeywell to be more responsive to customers in a time-sensitive manner.

In 2020, Bombardier delivered the first Global 7500 aircraft equipped with a dual heads-up display. The technology of advanced GA aircraft continues to improve, greatly reducing pilot workload and enhancing safety.

In 2020, Pipistrel, a Slovenian company, began taking orders for a hybrid electric eVTOL cargo aircraft capable of carrying up to 1,000 pounds over an unspecified distance. This announcement is further evidence of the disruption that eVTOL is having in the industry.

In 2020, Textron Aviation began offering a tank of sustainable aviation fuel (SAF) to customers accepting delivery of new Beechcraft and Cessna turboprops and Citation twinjets. The move toward SAF continues to gather momentum, and Textron Aviation is committed to moving SAF into the mainstream.

Due to the effects of COVID, GA aircraft shipments in 2020 compared to 2019 saw piston airplane deliveries decline 0.9 percent, with 1,312 units; turboprop airplane deliveries decline 15.6 percent, with 443 units; and business jet deliveries decline 20.4 percent, with 644 units. The value of airplane deliveries for 2020 was $20 billion, a decline of approximately 14.8 percent.

2021 Onward—A Period of COVID Recovery

Fortunately, by fall 2022, the recovery from COVID was mostly complete. All states had dropped restrictions on large gatherings and dining indoors. The federal mandate on wearing facial coverings on airline flights was lifted in April 2022. Fortunately, by late November 2022, 79 percent of the U.S. population had received at least one COVID vaccine dose, while 68 percent were full vaccinated. An ever-growing concern for those in the medical community are variants of COVID, such as the Delta and Omicron variants. Commercial air travel had returned in earnest during summer 2021, with the TSA screening record numbers of passengers on June 30 and July 1 in advance of the July 4 weekend. Specifically, more than 2.1 million passengers were screened each of these days, which was even higher than the number screened on these days in 2019 (pre-COVID). TSA reported screening numbers equal to pre-COVID totals for some of the travel days during the 2022 Thanksgiving holiday period (TSA 2022).

By late 2022, it was apparent that the worst of the pandemic was behind us. For the entire aviation industry, GA specifically, the importance of business continuity planning was obvious. Only by planning for future business disruptions can businesses be prepared to maintain operations in the midst of the next crisis.

According to Honeywell's 31st Annual Global Business Aviation Outlook, up to 8,500 new business jet deliveries worth $274 billion are forecast for 2023 to 2032. This is a 15% increase for the same 10-year forecast issued in the 30th Annual Global Business Aviation Outlook. "The business aviation sector is expected to recover to 2019 delivery and expenditures levels by 2023, which is much sooner than previously anticipated" (Honeywell 2022).

Summary

Although the GA industry has experienced ups and downs since the beginning, extensive efforts remain underway to advance GA. These include funding for research and development that is advancing avionics and computer technology for the next generation of technically advanced GA aircraft, and activities to grow the pilot population by promoting flying with "learn to fly" programs, such as the Experimental Aircraft Association's Young Eagles program as well as Girls in Aviation Day by Women in Aviation International. The industry is also developing programs to assist schoolteachers in bringing aviation into the classroom with the hope of encouraging students to pursue careers in the field of aviation.

In the end, GA advances when each of us develop a passion for GA and invest our talents into the industry, even in seemingly small ways. As we give back to the next generation, we can ensure decades of innovation and growth for GA into the future.

Key Terms

9/11. Reference to the terrorist attacks that occurred on U.S. soil on September 11, 2001.

ADS-B. Automatic Dependent Surveillance–Broadcast is a surveillance technology in which an aircraft determines its position via satellite navigation or other sensors and periodically broadcasts it, enabling it to be tracked. The information replaces the need for FAA secondary surveillance radar.

Advanced General Aviation Transport Experiments (AGATE). A consortium that provided a unique partnership between government, industry, and academia established to help revive the general aviation industry. The goal of AGATE was to utilize new technology to produce aircraft that are safer, easier to operate, and affordable. AGATE was founded in 1994 and dissolved in 2001.

Aero Club of America. The first licensing authority of pilots dating back to 1905, when it was initially founded as a social club to promote aviation. This organization had a number of state chapters, such as the Aero Club of New England and the Aero Club of New York, which were quite active in holding local conventions and air meets.

Air Commerce Act of 1926. Legislation that charged the Secretary of Commerce with fostering air commerce, issuing and enforcing air traffic rules, licensing pilots, certifying aircraft, and operating and maintaining aids to air navigation.

Air Mail Act of 1925. Commonly known as the Kelly Act for Congressman Clyde Kelly, it allowed the Post Office to contract with private airlines to establish feeder routes into the national system.

Aircraft Owners and Pilots Association (AOPA). An industry association representing aircraft owners and pilots and actively advocating for general aviation.

barnstormers. Skilled aviators and stunt artists known for entertaining crowds with tricks, such as wing walking and aerobatics, designed to impress people with the skills of pilots and sturdiness of aircraft. Barnstorming became popular in the 1920s.

Beech Aircraft Corporation. GA aircraft manufacturer established in 1932 by Walter H. Beech.

Cessna Aircraft Company. GA aircraft manufacturer established by Clyde Cessna, one of the original founders of Travel Air Manufacturing Company.

Cirrus Design. Began in 1984 as a kit airplane design and manufacturing company in Baraboo, Wisconsin. Today, the company is known as Cirrus Aircraft and has a number of aircraft in production, including the SR20, SR22, SR22T, and Vision Jet.

Civil Pilot Training Program. A flight training program from 1938 to 1944 sponsored by the United States government with the purpose of increasing the number of official pilots.

COVID-19. A contagious disease caused by severe acute respiratory syndrome coronavirus 2 (SARS-CoV-2) that became widely known in early 2020.

E.M. Laird Company. A manufacturer of GA and commercial aircraft, founded in 1923 by Emil Matthew Laird.

eVTOL. An electric vertical takeoff and landing aircraft that uses electric power to hover, take off, and land vertically. This is the newest segment of uncrewed aircraft systems and is playing a critical role in Advanced Air Mobility (AAM).

Federal Aviation Administration (FAA). The largest transportation agency of the U.S. government. It regulates all aspects of civil aviation and is housed in the Department of Transportation.

fractional ownership. A method in which multiple partial owners join a pool and share the cost of purchasing, leasing, and operating aircraft.

General Aviation Manufacturers Association (GAMA). An industry association representing GA aircraft manufacturers.

Gates Flying Circus. A traveling flying circus full of barnstormers. The Gates Flying Circus attracted some of the best stunt pilots and wing-walkers ever to thrill a crowd.

General Aviation Action Plan Coalition. Formed by eleven general aviation organizations to support implementation of the FAA's General Aviation Action Plan.

General Aviation Propulsion (GAP) Program. Under this program, two companies were selected to begin three-year design projects for new, smoother, quieter, and more affordable engines.

General Aviation Reservation (GAR) Program. Initiated after the air traffic controller's strike in 1981 for two years. This program put quotas on the number of IFR general aviation flights in each of the nation's ATC centers.

General Aviation Revitalization Act (GARA). This Act imposed an 18-year statute of repose, limiting product liability suits for aircraft having fewer than 20 passenger seats not engaged in scheduled passenger-carrying operations.

GI Bill. The Servicemen's Readjustment Act of 1944, known as the GI Bill, provided a range of benefits for returning WWII veterans.

Glenn Curtiss. American aviation and motorcycling pioneer, known as the winner of the first international air meet in France in 1909. Designer of the Curtiss *June Bug.*

Global Positioning System (GPS). A satellite-based radio navigation system owned by the United States government and operated by the United States Space Force. Consists of 32 satellites, with 24 active at any one time.

International Civil Aviation Organization (ICAO). A specialized agency of the United Nations with responsibility for developing principles and techniques of international air navigation and fostering the planning and development of international air transport.

Korean War. A war between North Korea and South Korea that began on June 25, 1950, after North Korea invaded South Korea. The United Nations created a UN force to support South Korea, with the U.S. providing 90 percent of the military personnel. Russia and China supported North Korea. The fighting ended on July 27, 1953, when the Korean Armistice Agreement was signed.

Local Area Augmentation System (LAAS). Consists of a reference station at or near an airport and a monitor station that make it possible to measure any GPS errors at that airport. LAAS can support CAT I, II, and III GPS approaches.

light-sport aircraft (LSA). A category of small, lightweight aircraft created by the FAA in 2004. An LSA has a maximum gross weight of 1,320 pounds; maximum stall speed of 45 knots; fixed landing gear; single, reciprocating engine; one- or two-person occupancy; and fixed or adjustable propellor.

Mooney Aircraft Corporation. An aircraft manufacturer established in 1929 by brothers Albert and Arthur Mooney. It produced a number of successful designs, including the Mooney Mite M-18. The company has filed numerous bankruptcies and had a number of different owners, and production was officially halted in November 2019. As 2021, the company had once again been resurrected, although mostly focused on supplying parts for the roughly 7,000 Mooney aircraft that are in service.

National Aeronautics and Space Administration (NASA). An independent agency of the U.S. federal government responsible for the civilian space program as well as aeronautics and space research.

National Business Aviation Association (NBAA). An industry association that represents business aircraft operators. It was founded in 1946 as the Corporate Aircraft Owners Association and was later renamed the National Business Aircraft Association and then the National Business Aviation Association.

Next Generation Air Transportation System (NextGen). The planning and implementation of innovative technologies and airspace procedures to make flying safer, more efficient, and predictable.

National Transportation Safety Board (NTSB). An independent U.S government investigative agency responsible for civil transportation accident investigation.

Piper Aircraft Corporation. An aircraft manufacturing company established by William T. Piper, possibly best known for the Piper Cub.

Reconstruction Finance Corporation. A government corporation administered by the U.S. federal government for the purpose of providing financial support to state and local governments that made loans to banks, railroads, mortgage associations, other businesses.

Small Aircraft Transportation System (SATS). Conceived by NASA as a safe travel alternative, freeing people and products from existing transportation system delays, by creating access to more communities in less time. The SATS concept of operations uses small aircraft for business and personal transportation for on-demand, point-to-point travel between smaller regional, reliever, general aviation, and other landing facilities, including heliports.

Swallow Airplane Manufacturing Company. Founded in 1920 by William Burke, Matthew Laird, and Jacob Moellendick. Famous for biplane designs.

Taylor Aircraft Company. Founded in 1935 by Clarence Taylor, and focused on building easy-to-fly machines at an attractive price. The E-2 Cub was an early design.

Travel Air Manufacturing Company. A GA aircraft manufacturer established in 1925 by Clyde Cessna, Walter Beech, and Lloyd Stearman.

very light jets (VLJs). Entry-level or personal jet typically seating 4–8 people and often with a maximum takeoff weight of under 10,000 pounds.

very high frequency omni-directional range (VOR). Type of short-range radio navigation systems for aircraft, enabling aircraft with a receiving unit to determine its position and stay on course by receiving radio signals transmitted by a network of fixed ground radio beacons.

Weaver Aircraft Company. Founded by George Weaver, Clayton Bruckner, and Elwood Junkin in 1920, it produced a number of Waco biplane designs. In 1923, the name was changed to Advance Aircraft Company after the departure of Weaver.

Wichita, Kansas. Considered the home of general aviation due to the numerous aircraft manufacturing companies historically (and currently) located here.

Wide Area Augmentation System (WAAS). Designed to provide corrections to GPS signals on a regional or national basis. It consists of a network of ground reference stations, master stations, and a geosynchronous communications satellite, which broadcasts corrections to the GPS signal to aircraft. WAAS can support CAT I approaches.

William "Bill" Lear. An American inventor and businessman. Best known for founding the Learjet corporation and developing the first light plane three-axis autopilot in 1950. Interestingly, he invented the 8-track music cartridge.

World War I (WWI). Occurring 1914 to 1918, this First World War involved the Central Powers (Germany, Austria-Hungary, Bulgaria, and the Ottoman Empire) fighting the Allied Powers (Great Britain, France, Russia, Italy, Romania, Japan, and the United States). More than 16 million people died in the conflict.

World War II (WWII). Occurring 1939 to 1945, the Second World War involved most of the world's countries forming two opposing alliances—the Allies and Axis powers. This was the deadliest conflict in human history with 70–85 million fatalities.

Wright brothers. Orville and Wilbur Wright were two American aviation pioneer brothers credited with the first sustained, heavier-than-air, powered flight in an aircraft—the *Wright Flyer*—on December 17, 1903.

Review Questions

1. How did Glenn Curtiss get started in manufacturing aircraft?
2. To what degree did the barnstormers contribute to the development of general aviation?
3. How did Wichita become the home for many of the light GA aircraft manufacturers?

4. What successful aircraft was developed in 1932 that brought the Beech name into prominence?
5. Cessna gained prominence in 1935 with the development of which aircraft?
6. Piper's Cub developed out of which aircraft?
7. Why did the manufacturers have such a feeling of optimism concerning market potential during the post-WWII period?
8. What were some of the developments that took place during the 1950s that helped general aviation grow?
9. Why can it be said that general aviation really matured during the 1960s?
10. Describe some of the new aircraft that were developed during the 1960s, including the first jet designed specifically for the general aviation market.
11. Describe some of the major events during the 1970s that impacted general aviation.
12. What are some of the reasons for the decline in general aviation aircraft sales during the 1980s?
13. Why did Cessna stop production of single-engine training aircraft?
14. Why did the light aircraft manufacturers begin concentrating on turbine aircraft?
15. Discuss the reasons for the downturn in the number of pilots from the late 1970s through the early 1990s.
16. How did the government agencies, manufacturers, and the general aviation community respond to industry challenges?
17. How was the general aviation industry revitalized during the 1990s?
18. What was the purpose of the General Aviation Revitalization Act (GARA) of 1994?
19. Describe the role that fractional ownership has played in revitalizing the industry.
20. What are the advantages and disadvantages of the very light jet category of aircraft?
21. Discuss the highlights of the 2000–2010 period.
22. Why is 2011–2020 considered a period of transformation?
23. In what ways has the industry recovered from COVID impacts?

Scenarios

1. You have been hired as the curator of a local aviation museum. Your goal is to develop a display to present highlights of the GA industry in the 1950s and 1960s. What might you include in this display?
2. You have decided to write a book on the history the GA industry. Provide the title and outline for the first three chapters of this book.
3. Your professor has asked you to develop a teaching tool to teach K–6 students about the history of GA. How might you convey the most interesting aspects of this history to these students?

4. If the news media requested a highlight video of GA since 2000, what might you include in this video?
5. GA aircraft manufacturing relies on flight training activity to stimulate aircraft sales. As owner of an FBO, you are writing a paper on the role of FBOs in stimulating aircraft sales. What might you include in this paper?

Bibliography

AOPA (Aircraft Owners and Pilots Association). 1992–1998. Annual AOPA member surveys.

Cessna Aircraft Company. 1943. "Texas won't be much bigger than Rhode Island." Advertisement. *Flying* 32, no. 1 (January 1943): 2.

Cessna Aircraft Company. 1962. *An Eye to the Sky: Cessna—First Fifty Years, 1991–1961.* Wichita: Cessna Aircraft Company.

Chant, Christopher. 1978. *Aviation: An Illustrated History.* New York: Crescent Books.

Christy, Joe. 1985. *High Adventure: The First 75 Years of Civil Aviation.* Blue Ridge Summit: TAB Books, Inc.

FAA (Federal Aviation Administration), U.S. Department of Transportation. n.d. *FAA Aerospace Forecasts.* Various years. FAA, APO-110. Washington, D.C: U.S. Government Printing Office.

FAA (Federal Aviation Administration). 1970s–1990s. *U.S. Civil Airmen Statistics.* Washington, DC: FAA.

GAMA (General Aviation Manufacturers Association). 2015. "On 45th Anniversary, GAMA Establishes New Associate Member Category for Electric and Hybrid Propulsion Aircraft." Press release, October 26, 2015. https://gama.aero/news-and-events/press-releases/on-45th-anniversary-gama-establishes-new-associate-member-category-for-electric-and-hybrid-propulsion-aircraft/.

Hedrick, Frank E. 1967. *Pageantry of Flight: The Story of Beech Aircraft Corporation.* Wichita: Beech Aircraft Corporation.

Honeywell. 2017. "Honeywell's Business Aviation Forecast Projects 8,300 Deliveries Valued at $249 Billion Through 2027." Press release, October 7, 2017. https://aerospace.honeywell.com/us/en/about-us/press-release/2017/10/honeywells-business-aviation-forecast-projects-8300-deliveries.

Honeywell. 2022. "Honeywell Forecast Shows Strong Growth for Business Aviation as Purchase Plans Increase Sharply." Press release, October 16, 2022. https://www.honeywell.com/us/en/press/2022/10/honeywell-forecast-shows-strong-growth-for-business-aviation-as-purchase-plans-increase-sharply.

Minijets. n.d. "Williams FJX-2." Accessed January 4, 2023. http://minijets.org/en/300-500/williams-fjx-2/.

Namowitz, Dan. 2018. "GA Welcomes 'Pivotal' Aircraft-Manufacturing Reform." AOPA, May 14, 2018. https://www.aopa.org/news-and-media/all-news/2018/may/14/ga-welcomes-pivotal-aircraft-manufacturing-reform.

Piper Aircraft. 2000. *The New Piper Aircraft, Inc.*: A History of the Legendary Company. Vero Beach: The New Piper Aircraft, Inc.

Prather, C. Daniel. 2009. *General Aviation Marketing and Management: Operating, Marketing, and Managing an FBO.* 3rd ed. Malabar, FL: Krieger Publishing Company.

TSA (Transportation Security Administration). 2022. "TSA Checkpoint Travel Numbers." Accessed January 5, 2023. https://www.tsa.gov/travel/passenger-volumes.

Williams International. 1997. "V-JET II." Press release, June 23, 1997. http://www.scaled.com/projects/v-jet_ii.

2

The Scope of General Aviation

In Chapter 2

Objectives

At the end of this chapter, you should be able to:

1. Define "general aviation."
2. Identify the many uses of GA aircraft.
3. Describe the size and scope of general aviation airports in the United States.
4. Discuss the economic role of general aviation airports.
5. Identify the primary FAA services provided to pilots.

6. Discuss the changing size and scope of the airframe manufacturers.
7. Understand the various aviation industry associations.
8. Understand the importance of e-commerce in the marketing and sales process.
9. Realize the value of digital GA.

What Is General Aviation?

In 1848, the English historian Thomas Babington Macaulay postulated that "Of all inventions, the alphabet and the printing press alone excepted, those inventions which abridge distance have done most for the civilization of our species" (Macaulay 1849, 1:370). The role aviation has played in helping America achieve its position of world preeminence can hardly be overstated. In fact, the growth and success of our nation during its 200-year existence have always been closely related to the innovative abilities of its various forms of transportation.

Land, water, and air transportation systems historically have provided the lines of communication and distribution required to unite the nation and foster the development of its commerce. Throughout history, progress has depended upon developing a better transportation system.

Air transportation is a purely twentieth-century phenomenon. It has developed with almost incredible swiftness from scarcely noted experiments on the hills of Kitty Hawk in 1903 to its role today as a vital public necessity that touches the lives of everyone. The Wright brothers' efforts enabled an industry that has made us globally connected.

Today, transportation as an industry, in its many public and private forms, accounts for 8.4 percent of the total gross national product of the United States. Air transportation makes a significant contribution to this total economic impact (BTS, n.d.).

General aviation (GA) refers to all civil aviation activity except that of the certificated airlines and the military. Together, general aviation and the airlines make up America's balanced air transportation system, which is the safest and most efficient aviation network in the world.

Air service in America is available to almost everyone because the airlines and general aviation fulfill separate but compatible transportation roles. The general aviation fleet of some 220,000 active aircraft—including amateur-built aircraft, rotorcraft, balloons, and turbojets—serve all of the nation's almost 20,000 airports, bringing the benefits and mobility of air transportation to virtually everyone, including millions of people who live outside of the metropolitan areas that the airlines serve through some 600 airports.

General aviation is air transportation on-demand. It moves millions of passengers a year and tons of cargo and mail faster and farther than any earthbound mode of transportation—and with almost unlimited flexibility. Statistically, the general aviation fleet represents the vast majority of all civil aircraft registered in the United States.

- General aviation aircraft range from two-seat training aircraft to international business jets.
- More than 90 percent of the roughly 220,000 civil aircraft registered in the United States are general aviation aircraft.
- An estimated 65 percent of general aviation flights are conducted for business and public services that need transportation more flexible than the airlines can offer.
- More than 80 percent of the 609,000 pilots certificated in the United States fly GA aircraft.
- General aviation annually generates more than $150 billion in economic activity, including $39 billion in direct economic output, and creates 7.6 million jobs according to the latest FAA analysis. (AOPA 2019)

Before general aviation became a factor in the nation's transportation system, most factories and distribution centers were located in or near large metropolitan areas. Over time, industrial decentralization located facilities away from major population centers to smaller communities—those communities served by a general aviation airport.

General aviation is a major reason why the map of United States industry is changing perceptibly and constantly. As a result, business flying is one of the largest categories in general aviation. General aviation aircraft are also used for instruction, to fight fires, carry medical patients, perform aerial mapping and pipeline patrol, fertilize crops, enhance law enforcement, and many other functions.

Today's general aviation aircraft, because of advances in technology that provide better speed, range, fuel efficiency, and flexibility, have become integral business tools—to both large and small companies alike. According to the National Business Aviation Association (NBAA), only about 3 percent of the approximately 15,000 business aircraft registered in the United States are operated by large Fortune 500 companies. The remaining 97 percent are operated by smaller organizations, including governments, universities, charitable organizations, and businesses (NBAA 2014).

The Uses of General Aviation Aircraft

The size and diversification of general aviation make it challenging to categorize for statistical purposes. General aviation has no reporting requirements comparable to those of the certificated air carrier industry. Aircraft flown for business during the week may be used for personal transportation on weekends, just as a family car is used. Instructional aircraft may be used for charter (air taxi) service or rented to customers for business or personal use. An air taxi aircraft may also be used for advanced flight instruction or for rental.

The various GA use categories, along with the number of active aircraft and hours flown (2008–2019) are presented in Table 2-1.

Table 2-1. Active Aircraft and Hours Flown per GA Use Category

	Number of active aircraft	% of total active aircraft	Hours flown	% of total hours flown
Personal	141,800	67.2%	7,849,000	30.7%
Business without paid flight crew	15,000	7.1%	1,635,000	6.4%
Business with paid flight crew	11,100	5.3%	2,362,000	9.2%
Instructional	18,000	8.5%	6,417,000	25.0%
Aerial application agriculture	3,100	1.4%	884,000	3.5%
Aerial observation	4,100	1.9%	946,000	3.7%
Aerial application other	1,100	0.5%	176,000	0.7%
External load	300	0.1%	158,000	0.6%
Other work	1,000	0.5%	246,000	0.9%
Sightseeing	1,000	0.5%	141,000	0.5%
Air medical	300	0.1%	66,000	0.2%
Other	5,000	2.4%	921,000	3.6%
TOTAL	**210,983**		**25,566,000**	

Source: FAA 2019.

The number of active aircraft and hours flown per aircraft type are shown in Table 2-2.

Table 2-2. Active Aircraft and Hours Flown per Aircraft Type

Aircraft type	Number of active aircraft	% of total aircraft	Hours flown	% of hours flown
Fixed-wing piston	141,396	67%	14,431,000	56.4%
Fixed-wing turboprop	10,242	4.9%	2,619,000	10.2%
Fixed-wing turbojet	14,888	7.0%	3,926,000	15.3%
Rotorcraft	10,199	4.8%	2,997,000	11.7%
Gliders	1,517	0.7%	71,000	0.3%
Lighter-than-air	2,617	1.2%	64,000	0.2%
Experimental	27,449	13.0%	1,269,000	4.9%
Light Sport	2,675	1.2%	189,000	0.7%
TOTAL	**210,983**		**25,566,000**	

Source: FAA 2019.

There were 210,981 active GA aircraft in 2019 that flew more than 25 million hours. Fixed-wing, piston-engine aircraft dominated the fleet, accounting for 67 percent of the total active fleet and 56.4 percent of total hours flown. Fixed-wing turboprops accounted for 4.9 percent of the fleet and 10.2 percent of total hours flown. Fixed-wing turbojets accounted for 7 percent of the fleet and 15.3 percent of total hours flown. Rotorcraft accounted for 4.8 percent of the fleet and 11.7 percent of the hours flown. From this data, it is apparent that utilization is greater for turboprops, turbojets, and rotorcraft than it is for piston-engine aircraft. Indeed, although piston-engine aircraft are more plentiful, it appears the turboprops, turbojets, and rotorcraft are the workhorses of the GA fleet.

PERSONAL

Figure 2-1. Personal flying. *(Harbucks/Shutterstock.com)*

Personal flying includes any use of an aircraft for personal purposes not associated with a business or profession, and not for hire. A personal aircraft is like a personal car. When the owner (or renter) uses a car or plane for a business trip, it becomes a business automobile or a business aircraft. It does not change its appearance. There is no way for anyone to tell whether a car or an aircraft is being used for business or pleasure just by looking at it. A high-net-worth individual may own a large aircraft for private transportation, with no business use. However, since the majority of privately owned (as distinguished from company-owned or corporate-owned) aircraft are of the light single or light twin-engine variety, it is appropriate to discuss this important segment of the general aviation industry.

Just as automobiles and boats are used for personal transportation and recreation, personal flying is a legitimate use of the sky. Flying is an efficient and effective business tool, but it is also a pleasant recreational vehicle. Many private pilots use their aircraft to visit friends and relatives, attend special events, and reach distant vacation spots.

These aircraft are also flown by doctors, lawyers, accountants, engineers, farmers, and small business owners in the course of conducting their business. Typically, such persons use their aircraft partly for business and partly for pleasure. They differ primarily from the purely business flier with respect to the type of aircraft flown. A much higher proportion of the aircraft they fly are single-engine piston aircraft. Aircraft flown primarily for personal purposes represented two-thirds of the general aviation fleet and 30.7 percent of the total flying hours in 2019 (FAA 2019).

BUSINESS WITH AND WITHOUT PAID FLIGHT CREW

Businesses may use aircraft to further the business (known as **business aviation**) and utilize either a paid or unpaid flight crew. For example, a manager may be a commercial pilot and fly the company airplane to a satellite facility without being paid for his or her flying services. On the other hand, a business may have an in-house flight department with hired flight crew to fly the company aircraft.

Whether utilizing unpaid or paid flight crew, business aviation is an important segment of the GA industry. These two uses of business aircraft represented approximately 12 percent of the active fleet and 15 percent of total hours flown (FAA 2019).

Business aircraft complement airline services in satisfying the nation's business transportation requirements. Although airlines offer transportation to the largest cities and business centers, business aviation specializes in many areas where major airlines cannot satisfy demand. These aircraft provided quick, safe, and reliable transportation whenever and wherever business needs required them, reaching 10 times the number of airports than the airlines.

Business aviation operators use all types of aircraft, including both single- and twin-engine piston-powered airplanes, helicopters, turboprops, and turbojets. Some two-thirds of NBAA member companies operate turbojets, approximately one-third operate turboprops, and about one-eighth use multi-engine piston powered aircraft. Further, 75 percent of companies that use business aircraft own only one aircraft. While most of these aircraft are operated domestically, an increasing number are utilized to expand markets overseas (NBAA 2021).

Figure 2-2. Business aviation. *(Tyler Olson/Shutterstock.com)*

Numerous examples of typical business executive and manager travel schedules demonstrate the advantages of business aircraft over use of the commercial airlines. Because of the proliferation of airline hub and spoke systems since deregulation, flying business aircraft directly between airports has become a big advantage. The monetary-equivalent savings in terms of executives' time—which would otherwise be spent in traveling to and from air carrier airports and in waiting for scheduled air carrier flights, plus hotel expenses, meals, and rental car expenses—loom large on the benefit side of such calculations. Also beneficial are the advantages of flexibility and the ability to work while en route by holding business meetings on the aircraft.

Today's business aircraft are quieter, more efficient, and safer than ever before. Much like the computer, business aircraft are powerful business tools that make a company more profitable by making better use of a company's most valuable assets—time and personnel. According to the NBAA, "Business aviation is essential to tens of thousands of companies of all types and sizes that are trying to compete in a marketplace that demands speed, flexibility, efficiency, and productivity" (NBAA 2014).

INSTRUCTIONAL

The **instructional flying** (or flight instruction) category includes any use of an aircraft for formal instruction, either with the instructor aboard or when the student is flying solo but is carrying out maneuvers according to the instructor's specifications, excluding proficiency flying. It is dominated by instruction leading to the Private Pilot Certificate, and close to 90 percent of the aircraft used for instruction are single-engine. Only 8.5 percent of the active fleet are used for instruction. However, 25 percent of total flight hours are instructional (FAA 2019).

Obtaining a Private Pilot Certificate for business or personal reasons is the primary goal for some students. Others use it as a stepping-stone to an airline or military aviation career. Most people learn to fly through the local FBO. Although not all FBOs offer flight instruction, many do, especially at less busy GA airports. These FBOs have one or more certified flight instructors (CFIs) on staff who provide ground and flight instruction. Many individuals may learn to fly through a local flying club that offers flight training. Such clubs are groups of individuals who own aircraft and rent them to members. They usually offer flight instruction and other flying-related activities to their members. Many vocational and technical schools, colleges, and universities may offer aviation programs that include flight training.

Figure 2-3. Instructional flying. *(Svitlana Hulko/Shutterstock.com)*

Figure 2-4. Aerial application agriculture. *(KDR In-Focus Productions/Shutterstock.com)*

AERIAL APPLICATION AGRICULTURE

Aerial application agriculture includes any use of an aircraft for work that concerns the production of foods, fibers, and timber production and protection. This category primarily includes aircraft that distribute chemicals or seeds in agriculture and reforestation.

The use of aircraft in agriculture is a major factor in the production of cotton, vegetables, and beef (by seeding and fertilizing grazing lands) and in the eradication of pests, such as the fire ant, screw worm, and gypsy moth. Countries such as Japan, Russia, and China are committing a large number of financial resources to developing aerial application of fertilizers to spread seeds in inaccessible locations, to control pests, and to harvest crops.

Aerial applicational agriculture is an expensive business. These specially designed aircraft can cost in excess of several hundred thousand dollars each. Needless to say, the operators, many of whom have fleets of as many as 50 aircraft, are involved in big business, requiring bank loans for equipment renewal, which in turn requires insurance coverage. Farmers then contract with these operators to apply fertilizer or pesticides to their crops.

AERIAL OBSERVATION

Aerial observation includes any aircraft engaged in aerial mapping/photography, surveillance, fish spotting, search and rescue, hunting, highway traffic advisory, ranching, oil and mineral exploration, and criminal pursuit. The aerial view of these areas provide significant benefits compared to traditional ground-based views.

Land-use planners, real estate developers, beach erosion engineers, and businesspeople seeking new industrial sites, as well as city officials and highway designers, are increasingly relying on photographs taken from aircraft in their deliberations. For years now, general aviation aircraft have been used to inspect pipelines and powerlines. These inspections must be made every couple of weeks. The locations of most pipelines and powerlines are remote and hard to reach by land, but general aviation aircraft can fill this vital need economically and efficiently, saving thousands of gallons of fuel and minimizing power outages by discovering undetected leaks or damage to pipelines or powerlines.

Geophysical survey pilots search for new sources of energy using general aviation aircraft. With sophisticated instruments in the aircraft, a general aviation aircraft can locate and identify oil and gas deposits, coal, diamonds, and even water below the earth's surface.

Commercial fishing fleets on both coasts have found that their operations are more productive and profitable when they can be directed to concentrations of fish schooling far from the shore. Hence, light aircraft for that purpose have evolved into making a major contribution to the industry.

Figure 2-5. Aerial observation. *(EB Adventure Photography/ Shutterstock.com)*

The **U.S. Fish and Wildlife Service** retains commercial operators to survey herd and flock movements and to count the size of herds as well as to air-drop food when natural forage is unavailable. Ranchers also use general aviation aircraft to inspect fences, round up strays, and check cattle for possible injuries. Because of the versatility of these aircraft, they can land and make necessary repairs or take care of cattle that may need treatment.

Major metropolitan police departments have found that road patrols by aircraft are highly effective for keeping watch over the flow of traffic during morning and evening rush hours and as an aid in apprehension of lawbreakers. Most police air patrols are performed in aircraft leased from general aviation operators.

Another specialized service usually performed on a contract basis is flying at very low levels along public utility rights-of-way to inspect the integrity of energy lines and check for transformer failures, broken insulators, short circuits, or line breaks. Inspection by air is frequently the only economical means of performing such service.

It should be noted that **uncrewed aircraft systems (UAS)**, or drones, are now providing the same level of observation at much lower cost. UAS have been adapted to many operations once performed by manned aircraft. In fact, experience has shown UAS to be extremely useful in dull, dirty, and dangerous operations. Although UAS have become more popular and have been adapted to a number of missions, including aerial observation, these platforms are generally supplementing manned operations, rather than completely replacing them.

AERIAL APPLICATION (OTHER)

Other aerial services include the use of aircraft for weather modification, firefighting, and insect control. Weather modification includes efforts by ski resorts to create snow and by governmental authorities in arid regions to create rain. Additionally, air-dropping chemicals and fire retardant by aircraft is a major weapon in the control of forest and brush fires. Very large aircraft, such as the McDonnell Douglas DC-10 and Boeing 727, have been retrofitted into tankers for this purpose.

Figure 2-6. Aerial firefighting. *(ShutterLibrary/Shutterstock.com)*

Resort operators have found that spraying light oils and suspensions by aircraft (as distinguished from agricultural use of similar aircraft) has enhanced their business by eliminating the irritations of small flying insects. In addition to the elimination of a nuisance, aerial application of pesticides has been highly effective in controlling and, in many cases, eliminating diseases transmitted by insects, such as malaria.

Cherry orchard farmers in California, Oregon, and Washington state have employed helicopters not so much to apply a chemical but to fly low and slow over the tops of cherry trees, using the helicopter's rotor downwash to blow moisture from the cherries to enable them to dry quickly—cherry drying. Otherwise, rainwater settles near the cherry stems, which can cause expansion and splitting of the fruit as well as mold and mildew. This is of greatest concern in the 3–4 weeks before harvest. This is quite an innovative use of helicopters, but it is heavily relied upon by these cherry farmers.

EXTERNAL LOAD

External load flying includes aircraft operating under 14 CFR Part 133. The majority of aircraft under this category are rotorcraft used for external load operations, such as hoisting heavy loads and hauling logs from remote locations. These heavy-lift helicopters can also transport heavy, expensive drilling equipment, transport wind turbine blades, and lift commercial air-conditioning units on top of high-rise buildings. There are times when external load operations are the only way to complete a task.

Figure 2-7. Helicopter external load. *(Stephen Duncombe/Shutterstock.com)*

OTHER WORK

The "other work" category includes research and development, testing, air shows, air racing, parachuting, towing gliders, and aerial advertising. For example, aerial advertising is a highly specialized—but very lucrative—part of GA. On the basis of "cost per thousand," key words in the advertising business, a towed banner or a message written in smoke over a city will draw a larger audience for less cost than any other form of advertising. A banner towed over a sports stadium or along a hundred miles of crowded beach is seen by more eyes than a similar message carried for the same price in any other communications medium. A message sky-written over Manhattan on a clear day can be seen by 10 million people at one time.

Figure 2-8. Helicopter sightseeing. *(ladyphoto89/Shutterstock.com)*

SIGHTSEEING

Sightseeing flying includes commercial sightseeing conducted under 14 CFR Part 91, whereas air tours are conducted under 14 CFR Part 135. More than one-half of the sightseeing flights are made in lighter-than-air aircraft (i.e., balloons). The majority of air tours are conducted in rotorcraft; for example, helicopter tours of the Grand Canyon, Hawaii, or Alaska glaciers.

AIR MEDICAL

The **air medical** category is dominated by helicopters, which transport ill patients for medical attention or donor organs for transplant. There are times when the American Red Cross needs to transport emergency supplies to disaster victims or transport blood of rare types or in large quantities. The entire medical emergency evacuation process was changed when state and local governments began establishing "medevac" units to respond to critically injured persons, such as those involved in auto accidents. The survival rate in life-threatening injuries has been greatly enhanced when people can be transported quickly to nearby hospitals.

PUBLIC USE

In addition to the standard uses previously discussed, **public-use** aircraft includes owned or leased aircraft operated by federal, state, or local governments. Government aircraft are an essential part of our national air transportation system. These more than 4,000 aircraft, most of which were designed for civilian use, are flown thousands of hours a year on government business, from firefighting and pest control to operations requiring high levels of security, such as prisoner transportation. Public-use aircraft also play a critical role in ensuring timely responses to disasters and emergencies, such as use by the National Transportation Safety Board (NTSB) and FAA.

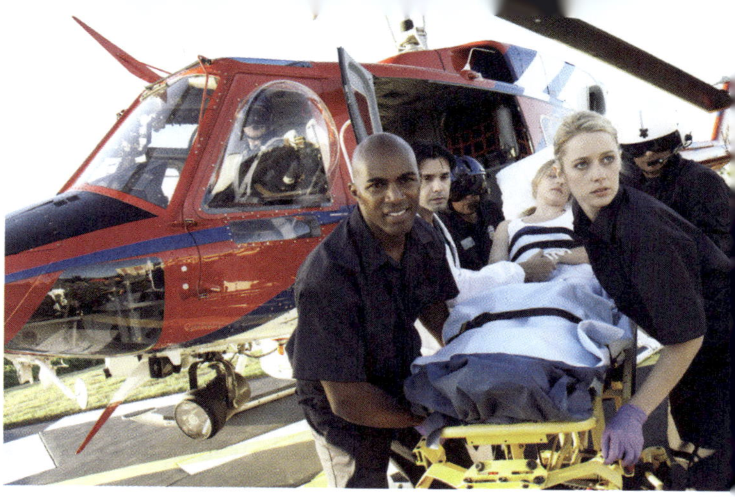

Figure 2-9. Air medical. *(Monkey Business Images/Shutterstock.com)*

Figure 2-10. FAA aircraft. *(FAA)*

Government aircraft are often configured for unique jobs. Some are fitted with firefighting apparatus; others are stripped of all furnishings to accommodate heavy equipment and cargo; and still others are equipped with communications equipment and modified with cameras, radar, or other specialized devices.

Government missions include:

- *Firefighting*—The air dropping of water, chemicals, and fire retardant by aircraft is a major weapon in the control of forest and brush fires, from the pine woods of New Jersey to the Florida Everglades, from the forests of the Big Sky country to the hills of Southern California.
- *Law Enforcement*—Several government agencies use aircraft to patrol borders; locate, chase, and apprehend crime suspects; transport prisoners; and play a major role in drug interdiction.
- *Scientific Research and Development*—Atmospheric research, especially severe weather prediction such as hurricanes, represents a major share of air operations in this category.
- *Flight Inspection*—Flight checking hundreds of navigational aids across the country to ensure safe and accurate readings is accomplished by government aircraft.
- *Surveying*—Aircraft operated by the Department of the Interior agencies, such as Fish and Wildlife Service and Park Service, help to conduct geological surveys such as wetlands mapping and volcano monitoring. Pilots conduct regular and annual wildlife surveys for certain mammals and waterfowl, such as migratory bird surveys.
- *Search and Rescue*—U.S. Coast Guard and other government agencies save many lives every year through search and rescue using aircraft.
- *Drug Interdiction*—To a great degree, the war on drugs is fought in the skies through the work of government pilots. These government pilots, flying air patrol, aircraft escort, and aerial spotting of suspect fields and plantings, help stop the flow of drugs into the U.S.
- *Transport of Government Personnel*—Because of security, timeliness, remote locations, and other reasons, government aircraft are often the only viable transportation choice. Safe and efficient transport of government officials is an important and legitimate use of public-use aircraft.

In summary, GA aircraft save time, lives, and money and provide efficient energy-saving transportation for people in all walks of life who are involved in all different kinds of activities. The ultimate value of general aviation is the flexibility and utility of the aircraft and the pilots. General aviation operates when the air carriers do not, and serve communities not served by air carriers. GA fills a critical gap in the aviation industry.

General Aviation Airports

In a broad sense, all airports are available to general aviation aircraft, even if an airport is designed to be served by certificated air carriers. The **National Plan of Integrated Airport Systems (NPIAS)** is the national airport plan produced by the FAA and updated every two years with a five-year outlook. The NPIAS categorizes airports based on levels of activity (Figure 2-11). Of the 3,304 existing airports included in the NPIAS, 76 percent (2,535) are GA airports (FAA 2020). To be included in the NPIAS, GA airports must meet certain thresholds. First, the GA airport must serve only GA traffic and/or less than 10,000 annual enplanements. Second, the FAA evaluates GA airports and includes those GA airports that are considered integral to the nation's air transportation system. Keep in mind that of the nearly 20,000 landing facilities in the United States (including both private-use and public-use airports, heliports, seaplane bases, ultralight, gliderports, and balloonports), only 3,304 are included in the NPIAS.

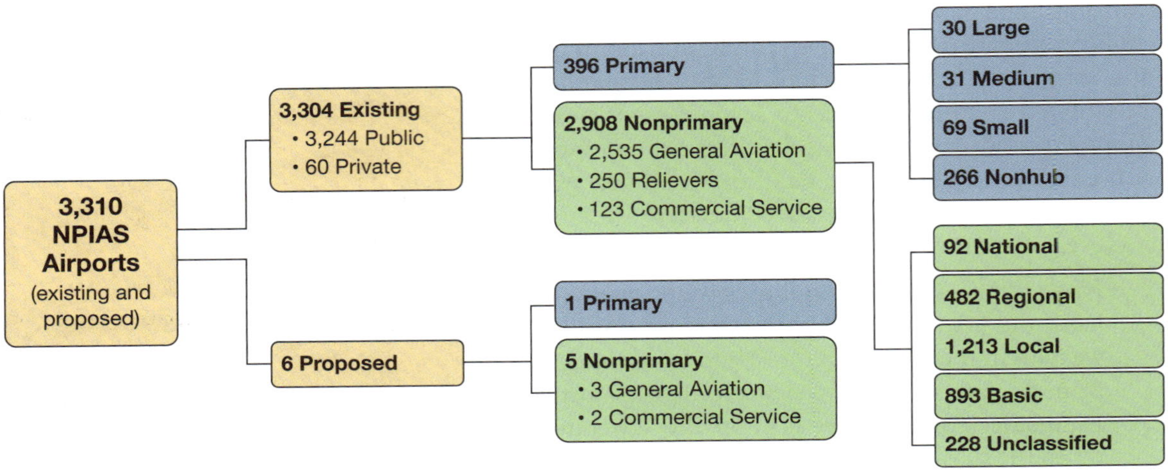

Figure 2-11. NPIAS airports (existing and proposed). *(FAA)*

These GA airports are categorized according to existing activity (e.g., the number and types of based aircraft and volume and types of flights), geographic factors, and public interest functions. GA airport categories include national, regional, local, basic, and unclassified. National GA airports are located in metropolitan areas near major business centers and support flying throughout the United States and the world. Regional airports, also located in metropolitan areas, support regional economies with interstate and some long-distance flying. Local airports are located near larger population centers and provide communities with access to local and regional markets. Local airports also accommodate flight training and emergency services. Basic airports serve communities by providing a means for private GA flying, linking communities with the national airport system, and making other unique contributions. In some cases, the airport is the only way to access the community, and it provides emergency response access, such as emergency medical or firefighting, as well as mail delivery (FAA 2020).

Most public-use airports in the United States are owned and operated by municipalities. GA airports are no exception. An airport owned by a government body can usually be regarded as permanent and stable, particularly if federal funding has been obtained for improving the facilities. Although the majority of airports in the U.S. are private-use, those that are public-use are commonly publicly owned as well.

ECONOMIC ROLE OF GENERAL AVIATION AIRPORTS

General aviation airports play an important role in the transportation network, but this fact is not publicized well. The United States has the finest scheduled air transportation system in the world.

The service points, equipment, personnel, and schedules are as excellent and as much in the public interest as it is humanly, mechanically, and economically possible to make them. This does not alter another fact: that unless the traveler is flying among the major metropolitan areas, many gaps in airline service still exist, including infrequent schedules requiring roundabout routes, time-consuming layovers, and frequent aircraft changes.

Since deregulation, many smaller cities have lost airline service from the major and national carriers, who simply find it uneconomical to serve these points with their jet equipment. Regional air carriers are now serving many of the smaller cities (sometimes subsidized by the **Essential Air Service** program), but voids in service throughout the nation continue to exist.

Thousands of smaller cities, towns, and villages also need air transportation service. There are close to 20,000 incorporated communities in the 48 contiguous states and an additional 15,000 unincorporated communities. Because the scheduled airlines serve less than 4 percent of the nation's 19,916 landing facilities with approximately 7,000 aircraft, many communities are without immediate access to the nation's commercial airline system.

The role of general aviation airports serving 220,000 aircraft, or 96 percent of the total active aircraft in the United States, in providing air access is increasing. By having air access to all the nation's airports, general aviation aircraft can bring the benefits and values of air transportation to the entire country.

Attracting Industry

Cities and towns that years ago decided not to build an airport have learned that lack of an airport jeopardizes community progress. Time and again, the lack of an airport has proven to be the chief reason that a community has been bypassed as a location for a new manufacturing plant or a new industry.

Although scheduled air service is concentrated in major metropolitan areas, business and industry are moving to less populated areas. Shifts in population, lower taxes, room for expansion, less congestion, and better access to highways are some of the factors causing this trend. With geographically diverse production plants, the source of production is nearer the distribution points, but management is farther away from its responsibilities. Without flexible transportation, industry faces the dangers of absentee management both in the widely spread branches and in the home office (because of extended trips).

The general aviation airport has become vital to the growth of business and industry in a community by providing access for companies that must meet the demands of clients, cope with competition, and capitalize on expanding market areas. Communities without general aviation airports place limitations on their capacity for economic growth and generally have a difficult time attracting business and the subsequent job opportunities created.

Flexibility is the key word in business flying—flexibility to go whenever and wherever necessary. The key to flexibility is airport facilities. The shorter the time between the office and the aircraft, the greater the benefits of the business aircraft. This flexibility in reaching destinations serves not only in direct point-to-point travel but also is a factor that has made business aviation one of the most significant suppliers of passengers to the airlines. Business and private aviation supply passengers to major airport terminals. Charter and air taxi services allow passengers to step from a long-distance, wide-body, commercial aircraft into a single-engine or twin-engine air taxi for swift completion of their travel to cities and towns hundreds of miles from airline hubs.

Time equals dollars to business executives who cannot afford the luxury of a long wait between business appointments or the rigidity of public transportation timetables. Between cities with frequent service, this is not a problem. It is easy to go from New York City to Chicago or Atlanta, but it is considerably more difficult to go with equal speed between Peoria, Illinois, and Rochester, Minnesota, or between Decatur, Illinois, and El Dorado, Arkansas.

The competitive nature of today's business and the value of an individual's time prohibits unproductive or uneconomical periods. A person who saves just 30 minutes a day will in one year accumulate 125 hours of productive time—more than three weeks' additional time on the job rather than in transit.

In most large metropolitan areas, business travelers can choose among several general aviation airports that are not available to the scheduled airlines. For example, Atlanta has 12 general aviation airports within a 30-mile radius of the city. One or more of these alternative airports are commonly used by the majority of business aircraft operators in the region and, in most instances, are chosen for their more convenient location to the business office. Such airports typically offer closer and more available parking, more rapid boarding, less airfield congestion, better security, and much shorter walking distances than a major airline terminal.

Stimulating Economic Growth

Airports and related aviation and non-aviation businesses located on the airports represent a major source of employment for many communities around the country. The wages and salaries paid by airport-related businesses can have a significant effect on the local economy by providing the means to purchase goods and services while generating tax revenues, as well. But local payrolls are not the only measure of an airport's economic benefit to the community. Indirectly, the employee expenditures generate successive waves of additional employment and purchases, which are more difficult to measure, but nevertheless substantial.

In addition to the local economic activity generated by the regular expenditures of resident employees, the airport also stimulates the economy through the use of local services for all cargo, food catering, aircraft maintenance, and ground transportation on and around the airport. Regular purchases of fuel, supplies, equipment, and other services from local distributors inject additional income into the local community. The airport retail shops, hotels, and restaurants further act to recycle money within the local community as dollars pass from one person to another, supporting many people and businesses. This beneficial multiplier effect operates in all cities as aviation-related dollars are channeled throughout the community.

Airports provide an additional asset to the general economy by generating billions of dollars per year in state and local taxes. These taxes increase the revenues available for projects and services to benefit the residents of each state and community. Whether the extra tax dollars improve the state highway system, beautify state parks, or help prevent a tax increase, airport-generated tax dollars work for everyone.

Cities with good airport facilities also profit from tourist and convention business. This can represent substantial revenues for hotels, restaurants, retail stores, sports clubs, nightclubs, sightseeing, rental cars, and local transportation, among others. The amount of convention business varies with the size of the city, but even smaller communities show a sizable income from this source.

Beyond the benefits that an airport brings to the community as a transportation facility and as a local industry, airports have become a significant factor in the determination of real estate values in adjacent areas. Land located near airports almost always increases in value as the local economy begins to benefit from the presence of the airport. Land developers consistently seek land near airports, and it follows inexorably that a new airport will inspire extensive construction around it.

Pilots

At the end of 2021, the FAA reported 720,605 active pilots in the United States, including 250,197 student pilots and 161,459 private pilots (FAA 2021). Although the numbers have varied year to year, the number of active pilots in the United States at the end of 2021 was the highest it has been during the previous ten years.

The flexibility of transportation offered by general aviation is not restricted to business use. Flying a light aircraft, a resident of the middle-Atlantic states or the Midwest can visit the warm climate of Florida for the weekend. Air transportation for vacationing is proudly advertised by the air carriers. It should not be overlooked as an aspect of general aviation.

Many pilots who start off as weekend pilots upgrade into high-performance equipment and obtain higher ratings and pilot privileges and eventually become business, as well as pleasure, air travelers in light aircraft. Others start out to obtain their Commercial and Airline Transport Pilot Certificates with the intention of making a career in aviation. Many pilots now flying for the airlines, business aviation, or the military once began in general aviation.

FAA Services to Pilots

Today's sophisticated air navigation network has its roots in the 1920s, when pilots relied on scattered radio stations and rotating light beacons to hop from one landing field to the next. During periods of poor visibility, however, the usefulness of light beacons was severely limited. Eventually, the federal government introduced the first of many navigational aids that could serve pilots day or night, fair weather or foul. This was the four-course radio range, a device that transmitted radio signals in four directions. The government installed a network of these facilities to guide pilots to their destinations.

As aviation grew, more than four paths were needed to handle the navigational needs of air traffic, and the original radio range was replaced by the very high frequency omnidirectional range (VOR), a device developed during World War II. VORs were deployed on the airways in large numbers after the war and became the foundation for Victor airways.

Today, the FAA has transitioned to **performance-based navigation (PBN)**, which is satellite (GPS) based. As a result, the VOR infrastructure is being repurposed to provide a conventional backup NAVAID during GPS outages. This backup infrastructure is known as **VOR MON** (very high frequency omnidirectional range Minimum Operational Network). VOR MON enables aircraft that have lost GPS service to revert to conventional navigation, using VORs and landing at an airport with an established **ILS (instrument landing system)**, **LOC (localizer)**, or **VOR approach**.

In addition to enroute navigation, NAVAIDs also help a pilot descend from cruising altitude to land on an airport runway, even under poor weather conditions. The instrument landing system (ILS) is the most widely used equipment in the world for making safe runway approaches in difficult weather, serving as the mainstay of precision approaches for more than 50 years. An ILS sends out two radio beams to approaching aircraft. One beam, the localizer, gives the pilot left-right guidance; the other, the glide slope, gives the pilot the correct angle of descent to the runway. Even when visibility from the approach end of the runway is only a few hundred feet, properly instrumented aircraft can land with pinpoint accuracy.

The air traffic control system is crucial to civil aviation, keeping airplanes safely separated from each other and regulating their flow into and out of airport terminal areas. Under instrument flight rules, standard separation between two airplanes depends on a number of factors, including the size of the airplanes being separated and the kind of airspace they occupy. Generally, airplanes close to an airport are kept apart by at least three miles horizontally and 1,000 feet vertically. When airplanes are flying between major terminal areas, standard separation is never less than five horizontal miles and 1,000 vertical feet.

Making this system work are the personnel who staff **air traffic control towers (ATCT)**, **terminal radar approach control (TRACON)**, **air route traffic control centers (ARTCC)**, and **automated flight service stations (AFSS)**. Each type of facility performs a different task. Tower and terminal-area controllers handle airplanes that are landing and taking off, taxiing on the ground, and flying in the vicinity of the airport. As of late 2021, 250 contract towers were operating under national contracts with Midwest Air Traffic Control Services, Serco Management Services Inc., and Robinson Aviation (RVA) Inc. (FAA, n.d.). With the exception of the major hubs that serve large metropolitan areas, general aviation airports are the primary users of contract towers.

The busier tower-controlled airports have an additional facility for the safe and expeditious movement of air traffic: radar. Many civil airports have Airport Surveillance Radar that is also available to general aviation pilots who operate in the areas of their coverage. When flying into airports with such equipment, most general aviation pilots use radar assistance because it is available, and in some cases, required.

Another service available to all pilots is the en route air traffic control complex, which consists of 21 air route traffic control centers (ARTCCs). These centers provide radar air traffic separation service to aircraft operating on an instrument flight plan within controlled airspace. No aircraft may be operated when the visibility or ceiling falls below prescribed limits unless they are operated on an instrument flight plan under **instrument flight rules (IFR).** Air carrier category aircraft, particularly those operated by certificated air carriers, operate under instrument flight rules all the time, no matter how good the actual weather may be, as a matter of course. General aviation pilots who are instrument qualified, or instrument "rated," tend to file instrument flight plans only when it is necessary to make a flight in adverse weather.

The most widely used service previously provided by the FAA to general aviation pilots was the Flight Service Station (FSS) network of 75 facilities for collecting and disseminating weather information, filing flight plans, and providing in-flight assistance and aviation advisory services. Although these services remain available to pilots, they are now offered by Leidos on contract to the FAA. This is due mainly to a **Government Accountability Office (GAO)** study in 2001, which revealed escalating costs to maintain the FSS program, the FAA's inability to effectively modernize the FSS computer system, and widespread inefficiencies in the FSS program. As a result, in 2005, Lockheed Martin was awarded a $1.9 billion, 10-year contract by the FAA to provide these flight services to pilots. In 2019, Lockheed Martin Flight Service was renamed Leidos Flight Service. "Flight Services 21" (FS21) refers to Leidos's modernization that retrofitted Leidos facilities and tied them together in a super network sharing a common database where all briefers have access to the same information.

Flight service stations are the sole means for general aviation pilots to file flight plans, which are required under actual instrument conditions and are optional in good weather. They are also the sole source from which to obtain an official weather briefing.

The FSS system is vitally important to general aviation operations, and it is used by pilots of every level, from student pilots to air transport-rated pilots of large business jets. Indeed, flight service is indispensable to all general aviation flight operations.

Airframe Manufacturers

The United States is a powerhouse of GA aircraft manufacturing. Manufacturers include Mooney International, Piper Aircraft, Textron Aviation, Cirrus Aircraft, and Gulfstream Aerospace. In 2020, of the 1,321 piston-engine aircraft produced worldwide, 885 (67 percent) were produced in the United States. Of the 443 turboprops produced worldwide in 2020, 317 (72 percent) were produced in the United States. Of the 1,087 turbine aircraft produced worldwide, 670 (62 percent) were produced in the United States. Additionally, U.S. operators purchased most of the GA aircraft manufactured worldwide. In 2020, 64.7 percent of all GA aircraft manufactured worldwide were delivered to U.S. operators (GAMA 2021).

SIGNIFICANCE OF PILOTS TO AIRCRAFT MANUFACTURING

The significance of pilots to the growth in airframe manufacturing cannot be overstated. Traditionally, the industry has perceived the impact of pilots two ways. First, as new pilots "earn their wings," they may acquire an aircraft. Whether new or used, through a flying club or FBO rental, the new pilot is acquiring use of an aircraft, whether purchased in full or by the hour. Second, manufacturers considered pilots as those who would fly their products for a living with the air carriers, military, corporate, utility, agricultural, air ambulance, state, local or federal government, or other operations.

Thus, as new pilots are created, future aircraft sales are positively impacted. Even in business aviation, manufacturers have recognized that one of the key indicators of aircraft usage or acquisition by a company is the presence of a pilot, even a noncurrent pilot, in the senior management ranks of a company. Thus, the industry is best served when new pilots begin training.

Associations

AIRCRAFT OWNERS AND PILOTS ASSOCIATION (AOPA)

The **Aircraft Owners and Pilots Association (AOPA)** is headquartered in Frederick, Maryland, and has been in existence since 1939. It exists to serve its approximately 400,000 members by protecting and growing "the incredible privilege that we call general aviation." The mission of AOPA "is to ensure that the sky remains within reach of everyone who dreams of becoming a pilot" (AOPA, n.d.[a]). The organization provides extensive resources to benefit general aviation pilots and aircraft owners, including its superb Air Safety Institute, which presents various webinars, podcasts, accident analyses, CFI renewals, and more. For more information about AOPA, see aopa.org.

EXPERIMENTAL AIRCRAFT ASSOCIATION (EAA)

Possibly best known for AirVenture held each summer in Oshkosh, Wisconsin, the **Experimental Aircraft Association (EAA)** was formed in 1953. According to the EAA, this organization "is the only association that offers the fun and camaraderie of participating in the flying, building, and restoring of recreational aircraft with the most passionate community of aviation enthusiasts" (EAA, n.d.[a]). The mission of the EAA is to "grow participation in aviation by promoting the 'Spirit of Aviation'" (EAA, n.d.[b]). Learn more about EAA online at eaa.org.

GENERAL AVIATION MANUFACTURERS ASSOCIATION (GAMA)

Representing the manufacturers of general aviation aircraft, the **General Aviation Manufacturers Association** is considered a trade association. The mission of GAMA is "to foster and advance the general welfare, safety, interests and activities of the global business and general aviation industry. This includes promoting a better understanding of general aviation manufacturing, maintenance, repair, and overhaul and the important role these industry segments play in economic growth and opportunity, and in serving the critical transportation needs of communities, companies and individuals worldwide" (GAMA, n.d.). GAMA was established in 1970 and today represents approximately 115 member companies. For further information, see gama.aero.

HELICOPTER ASSOCIATION INTERNATIONAL (HAI)

Founded in 1948 and headquartered in Alexandria, Virginia, the mission of the **Helicopter Association International (HAI)** is to "Internationally represent all aspects of the Vertical Take-off & Landing (VTOL) industry. Be the leading global voice in promoting safety, community compatibility, professionalism, innovation, and the economic viability of the industry" (HAI, n.d.). The organization currently represents 2,500-plus member organizations in more than 68 nations. For further information, see rotor.org.

NATIONAL AIR TRANSPORTATION ASSOCIATION (NATA)

The industry trade association most appropriate for FBOs is the **National Air Transportation Association (NATA).** Founded in 1940 and headquartered in Washington, DC, NATA represents aviation business service providers to policymakers and the aviation industry at large. NATA provides a number of resources, including the industry-leading Safety 1st program for FBO line service personnel, as well as Safety 1st Clean to advance facility cleaning, disinfecting, and operations best practices in response to the COVID pandemic. For further information, see nata.aero.

NATIONAL BUSINESS AVIATION ASSOCIATION (NBAA)

Headquartered in Washington, DC, the **National Business Aviation Association (NBAA)** was established in 1947. The NBAA represents business aviation operators and the vendors and manufacturers that support this segment of aviation. Approximately 4,300 member companies of NBAA operate aircraft for business purposes, relying on the organization's representation in Washington, DC, as well as the provision of numerous resources, such as the Compensation Survey, GA Desk at the FAA Command Center, and the Certified Aviation Manager (CAM) program. The annual NBAA Business Aviation Convention and Exhibition (BACE) is the fourth largest tradeshow in the United States, regularly attended by 25,000 business aviation professionals. For further information, see nbaa.org.

NATIONAL ASSOCIATION OF FLIGHT INSTRUCTORS (NAFI)

Established in 1967, the **National Association of Flight Instructors (NAFI)** exists for the purpose of "raising and maintaining the professional standing of the flight instructor in the aviation community" (NAFI, n.d.). Headquartered in Portage, Michigan, NAFI serves flight instructor members with a professional development program, Master CFI, MentorLIVE streaming broadcasts, and more. NAFI also stays abreast of FAA actions and proposals, coordinating with the FAA to ensure that flight instructors interests are considered. For further information, see nafinet.org.

NATIONAL AGRICULTURAL AVIATION ASSOCIATION (NAAA)

Established in 1966 and headquartered in Alexandria, Virginia, the **National Agricultural Aviation Association (NAAA)** represents approximately 1,900 members in 46 states. The organization exists to support to "the interests of small business owners and pilots licensed as professional commercial aerial applicators who use aircraft to enhance food, fiber and bio-energy production, protect forestry and control health-threatening pests." NAAA works with its partner organization, the National Agricultural Aviation Research & Education Foundation (NAAREF), to provide research and educational programs focused on enhancing the efficacy, security and safety of aerial application. NAAA is focused on "communicating the importance of aerial application to agriculture, forestry and the public welfare to the public" (NAAA, n.d.). For further information, see agaviation.org.

UNITED STATES PARACHUTE ASSOCIATION (USPA)

Headquartered in Fredericksburg, Virginia, and established in 1946, the **United States Parachute Association (USPA)** has a mission to "promote safe skydiving through training, licensing, and instructor qualification programs; ensure skydiving's rightful place on airports and in the airspace system; and promote competition and record-setting programs." In representing more than 40,000 members, USPA is "committed to promoting an atmosphere that allows our sport to be safe, inclusive and fun" (USPA, n.d.). For further information, see uspa.org.

OTHER ASSOCIATIONS

In addition to those discussed above, following are additional associations focused on different segments of the aviation industry and providing relevant information and resources to their members.

- Aerospace Industries Association (aia-aerospace.org)
- Aircraft Electronics Association (aea.net)
- Air Line Pilots Association (alpa.org)
- Airlines for America (airlines.org)
- Allied Pilots Association (alliedpilots.org)
- American Association of Airport Executives (aaae.org)
- Aviation Insurance Association (aiaweb.org)
- Canadian Business Aviation Association (cbaa-acaa.ca)
- Corporate Aircraft Association (corpaa.us)
- Corporate Angel Network (corpangelnetwork.org)
- European Business Aviation Association (ebaa.org)

- European Regions Airline Association (eraa.org)
- Flight Safety Foundation (flightsafety.org)
- International Business Aviation Council (ibac.org)
- National Air Traffic Controllers Association (natca.org)
- The Ninety-Nines (ninety-nines.org)
- Professional Aviation Maintenance Association (pama.org)
- Regional Airline Association (raa.org)
- Royal Aeronautical Society (aerosociety.com)
- SAE International (sae.org)
- Vertical Flight Society (vtol.org)
- Women in Aviation, International (wiai.org)
- Women in Corporate Aviation (wca-intl.org)

Digital General Aviation

The aviation industry, like most industries, has been affected dramatically by the digital evolution. Prospective customers for various GA products and services often begin with a quick internet search. Some may first turn to social media, such as Instagram, Twitter, or Facebook. Thus, to remain competitive in today's digital world, a digital presence is a necessity. Commonly, this includes a company website as well as some degree of social media presence. Although websites may be somewhat static once developed, a dynamic social media presence requires at least one company employee to be engaged daily on social media

Consider the broker/dealer of pre-owned aircraft. In the past, a handful of experts possessed an advantage simply because they had access to information that others did not. Being the first (and preferably the only) person to know where a certain aircraft type was available meant a competitive advantage, and it was to be protected at all costs. Today, with immediate access to information about pre-owned aircraft available at the click of a mouse, the monopoly on such information has been broken. In fact, information flows so freely that many buyers and sellers today complete a transaction without the assistance of a broker or dealer representative.

The internet has certainly brought about the convergence of information gathering and purchasing decisions. Customers are armed with data before they ever get in touch with the company and hence are more empowered than ever before. A business must learn to grapple with large amounts of fast-changing data and use that information to assist clients. An effective website and social media presence can be used to bridge time and distance to create new levels of customer intimacy.

Those who adopted the internet early (as in the mid-to-late 1990s) took risks and made mistakes from which others can learn. There is now less risk than ever in applying resources to a strong online presence. In some ways, the risks are higher for those few companies who have not implemented a **digital presence** strategy. In other words, effective digital marketing requires a digital presence.

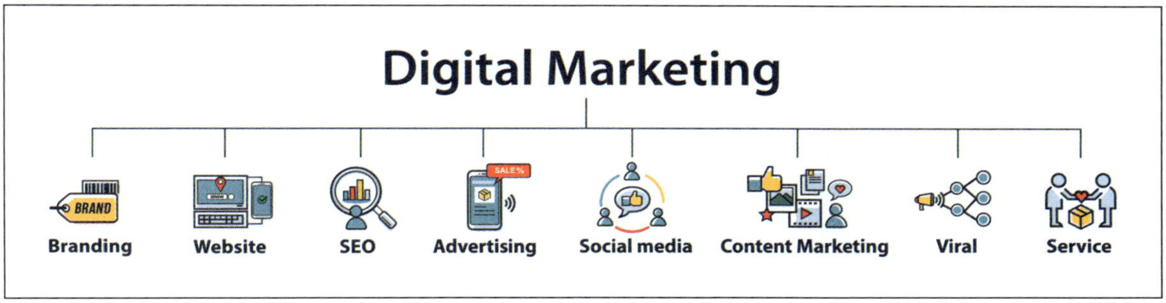

Figure 2-12. Digital marketing and presence. *(buffaloboy/Shutterstock.com)*

The main reason for conducting business online is to increase revenues and reduce transaction costs while enhancing customer engagement. E-commerce, used correctly, can strengthen the relationship between a company and its customers. Amazon, for instance, has proven the effectiveness of e-commerce. Consumers benefit from being able to use their computers or smart devices to enhance the overall buying experience. For example, customers can track the status of orders they have placed, get quick answers to technical questions, swiftly compare prices between multiple vendors, search online catalogs with ease, and solve product warranty issues. With the right interactive programming, an aviation website can be transformed into a sophisticated marketing and sales tool that offers every visitor a highly personalized and responsive experience. An effective social media presence creates higher levels of customer service.

Customers are struggling with the deluge of information they face in making decisions. Unfortunately, the internet has developed a lot of useless, redundant, and even wrong information. It is a company's responsibility to help its clients gain access to the right data and interpret and apply that data intelligently. This is where the true value of the Information Age lies, and smart customers are willing to pay to have access to it.

Gaining an edge today, therefore, will depend on leveraging internet technology and social media platforms to create niches based on a company's particular area of expertise and service delivery. For example, each dealer and broker must stake out a unique place in the new marketplace and stream critical information out to the audience most interested in it. Each FBO must market its services to existing and potential clients in a very tangible way, using multiple channels to do so. In this way, the company will become a valuable resource for clients and will realize tangible benefits through the unique networking opportunities made possible by a connected aviation community.

INTERNET SEARCHES

When conducting research on various aviation industry topics, it will be helpful to utilize an internet search engine. There are numerous companies engaged in airframe manufacturing, aircraft sales, avionics, charter services, aircraft completions, engine manufacturing, financial services, fractional ownership, flight planning, insurance, maintenance, publications, aircraft parts, and training. As companies' website URLs may change, an internet search of product or service areas or specific companies should yield current URLs for websites of interest.

AIRFRAME MANUFACTURERS

Airframe manufacturers face a dilemma when developing a digital presence. On the one hand, a website can be tremendously useful in disseminating information to operators; however, it can also generate a flood of casual queries from the general public as well as sales leads from dubious sources.

Each manufacturer with a website has attacked the problem differently, choosing either to deliver some information along with password-limited access to customer service areas or to simply use the website as a brochure-like publishing and distribution medium.

Websites have tremendous potential for saving manufacturers money by allowing them to distribute the kind of information their customers need. Sites can provide basic product information as well as links to sales and support personnel, including contact phone numbers and e-mail addresses. They can also be used to order parts or download technical information such as service bulletins. Customers who have clicked through online parts catalogs and updated their maintenance manuals over the web recognize that it can be a tremendous time saver. Not only does it save the customer time, but it also allows the manufacturer to devote its resources to other areas.

The greatest potential for aviation web utility is with customer-oriented aircraft manufacturers. Aircraft manufacturing does not stop after the product is delivered. There is a constant need for two-way communication between manufacturers and aircraft owners and operators, and the web is the perfect way to enable that type of dialogue.

AIRCRAFT SALES

In the world of web classifieds, Trade-A-Plane (trade-a-plane.com) is the dominant source. Searches can be performed for aircraft by type, manufacturer, model, location (by state), price, model year, total time, engine time, and keywords. This site also has parts and products, engines, real estate, and various services that are searchable.

Another excellent site is Aircraft Shopper Online (ASO, aso.com), a web-only directory of aircraft for sale, accessible free of charge. Using ASO's search function, visitors can look for airplanes and helicopters by manufacturer, price range, year built, and time on airframe. Links are provided to contact the seller by email or phone, and many listings have photos showing the exterior and interior of aircraft for sale.

Sales of pre-owned aircraft online may not be threatening traditional aircraft sales channels, but dealers and brokers are using it extensively to help develop leads. And for the buyer, the internet is a great place to comparison-shop for pre-owned aircraft.

OTHER AVIATION PRODUCTS, SERVICES, AND RESOURCES

Following are additional categories of providers in the aviation industry that utilize a digital presence to reach and provide support to customers.

- *Associations.* Numerous industry associations serve members in all segments of aviation. These commonly non-profit associations use the internet to provide news and pertinent resources for their members, as well as create a sense of community among members by announcing events and holding webinars online. Each association serves a specific market and typically represents that market to decision makers in the nation's capital.
- *Avionics.* For a glimpse into aviation's future, the avionics manufacturers provide excellent sites for advanced avionics that enable today's technically advanced aircraft. Some of the best websites for taking a look into the future are those maintained by Honeywell and Garmin.
- *Charter reservations.* Because the internet can provide a high level of interaction between buyer and seller, it is often the preferred tool for an array of online charter reservations services. It's possible to check prices and make inquiries online to complete a charter reservation.
- *Completion centers.* Aircraft completion centers are typically relied upon to create customer interior enhancements for business aircraft. Their full range of services are often displayed on their respective company websites.
- *Engine manufacturers.* Engine manufacturers utilize their websites to showcase their ingenuity and the products they offer.
- *FBO chains, fuel suppliers, and cards.* FBOs create websites to not only provide information to current and prospective customers, but an FBO chain can also use its website to highlight the benefits of joining the chain. Fuel suppliers use websites to present the benefits of purchasing their branded fuel.
- *Federal government.* The federal government maintains a number of websites, with some dedicated to aviation. These websites often contain a wealth of information, including quick links to regulations. The FAA website (faa.gov) is frequently visited; however, other agencies, such as the NTSB (ntsb.gov) and ICAO (icao.int) also have robust websites.
- *Financial services.* Financial services firms maintain websites that allow customers to check account information via a secure link, as well as learn about the financial services available. Commonly, financial products may be applied for online.
- *Fractional ownership providers.* Fractional ownership providers maintain websites to both serve existing owners and promote their offerings to prospective owners. Details about each company's fleet and business model can be found via the company's website.
- *Flight planning and weather.* There are excellent resources for professional online assistance for every facet of trip planning. Retrieval of weather information online has become the most

popular use of the web among pilots, either through commercial vendors or no-fee government and university-sponsored sites. Beyond that, it's possible to file flight plans, discover bargains on fuel, order parts, access federal regulations and safety-related information, schedule trips, and locate hotels, rental cars, and restaurants. Helpful sites include 1800wxbrief.com and aviationweather.gov.

- *Insurance.* Aviation insurance websites provide information to current customers, including the ability to check account information and coverage. These websites also serve as marketing portals to inform prospective customers of the range of insurance services offered by a company.
- *Maintenance/modifications.* Companies in the business of aircraft maintenance and modifications provide websites that promote their services.
- *Publications.* Because the internet is such an inexpensive communications medium, accessible by anyone with a computer and internet connection, hundreds of electronic-only (no print counterpart) publications have appeared online. Similarly, all the nation's major newspapers and magazines have launched sites of their own, resulting in a seemingly unending source of news and information available online, 24 hours a day. Aviation print publications have approached the internet in similar fashion, although there is some variation in how much content is delivered online for free versus requiring a subscription to access it. Popular sites include flyingmag.com, aviationweek.com, planeandpilotmag.com, ainonline.com, and avweb.com.
- *Parts suppliers.* There are websites that provide huge parts databases for technicians. One of the best known parts distributors, Boeing (formerly Aviall), provides its customers with full access to its entire inventory online. Users can search by part number to find out if specific parts are available, how much they cost (including discounts), and whether any parts are on back order or have been shipped. Once the desired parts are located, users can order them online.
- *Training.* Flight training organizations mainly use their websites to list course schedules and locations. CAE allows customers to sign up for training on its website (as do many other training organizations). All of CAE's simulators are listed, along with detailed specs for each aircraft type in which training is offered. Guidance on the types of pilot training providers and how to choose a pilot school can be found on the FAA's website at www.faa.gov/training_testing/training/pilot_schools.

Summary

The scope of general aviation is wide and varied. In this segment of the aviation industry, pilots get their start, FBOs service the largest corporate jets, helicopters lift heavy logs from the forest, advanced avionics are installed on small single-engine aircraft, helicopter tours are conducted over the Grand Canyon, cherry trees are dried in Washington state, and much more! GA is dynamic. GA is growing. GA is the future.

Key Terms

aerial application agriculture. Agriculture that includes any use of an aircraft for work that concerns the production of foods, fibers, and timber production and protection. This category primarily includes aircraft that distribute chemicals or seeds in agriculture and reforestation.

aerial observation. Any aircraft engaged in aerial mapping/photography, surveillance, fish spotting, search and rescue, hunting, highway traffic advisory, ranching, oil and mineral exploration, and criminal pursuit.

Aircraft Owners and Pilots Association (AOPA). An industry trade group that advocates on behalf of general aviation.

air medical. Any aircraft that serves medical purposes, such as transporting ill patients for medical attention or donor organs for transplant.

Air Route Traffic Control Center (ARTCC). FAA facility responsible for controlling aircraft flying in airspace of a given flight information region at high altitudes between airport approaches and departures.

air traffic control towers (ATCT). FAA facility (or contract tower) providing control of aircraft on the ground and in controlled airspace, as well as advisory services to aircraft in non-controlled airspace.

automated flight service station. A facility that communicates directly with pilots for pilot briefings, flight plans, inflight advisory services, search and rescue initiation, aircraft emergencies, and NOTAMs.

business aviation. The use of aircraft in the furtherance of a business.

digital presence. The concept of having a presence online, in the form of websites, social media accounts, video platforms, and other electronic, internet-based means.

Essential Air Service (EAS). A federal program that provides subsidies to air carriers to serve specific underserved communities. It dates back to the Airline Deregulation Act of 1978.

Experimental Aircraft Association (EAA). The industry association representing recreational pilots, builders, and restorers. Organizes AirVenture held in Oshkosh, Wisconsin, each summer.

external load flying. Aircraft operating under 14 CFR Part 133. Aircraft under this category are rotorcraft used for external load operations, such as hoisting heavy loads, hauling logs from remote locations, transporting heavy, expensive drilling equipment and wind turbine blades, etc.

fixed-base operator (FBO). A business that is granted the right to operate by an airport to provide commercial aeronautical services such as fueling, hangaring, tie-down and parking, aircraft rental, aircraft maintenance, flight instruction, aircraft sales, and more.

general aviation (GA). All civil aviation operations other than scheduled air services and non-scheduled air transport operations for remuneration or hire.

General Aviation Manufacturers Association (GAMA). An industry trade group that represents the manufacturers of general aviation aircraft and components.

Government Accountability Office (GAO). Legislative branch agency of the United States government that provides auditing, evaluation, and investigative services for the United States Congress.

Helicopter Association International (HAI). The industry association representing the vertical take-off and landing (VTOL) industry.

instructional flying. Flying in which instruction is provided to a student pilot.

instrument flight rules (IFR). Rules and regulations established by the FAA to govern flight under instrument conditions (less than 1,000-foot ceiling and/or visibility less than 3 statute miles).

instrument landing system (ILS). A precision approach aid consisting of a localizer, glide slope, marker beacons or distance measuring equipment, and high-intensity runway lights and approach lights.

localizer (LOC). Provides azimuth guidance to aircraft via radio signal. Generally used as part of ILS approach aids, although a localizer approach may exist.

National Agricultural Aviation Association (NAAA). The industry association representing the interests of small business owners and pilots licensed as professional commercial aerial applicators who use aircraft to enhance food, fiber, and bio-energy production, protect forestry, and control health-threatening pests.

National Air Transportation Association (NATA). The industry association representing aviation business service providers, such as FBOs, to policymakers and the aviation industry at large.

National Association of Flight Instructors (NAFI). The industry association representing flight instructors.

National Business Aviation Association (NBAA). An industry trade group representing companies that use aircraft for business purposes.

National Plan of Integrated Airport Systems (NPIAS). The national airport plan that is produced by the FAA, updated every two years with a five-year outlook.

performance-based navigation (PBN). Comprised of area navigation (RNAV) and required navigation performance (RNP) and describes an aircraft's capability to navigate using performance standards.

personal flying. Any use of an aircraft for personal purposes not associated with a business or profession, and not for hire.

public use. Public-use aircraft include owned or leased aircraft operated by federal, state, or local governments.

sightseeing flying. Commercial sightseeing conducted under 14 CFR Part 91 and air tours conducted under 14 CFR Part 135.

terminal radar approach control (TRACON). FAA facilities that guide aircraft approaching and departing airports.

U.S. Fish and Wildlife Service. A federal agency focused on conserving, protecting, and enhancing fish, wildlife, and plants and their habitats.

uncrewed aircraft systems (UAS). Uncrewed aircraft (drones) and associated systems, including autonomous or human-operated control systems and command and control systems.

United States Parachute Association (USPA). Industry association representing the skydiving industry.

very high frequency omnidirectional range (VOR). A ground-based electronic system that provides azimuth information for high- and low-altitude routes and airport approaches.

VOR approach. A non-precision aircraft approach utilizing the VOR NAVAID to provide horizontal navigation guidance.

VOR Minimum Operational Network (VOR MON). Designed to enable aircraft, having lost GPS service, to revert to conventional navigation procedures, such as VOR.

Review Questions

1. Define "general aviation."
2. What are the primary use categories of GA aircraft?
3. What are some examples of public-use aircraft?
4. Provide several reasons why businesses may use aircraft.
5. Personal flying is primarily for wealthy individuals who want aircraft for recreation. Do you agree? Why?
6. Discuss the importance of instructional flying to the industry.
7. What are some examples of aerial application flying activity?

8. What are the most significant advantages to chartering an aircraft?
9. Describe several uses of helicopters for carrying external loads.
10. Describe the important economic role played by general aviation airports.
11. Why is the growth in the number of student and private pilots so important to the continued health of the general aviation industry?
12. Discuss the types of flight services provided by the FAA (or designated contactor) to pilots.
13. How has the internet positively changed general aviation, from a pilot's perspective?
14. Why is it important for an FBO to have a digital presence?

Scenarios

1. As the chapter president of your local EAA chapter, you have decided to produce a brochure highlighting the benefits of general aviation. What five points will you make in this brochure?
2. As the manager of a small FBO, you are considering acquiring some additional aircraft to support additional uses. Your FBO currently offers only flight instruction and fuel sales. What additional uses of GA aircraft might you consider?
3. In recognition of your experience with social media, the FBO manager has asked you to develop a social media plan. Which platforms might you consider, and how will you plan to engage with current and prospective customers?
4. As the new manager of a GA airport, you would like to make a presentation to the airport board on the economic benefits the GA airport brings to the local community. Discuss, in general terms, the benefits you intend to include in your presentation.
5. As a web developer, you have been asked by a local FBO manager to develop a website for the FBO. Consider all the sections you will include on its website. Discuss these sections and the benefit of including them.

Bibliography

AOPA (Aircraft Owners and Pilots Association). n.d.(a). "About AOPA." Accessed April 19, 2022. https://www.aopa.org/about.

AOPA (Aircraft Owners and Pilots Association). n.d.(b). *General Aviation Explained: The Backbone of America's Aviation System.* https://download.aopa.org/Media/General-Aviation-Explained-r5.pdf.

AOPA (Aircraft Owners and Pilots Association). 2019. *State of General Aviation.* https://download.aopa.org/hr/Report_on_General_Aviation_Trends.pdf.

BTS (Bureau of Transportation Statistics). n.d. "Contribution of Transportation to the Economy: Final Demand Attributed to Transportation." https://data.bts.gov/stories/s/Transportation-Economic-Trends-Contribution-of-Tra/pgc3-e7j9/.

EAA (Experimental Aircraft Association). n.d.(a). "About EAA." Accessed April 19, 2022. https://www.eaa.org/eaa/about-eaa.

EAA (Experimental Aircraft Association). n.d.(b). "Who We Are." Accessed April 19, 2022. https:/v/www.eaa.org/eaa/about-eaa/who-we-are.

FAA (Federal Aviation Administration). n.d. “FAA Contract Tower Program.” Accessed January 10, 2023. https://www.faa.gov/about/office_org/headquarters_offices/ato/service_units/mission_support/faa_contract_tower_program.

FAA (Federal Aviation Administration). 2019. “General Aviation and Part 135 Activity Surveys—CY 2019.” https://www.faa.gov/data_research/aviation_data_statistics/general_aviation/cy2019.

FAA (Federal Aviation Administration). 2020. *National Plan of Integrated Airport Systems (NPIAS) 2021–2025.* September 30, 2020. https://www.faa.gov/sites/faa.gov/files/airports/planning_capacity/npias/current/NPIAS-2021-2025-Narrative.pdf.

FAA (Federal Aviation Administration). 2021. U.S. Civil Airmen Statistics. https://www.faa.gov/data_research/aviation_data_statistics/civil_airmen_statistics.

GAMA (General Aviation Manufacturers Association). n.d. “Who We Are.” Accessed April 21, 2022. https://gama.aero/about-gama/.

GAMA (General Aviation Manufacturers Association). 2021. *General Aviation Aircraft Shipment Report, 2020 Year-End.* Washington, DC: GAMA. https://gama.aero/wp-content/uploads/2020ShipmentReport-05202021.pdf.

HAI (Helicopter Association International). n.d. “The Leading Helicopter Organization.” Accessed April 21, 2022. https://rotor.org/about/our-mission/.

Macaulay, Thomas Babington. 1849. *The History of England.* 5th ed., vol. 1. Quoted in Federal Highway Administration. 2017. “Highway History: The Rambler’s Quote File.” Last modified December 18, 2017. https://www.fhwa.dot.gov/highwayhistory/quotes.cfm.

NAAA (National Agricultural Aviation Association). n.d. “About NAAA.” Accessed April 21, 2022. https://www.agaviation.org/aboutnaaa.

NAFI (National Association of Flight Instructors). n.d. “About NAFI.” Accessed April 21, 2022. https://www.nafinet.org/about.

NBAA (National Business Aviation Association). 2014. *Business Aviation Fact Book.* Washington, DC: NBAA.

NBAA (National Business Aviation Association). 2021. *Business Aviation Fact Book.* Washington, DC: NBAA.

Prather, C. Daniel. 2009. *General Aviation Marketing and Management: Operating, Marketing, and Managing an FBO.* 3rd ed. Malabar, FL: Krieger Publishing Company.

USPA (United States Parachute Association). n.d. "USPA's Values Statement." Accessed May 23, 2023. https://www.uspa.org/about-uspa/what-is-uspa#Values-Mission-185.

3

The Fixed-Base Operator

In Chapter 3

Objectives

At the end of this chapter, you should be able to:

1. Describe the size and scope of the FBO industry.
2. Discuss recent trends affecting FBOs.
3. Choose the correct legal structure for a new FBO.
4. Analyze the market for a new FBO.
5. Select a location for a new FBO.
6. List the basic facilities, equipment, and aircraft needed in establishing an FBO.
7. Discuss the role of airport minimum standards and their impact on an FBO's operation.
8. Discuss some of the advantages and disadvantages of joining an FBO chain.

Introduction

In the early days of aviation, most individuals who made their living by flying went from field to field putting on air shows, giving rides, and providing maintenance services for other operators. These barnstormers, as they became known, did not have a fixed base of operation and were not highly regarded from the standpoint of dependability or business knowledge. Some, however, became successful aviation businesspeople and established airport facilities to base their aviation service operations. These respected, down-to-earth, here-to-stay businesses became known as **fixed-base**

operators (FBOs). Although attempts have been made to re-name FBOs as flight support operations or aviation service businesses, the term FBO is now widely used all over the world. FBOs are called FBOs even in France.

Figure 3-1. FBO terminal building. *(D. Prather)*

Today, fixed-base operators are to the general aviation industry what service stations, repair garages, engine specialists, body and fender shops, paint shops, tire sales outlets, driver training schools, taxicabs, new and used automobile dealers, and auto supply stores are to the automobile industry. By the very nature of the aviation business, all of these services must be concentrated on or close to a designated airport, and usually at one or two locations on an airport, in many cases sharing the airport with air carrier operations and military operations.

Size and Scope of the FBO Industry

Past data indicated that as many as 10,000 FBOs were operating during the late 1970s. By the early 1990s, there were just over 4,000 FBOs. Consolidation and the effects of competition (as well as some airport closures) created this reduction in the number of FBOs. Recently, according to 2020 data from the National Air Transportation Association (NATA), there are currently 3,384 FBOs, 77 percent of which (2,595) sell both aviation gasoline (avgas) and Jet A (NATA 2020). Three-quarters of public-use airports with a 3,000-foot or longer paved runway have only one FBO. NATA defines an FBO as an organization that has a specific lease with an airport-owning entity and offers a minimum of two of the major services provided by FBOs.

In 2022, there were 5,069 public-use landing facilities (including airports, heliports, seaplane bases, ultralight ports, gliderports, and balloon ports) in the United States, of which 517 were certificated under 14 CFR Part 139 to serve air carriers, as well as general aviation. Of the remaining 4,552 airports, which might be called general aviation airports, plus several hundred privately-owned airports open for public use, not all are attended or have service all the time (FAA 2022). Many are attended seasonally (summer resorts, for example), and many are attended only during daylight hours. On the other hand, many offer services 24 hours a day, and many large airports have several FBOs competing for aviation business.

There are four types of FBO ownership, which occur with the following frequency at public-use airports (Kramer 2020):

1. **Publicly owned**—FBOs owned by municipalities, counties, authorities, schools, branches of the military, and other governmental units. These represent 43 percent of all FBOs at public-use airports.
2. **Independents**—Privately owned and independent FBOs. Operate one or two locations. These represent 46 percent of all FBOs at public-use airports.
3. **Small network**—Privately owned FBOs with 3–5 locations, often concentrated in a specific region. These represent 3 percent of all FBOs at public-use airports.
4. **Large network, franchises, and affiliates**—FBOs with more than five locations; each location in a network shares the same brand identity and service standards. These represent 9 percent of all FBOs at public-use airports.

FBOs fall into three major categories, according to size:

1. **Major fixed-base operators.** Major fixed-base operators are located on major commercial-service airports and are fully equipped to handle the servicing and maintenance of all types of aircraft, including large air carrier aircraft used by the airlines and major corporations.

Many of these full-service FBOs have multiplex operations, as do some of the medium-size FBOs, but most major operators have a single base of operations. Their investments run into hundreds of millions of dollars, including leaseholds and equipment. Being part of a chain may portray the image of a major FBO due to nationwide brand awareness, even if the particular location is not that large.

2. **Medium-sized fixed-base operators.** The primary difference between major and medium-sized operations is the amount of investment. Most medium-sized operators are also located at airports where air carriers are served. FBOs must be able (by contract with the lessor) to remove and repair any aircraft that may be expected to use their facilities in the event that such aircraft becomes disabled on the ramps or runways. The investment in a medium-sized FBO may run as high as $50 million, and annual sales volumes may run into multi-million-dollar ranges, principally on aircraft sales, fuel sales, and maintenance.
3. **Small fixed-base operators.** It is estimated that two-thirds of FBOs fall into the small category. Many small FBOs began with minimal investment and may have grown organically from a small aircraft maintenance shop or small flight school. By attracting a loyal following, these businesses are able to expand service offerings to include fueling, hangarage, and tie-downs. In a short time, the specialist becomes a generalist and evolves into a classic multi-service fixed-base operation, with many employees and increased investments in facilities, equipment, and services. Small FBOs may use the cash accounting system, in which receipts are recorded as they are received. A small FBO may or may not have extensive information management systems in place, and small FBO operators may have minimal, if any, business training.

In addition to the three main categories of FBOs, **specialized aviation service operations (SASO)** providers include extremely specialized aviation services but do not qualify as a fixed-base operation. Even so, these businesses are totally involved with and dependent upon general aviation. Examples of these specialized services include aircraft flying clubs, flight training, aircraft airframe and powerplant repair/maintenance, aircraft charter, air taxi or air ambulance, aircraft sales, avionics, instrument or propeller services, and other specialized commercial flight support businesses. Airport sponsors generally do not allow fuel sales alone as a SASO but instead usually require that fuel sales be bundled with other services. These operations are separate from and not competitive with true fixed-base operators at the same airport, but they fall within the category simply because they are located at the same airport. Oftentimes, there is a complimentary relationship between an FBO and the specialized aviation service provider.

General aviation air transportation cannot exist without a nationwide system of fixed-base operators to support it. Not only is the FBO the interface between the manufacturing business and the public, as well as the principal outlet for aircraft sales, but it also typically provides the fueling, routine (and major) maintenance, inspection and relicensing services, storage, and hangars. No one can plan a trip on a general aviation aircraft unless such support facilities, with at least fueling capabilities, are available at both the departure and arrival airports. FBOs fill a critical need for operators.

Recent Trends in the FBO Industry

As previously stated, the FBO industry went through a transitional stage from the early 1980s through the mid-1990s, characterized by mergers and failures. By the mid-1990s, NATA statistics showed a drop in the number of FBOs from a high of more than 10,000 to fewer than 5,000 with dire predictions of "2,000 in 2000" if something did not change (NATA 2017). But something did change. The U.S. economy remained strong during the latter half of the 1990s. The General Aviation Revitalization Act (GARA) was passed; Cessna resumed production of single-engine aircraft; new models entered the market; and fractional ownership served to increase aircraft sales. These factors have led to a stabilization in the FBO industry with the number now between 3,000 and 3,500.

Historically, FBOs have been driven by the rate of new aircraft deliveries. The explosive growth in FBOs and other industry segments during the 1970s was led by new aircraft sales. The contraction in the number of FBOs in the 1980s and early 1990s again reflected the rate of new aircraft sales. Present, but not visible in new aircraft delivery statistics, was a growing trend on the part of airframe manufacturers to seek after-market work such as repair, overhaul, and maintenance including refurbishing, painting, interior, and avionics work. In the past, this work was almost entirely the province of independent FBOs, modification centers, and maintenance facilities. This trend began in the early 1980s as aircraft sales declined and manufacturers looked to other markets to supplement declining revenues and profits.

Complying with the myriad federal, state, and local regulations has also added to the cost structure of many FBOs. Some of these costs include those arising from security requirements, fuel flowage fees, and Superfund. Many FBOs also incur costs in order to conform to Environmental Protection Agency (EPA) underground storage tank regulations. Added to these fees and charges are rising product costs, including large increases in Jet A and 100 low-lead fuels in recent years. Insurance premiums have also begun to rise since the fiercely competitive rates offered during the late 1980s to mid-1990s. These trends may add enough incremental costs to smaller or marginally profitable FBOs that they will fail. The larger FBOs—by their very nature, capital base, and size—are better able to absorb these costs.

The entry of airframe manufacturers has impacted those FBOs that in the past had derived significant income from completions, modifications, maintenance, and parts. New aircraft completions were profitable business, with significant margins available on material content and somewhat lower margins on interior and paint. Now virtually all of the business jet manufacturers have in-house completion capability. At the same time, manufacturers have been able to extend warranty periods due to improved quality. Some manufacturers now offer inclusive, long-term maintenance and parts packages with an aircraft purchase. This further erodes one of the FBO's traditional market opportunities.

Another trend is the move toward corporate self-fueling. Airports are required to permit self-fueling, although fire fuel safety standards must be adhered to and the airport may have additional requirements for self-fueling activities. Self-fueling is becoming more common at airports. Because most FBOs derive the highest percentage of their income from fuel service activities, this trend is very alarming. Corporate self-fueling is justified by corporate operators because it may result in a total fueling cost that is less than 50 percent of the neighboring FBO's retail fuel price. Ironically, that same corporate operator, when a transient, expects their destination FBO to have ground transportation, catering service, fuel trucks, line persons, lounges, telephones, and other services ready 24 hours a day. The host FBO now depends on retail fuel sales to pay for these services even if the transient purchases little or no fuel. These market forces will lead to a diversification of services on a pay-as-you-go basis. The purchase of fuel cannot remain the sole currency of the transient aircraft. This may actually be beneficial for both buyer and seller. A fairly priced menu of services allows the FBO to recognize and deal with the consequences of tankering, self-fueling, and fuel discounting. It also allows customers to buy what they need while not appearing to subsidize other transients.

Establishing an FBO

The simplest form of a fixed-base operator is a flight instructor who owns an airplane and is in business independently. The only reason this person is in business at all is due to enthusiasm about flying. Then, let's say this single flight instructor operation adds satisfied customers, allowing the business to grow and expand. A second aircraft is added and the instructor has the start of a fleet. While the instructor is flying one plane, the other remains on the ground. At this point, another pilot should be hired as a part-time instructor. Even with such simple acquisitions, business is suddenly becoming more complex. Now there is a payroll with tax deductions, additional insurance for the second plane, cost of maintenance of both planes, and hangar or tie-down charges.

The flying business, however, keeps both pilots and planes busy. The instructor begins to think further. By leasing a hangar and hiring a mechanic, the operation could handle its own maintenance and then take in other work for additional income. Soon, in this oversimplification of FBO growth, the enterprise is generating more work for more people and is paying wages that directly or indirectly contribute to the economy of the community.

Another example is the FBO at a major airport with an executive aircraft terminal that is the base for general aviation aircraft, as well as scheduled and charter air carriers. This location may provide phone and online access to weather information, Flight Service briefings, and filing of flight plans. Pilot lounges have high-speed internet, printers, and multi-function fax/copy/scan machines.

The firm has contracts with some scheduled airlines for fueling, cleaning, and supplying turbine-starting equipment to jet-powered aircraft. It operates a helicopter for charter/lease and light aircraft for air taxi. The same operator offers aircraft maintenance, avionics services, and an aircraft interior shop. The owner-manager holds FAA repair station certificates for various categories of large and small aircraft. The operation described here is obviously on a large scale. However, it was developed rather speedily at a time when the airport had decided to expand and upgrade its facilities.

Regardless of whether an FBO starts on a small or a large scale, its success will largely depend on how it plans for the future and responds to changing conditions. As the scope of services offered by the typical fixed-base operator grows, technical aviation knowledge will continue to be important, but this will become secondary to other qualifications needed to manage any successful enterprise. Management will have less direct contact with the aviation activities and more concern with running the FBO and problem-solving activities that accompany the growth of any business.

LEGAL STRUCTURE

The manner in which FBOs can be organized also varies. By selecting the correct legal structure, the owner(s) of the FBO can enjoy tax savings, increase profit, provide for orderly growth of the business, and plan for eventual ownership changes. Although the three main types of organization are discussed below, it is prudent to discuss any business start-up issues with competent attorneys and tax advisors. A business can be organized using one of four main forms: (1) sole proprietorship, (2) partnership, (3) corporation, or (4) LLC.

Sole Proprietorship

The **sole proprietorship** requires an individual who owns and operates the business. In community property states, the spouse also has an ownership interest.

Advantages of a sole proprietorship include:

- Ease of formation and dissolution
- Sole ownership of profits
- Control and decision-making vested in one owner
- Flexibility
- Relative freedom from regulation and special taxation

Disadvantages of a sole proprietorship include:

- Unlimited personal liability for business debts and liabilities
- Unstable business life, solely dependent on the health of the sole owner
- Difficult to acquire capital
- Relative lack of additional expertise and alternative perspectives

Partnership

A **partnership** is an association of two or more individuals for business purposes. In a best effort to avoid the typical conflict associated with numerous partners, it is best to execute a written articles of partnership prior to legally creating the business. These articles will typically address the duration of the agreement, nature of the partners' involvement with the business, how capital and ongoing expenses will be handled, the manner in which losses and profits will be shared, and the manner in which disputes will be settled. It is also recommended that each partner be subjected to an intensive background, credit, and character investigation to minimize any potential problems with this form of organization.

Advantages of a partnership include:

- Relative ease of organization
- Minimum capital required
- More capital available
- Broader management base and continuity

Disadvantages of a partnership include:

- Conflicts between partners
- Less flexibility due to need for agreement among partners
- Unlimited liability, as with sole proprietorship
- Size limitations
- Capital restrictions
- Firm bound by actions of only one partner
- Difficulty of transferring partnership interest

Corporation

The **corporation** has a separate and distinct legal life from its members and is an artificial being existing only in terms of the law. Corporations are typically formed under the authority of state governments. Although the state requirements vary, the formation of a corporation usually begins by filing articles of incorporation with a state's Division of Corporations. Some states are more corporation-friendly; thus, Delta Air Lines is incorporated in the state of Delaware, even though the corporate offices are in Atlanta, Georgia. A company must have a registered agent in each state in which they conduct business.

There are two main options available for forming a corporation. A company may be formed as either a C corporation (C corp) or an S corporation (S corp). These are differences recognized by the Internal Revenue Service (IRS) and allow smaller corporations the opportunity to experience tax advantages by avoiding the double taxation associated with C corporations. Double taxation occurs when corporate net income is taxed and then stock dividends and individual salaries are also taxed. The S corp can avoid this and allow shareholders to offset business losses against other income by forming as a Subchapter S corporation with the IRS. Not all corporations are eligible, however. The corporation must have fewer than 10 shareholders, all of whom are individuals or estates; there must not be nonresident alien shareholders; there must be only one class of outstanding stock; all shareholders must consent to filing as a Subchapter S corp; and a specific portion of the corporation's income must be derived from active business rather than from enumerated passive investments.

Advantages of incorporating include:

- Limitation of the stockholder's liability to the amount invested, with respect to business losses
- Readily transferable ownership
- Separate legal existence, even with the demise of all current owners
- Relative ease of obtaining capital
- Tax advantages
- Permits large size
- Easy expansion

- Delegated authority
- Potentially broad management base

Disadvantages of incorporating include:

- Close government regulation
- Cost and complexity to set up
- Activities limited by charter
- Manipulation of minority stockholders
- Double taxation—once on corporate income and again on individual salaries and stock dividends

LLC

A final form of legal structure is the **LLC**. Although many consider this a Limited Liability Corporation, it actually refers to a Limited Liability Company. It offers limited liability to its owners, is similar to a corporation, and is often a more flexible form of ownership, especially suitable for smaller companies with a limited number of owners. Unlike a regular corporation, a limited liability company with one member may be treated as a disregarded entity by the IRS. A limited liability company with multiple members may choose, generally at the time that the new entity applies for a U.S. federal taxpayer ID number, to be treated for U.S. federal taxation purposes as a partnership, as a C corporation, or (if it is otherwise eligible) as an S corporation. An LLC can elect to be member-managed or manager-managed.

Advantages of an LLC include:

- Much less administrative paperwork and recordkeeping than a corporation.
- Avoid double taxation.
- Limited liability, meaning that the owners of the LLC, called "members," are protected from some liability for acts and debts of the LLC but are still responsible for any debts beyond the fiscal capacity of the entity.
- An LLC can elect to be taxed as a sole proprietor, partnership, S corporation, or C corporation, providing much flexibility.

Disadvantages of an LLC include:

- Many states levy a franchise tax or capital values tax on LLCs for the privilege of that company having limited liability.
- It may be more difficult to raise financial capital for an LLC, as investors may be more comfortable investing funds in the better-understood corporate form with a view toward an eventual IPO.
- The LLC form of organization is relatively new, and as such, some states do not fully treat LLCs in the same manner as corporations for liability purposes.
- The principals of LLCs use many different titles—e.g., member, manager, managing member, managing director, chief executive officer, president, and partner. As such, it can be difficult to determine who actually has the authority to enter into a contract on the LLC's behalf.

ANALYZING THE MARKET AND SELECTING A LOCATION

Once the legal structure is selected, and before deciding upon a location for a fixed-base operation, a study of the potential market is needed. The process of studying the market is called **market analysis.** Information sought in a market analysis for a fixed-base operator (or any kind of business) includes the number of potential customers, where they are located, and what kind and what quantity of business they are likely to bring to the firm.

In studying the potential market, it is necessary to recognize that the aviation industry as a whole has been undergoing tremendous and rapid change. The introduction of very light jets (VLJs), light sport aircraft (LSA), and other innovative technologies have affected the kinds of products and services the flying public has come to expect.

One of the first questions in analyzing the potential market is what the firm has to offer the flying public to meet current demand. In other words, why is another FBO needed? Next, the firm must consider how useful and how popular its offerings will be with the people in the community in which it plans to locate.

Other important market factors to consider are population, weather conditions, income levels, the social and economic nature of the community, ground facilities to support efficient use of the aircraft, industrial developments and trends in the community, agricultural activities, traffic problems, and other ground transportation problems in the area. For example, weather conditions are important to any flight-related business. Is the area subject to snow on the ground for several months during the year? Does it rain steadily for months at a time? Will fog close the airport for long periods? These are important questions that prospective FBO owners must consider. A check with the FAA and National Centers for Environmental Information can determine the prevailing weather and the number of flying days in the past five years, which would indicate the number of business days the FBO can expect during an average weather year.

The Community

The characteristics of the community will greatly affect an operation. Is general aviation an established fixture of the community, or is it still considered a rich person's pastime? Is the airport on established commercial routes? Will there be an opportunity for charter flights to neighboring communities? These and other questions concerning the community should be answered in any complete market analysis.

Activities such as agriculture, aerial survey, and aerial exploration are also covered in a market analysis. Occupations and activities such as these provide increased opportunities for charter operations. On the other hand, if such activities are not carried on to any extent, a firm must determine whether there is enough other business to compensate for this deficiency.

Industrial and business activities constitute another area to be examined in the market analysis. Many businesses use airplanes as a daily part of their operations, while other corporations fly personnel to and from conferences to conserve time. If these business practices do not exist in the location under consideration, it may be a sign that the firm will have to depend upon other sources of revenue.

The market for an FBO is not just one group but consists of many segments, and each requires a separate analysis. Major segments include, but are not limited to, the following list:

1. Business and corporate market
2. Private or pleasure market
3. Agricultural market
4. Government aircraft sales and service market
5. Transient potential
6. Other operations or airline markets

Each of these areas should be thoroughly explored before a location is selected, and regardless of the FBO's size, possible sources of business must be considered regarding their potential. A large percentage of these possibilities should look promising or the chances for success will be slim.

Site Selection

The process of site selection should start with the choice of a geographical area. Having decided on a general area, the next step involves the selection of a specific airport. In making this choice, it is important to survey the competition of other FBOs and find out how well they are doing. A firm must also determine whether to locate on a private or publicly owned field.

In comparison with most other businesses, site selection for a fixed-base operator can be a difficult process because suitable locations are limited. A firm must think in terms of the entire airport and its future development plans. Moving into an existing facility has good and bad points. Choosing an established facility is certainly beneficial, but if the airport master plan calls for relocation of the center of activities, leaving the FBO isolated, the result could be disastrous. Additionally, the firm must consider why the established facility is currently vacant. The location on the airport has a significant effect on business both immediately and in the future. A few key factors include the distance to fueling facilities (if fuel service is not provided by the FBO); distance to the main terminal area (especially if the FBO will not include food services); distance from the nearest competitor (to avoid customer confusion); and ease of access to and from public roads. Consider also that the operator of an airport may not desire or have space for a new FBO.

A firm often must consider whether to buy or rent the facility site. Do financial arrangements make it advisable to own the property, or is it more desirable to lease? The firm must consider whether or not the site is likely to be permanent. Being forced to vacate on short notice could be a great inconvenience. These terms would be negotiated and spelled out in the lease agreement.

Another consideration in deciding whether to buy an existing facility is the matter of who the predecessors were. If a similar fixed-base operation existed, what was its reputation? A firm must consider whether its reputation will be favorably or unfavorably affected by the former tenant.

Getting Assistance

Individuals considering the establishment of an FBO typically need two main forms of assistance: informational and financial. Informational assistance can be obtained from a number of sources including local chambers of commerce, airport boards and local airport advisory committees, the Aircraft Owners and Pilots Association (AOPA), Federal Aviation Administration (FAA), **Internal Revenue Service (IRS),** National Air Transportation Association (NATA), **National Association of State Aviation Officials (NASAO),** and the **Small Business Administration (SBA).**

- Local chambers of commerce typically provide detailed information on the local economy and businesses in the local area.
- The airport governing board and any airport advisory committee and their past meeting minutes will prove helpful in learning more about the airport's business and any concerns that the community voices about the airport and/or businesses operating on the airport.
- AOPA is the main voice for GA aircraft owners and pilots and is a wealth of information on issues affecting the GA industry.
- The FAA and its **advisory circulars (ACs)** associated with issues such as minimum standards, aircraft fueling, and towing will be quite helpful sources of information for individuals starting an FBO (see Appendix B).
- Various services can be rendered by the FAA, including those of the FAA district airport engineer. However, because of the small staff of the airport district offices, its services are usually limited to preliminary discussions and advice and do not include the solution of complex operational problems.
- The Internal Revenue Service has many publications geared toward small businesses, which will assist entrepreneurs with issues such as establishing their legal structure and filing appropriate taxes.
- The National Air Transportation Association is an organization with a heart for corporate aviation. This organization makes available a large number of resources to members and non-members. Most helpful to FBOs is the Safety 1st line service training program.
- NASAO will assist with providing contact information for state aviation officials, which will be specifically knowledgeable on state aviation issues.
- Frequently, it may be necessary to obtain certification for a new FBO from the state aviation office.

- The airport manager or owner will, of course, have valuable information concerning the airport, such as statistics on aircraft movements, plans for future expansion of the facility, and much more information that will directly affect any proposed business.
- Lastly, the Small Business Administration provides a great deal of guidance to those establishing small businesses.

The second, and typically most important, type of assistance needed by those establishing an FBO is financial assistance. This is discussed in detail in Chapter 14, Financial Planning and Control. For now, the reader should understand that debt and equity are the two possible sources of start-up capital. Also known as seed funding, sufficient start-up capital is imperative for the business to have a chance at success. Debt (in the form of loans, bonds, and lines of credit) must be paid back, whereas equity does not. Why wouldn't everyone use equity financing to fund a new business? Equity is oftentimes difficult to secure, but also, the return for investors providing equity capital is a share in the ownership of the business. The individuals establishing an FBO must thoughtfully consider these two forms of financial assistance and make a strategic choice.

FACILITIES

After considering all airport requirements, the firm can narrow its sights to specific facilities for its own operation. While the facilities chosen will largely depend upon the size of the FBO and services offered, there are three categories to consider: aircraft storage areas, customer or public areas, and employee or work areas.

In a small operation, these facilities can easily be grouped together in one multi-purpose structure. Often, a hangar can be converted, by a little simple carpentry, into office space as well as storage and work areas. If the firm is planning a larger operation, it may have several large hangars, 20 or 30 smaller T-hangars, equipment and maintenance hangars, and a separate office building.

Aircraft Storage Areas

A common expectation by pilots is that an FBO will have various aircraft storage options, depending on whether the aircraft will be stored for several hours, days, or longer. Often, the capital costs of providing such options may dictate which options are available. A secondary concern is the specific aircraft storage needs of the primary customer. For example, corporate jet operators appreciate, and may demand, hangar storage, especially for overnight and longer-term storage. On the other hand, piston-engine aircraft customers may be pleased with convenient tie-down spots. There are three main types of storage for aircraft:

1. **Outdoor tie-down.** Is the area adequate for the expected number of aircraft to be based at the airport as well as for transient aircraft? Are the tie-downs spaced properly? Are the parking spaces clearly marked? Can the area be policed and kept clean easily? These are just some of the questions that must be considered regarding this important category.
2. **T-hangars.** This is a type of enclosed structure designed to hold aircraft in storage protected from environmental elements. Aircraft are typically nested in alternating fashion in the least amount of space. There are literally hundreds of designs and types of T-hangars available to meet a particular FBO's needs. Consideration must be given to having an adequate number, placed in locations convenient for customers.

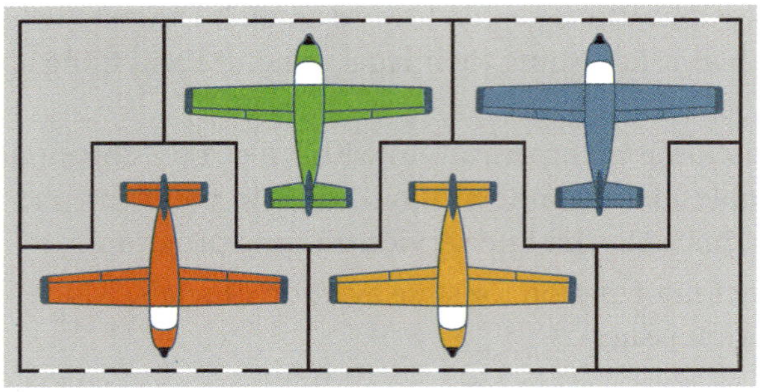

Figure 3-2. Nested T-hangar.

3. **Community hangars.** A community hangar is a large hangar that can hold many aircraft from different owners under one roof. It can also be used as a combination hangar—both for storing aircraft and for maintenance work.

Figure 3-3. Large community hangar. *(BoJack/Shutterstock.com)*

FBO Terminal

These facilities are designed primarily for customer use and should always be kept neat and clean. The first requirement is the reception area, with a place for registration, if necessary, and a pilots' service desk. Next is the pilot ready room, with maps, weather information, and phones and internet. Although it's not necessary for this to be a completely separate room, having a separate room is always an attractive feature. It must be fully equipped and functional from the pilot's standpoint. The exact location of maps, forms, weather information, and assorted pilot aids should be carefully planned. Adequate space must be provided for pilots to spread out sectionals, approach plates, and other items to properly plan a trip.

Other facilities include:

- *Pilot or crew sleeping quarters.* This may be considered a luxury facility, but it is certainly important if the firm expects to attract corporate business.
- *Restrooms.* Clean and modern restroom facilities, including showers and a dressing area with lockers, are a definite plus factor.
- *Waiting lounge.* People are always waiting for other people at any transportation facility, and airports are no exception. Whether traveling by airline or business aircraft, individuals appreciate a comfortable waiting area or lounge.
- *Classroom(s).* Providing classroom(s) is important, especially if offering flight instruction. This facility should be neat and well equipped.
- *Visitors' conference room.* The larger corporate aircraft are essentially flying offices. Conferences and meetings are often held while the plane is en route. For firms using intermediate-size business aircraft or for those firms meeting customers, a conference room can be a real asset. This facility can also be used by the FBO for meetings with employees and customers when it is not scheduled for use by corporate aircraft users.
- *Recreational facilities.* The FBO should consider whether outdoor or indoor recreational facilities would be appropriate for the kind of customer the FBO expects to attract.
- *Display case or room.* Whether it is simply a display case or an entire room devoted to pilot supplies and accessories, this can be a highly profitable area for an FBO.

Employee (or Work) Areas

The principal areas used by employees include:

- *Offices.* As required.
- *Line crew ready room.* This room should have a view of and be easily accessible to the transient aircraft ramp area.
- *Maintenance shops.* This area should include at least one small office for mechanics to order parts, write up job tickets, and talk to customers.
- *Parts and supply storage.* Parts and supplies require adequate shelves for access and inventory purposes. A separate storage area should be provided to place cartons, damaged parts, and other materials that can clutter up the main part of the hangar.
- *Fueling facilities.* Normally, this is one of the easiest of all facilities to plan because of the readily available assistance from the oil companies. The major decision here is whether to have

trucks or a fixed fueling facility. Both have advantages, but this decision largely depends upon the FBO's location on the airport and the airport's minimum standards. Mobile equipment has the advantage of being more flexible in allowing the line personnel to reach aircraft at various locations on the ramp area. Mobile equipment generally enables an FBO to stock a greater variety of octanes or jet fuel, if these are required. On the other hand, the initial cost and maintenance costs of mobile equipment is higher than that of fixed fueling equipment. Moreover, with mobile equipment, there is always the possibility of accidents, for which insurance must be carried. Also, evaporation and stock losses are higher with mobile equipment. For the average FBO, stationary facilities are dependable and economical to install and also require less personnel to operate.

- *Wash ramp.* A specific site with good drainage should be provided for washing aircraft. The size of the area largely depends upon the expected size of the aircraft to be washed and specific airport environmental requirements.
- *Vehicle storage areas.* Gasoline trucks, courtesy cars, and even scooters can get in the way and cause accidents unless they are parked in a designated area.
- *Employee showers and locker room.* This may seem like a luxury facility, but it is found at many successful FBOs and greatly enhances employee relations.

EQUIPMENT

The equipment needed is related to the services provided. Necessary equipment may include:

- *Fueling trucks.* The number of trucks and type of fuel required will depend entirely on the nature and volume of business expected. Typically, a minimum of one avgas and one Jet A truck would be expected.
- *Other vehicles.* These include courtesy cars, utility trucks, scooters, and trailers or carts.
- *Housekeeping needs.* Buckets, mops, brooms, carpentry tools, ladders, rags, and dust equipment fall into this category.
- *Shop tools.* The type of aircraft to be worked on will determine the shop tooling needs. Appropriate cabinets and hanging devices for storing tools must also be considered.
- *Supplies.* This area includes those items intended for resale as well as operating supplies used exclusively by the FBO.
- *Office equipment.* This includes desks, chairs, computers, file and storage cabinets, copying equipment, and desk supplies.

AIRCRAFT

Certainly one of the most important areas to consider is the type and quantity of aircraft in inventory. This may include aircraft intended for sale or operation, or both. The operational inventory would include aircraft used for charter, flight training, and other commercial work. Obviously, this category can prove expensive and may benefit from a staggered or multi-year phased plan for growing the aircraft inventory. For instance, an FBO may purchase two single-engine piston aircraft for flight training in the first year, add a twin-engine aircraft for flight training the following year, and purchase a turboprop for charter purposes in year three.

PASSENGER AND CREW HANDLING

FBOs must be prepared to accommodate both flight crews and passengers. This requires the following services:

- *Loading and unloading of crew and passengers*—Assisting with lowering the aircraft stairs or bringing air stairs for larger aircraft without stairs, often with a red carpet or rug placed on the ground at the bottom of the aircraft stairs.

- *Baggage handling*—Removing baggage from the aircraft and making it available, or even loading it into the ground transportation, creates convenience to passengers and crew.
- *Catering*—FBOs can create tremendous value for passengers and crew by providing catering, or at a minimum, working with a reputable catering company to make healthy food choices available.
- *Concierge services*—Arranging hotels, golf courses, theme parks, and visits to local landmarks and museums will benefit passengers and crew.
- *Ground transportation*—Passengers and crew will frequently require some form of ground transportation, such as a rental car, limousine, taxi, or shared ride service that can be arranged by the FBO. If an FBO offers rental cars on-site, passengers and crew will appreciate the added convenience.

FLIGHT SERVICES

FBOs may offer a number of flight services, depending on market demand. These services may include:

- *Flight training.* Providing Part 61 or Part 141 flight training for private pilot, commercial pilot, instrument rating, and more not only supports the flight training industry but may also create lifelong customers that eventually purchase aircraft, fuel, and aircraft maintenance. The FBO must consider the activity of the airport to gauge whether flight training activity will mix well with existing traffic.
- *Aircraft rental.* By renting aircraft to pilots, especially in combination with a flight school, an FBO can serve the private flight market, which may create synergies with other FBO services, such as fuel sales.
- *Aircraft charters.* Operating under a 14 CFR Part 135 charter certificate, an FBO can provide aircraft charter services for professionals, high-net-worth individuals, and businesses.
- *Aerial photography.* The use of aircraft for aerial photography has long been an accepted practice. Recently, uncrewed aircraft systems (UAS, or drones) are also being used for this purpose. By providing aerial photography services to clients, the FBO can possibly create a niche market with this service.
- *Aircraft management.* By providing management services for owners of aircraft, the FBO can generate income and meet the needs of aircraft owners that desire support in this area.
- *Aircraft sales.* By brokering the sale of aircraft, an FBO can generate significant income. Especially if multi-million-dollar jets are brokered, this can be quite lucrative for the FBO.

Airport Minimum Standards

Frequently, airports develop minimum standards that apply to commercial aeronautical activities, including FBOs. Although minimum standards are optional, the FAA highly recommends their use and implementation as a means to minimize the potential for violations of federal obligations at federally obligated airports (airports that have accepted Airport Improvement Program funds) and ensure certain levels of service by these providers. Airports with standards in place generally utilize FAA Advisory Circular (AC) 150/5190-7, *Minimum Standards for Commercial Aeronautical Activities,* in developing the standards (see Appendix B). This AC addresses specialized aviation service operations (SASO), independent operators, self-fueling, and through-the-fence operators.

An FBO may find they are subject to airport minimum standards in the following areas:

- Fuel sales
- Personnel
- Passenger services
- Flight training
- Aircraft maintenance
- Skydiving
- Ultralight activity
- Fractional ownership activity

Depending on the airport, the minimum standards that apply to an FBO can be very specific. For instance, the airport may require the FBO to be staffed a certain number of hours, employ a certain number of personnel, provide for flight instruction for specific certificates/ratings with a certain number (and type) of aircraft, make on-site rental cars available, etc. Thus, it is imperative to review an airport's minimum standards as part of the review process in deciding where to locate an FBO. This will help determine if the minimum standards in place would be too burdensome for the FBO to make a reasonable return on investment.

Chains versus Independents

To many FBOs, the question of remaining an **independent FBO** or becoming affiliated with an **FBO chain** is an important decision to be made. Which of these choices can increase the odds for surviving in today's industry?

The best year for the general aviation industry from an aircraft sales standpoint was 1978, when 17,811 general aviation aircraft were sold. From an FBO-industry historical perspective, during the very prosperous FBO industry years of the 1970s and early 1980s, any lack of attention or responsiveness to a specific problem area within the industry, or within an individual organization, would not necessarily have been catastrophic. During this period, an FBO could easily compensate for oversights in any one problem area by increasing product or service margins or increasing volume.

This all changed in the period from the early 1980s through the mid-1990s. It was a different marketplace and operating environment with dramatic declines in aircraft sales, fuel revenues, aircraft maintenance income, and revenues from the ancillary services provided by FBO organizations. During recent years, many FBOs have realized the importance of becoming part of a larger organization.

The most significant motivation for an FBO to become affiliated with a chain is the benefits and cost savings derived from marketing and identity and the resulting economies of scale inherent to such an organization. Belonging to a national or international chain is not for all FBOs. The chains are very selective, as are many independent owner/operators. The cost/benefit relationship may not be viable for some smaller FBOs. The approach of most chains is to support an individual operator as an independent business that has access to a well-financed and professionally developed marketing and identity program. This offers the best of both worlds, as operators receive assistance from the chain in marketing while making their own decisions regarding the FBO's operation.

The question of independence or affiliation can be a difficult decision for many FBO operators because of the confidence that founders and/or operating management have developed from having survived and even prospered during the previous tenuous periods in the evolution of the industry. For the most part, the strength and determination of many FBOs have given them the feeling that they can go it alone; however, this approach may not always be the most prudent.

By examining some of the basic issues when evaluating the question of affiliation or independence, readers can draw their own conclusions. Some considerations that might apply in deciding whether to remain independent include the following:

1. A desire to continue to operate as a totally independent business, thereby ensuring control when making marketing, management, and operational decisions.
2. Operating an FBO that already has a sound reputation for quality services and support, and a highly established and recognizable identity/image.
3. An established and profitable FBO that would have little or no potential incremental revenue impact from increased marketing exposure or networking with affiliated organizations.
4. Operating an FBO in a strong geographical location, or established destination marketplace, which would not benefit from increased network exposure.

Conversely, the process for deciding if a program of affiliation would be desirable for an FBO would involve examination of these same issues from a slightly different perspective:

1. The desire to operate with the support of a larger organization and to have access to a variety of resources and expertise.
2. Limited advertising budget and the need to gain national exposure to increase market share and sales volumes.
3. Being located in an underexposed geographical area. Need for national marketing and networked transient clientele, with additional high cost/benefit exposure to the marketplace to develop a larger customer base.
4. Desire to work with other FBOs with similar interests and operating objectives who are also affiliated with the franchise organization through an advisory council approach.

Although they are not literally franchise organizations, several oil companies also offer marketing programs for their dealers to stress the advantages of their programs for promoting their brand products. ExxonMobil, with more than 450 airport locations around the world, was the first to develop this concept more than 20 years ago and continues to add new designated dealers each year. Phillips 66 Aviation also has a large airport presence. It stands to reason that FBOs seeking broader identity or deeper market penetration for their fuel products and services may be well served to consider the support available as an authorized franchisee or specialized dealer.

Signature Flight Support is the world's largest fixed-base operator and distribution network for business aviation services. Headquartered in Orlando, Florida, Signature currently operates at more than 200 locations in the United States, Europe, South America, Africa, and Asia. Signature Flight Support provides refueling, hangaring, maintenance, repair and overhaul, and other services.

Founded in 1984 by the Mary Kay Cosmetics family, Million Air is a very successful chain with more than 30 locations. This FBO chain is focused on luxury and caters to executive travelers. By delivering genuine care and exceptional service, Million Air has been recognized as Best Large FBO Chain by the *Professional Pilot* PRASE Survey for a number of consecutive years (Singer, n.d.).

In any organized marketing program, such as those of Signature or Million Air, there is a large pool of ideas from which to draw, all within the same organization and all having the same objectives. There is no question that the chain concept has not only improved the outward appearance and perception of Signature and Million Air FBOs, but it has also markedly improved market share and sales volume for these operators as well.

The success enjoyed by Signature and Million Air franchisees is basically the same as that of any high-quality FBO. Operators are allowed maximum decision-making in running their business. However, in order to maintain the integrity of the system, there are specific requirements for standardized identity signage and uniforms, training, and certain other operations and procedures, which are mandatory from a customer-service standpoint.

Regardless of an operator's decision concerning independence or affiliation, these challenging economic times require the operator to be innovative and willingly adopt nontraditional approaches for increasing revenues in today's declining marketplace. Often, the degree of innovation means the difference between a successful FBO and one that experiences poor results, or even business failure.

The theory of maximum competition within the FBO industry was once highly regarded by the FAA and many airport operators. Competition was viewed as beneficial to the end user. And although the FAA prohibits the granting of an exclusive right at federally obligated airports, an allowance is made for a single FBO if traffic would only support one FBO at that airport.

Today, however, the theory of maximum competition is being challenged on the basis of pure economic survival. Competitors today may become partners tomorrow. The decision to remain independent, or alternatively align with a chain, may become clearer as traffic is considered and dollar/value tradeoffs become more important.

In many business dilemmas, while quick-fix solutions may be appealing at first, they may ultimately result in having to return to the basics of the business. Nevertheless, from a fundamental perspective, the decision of independence or affiliation may be more relevant now than ever.

Summary

The FBO business model is built on providing services with a focus on the end user. Success requires consideration of a number of factors in the formulation phase, to include legal structure, market analysis, location, facilities, equipment, and aircraft (for charter and/or flight instruction). Whether to remain independent or join a chain is also an important consideration. As the FBO business continues to evolve, the FBOs must also evolve. Regularly examining the FBO business model can ensure a greater likelihood of continued success.

Key Terms

advisory circular (AC). An FAA publication that provides guidance for compliance with airworthiness regulations, pilot certification, operational standards, training standards, and any other rules within Title 14 CFR.

community hangar. A larger hangar that houses multiple aircraft from different owners. Generally used to house more expensive corporate jets overnight, rather than parking them on the ramp exposed to environmental conditions.

corporate self-fueling. The process of a company fueling its own aircraft generally on its own ramp with its own personnel and fuel supply. This concept competes with the FBO, which loses sales to a corporate operator who is fueling its own aircraft and effectively bypassing the FBO's fuel services.

corporation. A form of legal structure with a separate and distinct legal life from its members. A corporation is an artificial being existing only in contemplation of the law. Corporations are typically formed under the authority of state governments.

FBO chain. An FBO with numerous locations, often in a franchise arrangement. The parent company controls standards among the various locations to ensure consistent brand awareness throughout the network.

fixed-base operator (FBO). An organization granted the right by an airport to provide commercial aeronautical services, such as fuel, aircraft hangaring, aircraft tie-down, aircraft rental, aircraft maintenance, flight instruction, and more.

independent FBO. An FBO that is privately owned and independent of any chain. Independent FBOs may operate one or two locations. They represent 46 percent of all FBOs at public-use airports.

Internal Revenue Service (IRS). An entity of the U.S. federal government responsible for collecting taxes and administering the Internal Revenue Code. It is part of the Department of Treasury.

large network, franchise, and affiliate FBOs. FBOs with more than five locations in which each location in the network shares the same brand identity and service standards. These represent 9 percent of all FBOs at public-use airports.

Limited Liability Company (LLC). A form of business legal structure that has limited liability to its owners, is similar to a corporation, and is often a more flexible form of ownership, especially suitable for smaller companies with a limited number of owners.

major fixed-base operator. An FBO located on a major commercial-service airport, fully equipped to handle the servicing and maintenance of all types of aircraft. Their investments run into hundreds of millions of dollars, including leaseholds and equipment.

market analysis. The process of studying the market, including the number of potential customers, where they are located, and what kind and what quantity of business they are likely to bring to the firm.

medium-sized fixed-base operator. An FBO often located at air carrier airports; requires an investment as high as $50 million, with sales volumes into multi-million-dollar figures annually, principally on aircraft sales, fuel sales, and maintenance.

National Association of State Aviation Officials (NASAO). An organization that represents state aviation divisions to policymakers at the federal level.

outdoor tie-down. A parking location on a ramp, typically equipped with ropes or chains to properly secure an aircraft.

partnership. A form of business legal structure consisting of an association of two or more individuals for business purposes. Articles of partnership define the partnership, including partner responsibilities and expectations.

publicly owned FBO. An FBO owned by a municipality, county, authority, school, branch of the military, or other governmental unit. Represent 43 percent of all FBOs at public-use airports.

site selection. The process of locating an FBO, including geographical area, specific airport, and site on the airport.

Small Business Administration (SBA). A U.S. government agency that provides support, including counseling, loans, and educational resources, to entrepreneurs of small businesses.

small fixed-base operators. The smallest of FBOs often established from a specialized service, such as maintenance or flight training. These generally consist of only one location and initially require the least investment of all FBO sizes.

small network FBO. A privately owned FBO with 3–5 locations, often concentrated in a specific region. These represent 3 percent of all FBOs at public-use airports.

sole proprietorship. The easiest of business legal structures, a business owned and operated by a single individual who also has personal liability.

specialized aviation service operations (SASO). A provider of extremely specialized aviation services that does not qualify as a fixed-base operation. Examples include aircraft flying clubs, flight training, aircraft airframe and powerplant repair/maintenance, aircraft charter, air taxi or air ambulance, aircraft sales, avionics, instrument or propeller services, or other specialized commercial flight support businesses.

T-hangar. A type of enclosed structure designed to hold aircraft in storage protected from environmental elements. Aircraft are typically nested in alternating fashion in the least amount of space.

Review Questions

1. How was the term "fixed-base operator" coined?
2. What are FBOs similar to?
3. Approximately how many FBOs are there in the United States?
4. How are FBOs categorized?
5. Discuss some of the problems experienced by small fixed-base operators.
6. What are specialized aviation service operations?
7. Discuss some recent trends affecting FBOs.
8. In establishing an FBO, what are the advantages and disadvantages of the four main forms of legal structure?
9. Describe the importance of analyzing the market and selecting a location.

10. What is market analysis?
11. Discuss the importance of the community in locating an FBO.
12. Describe the factors that must be considered in selecting a site for an FBO.
13. Where can a prospective FBO get assistance?
14. List the basic equipment needed to establish an FBO.
15. What specific facilities and equipment are needed for an FBO?
16. Why have many independent FBOs joined a chain?
17. What are some advantages and disadvantages of joining a chain?
18. Why would an FBO choose to remain independent?
19. What are some advantages and disadvantages of remaining independent?

Scenarios

1. Your FBO is located at a small GA airport and is currently the only FBO on the field. At present, you do not offer Jet A fuel. Your avgas sales have always been your highest source of revenue, and your airport generally sees very little, if any, turbine (jet or turboprop) traffic. This is mainly due to your airport's short, single runway (3,000 feet). However, you have been reading about a new air-taxi operator of very light jets. This operator indicated they would begin serving airports in your state in the near future. However, your FBO is not currently prepared to handle these VLJs (mainly because you do not have jet fuel). How do you evaluate the need to begin offering jet fuel? What must you consider? In essence, will your FBO choose to cater to VLJs?
2. Your best friend and you decide to start an FBO together. A request for proposal (RFP) was recently issued by a local GA airport to find an FBO operator to take over the existing airport-managed FBO on the field. You closely examine this opportunity and determine that it is the only FBO on the field, has a solid customer base, and is located in a growing area and at a popular GA airport. As you both work on your proposal, you must consider how you will legally structure your business. Which of the four forms of business structure will you choose, and why?
3. You have been working at an FBO for five years. You started out in line service and then spent time in administration as the director of line service. You feel you know the FBO business inside and out. Thus, you have decided to start your own FBO. After analyzing the market, you have decided upon two possible locations for your FBO. The first location is at a small GA airport where there currently is no FBO. This airport is not very active and only has 10 T-hangars, but you feel there is potential for an FBO to offer fueling, aircraft rental, and flight instruction. Your second option is to join an existing FBO at a larger GA airport where there are 60 based aircraft and an active GA pilot community. Of course, if you select this location, you'll have direct competition starting on the first day of business. Which location do you choose: The smaller GA airport with fewer tenants but with possibly greater growth potential, or the larger GA airport with many more tenants but also with direct competition? Why?

4. You recently prepared a bid to operate an FBO at a busy GA airport near your hometown. Your firm was selected, and you are excited as you and a longtime friend begin this venture together. Fortunately, you'll be housed in an existing terminal building, which has a community hangar. However, what additional facilities and equipment might you need? You do plan to offer flight instruction (as your friend is a CFII), but how many aircraft (and what type) should you acquire? What type of customer/public facilities will you need? What about employee facilities?

5. You have owned a small FBO for the past 10 years. It has been successful, but you feel revenues could always be higher. You are considering adopting an aggressive marketing campaign when you are approached by a nationwide FBO chain. They would like you to consider joining their chain. This would require you to pay franchise fees and sacrifice a percentage of your gross revenues. At the same time, however, you would have access to their name (brand recognition) and national marketing, as well as standardized procedures and improved efficiencies. Do you remain independent or become part of the chain? What is your thought process in making this decision?

Bibliography

FAA (Federal Aviation Administration). 2022. *National Plan of Integrated Airport Systems (NPIAS) 2023-2027.* September 30, 2022. https://www.faa.gov/sites/faa.gov/files/npias-2023-2027-narrative.pdf.

Kramer, Lois S. 2020. *ACRP Synthesis 108: Characteristics of the FBO Industry 2018–2019.* Washington, DC: Airport Cooperative Research Program, National Academy of Sciences. http://www.trb.org/Main/Blurbs/180833.aspx.

NATA (National Air Transportation Association). 2017. *The State of the FBO Industry.* March 31, 2017. https://www.nata.aero/data/files/gia/nata%20formal%20response%20on%20state%20of%20the%20industry.pdf.

NATA (National Air Transportation Association). 2020. *FBO Statistics.* May 2020. https://www.nata.aero/assets/Site_18/files/GIA/CBP%20Monthly/FBO%20Statistics%20May%202020.pdf.

Prather, C. Daniel. 2009. *General Aviation Marketing and Management: Operating, Marketing, and Managing an FBO.* 3rd ed. Malabar, FL: Krieger Publishing Company.

Singer, Melissa. n.d. "Best FBO Practices: Award-Winning Fixed Base Operators Share Their Secrets." *Professional Pilot.* Accessed April 27, 2022. https://www.propilotmag.com/best-fbo-practices/.

4

Line Service

In Chapter 4

Objectives

At the end of this chapter, you should be able to:

1. Identify the role of a line service specialist.
2. Understand the importance of safety for the line service specialist.
3. Provide directions from the pilot's point of view.
4. Convert local time to Zulu time.
5. Recite the phonetic alphabet.
6. Describe the components of an aircraft.
7. Describe the various classes of fires and properly use a fire extinguisher.
8. Understand the refueling process for piston, turboprop, and jet aircraft.
9. Describe various types of fuel contamination.
10. Describe the types of aviation fuel and their colors.
11. Discuss the proper manner in which to tow an aircraft.

12. Recognize proper marshalling signals.
13. Describe the many possible services of the line service specialist.
14. Discuss the importance of foreign object debris (FOD) management.

The Most Visible Aspect of an FBO

The most visible and important aspect of an FBO's operation can be characterized simply as **line service**. "Line" refers to the aircraft flight line, which is active with aircraft taxiing inbound and outbound, passengers and pilots walking to and from aircraft, aircraft being towed, aircraft being fueled, and aircraft being marshalled to their parking area. When you visit an FBO and look out the terminal building window, you are looking at the line; thus, this is the most visible aspect of an operating FBO. It is imperative for the beginning FBO manager to fully understand the line before being tasked with managing this aspect of an FBO's operation.

Figure 4-1. Line service specialist. *(Svitlana Hulko/ Shutterstock.com)*

The Role of Line Service Specialists

The role of the **line service specialist** cannot be overstated. Indeed, these individuals are typically the first contact a flight crew has with an FBO. As such, these individuals must be well-trained and act with professionalism and a safety mindset at all times. If the FBO is not operated in a safe manner, financial difficulty will likely result. Additionally, the line service specialist must display positive work habits and treat everyone, whether the pilot of a Cessna 152 or a Gulfstream G650, with courtesy and respect. A wise line service specialist realizes that the weekend pilot of a Cessna 152 may be the chief pilot for a large corporation.

Although it may not be obvious to the beginning line service specialist, this position plays a large role in supporting the overall health of the FBO. Primarily, the line service specialist pumps many gallons of fuel on a daily basis. For many FBOs, fuel sales are the largest single source of revenue. Depending on the size of the FBO and the type and size of aircraft being serviced, an FBO may sell hundreds of thousands of gallons of fuel daily. For example, a Cessna 172 holds 43 gallons, while a Gulfstream G700 holds 7,400 gallons. Fueling several large business jets can easily generate $125,000 in gross fuel sale revenues in one day (estimating 25,000 gallons at price of $5.00 per gallon). That being said, the smallest FBOs may sell only 25,000 gallons in an entire year. Generally, avgas sales are more limited in nature (often used in smaller aircraft with smaller fuel tanks), while Jet A sales are more robust (often used in larger aircraft with larger fuel tanks). For that reason, many FBO managers endeavor to attract more corporate aircraft to increase fuel sales.

The safety posture exhibited by line service specialists leads to a safer FBO, fewer incidents, and lower insurance premiums. Lastly, line service specialists are the front door to most FBOs, which allows these individuals to single-handedly make a positive or negative first impression on customers flying into the facility.

Knowledge Base

As with any position within the aviation industry, it is imperative that line service specialists possess the knowledge necessary to successfully perform their job. An FBO employing line service specialists without this specialized knowledge is making a mistake that may have serious consequences. On the other hand, wise FBO managers realize the specialized nature of the business and insist on hiring line service specialists with at least basic aviation knowledge. On-the-job training is provided to all employees to ensure standardized job performance. In this way, individuals in these positions feel more competent and are able to positively contribute to the success of the organization.

SAFETY

Prior to first stepping onto the ramp, line service specialists must be fully aware of the hazards involved. Airport ramps contain jet blast, spinning propellers, helicopter main and tail rotor blades, tie-down cables, chocks, various parts of aircraft that protrude, high levels of noise, and vehicles moving in all directions. Lives have been lost due to careless behavior on the ramp. First and foremost, safety must be a way of life for the line service specialist. It is important that they keep their heads up and eyes moving. Many airport employees are taught to keep their head on a swivel to allow the early detection of an oncoming hazard. This is good advice and practiced by the experienced line service specialist. Line service specialists must also protect themselves with gloves, hearing protection, and proper clothing, and in many parts of the country they would likely add sunscreen, a cap, and sunglasses to that list as well. Safe line service specialists don't rush into performing a task. Although time will be of the essence, it is more important to be safe and perform a task properly than to speed things up and make mistakes. Lastly, beginning line service specialists with any questions about a task will ask their supervisor for guidance. Accuracy is important and verification of instructions may be necessary.

Figure 4-2. Fueler adhering to Safety 1st principles. *(iStock.com/SkyF)*

Figure 4-3. NATA's Safety 1st Clean logo. *(NATA)*

The National Air Transportation Association (NATA) offers a **Safety 1st** program that is designed to train line service personnel in safety best practices. The training, which is online-based, trains line service personnel in the proper techniques of aircraft fueling, aircraft handling, and more. Many FBOs across the nation have 100 percent of their line service personnel possessing the Safety 1st designation. This credential provides aircraft operators peace of mind.

Safety 1st Clean was developed by NATA in response to the COVID-19 pandemic. This program was designed to provide guidelines to FBOs in ensuring proper cleaning and disinfection to minimize spread of contagious diseases. Specifically, it provides guidelines on facility cleaning, disinfecting, and facility operations during a pandemic.

DIRECTIONAL TERMINOLOGY

One of the most basic pieces of knowledge that a line service specialist must have is that of directional terminology. For instance, if a pilot requests to have maintenance check on the oil pressure in the number one engine, what must be done? Which is the number one engine? Aircraft engines are numbered from the pilot's point of view, left to right. Thus, the number one engine is the engine to the pilot's left as he or she is seated in the cockpit. On a Boeing 747, engine number one is the outboard engine to the pilot's left, while engine number four is the outboard engine to the pilot's right (Figure 4-4). Don't be mistaken, FBOs may actually serve a B747 on a charter operation. Air Force One (B747) typically utilizes an FBO to ensure a more secure operation away from airlines and their passengers.

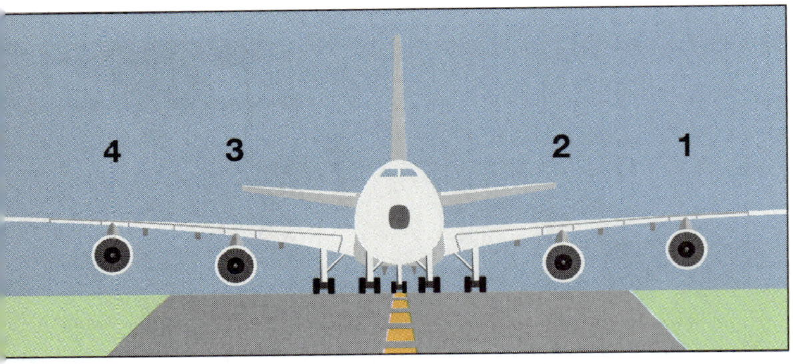

Figure 4-4. Engine numbering.

All directional terminology is oriented from the pilot's point of view from the cockpit. For instance, the left wing is always the wing to the pilot's left. If a pilot calls inbound to ask for directions to the FBO, these directions must be provided from the pilot's point of view. By explaining that the FBO is "on the right as you taxi off the runway," the employee providing directions must be certain that this takes into consideration the active runway and the pilot's point of view.

COORDINATED UNIVERSAL TIME

Yet another unique aspect of the aviation industry is the need to coordinate time on a worldwide basis. As a flight leaves New York and flies to London, it departs from one time zone, flies through several other time zones, and then lands in yet another. If time were not coordinated, this would wreak havoc on flight times and on the job of the airline dispatcher. As a result, the aviation industry operates under **Coordinated Universal Time (UTC)**. Also designated as Greenwich Mean Time or Zulu time, this is the time at the meridian of the globe or zero degrees longitude, which passes through Greenwich, England.

To convert either from local time to UTC or vice versa, the rules shown in Table 4-1 must be followed. For example, if an airport is located in the Central Daylight Time zone, five hours must be added to local time to arrive at UTC. If it is 8:00 a.m. local time, the addition of five hours results in 1:00 p.m., or more accurately, 1300(Z). As shown in this example, the aviation industry also operates on a 24-hour clock. Familiar to those in the military, the 24-hour clock contributes to the effectiveness of UTC. A time of day in 24-hour notation is simply the amount of time that has passed since midnight. In order to convert an afternoon time from the regular 12-hour notation to the 24-hour clock, simply add the p.m. time to 12:00 (noon). For instance, 6:00 p.m. local time, when added to 12:00, results in 18:00. In aviation, times are typically represented without the colon or a.m. or p.m., which also signifies the 24-hour clock. Additionally, the letter in parentheses after the numbers will signify whether the time refers to local time (L) or Zulu (Z) time.

Table 4-1. UTC Time Conversion

Converting from UTC to a local time		When Daylight Savings Time is in effect	
Eastern Standard Time (EST)	= UTC–5 hours	Eastern Daylight Time (EDT)	= UTC–4 hours
Central Standard Time (CST)	= UTC–6 hours	Central Daylight Time (CDT)	= UTC–5 hours
Mountain Standard Time (MST)	= UTC–7 hours	Mountain Daylight Time (MDT)	= UTC–6 hours
Pacific Standard Time (PST)	= UTC–8 hours	Pacific Daylight Time (PDT)	= UTC–7 hours

PHONETIC ALPHABET AND NUMBERS

In addition to the unique way to signify time, aviation uses the International Radiotelephony Spelling Alphabet, known as the **phonetic alphabet**, to pronounce letters (Table 4-2). It is easy to discern if someone is knowledgeable of the phonetic alphabet when they say "B, as in Bravo." Otherwise, you'll likely hear, "B, as in Boy." It is imperative for all line service personnel to memorize the phonetic alphabet. If not, it will likely lead to a recognition by others that an individual is not very knowledgeable about aviation and possibly lacks the skills and knowledge necessary to effectively perform the job of a line service specialist. It may also result in miscommunication, as "D" and "B" sound alike, for example.

Table 4-2. Phonetic Alphabet

Character	Telephony	Pronunciation
A	Alfa	al-fah
B	Bravo	brah-voh
C	Charlie	char-lee *or* shar-lee
D	Delta	dell-tah
E	Echo	eck-oh
F	Foxtrot	foks-trot
G	Golf	golf
H	Hotel	hoh-tel
I	India	in-dee-ah
J	Juliett	jew-lee-ett
K	Kilo	key-loh
L	Lima	lee-mah
M	Mike	mike
N	November	no-vem-ber
O	Oscar	oss-cah
P	Papa	pah-pah
Q	Quebec	keh-beck
R	Romeo	row-me-oh

Character	Telephony	Pronunciation
S	Sierra	see-air-rah
T	Tango	tang-go
U	Uniform	you-nee-form *or* oo-nee-form
V	Victor	vik-tah
W	Whiskey	wiss-key
X	Xray	ecks-ray
Y	Yankee	yang-key
Z	Zulu	zoo-loo
1	One	wun
2	Two	too
3	Three	tree
4	Four	fow-er
5	Five	fife
6	Six	six
7	Seven	sev-en
8	Eight	ait
9	Nine	nin-er
0	Zero	zee-ro

Each letter of the alphabet has a word associated with it. The use of this alphabet plays an important role in preventing miscommunication between pilots and air traffic control, pilots and FBO staff, and all aviation industry personnel. Typically, ATC and pilots will refer to their tail number (discussed next) using the phonetic alphabet; for example, "November One Three Charlie Bravo Kilo." Without knowledge of the phonetic alphabet, this will leave an individual scratching their head. However, once the phonetic alphabet is memorized, it becomes a second language and is very effective at improving communication in aviation.

Likewise, a knowledgeable line service specialist will effectively communicate numbers (Table 4-2). Only several rules are applicable. First, each number must be enunciated clearly. The number nine is spoken as "niner," and zero is spoken as "zero" rather than "oh." Lastly, numbers above 9,900 are spoken by saying each digit before the word "thousand." For instance, 13,000 is spoken as "one three thousand."

Table 4-3. Country Registration Prefixes

COUNTRY	REGISTRATION
Afghanistan	YA
Algeria	7T
Angola	D2
Antigua and Barbuda	V2
Arab Air Cargo (Jordan)	4YB
Argentina	LQ, LV
Armenia	EK
Australia	VH
Austria	OE
Azerbaijan	4K
Bahamas	C6
Bahrain	A9C
Bangladesh	S2
Barbados	8P
Belarus	EW
Belgium	OO
Belize	V3
Benin	TY
Bhutan	A5
Bolivia	CP
Bosnia-Herzegovina	E7
Botswana	A2
Brazil	PP, PR, PT, PU
Brunei Darussalam	V8
Bulgaria	LZ
Burkina Faso	XT
Burundi	9U
Cambodia	XU
Cameroon	TJ
Canada	C, CF
Cabo Verde	D4
Central African Republic	TL
Chad	TT
Chile	CC
China	B
Colombia	HJ, HK
Comoros	D6
Congo	TN
Cook Islands	E5
Costa Rica	TI
Ivory Coast	TU
Croatia	9A
Cuba	CU
Cyprus	5B
Czech Republic	OK
Dem. People's Rep. of Korea	P
Dem. Rep. of the Congo	9Q
Denmark	OY
Djibouti	J2
Dominica	J7
Dominican Republic	HI
Ecuador	HC
Egypt	SU
El Salvador	YS
Equatorial Guinea	3C
Eritrea	E3
Estonia	ES
Ethiopia	ET
Fiji	DQ
Finland	OH
France	F
Gabon	TR
Gambia	C5
Georgia	4L

COUNTRY	REGISTRATION
Germany	D
Ghana	9G
Greece	SX
Grenada	J3
Guatemala	TG
Guinea	3X
Guinea-Bissau	J5
Guyana	8R
Haiti	HH
Honduras	HR
Hungary	HA
Iceland	TF
India	VT
Indonesia	PK
Iran	EP
Iraq	YI
Ireland	EI, EJ
Israel	4X
Italy	I
Jamaica	6Y
Japan	JA
Jordan	JY
Kazakhstan	UP
Kenya	5Y
Kuwait	9K
Kyrgyzstan	EX
Lao People's Dem. Rep.	RDPL
Latvia	YL
Lebanon	OD
Lesotho	7P
Liberia	A8
Libya	5A
Liechtenstein	HB[1]
Lithuania	LY
Luxembourg	LX
Madagascar	5R
Malawi	7Q
Malaysia	9M
Maldives	8Q
Mali	TZ
Malta	9H
Marshall Islands	V7
Mauritania	5T
Mauritius	3B
Mexico	XA, XB, XC[1]
Micronesia	V6
Monaco	3A
Mongolia	JU
Montenegro	4O
Morocco	CN
Mozambique	C9
Myanmar	XY, XZ
Namibia	V5
Nauru	C2
Nepal	9N
Netherlands	PH
NETH: Aruba, Antilles	P4, PJ
New Zealand	ZK, ZL, ZM
Nicaragua	YN
Niger	5U
Nigeria	5N
Norway	LN
Oman	A40
Pakistan	AP

[1] Plus national emblem.

COUNTRY	REGISTRATION
Palau	T8
Panama	HP
Papua New Guinea	P2
Paraguay	ZP
Peru	OB
Philippines	RP
Poland	SP
Portugal	CR, CS
Qatar	A7
Republic of Korea	HL
Republic of Moldova	ER
Romania	YR
Russian Federation	RA
Rwanda	9XR
Saint Kitts and Nevis	V4
Saint Lucia	J6
Saint Vincent and the Grenadines	J8
Samoa	5W
San Marino	T7
Sao Tome and Principe	S9
Saudi Arabia	HZ
Senegal	6V,6W
Serbia	YU
Seychelles	S7
Sierra Leone	9L
Singapore	9V
Slovakia	OM
Slovenia	S5
Solomon Islands	H4
Somalia	6O
South Africa	ZS, ZT, ZU
Spain	EC
Sri Lanka	4R
Sudan	ST
Suriname	PZ
Swaziland	3D
Sweden	SE
Switzerland	HB[1]
Syrian Arab Republic	YK
Tajikistan	EY
Thailand	HS
The former Yugoslav Rep. of Macedonia	Z3
Togo	5V
Tonga	A3
Trinidad and Tobago	9Y
Tunisia	TS
Turkey	TC
Turkmenistan	EZ
Uganda	5X
Ukraine	UR
United Arab Emirates	A6
United Kingdom	G
United Rep. of Tanzania	5H
United States	N
Uruguay	CX
Uzbekistan	UK
Vanuatu	YJ
Venezuela	YV
Viet Nam	XV
Yemen	7O
Zambia	9J
Zimbabwe	Z

Source: FAA 2022, 4-2-1.

TAIL NUMBERS

Figure 4-5. Tail number. *(C. Daniel Prather)*

Every aircraft is registered in its country of ownership by the country's equivalent to the Federal Aviation Administration (FAA). As part of this registration, each aircraft has a given **tail number**, referred to as such because it is typically painted on the tail of the aircraft, either on the vertical stabilizer or the engine nacelle (Figure 4-5). As expected, whether it includes numbers or letters, the tail number is referred to using aviation-speak (phonetic alphabet and numerals). Although tail numbers in the United States are referred to as N-numbers, this is not true for any other country. Table 4-3 presents the registration prefixes from other countries. For instance, Canada, rather than having N-numbers, has "CF-numbers."

AIRCRAFT COMPONENTS

It is also important for line service specialists to fully understand the typical components of an aircraft. Although almost anyone interested in aviation has a basic understanding of these components, they are presented here for clarification purposes (Figures 4-6 and 4-7).

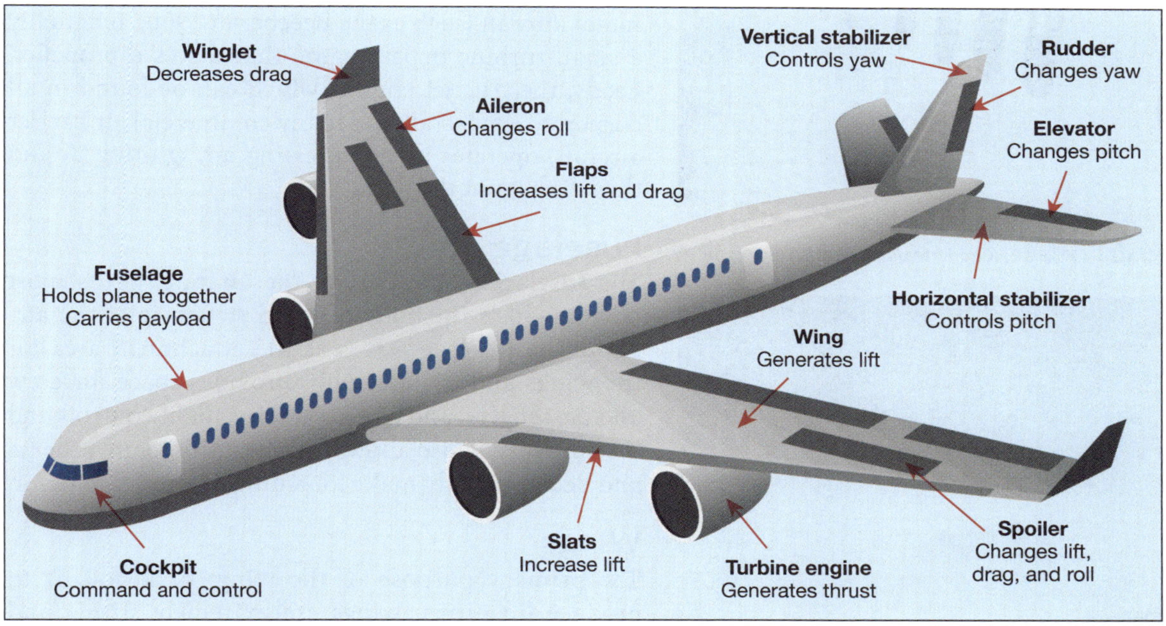

Figure 4-6. Parts of a large aircraft.

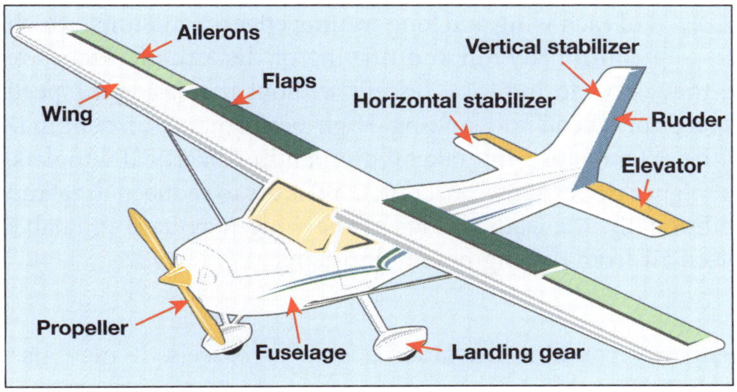

Figure 4-7. Parts of a small aircraft.

Figure 4-8. Aircraft turbine engines. *(balipadma/Shutterstock.com)*

Figure 4-9. Aircraft fuselage. *(Charlotte Ulrich/Shutterstock.com)*

Figure 4-10. Aircraft wing with winglet. *(itlada/Shutterstock.com)*

Engine or Powerplant

The **engines** or powerplants on an aircraft are the driving force behind powered flight. These may consist of an engine-propeller combination, or in the case of jet aircraft, just the engine itself. In addition to the engine, propeller-driven aircraft have a cowling (used to enclose the engine and provide cooling by ducting the air around the engine) and a nacelle (providing protection, as well as improved aerodynamics, and located aft of the engine).

The three types of engines typically encountered at an FBO include (a) **reciprocating piston engine**, (b) **turboprop engine**, and (c) **jet engine**. Common to a large majority of single-engine aircraft and light twin-engine aircraft, the reciprocating piston engine is similar to an automobile engine and operates by moving pistons, which in turn move a crankshaft, which then in turn spins the propeller. The turboprop engine, which is found in many large twins and commuter aircraft (such as the Beechcraft 1900), is actually a small turbine or jet engine that drives a propeller. Lastly, the true jet engine, which can be found in all corporate jet aircraft and many commercial air carrier aircraft, operates by compressing air, igniting it, and thrusting it out the back.

Fuselage

The **fuselage** is the part of the aircraft that is most obvious—it is the body or main structure of the aircraft. The fuselage serves as the attachment area for the wings and tail assembly, provides space for crew and passengers, and houses various flight controls and instruments. It also allows for a beautiful paint scheme and decals to truly make for a unique aircraft exterior.

Wings

The primary purpose of the **wing**, or airfoil, is to produce lift. Thus, wings are extremely strong and lightweight. On conventional aircraft, wings will contain most of the usable fuel on board. At the end of each wing and long trailing edge are ailerons, which control the roll and turning of the aircraft. Flaps are located on the inboard trailing edge; they serve to increase descent without increasing airspeed and allow for improved lift at slower speeds of takeoff and landing. High-performance aircraft may also have leading-edge slats that may be extended during takeoff and landing. Vertical winglets, which may be found on the wingtips of higher performance aircraft, contribute to reduced drag and improved efficiency (Figure 4-10). Additionally, the leading edge of the wing may have inflatable boots for deicing or be heated using bleed air from the engines for anti-icing.

Undercarriage

The **undercarriage** of an aircraft primarily contains the landing gear or wheels. It may also include cowl flaps, landing lights, and antennas. Most aircraft have a tricycle gear configuration, allowing for a steerable nose wheel and two main wheels (Figure 4-11). Taildragger aircraft contain two main wheels and a tail wheel (such as found on a Piper Cub or a Douglas DC-3). Complex aircraft have retractable landing gear, while lower performance (and most trainer) aircraft have fixed landing gear.

Figure 4-11. Aircraft undercarriage of a tricycle-gear aircraft. *(JITD/Shutterstock.com)*

Empennage (Tail)

The **empennage**, or tail, can be configured in one of several ways. Most common is the vertical stabilizer with an attached movable rudder (controlling yaw or side-to-side motion) and the horizontal stabilizer with hinged, movable elevators (controlling pitch or up-and-down movement). An aircraft may also have a pivoting, one-piece horizontal stabilizer referred to as a stabilator. Trim tabs are commonly found and consist of small, hinged sections on the rudder and elevator.

When on the ramp, one may hear of a T-tail, V-tail or canard. These unique configurations deserve special explanation. A T-tail aircraft has a horizontal surface (typically the horizontal stabilizer) at the top of the tail, such as that found on a Piper Turbo Arrow IV. A V-tail aircraft has movable surfaces on the tail used in combination as both rudder and elevator (such as on a V-tail Beechcraft Bonanza). Lastly, a canard is an elevator assembly found at the front of an aircraft. Although unique in appearance, these work in the same manner as an elevator in a conventional tail assembly.

Figure 4-12. Aircraft empennage/tail. *(vaalaa/Shutterstock.com)*

Fire Safety

Prior to handling any fuel, the line service specialist must be taught the importance of proper handling of these fuels and of **fire safety**. An awareness of fire safety requires knowledge of the **fire triangle** (Figure 4-13). This triangle contains the following three elements: heat, fuel, and oxygen. Remove any of these elements and the fire will be extinguished. In general terms, heat may be removed by cooling the fire, as is possible with the use of water on Class A fires. The fuel source may also be removed, such as by eliminating the wood or paper fueling a Class A fire (for example, making a fire break ahead of a forest fire). Oxygen can be removed by use of certain chemical fire extinguishers, such as carbon dioxide (which displaces oxygen).

Figure 4-13. Fire triangle.

Although the fire triangle is appropriate for learning the components necessary to start a fire, the **fire tetrahedron** is necessary to learn how a fire continues to burn (Figure 4-14). The fourth side is a chemical chain reaction. If uninterrupted, this chemical chain reaction will maintain a fire. The chemical chain reaction can only be interrupted by application of certain extinguishing agents.

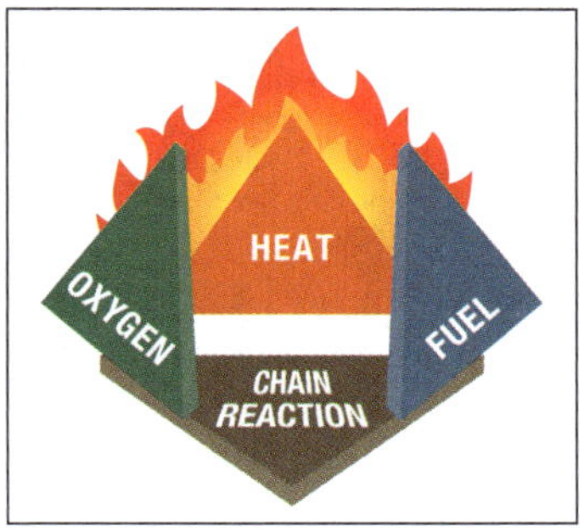

Figure 4-14. Fire tetrahedron.

Prior to applying an **extinguishing agent**, however, the individual fighting the fire must know which class of fire is involved. **Class A fires** are composed of ordinary combustibles (such as wood or paper). **Class B fires** are composed of flammable and combustible liquids (such as greases and gas). **Class C fires** are composed of energized electrical equipment. **Class D fires** are composed of combustible metals (magnesium and sodium). Water, which has a cooling effect, is used only on Class A fires. Carbon dioxide, which smothers the fire as it displaces oxygen, is effective on Class B or C fires. Dry chemical, which is a mixture of specially treated sodium bicarbonate, also deprives the fire of oxygen and is effective on Class B and C fires.

Foam, also known as **aqueous film forming foam (AFFF)**, is a blend of bicarbonate of soda and aluminum sulfate. AFFF effectively blankets a fire with a layer of foam, thus cooling the fire and starving it of oxygen. It is primarily used on Class B fires, such as on-airport fuel fires, but may also be effective on Class A fires. Foam, however, is not effective on vertical surfaces or pressure fires (such as a broken fuel line). Aircraft rescue and firefighting (ARFF) trucks generally always carry AFFF as well as some dry chemical. Halon is a liquefied gas that breaks the chemical reaction by interrupting the supply of oxygen. Although it has negative environmental implications due to its ability to degrade the ozone layer, it is effective on Class B and C fires. For Class D fires, only specialized agents such as METL-X and G-1 powder are effective. In May 2023, the FAA introduced an Aircraft Firefighting Foam Transition Plan to transition away from AFFF in recognition that AFFF can cause serious health problems, including cancer, if people are exposed to it over a long period of time, and it can also be harmful to aquatic and terrestrial organisms. The Transition Plan is designed to gradually replace AFFF with a new fluorine-free foam. The new foam lacks a fluorinated surfactant and therefore does not have the film forming properties of AFFF. This will require training of fire crews to include a change in how fires are suppressed at airports with the new foam (FAA 2023).

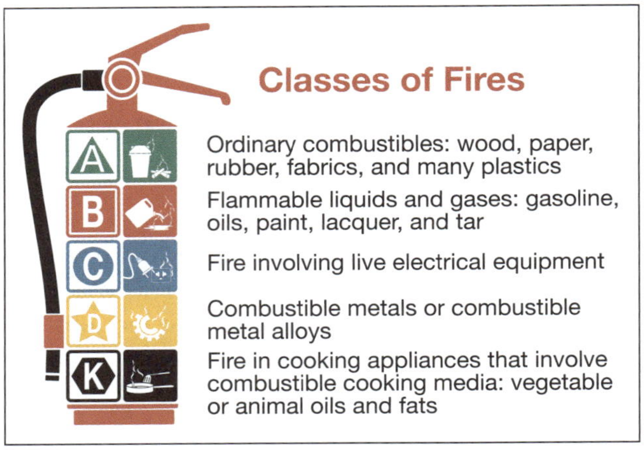

Figure 4-15. Classes of fires. *(Heavypong/Shutterstock.com)*

The principles used in fighting a fire begin with interrupting the fuel source if at all possible. If this is a fuel fire, this can be done with an emergency fuel shutoff or the releasing of a **deadman control** (Figure 4-17). Before reaching for the proper fire extinguisher, the person must evaluate the fire to determine if it is of a small enough size to extinguish. If not, 911, the airport fire department, or a supervisor must be notified. If so, the individual selects the proper fire extinguisher, positions themselves upwind, and approaches the fire. Next, the fire extinguisher safety seal must be broken, the pin must be removed, and the nozzle must be pointed at the base of the flame. Next, the individual fighting the fire pulls the nozzle trigger to begin releasing the agent while moving

Figure 4-16. Aqueous film forming foam (AFFF). *(U.S. Air Force Senior Airman Jarad A. Denton, flickr.com/photos/36281822@N08/6119569867, CC BY 2.0, creativecommons.org/licenses/by/2.0/)*

Figure 4-17. Deadman control. *(A1C Jonathan McElderry/ Minot Air Force Base)*

the extinguisher with a rapid sweeping motion, and steadily advances toward the flame. PASS is an acronym used to aid in remembering this process: Pull, Aim, Squeeze, Sweep.

Certain measures should be taken to regularly minimize the risk of fire. Keep in mind that liquid fuels, such as avgas and Jet A, emit vapors that can ignite when the flashpoint is reached. **Flashpoint** is the lowest temperature at which the liquid fuel will form a vapor in the air near its surface that will "flash" or briefly ignite on exposure to an open flame. The flashpoint of avgas is −50 degrees Fahrenheit, while Jet A has a 100-degree Fahrenheit flashpoint. As a result, the vapors released from these two fuels will be at or above the flashpoint in almost every circumstance in which they will be handled.

The first measure that should be taken is to ensure the engines of all mobile fuelers are equipped with air filter/flame arrestor equipment and a leak-free exhaust system that terminates into a standard baffle muffler at the front of the vehicle. Next, line service personnel should only wear clothing composed of 100 percent cotton. Fabrics such as silk, polyester, nylon, and wool generate static, which can produce a spark that may ignite fuel or fuel vapors. Additionally, refueling personnel should not carry any type of igniting device on their person or within 100 feet of any fuel tank or refueler. Next, plastic funnels or buckets should not be used to handle fuel. Rather, a high-quality, non-galvanized metal funnel should be used. **Bonding** is also extremely important during fueling procedures. Static can build up on an aircraft during flight and while fuel is flowing through a hose and nozzle. Bonding consists of connecting a cable between the fueling vehicle and aircraft (Figure 4-18). Bonding is necessary to equalize any static charges and prevent an errant spark. Additional ignition sources include hot brakes, hot engine surfaces, jet engine exhaust, thunderstorms and lightning, portable electrical devices, fixed electrical equipment, and exposed light bulbs.

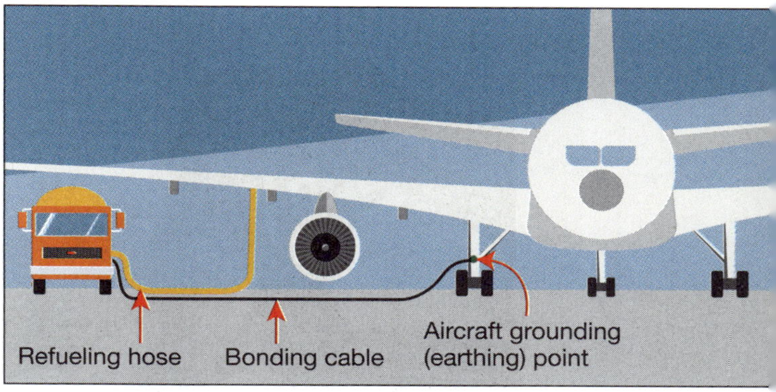

Figure 4-18. Bonding during aircraft fueling.

Even with proper measures in place, a **fuel spill** may occur. Typically, fuel spills may happen if a fueler has been filled beyond its capacity at the fuel farm, an aircraft has vented a significant amount of fuel, or a fueler has been moved while connected to an aircraft or fuel farm. If a spill does occur, the first step is to stop the flow of fuel. If possible, a fire extinguisher must be placed upwind of the spill. Next, a supervisor or the airport fire department must be notified. Third, it is important not to move a fueling vehicle or start or turn off any equipment (due to a possible backfire). If trained and properly equipped, personnel may begin cleaning up the spill. Typically, a **spill cart** will need to be brought on scene to enable proper spill clean-up. It is important to have ARFF or fire extinguishers standing by, as the vapors may ignite.

The fire fuel safety standard that is commonly utilized by FBO line service personnel is produced by the **National Fire Protection Association (NFPA)**. Specifically, NFPA 407, *Standard for Aircraft Fuel Servicing*, provides guidance on the safe refueling of aircraft and applies to fuel farms, self-serve fueling, mobile fuelers, and other fueling operations (NFPA 2022). NFPA 407 is revised occasionally. For example, a 2017 revision required new and existing equipment to have automatic overfill devices.

Aircraft Refueling

The sale of aircraft fuel is the lifeblood of many FBOs. General aviation fuel is a small, niche market. GA jet fuel (**Jet A**) accounts for just 1.3 billion gallons annually, or just 6 percent of the total U.S. jet fuel market. **Avgas** is confined to the 167,000 piston-engine aircraft operating in the United States that consume an average of 150–190 million gallons annually.

Avgas 100LL and Jet A, the two primary fuels used in aviation, are priced differently due to their differences in production and distribution. For example, Jet A distribution efficiencies are due to pipelines, whereas the lead content of 100LL requires shipment by truck. It would cost only a few cents to move 8,000 gallons of Jet A 500 miles, but it would cost about $2,000 to ship the same amount of 100LL. It is also more labor intensive to provide 100LL compared to Jet A. Line service personnel must constantly monitor the fuel farm and fuel truck filters, drains, and overall fuel systems that are used for 100LL. Further, there is great demand for Jet A both within GA and commercial aviation (airlines). However, the demand for avgas is confined to GA, which affects pricing. It can cost more to provide a small piston aircraft ten gallons of avgas than to provide 500 gallons to a jet aircraft, due to the labor-intensive nature of over-the-wing refueling compared to single-point refueling. On a revenue basis, the jet fuel transaction is far more profitable to the FBO owner (NATA 2017).

Aircraft can be refueled by one of two primary methods—over-the-wing and single point. **Over-the-wing refueling** is most common on piston-engine aircraft (Figure 4-19). This method is similar to refueling an automobile. Aircraft equipped with one fuel cap on the upper surface of each wing just outboard of the engine(s) likely require over-the-wing refueling. In this method, after bonding the fuel vehicle to the aircraft, the line service professional uses a step ladder to access the fuel cap, removes the fuel cap, and inserts the fuel nozzle into the filler opening, depressing the handle to begin the flow of fuel.

Single-point refueling uses a pressurized, closed system to deliver fuel (Figure 4-20). This has obvious advantages. Generally, aircraft that use jet fuel also utilize a single-point system. The single-point refuel/defuel control panel will be located either on the landing gear fairing or under a wing. The control panel consists of a fuel/refuel connection point (receptacle). In this method, after bonding the fuel vehicle to the aircraft, the line service professional removes the adaptor cap (using a step ladder for access as needed on large jets), inserts the refueling nozzle into the receptacle, turns it clockwise to latch it into place, then opens the nozzle to start the flow of fuel.

Figure 4-19. Over-the-wing refueling. *(Isaiah Shook/ Shutterstock.com)*

Figure 4-20. Single-point refueling. *(Skycolors/ Shutterstock.com)*

A line service professional is not needed in all refueling situations. Indeed, fuel can be delivered through two primary methods: full-serve or self-serve. Full-serve does require a line service professional to fuel the aircraft, similar to full-service gas stations requiring an attendant to fuel the automobile. Self-serve, however, does not. With self-serve, the operator of the aircraft fuels their own aircraft.

Generally speaking, 30 percent of FBOs provide full-serve and self-serve Jet A only, and 22 percent of FBOs provide self-serve 100LL only. The third most popular delivery method mix is full-serve Jet A, self-serve Jet A, and self-serve 100LL, provided by 12 percent of FBOs. Ten percent of FBOs provide full-serve and self-serve 100LL only. Only 36 FBO locations nationwide do not provide fuel (Kramer 2020).

Whether delivering avgas or Jet A to an aircraft, learning how to properly fuel an aircraft is most effectively conducted through on-the-job training at the FBO. However, the beginning line service specialist should be aware of the basic terminology and procedures utilized when fueling aircraft.

FUEL SUPPLIER

FBOs that sell fuel must purchase the fuel in bulk from a fuel supplier. Although some fuel suppliers only operate in specific regions of the country, commonly fuel suppliers serve both national and international markets. The top three fuel suppliers in terms of market share are Phillips 66 (23 percent market share), Avfuel (18 percent), and Shell (15 percent) (Kramer 2020). FBOs generally advertise branded fuel so customers know what fuel brand they are purchasing. However, almost one-third of FBOs have opted not to sell branded fuel. These FBOs list their fuel as either undesignated or independent. For example, Signature Flight Support lists its fuel brand as independent but likely purchases fuel from multiple well-known fuel suppliers.

FUEL TRUCKS

The majority of FBOs lease fuel trucks from the supplier of their fuel, such as Phillips 66, Avfuel, Shell, or World Fuel. By providing fuel truck and equipment leasing to FBOs, the fuel supplier can ensure that a branded truck refuels aircraft and that consistency of their product is maintained (with regular fuel testing). It also minimizes the FBO's financial investment in such equipment. Generally, it is a win-win relationship.

Figure 4-21. Fuel truck. *(Lawrence Glass/Shutterstock.com)*

PISTON AIRCRAFT

Piston aircraft have reciprocating engines, which is nothing more than an internal combustion engine with pistons that move back and forth, or reciprocate. This reciprocating motion spins a crankshaft that is connected to the propeller, which produces the thrust to propel the aircraft. Although some higher performance piston aircraft may use a turbocharger to increase manifold pressure, and thus high-altitude performance, be aware that those aircraft remain piston aircraft utilizing avgas and should not be confused with a turboprop aircraft. Thus, the line service specialist must use caution when fueling aircraft such as a Piper Turbo Arrow.

There are three types of aircraft fuel filler caps. First, with a simple twist-off, surface-mounted cap, the grip must remain parallel to the airflow. A second type has an inner cap located under a secure access door. A pop-up lever releases the cap for removal. The most common type involves a flush-mounted filler cap with a pop-up tab that must be rotated counterclockwise for removal. Regardless of the type, the line service specialist must ensure that the cap is properly secured at the completion of fueling.

The entire process of refueling a piston aircraft can be summarized in the following eleven steps:

1. Understand the service order.
2. Choose the correct refueler.
3. Properly position the refueler.
4. Review the service order.
5. Set up to refuel.
6. Refuel the aircraft (see details below).
7. Check the oil.
8. Clean the windshield.
9. Stow and check.
10. Complete paperwork.
11. Perform a final visual check.

Step 6, which involves actually refueling the aircraft, includes additional substeps. First, protect the wing's leading edge by placing the appropriate wing mat. Next, connect the bonding cable to the aircraft. Additionally, be sure to touch the nozzle to the filler cap prior to beginning the flow of fuel. This will discharge any remaining static electricity. Next, as the nozzle is inserted into the tank, remember not to insert the nozzle deeper than 3 inches, and ensure contact is maintained between the filler neck and nozzle. As you begin the flow of fuel, maintain vigilance so as not to allow contaminants into the tank (such as pens or sunglasses). Once complete, replace the filler cap immediately to prevent any contaminants from finding their way into the tank. Be aware that during the summer, the service order may request fuel to be at a level below a full tank to allow room for the fuel to expand. If refueling a multi-engine aircraft, the process is essentially the same, albeit with additional filler locations.

If refueling a reciprocating engine helicopter, care must be exercised around the rotor blades. Specifically, always park the refueler outside the circle of blade rotation even if the blades are not turning. Also, never walk behind a helicopter. Remain in the pilot's field of vision away from the tail rotor. Refueling of helicopters "hot," or while the blades are turning, is not recommended, as it increases risks to both the fueler and the helicopter. Due to the large amount of static generated by helicopter blades, several minutes must pass for static to dissipate after bonding the refueler to the aircraft. Lastly, as with refueling piston aircraft, always touch the refueler nozzle to the filler cap prior to opening the fuel tank.

TURBOPROP AND JET AIRCRAFT

The word *turboprop* refers to an aircraft with propellers, but also equipped with a jet engine or turbine, and as a result, it requires jet fuel. A turboprop engine takes in air, which is routed through a series of spinning turbine blades. This process compresses the air, which is then mixed with jet fuel and ignited. Gases are produced, which spin a shaft that is attached to the propeller. Similarly, once the air is compressed within a jet engine, it is mixed with fuel and ignited, which produces a jet blast which propels the aircraft forward. The most common type of fuel for these aircraft is Jet A.

Fuel additives, including those specifically intended to prevent icing, may be called for. For example, Prist is an anti-icing fuel additive that is commonly used. These additives are either pre-blended by the manufacturer or supplier, injected through a closed system on the refueler, or delivered over the wing via an aerosol spray can during refueling. If using an aerosol spray can, certain steps must be followed to ensure proper mixing of the additive. One must start the flow of fuel before beginning the flow of additive and then shut off the flow of additive before refueling is completed. This process will ensure proper mixing and avoid any areas of concentration of the additive in the fuel.

Jet fuel refuelers typically have larger tanks and additional fuel hoses, nozzles, and meters. There are three delivery hoses: two overwing hoses and nozzles and one single-point (pressure) hose and nozzle. The overwing nozzles will have a J spout, which will prevent inadvertent delivery of Jet A into a piston-engine aircraft. Refuelers providing jet fuel will have both types, as any aircraft with a single-point refueling system will also have overwing filler caps to be used if the pressure system is not operational. Single-point systems, which are common on many business jets, are easy to use, safe, and more efficient than overwing refueling, as they produce a closed, pressurized system which should reduce the opportunity for fuel spills. These systems have an automatic shutoff that terminates the flow of fuel when the tanks are full.

Unique to the single-point system, the deadman control allows delivery of fuel from a position slightly away from the aircraft and will only start the flow of fuel when the deadman control is held open. The deadman control consists of a control valve with a handheld electric or hydraulic deadman handle (switch) deployed via a cable or hose reel assembly. After the underwing nozzle is locked onto the aircraft receptacle, fuel flow begins only after the deadman handle is depressed. When released, the flow of fuel stops

The single point is typically located in the vicinity of the wing root, either fore or aft, and either above or below wing. A fuel control panel will have the master fuel power switch, tank valve on/off switches, refuel/defuel switches, fuel tank configuration diagram, and possibly fuel quantity gauges. The closed, single-point system must also have a way for air that is being displaced by fuel in the tanks to escape. This is accomplished through a fuel vent system. Vents are commonly located on outboard, underside sections of wings, near the wingtips. Connecting a single-point nozzle simply involves making contact at the appropriate connection point and rotating the handles of the nozzle clockwise for proper connection. Once refueling is complete, the nozzle is removed by rotating handles counterclockwise.

Special precautions must be taken when filling aircraft with **tip tanks**. A prime example is the Mitsubishi MU-2 (Figure 4-22). The aircraft's wingspan is 39 feet, 2 inches, yet the wheelbase is less than five feet wide. This makes the aircraft susceptible to a tip over if the aircraft is improperly refueled, resulting in an unbalanced situation. The proper procedure to refuel a Mitsubishi MU-2 begins with approaching the aircraft from the nose in a safe manner (generally approaching parallel with the wings, and waiting until the aircraft's engines have ceased operating before approaching). Next, line personnel should attach the bonding cable to the designated grounding point and, after the bonding cable is secure, locate the left inboard tank to begin refueling operations. Line personnel must start with the left inboard tank due to the aircraft's baffling within the wing. After refueling the left inboard tank, the line personnel should proceed to refuel the aircraft via the right inboard tank, followed by the right outboard tank and then the left outboard tank.

Figure 4-22. Mitsubishi MU-2 aircraft. *(Tomás Del Coro, flickr.com/photos/tomasdelcoro/48725547427/, CC BY-SA 2.0, creativecommons.org/licenses/by-sa/2.0/)*

Once the main wing tanks have been fueled, the line personnel should proceed to the left tip tank. The Mitsubishi MU-2's tip tanks are different than the inboard/outboard wing tanks on the aircraft. The tip tanks are pressurized, which means the line personnel refueling the aircraft should take great care in opening the tank's filler cap, to prevent personal injury as well as damage to the aircraft. A good general rule of thumb is to pull the filler cap's tab and wait for the pressure to stabilize before removing the cap completely. When filling the MU-2's tip tanks, it is important to remember that the tanks cannot exceed 45 gallons per tip tank (maximum capacity is 90 gallons) in order to keep the aircraft from tipping over. To properly complete the refueling procedure, the line personnel must move from the left tip tank (after adding no more than 45 gallons) to the right tip tank (again taking care to depressurize the system), adding the desired amount of fuel. After the right tip tank is fueled, the left tank can be completed (unless the desired amount of fuel in the tip tanks is less than 45 gallons, in which case the left and right tip tanks are now finished). After refueling, the line personnel removes the bonding cable from the aircraft and proceeds away from the aircraft to complete the process.

It is also important to understand that the Mitsubishi MU-2's wings have a tendency to flex downward, or droop, under the added weight of the fuel. The wings have been known to flex anywhere from a few inches to roughly a few feet. If line personnel place an access ladder underneath the wing, the wing itself could flex and lodge itself onto the ladder, making it impossible to remove the ladder without transferring the fuel load to change the flex of the wing. Of course, the best scenario when refueling a Mitsubishi MU-2 is to have two line personnel, each with a separate refueling hose, working independently on each side of the aircraft. This scenario makes refueling the aircraft faster, more efficient, and less likely to result in an unbalanced situation.

When refueling an aircraft that appears to be unbalanced, additional considerations are necessary. It is important to exercise extreme caution in opening filler caps on the lower wing, as fuel may rush out, resulting in a fuel spill.

Fuel Farm Management

Figure 4-23. Fuel farm. *(Oxanaso/Shutterstock.com)*

Fuel farms are areas where fuel is stored in bulk at airports. It may indeed appear to be a farm, as there are typically several aboveground storage tanks containing avgas and Jet A fuels. Pilots expect high-quality fuel that is of the correct type and grade and free of any contamination. As a result, the fuel farm must be properly managed to ensure the delivery of quality fuel meeting these standards.

Fuel must be regularly checked for **contaminants**. Different types of contaminants may exist in fuel, including water, particulate, microbial organism growth, surfactants, and improper fuel mixing. Water, which appears as a cloud, haze, or droplets at the bottom of the fuel sample, must be eliminated by draining, extracting with a sump pump, or using monitor elements and filter separators. Free water can cause many complications for an aircraft. It can freeze in fuel lines and filters, stimulate the growth of microorganisms that can block fuel lines and filters, or if it's severe enough can cause engine shutdown or flameout. In contrast to free water, if fuel contains dissolved water, this refers to water occurring in such trace amounts that fuel is not considered contaminated. Next, particulates such as sand, fiber, particles, and metal shavings can contaminate fuel and may result from damaged filters and rust and scale from storage tanks, hatches, pipes, and nozzles. Particulates are best removed by micron filters, monitors, and filter separators. Microorganisms, including bacteria, fungi, and yeast, are another form of contamination. These can damage or obstruct fuel filters, corrode engine components, and cause fuel deterioration. The most effective way to minimize the presence of microorganisms is to eliminate free water in the fuel. Surfactants, such as soap, can enter the fuel system through inadvertent chemical contamination, such as improperly cleaned tanks or motor gasoline residue. Finally, mixing of different types and grades of aviation fuels is also a form of contamination. This can be prevented by segregating each type and grade of fuel and properly marking tanks and fueling trucks. To ensure high-quality fuel, filtration is performed at three stages: as fuel is loaded into storage tanks, when it is loaded onto the refueler, and when it is delivered to the aircraft.

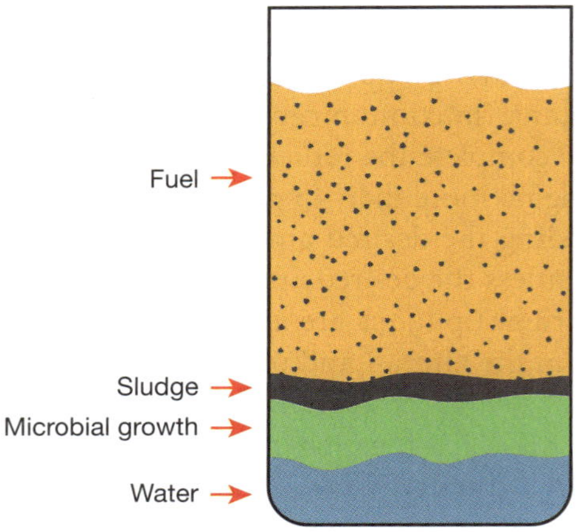

Figure 4-24. Fuel contamination.

Each type and grade of aviation fuel has a unique color. Avgas may be in 80/87 octane (red in color), 100/130 (green in color), or 100 Low Lead (blue in color). Although 80/87 octane is used in lower-powered piston engines, and 100/130 is used in high-performance piston engines, 100LL is most common, is compatible with all reciprocating engines, and is offered by the majority of FBOs. Jet fuel, most commonly in the form of Jet A, is clear or occasionally straw in color. Additionally, each fuel has a universal marking and coding system. All tanks, pipelines, filter vessels, valves, and fittings must be marked with the appropriate grade, ID, and color banding. Avgas has white letters on a red background. Additionally, 100LL has a blue band, 80 octane has a red band, and 100 octane has a green band. If the entire system is painted the appropriate color, no colored banding is required on the valves and fittings. Jet A has white letters on a black background, next to a single black band. The entire Jet A system may be painted white, silver, or aluminum colored with black joints, fittings, and valves.

Fuel at fuel farms may be stored in either underground tanks or above-ground tanks. Although there are strict requirements for underground storage tanks (including leaking underground storage tanks [LUST]), there are some advantages to locating tanks underground, including minimizing sabotage and making more ramp space available. Typically, however, FBOs have above-ground tanks at their fuel farms. All successful FBOs have accurate recordkeeping and clean, well-maintained fuel farms. Security is also important to protect the fuel farm area. Most commonly, this is in the form of chain-link fencing with three strands of barbed wire on top. Additionally, "No Smoking" and "Flammable" signs should be posted. Emergency shutoff controls must be properly marked, fire extinguishers must be present, and bonding cables must be available at all loading and unloading locations.

To ensure high-quality fuel, periodic testing and monitoring must be performed. There are four main types of tests that are performed.

1. The *clear and bright test* is utilized for both jet fuel and avgas to determine clarity and the presence of particulates or water in the fuel. Also, the proper color of the fuel can be verified.
2. The *white bucket test* is used for testing jet fuel and provides the ability to identify water, particulates, and microorganisms in the fuel. A water finder and sump check may be used to detect water in fuels. Water is heavier than aviation fuel and will settle to the bottom of all storage tanks and piping.
3. The *millipore test* is used to evaluate particulate contamination of aviation fuels. Named after the Millipore Corporation—the company that originally manufactured the membrane—this test requires drawing a fuel sample through a filter membrane with a pore size of 0.8 microns. Samples can be analyzed using three different methods: colorimetric, gravimetric, or microscopic. Of these, colorimetric is most common and allows a comparison of the color and intensity of the membrane to established standards.
4. *The differential pressure check* is conducted by measuring the difference between the inlet pressure and the outlet pressure with fuel flowing through the filtration vessel. A drop between inlet and outlet pressure is normal with a new filter, ranging between 2–7 psi. However, as fuel flows through the filter and collects contaminants, the differential pressure will increase. The filter elements need replacing when (a) the corrected differential pressure equals or exceeds 15 psi, (b) a drastic drop in differential pressure is experienced, (c) no differential pressure is shown, or (d) free water is found downstream of the filter vessel.

Figure 4-25. Fuel test. *(U.S. Navy photo by Mass Communication Specialist 3rd Class Jerine Lee, public domain)*

Daily fuel farm checks consist of:

- Storage tanks
  - › Clear and bright test on avgas
  - › White bucket test on jet fuel
  - › Water detection test on each storage tank
- Filter separators
  - › Clear and bright or white bucket test on each filter separator sump drain
  - › Monitor differential pressure on the direct reading gauge
- Overall
  - › Fuel tank quantity, tank vents and hatches, bonding wires, hoses and connections, pumps and motors, overall storage area, fire extinguishers

Weekly fuel farm checks consist of:

- Emergency shutoff and deadman controls
- Floating suction on storage tanks
- Signage and placards

Monthly fuel farm checks consist of:

- Millipore/membrane testing
- Hoses (working pressure test)
- Pumps, reels, and motors (oil level)
- Water slug test (if equipped with water slug shutoff valves)
- Month-end fuel inventory
  - › A full inventory of fuel ordered and delivered is compared to the fuel levels in each storage tank and each refueler. Keep in mind that fuel consumed in testing may have an impact on monthly inventory.

Ground Services and Handling

Each FBO provides a certain menu of services, and various ground services and handling are usually at the top of the list.

Figure 4-26. Aircraft towing. *(Media_works/Shutterstock.com)*

TOWING

Towing is the movement of an aircraft with a specialized vehicle. This task requires hand–eye coordination and skills that are developed with practice. Prior to towing any aircraft, however, the line service specialist must be aware of proper aircraft care and handling. All aircraft components can be delicate and subject to damage if they come into contact with any ground equipment, other aircraft, or objects. What appears to be minor damage can cause catastrophic failure in flight. Therefore, it is important that line service personnel notify their supervisors of any aircraft damage, no matter how insignificant. Keeping quiet in hopes of avoiding negative consequences is not an option.

When moving aircraft, the line service specialist must be certain of clearances. If in doubt, the specialist must stop the vehicle and check clearances. If there is concern about the amount of clearance, the use of **wing walkers** is highly recommended. Wing walkers assist on each wingtip in ensuring proper clearance. Remember, it is the line service specialist's job to ensure the safety of a customer's aircraft.

Tow vehicles include tugs, tractors, electric towing units, gas-powered walk-behind units, remote-controlled units, handheld towbars, and nose cradles on vehicles without towbars. These may be operated from a standing, seated, or remote position depending on the vehicle. Tugs that allow the driver to be seated are typically the most common tow vehicle in use at FBOs.

Figure 4-27. Wing walker in position. *(Rebius/Shutterstock.com)*

Tugs connect at either the nose gear (for tricycle gear aircraft) or the tail wheel (for taildragger aircraft). The connection point may be the nose gear wheel axle, nose gear shear pins, or towbar connection points. Prior to towing, the proper towbar (if required) must be selected. Options include a universal-fit towbar or a custom towbar. Typically, larger turboprop and jet aircraft require use of a unique towbar head. Be aware that once underway, aircraft develop momentum that can cause difficulty in stopping. Larger corporate jet aircraft can weigh 35 tons. Thus, speed must be kept to a minimum, with plenty of space to bring the aircraft to a complete stop. Likewise, if an aircraft becomes disconnected from the tow vehicle during a towing operation, move the vehicle away from the aircraft and allow the aircraft to stop on its own. Never attempt to stop the moving aircraft.

What is the typical process for towing an aircraft? First, the preferred route of travel must be determined. This should be the safest and most direct route available. After performing a vehicle safety check (including making sure the correct towbar is available), the tug is started and the brakes are tested as the front of the (tricycle gear) aircraft is approached. Once in position, the engine is turned off and the parking brake is set. Next, the towbar is attached to the aircraft. Be sure to check for any turning limit markers on the nose gear. Next, the towbar is connected to the tug. Prior to towing the aircraft, an aircraft walk-around should be performed. Are chocks removed? Are the aircraft tie-down cables removed? Is the aircraft parking brake off? As the tug is started, check for clearance around the aircraft and in the intended direction of travel, slowly and smoothly beginning to move the aircraft. While towing, the driver must stay alert and keep their eyes moving. When pulling the aircraft into position, the driver must slowly and smoothly come to a stop. The tug is placed in park, the engine is turned off, and the parking brake is set. Chocks are positioned to secure the aircraft and the towbar is disconnected first from the tug and then from the aircraft. Safe line service specialists know to never remove the towbar without first securing the aircraft with chocks; otherwise, the aircraft may roll into the tug.

When towing into a hangar, additional considerations apply. In these confined areas, hazards such as wing clearances, tail height in relation to ceiling limits, hangar door openings, and various obstructions must be considered. Wing walkers are very important when moving aircraft in or out of a hangar. The wing walker and tug driver should always maintain eye contact to ensure a successful operation. When pushing an aircraft back, the driver always steers the tug in the same direction intended for the aircraft. When moving the aircraft over hangar door tracks, it is important to avoid stopping the aircraft while the landing gear wheels are over the tracks. Further, the hangar door should be approached so that both wheels cross over the track at the same time. An aircraft with a red maintenance tag on the nose gear should never be moved. Also, avoid overlapping wing surfaces in a hangar; if a landing gear strut collapses, substantial damage may result. Also, avoid parking aircraft within the propeller arc of another aircraft. By following these guidelines, the line service specialist can ensure a safe towing operation within the hangar environment.

The **International Business Aviation Council (IBAC)**, in collaboration with the National Air Transportation Association (NATA), has produced the **International Standard for Business Aircraft Handlers (IS-BAH)** to provide a global set of industry best practices for business aviation ground handlers. If followed, these standards provide for safe and efficient aircraft ground handling. IS-BAH uses **safety management system (SMS)** concepts as a foundation. In reality, these standards can be adopted by any FBO, with line service personnel trained accordingly.

GROUND POWER

Yet another service provided by line service specialists is **ground power unit (GPU)** support. The GPU is used to provide a source of electricity to power aircraft systems while the aircraft is on the ramp without engines running (Figure 4-28). GPUs are typical at FBOs, although they are much less so at main air carrier terminals because a 400 Hz power cord is usually provided by the airport at the jet bridge. GPUs can be used for starting engines and provide a power output of 12, 28, or 115 volts. Caution must be exercised, as delivering the wrong voltage to an aircraft will damage the aircraft's electrical system. The procedures for using a GPU are as follows:

1. Determine aircraft power requirements and select proper GPU.
2. Position power unit at rear of aircraft.
3. Do not position within 10 feet radius of fuel tank vents.
4. Set GPU parking brake.
5. Start GPU engine and allow it to warm up to normal operating temperature.
6. Verify generator switch is off and connect the cable to the aircraft. Never connect the GPU to the aircraft with the generator running, as a dangerous electrical arc may occur.
7. Once the pilot is ready, bring the GPU up to operating speed, check voltage and amperage, and switch generator on.
8. Remember to switch the generator off prior to disconnecting the cable from the aircraft to avoid an electrical arc.

Figure 4-28. Ground power unit. *(Longfin Media/Shutterstock.com)*

Figure 4-29. Aircraft deicing. *(Gulliver20/Shutterstock.com)*

DEICING

Depending on the climate, aircraft may need to be deiced prior to a flight operation. Although the airport may have a central aircraft deicing pad with either mobile or fixed deicing equipment, the FBO may need to provide these services. The key is to ensure all customer aircraft are prepared for safe flight, even during winter operations.

Technically, deicing removes snow and ice from the aircraft surfaces, while anti-icing provides holdover protection for the aircraft until it can get airborne. This is especially true for current winter conditions, such as freezing rain, that the aircraft will be exposed to once deiced and prior to takeoff. Deicing and anti-icing fluids are typically glycol-based with dye and polymers. Although ethylene glycol may be more effective in colder temperatures, propylene glycol has less environmental impacts.

Deicing and anti-icing fluid is commonly applied using mobile applicators, unless the airport has a dedicated aircraft deicing facility, such as at Philadelphia International Airport. The deicing process can be either a one- or two-step procedure. The one-step procedure can deice and apply anti-ice in a single step using a heated mixture. The two-step procedure first requires deicing fluid to be applied, and then within three minutes an anti-ice fluid is applied. The specific process and chemicals used varies among airports. The FBO will want to ensure that it complies with airport rules and regulations and minimizes environmental impacts during deicing operations.

LAVATORY

Aircraft arriving into an FBO may be equipped with a lavatory on board. An aircraft lavatory is one of two types—a portable lift-out system or a permanently installed internal system. Both types may require servicing upon landing. While servicing any lavatory, personnel must wear protective gloves and goggles to prevent inadvertent exposure to bacteria and disease. Portable systems can be lifted out and taken to a remote fill and disposal location. These systems should be flushed and refilled with clean water. It is best to wait until the unit is reinstalled in the aircraft prior to adding blue deodorant tablets. If not, a spill upon entering the aircraft may result in blue water being spilled inside the cabin.

Fixed internal lavatory systems may also need to be serviced. These systems must be serviced with a lavatory service truck or a service cart. Servicing these systems involves connecting a discharge hose and water fill line to the aircraft. Once the waste is discharged and the system is flushed, blue deodorant water is pumped into the holding tank to the recommended fill level. The flight crew should be notified of any leaks and the waste should be disposed of at approved locations.

Figure 4-30. Lavatory servicing. *(ungvar/Shutterstock.com)*

Figure 4-31. Potable water servicing. *(letspicsit/Shutterstock.com)*

POTABLE WATER

Potable water servicing may also be necessary. Potable water is the term given to sanitary drinking water. Aircraft with potable water on board will have one of two systems. A portable lift out container is serviced from a potable water faucet at the FBO. An installed tank is filled from a remote location outside the aircraft and is serviced with a water truck or pull-behind cart.

LUBRICANTS

All aircraft engines utilize oil. It is this oil that provides a fluid barrier between moving parts to prevent friction and wear. Oil also provides up to 40 percent of an aircraft's air-cooled engine's cooling. Due to its importance, an aircraft may need to have oil added.

The line service specialist will first ensure that the correct oil viscosity is being used. Monograde oils are a petroleum-based lubricant with a single viscosity grade, such as SAE 30, SAE 40, SAE 50, or SAE 60. Multigrade oils are either full mineral-based or a synthetic blend; these include 15W-50, 20W-50, and 25W-60. Straight mineral oil is usually recommended by manufacturers for the first 50 hours of engine break-in. This oil allows for faster piston ring seating. Ashless dispersant oils can be in multigrade and monograde and are additives designed to minimize deposit formation, prevent contaminants from forming sludge, and keep combustion byproducts suspended in the oil until draining and replacement.

AIRCRAFT CLEANING

A clean aircraft is more likely to hold its value, be more efficient in flight, and provide a pleasing experience for both passengers and crew. Therefore, the line service specialist may be called upon to clean either an aircraft exterior or interior. The aircraft exterior is typically washed as one would wash an automobile, using special cleaning solutions and drying the aircraft after washing. A clean exterior is critical to maintaining efficiency in flight, as a clean surface produces less drag than a dirty surface. More likely, the line service specialist will be asked to clean the interior of an aircraft. Interior cleaning includes vacuuming the interior, washing galley and lavatory surfaces, removing trash, and straightening seat belts. No one should ever enter the cabin without flight crew permission, however. Prior to cleaning, the attendant will make sure to have the proper supplies and protection (including gloves), and have clean shoes (rather than oily boots). It is important to be efficient yet thorough, which will please both passengers and crew.

Figure 4-32. Aircraft windshield cleaning. *(iStock.com/andresr)*

Yet another service provided by line service is windshield cleaning. Although this sounds fairly basic, certain rules unique to aircraft must be adhered to. Whether cleaning a glass or plexiglass windshield, shop rags should never be used, as small metal particles may be present that could scratch the windshield. Most cleaners are designed for either glass or Plexiglas, but not both. Additionally, it is important to use plenty of solution and wipe in the direction of airflow (never in a circular motion).

Guidance and Parking

Marshalling of aircraft is yet another role of the line service specialist. Pilots need assistance in knowing where to park at unfamiliar FBOs. The role of the marshaller is to provide this direction and ensure adequate wingtip clearances using common hand signals, shown in FAA Advisory Circular 00-34A, *Aircraft Ground Handling and Servicing*, Appendix 1 (FAA 1974). When acting as a marshaller, the individual is considered an extension of the pilot and is there for the pilot's benefit. A marshaller has an unobstructed view and better perspective than the pilot sitting in the cockpit.

Marshallers are typically located in front of the aircraft nose and in full view of the pilot. If the marshaller can't see the pilot, the pilot will not be able to see the marshaller. The marshaller must also wear hearing protection and have illuminated wands for night operation. Orange wands are typically used during daytime operations to enhance visibility of hand signals. The following is a list of typical safety procedures utilized by marshallers.

1. Always remain visible to the pilot.
2. Use standard aviation hand signals.
3. Fully extend arms and provide clear signals.
4. When directing arriving aircraft to a parking position, establish and remain in the proper position prior to the aircraft arriving on the ramp.
5. Be aware of the pilot's reaction and adjust hand signals if necessary.
6. Use additional personnel to assist in congested areas or provide additional clearance guidance.
7. Never position a small aircraft where it will be in danger of jet blast.
8. Remain clear of propellers and rotors.
9. Secure the aircraft using appropriate chocks and tie-downs.

Figure 4-33. Aircraft marshalling signals. *(Denis Dubrovin/Shutterstock.com)*

Fixed-base operators also have facilities for storing planes. Several storage options are usually available for both based and transient aircraft, and these options can be divided into two categories—hangar and tie-down. Hangars, offering protection from the elements, are often available for an individual or corporation to rent and can be found in a variety of sizes, from those designed for a small, single-engine airplane to large buildings that can house a corporate fleet. Also, many aviation businesses offer storage options in a general or community hangar. This is usually where any transient aircraft will be kept overnight, and this option can be less expensive for the aircraft owner than a single-user hangar. A tie-down space is generally less expensive than hangar storage. Tie-downs are open areas on the airport ramp that allow an airplane to be secured to the ramp via ropes, chains, or other means.

FOD Management

Although not necessarily a specific task, the line service specialist must always be aware of and on the lookout for **foreign object debris (FOD)**. FOD may appear both on the line and the ramp, including near hangars, the FBO terminal building, and the fence line. FOD can cause severe damage to persons on the ramp and aircraft as objects are picked up by jet blast or propwash and propelled into the air or ingested into the engine. As a result, persons on the ramp must always be on the lookout for pieces of metal, trash, or other items that simply don't belong.

Figure 4-34. FOD on taxiway shoulder. *(U.S. Air Force, public domain)*

An employee attitude expecting someone else to pick up this debris is simply not one that a successful FBO can afford to have.

An example of the effects of FOD (although on a runway) occurred on July 25, 2000. On this unfortunate day, a piece of titanium from an earlier departing aircraft remained on the runway and was rolled over by a Concorde on its departure roll. A tire blew, spraying the fuselage with pieces of rubber that then shattered a fuel tank and eventually brought down the aircraft, resulting in the deaths of 100 passengers and 9 crew on board and 4 people on the ground. Obviously, the important role of the line service specialist in detecting and retrieving FOD, even before it gets to the movement area, cannot be overstated.

Summary

With the growth of the regional airlines in recent years, many FBOs have established contractual services with the air carriers, including fueling, exterior cleaning, interior cleaning, deicing, turbine starting, minor maintenance, and in some cases even baggage handling and screening passengers and their baggage. Thus, line service specialists are increasingly called upon to fulfill these requests for additional services. Rather than detracting from the line service profession, this simply enforces the importance of line service at FBOs.

Line service, as the bread and butter of the FBO, requires highly skilled personnel working in a professional, safety-focused environment. By using proper terminology, proper fueling techniques, and proper towing techniques, line service personnel can make significant contributions to the success of the FBO.

Key Terms

aqueous film forming foam (AFFF). A fire suppressant used to extinguish flammable liquid fires such as fuel fires.

avgas. Fuel (typically 100LL) used in piston-engine aircraft.

bonding. Use of a cable to connect a fueler to an aircraft for the purpose of providing a conductive path to equalize the potential so that no spark will jump from one to the other.

Class A fire. A fire involving ordinary combustibles, such as wood, paper, cloth, etc.

Class B fire. A fire involving flammable liquids, such as grease, oil, paint, solvents, etc.

Class C fire. A fire involving live electrical equipment, such as an electrical panel, motor, wiring, etc.

Class D fire. A fire involving combustible metal, such as magnesium, aluminum, etc.

contaminants. Contents that degrade the quality of fuel. Types of fuel contaminants include water, particulates, microbial organisms, surfactants, and improper fuel mixing.

Coordinated Universal Time (UTC). The time at the meridian of the globe or zero degrees longitude, which passes through Greenwich, England. Also designated as Greenwich Mean Time or Zulu time, it allows standardization of time worldwide.

deadman control. Unique to the single-point system, this control allows delivery of fuel from a position slightly away from the aircraft and will only start the flow of fuel when the deadman control is held open. It consists of a control valve with a handheld electric or hydraulic deadman handle (switch) deployed via a cable or hose reel assembly.

empennage. Also referred to as the aircraft tail, this part of the aircraft generally contains the rudder and elevator.

engine. The powerplant(s) on an aircraft providing the driving force behind powered flight, propelling the aircraft forward and allowing lift to be created by the wings.

extinguishing agent. An agent (substance) that extinguishes a fire by removing the heat element (and possibly disturbing the chemical reaction).

fire safety. Knowledge of the elements of the fire triangle and fire tetrahedron as well as knowledge in preventing and extinguishing fires.

fire tetrahedron. Represents the four elements required in proper proportion to ignite and sustain a fire, which are oxygen, heat, fuel, and a chemical reaction.

fire triangle. Represents the three elements required in proper proportion to ignite a fire, which include oxygen, heat, and fuel.

flashpoint. The temperature at which the fuel produces sufficient vapors to form an ignitable mixture with air near the surface of the container, but will not sustain combustion.

foreign object debris (FOD). Any object, live or not, located in an inappropriate location in the airport environment that has the capacity to injure airport or air carrier personnel and damage aircraft.

fuel farm. Areas where fuel is stored in bulk at airports. An efficient way to provide storage and dispensing of aviation fuels to multiple users at an airport.

fuel spill. Accidental release of fuel, typically on an airport that requires cleanup and environmental remediation.

fuselage. The body or main structure of the aircraft. The fuselage serves as the attachment area for the wings and tail assembly, provides space for crew and passengers, and houses various flight controls and instruments.

ground power unit (GPU). A unit used to provide a source of electricity to power aircraft systems while the aircraft is on the ramp without engines running.

International Business Aviation Council (IBAC). An international trade association that provides advocacy and intelligence for business aviation.

International Standard for Business Aircraft Handlers (IS-BAH). A set of global industry best practices developed by IBAC to provide standard safety protocols for the ground handling of business aircraft.

Jet A. Kerosene-based fuel used in turboprop and turbine engines.

jet engine. An engine that operates by compressing air, igniting it, and thrusting it out the back.

line service. Service provided to aircraft on the line, which includes marshalling, fueling, etc.

line service specialist. Personnel responsible for providing service to aircraft on the line.

marshalling. The job of providing direction to aircraft for parking and taxi out by ensuring adequate wingtip clearances using common hand signals.

National Fire Protection Association (NFPA). A nonprofit organization that developed NFPA 407, *Standard for Aircraft Fuel Servicing*, that provides guidance on the safe refueling of aircraft and applies to fuel farms, self-serve fueling, mobile fuelers, and other fueling operations.

over-the-wing refueling. Aircraft refueling accomplished through fuel tank caps on the upper surface of the wing; this method is most common on piston-engine aircraft.

phonetic alphabet. The International Radiotelephony Spelling Alphabet used in aviation to pronounce letters and avoid miscommunication.

reciprocating piston engine. Common to a large majority of single-engine aircraft and light twin-engine aircraft, this engine type is similar to an automobile engine and operates by moving pistons, which in turn move a crankshaft, which in turn spins the propeller. This engine commonly uses 100LL avgas.

Safety 1st. A program developed by the National Air Transportation Association (NATA) to present industry best practices for safe line service operations.

Safety 1st Clean. A standard developed by NATA in response to the COVID-19 pandemic to provide guidelines to FBOs in ensuring proper cleaning and disinfection to minimize spread of contagious diseases. It provides guidelines on facility cleaning, disinfecting, and facility operations during a pandemic.

safety management system (SMS). A proactive safety system that consists of safety policy and objectives, safety risk management, safety assistance, and safety promotion.

single-point refueling. A method of refueling an aircraft from a single point, commonly via a pressurized system, often under the wing.

spill cart. A mobile cart that provides absorbent materials that contain a fuel spill and prevent it from spreading into drains or other areas.

tail number. An identification number typically painted on the tail of an aircraft, either on the vertical stabilizer or the engine nacelle. It is typically referred to as N-number in the U.S and is provided as part of aircraft registration.

tip tank. Fuel tanks at the tip of the wing commonly used when the wing volume is insufficient to carry needed fuel or to extend aircraft range beyond what is possible with wing tanks.

towing. Using a tug to move aircraft not under power, either for pushback or into or out of a hangar.

turboprop engine. Turbine engine that drives an aircraft propellor. Utilizes Jet A fuel.

undercarriage. The area underneath the main fuselage and wing sections of an aircraft that primarily contains the landing gear or wheels. It may also include cowl flaps, landing lights, and antennas.

wing walker. Role of a line service personnel to add assurance to pilots as they taxi in and out of parking areas, ensuring adequate wingtip clearance with other aircraft and equipment.

wing. The primary purpose of the wing, or airfoil, is to produce lift. Thus, wings are extremely strong and lightweight. On conventional aircraft, wings will contain most of the usable fuel on board.

Review Questions

1. What is the most visible aspect of an FBO?
2. What is the role of the line service specialist?
3. What makes up the knowledge base for a line service specialist?
4. Why is fire safety important for the line service specialist?
5. What are the four classes of fires?
6. What principles are used in extinguishing a fire?
7. What measures should be taken by FBOs to minimize the risk of fire?
8. What are the three types of aircraft fuel filler caps?
9. What are the proper steps in refueling an aircraft?
10. Explain the three different types of aircraft engines that a line service specialist would expect to service.
11. Describe the types of fuel contamination.
12. What are the different types and colors of aviation fuel?
13. What are the procedures to follow in towing an aircraft?
14. What are the safety procedures typically utilized by marshallers?
15. What are two categories of aircraft storage?
16. What services, in addition to fueling, may a line service specialist be expected to carry out?

Scenarios

1. An MU-2 aircraft just taxied into your ramp and requested to be "topped off." As you approach the aircraft, it appears to be leaning toward one side. What do you do?
2. This is only your second day as a line service specialist at a full-service FBO. The line service manager, who has been quizzing you on various aspects of line service, recently handed you a quiz. You were instructed to answer the following questions and have it back to her before lunch.
   a. What color is 100LL?
   b. If it is 1400(L), and we are in EDT, what time is it in Zulu time?
   c. A pilot in a King Air just called in and requested maintenance to look at the oil pressure in the number two engine. Which engine is he referring to?
   d. Your co-worker just rushed in to say there was a fire behind the hangar. Upon arriving on scene, you see some cardboard burning. What class of fire is this and what is the preferred extinguishing agent?
   e. What is a J spout?
3. You are underway towing a Piper Seminole toward the hangar. As you near the hangar door, you realize that it will be a tight fit getting between two aircraft parked near the entrance. What do you?

4. A pilot that just arrived into the ramp is concerned about your ability to correctly fuel his aircraft. He starts quizzing you to determine your level of knowledge, asking, "What types of testing do you do for quality control at your fuel farm?" If your FBO followed the guidance in this chapter, what would you tell him?

5. You have three years of experience as a line service specialist. Your FBO just hired a new line service specialist whom you have been instructed to train. After fueling a King Air, the new employee asks, "Why didn't you put avgas in that aircraft? It has props just like that Seminole you fueled over there." How do you answer the new employee and explain the differences?

Bibliography

FAA (Federal Aviation Administration). 1974. *Aircraft Ground Handling and Servicing.* AC 00-34A. July 29, 1974. https://www.faa.gov/documentLibrary/media/Advisory_Circular/AC_00-34A.pdf.

FAA (Federal Aviation Administration). 2022. *Contractions.* Order JO 7340.2L, Change 3. November 3. 2022. https://www.faa.gov/documentLibrary/media/Order/7340.2L_CNT_Bsc_w_Chg_1_2_and_3_dtd_11_3_22.pdf.

FAA (Federal Aviation Administration). 2023. *Aircraft Firefighting Foam Transition Plan.* May 8, 2023. https://www.faa.gov/sites/faa.gov/files/FAA_Aircraft_F3_Transition_Plan_2023.pdf.

Kramer, Lois S. 2020. *ACRP Synthesis 108: Characteristics of the FBO Industry 2018–2019.* Washington, DC: Airport Cooperative Research Program, National Academy of Sciences. http://www.trb.org/Main/Blurb/180833.aspx.

NATA (National Air Transportation Association). 2017. *The State of the FBO Industry.* March 31, 2017. Washington, DC: NATA. https://www.nata.aero/data/files/gia/nata%20formal%20response%20on%20state%20of%20the%20industry.pdf.

NFPA (National Fire Protection Association). 2022. *NFPA 407: Standard for Aircraft Fuel Servicing.*

Prather, C. Daniel. 2009. *General Aviation Marketing and Management: Operating, Marketing, and Managing an FBO.* 3rd ed. Malabar, FL: Krieger Publishing Company.

5

FBO Services

In Chapter 5

Objectives

At the end of this chapter, you should be able to:

1. Discuss the benefits of having a maintenance department at an FBO.
2. Discuss the various Federal Aviation Regulations applicable to aircraft maintenance.
3. Realize the differences between Aviation Mechanics possessing an Airframe Rating, Powerplant Rating, A&P Rating, and Inspection Authorization (IA).
4. Explain what 100-hour and annual inspections are.
5. Explain a progressive inspection program and continuous inspection program.
6. Discuss the avionics typically requiring inspection.
7. Discuss the benefits and considerations in offering flight instruction, aircraft rental, and charter services.
8. Discuss the aircraft sales process and considerations necessary in forming an aircraft sales division at an FBO.
9. Discuss aircraft management services.

Introduction

As noted in chapter 4, the principal business of fixed-base operators is line service, which includes the retail sales of fuel and oil, minor repairs, emergency service, and other minor services for general aviation aircraft, including lavatory service, cleaning, etc. In addition to line service, FBOs may also maintain storage facilities for private aircraft, provide major maintenance and overhaul services, and offer flight instruction and charter services. Some of the larger FBOs are also active in selling new and used aircraft. A few of the larger operators offer aircraft management services, which allow high-net-worth individuals and corporations the ability to own an aircraft, with all maintenance, fueling, and even crewing taken care of by the FBO.

Maintenance

OVERVIEW

The proper maintenance of aircraft is necessary so that aircraft can be maintained in an airworthy condition, as required by the **Federal Aviation Regulations (FARs)**. The aircraft owner/operator is responsible for ensuring that maintenance personnel, upon completion of necessary maintenance, make appropriate entries in the aircraft maintenance records indicating the aircraft has been approved for return to service. It is the responsibility of the owner and operator to have maintenance performed that may be required between scheduled inspections.

Inspection of airframes, powerplants, propellers, and appliances is the single most effective way to identify potential problems with aircraft and ensure safe operations. The FAA requires aircraft and their associated components to be inspected at regular intervals. The frequency of these inspections varies depending on the type of aircraft, primary use, and components installed. As a result, inspections, maintenance, and repairs can be a primary business function of an FBO.

Although corporate-owned aircraft may be maintained by an in-house maintenance department, there are many aircraft owners that utilize FBOs for aircraft maintenance. FBOs that present a complete offering of services will include maintenance in those services. At a minimum, these maintenance services will cover piston-engine aircraft. Larger FBOs with the proper equipment and personnel will also have larger aircraft maintenance departments that are capable of maintaining turboprop and jet aircraft.

Figure 5-1. Aircraft maintenance in progress. *(industryviews/Shutterstock.com)*

Any maintenance performed on an aircraft today must comply with the FARs. When it becomes necessary to implement a new rule or change an existing FAR, the FAA creates a statement of reason and support called a **notice of proposed rulemaking (NPRM)** for publication in the ***Federal Register.*** After a predetermined period for public comments, proposals are adopted in Title 14 of the **Code of Federal Regulations (CFR)**, thus becoming a federal statute.

The FARs are organized into separate sections or parts. For example, Title 14 CFR Part 65 describes the requirements, privileges, and limitations for certification of airmen other that flight crewmembers, which includes aviation maintenance technicians and repairmen.

There are numerous regulations that are of vital importance to the aircraft maintenance industry, whether for experimental, private, commercial, or air cargo aircraft. Some of the regulations that specially concern general aviation are listed and discussed below:

- 14 CFR Part 1: Definitions and Abbreviations
- 14 CFR Part 21: Certification Procedures for Products and Articles
- 14 CFR Part 23: Airworthiness Standards: Normal Category Airplanes
- 14 CFR Part 39: Airworthiness Directives
- 14 CFR Part 43: Maintenance, Preventive Maintenance, Rebuilding, and Alteration
- 14 CFR Part 65: Certification: Airmen Other Than Flight Crewmembers
- 14 CFR Part 91: General Operating and Flight Rules
- 14 CFR Part 145: Repair Stations

14 CFR PART 1

14 CFR Part 1 is an official listing containing the definitions of words and their abbreviations and associated symbols. Maintenance personnel utilize Part 1 terminology to distinguish between types of maintenance performed, such as **maintenance** (inspection, overhaul, repair, replacement of parts, and preservation) and **preventive maintenance** (oil and filter changes, and the replacement of small standard parts such as brakes, tires, or tubes).

14 CFR PART 21

14 CFR Part 21 details the requirements for establishing and maintaining the certification of aircraft and components. When an aircraft is assembled and test flown, an authorized representative must decide if it conforms to the appropriate model's FAA-approved **type certificate**. The type certificate lists all the essential information about the aircraft and its accessories. If the aircraft is in conformity to the type certificate for safe and reliable operation, it is then issued an **airworthiness certificate**, which signifies the aircraft meets acceptable standards for service. The airworthiness certificate remains with the aircraft during its service life, regardless of owner. However, proper and timely maintenance must be performed on the aircraft for the airworthiness certificate to remain valid.

14 CFR PART 23

14 CFR Part 23 describes the precise performance-based airworthiness standards that normal category airplanes and their related systems must demonstrate to be certified airworthy. It details the requirements for every component and system installed on the aircraft, down to the slightest detail. For example, whenever a cockpit instrument is repaired or replaced, technicians installing the instrument must ensure that the range markings on the instrument dial are correct according to the FAA approved aircraft flight manual.

14 CFR PART 39

Whenever an unsafe condition develops on an aircraft, engine, propeller, or accessory and is likely to exist in other products of a similar design, the FAA issues an **airworthiness directive (AD)** as an amendment to **14 CFR Part 39** to notify concerned parties or aircraft owners of the condition. FAA ADs are legally enforceable rules for anyone who operates a product for which an airworthiness directive applies. Airworthiness directives specify inspections the aircraft owner or operator must carry out, conditions and limitations that must be complied with, and any other actions that must be taken to resolve the unsafe condition. Airworthiness directives are part of the FARs but are not published in printed editions. The FAA publishes airworthiness directives in full in the *Federal Register* as an amendment to 14 CFR §39.13. Consequently, anyone who operates a product that does not meet the requirements of an applicable airworthiness directive is in violation of the FARs.

14 CFR PART 43

14 CFR Part 43 outlines the fundamental standards for general aviation aircraft inspection, maintenance, and repair, as well as all recordkeeping requirements. A **repair** is an operation that restores an item to a condition of useful operation or to original condition, whereas an **alteration** is a change in the configuration or design of an aircraft. Under 14 CFR Part 43, the FAA divides aircraft repairs and alterations into two categories: major and minor. A **major repair** is one that, if performed incorrectly, might significantly affect weight, balance, structural strength, performance, powerplant operation, flight characteristics, or other airworthiness factors. A **major alteration** is any change or alteration not listed in the aircraft, powerplant, or accessory specifications that might affect the product's performance in a fashion similar to a major repair. Part 43 defines **minor repairs and alterations** as those that are not considered major repairs or alterations. Since this definition is not very specific, it is sometimes difficult to distinguish in which category a repair or alteration is considered to be.

Preventive maintenance consists of preservation, upkeep, and the simple replacement of small parts. In some situations, the FARs allow licensed airmen other than maintenance technicians to perform preventive maintenance tasks. Specifically, the individual performing preventive maintenance must be the holder of at least a private pilot certificate issued under 14 CFR Part 61, must be the registered owner (including co-owners) of the affected aircraft, and must hold a certificate of competency for the affected aircraft issued by the holder of the production certificate for that primary category aircraft that has a special training program approved under 14 CFR §21.24 or issued by another entity that has a course approved by the FAA. Once the individual meets these qualifications, the owner can, among other things, change the aircraft's engine oil and replace a landing gear tire. A comprehensive list of items that are considered preventive maintenance are included in Appendix A of 14 CFR Part 43.

Section 43.15 catalogs the performance criteria for performing inspections on most general aviation aircraft types, and specifically states that a checklist that meets the minimum requirements listed in 14 CFR Part 43 Appendix D must be used for all annual and 100-hour inspections. This does not preclude the operator developing a more comprehensive checklist or using one prepared by a repair station or manufacturer. As long as the checklist covers all the items in Appendix D, and is approved by the local FAA office, it may be used. Most aircraft, powerplant, and propeller manufacturers provide inspection checklists for their equipment type. These forms are readily available through the particular manufacturer and often include references to service bulletins and information letters that contain important product service and improvement information.

14 CFR PART 65

Airframe and Powerplant

14 CFR Part 65 discusses the certification requirements, as well as the privileges and limitations, for aviation maintenance technicians. Under current regulations, there are two certificates for maintenance personnel described in part 65, each with different privileges and limitations. They are the Mechanic Certificate and the Repairmen Certificate. In addition, there are two ratings issued to certificated mechanics, the **Airframe Rating** and the **Powerplant Rating**.

The FAA requires at least 18 months of practical experience with the procedures, practices, materials, tools, machine tools, and equipment generally used in constructing, maintaining, or altering airframes or powerplants for a Mechanic Certificate with an Airframe or Powerplant Rating. For a combined **Airframe and Powerplant (A&P) Rating**, at least 30 months of practical work experience concurrently performing the duties appropriate to both the airframe and powerplant ratings is required. All applicants must be at least 18 years old and able to read, write, speak, and understand English. In addition, they must pass a series of written and oral tests as well as a practical examination to demonstrate that they can perform the work authorized by the A&P certificate.

An Airframe and Powerplant Certificate remains in effect until it is surrendered, suspended, or revoked. A certificated mechanic may not exercise the privileges of his certificate and rating unless, within the preceding 24 months:

1. The Administrator has found that he is able to do that work; or
2. He has, for at least 6 months:
   a. Served as a mechanic under his certificate and rating;
   b. Technically supervised other mechanics; or
   c. Supervised, in an executive capacity, the maintenance or alteration of aircraft.

Privileges and Limitations

A certificated mechanic may perform or supervise the maintenance, the preventive maintenance, or an alteration of an aircraft, appliance, or part for which the technician is appropriately rated. A Mechanic Certificate with an Airframe Rating allows a mechanic to approve and return to service an airframe, or any related component or appliance, after performing, supervising, or inspecting its maintenance or alteration. An airframe-rated mechanic can perform 100-hour inspections on airframes and related parts or appliances and approve them for return to service. However, a technician with an Airframe Rating may not inspect or return to service an airframe or related part or appliance that has undergone a major repair or alteration.

A mechanic holding a Powerplant Rating can approve and return to service powerplants, propellers, and accessories after performing, supervising, or inspecting their maintenance or alteration. A powerplant-rated mechanic is allowed to perform 100-hour inspections on powerplants and propellers and return them to service. However, like the Airframe Rating, a Powerplant Rating does not permit a mechanic to inspect or return to service a powerplant, propeller, or accessory that has undergone a major repair or alteration.

Mechanics that possess both Airframe and Powerplant Ratings can perform minor repairs and alterations to airframes, powerplants, propellers, and components and approve these items for return to service. In addition, an A&P can perform major repairs and alterations to airframes, powerplants, and components. However, an A&P cannot perform major repairs or alterations to propellers or perform any type of repairs or alterations to instruments. An A&P can, however, perform 100-hour inspection procedures on airframes, powerplants, propellers, accessories, and instruments and approve them for return to service. It is important to note that an A&P cannot delegate their inspection duties while performing a 100-hour inspection. In addition, an A&P cannot perform annual inspections. However, they can correct discrepancies an authorized inspector discovers during an annual inspection.

Inspection Authorization

Technicians who have held a Mechanic Certificate with both an Airframe and Powerplant Rating for a minimum of three years and who have been actively involved in maintaining general aviation aircraft for at least two years can apply for an **Inspection Authorization (IA)**. In addition to all the privileges of an Airframe and Powerplant Rating, an IA permits a technician to perform an annual inspection on aircraft and approve it for return to service. Furthermore, an IA can perform major repairs and alterations made on airframes and powerplants and approve the work for return to service. However, an IA cannot perform major repairs and alterations to propellers or make repairs or alterations of instruments. Under current federal regulations, these tasks must be performed by an appropriately rated repair station.

Unlike an A&P rated technician, an IA's privileges expire on March 31 of each odd-numbered year. To renew the rating, the FAA requires that the IA achieve certain recurrency levels on an annual basis. For an IA's certificate to remain active, evidence must be shown that the IA has performed at least one annual every 90 days, inspected at least two major repairs or alterations every 90 days, performed or supervised at least one progressive inspection, completed an approved IA refresher course, or passed an oral test given by an FAA inspector.

Repairman Certificate

Many aircraft repair facilities work on aircraft components, accessories, and instruments. Technicians employed in these facilities performing maintenance-related activities such as component overhaul and rebuilding do not require the broad training required for an Airframe and Powerplant Certificate. However, the FAA does require training on the specific duties the technicians are expected to perform. Once a person satisfactorily completes the appropriate training, they can be issued a **Repairman Certificate**. 14 CFR Parts 65 and 145 identify the requirements for a Repairman Certificate for technicians performing specialized maintenance functions at certificated repair stations.

The holder of a Repairman Certificate can perform and supervise the maintenance, preventive maintenance, and alteration of an aircraft or its components for which the employer is certified. The Repairman Certificate is issued to a technician for the repair station at which they are employed. Therefore, if a repairman leaves the employment of the designated repair station, the certificate is surrendered.

14 CFR PART 91

Annual Inspection

One segment of aircraft operations, known as general aviation, are conducted under 14 CFR Part 91. As previously discussed, general aviation refers to all aviation other than commercial (scheduled and non-scheduled) airline operations and military aviation. Although general aviation usually involves small aircraft, the definition depends on the nature of the operation, not the size of the aircraft. The FAA requires aircraft and their associated components to be inspected regularly. The frequency of these inspections depends on the type and use of the aircraft or component.

Part 91 states that all general aviation aircraft must go through an **annual inspection** to remain airworthy. Annual inspections are based on calendar months; therefore, annuals are due on the last day of the 12th month after the last annual was completed. For example, if the preceding annual was completed on July 8, 2021, the next annual inspection would be due by July 31, 2022.

Annual inspections must be performed regardless of the number of hours flown in the preceding year. Annual inspections may only be performed by airframe and powerplant mechanics possessing a valid Inspection Authorization. If the person performing the annual inspection finds a discrepancy that makes the aircraft unairworthy, the mechanic is required to provide the aircraft owner with written notice of the discrepancy. Additionally, the defect must be corrected before the aircraft is approved for return to service. In special situations where the aircraft needs to be flown to a different location for repairs to be made, a special flight or ferry permit may be obtained to fly the aircraft to another location for repairs.

Figure 5-2. Aircraft annual inspection in progress. *(Delta Studio/Shutterstock.com)*

100-Hour Inspection

General aviation aircraft operated for flight instruction or hire must be inspected every 100 flight hours. For most types of general aviation aircraft, the **100-hour inspection** is in addition to the annual inspection check and often covers the same parameters as the annual inspections. A 100-hour inspection may be performed by an Aviation Mechanic whereas an annual inspection must be performed by an Aviation Mechanic who holds Inspection Authorization.

As the 100-hour inspection implies, actual flight hours are the primary consideration for determining when a 100-hour inspection is due. Simply, a 100-hour inspection is required in 100-hour increments after the last 100-hour inspection was completed, regardless of the calendar date. If the aircraft is away from the place where its regular maintenance is performed, there is a provision for extending the 100-hour interval up to 10 hours to allow the aircraft to be flown to its base. However, whenever this is required, the numbers of hours in excess of the 100-hour interval are deducted from the next inspection interval. For example, if it is necessary to fly the aircraft to a facility where a 100-hour inspection can be performed and the flight takes 5 hours to complete beyond the 100-hour interval, the next 100-hour inspection is due in 95 hours. Simply, the next inspection interval is shortened by the exact amount of time the previous inspection was extended.

Progressive Inspection

A **progressive inspection program** is an option for aircraft owners or operators routinely flying more than 400 hours and who do not wish to have their aircraft out of service for several days to complete a 100-hour or annual inspection. It must be approved by the FAA. For example, Phase 1 would require an in-depth inspection of the engine and propeller and a brief inspection of the rest of the aircraft. Then after a specified number of hours or calendar months, the next phase would include a quick inspection on the engine and fuselage but require a detailed inspection of wings and landing gear, and so on until the whole aircraft has had a detailed inspection. Usually, a progressive or phase inspection program requires the entire aircraft and all components be inspected within 12 calendar months.

Continuous Airworthiness Inspection Program

A **continuous airworthiness inspection program** is designed for operators of large commercial aircraft currently in use by a person holding an air carrier operating certificate issued under 14 CFR Part 121 or an operating certificate issued under 14 CFR Part 135. Like the progressive inspection program, the continuous airworthiness inspection program must be approved by the FAA and allows the owner/operator to maximize aircraft availability and reduce maintenance costs by dividing inspection requirements into regularly scheduled blocks.

Avionics

Modern aircraft navigation and communication systems are a complex mix of computers, sensors, actuators, and control and display units interconnected with many aircraft flight control and other systems. As aircraft systems have increased in sophistication, the avionics component accounts for an increasing proportion of the value of the aircraft. As part of an FBO's aircraft maintenance services, several important avionics checks and inspections must be performed.

ALTIMETER AND PITOT-STATIC SYSTEM

14 CFR §91.411 requires periodic **altimeter and pitot-static system** checks for aircraft that operate in controlled airspace under instrument flight rules (Figure 5-3). These checks must be completed in accordance with the guidelines of 14 CFR Part 43, Appendices E and F, and performed every 24 calendar months. Additionally, tests must be performed any time the static system is opened or otherwise disturbed.

TRANSPONDER

A **transponder** is an electronic device that detects incoming radar signals and broadcasts an encoded radio signal to the air traffic control system, providing aircraft identification, altitude, airspeed, and destination. Because of their critical safety role, transponders must be checked every 24 months. Transponder checks are complied with under 14 CFR §91.413 in accordance with Part 43, Appendices E and F.

EMERGENCY LOCATOR TRANSMITTER

Emergency locator transmitters (ELTs) are essential safety devices that have been used in aircraft for decades. In the event of an aircraft accident, these devices are designed to transmit a distress signal on 121.5 and 243.0 MHz frequencies, and for newer ELTs, on 406 MHz. ELTs are required to be installed in all U.S.-registered civil aircraft, including general aviation aircraft, as a result of a congressional mandate. When activated, these distress beacons send a signal to FAA air traffic control centers and towers that can pinpoint an aircraft's location. ELTs are automatically activated when the aircraft impacts the ground or water above a certain G-force or can be manually activated by the pilot. Section 91.207 requires that all U.S. aircraft be equipped with an ELT. These devices must be inspected every 12 calendar months for proper operation of the crash sensor, battery condition, and radio strength.

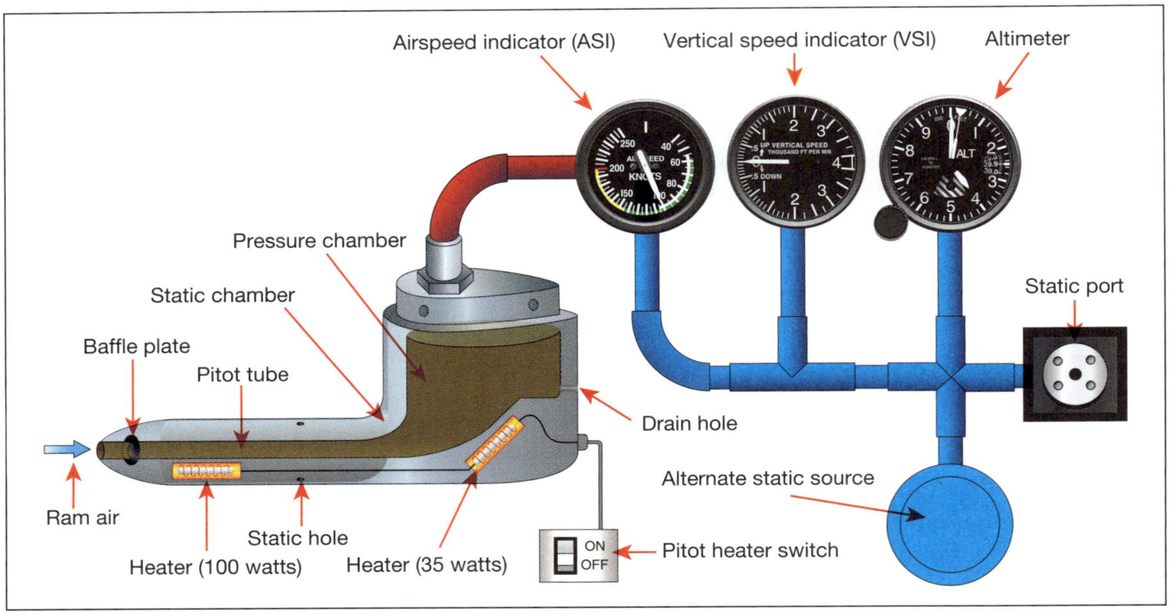

Figure 5-3. Pitot-static system and instruments. *(FAA Pilot's Handbook of Aeronautical Knowledge)*

14 CFR PART 145

FBOs located at major airports are often affiliated with aircraft manufacturers to provide aircraft maintenance and other services such as painting, interior improvements, or engine and component overhauls. In addition to providing flight training, fuel, and crew rest facilities, many FBOs also hold a **repair station certificate** issued by the FAA under 14 CFR Part 145. These certificates are the FBO's version of a "license to do business as a repair station." Authorized repair stations perform maintenance and alterations on civil aircraft, which includes engine overhauls, propellers, and the component parts installed on these products. These repair stations can also perform maintenance for airlines and air taxi or charter operators.

Today, many low-cost air carriers do not perform their own heavy maintenance on their respective aircraft fleets. As a result, several large repair stations have emerged, or existing repair stations have expanded, to accommodate the increased work from these air carriers. In an effort to reduce workforce numbers and expenses related to heavy maintenance work, there has been a trend for established air carriers to contract out heavy maintenance work to overseas repair stations that can perform the necessary procedures at substantially reduced costs.

To operate in the civil aviation maintenance industry, certificated repair stations must demonstrate to the FAA that they possess the facilities, equipment, personnel, technical data, and quality control systems necessary to perform maintenance in an airworthy and safe manner. A repair station is rated to perform certain types of maintenance on specific aircraft, engines or propeller types, and components such as generators or governors. Not all repair stations are alike, and their capabilities can vary significantly. Some repair stations provide line maintenance, or routine work necessary to keep an aircraft operating safely. Some perform substantial maintenance, which includes more comprehensive or progressive inspections and repairs on airframes and overhauls of aircraft engines. Some repair stations offer specialized services such as fuel cells, landing gear overhauls, or aircraft paint.

FAA MOSAIC

In late July 2023, the FAA published a notice of proposed rulemaking (NPRM) in the *Federal Register* entitled "Modernization of Special Airworthiness Certification" (**MOSAIC**). Through this proposed rule, the FAA is proposing reforms that, if adopted, would provide major benefits to GA. Specifically, MOSAIC would redefine the light-sport aircraft (LSA) category and significantly raise the size and performance capabilities of airplanes that can be flown by sport pilots. For instance, MOSAIC will replace the current LSA weight limit of 600 kilograms (1,320 pounds) with performance-based measures, including a 54-knot maximum clean stall speed (V_{S1}) that will allow sport pilots to operate aircraft that weigh as much as approximately 3,000 pounds. Additionally, MOSAIC will eliminate the current 120-knot LSA speed restriction and allow controllable-pitch propellers and retractable landing gear on LSA. Also, LSA will be permitted to have up to four seats and travel at a top speed of 250 knots calibrated airspeed. In anticipation of vertical takeoff and landing (VTOL) aircraft, MOSAIC will replace the current requirement that LSAs have a "single, reciprocating engine" with "any number and type" of powerplants. In addition to changes in LSA, sport pilots will also directly benefit. For instance, sport pilots will be allowed to fly at night and operate the more capable aircraft with appropriate training and instructor endorsements.

The changes that are proposed by MOSAIC will provide significant benefits to GA pilots, aircraft owners, instructors, technicians, and manufacturers. Several industry organizations, such as AOPA and EAA, have promoted these changes and are pleased to see the proposed rule.

Flight Operations

In addition to providing maintenance, FBOs are obviously also involved in various aspects of flight operations. Without flight operations, FBOs can only fuel and maintain aircraft. However, the heart of the GA industry originates at FBOs in the form of flight training. Even the smallest of FBOs tend to offer flight instruction and aircraft rental. Additionally, some FBOs also offer charter services. Regardless, flight operations, in one form or another, allow an FBO to capitalize on another area of demand and diversify service offerings.

FLIGHT INSTRUCTION

Flight instruction is offered by many FBOs, although it tends to be concentrated at smaller FBOs that lie outside busy Class B airspace. This is due to the inherent problems with conducting flight training at busy commercial service airports. Although learning about wake turbulence is important, a first-hand experience behind a B747 will likely be more than a student bargained for!

Figure 5-4. Flight training in progress. *(RGtimeline/Shutterstock.com)*

Flight instruction at an FBO can be conducted either as **Part 61 flight training** or **Part 141 flight training**. A Part 61 flight school operates under 14 CFR Part 61, which is the regulation that outlines certificate and rating requirements for pilot certification through non FAA-certificated schools and individual flight instructors. A Part 61 flight school can begin offering flight instruction on day one without needing FAA inspections or FAA approvals. An advantage of pilot training in the Part 61 flight training environment is flexibility. Flight lessons can be tailored to each individual student, as a long as Part 61 minimums are met for flight experience and knowledge areas. Unfortunately, this flexibility may also be detrimental for students if the flight instructor is disorganized and repeats lessons rather than allowing students to progress according to their proficiency.

A Part 141 flight school operates under FAA approval and provides a structured flight training environment. To obtain a Part 141 certificate, the flight school undergoes an FAA inspection and must meet stringent requirements for personnel, equipment, maintenance, and facilities. It must also create a training course outline (TCO) that the FAA approves and which then serves as a guide for all flight instruction. A Part 141 certificate can be issued for flight instruction or ground instruction, or both. An advantage to training in a Part 141 flight training environment is quality, continuity, and structure. All flight training is documented in each student's Part 141 folder, and these folders are available for inspection by the FAA. Additionally, FAA certificates and ratings may be earned in fewer flight hours, thus saving students time and money. On the other hand, certain flight students may not desire a structured flight training environment and instead may opt for a Part 61 flight school.

New in 2013, and partly in response to the February 12, 2009, Colgan Air crash in Buffalo, New York, Part 121 airline pilots were required to obtain 1,500 flight hours to obtain the **Airline Transport Pilot (ATP) Certificate**. A **Restricted ATP (R-ATP) Certificate** could be obtained at 1,250 flight hours through an associate's degree program, 1,000 flight hours through a bachelor's degree program, and 750 flight hours through the military. For these academic programs, flight training is required to be conducted under Part 141, thus making the Part 141 certificate even more valuable. In essence, if a student pilot desires to become an airline pilot, any flight training beyond the Private Pilot should be conducted at a Part 141 flight school approved by the FAA to offer the R-ATP.

Depending on the FBO, flight training may be provided for Sport Pilot, Recreational Pilot, Private Pilot, Commercial Pilot, Airline Transport Pilot, Instrument Rating, Multi-Engine Rating, Certified Flight Instructor (CFI), Certified Flight Instructor Instrument (CFII), Multi-Engine Instructor (MEI), tailwheel endorsement, and high-performance endorsement. Whether Part 61 or Part 141, all flight training must be provided by FAA-certificated CFIs, and, if advanced training is offered, by CFIIs and/or MEIs. While not all FBOs offer flight training, those that do play an integral role in the continued growth of GA.

AIRCRAFT RENTAL

Most fixed-base operators, even relatively small ones, own at least a few aircraft that can be rented for short periods of time. Most facilities offer several single-engine piston aircraft with varying degrees of complexity, from basic two-seat trainers to larger aircraft with retractable gear and an adjustable propeller. Some FBOs offer multi-engine aircraft, as well.

A rental agreement and inspection of the pilot's certificate and currency are always required. Many businesses also require a check-out before renting. In an aircraft check-out, one of the school's flight instructors reviews the performance aspects of the aircraft with the renter and then conducts a flight to evaluate the renter pilot's ability to operate the aircraft safely. Aircraft can be rented by the hour, day, or week, or for specific trips. Typically, overnight trips require the renter to pay for a minimum number of hours per day (typically four), whether or not the aircraft was actually used. In this way, the FBO is able to ensure a minimum number of rental hours per day (with subsequent revenue) even if the aircraft is away for an extended period.

Figure 5-5. Aircraft rental. *(EB Adventure Photography/Shutterstock.com)*

AIRCRAFT CHARTER

Aircraft charter is a significant FBO service that can generate sizable revenue. Aircraft may be chartered for the transportation of executives or high-net-worth individuals, cargo transportation, emergency medical flights, and air tours. Accordingly, a wide range of aircraft is necessary to complete these missions—including single-engine piston aircraft; large, turbine-powered, corporate aircraft; and helicopters.

Many businesses, including those that own their own planes, utilize aircraft charter on a regular basis. Some companies may prefer to own only one aircraft and charter additional aircraft as necessary for special occasions or periods of peak load. This **supplemental lift** allows the business to benefit from more aircraft than it owns in-house. Some firms chartering aircraft use only their own crews, but an FBO can provide complete aircraft charter secrecies, which will include flight crew. (See chapter 11 for an in-depth discussion of aircraft charter.)

There are more than 3,000 on-demand air charter operators nationwide. All operators must hold an Air Carrier Operating Certificate issued by the Federal Aviation Administration (FAA) and are regulated under **14 CFR Part 135**, which sets forth operational, maintenance, training, and other safety requirements. Additionally, pilots and management personnel are subject to minimum qualification standards. A series of regular inspections, spot inspections, routine surveillance, and in-depth inspections are all performed by the FAA to ensure compliance with applicable regulations.

Charter brokers represent buyers who need on-demand air transportation. Air charter brokers are regulated under **14 CFR Part 295**. The regulation requires brokers to make their role clear and to identify the Part 135 air charter company that will operate each flight before the customer signs the contract. Part 295 also addresses business relationships between brokers and air charter operators, prohibiting unfair or deceptive business practices. The National Business Aviation Association (NBAA) has produced an Aircraft Charter Consumer Guide, which may be helpful to individuals intending to charter an aircraft and possibly secure the services of an charter broker.

Figure 5-6. Aircraft charter customer. *(Hurst Photo/Shutterstock.com)*

Sales

The sale of parts and supplies, as well as aircraft, are yet another form of revenue stream for FBOs.

AIRCRAFT

The addition of an aircraft sales division to an FBO can create many new and different opportunities for enhancing revenue. A sales department typically has the best overhead-to-profit ratio of the entire company. There is no need for a large staff or expensive equipment and materials. The salespeople are typically all commission-based, and basic office supplies and some initial marketing money are the main costs involved with the startup. This allows an FBO to grow a sales

Figure 5-7. Aircraft for sale. *(Richard Thornton/Shutterstock.com)*

department from one current employee performing the task on the side to a department that moves millions of dollars in inventory per year.

The benefits of having a sales department fall into two main categories. The first category consists of the ways in which a sales department functions as its own profit center. The second category relates to the many ways in which the activities of the sales department are able to feed all of the other FBO divisions.

One of the best ways to understand how aircraft sales works as its own profit center is to compare it to the more commonly known business of real estate. Real estate companies acquire listings on houses, sell houses, find houses for people, and even purchase property for investment purposes. The reason people go through a real estate agent is that agents are experts in the market, know about the pitfalls in buying a house, advise prospective home buyers on their best course of action, and orchestrate a smooth transaction. For each type of transaction, a percentage of the closing sales price is paid to the real estate company as a fee for professional services rendered. The business of aircraft sales works the same way, only with aircraft.

Although new aircraft could be sold at an FBO, one typically finds only used aircraft available for sale. The used aircraft market remains strong, and although new aircraft are also in demand, used aircraft are more affordable and typically available at local FBOs. The FBO may own the aircraft outright that is being sold, but more commonly it sells aircraft on consignment. A sale earns the FBO a commission based on the sales price.

The percentage commission on an aircraft transaction varies with the price of the aircraft. All percentages are negotiable, but Table 5-1 provides a general breakdown of the brokerage fees associated with selling an aircraft.

Table 5-1. Typical Aircraft Brokerage Commissions

Price of aircraft	Brokerage fee
$0–$500,000	8–10%
$500,001–$1,000,000	6–8%
$1,000,001–$3,000,000	4–6%
$3,000,001–$4,000,000	3–4%
$4,000,001–$5,000,000	2–3%
$5,000,001 and up	1–2%

These percentages charged by the aircraft sales department will vary, based on different situations. For example, if there is competition over an exclusive brokerage on a $6.5 million Citation, it may be wise to offer brokerage services at a 1 percent commission instead of the 2 percent that might typically be charged, as a $65,000 profit minus expenses will still be well worth the resources required to make the sale. Ultimately, a sales department exists to create lucrative deals using the best strategy for the given scenario. Skilled negotiation combined with this ability to find the profit in any deal are the ingredients that can turn an aircraft sales department into the most lucrative profit center within an FBO.

In addition to being a very lucrative profit center with relatively low overhead, a sales department creates an increase in the revenues of all other profit centers of the FBO. The number of ways that an aircraft sales department can create revenue for an FBO are almost endless. In fact, one would be hard-pressed to think of an area of an FBO's business that could not benefit from the activities of the sales department.

The maintenance department typically benefits the most, as an aircraft transaction provides opportunities for performing logbook reviews, inspections, squawk repairs, and many different upgrades. Often, deals will hinge on what the potential buyer can be provided concerning maintenance. Many long-term relationships are created with an FBO's maintenance shop as a direct result of an aircraft purchase.

Speculative purchases of aircraft are another way that an aircraft sales department can help create revenues. The sales department's ability to locate aircraft well below retail can result in lucrative investments for the FBO, as the sales department can then sell the aircraft to create profit for the FBO as well as sales. This scenario can be taken a step further if an FBO purchases a group of aircraft that are in need of maintenance at a very good price. This would provide income for the maintenance department, the sales department, and the FBO as a whole.

Charter departments can also benefit, as a sales department can encourage the buyer of an aircraft to place the aircraft into the charter fleet of the FBO to offset expenses. This creates a low-risk scenario for the charter department since there is less risk in chartering another person's aircraft versus one owned by the FBO. This increase in charter activity increases traffic through the FBO, creating more opportunity for selling other services.

As an FBO considers offering aircraft sales, a few considerations must be kept in mind. First, is the FBO simply going to offer aircraft brokering or will it also sell aircraft from its own inventory? FBOs can make money on aircraft sales by simply serving as the broker (buyer's agent/seller's agent) of someone else's aircraft. Taking aircraft on consignment can be quite lucrative. An FBO may also choose to be a dealer and purchase aircraft for its own inventory to sell. Another consideration is that the aircraft sales business is completely unregulated. Anyone claiming to be an aircraft broker or acquisition specialist can perform those services without any training or knowledge of the aircraft sales process. Therefore, FBOs must be cautious in hiring individuals to staff a new aircraft sales division. Experience and references are important considerations.

If an FBO decides to offer aircraft sales, what are the keys in selling an aircraft to a client? First, the salesperson must spend a great deal of time understanding the client's needs, travel history, missions, and the amount of money budgeted for the purchase. A reputable broker will also encourage the buyer to build a team of professionals, including a CPA or tax specialist, an attorney for LLC formation and asset protection issues, an insurance professional, an escrow agent, a banker/lender, an inspection facility to conduct pre-purchase inspections, and possibly a pilot(s) to perform a thorough in-flight evaluation of the aircraft. The broker will also assist the buyer in answering the following preliminary questions:

- What is the primary purpose for the aircraft?
- Do you have an aircraft in mind?
- What is your mission?
  - How many passengers will you typically take?
  - How far will you fly?
  - To which cities/airports will you fly?
  - How long will you stay?
  - How often will you use the aircraft?
- Will the aircraft you're considering work on 80–90 percent of your missions?
- What is your budget?
- Will you be the pilot or the passenger?
- Will you hire your own crew and manage your own aircraft or hire a professional management firm to manage the aircraft for you?
- If the aircraft will be used for both business and pleasure, what percentage for each?
- Are you trading an aircraft?
- When would you like your new aircraft to be in service?

Buyers must also be encouraged to think outside the box. For instance, maybe two smaller aircraft will make more sense than one larger aircraft. If the new plane is not well suited for a few of the buyer's anticipated trips, chartering the right aircraft to meet those needs may be a good alternative.

Even the largest companies find that alternative methods for supplemental lift may make more sense than a larger aircraft or more extensive fleet. Lastly, flying on a major air carrier should also be considered an option if necessary.

AIRCRAFT PARTS AND AVIATION SUPPLIES

In addition to the sale of aircraft, the sale of parts and accessories is an important segment of business for most FBOs. FBOs with maintenance services tend to make aircraft parts available for sale, as this becomes part of the necessary support for aircraft maintenance, especially if much repair work is done. The items carried by a well-stocked operator include engines, airframe parts, tires, and avionics components, as well as a wide variety of accessories. All parts are subject to strict FAA standards for tracking, storage, sale, and installation to prevent the introduction of fraudulent parts into the market.

As discussed earlier, offering aircraft parts and aviation supplies can significantly contribute to a diverse revenue stream for an FBO. Aircraft owners and operators will oftentimes not have a choice in having non-scheduled maintenance performed at an FBO, but they may also choose to have scheduled maintenance performed if the facilities are clean and modern, if the timeframe for having the work performed is reasonable, and if the price is right. Many FBOs become known in their local areas as the experts in certain aircraft (Cessna, for instance), and word of mouth will assist these FBOs in continuing to gain more maintenance work on these aircraft. Pilots will purchase aviation supplies if prices are competitive simply due to the convenience of having these items available at the FBO. The FBO must remain competitive with internet and mail-order sources, such as Aircraft Spruce and Sporty's Pilot Shop.

Aircraft Management Service

Many of the larger fixed-base operators offer a complete **aircraft management service** for high-net-worth individuals and business customers. Under such an arrangement, the aircraft owner supplies the aircraft, and the aircraft management company (or FBO) provides the flight, maintenance, and administrative personnel while assuming responsibility for conducting flight operations, performing maintenance, and handling administrative matters. Thus, the owner is relieved of the responsibilities of running an aviation department and all of the workload associated with it. The client company normally is billed monthly for the actual cost of the service, plus an agreed-upon management fee, which is usually a specified percentage of the cost of the services rendered.

The FBO managing the aircraft can also supervise the installation of the appropriate avionics and passenger cabin accommodations. The FBO obtains the hull and liability insurance coverages on the aircraft, in accordance with minimums of liability coverage that are normally specified by the operator. The FBO handles the assignment of pilots and copilots, either selecting crews from among its own personnel or hiring new personnel especially for the customer's operation. In either event, the flight crews are assigned to the customer company full time, though they remain the employees of the FBO. The operator is responsible for checking out pilot and copilot qualifications, ensuring that they receive the appropriate recurrent flight and ground school training, and arranging for the periodic medical examinations required.

The FBO is completely responsible for flight operations, maintenance, and whatever administrative services and personnel are required to provide full service. This responsibility includes establishing safe operational standards for the aircraft and crews regarding such factors as aircraft performance, weather conditions, airport facilities, and crew duty times as well as providing employees to handle scheduling, clerical, and secretarial duties. The FBO also provides office space, with furnishings and equipment for the use of the flight and administrative personnel and the customer company's passengers. Maintenance supervision is provided in the typical contract, though the supervisor usually does not work full time for a customer unless the size of the customer's fleet warrants such full-time assignment.

Other Specialized Commercial Flight Services

Some FBOs have arrangements with private and public organizations to provide various specialized commercial flight services. These include aerial advertising, aerial photography, firefighting, fish spotting, mosquito control, pipeline and powerline surveillance, and wildlife conservation. Partnerships such as these can create a one-stop shop for FBO customers in need of such services.

Summary

Not all FBOs perform all the functions set forth above; indeed, some FBOs may elect to participate as specialists in only one or two categories. However, it is normal for FBOs to perform at least four of the services listed, either as part of their own business or by leasing space to specialists who perform the functions on their own (or leased) premises. An FBO has been compared to a shopping mall manager who is charged with making a profit on each of the many widely diversified individual businesses within the orbit of the overall operation.

Key Terms

100-hour inspection. An aircraft inspection that must be conducted every 100 hours of flight time for aircraft used for flight instruction or hire.

14 CFR Part 1. FARs: Definitions and Abbreviations.

14 CFR Part 21. FARs: Certification Procedures for Products and Articles.

14 CFR Part 23. FARs: Airworthiness Standards: Normal Category Airplanes.

14 CFR Part 39. FARs: Airworthiness Directives.

14 CFR Part 43. FARs: Maintenance, Preventive Maintenance, Rebuilding, and Alteration.

14 CFR Part 61 flight training. A Part 61 flight school operates under Part 61, which is the regulation that outlines certificate and rating requirements for pilot certification through non-FAA-certificated schools and individual flight instructors. A Part 61 flight school can begin offering flight instruction without needing FAA inspections or FAA approvals.

14 CFR Part 65. FARs: Certification: Airmen Other than Flight Crewmembers.

14 CFR Part 135. FARs: Operating Requirements: Commuter and On Demand Operations and Rules Governing Persons on Board Such Aircraft.

14 CFR Part 141 flight training. A Part 141 flight school operates under FAA approval and provides a structured flight training environment. To obtain a Part 141 certificate, the flight school undergoes an FAA inspection and must meet stringent requirements for personnel, equipment, maintenance, and facilities. It must also create a TCO (training course outline) that the FAA approves and that then serves as a guide for all flight instruction.

14 CFR Part 295. FARs: Air Charter Brokers.

aircraft charter. Flights that operate based on the passenger's schedule under a Part 135 certificate.

aircraft management service. An arrangement whereby the aircraft owner supplies the aircraft and the aircraft management company (or FBO) provides the flight, maintenance, and administrative personnel while assuming responsibility for conducting flight operations, performing maintenance, and handling administrative matters.

Airframe and Powerplant (A&P) Certificate. The holder of an A&P certificate, also known as an aviation mechanic or aviation maintenance technician, is permitted to maintain the airframe and powerplant parts of an aircraft. An A&P can perform a 100-hour inspection on airframes, powerplants, propellers, accessories, and instruments and approve them for return to service, but cannot perform annual inspections.

Airframe Rating. The airframe-rated mechanic can approve and return to service an airframe, or any related component or appliance, after performing, supervising, or inspecting its maintenance or alteration. An airframe-rated mechanic can perform 100-hour inspections on airframes and related parts or appliances and approve them to return to service but cannot perform annual inspections.

Airline Transport Pilot (ATP) Certificate. The highest level of aircraft pilot certificate, required to act as pilot-in-command of an aircraft operated under 14 CFR Part 121.

airworthiness certificate. A certificate signifying an aircraft meets acceptable standards for service. The airworthiness certificate remains with the aircraft during its service life, regardless of changes in ownership.

airworthiness directive (AD). Legally enforceable regulations issued by the FAA in accordance with 14 CFR Part 39 to correct an unsafe condition in an aircraft, engine, propeller, or appliance.

alteration. A change in the configuration or design of an aircraft that may be in the form of a minor alteration or major alteration.

altimeter and pitot-static system. The altimeter is an instrument that measures the height of the aircraft above a given pressure level, whereas the pitot-static system includes a pitot tube (which measures ram air pressure) and one or more static ports (which provide static air pressure). This entire system must be inspected for proper operation every 24 calendar months.

annual inspection. A comprehensive inspection required of GA aircraft once annually that must be conducted by an A&P with Inspection Authorization (IA).

Code of Federal Regulations (CFR). The codification of regulations published in the *Federal Register*. The CFR is divided into 50 titles that represent broad areas subject to federal regulation. Title 14 is Aeronautics and Space.

continuous airworthiness inspection program. A program designed for operators of large commercial aircraft currently in use by a person holding an air carrier operating certificate issued under 14 CFR Part 121 or an operating certificate issued under 14 CFR Part 135. The program must be approved by the FAA and allows the owner/operator to maximize aircraft availability and reduce maintenance costs by dividing inspection requirements into regularly scheduled blocks.

emergency locator transmitter (ELT). An emergency transmitter that is carried aboard most GA aircraft and designed to be activated in the event of an aircraft accident.

Federal Aviation Regulations (FARs). Rules prescribed by the FAA governing all aviation activities in the United States.

***Federal Register*.** The official journal of the U.S. federal government that contains rules, proposed rules, and public notices.

Inspection Authorization (IA). An IA may inspect and approve for return to service any aircraft or related part or appliance after a major repair or major alteration. The IA may perform an annual inspection and may supervise a progressive inspection. The IA expires every odd-numbered year on March 31.

maintenance. Inspection, overhaul, repair, preservation, and replacement of parts, excluding preventive maintenance.

major alteration. An alteration that might appreciably affect weight, balance, structural strength, performance, powerplant operation, or flight characteristics, or one that is not done according to accepted practices or cannot be done by elementary operations.

major repair. A repair that if improperly done might appreciably affect weight, balance, structural strength, performance, powerplant operation, or flight characteristics, or a repair that is not done according to accepted practices or cannot be done by elementary operations.

minor repairs and alterations. An alteration or repair other than a major alteration or major repair.

MOSAIC. FAA Modernization of Special Airworthiness Certification (MOSAIC) that proposes significant changes for light-sport aircraft.

notice of proposed rulemaking (NPRM). A public notice that is issued by law when an independent agency of the federal government (such as the FAA) wishes to add, remove, or change a rule or regulation as part of the rulemaking process. Each NPRM is published in the *Federal Register.*

Powerplant Rating. The powerplant-rated mechanic can approve and return to service powerplants, propellers, and accessories after performing, supervising, or inspecting its maintenance or alteration. A powerplant-rated mechanic is allowed to perform 100-hour inspections on powerplants and propellers and return them to service but is not permitted to perform annual inspections.

preventive maintenance. Maintenance consisting of preservation, upkeep, and the simple replacement of small parts.

progressive inspection program. A program that allows for more frequent but shorter inspection phases.

repair. An operation that restores an item to a condition of useful operation or to original condition.

Repairman Certificate. The holder of a Repairman Certificate employed by a certificated repair station, or the holder of an air carrier operating certificate, may perform or supervise the maintenance, preventive maintenance, or alteration of aircraft or aircraft components appropriate to the job for which the repairman was employed and certificated.

repair station certificate. A certificate issued by the FAA under 14 CFR Part 145 to a repair station authorizing it to engage in the maintenance, inspection, and alteration of aircraft and aircraft products.

Restricted Airline Transport Pilot (R-ATP) Certificate. Allows the holder to exercise privileges as co-pilot in a Part 121 operation at 750 flight hours (military), 1,000 hours (bachelor's degree), or 1,250 hours (associate's degree) prior to obtaining an ATP without restriction at 1,500 flight hours.

supplemental lift. The concept of utilizing charter and other options to allow a business to benefit from more aircraft than it owns in-house.

transponder. An electronic device that produces a response when it receives a radio-frequency interrogation.

type certificate. Signifies the airworthiness of a particular category of aircraft, according to its manufacturing design.

Review Questions

1. Why is maintenance necessary for aircraft?
2. Explain what FARs concern aircraft maintenance.
3. What are the privileges and limitations of aircraft mechanics under 14 CFR Part 65?
4. What is an A&P mechanic? What is required to become one?
5. What is an IA? What is required to become one?
6. Explain why an annual inspection and 100-hour inspection are necessary.

7. Why would a progressive inspection program or a continuous airworthiness inspection program be adopted?
8. What avionics require regular inspections?
9. Explain the difference between 14 CFR Part 61 and Part 141 flight programs.
10. Explain why the addition of an aircraft sales department to an FBO can be beneficial.
11. What are typical commissions charged by aircraft brokers?
12. What must be considered in assisting a buyer with purchasing an aircraft?

Scenarios

1. As manager of the maintenance department at a full-service FBO, you are constantly seeking ways in which to cover costs, make a profit, and still price repair and maintenance services competitively with a competing FBO on the field. What are some ideas to accomplish these objectives?
2. It is true that not all FBOs provide aviation maintenance services. Of those that do, however, certain Federal Aviation Regulations must be complied with. You are currently starting an FBO at a GA facility with no aviation maintenance services currently available. Do you feel it is in your best interest to include aviation maintenance in your start-up plans? If so, what are some considerations you must keep in mind in opening an aviation maintenance shop?
3. In deciding to offer flight instruction at your FBO, you must consider whether to offer these services under 14 CFR Part 61 or Part 141. What are the pros and cons of each? Which will you choose?
4. You were recently hired by FastFlight FBO as an aircraft sales associate. What process would you use in assisting someone with their first purchase of an aircraft? What types of questions would you ask? What commission would you charge based on the customer's budget and preferred aircraft? How would you see the sale through to completion?
5. As the new manager of a small but growing FBO, you have decided to diversify your offerings. Specifically, you feel that aviation supplies need to be offered for sale. What types of supplies will you offer and how will you cater to your existing customers?
6. Quality control is a necessary component of a good FBO maintenance facility. At a minimum, the FARs must be complied with. However, as an FBO manager trying your best to control costs, you are hesitant to spend a great deal on quality control. When is it advantageous to adopt various quality control procedures? Is it possible to spend more on quality control than you receive in either direct or indirect benefits?

Bibliography

FAA (Federal Aviation Administration). Continually updated. *Code of Federal Regulations, Title 14: Aeronautics and Space.* Accessed November 7. 2022, https://www.ecfr.gov/current/title-14.

Prather, C. Daniel. 2009. *General Aviation Marketing and Management: Operating, Marketing, and Managing an FBO.* 3rd ed. Malabar, FL: Krieger Publishing Company.

6

Customer Service

In Chapter 6

Objectives

At the end of this chapter, you should be able to:

1. Identify both internal and external customers.
2. Describe methods of effective customer service.
3. Properly handle complaints received via email, online, telephone, radio, and face-to-face.
4. Discuss the attributes of a high-quality FBO.
5. Discuss the attributes of a low-quality FBO.
6. Highlight various customer service initiatives.
7. Discuss the components of an FBO customer services checklist.
8. Propose how an FBO in your community could enhance its customer service.

Customers

Customers are at the core of every business, FBOs included. As discussed in this chapter, customers can be internal and external. They can experience the best a business has to offer or, unfortunately, the worst as well. Customers are the group to which FBOs owe their success, for without them, there is no reason to offer services and truly no demand to meet. At the same time, customers can be quite particular regarding their needs and desires. At times, it may seem impossible to meet the needs of every customer. As the saying goes, "You can't be all things to all people." Just as an FBO doesn't cater to every individual in the local area, this quote also provides some insight into the difficulty of attempting to please every customer that walks through the front door of an FBO.

Customer service, and the goal of complete **customer satisfaction,** is truly an art. Customer service is more than just being nice or smiling. The commitment to customer service is an important component of an FBO's success. Many of us have either directly experienced or heard of poor examples of customer service, including not meeting customer needs, not being knowledgeable about the products available, or simply lacking a professional attitude and courteous manners. News of these negative experiences spread fast in any industry, and this includes aviation. Pilots speak to each other, and with social media today, word will quickly spread about an FBO's lack of customer service and poor customer satisfaction. It is probably even easier to recall personal experiences of poor customer service than positive experiences. Whatever the reason, all FBO managers must be aware of this and realize it is much more efficient to retain a customer than acquire a new one. Retaining a customer begins with a proactive focus on customer service.

INTERNAL

When considering the typical customer of an FBO, we likely picture pilots taxiing their aircraft to the ramp upon landing. While this is true, there is another important customer base as well: **internal customers**. This customer group includes the individuals working within the company—more specifically, those working by your side and in other departments. Consider this: John's FBO has three main departments: flight operations (which includes line service, aircraft charter, maintenance, and flight instruction), aircraft sales, and administration (which includes finance, marketing, and public relations). Flight operations does a good job of handling its daily tasks and earning revenue for the company. The aircraft sales division does a great job of enhancing revenue, but it rarely communicates with the flight operations department. Lastly, employees in administration (including the FBO manager) usually stay on the second floor of the terminal building all day and rarely communicate with the department directors or shift supervisors. In fact, corporate communication is lacking, and those in flight operations do not understand why they have to fire two flight instructors and delay their acquisition of another training aircraft. The aircraft sales department feels things are great but has recently been told it must increase gross sales 10 percent next fiscal year. Over time, this FBO begins experiencing major problems internally simply due to lack of communication and lack of internal customer service.

Internal customers are as important as external customers, because if the business does not communicate effectively, with all departments working toward the same goals and objectives, the business will suffer. Employee morale will decline, employee productivity will suffer, and the achievement of company goals will be delayed if not sidelined altogether. As this occurs, it will become obvious to external customers, and it will prove extremely difficult to offer superior levels of customer service to these external customers. In essence, people make up the industry. They fly the planes, travel on the planes, service the planes, and maintain the planes. Therefore, without a clear, concerted effort to focus on people (customer service, in other words), any FBO, or any company, will likely experience financial difficulty as a result.

EXTERNAL

In addition to the internal customers of an FBO, **external customers** are also important. In fact, it is sometimes easier to focus on external customers because they are the typical customers for which the FBO operates. The two main customer groups of an FBO are pilots (or flight crews) and their passengers. These external customers serve as the core customer base for an FBO. In instances in which people remember experiencing either positive or negative customer service, they most likely were an external customer interacting with a company.

Let's consider a negative customer service experience at an FBO—Bob's FBO, for example. You just landed and are taxiing your Cessna 172 up to the only FBO on the field. You don't see a line service specialist and really have no idea where to park. You find the FBO frequency and give them a call on the radio. No answer. You call ground control and are told, "They're hardly ever there. Just park wherever." Disappointed, you taxi a bit further and pull into a tie-down spot on the ramp. Just as you shut down your engine and are about to exit the aircraft, a line service specialist runs up to your aircraft and says, "You should have parked over there!" As he points to another tie-down spot, you can't help but wonder how you were supposed to know this. After all, they didn't answer your radio call and had no one on the ramp to direct you to a proper parking spot. This first impression of this FBO is obviously a negative one. What do you do? You tell your pilot friends, most likely. "Stay away from Bob's FBO."

As an important external customer, you were poorly treated and will likely not return to this FBO. However, the wise FBO manager realizes how important external customers are and will focus a great deal of effort on continuously improving customer service to meet the needs of external customers. Without positive customer service, an FBO may see the number of based aircraft decline, hangar rentals not renewed, fuel sales decline, employees resign, and a number of other consequences of poor customer service. Truly, customer service—and specifically, external customer service—is becoming one way in which successful FBOs are able to differentiate themselves from the competition. In fact, *Aviation International News* regularly conducts an annual FBO Survey that includes areas such as line service, passenger amenities, pilot amenities, and facilities (AIN, n.d.). Interestingly, when examining the results and specific comments received from survey participants, much of the ratings center around customer service. It is clear that the highly rated FBOs offer excellent customer service and place an emphasis on their external (and likely internal) customers. Likewise, FBOs with poor customer service are not highly rated in this annual survey.

What are the main external customer groups of an FBO? Obviously, pilots and their passengers are the largest group. This group will expect aircraft fueling, aircraft marshalling, aircraft cleaning, catering, clean and convenient facilities, and information. Specifically, upon arriving on the ramp, flight crews may wonder the following:

- Will anyone be available to show me where to park?
- Will ground transportation be waiting?
- Will anyone be available to assist with offloading baggage?
- Will the catering be available for the departing flight?
- Will the line service specialists be knowledgeable in handling my aircraft and taking care of our aircraft servicing needs?

The successful FBO will anticipate these questions and meet these needs without delay.

Yet another group of customers with which an FBO may interact include potential flight training students. These are individuals who are interested in aviation and have decided (or are considering) to start flight instruction. They may be apprehensive about the financial requirements, their abilities, and the physiological effects of flight. Therefore, these customers must be treated with respect and taught about aviation as they are entering the process of flight instruction. They will expect clean, modern aircraft, competent and friendly flight instructors, and clean and adequate facilities. Yet another external customer group is the potential aircraft sales customers. These individuals (or organizations) will be in the market for an aircraft and will demand knowledgeable salespeople, well-priced and well-maintained aircraft, and the ability to investigate their many options without being hassled or pressured into making a premature purchase.

Clearly, the wise FBO manager realizes the diverse customer groups and their many needs. This person will understand the importance of customer service (both internal and external) and conduct **customer service training** for employees. Some FBOs have utilized programs offered by the Disney Institute, Ritz-Carlton, or Dale Carnegie for specific customer service training. This training is beneficial in that it requires employees to consider the importance of customer service and learn the skills necessary to provide exemplary customer service within the FBO environment. Training will seem ineffective, however, if management does not model appropriate customer service skills. Management should be aware of the internal and external customers of the FBO and focus on providing excellent customer service both internally and externally. Additionally, it will seem ineffective if employees are not empowered to exceed customer needs. Employees should be given the ability to think outside the box and, within reason, utilize company resources to address customer concerns and exceed expectations. Most likely, this will require guidance so that employees understand the boundaries of this empowerment. However, once employees are empowered, the manager will likely be surprised at the ability of employees to resolve concerns and complaints before they ever reach the desk of the FBO manager.

Methods of Effective Customer Service

Just as there are proper ways to fuel an aircraft, there are also proper ways to interact with customers to ensure a delightful experience. While some of these methods may seem obvious, it is amazing how many companies today lack employees who exhibit these basic customer service skills. As stated before, companies without a proactive position on customer service will likely see sales and customers decline. This can be so severe that the FBO is unable to prosper and eventually goes out of business.

Figure 6-1. Telephone customer service. *(istock.com/ Maksym Belchenko)*

TELEPHONE PROCEDURES

As with many businesses, the first point of contact with an FBO may be via a telephone call. Thus, it is extremely important for those answering the phone to do so in a professional and courteous manner. Although this may seem obvious, the wise FBO manager does not assume that every employee answers the phone properly. Indeed, training in telephone etiquette is recommended.

First, employees must be taught to answer the phone professionally and with a smile in the voice. How does one smile through the telephone? In simple terms, they speak in an upbeat manner with a positive tone in their voice. It is easy to tell if someone is having a bad day just by speaking to them on the phone. Obviously, even if an employee is not having the best day, this should not be discernable in their voice.

Next, in answering the telephone, employees should identify their company and themselves. You have likely called a business before only to find yourself asking, "Is this Bob's Pizza Palace?" If the employee had answered the phone properly, there would have been no question. Thus, the proper manner in which to answer the telephone is as follows: "Hello. Thank you for calling Expert FBO. This is Wendy." The employee may also offer assistance to the caller but should avoid speaking a paragraph as they answer the phone. In busy times, the employee answering the phone may simply say, "Expert FBO; This is Wendy." Even so, she has followed proper telephone protocol by identifying the company and herself.

While on the telephone, it may be helpful to take notes. This is especially important if the caller is giving specific directions or making a long request that may be difficult to remember. With experience, employees will develop a shorthand method to use in copying down the most pertinent information in each phone call. Although jotting down a few notes takes time and may take the employee away from other duties, it is important to avoid the tendency to check emails or listen to other employees while listening to a customer on the telephone. These distractions will make it obvious to the caller that they are not important and will be perceived by the caller as poor customer service.

Additionally, an employee must use caution when receiving another phone call while currently on the phone. It is best to ask the caller if they can hold, greet the second caller and ask them to hold, and then return to the first caller to finish the initial conversation. In this way, the second caller won't be lost (unless the hold time grows much longer than one minute) and the first caller will likely not be offended.

In summary, proper telephone procedures require a positive mental attitude, good listening skills, an enthusiastic and knowledgeable employee, and a customer focus. Clearly, the employees answering incoming telephone calls can have a positive impact on the company image. Conversely, if these employees don't follow proper telephone procedures, they may have a substantial negative impact on the company. Thus, FBO managers must educate employees about proper telephone etiquette and explain that current and potential customers can be won or lost on the telephone.

RADIO COMMUNICATIONS

In addition to interacting with current and potential customers on the telephone, FBO personnel will likely also interact with customers (both internal and external) via a radio. This includes company radio, air traffic control (ATC) ground radio, and air-to-ground radio. Company radio will be used most often to communicate with fellow employees. This is especially useful in the ramp environment as line service specialists are busy fueling aircraft and towing aircraft. Occasionally, a line service specialist may need to communicate with the ATC ground control. Normally, if the line service specialist has the need to be on the movement area (to retrieve a disabled aircraft, for example), an escort would be provided by airport operations, who would also make all necessary ATC radio calls. Most often, the air-to-ground radio will be used. This allows people on the ground to communicate directly with an aircraft in flight. This radio call is initiated by the flight crew in advance of their arrival to express their needs and coordinate aircraft servicing.

The key to effective radio communication is to relay information with a minimum number of words. Lengthy requests only create frequency congestion, which only interferes with others attempting to speak on the same frequency. Prior to speaking, it is important to listen momentarily to avoid "stepping on" another conversation. The following is a typical radio conversation one would expect to hear at an FBO:

Pilot: "Tampa Jet Center, this is Eclipse 586 golf hotel."

FBO: "586 golf hotel this is Tampa Jet Center."

Pilot: "586 golf hotel will be landing at Tampa International in 15 minutes and we will need fuel and a courtesy car. Our passenger states he has your boardroom reserved as well."

FBO: "586 golf hotel, understand 15 minutes to arrival and we'll be ready with fuel and courtesy car. Boardroom is reserved for Mr. Hanes."

Pilot: "Roger, 586 golf hotel."

This radio transmission is typical, and although the actual requests may vary, you can see how a great deal of information was relayed in a short period of time by using few words and focusing on the conversation.

HANDLING COMPLAINTS

Inevitably, regardless of the superior level of customer service being provided, customers may complain about something. These complaints, no matter how trivial, must be treated seriously and with utmost professionalism. Often, a customer may simply be having a bad day and may be angry with circumstances that are completely out of the employee's control. Sometimes the complainant may be quite agitated and confrontational. The FBO employee should never place themselves in a dangerous situation. If necessary, assistance should be requested. By listening to customer needs and striving to satisfy those needs, the employee can effectively resolve complaints and maintain high levels of customer relations. Complaints may be received in the form of verbal or written communication.

If the complaint is received via verbal communication (most likely the telephone), it is best to simply listen and do so carefully. As mentioned, the complainant may simply need to blow off some steam. By simply listening, the customer will be allowed to vent their frustrations. While doing this, the individual answering the call should be taking some notes. This will enable a specific response to the caller's concerns, rather than saying, "I know how you feel" (which, most likely, isn't true). This leads to the need to show empathy. The employee must try to look at the situation from the caller's perspective but should not claim to know how the caller feels—for example, about aircraft flying over their house every few minutes. Also, it is important to avoid placing blame. "It's not our fault, it's the pilot's fault" is not a satisfactory response. The FBO employee answering the complaint is not there to place blame. Rather, the employee is there to listen to the customer's complaint and resolve it as best as possible. In particular, the employee must avoid being defensive and must remain calm and not take the complaint personally. Once the caller has expressed the problem, the employee must clarify understanding of the actual complaint, thank them for bringing it to the company's attention, and be sure to follow through on any agreed-upon solution or response to the situation.

An in-person complaint will be handled similarly to a telephone complaint, with minor differences. First, the employee must remember to maintain eye contact while listening to the complaint. If able, the employee should take some notes but not become preoccupied with this. If note-taking seems excessive, the complainant will likely feel as if they are being ignored. That, of course, will simply make the situation worse. Actually, when responding to an in-person complaint, employees have the advantage of using body language to positively impact the situation. A warm smile and non-defensive gestures will go a long way in easing the tension and positively resolving the complaint.

GOING ABOVE AND BEYOND

What does it mean to "go above and beyond?" It means doing more than what is expected of you, either by your manager or the customer. This is not easy to teach, as employees will likely feel that doing the minimum is all that is expected. Therefore, the wise FBO manager will create a corporate culture that supports going above and beyond in all situations. Although a manager may be tentative about doing so at first, if such an environment is properly developed, it will positively impact the business and level of customer service offered by the business.

Several things are necessary to create a culture of going above and beyond. First, employees must truly sense this culture by observing management model this behavior. If management is apathetic about the company or does the minimum to address employee concerns or customer concerns, employees will sense that the "above and beyond" talk is only that—talk. Therefore, managers and supervisors must model this high level of customer service for both internal and external customers.

Additionally, once employees understand the focus on going above and beyond, they need another tool. This tool is referred to as empowerment. Employees must know they are empowered to handle any situations that arise in their daily work. Even extraordinary circumstances should not derail a well-intentioned employee. This, of course, requires management trust and the confidence that employees are knowledgeable and well-equipped to provide such superior levels of customer service. Empowerment is more than simply telling employees to do whatever is necessary to please the customer. This may result in inappropriate use of company resources. For instance, an employee may decide to give a tenant free hangar rent for one month because the hangar was dirty upon move-in. Specifically, management must create guidance for employees so that any limits are known about the use of company resources. This guidance, typically in the form of a standard operating procedure, will inform employees of the expectation by management that employees will handle and address most, if not all, customer concerns. It may give examples of ways to handle certain situations and give specific guidance on dollar amounts or maximum uses of company resources. It will likely also educate employees about the need to involve management if a customer cannot be satisfied within these boundaries.

NON-INCOME SERVICES

In addition to positively interacting with customers and effectively addressing customer concerns, customer service at an FBO can be enhanced by offering non-income services. In addition to income-producing services (such as fuel sales and aircraft rental), these non-income services create convenience and enhance the well-being of customers.

Indeed, these services typically figure highly into the level of customer satisfaction at an FBO. Depending on location, market, and customer demands, any or all of these services discussed below may be available. One of the most rapidly emerging of these amenities is the provision of designated areas for business travelers. Many aviation businesses now offer private meeting rooms, phones, fax machines, photocopiers, high-speed internet access, and plenty of electrical outlets to recharge the many electronic gadgets in use today. Conference rooms may also be made available to allow interactive presentations with clients. Wireless internet (Wi-Fi) is becoming more popular and allows customers to access the internet from their laptops, tablets, or smartphones anywhere in the FBO.

Other commonly provided services include:

- Clean rest rooms and showers
- Pilot lounges and sleeping quarters
- Preflight planning rooms
- Pilot supplies
- Recreational facilities
- Vending machines and/or restaurant
- Rental and/or courtesy cars
- In-flight catering
- Hotel accommodations
- Tourist/visitor activities

Clearly, these services cost the FBO money, but not all of these services bring in revenues. For example, although a restaurant generates revenues, providing a pilot lounge or preflight planning rooms might not. Even so, by spending money on these services, the FBO will likely attract additional customers and see an increase in revenues as a result. Specifically, when referring to business aviation, the flight crew and passengers flying in a $20 million private aircraft will expect these services at an FBO. If these services are not available, it will certainly be noticed by the customer. As such, non-income services are proving to be a major competitive factor among FBOs today.

What Makes a High-Quality FBO?

Clearly, some FBOs do a much better job of meeting customer needs and going above and beyond customer expectations than others. What exactly makes a good FBO? The following comments provided by FBOs were obtained by *Aviation International News* (AIN) during its 2021 FBO survey (AIN 2021):

- "We are the first and last people our guests see when they visit this area."
- "Our team is always looking for ways to exceed the needs and expectations of our customers."
- "[Our] trained professionals . . . appreciate the value of our clients' time and remain focused on optimizing their efficiency and productivity when utilizing our services."
- "Our greatest strength is our ability to flex to our customers' needs."
- "Every customer is important to us and we try to show it in our services every day."
- "We are a safety first, service and solutions-oriented team, backed by literally centuries of experience."

- "We drive customer loyalty by delivering a recognizable, elevated customer service offering and by making it easy to do business with us. We don't believe in the word 'no,' and always find a solution."
- "Our team will go above and beyond to meet a customer's request."
- "Under-promise and over-deliver, while always offering exceptional, quality, safe service with a smile."

Although these comments point to many things, the essence of most of the comments pertain to customer service. FBOs offering excellent customer service are those FBOs most preferred by customers and more likely to be rated very high in terms of customer satisfaction.

What Makes a Low-Quality FBO?

At the same time, there are specific things that make a poor impression on customers and translate into being considered an FBO of low quality. The following comments by FBO customers were obtained by *Aviation International News* during past FBO surveys (AIN, n.d.):

- "Linemen who don't really care and are going through the motions. Customer service that comes across like they are doing me a favor. A place that charges premium prices and thinks it is doing a better job than the guy down the ramp."
- "One that doesn't understand that customer service and presentation are most important. They are the gateway to their communities in some cases, and the impression they show can make or break the experience."
- "If there is no place for the pilots to relax and take care of business (internet and phone service), it makes for a very long day for a crew that has a several-hour layover."
- "Dumpy facility, indifferent service, poor flight planning amenities. Internet is nice to have for flight-planning these days, too."
- "One bad encounter with an FBO employee will stick in your mind for years, no matter how good the FBO has been in the past. Rude, unfriendly and unhelpful associates will kill an FBO faster than anything. The FBOs that make you feel like you're the most important aircraft on the field are the ones I remember forever."
- "A rigid 'can't do' attitude. A cold, sterile, indifferent environment and an unwillingness to help the crew with their special needs coupled with poor crew facilities."
- "I go to great lengths to notify an FBO of my arrival and requests. If I get there and I seem to be a surprise, nobody is there to marshal me in and out, and/or I'm dealing with people who don't seem to know anything about aviation, then I get a bit disappointed."
- "Unfriendly CSRs, absentee line techs and unfulfilled requests are at the top of the list. At some FBOs, you'd think that it was their first time to fuel an airplane."
- "Poor supervision. You can't manage an FBO if you don't know what goes on outside your office."
- "Distracted CSRs (personal phone calls, issues, and so on) who delay transmittal of information to ramp personnel regarding needed crew/aircraft services."
- "Discounts only to large fleet operators while gouging smaller operators with exorbitant handling fees even if that operator doesn't use any of their facilities."
- "Not open at published hours, won't answer the radio, telephone long hold time, slow service, theft."
- "Requiring me to sign a hold harmless [agreement] before they will tow or store my aircraft."
- "A business that gives line people minimal training and turns them loose on the line by themselves."

- "Walking up to the counter and no one wanting to even look at you because they are chatting amongst themselves, and then after pulling themselves away with great effort (and usually a sigh), not even asking if I need something, or a hello or a greeting, only a blank stare."
- "Absence of safety."
- "Slow service, long faces, unclean facilities."

Although many complaints about FBOs concern high jet fuel prices, high ramp fees, and outdated and unclean facilities, most of the complaints stem from poor customer service. Clearly, it is a challenge for FBOs to hire and retain top-notch personnel. Yet, it is imperative if the FBO wants to experience success and high customer satisfaction. By reviewing the comments above, future FBO managers can learn what not to do and instead focus on the correct things to do to ensure success.

Customer Service Initiatives

As indicated in the AIN survey results, amenities are important among pilots, but service remains the most important factor among FBO customers. As one FBO manager said, "People make the biggest difference." As FBOs are trying to differentiate themselves in the comparative market, it is apparent that success stems from a proactive effort to enhance customer service. This effort, in the form of customer service initiatives, is increasingly important.

Excellent customer service begins with hiring the right employees. As discussed in Chapter 15, this process can be time consuming but very rewarding for the organization. Even if housed in temporary facilities, if employees are providing excellent customer service and knowledgeable and efficient in their tasks, fuel sales may increase. How are FBOs able to continually improve in this area? An FBO may check rental and courtesy cars upon return to check for cell phones or other items left behind. This, in the words of one FBO manager, is about having "proactive customer service."

As any FBO manager would know, employees do not automatically begin providing excellent customer service the day they are hired. Thus, it is important for FBOs to train and educate employees in safety and customer service to ensure that this culture of positive customer service continues. There are companies that specialize in providing such training to FBOs. This training focuses on teaching employees how to focus on the customer and simplify the customer interaction. For example, rather than waiting on a customer to request something, employees are taught to be proactive and attempt to meet these needs before they are voiced. Whether contracting with a company specializing in service or conducting in-house training on this issue, successful FBOs realize that providing excellent customer service is a journey, not a destination. This requires continual training, education, and emphasis on the employee–customer interaction.

In addition to providing employees the resources they need to provide excellent customer service, it is imperative that an FBO gauge the level of customer satisfaction on a regular basis. Otherwise, how will an FBO manager know what level of customer service is being provided or if customers are satisfied with this level of service? One way to accomplish this objective is to employ mystery shoppers. This mystery shopper would generally fly into the airport, land, and taxi to the FBO just as a typical customer would. This person would also request services and shop like the typical customer, all the while paying particular attention to the level of customer service they are experiencing. This information would then be relayed to the FBO manager for data analysis to gauge the actual levels of customer service at the FBO. Another way to gauge customer service levels is to conduct surveys with customers. Similar to the nationwide survey by *Aviation International News* discussed earlier, an FBO would conduct a local survey with customers and tenants to gauge levels of satisfaction and recognize areas for improvement. Typically, customers only voice comments if something needs to be improved, but a survey with all customers would allow both kudos and concerns to be voiced, which would allow the FBO to improve in certain areas and give praise in other areas.

FBO Customer Services Checklist

Exemplary service to customers is going to take on added significance for FBOs wishing to survive competition in the future. Whether the customer is a prospective student pilot seeking flight instruction, a business requesting a charter flight, or a corporate operator looking for a maintenance or line service facility, service becomes an important element in distinguishing among competitors.

The following section provides a checklist of accepted practices and procedures designed to improve service to customers.

RAMP AREA

A well-thought-out ramp area will not only enhance the appearance of an FBO, but it will also reduce the possibility of ramp accidents and increase the utilization of equipment. Good ramp planning can also improve fuel service and tie-down business. A ramp area checklist should include the following considerations.

1. Training aircraft should be parked for easy access from the flight office. Parking should be arranged to place the most active aircraft in the most accessible spots. There should be adequate room for students to taxi safely in and out of parking areas.
2. When possible, one-way, flow-through taxi routes should be provided. Lead-in stripes to guide aircraft into parking spots should be painted brightly. All obstructions close to taxi routes should be marked with high-visibility caution signs or symbols, according to standard airport markings and signage.
3. One-way, flow-through traffic paths to fuel islands should be used. A refueling parking spot for fuel truck operations should be designated so that it does not conflict with normal traffic flow.
4. If flood lighting is impractical or causes glare, a series of low (below wing level) ground illuminating lights should be considered. Warning lights on all obstructions close to taxi routes should be used. The refueling area should be well lit.
5. To attract transient aircraft, high-visibility signs should be positioned to be seen from taxiways, announcing transient fuel service. Lead-in signs and/or taxiway markings with lead-in stripes should indicate the route to refueling and parking areas.
6. The following items of ramp equipment should be provided in sufficient number, in good repair, and conveniently located:
   - Tugs
   - Tow bars
   - Ladders and stands
   - Power units
   - Jacks
   - Nitrogen, oxygen, and air tanks
   - Deicing equipment
   - Lavatory flush carts
   - Survival gear (life rafts, radios, etc.) at ports of debarkation
   - Avionics and component repair equipment to the extent that such service is offered or intended
   - Windshield cleaner and cleaning cloths
   - Oil wipe cloths
   - Chocks numbered to tie-down spots
   - Equipment lockers at strategic points on the flight line
   - Covered trash containers

GROUND PERSONNEL

Dispatcher and/or receptionist personnel should fulfill these checklist requirements:

1. Have a complete understanding and be able to explain the following:
    - Company rental policy and agreements
    - FAA pilot certificates, medical certificates, and Federal Communications Commission (FCC) radio license
    - Federal Aviation Regulations (FARs) currency requirements
    - Company insurance policies
    - Student enrollment procedures
    - Part 141 student record requirements
    - FAA, FCC, and Veterans Affairs (VA) forms
    - Flight training and services fee schedule
    - Information regarding rental car service and hotel or motel facilities, including rates, discounts, and distances
2. Be familiar with all UNICOM procedures and responsibilities.
3. Reschedule customers after each flight.
4. Call customers who have become inactive.
5. Be skilled in professional telephone sales techniques.
6. Regularly use an inquiry form to record the maximum amount of data from incoming phone inquiries.
7. Assume duties that relieve flight instructors from routine tasks and allow more time for training.
8. Monitor student progress (ground school and flight training).

Line personnel are often the first interaction customers have with an FBO. As a result, they must be professional and well-qualified to perform their jobs. Line personnel should:

1. Be thoroughly trained in the following aspects of line service (see Chapter 4):
    - The nature, coding, and handling of all aircraft servicing materials
    - All aircraft servicing procedures
    - Aircraft towing and ground handling procedures
    - Ramp safety procedures
    - Aircraft spotting and parking techniques
    - All ramp signaling techniques
2. Be in uniform or dress that is immediately identifiable to transient pilots.
3. Be ready to jump into action with inbound aircraft.

All employees should be instructed on the importance of a safe, prompt, efficient, dependable, and courteous service attitude to all customers. Some larger FBOs employ a customer service representative to meet all incoming business aircraft, their passengers, and crews.

AIRCRAFT

Aircraft must not only be airworthy but must also look airworthy. Nothing can add to the apprehension of a student or renter pilot more than an aircraft that looks unsafe to fly. The following list includes those items which demonstrate care and professionalism.

1. A clean and polished exterior finish
2. A clean engine compartment
3. Tires in good condition and properly inflated

4. Windows clean inside and out
5. A clean interior (trash removed, seat belts straightened, etc.)
6. All interior trim panels in good repair
7. Carpeting clean and in good repair
8. Instrument panel and anti-glare shield finish in good repair
9. Upholstery clean and in good repair
10. All knobs, levers, and switches in place and functioning
11. All unused instrument cutouts, avionics bays, etc., properly covered or blanked out
12. All loose equipment properly stowed and secured
13. All checklists, frequency reminders, etc., professionally printed and durable
14. All manuals and required paperwork on board and properly stowed or displayed

FLIGHT PERSONNEL

The demands on flight instructors should go far beyond pilot skills. The instructors must have ability in teaching, consulting, customer relations, and salesmanship. Flight instructors should be responsible for, or be subject to, the following:

1. Maintaining a professional attitude about teaching.
2. Currency in the following:
   - All applicable FARs.
   - All FAA-recommended flight procedures and techniques.
   - Latest teaching techniques. Many FBOs require instructors to attend recurrent training seminars. Regularly scheduled meetings with instructors to review recent changes and developments are also utilized. Information bulletins explaining recent changes and developments are distributed on a regular basis.
3. Adhering to standards in the following areas:
   - Teaching methods.
   - Flight procedures and maneuvers.
   - Student evaluation.
   - Flight and ground curriculum. A program of standardization flights with the chief pilot can be established so that all instructors are teaching from the same syllabus.
4. Ensuring no conflict between student instruction and charter flights. Some FBOs schedule a specific day for each instructor to fly charter. The manager or chief pilot can fly all charters that conflict with an instructor's training schedule.
5. Continued upgrading of the instructor's image and prestige, including an area for student briefings and conferences (preferably including an office, cubicle, or desk with nameplate). Some FBOs provide business cards for each instructor as well as company shirts and/or jackets with the FBO logo and instructor's name. If aircraft utilization permits, one aircraft could be assigned to each instructor with the individual's name on the door.
6. An incentive system to increase instructor wages. This might include incremental increases for such items as night instrument and multi-engine training. A higher rate could be established for total hours after a pre-selected weekly minimum.
7. An understanding of sales and customer relations. Some FBOs pay bonuses to instructors whose students complete an entire course. Finders' fees are sometimes paid to instructors who recruit students. A small override fee is often established for a student's solo time.

The responsibilities of the chief pilot vary depending on the size and complexity of the fixed-base operation and whether the chief pilot is also the manager. However, the following responsibilities should apply to most operations.

1. Maintain a close liaison with local FAA personnel.
2. Develop flight and ground school curricula.
3. Conduct standardization flights for staff instructors.
4. Conduct student phase check flights.
5. Conduct regular instructor meetings to maintain standardization, review problem areas, and develop new methods.
6. Provide written information for instructors and students on operational techniques and procedures.
7. Maintain student records and FAA reports.
8. Provide monthly status reports to management.
9. Maintain a list of available local CFIs.
10. Maintain an open-door policy to listen to student or instructor problems.
11. Make regular checks on student attitudes.
12. Conduct introductory flights and tours of the facility.
13. Establish a program to recruit new students and improve attrition.

Summary

Clearly, many things must be considered when committing to an environment of excellent customer service. Training, non-income services, and proper facilities all require financial commitments by the FBO, but these are essential for maintaining a competitive position and ensuring "above and beyond" customer service well into the future.

Key Terms

customer satisfaction. A measure of how pleased customers are with a company's products and services.

customer service. The act of supporting and advocating for customers in their discovery, use, optimization, and troubleshooting of a product or service.

customer service training. The methods to teach employees the knowledge, skills, and competencies required to increase customer satisfaction.

external customers. Customers external to the organization. The main FBO external customers are flight crews and passengers.

internal customers. Customers internal to the organization. This includes coworkers, supervisors, and subordinates.

Review Questions

1. What are the differences between internal and external customers? Are both groups important? Why?
2. What are some considerations in effectively answering the telephone?
3. What are some considerations when communicating via the radio?
4. What are some considerations in handling complaints?
5. What does it mean to "go above and beyond?"
6. What are non-income services? Discuss their importance.
7. Summarize what makes a high-quality FBO.
8. Summarize what makes a low-quality FBO.
9. Discuss some recent customer service initiatives adopted by FBOs.
10. What can an FBO do to improve efficiency and customer service in the ramp area?
11. Describe some of the areas that ground personnel should be responsible for in carrying out their duties efficiently.
12. Explain some of the little things that can be done to make aircraft look better.
13. The demands of flight instructors should go far beyond pilot skills. Explain.
14. Describe some of the responsibilities of the chief pilot.

Scenarios

1. As the manager of a full-service FBO at a large GA airport, you are aware of the need to remain competitive. A pilot just taxied into your FBO and complained to the line service specialist that fuel prices were too high. He is about to purchase 500 gallons and is demanding a discount. How do you handle this?
2. You are working the front desk at the FBO where you have been employed for the past year. As you answer the phone, you hear, "These planes are driving me crazy! They are too noisy, and I want you to make them stop! If not, I'll be calling Channel 10!" This is a typical day at your FBO and airport. How do you address this caller's concern and handle this complaint?
3. Your FBO manager recently held a customer service training class for all employees. In that class, he explained that the FBO is subscribing to a new standard of customer service: "Going above and beyond." In class, he presented some scenarios and asked you to explain how you would address each of the following situations:
   a. A long-time customer of your FBO, Mark Jenkins, is planning a trip out on Saturday at 0600 (L). Mr. Jenkins has a Lear 35 in your community hangar that will need to be out and ready to go. You and another coworker also remember that this Saturday is Mr. Jenkins's 40th birthday. How could you "go above and beyond" for Mr. Jenkins?
   b. A pilot taxiing in calls on the radio and asks if a rental car could be reserved for his two passengers. You realize that a car is available and decide to go above and beyond in meeting this pilot's needs. How can you do that?

c. Three passengers just arrived on a King Air and would like to use the FBO conference room to conduct some business. Unfortunately, the conference room is already in use by another customer. What are your options?

4. Your manager just asked you to develop some customer service guidelines for the line service division. He says, "Our crew is typically the first to interact with a customer on the ramp and we need some guidelines so each of these employees understands the value of customer service and knows what excellent customer service on the ramp looks like." What are some guidelines you could develop to assist these employees?

5. As an assistant FBO manager, you know how important excellent customer service is to your FBO. Recently, you have been studying the non-income services offered by a competitor and feel that your FBO needs to begin offering more non-income services for pilots and their passengers. However, your boss (the FBO manager) feels these things are a waste of money. "If it doesn't make us money, we're not paying for it!" How do you persuade your manager of the need to adopt more non-income services to enhance your FBO's image and create more customer satisfaction?

6. While working the front desk, an irate customer (the chief pilot of a Hawker 850XP) confronts you about lack of service personnel on the ramp. He has waited 30 minutes for jet fuel, and his departure will be delayed as a result. "I will never return to this FBO. Your lack of service is unacceptable," he states. As you listen to him, you formulate your response. What do you say?

7. The FBO at which you are the manager recently conducted a survey of based and transient customers. Overall, the results were disappointing. Particularly, customer service (in all areas) was ranked quite low. As FBO manager, what is your next step?

8. You have been anxiously awaiting this day—the grand opening of your FBO. It's not going to be easy, though, because there is an established FBO already on the field. What can you do to differentiate your FBO from the competition?

9. In an effort to enhance the FBO you currently manage, you asked an aviation consultant to conduct an independent audit of your facility. In the report, it was noted that customer service could be improved upon. Specifically, the consultant stated that "employees are lacking on customer service skills. Consequently, additional training and support is needed in this area." What are some of your options to address this?

10. You are the new manager of a full-service FBO that has a record of poor customer service. As part of your effort to improve in this area, you ask the employees about their ideas. Many say that they would do more, if only they could. They explain the former manager did not give them much latitude at all when it came to dealing with customers and handling their concerns/complaints. You conclude that the employees just need to be empowered. How do you do this?

Bibliography

AIN (Aviation International News). n.d. "AIN's FBO Survey." Accessed August 18, 2022. https://www.ainonline.com/aviation-news/fbo-survey.

AIN (Aviation International News). 2021. *FBO Survey 2021: The Americas.* https://www.ainonline.com/sites/ainonline.com/files/pdf/fbo_survey_2021_the_americas_online.pdf.

Prather, C. Daniel. 2009. *General Aviation Marketing and Management: Operating, Marketing, and Managing an FBO.* 3rd ed. Malabar, FL: Krieger Publishing Company.

7

The Role of Marketing

In Chapter 7

Objectives

At the end of this chapter, you should be able to:

1. Define marketing.
2. Trace the evolution of marketing through three distinct periods of development.
3. Define the marketing concept and explain its importance to an organization's success.
4. Explain the importance of determining objectives in quantifiable terms.
5. Identify and highlight the steps in the process of segmenting the market.
6. Differentiate the three approaches to target marketing.
7. Describe each of the four Ps in the marketing mix.
8. Discuss the factors involved in implementing and controlling marketing plans.
9. Describe the uncontrollable variables that can affect a firm's marketing efforts.

Marketing Defined

Every day throughout the world, immeasurable goods and services trade hands. Why do individuals and businesses purchase particular products and services? In a simple word—**marketing.** The role of marketing in our modern society is much greater than many appreciate. Some even suggest that the price of products and services could be reduced by 30 percent to 50 percent if all marketing activities were eliminated. Is this elimination a viable alternative? Marketing is a powerful force in the world economy. Marketing is responsible for creating demand, goods and services, and jobs in many related fields like research, advertising, wholesaling, retailing, and transportation. Marketing has been a major factor in the increased quality of life enjoyed by developed countries throughout the world.

Contemporary marketing efforts are far different from those used in the past. The evolution of marketing can be traced through three distinct periods of development. The first period, known as the **production era,** covered the period from about 1870 to 1930. This era was characterized as a seller's market, where demand for products exceeded the supply. Firms concentrated on efficient production to offer products that were well made. This production thinking worked due to limited competition and the imbalance between demand and supply. During this production era, marketing was not needed.

By 1930, however, technology had drastically changed and allowed manufacturers to produce more goods than they could sell. This created a buyer's market, where supply exceeded demand, and it was referred to as the sales era. During the **sales era,** manufacturers focused on aggressively selling the oversupply of their products. Their philosophy was to "sell what the firm could efficiently make, rather than making what the firm could sell." The initial marketing function that was introduced was one of aggressive sales tactics, which often had the opposite of the desired effect because the customer was offended and refused to purchase the product. The sales era continued until the mid-1950s when customers became more selective and demanded products that better fit their needs.

The third and current era is best known as the **marketing concept era** and emphasizes customer need fulfillment and customer satisfaction. The marketing concept is a customer-oriented, integrated, goal-oriented philosophy for the firm. It means that a firm aims all its efforts at satisfying its customers—for a profit. Instead of just trying to persuade customers to buy what the firm is selling, a firm implementing the marketing concept tries to produce what customers need and want. Market research (discussed in Chapter 9) plays an important role in assisting the firm to identify and monitor customer satisfaction. The three components of the **marketing concept** are (1) a customer orientation, (2) a total company effort, and (3) a profit, not just sales, as an objective.

Today, goods and services move through many different channels of distribution efficiently, which allows consumers to satisfy their needs and wants on demand. The economic justification for a business firm today is that it has the ability to create utility or value for its customers. **Utility** is the want-satisfying ability of a good or service. From a marketing perspective, there are three forms

Figure 7-1. Elements of marketing. *(wowomnom/Shutterstock.com)*

of utility: time, place, and possession. **Time utility** involves making the goods available when the customer wants them. Having line service available 24 hours each day is an example of time utility. **Place utility** involves making products available where the customer wants them. Place utility helps bring buyers and sellers closer together. Locating an FBO at a preferred location may enable place utility for customers in that area. **Possession utility** involves transferring of the title for a product between the parties. The use of trade credit among marketing intermediaries and credit cards with consumers have greatly enhanced this utility.

This chapter views marketing from a micro-perspective and will investigate the role of marketing in a firm and demonstrate how essential marketing is to the long-term survival of an organization. What does the term *marketing* mean? Most people mistakenly equate the term with selling and promotion. Marketing is much more than selling and promotion and is more commonly defined as the performance of business activities or functions that direct the flow of products and services from the seller to the buyer in order to satisfy customers and accomplish the company's objectives.

Clearly, a variety of business activities must be performed to accomplish the overall objective of marketing, which is to develop exchange relationships with customers. The three categories of marketing activities are exchange, physical distribution, and facilitating functions. **Exchange functions** involve buying and selling on the part of various channel members, like wholesalers and retailers, and the final customer. Logistical or **physical distribution functions** help satisfy time and place utilities by efficiently combining the components of warehouse locations, inventory strategies, material handling, and transportation modes that provide a satisfactory service level for the customer. **Facilitating functions** include financing, risk-taking, providing information through market research, and standardizing and grading products. It is important to note that each of these functions must be performed for exchange to take place. Who performs these functions and how they are performed depends on the type of product, type of customer, geographical location, and urgency of the need.

The second part of the marketing definition deals with satisfying customers. Customer satisfaction is the ultimate objective of the marketing process. Marketing attempts to build stronger relationships with existing customers and to discover new target markets that fit well with the firm's expertise and objectives. Customers, not marketers, primarily determine what they need, want, and are willing to buy. It is the responsibility of marketing to identify and to satisfy customers' needs.

The final portion of the definition indicates that accomplishing the company's objective is an essential part of marketing. Just as the customers must be satisfied, the marketing plan must also achieve company objectives. The primary objective of the marketing plan is to make a satisfactory profit while meeting customers' expectations. Other objectives may include increasing market share, expanding into the global market, introducing new products, or increasing distribution efficiencies.

Marketing Management

Marketing management is a three-phase process that includes planning marketing activities, directing the implementation of the plans, and controlling these plans. This process is so central to the activities of most organizations that they formalize it as a marketing plan, which is a road map to guide the marketing activities for a specified future period of time, such as one year.

PLANNING

Marketing planning involves making decisions that commit the firm to actions in order to reach organizational and marketing objectives effectively. Planning includes determining objectives, segmenting the market, selecting target markets, and establishing a unique marketing mix aimed at the particular audience. The marketing mix includes the product or service, price, channel of distribution (place), and promotion (advertising, sales promotion, personal selling, and publicity). These so-called controllable variables are referred to as the *four Ps of marketing.*

Although not generally taught, a fifth "P" could be referred to as passion. Another controllable variable, passion is the fifth ingredient in a successful marketing mix. Typically, passion is always present in the marketing mix of aviation businesses. Those in aviation are usually passionate about aviation and as a result, product, price, place, and promotion are more effective. Without passion, the four Ps lack a key component of the marketing mix.

Determining Objectives

Marketing objectives should clearly state the intended outcomes of the marketing effort. These objectives should complement and be set within the framework of the larger company objectives. For example, the firm's objectives might include increasing flight school revenues. A marketing objective would be to increase the number of students or to improve the student pilot retention rate. Because objectives are not equally important, a hierarchy of objectives should be specified for the marketing personnel.

Marketing objectives should be quantified and stated in understandable terms. Ideally, the attitudes of upper management toward the achievement of these objectives should also be ascertained. Top management must guide each department manager of a product service area. For example, should a 20 percent increase in charter business be attained regardless of cost or only sought if the return on investment is 18 percent or better? Even more important—but less quantifiable—should a 20 percent increase be obtained even if it requires high-pressure selling, reduced availability or reliability, or other possibly unethical actions? Clearly, these costs would not be worth any potential benefits.

Each department manager is responsible for generating a certain amount of revenue so that the profit objective can be reached. The sales force has the objective of achieving a designated sales quota. Advertising has the objective of creating a level of awareness of product-service areas within the target markets. Prices must be competitive and achieve a specific market share or target rate of return. Marketing research must be completed on time and within budget.

Objectives at all levels of the firm should be operationally specified. Each department manager should understand what activities must be undertaken and what operations must be performed in order to accomplish the objectives. Quantification is usually helpful; for example, "increase sales by 10 percent" is more precise than asking the department manager to get "more sales than last year." Managers should not focus their efforts exclusively on objectives that can be quantified, however. It is fairly easy, for example, to measure the cost savings of holding parts inventory to a minimum, but it is very difficult to determine the degree of customer dissatisfaction that might be created when that minimum inventory results in being out of stock of required parts, resulting in delayed repairs to a customer's aircraft.

Segmenting the Market

Market segmentation is the process of breaking down the total market into smaller, more homogeneous groups with similar needs that the firm can satisfy. A market segmentation approach aims at a narrow, specific consumer group (market segment) through one specialized marketing plan that caters to the needs of that segment. Market segmentation has emerged as a popular technique for FBOs with highly specialized products and limited resources. The consumers within a market segment should be as similar to each other as possible with respect to their needs. There also should be significant differences among

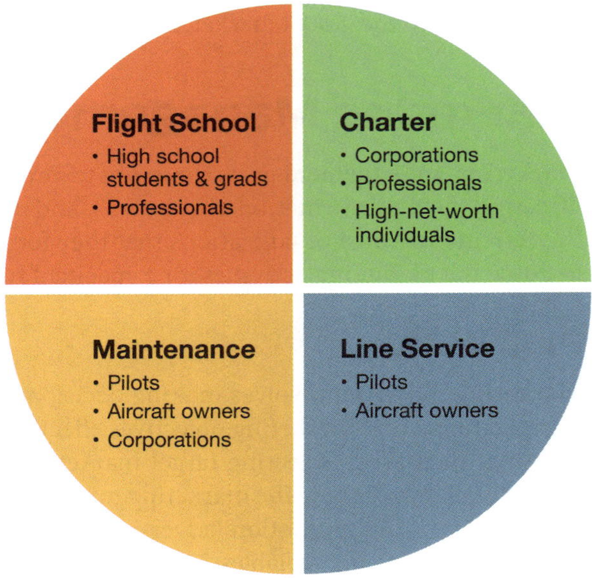

Figure 7-2. Sample market segmentation.

segments, and the segments should be large enough to be profitable. Segmenting assists the firm in deciding which market to target and also in planning marketing mixes. A sample market segmentation is shown in Figure 7-2.

Market segmentation includes the following steps:

1. *Identify the product-service areas to be segmented.* The first step involves identifying all of the product-service areas presently offered by the firm. This might include the following:
   - Flight school
   - Aircraft sales
   - Rental: by hour or by trip
   - Charter: scheduled and non-scheduled
   - Overhaul: major and minor
2. *Identify all of the possible market segments.* This step includes an identification of all markets for the firm's product-service areas. These might include the following:
   - Pilots
   - Aircraft owners
   - High school students
   - High school graduates
   - Community college flight program students
   - Corporate fleet operators
   - Physicians
   - Engineers
   - Managers
   - Professionals
   - Proprietors
   - Salespeople
   - Commuter airlines
3. *List all needs for the possible market segments that have been identified.* This is a brainstorming step. For each of the product-service areas, it is now important to identify the needs for all the possible market segments. For example, using the flight school as the product-service area, what are the particular needs of high school students? Their needs include availability of an evening ground school, instructor availability from 3:00 p.m. to 6:00 p.m., competitive prices, an installment payment plan, college credit for attainment of the private pilot certificate, and counseling with parents.

At this point, it is helpful to develop a matrix as shown in Table 7-1 (see next page). This table shows the product-service areas on the left side and possible target markets across the top. The table includes evaluations of each product-service area against each market with a judgment of whether that will be of major or minor interest to the firm.

Another helpful analysis in determining possible market segments is to compare product-service areas with competitors. In this case, product-service areas would be shown across the top of the table, and a listing of the firm's chief competitors would be listed on the left side. Again, a matrix is formed in which the firm can rate competitors' strengths and weaknesses using a scale of one to five, with five being excellent and one being poor.

The ratings reflect how well each competitor delivers that product-service. The firms can also rate themselves. In order to check their findings, some firms poll customers who are familiar with the competitive operations to evaluate both the firm and its competitors. Customers may come up with completely different perceptions of the firm and its competitors for the various product-service areas.

Table 7-1. Market Segmentation

Product-service areas		Pilots	Aircraft owners	HS students	HS graduates	CC flight progs.	Corporate fleet	Physicians	Engineers	Managers	Professionals	Proprietors	Salespeople	Commuter airlines
Flight school		O	O	X	X	X		X	X	X	X	X	X	
Airplane sales		X	O		O		X	X	X	X	X	X	X	O
Rental:	Hour	X		X	X	X		X	X	O	X	O	O	
	Trip	X		O	X	X		X	X	X	X	X	X	
Charter:	Scheduled						X							O
	Non-scheduled						X			X	X	X	X	
Overhaul:	Major		X				X							O
	Minor	O	X				O							
Hangar rental		X	X			X								
Sale of gas and oil		X	X	X	X	X	X	X	X	X	X	X	X	X
Accessories:	Plane		X				X							O
	Pilot	X	X	X	X	X		X	X	X	X	X	X	X
Services		X	X	X	X	X	X	X	X	X	X	X	X	X

X = Major interest
O = Minor interest

The objective of these exercises is to try to identify possible target markets and also point out a firm's strengths and weaknesses. Too many FBOs fall into the trap of trying to be all things to all markets, with the result of not excelling at anything. The better approach is to do fewer things but to do them well.

The process of identifying segments and determining their accessibility necessitates focusing on customer needs. This, of course, is the essence of marketing management. It encourages the firm to track who buys its products—and where, when, and how. Segmentation keeps the organization alert to changes in market conditions and competitors' actions. Competitive analysis may indicate which segments of the market are controlled by strong, entrenched competitors and which segments' needs are not fulfilled by present product-service areas.

Establishing Target Markets

Once the market segments are determined and the segmentation criteria are satisfied, the firm is ready to direct its effort toward one or more market segments. A **target market** is a segment that is the object of a firm's marketing mix. It is the opposite of mass marketing, which does not attempt to differentiate between the market segments but instead designs and aims its marketing mix at all segments.

A single target market approach means that there is one primary market segment selected as the firm's target market. This concentrated marketing is a cost-effective way to market because there are no expensive variations of the marketing mix. Marketers narrow their sales potential by concentrating on a single market segment, but they are exposed to more financial risk by not diversifying efforts into multiple target markets. A multiple target market approach means selecting two or more market segments; each will be treated as a separate target market, and each will require a unique market mix. A combined target market approach means aggregating two or more similar market segments into one larger target market.

Most successful FBOs utilize the multiple and combined target market approaches. Mass marketing is not appropriate for the highly specialized product-service areas of the average FBO.

Establishing a Marketing Mix

Once the firm has determined its objectives and selected its target market(s), it is ready to begin planning the details of the marketing mix. The **marketing mix** was previously defined as the set of controllable marketing variables that the firm blends to produce the desired response in the target market. The marketing mix consists of everything the firm can do to influence the demand for its product. The many possibilities can be collected into four marketing mix variables: product, price, place, and promotion (with passion an always present member of the marketing mix).

THE PRODUCT

A product is a combination of benefits, physical features, and services, designed to satisfy the needs/wants of identified target markets. This definition includes both tangible products and intangible services. The ability of a firm's product to satisfy wants is the key to developing exchange relationships. Purchasers of aircraft are vitally concerned with parts and service availability, warranties, image of the brand name, and other intangible benefits that contribute to the total satisfaction of owning an aircraft. Flight students purchase an intangible service but are also concerned with other benefits such as quality, reputation of the school, and professionalism of the instructors.

There are four unique characteristics of services that offer marketers challenges different from marketing tangible products like aircraft. These four elements are referred to as the *four I's of services.*

1. Services are **intangible**. The buyer must purchase a service on faith because it is often only after the sale that quality, benefits, and dimensions can be evaluated. Service marketers should stress the benefits of the service instead of the service itself. Many aviation firms today are successful because they have differentiated their product by including key benefits that are sought out by their market. For example, an FBO may build its line service business by including a complimentary aircraft wash with the purchase of 100 gallons of aviation fuel.
2. Services are **inconsistent**. Since services depend on the people who provide them, their quality varies with each person's training, capabilities, and attitudes.
3. Services are **inseparable**. In most cases, the provider of the service cannot be separated from the service itself (e.g., A&P mechanic repairing an aircraft).
4. The fourth characteristic identifies the **inventory** problems of services, which is that no inventory can be maintained for services. Marketers must implement strategies that will assist in managing the level of demand for a service in line with the firm's ability to provide the service. For example, FBOs have a continuing challenge in providing quality and timely maintenance while keeping overhead at profitable levels.

THE PRICE

Price represents the exchange value of a good or service. Since customers perceive price as the sacrifice or cost they must pay, marketers must maintain the price level equal to or less than utility (satisfaction level). This cost-benefit relationship plays a major role in pricing strategies.

Price planning is systematic decision-making by a firm regarding all aspects of pricing. A price contains all the terms of purchase: monetary and nonmonetary costs, discounts, handling and shipping fees, credit charges and other forms of interest, and late-payment penalties.

With **price competition**, sellers influence demand for their products primarily through changes in price levels. Non-price competition minimizes price as a factor in customer demand. This is accomplished by creating a distinctive product or service as expressed through promotion, customer service, availability, and other marketing factors. The more specialized a product or service offering is perceived to be by customers, the greater is the freedom of the firm to set prices above those of competitors.

Price competition is a flexible marketing tool because prices can be adjusted quickly and easily to reflect demand, cost, or competitive factors. However, of all the controllable marketing variables, pricing strategy is the easiest for a competitor to duplicate. For instance, if an FBO lowers the price for avgas to $4.75 per gallon, the competing FBO across the field can do the same.

Before a firm develops a pricing strategy, it must analyze the outside factors affecting price decisions. Price decisions depend heavily on elements external to the firm. This contrasts with product and promotion decisions, which are more directly controlled by the firm. The major factors affecting price decisions are customers, competition, costs, and products.

1. *Customers.* A firm must understand the relationship between price and customer purchases and perceptions. This relationship is explained by two economic principles: the law of demand and the price elasticity of demand. The law of demand states that customers usually purchase more units at a low price than at a high price. The price elasticity of demand defines the responsiveness of buyers to price changes in terms of the quantities they will purchase. Price elasticity is computed by dividing the percentage change in quantity demanded by the percentage change in price charged:

   $$\textit{price elasticity of demand} = \frac{\textit{percentage change in quantity demanded}}{\textit{percentage change in price}}$$

   Elastic demand occurs if relatively small changes in price result in large changes in quantity demanded. Numerically, price elasticity is greater than one. With elastic demand, total revenue increases when prices are lowered and decreases when prices rise. For example, if flight instruction rates decreased by 10 percent and the number of students increased by 15 percent, then demand is elastic and total revenue would increase.

   Inelastic demand takes place if price changes have little impact on quantity demanded. With inelastic demand, price elasticity is less than one. Total revenue increases when prices are raised and decreases when prices decline. If fuel prices increased by 5 percent and the quantity demanded decreased by 2 percent, demand is inelastic. Total revenue would increase in such a case. Unitary demand exists if changes in price are exactly offset by changes in quantity demanded, so that total revenue remains relatively constant. In that case, price elasticity is one.

   Elasticity of demand depends primarily upon three criteria: (a) the price, (b) the availability of substitutes, and (c) the urgency of need. In general, customers tend to be more responsive to price changes of high-ticket items, such as aircraft, than they are to low-priced items, such as approach plates or FBO t-shirts sold over the counter. The more substitute products are available, the more responsive customers tend to be. Lack of substitutes is generally associated with inelastic demand. The more time that customers have to shop around, the more elastic their demand. If a customer has an urgent need for a product, such as an aircraft part for which they cannot afford several days' delay, this customer will tend to be inelastic with regard to price.
2. *Competition.* Another element contributing to the degree of control a firm has over prices is the competitive environment within which it operates. An oligopolistic market has only a few firms that offer homogeneous products and have limited control over market pricing. Firms attempting to charge more than the current competitive price would attract few customers, because demand for any particular firm's product is not strong enough to prevent customers from switching to competitors when prices are increased. Similarly, a firm would actually lose revenue by selling for less than the market price because competitors would immediately match any price reduction, thus establishing a lower market price.

A **monopolistic competitive market** contains many sellers and is characterized by a moderate level of competition, well-differentiated product-service areas, and strong control over price by individual firms. In this environment, firms may succeed with higher prices because customers view their products as unique. Differentiation among FBOs may be based on reputation, professionalism of personnel, newness of aircraft, attractiveness of facilities, services offered, or other factors. Marketers desiring to sell below market price can carve out a niche in this environment by attracting customers interested in the lowest price. The choice of price level depends on the firm's strategy, target market, and competitive environment.

3. *Cost-oriented pricing*. This method is most commonly used because it has the advantage of simplicity. The price of a product must cover costs of manufacturing, promotion, and distribution, plus a reasonable profit. There are at least three variations of this approach: mark-up pricing, cost-plus pricing, and rate of return pricing. Markup pricing is appropriate when the seller is not the manufacturer. A reseller will add a percentage of the invoice cost to determine the selling price. The size of the percentage markup will depend on such factors as inventory turnover rate, competition, and degree of elasticity.

   Manufacturers of tangible products use cost-plus and rate of return pricing methods. Total unit costs are determined, and then a profit dollar amount or a desired rate of return percentage is added to arrive at the selling price. Cost-oriented approaches have a major disadvantage in that they give little or no consideration to customer demand. The price determined using this method only looks at internal factors (costs) rather than the market forces of supply and demand and the willingness of target markets to pay the asking price.
4. *Products*. There are numerous product characteristics which influence pricing, including:
   - *Perishability*. Products that are perishable in a physical sense must be priced attractively to promote sales without costly delays. Intangible products, which cannot be stored, are also very sensitive to the right price level to ensure a match between supply and demand. Perishability is also a concern as it applies to the consumption rate. Products that have a long life, like airplanes, tend to have an initial high cost. Second, owners of these types of products have a great deal of time to make replacement purchase decisions, which reduces the persuasiveness of price.
   - *Distinctiveness*. One of the major challenges facing marketing managers is to make their products different from their competitors. If unsuccessful, pricing becomes a matter of meeting the market price. Distinctiveness can be achieved in many products through design changes, packaging, services provided, warranties, etc. Being able to charge higher prices for these differentiated products rewards the seller.
   - *Life cycle*. The four stages of the product life cycle—introduction, growth, maturity, and decline—have an important impact on pricing decisions. During the introductory stage, a skimming policy or a penetrating policy is followed. Skimming is particularly useful when introducing a unique product for which the initial price is very high and which appeals to the innovators. As competitors enter the market, price is reduced. Penetrating is setting a below-competition price in order to capture an immediate share of the market. Prices will be raised as some brand loyalty has been attained. Growth and maturity stage pricing is driven by the aggressiveness of competitors and a firm's ability to remain distinctive in product lines. Decline stage pricing is usually geared to harvest the most revenue prior to the elimination of the product.

THE PLACE

Place is concerned with delivering the product and services to customers in a timely manner. In addition to a convenient location on the airport, the appropriate products and services must be available for each target market in the correct amount when customers need them. For example, aircraft used for flight instruction must be available when members of a target market need them and not off on a charter flight or down for maintenance.

Place decisions are directly related to a firm's desired customer service level. Customer service level is a measure of how rapidly and dependably a firm can deliver what customers want. For an FBO, it might mean having the appropriate parts in inventory. If a firm decides to lower overhead costs, it may also be settling for a lower customer service level by handicapping employee's ability to efficiently handle customer requests. On the other hand, obtaining a higher service level might increase sales that would in turn offset the increased costs. Clearly, a marketing manager has a decision to make about what service level to offer. Minimizing cost is not always the right answer.

THE PROMOTION

Promotional planning is systematic decision-making relating to all aspects of the development and management of a firm's promotional effort. Promotion is any form of communication used by a firm to inform, persuade, or remind people about its products, services, image, ideas, or community involvement.

The promotional mix consists of the following four major tools:

1. **Advertising**—Any paid form of nonpersonal presentation and promotion of ideas, products, or services by an identified sponsor.
2. **Sales promotion**—Short-term incentives to encourage the purchase or sale of a product or service.
3. **Personal selling**—Oral presentation with one or more prospective purchasers for the purpose of making sales.
4. **Publicity**—Nonpersonal stimulation of demand for a product or service by placing commercially significant news about the firm in a publication (e.g., *Business and Commercial Aviation*) or obtaining favorable presentation on radio or television that is not paid by the sponsor. Publicity can be positive or negative. For example, media coverage of an FBO after a plane crash is negative publicity.

Within the advertising and sales promotion categories are specific communication tools, such as mass media advertising, displays, print and specialty advertising, trade shows, brochures, literature, posters, contests, and flight training coupons. Many products, like aircraft, require the use of personal sales to first initiate contact and then use of sales skills to turn the prospect into a satisfied customer.

Promotional activities such as these are often thought to be the major, if not the total, thrust of marketing at any FBO. Promotion is important, but no more important than the other three marketing mix variables. The firm's products and services, prices, and distribution strategies all communicate important information to buyers. The whole marketing mix, not just promotion, must be coordinated for the maximum communication impact.

IMPLEMENTATION OF PLANS

Marketing implementation is the process that turns the marketing plan into action assignments and ensures that such assignments are executed in a manner that accomplishes the plan's stated objectives. No matter how well the marketing program has been planned, nothing happens until a product has been sold or a service performed. All department managers must not only have input into the marketing plan, they also must enthusiastically endorse the plan and play an important role in its implementation. Specific skill areas required for successful marketing implementation include organization and execution.

Organizing for Implementation

An organization is a group of people with a common purpose or mission. This mission can best be achieved if each person has a specific responsibility, and all are joined in such a way as to facilitate and reinforce each other. All members of the organization must be guided by the marketing concept. This **customer orientation** requires a thorough understanding of customer needs, wants, and behavior. The focal point, then, is the customer. Ideally, all members of the organization should attempt to learn more about customers' needs and work to develop products and services to satisfy those needs.

Another important element is coordination. First, there should be coordination within the marketing mix variables. Second, marketing efforts must be coordinated within each department and among departments. Unless all departments see themselves working toward a common goal of satisfying customers, they will not be able to assist in adhering to the marketing concept.

Executing Marketing Plans

Another ingredient to successful implementation of the marketing plan is management of the execution phase by all members of the firm. Implementation responsibilities fall into three areas: delegation, communication, and motivation.

1. **Delegation**. It is necessary in organizations to delegate responsibilities to various people. Delegation is done both formally through organizational structure and informally. In addition to determining appropriate duties, delegation also means matching people's capabilities and preferences to those duties. In other words, delegation will not result in successful implementation unless (1) the duties to be performed have been clearly specified and (2) appropriate personnel have been assigned to perform those duties.
2. **Communication**. After responsibilities have been delegated, they must be coordinated to achieve the firm's objectives, and the information must be communicated. Communication involves written or verbal means to create shared understanding among individuals. Ideally, information should flow throughout the firm—not just down the organizational hierarchy, but also across the organizationally hierarchy (among departments). Marketing plans are best implemented in a work environment that fosters complete and open information flow. Here are examples of several ways to improve communications:
   - *Information dissemination*—Up-to-date organizational charts, telephone directories, a company newsletter, an in-house library of industry material, and a policy for releasing information as quickly as possible to avoid rumor.
   - *Instruction*—Training programs, formal performance appraisals, sessions with supervisors, and financial assistance for educational pursuits.
   - *Interaction*—Informal company gatherings and interdepartmental committees.
3. **Motivation**. Delegation and communication will be to no avail unless someone in a leadership position takes the responsibility to motivate people to perform the tasks expected of them. Perhaps the most succinct method of motivating people is to reward them for a job well done. An aircraft salesperson can be rewarded with a bonus or week of vacation once a certain number of aircraft are sold each quarter or year. The salesperson on commission, for example, will devote more time to making new sales than to handling old complaints. A flight instructor can be rewarded for a good student retention rate by giving the instructor the next charter flight. Prizes can be given to the line person of the month. All of these are motivating factors designed to reward exemplary performance in carrying out the marketing objectives of the firm.

CONTROL

Marketing control is the process of translating organizational objectives into quantifiable standards, periodically analyzing marketing results, and taking actions that will correct the deficiencies affecting the FBO's ability to reach stated marketing objectives. It starts after the marketing program has been implemented and is monitored on a continuous basis. Generally speaking, control is the process that attempts to reconcile performance of the marketing plan with marketing objectives. The types of activities and standards differ across the four marketing mix variables. Thus, control is intertwined with planning. Some marketing authorities refuse to draw a precise distinction between planning and control, preferring instead to see them as two sides of the same coin.

Setting Standards and Measuring Results

The first step in marketing control is to translate organizational objectives into standards against which performance can be measured. In general, there are three bases for performance standards—industry norms, past performance, and managerial expectations.

Industry norms can be obtained from manufacturers, trade publications, and industry organizations. They can be quite useful as guidelines for marketing performance standards. Industry sales, pricing policies, and advertising strategies are examples of the types of information included. The underlying assumption of this kind of standard is that if the firm's performance is comparable to others in the industry, things "can't be too bad." This is not necessarily true. For example, an organization's market share may hold steady while the total market declines, as in the case of single-engine aircraft sales in the 1980s and 1990s. On the other hand, the firm's market share may fall while the total market is expanding. In essence, industry norms provide comparisons with average performance.

A second basis for performance standards is past performance: how do this month's or year-to-date sales compare to those of last month or last year? This information should be available from departments within the company. Past performance measures provide a minimum standard, a benchmark by which to measure subsequent efforts. Also, trends of performance over a period of time can be analyzed. However, the use of past performance assumes that historical patterns have relevance for future decisions. It may be misleading to measure current performance on the basis of these results.

The third basis for performance standards is managerial expectations. Forecasts, budgets, schedules, and policy decisions become standards against which actual performance is measured. These standards may involve both industry norms and past performance, but they also take estimates of future conditions into account. To the extent that managerial expectations are realistic, they probably provide the most useful standards for measuring performance. Assessments of future conditions, based on the manager's intuition, experience, and information, provide perhaps the most feasible standards for the situation. Of course, compared with industry norms or past performance, managerial expectations are more subjective and uncertain. Consequently, they are more open to criticism.

Corrective Action

Efforts at marketing control will meet with little success if the actions necessary to bring actual performance into line with standards are not taken. The first problem facing a manager contemplating corrective action is identification of specific causes for the deviation from the standard. This is sometimes easier said than done. Another difficulty is one of time lags associated with the desired corrective action. Sometimes, a manager finds that because of the time lag between recognition of a problem and a decision about corrective action, the problem has changed before it has been addressed. Perhaps a salesperson's poor performance during a given period, for example, was the result of a personal problem that has now been resolved. There are no easy answers to guide corrective action.

Perhaps performance is not faulty. It may be that the objectives set by the plan were inappropriate due to totally unexpected competitive, economic, or governmental actions. If this is the case, the proper corrective action involves adjusting the plans rather than performance.

Figure 7-3. Marketing management process.

SUMMARY OF MARKETING MANAGEMENT

It is clear that the marketing management process is one of planning marketing activities, directing the implementation of the marketing plan, and controlling the plan.

In Figure 7-3, all the steps are connected to show that the marketing management process is continuous. The planning job sets guidelines for implementation and specifies expected results that are compared in the control function to see if everything has worked out as projected. This feedback is especially important and can lead to changes. A manager should not only be concerned with the present plan but must also be proactive by always looking for attractive new opportunities and creating new strategies.

Uncontrollable Variables

The **uncontrollable variables** are those factors affecting a firm's performance that cannot be directed by marketing efforts. It must be recognized that any marketing plan, no matter how well conceived, might fail if adversely influenced by uncontrollable factors. Therefore, the external environment must be continually monitored and its effects incorporated into any marketing plan. The process of continually acquiring information about the trends occurring externally to the firm in order to be more efficient in planning, as well as to be proactive, is called **environmental scanning**. Uncontrollable variables that must be monitored and their trends analyzed are consumer demographics, competition, government regulations, the economy, technology, media, and public interest groups.

CONSUMER DEMOGRAPHICS

Although a firm has control over the selection of a target market, it cannot control the characteristics of the population. Firms can react to, but not control, these consumer demographics: age, income levels, marital status, occupation, race, education, and place and type of residence. The U.S. population will continue to grow, and there will be major changes in the country. In 2021, the population of the United States was more than 330 million people. As the population ages, the average age is rising. In 1970, the average age of the population was 28. In 2000, the average age was 37. By 2021, the average age was 38.1.

Since most marketers use age groups as one of the criteria in selecting homogeneous target markets, the change in the percentage of the population in different age groups will affect marketing strategies. For example, in the 18–24 age group, there were 29.4 million people in 2005, 30.6 million in 2010, 30.9 million in 2015, and 30.8 million in 2020. The major reason for the changing age distribution in different age groups is the U.S. birthrate. Expressed as the number of babies born per 1,000 people per year, the U.S. birthrate over the last 50 years indicates a major rise from 18.7 in 1935 to a high point of 25.0 in 1955. From this point forward, the birth rate has declined to the current 2000 level of 14.0. The post-World War II baby boom (1947 to 1957) produced about 43 million babies. This is about one-sixth of the present U.S. population. This large group crowded into the schools in the 1950s and 1960s and then entered the job market in the 1970s. Many of this group started to have children in the late 1970s and early 1980s, which caused another ground swell at the elementary school level. In the 1980s and 1990s, the baby boomers were middle-aged. By the early twenty-first century, this group reached retirement age. Because the baby boomers account for a large percentage of the population, they have been extremely important to marketers. This generation has a distinct profile compared with that of other age groups.

Millennials have the highest education level, with one-fourth of those between the ages of 25 and 35 having college degrees; they have high incomes and are commonly responsible for about half of all consumer expenditures. Many companies are designing products and developing marketing strategies to target this very important group.

Birth rates were very low during the 1960s and early 1970s, causing a significant drop in the number of individuals entering college in the mid-1980s. This factor might be one of the major causes of the decline in student pilot starts in the early 1990s.

Another significant trend is the increasing number of women in the workforce and the types of jobs they are performing. In 1950, only 24 percent of women worked outside the home. In 2019, 57.4 percent of all women participated in the labor force. Women are entering many nontraditional career paths, and income levels for this target group are rising, which gives them independence and purchasing power. Although only 6 percent of the total number of pilots in the country were women in 2006, by 2021, 8.5 percent were women. It is anticipated that these percentages will grow in the years ahead as more and more women become interested in flying (BLS 2021).

COMPETITION

A firm's competitors frequently affect its market planning and its success in attracting those in the target market. There are three types of competition. The first is **direct competition** between companies offering similar products and services. Two charter companies on the same airport compete directly for that area's charter business. The second type of competition (**indirect competition**) occurs between companies that offer products or services that can be substituted for one another. Automobiles are competitors for general aviation aircraft, as are commuter airlines, because they both can be used to transport company personnel. The third type of competition occurs because customers have limited financial resources (**replacement competition**). Marketers of dissimilar products and services are in competition with each other. The salesperson must help the customers prioritize their wish lists to accomplish immediate sales. A business aircraft salesperson, for example, may have to persuade the prospect to defer using credit to make a large company purchase so that credit resources will be available to secure an aircraft loan.

A firm must evaluate the marketing strategies of its competitors. Specifically, the firm must determine which markets are saturated and which are unfulfilled. The marketing plans and target markets of competitors, the images of competitors and their products, the strengths and weaknesses of competitors, and the extent to which consumers are satisfied with the level of service provided by the competition must also be considered.

GOVERNMENT REGULATIONS

A third uncontrollable variable affecting market planning is governmental regulation. In addition to the federal laws involving antitrust, discriminatory pricing, unfair trade practice, and occupational health and safety, the aviation industry is faced with numerous regulations promulgated by the Federal Aviation Administration. The FAA is charged with the safe operation of aircraft in the National Airspace System. In carrying out this responsibility, it develops many regulations that can have an impact on a firm's marketing plans.

In addition to federal legislation and agencies, each state and local government has its own legal environment for firms operating within its boundaries. State laws and local ordinances will vary across the country.

The political climate also affects legislation. Consumerism, nationalism, foreign trade, zoning, wage rates, and other items are discussed and debated through the political process before legislation is enacted.

THE ECONOMY

Markets require purchasing power as well as people. Total purchasing power is related to current income, profits, prices, savings, and credit availability. An economic recession, high unemployment, and the rising cost of credit all affect purchasing power. A high rate of growth means the economy in the region or country is usually good and the marketing potential large.

Of prime importance to firms are the perceptions of consumers regarding the economy. If consumers believe the economy will be favorable, they will increase spending. If they believe the economy will be poor, they will cut back on spending.

Some costs of doing business are often beyond the control of the firm. These include aircraft, parts and equipment, insurance, and interest rates. If costs rise substantially, marketing inflexibility is limited, and lower profit margins may be necessary. When costs are stable, firms have greater opportunities to differentiate their strategies and expand sales.

When widespread cost increases, such as premiums for product liability insurance, drive the price of aircraft up, the result is a high rate of inflation. Thus, the prices of some products and services may go beyond the reach of many consumers, or consumers may be forced to alter their spending habits.

Of importance is what happens to consumers' real income (income adjusted for inflation) over time. The level of corporate profits after taxes can also affect the number and type of aircraft purchased by corporations. A high rate of unemployment adversely affects firms because people cut back on discretionary spending.

TECHNOLOGY

Our society is characterized as being in the age of technological change. Technology refers to the inventions or innovations from applied science or engineering research. The aviation industry has always been on the leading edge of technological change. Many technological advances are beyond the control of individual firms, especially smaller ones. However, unless firms keep pace with improved technology, they will no longer remain competitive.

MEDIA

Firms do not control the media, yet they can influence the perceptions of the government, consumers, and the public about an industry or a company's products and overall image. The media can provide positive or negative coverage of a company or an industry. Whenever an aircraft crashes or a drug smuggler using an aircraft is captured, the industry receives bad press. Realizing the media's job is to distribute news, companies should willingly produce positive news releases.

PUBLIC INTEREST GROUPS

The number and power of public interest groups have increased during the past two decades and represent another uncontrollable variable. The most successful is Public Citizen, a consumer rights advocacy group. Hundreds of other consumer interest groups—private and governmental—operate at the national, state, and local levels. Other groups to consider are those seeking to protect the environment or advance the rights of minority groups.

Summary

An organization's level of success or failure in reaching its objectives depends on how well it directs and implements its controllable factors (marketing mix) and observes the impact of uncontrollable factors on the marketing plan. In order to improve the marketing effort and ensure long-run attainment of objectives, the firm needs feedback regarding the uncontrollable environment, the firm's performance, and how well the marketing plan is received. Feedback is obtained by measuring consumer satisfaction, looking at competitive trends, evaluating the relationship with government agencies, monitoring the economy, reading and reviewing the media, responding to public interest groups, analyzing sales and profit trends, talking with industry analysts, and employing other methods of gathering and assessing information.

After evaluating feedback, the firm needs to adapt its strategy to the business environment while continuing to utilize its distinct advantages. To ensure long-term success, the firm must continually look for new opportunities that are attainable and fit into its overall corporate objectives while responding to potential threats by revising marketing strategies.

Key Terms

advertising. Any paid form of nonpersonal presentation and promotion of ideas, products, or services by an identified sponsor.

communication. Written or verbal means to create shared understanding among individuals.

customer orientation. A focus on, and orientation toward, the customer. This requires a thorough understanding of customer needs, wants, and behavior.

delegation. The shifting of authority and responsibility for particular functions, tasks, or decisions from one person to another.

direct competition. Competition that occurs between companies offering similar products and services.

elastic demand. Occurs when the quantity demanded for a product or service changes by a greater percentage than the changes in price. With elastic demand, consumers are very sensitive to changes in price.

environmental scanning. The process of gathering information about events and their relationship within an organization's external environments.

exchange functions. A category of marketing activity that involves buying and selling on the part of various channel members, like wholesalers and retailers, and the final customer.

facilitating functions. A category of marketing activity that includes financing, risk-taking, providing information through market research, and standardizing and grading products.

inconsistent services. One of the four I's of services; it means that since services depend on the people who provide them, their quality varies with each person's training, capabilities, and attitudes.

indirect competition. Competition that occurs between companies that offer products or services that can be substituted for one another.

inelastic demand. Occurs when the quantity demanded for a product or service changes by a lesser percentage than changes in price. With inelastic demand, consumers are not price-sensitive, purchasing a product or service regardless of price.

inseparable services. One of the four I's of services. It means that the provider of the service cannot be separated from the service itself.

intangible services. One of the four I's of services; it means that the buyer must purchase a service on faith because it is often only after the sale that quality, benefits, and dimensions can be evaluated.

inventory of services. One of the four I's of services, representing the characteristic that many services are perishable in the sense that they cannot be stored.

marketing. The activities of promoting and selling products or services, including market research and advertising.

marketing concept. A customer-oriented, integrated, goal-oriented philosophy for a company in which the company aims all its efforts at satisfying its customers—for a profit.

marketing concept era. Occurring in the 1950s to 1990s, the marketing era that emphasizes customer need fulfillment and customer satisfaction.

marketing control. The process of translating organizational objectives into quantifiable standards, periodically analyzing marketing results, and taking actions that will correct the deficiencies affecting the company's ability to reach stated marketing objectives.

marketing implementation. The process that turns the marketing plan into action assignments and ensures that such assignments are executed in a manner that accomplishes the plan's stated objectives.

marketing management. A three-phase process that includes planning marketing activities, directing the implementation of the plans, and controlling these plans. This process is so central to the activities of most organizations that they formalize it as a marketing plan, which is a road map to guide the marketing activities for a specified future period of time, such as one year.

marketing mix. The mix of marketing variables that include the product or service, price, channel of distribution (place), and promotion (advertising, sales promotion, personal selling, and publicity). These controllable variables are referred to as the four Ps of marketing.

marketing objectives. The intended outcomes of the marketing plan. These objectives should complement and be set within the framework of the larger company objectives.

marketing planning. Making decisions that commit the firm to actions in order to reach organizational and marketing objectives effectively. Planning includes determining objectives, segmenting the market, selecting target markets, and establishing a unique marketing mix aimed at the particular audience.

market segmentation. The process of breaking down the total market into smaller, more homogeneous groups with similar needs that the firm can satisfy.

monopolistic competitive market. A market that contains many sellers and is characterized by a moderate level of competition, well-differentiated product-service areas, and strong control over price by individual firms. In this environment, firms may succeed with higher prices because customers view their products as unique.

motivation. The process that initiates, guides, and maintains goal-oriented behaviors.

personal selling. Occurs when a sales representative meets with a potential client for the purpose of transacting a sale.

physical distribution functions. A category of marketing activity that helps satisfy time and place utilities by efficiently combining the components of warehouse locations, inventory strategies, material handling, and transportation modes that provide a satisfactory service level for the customer.

place utility. Making products available where the customer wants them.

possession utility. The utility derived from transferring the ownership of a product between parties.

price competition. Competition in which sellers influence demand for their products primarily through changes in price levels.

price planning. Systematic decision-making by a firm regarding all aspects of pricing. A price contains all the terms of purchase: monetary and nonmonetary costs, discounts, handling and shipping fees, credit charges and other forms of interest, and late-payment penalties.

production era. The first era in the development of marketing, which occurred from 1870 to 1930. This era was characterized as a seller's market, where demand for products exceeded the supply. Firms concentrated on efficient production to offer products that were well made.

promotional planning. Systematic decision-making relating to all aspects of the development and management of a firm's promotional effort. Promotion is any form of communication used by a firm to inform, persuade, or remind people about its products, services, image, ideas, or community involvement.

publicity. Nonpersonal stimulation of demand for a product or service by placing commercially significant news about the firm in a publication or obtaining favorable presentation on radio or television that is not paid by the sponsor. Publicity can be positive or negative.

replacement competition. A type of marketing competition where customers have limited financial resources, and marketers of dissimilar products and services are in competition with each other.

sales era. A marketing era from the 1920s to 1950s defined by a buyer's market, where supply exceeded demand. During the sales era, manufacturers focused on aggressively selling the over-supply of their products.

sales promotion. Short-term incentives to encourage the purchase or sale of a product or service.

target market. A segment that is the object of a firm's marketing mix. By determining the target market, a company can tailor marketing toward those potential customers most likely to purchase the company's products/services.

time utility. Utility that occurs when a company makes goods available when the customer wants them.

uncontrollable variables. Variables affecting marketing that cannot be controlled by the company. Uncontrollable variables include consumer demographics, competition, government regulations, the economy, technology, media, and public interest groups.

utility. The want-satisfying ability of a good or service. From a marketing perspective, there are three forms of utility: time, place, and possession.

Review Questions

1. Define marketing and explain the three periods in the evolution of marketing.
2. Why is the ability to create utility the economic justification for a firm to be in business?
3. What is meant by segmenting the market?
4. Why would it be helpful for a firm to compare its strengths and weaknesses against its immediate competitors?
5. Do different target markets have different needs?
6. Why is it preferable to express objectives in quantifiable terms?
7. A product may include more than a physical item. Explain.
8. Name and explain the four I's of services.
9. What are the major factors affecting price?
10. Define elastic and inelastic demand.
11. Differentiate between an oligopolistic market and a monopolistic competitive market.
12. Discuss the three types of cost-oriented pricing.
13. What is meant by customer service level?
14. Define the four major tools in the promotional mix.
15. Implementing marketing plans involves delegation, communication, and motivation. Describe the importance of these functions.

16. How can workers be motivated?
17. How does control differ from implementation?
18. Describe several ways in which a firm can set standards.
19. What are the so-called uncontrollable variables that can affect a firm's marketing efforts?
20. Why should a firm be aware of consumer demographics?
21. Discuss several social trends that affect the marketing process.
22. Explain the three types of competition faced by an FBO.

Scenarios

1. As marketing manager for a start-up FBO, you have been tasked with establishing a marketing mix for flight instruction. Considering the four Ps, how would you do that?
2. You are the marketing manager of a new FBO, and the FBO manager has asked for your help in establishing target markets for the flight school, aircraft sales, and maintenance. Target markets will be important in your marketing plan, so what are some potential target markets for these three FBO services?
3. As marketing manager for a busy FBO, you were recently asked to consider the services offered by the FBO. The FBO manager feels that the services offered by the FBO need to be more fully developed. Specifically, you need to consider the "four I's" of services. Fully develop and explain these four I's for each of the following services: washing aircraft, fueling aircraft, and towing aircraft.
4. The FBO that you manage has decided to begin offering aircraft maintenance. What type of promotional mix can you develop to promote this new activity?
5. As the new manager of an existing FBO, you decided six months ago that a new marketing plan was necessary. Once developed, the plan was implemented. One goal was to increase new student pilot starts by 5 percent during the quarter. During the past month, your FBO has advertised for flight instruction via radio ads and billboards. How will you set standards and measure results of this effort?
6. As marketing manager of a full-service FBO, you have been asked by the FBO manager to evaluate competition faced by the firm. Clearly, there is a competing FBO across the field, but is this the only competition for the FBO? The FBO currently offers flight instruction, aircraft rental, charter services, aircraft sales, and aircraft maintenance.

Bibliography

BLS (Bureau of Labor Statistics). 2021. "Women in the Labor Force: A Databook." BLS Reports, Report 1092. https://www.bls.gov/opub/reports/womens-databook/2020/home.htm.

Prather, C. Daniel. 2009. *General Aviation Marketing and Management: Operating, Marketing, and Managing an FBO.* 3rd ed. Malabar, FL: Krieger Publishing Company.

8

Promotion and Sales

In Chapter 8

Objectives

At the end of this chapter, you should be able to:

1. Name and describe the four components in the promotional mix.
2. Discuss the objectives of advertising.
3. Distinguish between the following types of advertising: product, institutional, pioneering, competitive, comparative, and reminder.
4. Explain the importance of an advertising budget and message.
5. Summarize the advantages and disadvantages of the leading advertising media.
6. Describe several methods of measuring advertising effectiveness.
7. Give four examples and describe the purpose of sales promotion.
8. Describe several publicity techniques that may be used by an FBO.
9. Explain prospecting.
10. List four aircraft prospecting sources and describe the type of information given.
11. Highlight some of the basic business information needed by an aircraft salesperson to qualify a prospect.
12. Discuss the approach, presentation, handling objections, close, and follow-up steps in the selling process.

The Promotional Mix

In order to communicate the availability of its products, a firm can use one or more of four promotional activities: advertising, sales promotions, publicity, and personal selling. The **promotional mix** is the combination of one or more of these four activities.

Advertising is any paid form of nonpersonal communication about an organization, product, or service by an identified sponsor. The paid aspect of this definition is important because advertising normally must be purchased. The nonpersonal component of advertising is also important. Advertising involves mass media that are many and varied, including online ads, social media posts, email advertising, magazine and newspaper space, outdoor posters, signs, banner towing, direct mail, radio, television, catalogs, directories, and circulars.

Although advertising lacks the immediate feedback of personal selling, it can reach large numbers of potential customers at a relatively low cost. By using advertising in a promotional mix, a company can control what it wants to say and, to some extent, to whom the message is sent. For example, if an FBO wants college students to receive its message on flight training, advertising space can be purchased in a college campus newspaper.

Sales promotion involves marketing activities other than advertising, publicity, or personal selling that stimulate customer purchases and company effectiveness. Sales promotion activities include trade shows, coupons, contests, premiums, and free samples that are basically aimed at increasing sales. A $50 coupon for an introductory flight that appears under an FBO's advertisement in a local newspaper is an example.

Figure 8-1. Sample flight school advertisement. *(Vector Tradition/Shutterstock.com)*

Publicity is an unpaid form of nonpersonal communication about any organization, product, or service by an identified sponsor, which can take the form of a news story, editorial, or product announcement. An announcement in the local activities section of the newspaper, informing the public that the local aircraft model builders club meets in the conference room of Ace Flying Service at 7:00 p.m. on the last Thursday of each month, is a form of publicity. Publicity is generally thought of as favorable and is planted by the firm or its advertising agency to promote the company by informing or reminding the public about its products and/or services. Negative publicity can occur, however, such as when an airplane crashes or when local citizens complain about noise created by airplanes taking off and landing at the local airport. Publicity can occur without the urging of a firm, simply for its news value.

Personal selling is a two-way flow of communication between a representative of the firm and a customer for the purpose of making a sale. The two-way flow of communication distinguishes personal selling from other forms of promotion.

Costs associated with personal selling are high, but it has distinct advantages. A representative can control to whom the presentation is made and can also see or hear the potential buyer's reaction to the message. If the reaction is unfavorable or not completely understood, the salesperson can modify the message. The flexibility of personal selling also can be a disadvantage because different salespeople can change the message regarding the product or service so that no consistent communication is given to all customers.

In developing the promotional mix, a firm must consider the balance of elements to use. There is no one right blend of promotional activities. Each must be developed as part of a unique marketing mix (four Ps) for each target market.

ADVERTISING

Advertising can play an important role in the promotion blend. In contrast to personal selling, advertising is a form of mass selling that attempts to make potential buyers aware of and interested in a firm's products and services. In other words, it takes a shotgun approach, whereas personal selling zeroes in on individuals with more of a "rifle-like" approach.

While the level of advertising as a percentage of sales varies among industries, U.S. corporations on average spend about 3 percent of their sales dollars on advertising. Unfortunately, many smaller firms such as FBOs pay very little attention to this important ingredient in the marketing mix.

Few companies, big or small, have the in-house expertise to develop their own advertising programs. Consequently, they turn to advertising agencies who are specialists in planning and handling mass selling details. Some agencies are one-person operations, while at the other extreme are agencies that may have as many as 8,000 employees. Some agencies specialize in business advertising and others in retail advertising.

Basically, an advertising agency carries out the following functions:

1. Plans advertising.
2. Selects media and contracts for space and time.
3. Prepares the advertising, including copy, layouts, and other creative work.
4. Produces finished advertisements in the physical form required by different media.
5. Creates and produces direct-mail pieces and other collateral material.
6. Checks invoices and evidence that advertising has appeared as scheduled (such as tear sheets from publications and affidavits from broadcasting stations). The bills from vendors who supplied materials and services for preparing the advertising are reviewed by the agency.

An advertising agency begins by becoming familiar with the company and what it sells. Perhaps the agency's members already have a background of experience with similar businesses. If so, they concentrate on learning about the specific operation. They study promotional objectives and determine the role advertising can play in helping accomplish the objectives. Then the agency recommends an approach for the advertising message and the specific media to use. Online advertising, to include videos and social media posts, are quite common, but radio, magazines, and newspapers may also be part of the advertising strategy.

Agencies are paid in four ways: (1) commissions allowed by media; (2) fees paid by the firm; (3) service charges on materials and services purchased for preparation of advertising; and (4) charges for advertising not involving commissions, such as direct mail.

Commissions allowed by media to advertising agencies are usually 15 percent of the cost of advertising space or time purchased. Most media have two rate schedules: national and local. National rates are higher and include agency commissions. When the lower local rates apply, with a few exceptions, agencies are not allowed to deduct commissions. The commissions included in the national rates are allowed only to agencies. Commissions received from media are the major source of income for most agencies.

When an advertising agency is used, an individual from the firm, working along with the agency account executive, is responsible for coordinating the agency's activities with related company activities. This individual participates in the agency's planning and conduct of advertising campaigns, thus ensuring that the campaigns are consistent with the firm's overall marketing strategy.

Advertising Objectives

Every advertising campaign should have clearly defined objectives that must flow from prior decisions on the market to be targeted and the marketing mix. Accurate measurement of stated objectives such as sales, market share, and profits should be taken before and after the campaign. Firms who fail to do this will only have an intuitive feeling about the effectiveness of their campaigns.

Advertising objectives should specify the following:

1. The objective to be accomplished and the target market. Some examples are:
    - To increase line service business (target market: NBAA members)
    - To increase the number of flight students (target market: college students)
    - To develop charter business (target market: local businesses with more than 100 employees)
    - To increase maintenance business (target market: local, single-engine aircraft owners)
2. The time period for accomplishing the objectives.

The objectives listed above are not as specific as they could be. A firm may want to sharpen them for its own purposes. For example, a general objective, such as "To increase the number of flight students," could be rephrased more specifically as "To increase the number of student pilots by 20 percent during the next three months."

Setting reasonable advertising objectives is part of the art of marketing. The first time a manager sets objectives, they will probably be based on an educated guess, despite logical analysis that may have gone into the choice. In time, however, experience in setting objectives and observing the actual results of particular advertising campaigns will allow the manager to select more realistic objectives.

The advertising objectives largely determine which of two basic types of advertising to use: product or institutional. **Product advertising** takes three forms: (1) pioneering, (2) competitive or comparative, and (3) reminder. Product advertising tries to sell a product or service to final users or middlemen. **Institutional advertising** attempts to develop good will for the company and enhance its image, instead of promoting a specific product or service. In practice, a firm may employ both of these two basic types of advertising simultaneously.

Pioneering advertising tries to develop demand for a product or service category rather than for a specific company. It informs the target market what the product or service is, what it can do, and where it can be found. An example is FBOs placing a print advertisement describing charter services in the local chamber of commerce newsletter.

Advertising that promotes a specific company's products or service is **competitive advertising.** The objective of this advertising is to persuade the target market to select the firm's offerings rather than those of a competitor. An increasingly common form of competitive advertising used by the airlines and other segments of the aviation industry is comparative advertising. This form of advertising shows one firm's strengths relative to competitors.

Reminder advertising is used to reinforce prior knowledge about a product or service, such as by sending a brochure to a business aircraft owner who recently had aircraft serviced at the local FBO. The message might be: "The next time you are in Fort Lauderdale, drop by and see us. It was a pleasure serving you."

Establishing an Advertising Budget

Once the advertising objectives have been determined, a budget must be established for each product or service. Deciding on the ideal amount is a difficult task because there is no precise method to measure the results of advertising spending. There are five traditional approaches to deciding how much to spend for advertising: (1) spending all the firm can afford; (2) allotting a certain percentage of net sales; (3) matching the advertising expenditures of competitors; (4) investing for future profits; and (5) using the objective-and-task method.

The all-we-can-afford approach treats advertising as a luxury. This is a financial rather than a marketing approach. It does not consider what advertising can or should accomplish.

An approach that spends a percentage of sales is popular because it provides a formula—for instance, a certain percent of past sales—and it is simple and easy to use. Using the previous year's sales as the base seems to assume that advertising is the result of sales rather than sales the result of advertising. Furthermore, it makes no provision for increasing business and may not even allow enough money to maintain the current level of advertising. A variation of the percentage approach is the unit-of-sales method. This method establishes the amount of advertising on the basis of unit quantities of goods instead of dollar sales. This method is suitable for a firm with a narrow product line.

Trying to match the advertising of competitors is a defensive rather than an aggressive approach. It tends to produce advertising programs that are not tied to stated objectives and result in inefficient expenditures. This is reactive rather than proactive advertising.

Under the next approach, advertising is considered an investment for future profit. This approach is primarily used for introducing new products or services when extensive advertising dollars are required to get the product adopted. Any possible profits are plowed back into advertising and other promotional and sales activities.

The last of the five methods for creating advertising budgets is regarded by many as the best. The objective-and-task method builds a budget by first deciding what type of advertising is needed to accomplish the stated objectives. The principal problem with this method is the danger of being too ambitious. When the budget is totaled, the cost of the campaign may be more than the firm can possibly afford. The solution is usually to revise the objectives and/or modify the time for reaching them.

Common decision rules that can be used to determine the size and focus of a firm's advertising budget include the following:

- *Market share*—A company that has a higher market share must generally spend more on advertising to maintain its share.
- *Sales from new products*—If a company has a high percentage of its sales resulting from new products, it must spend more on advertising compared to companies that have well-established products.
- *Market growth*—Companies competing in fast-growing markets should spend comparatively more on advertising.
- *Unit price (per sales transaction)*—The lower the unit price of a company's products, the more it should spend on advertising because of the greater likelihood of brand switching.
- *Product price*—Both very high-priced (or premium) products and very low-priced (or discount) products require higher advertising expenditures because, in both cases, price is an important factor in the buying decision and the buyer must be convinced (through advertising) that the product is a good value.
- *Product quality*—Higher-quality products require a greater advertising effort because of the need to convince the customer that the product is unique.
- *Degree of standardization*—Standardized products produced in large quantities should be backed by higher advertising outlays because they are likely to have more competition in the market.

Most FBOs are small and have limited resources for advertising. Repeating advertisements can stretch advertising dollars. Savings occur through reduced preparation costs, both creative and mechanical. A number of studies have shown that advertisements repeated as many as four times do not lose their effectiveness. A later insertion attracts about the same number of readers as the first one.

For FBOs with limited financial resources, engaging customers via free social media platforms can be very effective. Although online ad impressions may be purchased, with an appropriate monthly budget set, an effective reach can be created for free by the digitally-savvy FBO. Consider sites such as Facebook, Twitter, Instagram, and Snapchat.

Advertising Message

Next, the firm develops its **advertising message,** the overall appeal for its campaign. The message in an advertisement is often called the copy. Copy results from a combination of analytical thinking based upon a clear understanding of the firm's products and services with a liberal use of imagination. The actual advertisements are produced by creative individuals at the advertising agency—the copywriters and artists—but the overall evaluation and approval of copy is the responsibility of marketing management.

The copy must fit both company and advertising objectives; it must be consistent with the target audience and the product or service itself. Generally, an early step is to develop a campaign theme—a keynote idea or unique selling proposition—as some marketing people refer to it. This keynote idea should provide continuity and have significant impact upon target market segments. For example, business aircraft have frequently been referred to as time machines—the theme being that they save time and increase productivity.

Language or visual messages projecting the central theme must be created; most advertisements use both. An effective message (1) attracts the market's attention, (2) is understandable, and (3) is believable.

Media Selection

The firm's next step is choosing the advertising media to carry the message. There is a wide variety of media from which to choose, and this decision is primarily related to the target audience, the product or service, available budget, and campaign objectives.

Table 8-1 summarizes the advantages and disadvantages of the leading media.

Table 8-1. Advantages and Disadvantages of Advertising Media

Medium	Advantages	Disadvantages
Newspaper	Short lead time, flexible, good local market coverage, inexpensive	Short life, poor reproduction quality, general audience, limited creativity, heavy ad competition
Magazines and trade journals	High geographic selectivity, long life, high-quality reproduction, good pass-along readership	Long lead time, poor frequency, ad clutter, expensive
Direct mail	Audience selectivity, no ad competition, personal approach, inexpensive	High throwaway rate, receipt by wrong person, low credibility
Radio	Selective market, high frequency, low cost	No visual contact, customer distractions
Television	Combines sight, sound, and motion; high attention; persuasive	General audience, relatively expensive, long lead time, short message
Billboard	High repeat exposure, low cost, low competition, color and creative options	General audience, legal restrictions, inflexible
Telephone/business directory	Low cost, coverage of market, specialized listings	Clutter of ads, limited creativity, long lead time
Digital	High degree of selectivity, interactive	Large competition

Possibly the most effective advertising medium for many advertising campaigns is digital. As of 2021, there were 284 million internet users in the United States and 3.97 billion users worldwide. Fully 79 percent of the U.S. population had a smartphone in 2021, representing 280 million users. Whether on a desktop computer or handheld smartphone, the vast majority of the population is digitally connected. This is even more true for that segment of the population serving as the FBO's target market. FBOs must consider this advertising media as the premier platform to reach existing and prospective customers.

Social media is another aspect of the digital advertising medium. Social media platforms such as Instagram, Twitter, LinkedIn, and Facebook are commonplace. It is important to consider the target audience and which platforms they are more likely to use. For example, teens are on TikTok, while people over 40 years old are more likely on Facebook. Instagram has a wide following from among many age groups. Interestingly, Facebook owns Instagram, so there are some commonalities between these two platforms. YouTube is another option for video ads. Internet and social media advertising offers a variety of advantages. It offers an exceptional ability to target specific customers, can be interactive, and can be customized to unique target markets. Depending on the platform, rates may average $10 to $40 per 1,000 viewers, which is in line with the cost of national magazine rates.

Specific types of internet and social media advertising include:

- *Banner ads*—Typically, static banner ads that can appear on a website, with pay per impression.
- *Photo ads*—Similar to a banner ads, but often specific to a social media platform. An ad with a photo that often contains a call-to action button.
- *Video ads*—Range from short video clips to longer videos.
- *Collection ads*—Highlights products in a social media feed, appearing somewhat like a digital storefront.
- *Carousel ads*—Include a number of images or videos, each with their own link.
- *Slideshow ads*—A video created from several static images.
- *Messenger ads*—Ads that appear in the chats tab of a messenger app, such as Facebook Messenger.
- *Search engine optimization (SEO)*—Improving the quality and quantity of website traffic to a website or a web page from search engines.
- *Search engine advertising*—Placement of ads with specific monthly budgets and market segments specified on search engines, such as Google.

The key for effective social media and internet advertising is to determine the digital location of the target market and try several innovative approaches to reach that market. Relying only on one platform or one type of ad may not generate the best results.

Newspapers are an important local medium with an excellent potential for reaching a large audience. They also allow great flexibility in the size of ads, which may be a few lines or a complete page. Very little lead time is needed to place or change an ad, and it can be tailored to current developments. The short life of a newspaper ad is a drawback, along with the inability to tailor the message to a specific target market.

Magazines and trade journals are certainly some of the fastest growing media. Color is used most effectively in magazines, and the big advantage of this medium is the great number of special interest publications that appeal to target markets. The long lead time required for magazine ads results in more general and less timely information. The high cost of magazine and trade journal advertisements compared with other media is another disadvantage.

Direct mail advertisements can reach a very homogeneous market and convey a great deal of information. Mailing lists can be obtained for specific aircraft owners in a particular geographic area. Direct mail advertising is a relatively inexpensive form of advertising, although many people view direct mail as junk. The challenge is to get the recipient to open the letter or brochure. In an effort to increase readership, some companies sending direct mail structure the envelope to appear official, as if it is from the IRS. This tactic, however, misleads the recipient and is not recommended.

Radio advertisements are fairly inexpensive and are particularly effective for local messages. Radio stations can be valuable in target marketing because of the different listening audiences. The lead time for developing radio ads is short. The main disadvantage of radio is the inability of the prospective customer to review the message. Another problem is the ease with which customers can switch stations and tune out a commercial. Radio also competes with people's attention as they do other activities, like driving or working. If used, however, a decision will need to be made whether AM, FM, or satellite radio is more appropriate, considering cost and the target market.

Television has a major advantage over all of the other media in that it combines sight and sound. Its primary disadvantage is cost. The combination of a general audience and cost are sufficient detriments to eliminate this medium from most FBO's promotion mix.

An effective medium for reaching a general audience in a specific locale is billboard advertising. The drawback in billboards is the inability to present lengthy advertising copy. Also, in many areas, laws have been passed to restrict the use of this medium.

Advertising in telephone and business directories is used by all firms and can be very effective because prospective customers seek out the firm. The cost is rather inexpensive, but its weakness is that directory ads compete with so many other similar ones. This medium is often called directional advertising. The prospect has already established the need and is looking for the best alternative to satisfy the need.

Measuring Effectiveness

The final element in the advertising campaign is measuring its effectiveness, which should be measured in terms of criteria derived from the firm's overall advertising and marketing objectives.

If advertising objectives are sales-related (e.g., to increase sales or improve market share) then it is possible to determine whether the advertising has been effective in reaching customers. However, advertising is only one cause of sales. Other aspects of marketing, including improved product or service and other forms of promotion such as personal selling and pricing, all contribute to sales performance.

Some firms pre-test advertising effectiveness before starting the campaign. Focus groups (composed of a panel of customers or knowledgeable individuals) might be asked to rate which ad would most influence them. Customers might be asked to evaluate several ads and then recall the source and as much of the content of the message as they can. The uniqueness of an ad can be best measured by this method. Post-testing an advertisement can also be used. For example, results can be measured by the number of orders mailed back, coupons brought in, or customers who responded to an ad for a sale. Recall tests can be used in which customers are asked to recall everything about an ad in a trade magazine or newspaper to which they subscribe. This test measures an ad's ability to be noticed and remembered.

SALES PROMOTION

Sales promotion activities supplement both advertising and personal selling. It is usually not directed at as large an audience as advertising but at much larger groups than a typical personal selling effort. Included are such activities as trade shows, exhibits, coupons, trade allowances, demonstrations, and dealer incentives.

Given the diversity of sales promotion activities, it is apparent that they are designed to reach many target markets and to achieve a variety of objectives, such as the following:

1. Identifying sales leads (trade shows)
2. Inducing prospective customers to try a new service (flight instruction coupons)
3. Increasing the share of an established market (price breaks on a block of charter hours)
4. Improving name recognition (calendars, matchbooks, T-shirts, pens, and posters with the firm's name)

Sales promotion has several distinct advantages. First, it involves the prospective customer. Customers must return the flight coupons to receive instruction, or they must use free samples or discard them. Additionally, sales promotion activities can offer true value to the user; money can actually be saved. Finally, sales promotions can be directed to narrowly defined market segments. For example, flight coupons can be mailed to prospective users in high-income areas, or a brochure announcing a specially priced maintenance package can be directed to particular aircraft owners.

The following sales promotion activities are typically used by FBOs:

- *Coupons.* Coupons are certificates entitling the bearer to a stated savings on the purchase of a specific product or service. Coupons can be mailed, enclosed with other products, or inserted in ads. They can be effective in stimulating sales and getting a customer to try a new product or service.

- *Price incentives or deals.* Short-term price reductions are commonly used to increase trial among potential customers or to counter a competitor's actions. These special deals generally work best when they are used infrequently or when the product or service being offered is relatively new.
- *Promotional contests and sweepstakes.* Promotional activities that involve customers in games of skill are called contests, while those involving customers in games of chance are called sweepstakes. For example, in the case of a contest, customers (present or prospective) may be required to complete a puzzle, identify a vintage aircraft, or complete a sentence for a prize. Sweepstakes are often used to increase fuel sales or to sell aircraft. The aircraft manufacturers and organizations such as AOPA and Sporty's Pilot Shop have sponsored a number of sweepstakes over the years with the winner receiving a new or restored aircraft.
- *Premiums.* Premiums are the offerings of merchandise at a low cost or free as an incentive to purchase those products or services or as a suggestion to visit the locations where the products or services can be obtained. Premiums serve as reminders and include such items as calendars, miniature flashlights, key chains, business card holders, T-shirts, pens, posters, and a host of other promotional items with the firm's name displayed.
- *Demonstrations.* Demonstrations are sometimes used by FBOs selling aircraft or charter services. A price break may be given to a prospective customer on a demonstration flight of an actual trip. Demonstrations involve a personal presentation of how the service works. It is often effective but is an expensive technique and has limited application.
- *Point-of-purchase promotions.* Point-of-purchase promotions are special displays, signs, banners, and exhibits that are set up in locations such as schools, stores, or mall entrances to promote a product or service. These promotions serve to remind customers that a product or service is available at a given location (e.g., a sign next to the cash register at the local flight shop advertising an FBO).
- *Trade shows.* Many firms use trade shows, such as the annual NBAA convention, to advertise their products and services. Participating companies expect several benefits, including generating new sales leads, maintaining customer contacts, introducing new products and services, meeting new customers, and selling more to present customers.

Another form of sales promotion is cooperative advertising. This is an agreement in which a manufacturer, like Cessna, pays a portion of an FBO's local advertising costs. These costs are shared on a fifty-fifty basis up to a specified limit. Sales promotion efforts can also be directed at a firm's employees. Awards or gifts might be given to employees for exemplary service. Many firms pick up the cost of uniforms and jackets with the company logo. Line personnel, pilots, instructors, mechanics, salespeople, and office personnel all could be considered for appropriate apparel. These items not only add to the professional image the company hopes to project but also create a feeling among employees that they are part of a team.

PUBLICITY

Publicity is the last component of the promotional mix and is another means firms can use to promote their products and services to mass audiences. It involves free promotion about the product, service, or organization in the media. Publicity is generally considered to be a part of a larger concept, that of public relations. Company public relations has several objectives, including obtaining favorable publicity for the firm, building a good image in the community, and handling adverse rumors and stories that circulate.

FBOs generally have many topics available to them with potential for publicity. Some possibilities are listed below:

- New products or services
- Product donations

- Special events, such as air shows, open houses, and presentations of construction and expansion plans
- Airport planning activities
- Athletic sponsorships
- Charitable activities, such as providing an aircraft for emergency purposes
- Personnel news such as promotions, service anniversaries, retirements, new student solos and pilot certificates, contest winners, and management participation in local service clubs

Several publicity techniques are available. These include the following:

- *News releases.* News releases are short statements about the firm's products, services, or organization released to the news media.
- *Feature articles.* Feature articles, usually containing up to 3,000 words, are prepared for a specific publication such as a trade journal.
- *Press conferences.* Press conferences involve inviting news people to hear a specific announcement and ask questions.
- *Online videos.* In addition to possibly creating videos in-house or through a contracted vendor, industry organizations such as GAMA and NBAA have created high-quality online videos that may be useful to reach schools and social/civic groups.

Publicity needs to be managed carefully and in a way that is effective; it must be integrated into the total promotional campaign. In this way, the full force of advertising, sales promotion, publicity, and personal selling can complement one another.

The Personal Selling Process

Unlike the other promotional activities, personal selling is a distinctive communication form because it utilizes two-way rather than one-way communication. Personal selling involves social interaction, with the prospect and salesperson influencing each other by what they say and do. The outcome of each sales situation depends upon the success of both parties in communicating with each other and reaching a common understanding of goals and objectives. A salesperson should tailor the communication to fit the prospect's needs.

Many position titles are used to identify people in the field of sales. The titles indicate the amount of selling done and the amount of creativity required to perform the sales task. Three types of personal selling exist: inside sales, executive sales, and sales support activities. Typically, inside salespeople process routine orders, engage in telemarketing, and facilitate the exchange of products with face-to-face customers. Executive salespeople operate outside in assigned territories, when appropriate, and identify prospective customers, provide these prospects information, influence prospects to purchase products, close sales, and follow-up after the sale to build lasting customer relationships. Sales support salespeople assist executive salespeople by performing promotional activities and providing technical expertise.

As products and services become more complex and expensive, personal selling becomes more important in the promotional mix. Highly technical products such as aircraft require greater emphasis on personal selling than other less sophisticated products. The task of an aircraft salesperson best fits the executive sales category, and the seven-step selling process will illustrate the format used to create sales by these salespeople.

Personal selling can be represented as a seven-step sequence that must be accomplished for success.

1. *Prospecting*—Searching for and identifying potential customers. Identifying primary and secondary sources.
2. *Pre-approach*—Qualifying the prospects.
3. *Approach*—Securing an interview to perform a travel analysis.

4. *Presentation*—Developing additional information. Performing a value analysis. Making a formal presentation to the prospective firm's decision makers.
5. *Handling objections*—Anticipating buyer resistance and developing effective responses.
6. *Closing*—Finalizing the details of the transaction and asking for the order.
7. *Follow-up*—Establishing a good relationship, reassuring the customer, and handling questions. Setting the stage for repeat sales.

PROSPECTING

Just as firms analyze markets seeking opportunities for their products and services, salespeople seek potential customers. **Prospecting** is the first step in the selling process. It involves the continuing search for potential buyers. This search for prospects is generally the sole responsibility of the salesperson. Firms may assist by engaging in direct mail or print advertising, which invites readers to inquire about the firm's products and services. These leads would then be turned over to the sales force for follow-up. Qualified prospects are the raw material for future sales. Salespeople must develop skills in this area to ensure that presentations are made only to those prospects that have an unfilled need and the financial ability to satisfy that need. The process begins with an in-depth macro view of the total potential market of those interested in acquiring an aircraft, charter, or other FBO services and then is refined to organizations that fit the following profile:

- The company's operations require frequent trips beyond a 300-mile radius to destinations not well served by commercial aviation.
- These frequent trips require two or more persons to travel together.
- The financial health of the company would allow the purchase or lease of an aircraft.
- The company's business operations presently require the use of air transportation to accomplish sales and marketing objectives.

Size and Scope of Markets

Most of the resources and reasons to buy general aviation airplanes lie within the business and government sectors of the economy. The best prospects for aircraft and associated services are organizations that can use them to make their own business efforts more productive and more profitable.

Businesses and governmental units include all the buyers in the nation except the final consumers. These buyers purchase and lease tremendous volumes of capital equipment, raw materials, manufactured parts, supplies, and business services. The aggregate purchases of business and government buyers in a year are far greater than those by final consumers. There are more than 23 million businesses in the United States. The first four categories of businesses (agricultural, forestry and fishing, mining, and construction and manufacturing) sell tangible products and represent approximately 20 percent of the firms. Transportation, communications, and public businesses represent approximately 4 percent of the total businesses. Resellers (wholesalers and retailers) account for approximately 19 percent of the firms, and the service industry (finance, insurance, real estate, and services) represent approximately 57 percent. Governmental units are the federal, state, and local agencies that buy goods and services for the constituents they serve. About 88,000 of these governmental units exist in the United States.

Measuring Business and Government Markets

Measuring the business and government markets is an important first step for an aircraft salesperson interested in gauging the size of these markets. Fortunately, information is readily available from the federal government to do this. The federal government regularly collects, tabulates, and publishes data on these markets using its **Standard Industrial Classification (SIC) System**. The SIC system groups organizations on the basis of major activity or the major product or service provided, which enables the federal government to list the number of establishments, number of employees, and sales volumes for each group, designated by a numerical code. Geographic breakdowns are also provided where possible.

The SIC system begins with broad, two-digit categories such as food (SIC code 20), tobacco (SIC code 21), and apparel (SIC code 23). Often, each of these two-digit categories is further divided into three-digit and four-digit categories, which represent sub industries within the broader two-digit category. The SIC system permits a firm to find the SIC codes of its present customers and then obtain SIC-coded lists for similar firms that may want the same type of products and services. Also, SIC categories can be monitored to determine the growth in the number of firms, number of employees, and sales volumes to identify promising market opportunities.

The **North American Industry Classification System (NAICS)** replaced the SIC in 1997 and was developed jointly by the United States, Canada, and Mexico. The NAICS allows for better comparisons between the three countries. Today, NAICS codes are the official codes used by the U.S. government and internationally. SIC codes are still commonly used by companies that often add numbers to the end of the original codes to expand or update the original classifications. SIC codes are more common in the private sector and are used to analyze the economy, segment markets for marketing purposes, and allow companies to identify competition. Whether the SIC or NAICS is referenced, the intent is the same—to classify firms based on their business activities to support the analysis and publishing of statistical data related to the U.S. business economy.

Prospecting Sources

The total prospective business aircraft market can be thought of as an iceberg. Above the waterline are the highly visible corporations appearing in Fortune's top 500 or top 1,000 lists. These include such companies as General Motors, ExxonMobil, IBM, Procter and Gamble, and General Electric. Over one-half of the Fortune top 1,000 firms own or operate aircraft for business purposes. Each year, *Business and Commercial Aviation* magazine, using data supplied by Aviation Data Service, Inc., breaks down the Fortune top 1,000 firms by SIC code and compares the number of aircraft operators and nonoperators for each category. There is no problem compiling information on these publicly owned firms or for that matter, on the next 25,000 leading U.S. corporations. Detailed information concerning these firms can be found in business directories such as Dun & Bradstreet, Moody's, and S&P Global Ratings.

There is still another layer of businesses, not listed in any national business directory, representing the balance of the 23 million companies. It is the upper one million companies of this business stratum that represents about 80 percent of the owners of general aviation aircraft. These businesses form part of the iceberg market profile that is immediately below the waterline. These are the companies listed in the telephone book, chamber of commerce directories, civil club rosters, state chamber of commerce directories, individual industry directories, medical society directories, and professional society rosters. They are companies, associations, and partnerships run by successful businesspeople in any city or area. Some major categories include the following:

- Automobile dealers
- Banks
- Food product manufacturers and distributors
- General contractors
- Insurance agents, brokers, and companies
- Machinery manufacturers
- Petroleum and natural gas companies
- Pharmaceutical companies
- Printers and lithographers
- Retailers
- Transportation equipment manufacturers
- Utility companies
- Wholesalers

Under each business type, there are hundreds of subcategories and many companies listed. The objective is to prepare the most thorough list of business prospects who logically could use private air transportation to accomplish one or more of the following objectives:

- Expand sales territory.
- Make faster on-the-spot management decisions at remote branches.
- Expedite service to customers.
- Use a faster mode of travel without being subject to airline routes and schedules.
- Utilize a quicker way to get raw materials.
- Expedite shipment of parts.
- Expand medical service to outlying areas.
- Bring customers/clients to the manufacturing plant.
- Go to buying markets.
- Develop far-reaching real estate prospects.
- Manage big farms and ranches.
- Put new marketing plans into action.

With this understanding of the various types and sizes of business prospects and the answers to the above specific operational needs that air transportation can efficiently satisfy, the salesperson can employ the traditional prospecting tools to build an inventory of company names. These prospects would then be qualified prior to actually attempting to make an appointment. Traditional sources of prospects would include the following:

1. *Existing customers.* A salesperson's customer base is an excellent source of leads. Frequent contacts with customers will not only provide new additional sales but if the customer is pleased with the product and service, referrals will be gladly given.
2. *Interview replacement.* This technique is often referred to as the Endless Chain Method, because if applied correctly, it becomes the primary source of leads. Prior to leaving the closing interview, successful or unsuccessful, the salesperson attempts to secure the names of three or four individuals or businesses that could benefit from the use of their own aircraft. Experience shows that out of these leads, one interview will be secured. The interview-to-leads ratio will be greatly enhanced if the salesperson obtains permission to use the name of the person who provided the lead.
3. *Acquaintances and friends.* Salespeople usually enjoy being with others socially and in church and community activities. These contacts often result in good leads.
4. *Direct mail.* This technique is used to supplement the methods identified above. Lists of names, which meet predetermined criteria, are purchased and processed either internally or by a company specializing in direct marketing. Leads are generated whenever a prospect requests additional information as a result of a direct marketing communication. A study by Posner and Walcek (1985) indicates that for every 100 responses:
   - 3 will purchase the advertised product within 3 months.
   - 20 have a legitimate need, authority, and intention to buy within 12 months.
   - 37 are gathering information to support a future purchase decision.
   - 40 are collecting information or are simply curious.

PRE-APPROACH

The qualifying stage of prospecting, known as the **pre-approach** in the selling process, is extremely important. The pre-approach step involves the selection of prospects who warrant further attention. It is this smaller group that becomes the prospect group, because the salesperson determines that each company needs the product or service, can finance the purchase, and has the authority to buy.

In qualifying prospects, a sales representative will attempt to develop information regarding the following questions:

1. Who are the decision-makers and what are their hobbies?
2. Are these individuals involved in the ownership or management of any other businesses? Are they located in one area or decentralized?
3. If they are involved in other businesses, what are these businesses and what is their size?
4. What has the company's sales performance been in recent years? Is it growing, diminishing, or staying the same?
5. What is the company's competitive position? (Number one, trying to be number one, smallest, newest, oldest?)
6. Do other firms in their industry use business aircraft? (Get examples.)
7. What is the company's financial position and what is the outlook for growth in its business?
8. How would you describe the marketing, distribution, and field sales organizations?
9. Who are some of the company's major customers?
10. Do customers have branch offices that need to be contacted regularly? Where are they, and how many?
11. Does the company ever use scheduled airlines for executive and sales travel? Shipping goods and equipment? Receiving raw materials? Moving parts and service personnel?
12. Does the company ever use air charter service?
13. Which department or division of the company utilizes scheduled air transportation the most?
14. Do any employees in the company fly themselves? How many? What kind of aircraft do they fly?
15. Has the company ever rented aircraft? For what purposes?
16. In the operation of the business, do they travel primarily to large metropolitan areas or to rural or outlying areas? (Get examples of some of these places.)
17. Does the company transport major customers to its plants and offices? Would an aircraft do this job better?
18. What is the length of trips that the company makes?
19. What is the average number of people who travel together?
20. If the prospect is a manufacturing company, what raw materials does it use? Where do they come from?

From this information, the sales representative attempts to determine the following:

1. Is there any possible direct relationship between an airplane and increased sales territory or sales volume? Could the prospect quickly and efficiently reach otherwise inaccessible customers with a private airplane?
2. How will the use of aircraft relate to overall expansion and growth for the prospect?
3. How will the aircraft increase the performance of the sales staff? Management personnel? Outline some examples.
4. Considering the company's financial strength and profitability, how important are tax and depreciation considerations to the prospect in the purchase of an aircraft?
5. Would a finance or lease plan be of benefit to the prospect?
6. Would the prestige factor of aircraft ownership be of any value to the business?
7. What additional use might there be for aircraft in the prospect's business?
8. Is there a flying group or association this company could belong to that might help it decide to fly its own aircraft? For example, Flying Physicians Association, Organization of Flying Adjusters, Lawyer-Pilots Bar Association, and Flying Funeral Directors Association are some specialized groups.

Qualifying information is necessary before detailed plans for visiting the prospect can be formulated. Such knowledge permits the customization of selling strategy. The sources of qualifying information are, for the most part, the same as the sources already mentioned for identifying prospects and developing basic information. Qualifying, however, involves deeper research and indicates more detailed questioning of sources who know more than just basic information. Chambers of commerce personnel may have particular knowledge about operations of important area businesses. Trade association personnel often keep clippings with details about successes and problems of industry firms. Certainly, employees of the prospective firm may be in a position to give information about who makes buying decisions and how they are made. Executive assistants of prospective companies may be in a position to reveal strategic facts. They are also in an excellent position to know about a buyer's problems and competitive activity. Analysis of credit ratings and annual reports show financial strength, company plans, and buying-power information.

Sometimes it is necessary to call on prospects to gain qualifying information before setting up a formal interview. Prospects themselves are usually the best sources of information about their companies. In these cases, the salesperson must first sell the need for qualifying information or fact-finding interview because asking for management time is like asking for money. Some prospects resist preliminary surveys, feeling that they may disrupt normal activities, constitute a threat to the firm's right to privacy, or create an obligation for a detailed survey or even a purchase. Most potential aircraft users, however, realize that a sales representative selling major capital goods is unable to analyze their problems and serve their needs without detailed operational information.

APPROACH

The strategies used by the salesperson to secure an interview and establish rapport with the prospect is called the **approach.** The use of the travel analysis in aircraft sales necessitates that the first interview be a fact-finding one where data is gathered in order to perform an analysis of the prospect's air transportation needs. One of the following three approach strategies are used to secure this first fact-finding interview:

1. *Direct personal contact.* In making a personal visit, the salesperson has the opportunity to evaluate the business premises, talk to company personnel, and to become better prepared for the prospect. The advantage of this strategy is that if the prospect is available, the interview can take place immediately. The major disadvantage is the inefficient use of time caused by either having to wait to see the prospect or finding that the prospect is out or too busy to be seen that day.
2. *Telephone call.* Using the telephone has many advantages over the direct personal contact. By calling ahead, the prospect will be available at the appointed time, thus resulting in more efficient use of the salesperson's time. This method allows the salesperson to efficiently schedule appointments so that daily and weekly activity quotas can be met. The major disadvantage of telephoning is that it is easy to be turned down over the telephone. Success with this approach requires skillful telephone techniques to be able to navigate through the screeners or gatekeepers and to persuade the prospect to grant an interview.
3. *Personal letter.* Personal letters or emails individually signed by the salesperson may be the best and most professional method to use to secure an interview. Letters introduce the salesperson and the selling company, the product, or service being offered, and specifically state that a telephone call will be made in a few days to arrange a convenient time for an interview. Colorful brochures may be included that describe the product or service in more detail. During this promised telephone call, the salesperson suggests alternative times for the interview. In doing so, the prospect's attention is focused on the issue of when to meet, rather than whether to meet at all.

PRESENTATION

Prior to the first face-to-face meeting with the prospect, the salesperson should understand that the success of that interview will depend upon understanding the following assumptions concerning the prospect and his or her environment:

1. The salesperson is interrupting the prospect. The salesperson must redirect the prospect's attention from what that person was doing immediately prior to the interview to the salesperson's objective of the meeting.
2. The salesperson must use the prospect's time wisely. The interview format must be carefully organized and well prepared. If the salesperson is talking to the right person in the company, that person's perception of the worth or value of the interview will probably determine future success or failure.
3. Generally, since the salesperson initiated the interview, the prospect is satisfied with the company's current usage of air transportation.
4. The prospect wants to purchase profitability.

The type of presentation used by the salesperson depends upon the nature of the product or service. If the needs of the prospect are obvious, the product offered is standardized, and the salespeople are new and not well-trained, then the organized approach is recommended. With this method, the salesperson follows a company prepared outline—a canned sales presentation. This approach has the weakness that all potential customers are treated alike, so whether successful or not, the salesperson probably won't know why or learn from the experience. The organized approach may be suitable for simple selling tasks, but for complicated situations like selling business aircraft, it is not a satisfactory strategy.

The unstructured approach is a problem-solving one in which the salesperson and the prospect define needs and problems and then collect supporting data. The exploration of needs using the fact-finding interview technique is the first of a two-interview system used by aircraft salespeople. After the data has been analyzed to determine the best fit between the prospect's requirements and the selling company's product, a second interview is requested to make a presentation of recommendations.

The format for the organized approach and the second interview of the unstructured approach is centered around the following five steps:

1. *Gaining the prospect's attention.* Talk to prospects about something that interests them.
2. *Arousing the prospect's interest.* Tell the prospects what the product will do to benefit or serve them.
3. *Convincing the prospect that it is an intelligent action to purchase the product.* Give the prospect sufficient information about the product to prove that purchasing the product is justifiable.
4. *Arousing the prospect's desire to purchase.* Determine the prospect's primary buying motive and then explain how the product will satisfy the unfilled need. Finally, paint a word picture of the satisfaction to be derived from the purchase.
5. *Closing the sale successfully.* Get a positive decision by weighing the advantages against the disadvantages.

Sales presentations can be enhanced with various aids such as video and PowerPoint presentations. Booklets, pamphlets, and computer software demonstrations may be beneficial. A demonstration trip is often arranged so that the prospect can learn first-hand how the use of a business aircraft can fulfill the company's transportation needs. These types of demonstrations are particularly effective in showing what the aircraft will do for the prospect and proving that the business aircraft is truly a business tool that will help solve problems and open many opportunities not presently available to the prospective company.

HANDLING OBJECTIONS

Objections by the prospect are a natural occurrence during any sales presentation and should be welcomed as a chance to get the prospect involved and to expand the discussion into areas of concern. An objection does not mean that the prospect does not want the product. In the majority of cases, prospects object because they lack information.

The best way to handle objections is to minimize them by covering the common questions adequately in the sales presentation. The answers to the most common objections, complaints, and criticisms should be in the form of positive selling points. When objections are anticipated and minimized, it is more difficult for the prospect to form negative opinions about the proposal that might result in a fixed position or issue.

Experienced salespeople realize that selling is made easier when objections surface because it is much easier to deal with a prospect who talks than with one who doesn't. Objections shed light on the prospect's thinking and tell the salesperson what subjects need amplification before attempting to close the sale.

Successful salespeople use the basic principles of handling objections skillfully during the sales presentation. Many prospects offer excuses that are not real obstacles to buying. When the objection is identified as an excuse, the actual reason why the prospect is unwilling to buy must be established. Tactful questions can penetrate the excuse smoke screen and probe for valid objections that the prospect may have concealed. Another technique to deal with objections is called the boomerang. This technique turns an objection into a reason for buying. A prospect states, "Your organization is entirely too small to provide the service we will require." The response by the salesperson might be, "Our small size is one of our assets—it permits us to give personalized service." The skillful use of these techniques will keep the presentation positive and moving toward a successful conclusion.

CLOSING

The **closing** step is the logical conclusion to a well-organized sales presentation and involves obtaining a purchase commitment from the prospect. This step is the most important, as well as the most difficult, because it is often unclear when the prospect is ready to buy. Closing clues are signals that indicate that a close should be attempted. Closing clues can be either physical or verbal. Physical signals are actions by the prospect such as nodding or smiling in agreement to the proposal. Verbal closing clues may be questions or comments such as: "What kinds of financing are available?" or "That aircraft is certainly modern looking." A number of different closing techniques can be employed. Salespeople can simply ask for the order or go over the points of agreement and offer to clarify any questions the buyer may have. Another closing approach assumes that the prospect is ready to buy and the salesperson asks, "Did you decide on the special avionics package or do you prefer the standard equipment?" This technique is called the alternative choice method.

Asking the prospect, "Which paint scheme did you decide upon?" is an example of the salesperson using the decision on minor points method. This technique is used when the prospect is reluctant to make the big decision, which is to buy or not buy, but is comfortable in making a series of minor ones. Offering the prospect specific inducements, such as attractive interest rates, a special price on a particular item of equipment, or a one-year extension on the new warranty can be effective in getting immediate positive results.

FOLLOW-UP

The last and very important step in the selling process is the **follow-up** after the sale. Salespeople depend upon repeat sales that are enhanced by post-sales activities. These activities include making sure that promises made at the time of the sale concerning delivery, equipment packages, training for employees, and others are met to the customer's satisfaction. Continuing to stay in contact with the customer will usually pay dividends in the form of referrals and additional sales.

Summary

The process of promoting an FBO's products and services should adhere to the process outlined in this chapter. Developing a robust and balanced promotional mix will enable the FBO to increase revenues by attracting new customers and maintaining existing customers.

Key Terms

advertising. Any paid form of nonpersonal communication about an organization, product, or service by an identified sponsor.

advertising message. The idea that an advertiser wants to communicate to the target audience.

approach. The strategies used by the salesperson to secure an interview and establish rapport with the prospect.

closing. The logical conclusion to a well-organized sales presentation, which involves obtaining a purchase commitment from the prospect.

competitive advertising. Advertising that promotes a specific company's products or service, designed to persuade the target market to select the firm's offerings rather than those of a competitor.

follow-up. The last and very important step in the selling process. Salespeople depend upon repeat sales that are enhanced by post-sales activities, so follow-up maintains a relationship and creates continued customer satisfaction.

institutional advertising. Advertising that attempts to develop good will for the company and enhance its image, instead of promoting a specific product or service.

North American Industry Classification System (NAICS). The standard used by federal statistical agencies in classifying business establishments for the purpose of collecting, analyzing, and publishing statistical data related to the U.S. business economy.

objections. A natural occurrence during any sales presentation that should be welcomed as a chance to get the prospect involved and to expand the discussion into areas of concern. In the majority of cases, prospects object because they lack information.

personal selling. A two-way flow of personal communication between a representative of the firm and a customer for the purpose of making a sale.

pioneering advertising. Advertising aimed at developing demand for a product or service category rather than for a specific company. It informs the target market what the product or service is, what it can do, and where it can be found.

pre-approach. The qualifying stage of prospecting that involves the selection of prospects who warrant further attention.

product advertising. Advertising that attempts to sell a product or service to final users or middlemen using one of three forms: (1) pioneering, (2) competitive or comparative, or (3) reminder.

promotional mix. The combination of one or more of four promotional activities: advertising, sales promotions, publicity, and personal selling.

prospecting. The first step in the selling process that involves the continuing search for potential buyers.

publicity. An unpaid form of nonpersonal communication about any organization, product, or service by an identified sponsor, which can take the form of a news story, editorial, or product announcement.

reminder advertising. Advertising that is used to reinforce prior knowledge about a product or service, such as a brochure sent to a business aircraft owner who recently had aircraft serviced at the local FBO.

sales promotion. Marketing activities other than advertising, publicity, or personal selling that stimulate customer purchases and company effectiveness. Sales promotion activities include trade shows, coupons, contests, premiums, and free samples aimed at increasing sales.

Standard Industrial Classification (SIC) System. A system for classifying industries by a four-digit code, in existence in the U.S. since 1937.

Review Questions

1. What is the promotional mix?
2. Distinguish between advertising and sales promotion.
3. Why do firms use advertising agencies?
4. Provide some examples of advertising objectives.
5. Distinguish between product and institutional advertising.
6. Explain several methods of establishing an advertising budget.
7. What is the advertising message and how is it developed?
8. Summarize the advantages and disadvantages of the following media: digital media, newspapers, magazines and trade journals, direct mail, radio, television, billboards, and telephone/business directories.
9. Provide several examples of how the effectiveness of advertising can be measured.
10. What is the purpose of a firm's sales promotion activities?
11. Identify and briefly describe five sales promotion activities used by FBOs.
12. What is cooperative advertising?
13. How does publicity differ from public relations?
14. Identify some of the topics available to an FBO that have potential for publicity.
15. Describe several publicity techniques.
16. Name and describe the three types of sales positions.
17. Define prospecting.
18. What is the North American Industry Classification System (NAICS)?
19. Name four aircraft prospecting sources.
20. What is the objective of qualifying the prospect?
21. What is the objective of the approach stage?
22. Discuss some of the techniques used by sales representatives in presenting a product or service to a prospective buyer.
23. Describe several closing techniques.
24. What is the importance of the follow-up stage?

Scenarios

1. As the newly promoted marketing manager at a full-service FBO, you have been asked by the FBO manager to develop a new advertising campaign for the FBO. To begin, the manager asks you to present all of the advertising media that may be used and to create a table with the advantages and disadvantages of each type. Next, the manager wants you to recommend a specific advertising plan for the FBO. How would you do that?
2. You have been asked to create some specific advertising objectives for the following departments: aircraft rental, flight instruction, aircraft sales, fuel sales, and aircraft maintenance. What are some specific objectives you could create that would lead to increased numbers in these areas?
3. Previously, Easy Aviation had no formal marketing/promotional plan. Additionally, this FBO did not even have a budget for these activities. However, the new owners plan to change this. As the newly hired marketing manager, you have been asked to establish an advertising budget. Explain the five approaches to advertising budgeting and recommend one to the new management.
4. As a marketing assistant intern at a full-service FBO in your hometown, you have been asked to assist with the advertising campaign for the FBO. Specifically, the FBO is embarking on an advertising campaign for flight instruction, aircraft sales, and aircraft maintenance. You have been asked to develop the adverting message for each of these three campaigns. What do you propose?
5. Executive FBO has been trying to increase its aircraft sales revenue. It mainly deals with high-end business jets. For the past three months, the FBO has advertised on a Sunday afternoon AM radio show entitled *Your House, Your Money*. This advertising is not paying off. In fact, aircraft sales have actually declined slightly. Based on your knowledge and experience with FBO marketing, the FBO manager has contracted with you to provide some guidance on their advertising campaign. Specifically, the FBO manager has asked you to recommend a proper advertising media for their aircraft sales campaign. What do you recommend, and why?
6. The FBO you manage is planning an air show and fly-in next September. The key for a successful event will be getting the word out. You want to attract not only the general public but also pilots. Develop a publicity campaign for this event.
7. As an intern in the aircraft sales division at Myers FBO, you have been shadowing the more experienced aircraft salespeople and learning as much as possible during the past month. The manager of aircraft sales has asked you to study the seven steps of the personal selling process and be prepared to engage in person selling with the executive director of the local Chamber of Commerce. How do you prepare for this? For each of the seven steps of the personal selling process, what will you plan to do?

Bibliography

Posner, Gerald, and Emil J. Walcek. 1985. "Implement Lead Follow-up System for More Business-Marketing Sales." *Marketing News* 19, no. 22 (October 25, 1985): 22.

Prather, C. Daniel. 2009. *General Aviation Marketing and Management: Operating, Marketing, and Managing an FBO*. 3rd ed. Malabar, FL: Krieger Publishing Company.

9

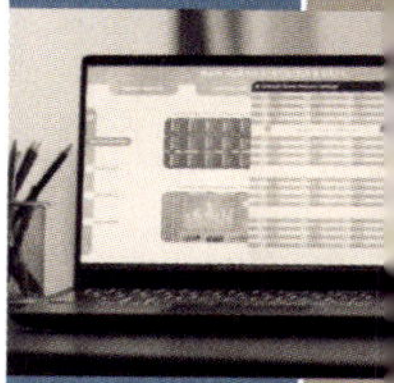

Marketing Research

In Chapter 9

Objectives

At the end of this chapter, you should be able to:

1. Define marketing research and explain its purpose within an organization.
2. Give examples of different types of marketing research studies categorized as market measurement, marketing mix, competitive situations, and the uncontrollable variables.
3. Describe the steps involved in the marketing research process.
4. Distinguish between primary and secondary data.
5. Identify five major sources of secondary data.
6. Discuss how to design a research project, including research designs, types of research instruments, and sampling procedures.
7. Discuss various methods of collecting data.
8. Discuss the importance and methods of data analysis.
9. Discuss considerations in presenting results.

Marketing Research Defined

Marketing decisions are often complex ones that have major impact upon the firm's ability to reach its market share and profitability goals. There are many variable factors in the external environment, such as increasing competition, technology, governmental regulations, changes in the macro economy, and the constantly changing opinions, attitudes, and values of customers. The ultimate objective for engaging in marketing research is to assist managers in decision-making, which is the essence of management. Managers at all levels spend more time defining, making, and implementing decisions than in any other activity. It is essential, therefore, that systematic information gathering and analytical procedures contribute to effective and efficient decision-making. Through research, management can reduce uncertainty in decision-making.

Marketing research is also a vital business activity, providing a foundation for the planning, implementation, and control of marketing programs. It is an integral part of any management information system that provides a flow of inputs useful in marketing decision-making.

Marketing research is the systematic process of gathering, recording, analyzing, and utilizing relevant information to aid in marketing decision-making. Marketing managers today should understand that marketing research is an aid to decision-making, not a substitute for it. Having the right kind of information available can greatly increase the probability that the best decision will be made.

Figure 9-1. Marketing research. *(buffaloboy/Shutterstock.com)*

Scope of Marketing Research

Marketing research has a broad scope that includes various types of studies. These studies can be grouped into four major categories: market measurement, marketing mix, competitive, and uncontrollable variables.

1. Market measurement
   a. Demand research
      i. Determination of market characteristics
      ii. Measurement of market potential
      iii. Short-range forecasting (up to one year)
      iv. Long-range forecasting (more than one year)
      v. Buyer motivation
   b. Performance research
      i. Market share analysis
      ii. Sales analysis
      iii. Establishment of sales quotas
      iv. Evaluation of test markets
      v. Customer surveys
2. Marketing mix—controllable variables
   a. Product or service research
      i. New product or service acceptance and potential
      ii. Existing products or service in new markets
      iii. Diversification of products
   b. Place research
      i. Methods of delivering product or service to customers
      ii. Facility location
   c. Price research

d. Promotion research
   i. Studies of advertising effectiveness
   ii. Sales compensation studies
   iii. Media research
   iv. Studies of sales promotion effectiveness

3. Competitive
   a. Competitive product or service studies
4. Uncontrollable variables
   a. Studies of business trends
   b. Studies of legal constraints—rules and regulations
   c. Environmental impact studies
   d. Demographic studies

MARKET MEASUREMENT STUDIES

Market measurement studies are designed to obtain quantitative data on potential demand—how much of a particular product or service can be sold to various target markets over a future period, assuming the application of appropriate marketing methods.

This data relates to market potential, sales potential, or both. Market potential is the maximum possible sales opportunity open to all sellers of a product or service during a stated future period to a target market. Sales potential is the maximum possible sales opportunity open to a particular company selling a product or service during a stated future period for a target market. For example, consider the business jet market. A predicted 8,400 to 8,500 new business jets will be delivered between 2022 and 2031. That amounts to an estimated total dollar value of $264 billion to $274 billion. This has resulted in order backlogs. For example, anyone placing an order for a new aircraft with Bombardier, Dassault, Embraer, Gulfstream, or Textron will have a wait of two years or so until they can take delivery (Young-Brown 2022).

Market measurement data is especially helpful in planning overall marketing strategy. In evaluating a proposed new twin-engine charter service, for example, management must estimate its probable marketing success. Analysis of market measurement data provides insights as to whether a potential market exists and, if so, its size. If management decides to add a new product, such as flight simulators, market measurement data is again helpful in determining target markets. In addition, breakdowns of potential sales by types of customers make it possible to ascertain which groups should be the targets for promotional efforts of varying amounts, and in what order they should be pursued. Management makes similar use of market measurement data in resolving questions of whether to drop certain services (for example, closing its avionics shop) or de-emphasize promotion to particular market segments.

Buyer motivation research studies probe the psychological, sociological, and economic variables affecting buyer behavior. Trained psychologists, sociologists, and economists are required to undertake these studies and interpret the resulting data. Few companies employ such people, and most motivation research is handled by outside consultants.

MARKETING MIX STUDIES

Most marketing research studies focus on the elements of the marketing mix: product, place, price, and promotion. Management uses studies of these controllable variables to determine the effectiveness of current product, service, pricing, and promotion policies, as well as to plan future policies and practices. Many firms make frequent studies of the effectiveness of advertising and other promotional devices, individual salespeople, existing sales methods, and sales compensation plans. Management can change the controllable variables with any formal study, but change is more effective with the added insight gained from research.

STUDIES OF THE COMPETITIVE SITUATION

More firms emphasize studies of the competitive position of their own products and services than they do studies of the nature and impact of their competitors' activities. Specifically, a study measuring the market share of a firm's products and services is more common than one which appraises the strengths and weaknesses of a competitor's products and services, evaluates the effects of a competitor's service improvement, measures the impact of a competitor's price change, or checks the effects of a competitor's revised advertising approach. Most companies could benefit by delving into competitors' marketing practices and policies. Management needs this information to understand how competitors' actions affect marketing strategy.

STUDIES OF INFLUENCES OF UNCONTROLLABLES

The studies of business trends, economic data, and industry statistics through the process of environmental scanning are the most widely used type of study in this category. Published information is available on such uncontrollables as interest rates, level of consumer credit, corporate profits, business expansion plans, and age and income distribution trends.

Federal government sources such as the Bureau of Economic Analysis, Bureau of Transportation Statistics, and the *Federal Reserve Bulletin* contain a great deal of information on the uncontrollables. The U.S. Census Bureau's Annual Survey of Manufactures lists the number and size of manufacturing firms by industry group (Standard Industrial Classifications—SIC Codes). The Annual Retail Trade Survey published by the U.S. Census Bureau provides comparable detailed information on retailers. The U.S. Department of Commerce gathers and publishes data on the national economic outlook. The Department of Commerce also maintains field offices to help firms looking for specific types of information.

Aerospace Facts and Figures, an Aerospace Industries Association (AIA) databook, provides statistical data on an annual basis. In addition, aviation trade associations such as General Aviation Manufacturers Association (GAMA) and National Business Aviation Association (NBAA), universities, and aviation and business periodicals provide detailed data of value to firms doing marketing research. *Business and Commercial Aviation, Air Transport World, Bloomberg Businessweek, The Wall Street Journal,* and *Sales and Marketing Management* are sources with considerable information on uncontrollables.

Marketing Research Process

The marketing research process consists of a series of activities: defining the problem and research objectives, designing the research, collecting the data, preparing and analyzing the data, and presenting the findings.

DEFINING THE PROBLEM AND RESEARCH OBJECTIVES

The first step in research requires management to carefully define the problem and clearly state the research objectives. If the president of an FBO asks the flight department manager to "Go and develop data on the charter market or flight training market," the results will be disappointing. Hundreds of subjects can be researched about those two markets. If the research findings are to be useful, they must relate to a specific problem or opportunity facing the firm. The president and the researcher, in this case the flight department manager, must agree on the problem. "How can we attract more charter business, or how can we improve the student pilot retention rate?" Collecting information is too costly to allow the problem to be defined vaguely or incorrectly.

At this point, management needs to set the research objectives. A well-defined problem statement gives direction to the research and assists in the formulation of research objectives. Some form of exploratory research is often needed to both refine and clearly state the problem and set research objectives. This informal investigation will attempt to uncover as much relevant information as possible. Sources for the investigation include knowledgeable employees who are directly involved in the situation, customers and current flight students who are directly affected by the problem, and internal sales and financial reports that pertain to the situation. Questions to be answered are: What is the frequency of use of our existing charter customers? What percentage of target businesses in the area are even aware of aircraft charter services? What is their perception regarding the cost of this service? At what stage in the flight-training program are students dropping out? What are their reasons? At the end of this first step, the researcher should know (1) the current situation; (2) the nature of the problem; and (3) the specific question or questions the research will be designed to answer.

SECONDARY DATA

Secondary data consists of information that already exists, having been collected for another purpose. Researchers usually start their investigation by collecting secondary data that can be obtained from internal or external sources. Internal secondary data is available within the company. External secondary data must be extracted from sources outside the firm. Secondary data sources include the following:

- Internal sources
  - Financial statements
  - Training records
  - Safety reports
- External sources
  - Government publications
  - Industry associations
  - Periodicals
  - Books
  - Online databases
  - Consultants
  - Nonprofit foundations
  - Commercial sources

PRIMARY DATA

Primary data is data collected from original sources for a particular study. Some researchers, unfortunately, collect primary data by developing a few questions and finding some businesses to interview. Data gathered this way might be useless or, even worse misleading. Instead, a plan should be created for collecting credible (valid and reliable) primary data, with specific attention to the following:

- Research designs
  - Survey method
  - Observation method
  - Experiment method
- Types of research instruments
  - Questionnaire
  - Mechanical instruments
- Sampling procedures
  - Sampling unit
  - Sample size
  - Sample group
- Methods of collecting data
  - Personal interview
  - Telephone interview
  - Mail questionnaire
  - Electronic/online questionnaire
  - Focus group interview

Designing the Research

RESEARCH DESIGN

Once the research problem has been defined and objectives stated, the next step is to select a research design. A **research design** is a master plan that specifies the methods and procedures for collecting and analyzing the required information. It is a blueprint of the research plan of action. The stated objectives of the research are included in the design to ensure that information collected is germane to solving the problem. There are three basic design techniques for descriptive and causal research: survey, observation, and experiment. The most common is the survey.

In the **survey method**, information is obtained directly from individual respondents through personal interviews, telephone interviews, mail questionnaires, electronic questionnaires, or focus groups. Questionnaires are used for specific responses to direct questions or for general responses to open-ended questions. The survey method has two main uses: (1) to gather facts from respondents, and (2) to report their opinions. The survey method's accuracy and reliability vary in each application. Generally, it is most accurate and reliable when gathering facts and less so when recording opinion.

In the factual survey, respondents are asked to report actual facts such as, "Have you ever used a charter flight service? During an average month, how many times do three or more employees travel to a meeting location within 300 miles of your office? How often does your present travel mode or modes cause you to remain overnight or travel long hours?" Even the answers to factual questions are subject to error because some respondents have faulty memories, are unable to generalize about personal experiences, or may give answers they believe interviewers want.

The opinion survey is designed to gather expressions of personal opinion and record evaluations of air travel matters. For example, the survey might include questions such as "How do you feel about the quality of flight instruction received?" "What were your instructor's strengths and weaknesses?" "What was the most difficult problem you encountered in using the self-paced learning materials?" Opinion surveys share the potential errors of factual surveys and, by forcing immediate answers to questions on subjects that the respondents possibly have not thought about lately, may produce answers that do not accurately reflect real opinions. In addition to response errors, survey results can be biased by excluding people who were not contacted (e.g., they were not at home) or who refused to cooperate. The statistical differences between a survey that includes only those people who responded and a survey that also includes those who failed to respond are referred to as nonresponse error. This problem is especially important in mail and telephone surveys because of the normally low response rate. To be able to use the survey results, the researcher must be sure that those who did respond were representative of those who did not. By selecting a group of nonrespondents and then contacting them, a researcher can determine the extent of the nonresponse error.

FBOs that rely on self-administered questionnaires must be aware of the self-selection bias that makes the survey results less useful. Surveys left for charter customers to fill out at the end of the trip fall into this category. A man who suffered minor injury due to turbulence or had coffee spilled on his suit is more likely to fill out the questionnaire than those passengers who were indifferent about the trip. Self-selection biases the survey because it tends to be overweighted by passengers with extreme positions and underweighted by those who were indifferent about the charter experience.

The second basic design technique is the **observation method**, where marketing research data is gathered not through direct questioning of respondents, but by observing and recording consumers' actions in a marketing situation. For example, line personnel are observed while they greet and service customers' aircraft. Students' questions and reactions are observed during preflight and postflight discussions with instructors.

The **experiment method** is the third technique and calls for selecting matched groups of subjects, giving them different treatments, and checking on whether observed differences are significant. For example, an FBO may run two versions of a proposed advertisement (ad A and ad B) in a city newspaper, with half the circulation carrying ad A and the other half carrying ad B. This experiment might be used to determine the more effective advertisement in different markets, and that ad could then be placed in all newspapers and other direct mailings in the area.

TYPES OF RESEARCH INSTRUMENTS

Marketing researchers have a choice of two main research instruments in collecting primary data—questionnaires and mechanical devices.

The questionnaire is by far the most common instrument used in collecting primary data. It consists of a set of questions presented to respondents to gather their answers. A questionnaire is very flexible in that there are many ways to ask questions. Questionnaires need to be carefully developed, tested, and debugged before they can be used on a large scale.

Prior to the actual start of constructing a questionnaire, the researcher must identify the questionnaire objectives, type, and method of collecting the data. Since the purpose of a questionnaire is to formulate questions to carry out the research objectives, it is imperative that these objectives be clearly understood. Questionnaires can be either highly structured or unstructured. Unstructured questions allow the interviewer to probe respondents and guide the interview according to the answers received. Most questionnaires are highly structured so that responses can be summarized in numbers, such as percentages, averages, or other statistics. The structured format provides fixed responses to questions that elicit uncomplicated answers that the respondent is both willing and able to provide. Five methods can be used to collect data: personal interview, telephone, mail, internet, and focus groups. The method selected will have a major impact on the format of the questionnaire.

In constructing a questionnaire, the marketing researcher carefully chooses what questions to ask, the form of the questions, the wording of the questions, and the sequencing of the questions. Common errors that occur in developing questions are including those that cannot be answered, would not be answered, or need not be answered, and omitting questions that should be answered. Each question should be checked to determine whether it contributes to the research objectives. Questions that are merely interesting should be dropped because they lengthen the time required and try the patience of respondents.

The form of a question can influence the response. There are four types of question formats available for communicating question content: open-ended, multiple choice, dichotomous, and attitude-rating scale questions.

Open-ended questions allow respondents to answer in their own words. Open-ended questions tend to reveal more because respondents are not limited in their answers. This form of question is especially useful in the exploratory stage of research where the researcher is trying to determine how people think, rather than measuring how many people think in a certain way. A major disadvantage of open-ended questions is that the responses are difficult to record and tabulate, which makes them very expensive and time-consuming to process. Content analysis is typically used with open-ended responses. This allows the researcher to look for common themes among respondents.

Multiple-choice questions offer respondents a number of alternatives. Multiple-choice questions require less interviewer skill, take less time, and are easier for the respondent to answer. The standard number of response choices offered is four, and the respondent should be informed if more than one alternative can be selected. Researchers should rotate the response sequence to help alleviate position bias, the tendency of respondents to select the first alternative in this type of question format.

Dichotomous questions require the respondents to choose one of two alternatives. The answer can be a simple "yes" or "no," and this is the most widely used of all question formats. Like multiple-choice questions, dichotomous questions eliminate interviewer bias and are easy and inexpensive to tabulate.

When the objective of a survey is to measure subjective variables like attitudes, motives, and perceptions, researchers use attitude-rating scales. The two most common rating scales are the Likert scale and the semantic differential scale. The Likert scale allows the respondents to indicate their attitudes by checking how strongly they agree or disagree with statements about products or services on a scale that ranges from very positive to very negative.

An FBO might use the following statement in a survey concerning the quality of its maintenance department:

The use of online maintenance scheduling has been a great improvement.

Strongly Agree	Agree	Neutral	Disagree	Strongly Disagree

Researchers assign weights to the alternative responses to be able to quantify the measurement of the attitude. For example, a weight of 5 is assigned to the very positive attitude (strongly agree). The weightings typically do not appear on the questionnaire itself.

The semantic differential is a popular attitude-measuring scale that asks people to rate a product, company, brand, or firm within the frames of a multi-point rating option. The options are grammatically on opposite adjectives at each end. An FBO attempting to measure prospective students' attitudes about the price of a proposed new flight option might ask:

To what degree does the new flight simulator enhance your flight training experience?

Greatly	Somewhat	Neutral	Minimally	None

Care must be given to the wording of questions. The respondent alone fills out most surveys (self-administered), so there is no opportunity to ask for clarification. The semantics problem in communication is always an area that needs attention. Words mean different things to different people depending on culture and geographical location. Words to avoid include often, frequently, many, some, good, fair, and poor. The researcher should use simple, specific, unbiased wording, and the questions should be tested before they are widely used. Attention should also be given to sequencing. When lead questions are simple to comprehend, interesting, and easy to answer, respondents' cooperation can be maintained throughout the questionnaire. Respondents whose curiosity is not piqued early will get discouraged and not complete the survey. Difficult or personal questions should be asked toward the end of the interview, and they should be presented in logical order.

Mechanical instruments include eye cameras, tachistoscopes, and galvanometers. An eye camera measures how long the eye lingers on a particular item in an advertisement. The tachistoscope flashes an advertisement to a subject with a predetermined interval; then the respondent describes what he or she remembers. A galvanometer measures a respondent's interest in or emotional reaction to a particular advertisement or picture based on body response. The use of these instruments is typically more time consuming and expensive and often lacks the quality data researchers are interested in.

SAMPLING PROCEDURE

A **sample** is a portion or subset of the population from which it is drawn. A population or universe is any complete group of people or businesses that share some set of characteristics. Since only a small number of people in the population are surveyed, sampling cuts costs, reduces labor requirements, and gathers vital information quickly. Marketing researchers must develop a procedure that will help them find the appropriate sample for their research. First, who is to be surveyed? This is not always obvious. In the case of the charter services survey, should the sample be made up of businesses in any industry or businesses in selected industries with more than 100 employees? In rating flight instructors, should only students who have dropped out of the program be surveyed? Should all students be surveyed at a certain stage in the flight program or only after completion? The researcher must decide what information is needed and what population or subset should be targeted.

Second, how many people or firms should be polled? Large samples are more reliable than small samples, but, depending on the population size, a researcher typically does not have to survey more than 5 percent of the actual or estimated population to get accurate answers.

Third, how should the people or firms in the sample be chosen? Sampling techniques fall into two categories: probability samples and nonprobability samples. The choice of sampling technique depends on the accuracy needed, cost, available information, research objectives, and other factors.

All samples observed or surveyed during marketing research studies are either probability or nonprobability samples. A **probability sample** is one in which every person or firm in the identified population being surveyed has a known chance of being sampled. An example of a probability sample is a simple random sample in which all members in the population have an equal probability of being chosen to participate in the sample. If you know, for example, that there are 500 Bonanza aircraft owners in your state, and you use a simple random sample, each owner is assigned a number from 1 to 500. Then you select, using a table of random numbers, the actual owners to be questioned.

When the selected population contains disproportionate demographics like gender, researchers may choose to use a stratified random sample to eliminate the bias. The population is divided into strata, such as two subgroups (males and females), and then a random sample is selected from each group. This method is an efficient procedure in situations in which subgroups hold divergent opinions. Probability sampling prevents the researcher's bias from influencing who is sampled, because the makeup of the sample is determined not by the researcher but by chance. The use of this technique allows the researcher to assign a statistical level of confidence. A 95 percent level of confidence means that the estimate will include the true value of what is being estimated 95 percent of the time.

Researchers using **nonprobability sampling** techniques arbitrarily select the sample according to their own convenience or judgment. Examples of nonprobability sampling include (1) convenience samples—any population member who is available; (2) judgment samples—individuals who are known to have a common interest in a type of product or service; and (3) quota samples—population is divided into subgroups and a certain number of individuals from each subgroup are included. Savings in time and money are the major advantages of using this type of sampling. It is, however, inappropriate to apply standard statistical testing to nonprobability samples.

Methods of Collecting Data

Sampling is one of the most important aspects of marketing research because it involves identifying the respondents upon which conclusions will be based. After identifying the population to be surveyed, a researcher will select a representative (sample) group.

Personal interviewing is the most versatile of the five methods. The interviewer can ask more questions and can supplement the interview with personal observations. Generally, the interviewer follows a questionnaire and accurately records the responses. Personal interviewing is the most expensive method and requires a great deal of planning, training of interviewers, and supervision. The face-to-face interview can be plagued with inaccurate responses because the respondent desires to please or impress the interviewer, or the respondent feels obligated to give an immediate response rather than a carefully considered reply.

The telephone interview consists of an interviewer asking questions of a respondent over the telephone. After self-administered surveys, telephone interviewing is the most widely used method of collecting data. Its popularity derives from its low cost and rapid response. The telephone method is less versatile than face-to-face interviewing. The interviewer is less likely to be able to ask detailed, open-ended questions on the telephone than in a face-to-face interview, but at the same time its anonymity allows the interviewer to ask questions that could not be asked face-to-face. A telephone interview is also limited because some members of the sample may not have telephones, may have unlisted numbers, may not be available, or simply may not care to be interviewed.

The mail questionnaire may be the best method for reaching people who will not give personal interviews or who may be biased by interviewers. It consists of a questionnaire sent to the respondent to be completed and returned by mail to the researcher. The primary problem with mail questionnaires is the low percentage of returns, which results in a possibility of nonrespondent error. Nonrespondent error is the possibility that the people who did respond are different from the people who did not respond; therefore, the data would not represent the population. Low response rates can be enhanced with a successive number of contacts.

With the growing number of available e-mail addresses, the electronic questionnaire is becoming more popular. Researchers can purchase a list of e-mail addresses of people or businesses that fit the intended survey population and send them a link to an online questionnaire. Follow-up is inexpensive and often involves sending a follow email to those who have not yet responded. Many companies and survey research firms (such as SurveyMonkey) utilize the web to post questionnaires. Respondents can select their answers from drop-down menus or easily type responses to open-ended questions.

Focus group interviewing consists of inviting from six to ten people to gather for a few hours with a trained interviewer to discuss a product, service, organization, or other marketing topic. The qualified interviewer has objectivity, knowledge of the subject matter and general aviation industry, and understanding of group dynamics and consumer behavior. An unqualified interviewer's results can be worthless or misleading. The interviewer encourages free and easy discussion among the participants, hoping that the spontaneous discussion will disclose attitudes and opinions about a situation that would not be revealed by direct questioning. The comments and reactions by participants may be recorded via video or note-taking.

Analyzing the Findings

After the information has been gathered, it must be analyzed. The purpose of this **data analysis** step is to extract the important information and findings from the data. A variety of analytical software programs are available ranging from simple descriptive statistics (means, medians, modes) to complex multivariate analyses. Microsoft Excel can accomplish simple statistics, while programs such as SPSS are capable of a full range of statistical analyses. Coverage of these topics is beyond the scope of this discussion. The researcher computes such statistics as frequency distribution and averages in preparing the findings. Tables, figures, and charts are often used to illustrate the findings.

Presenting the Findings

The last step in the marketing research process is presenting results. This may require a written report, an in-person or virtual presentation, or both. It is important to present results in an easy-to-understand fashion, generally avoiding the presentation of heavy statistical analyses. Visuals go a long way in conveying a point. However, it is important to know your audience. If presenting to a group of scholars, they would appreciate these statistical analyses. Company management, on the other hand, may not. The researcher should present relevant findings that are useful in major marketing decisions facing management. Often, this presentation will greatly affect decision-making and impact large financial decisions. Therefore, in preparing the presentation, emphasis must be placed on presenting data that is both reliable and valid in a professional manner.

Summary

The importance of conducting marketing research is clear. By understanding the market, an FBO can make more effective decisions, thereby better ensuring business success. Data-based decisions are possible because of insight gained through marketing research. Thus, the wise FBO manager will not only commit to conducting marketing research but will ensure that this marketing research is performed properly.

Key Terms

data analysis. The use of various tools to inspect, cleanse, transform, and model data to extract meaning from the data.

experiment method. A research technique that involves manipulating one variable to determine if changes in one variable cause changes in another variable.

marketing research. The systematic process of gathering, recording, analyzing, and utilizing relevant information to aid in marketing decision-making.

market measurement study. A study designed to obtain quantitative data on potential demand—how much of a particular product or service can be sold to various target markets over a future period, assuming the application of appropriate marketing methods.

nonprobability sample. A sample that is not selected randomly. It is used when random sampling is not feasible.

observation method. A research technique in which data is gathered by observing and recording participants' actions.

primary data. Data that is collected directly from the data source without going through any existing sources.

probability sample. Any method of sampling that utilizes some form of random selection, which means that each member of the population has an equal probability of being selected.

research design. The overall strategy utilized to carry out research that defines the plan to answer research questions/hypotheses through collection and analysis of data.

sample. A portion or subset of the population from which it is drawn.

secondary data. Data that has been collected in the past for another purpose but is made available for others to use.

survey method. A research method in which information is obtained directly from individual respondents through personal interviews, telephone interviews, mail questionnaires, electronic questionnaires, and focus groups.

Review Questions

1. What is the purpose of marketing research?
2. Provide several examples of market measurement studies.
3. Distinguish between market potential and sales potential.
4. Provide an example of a market research study involving a competitive situation.
5. Why are defining the problem and determining the research objectives so critical for effective market research?
6. Distinguish between primary and secondary data.
7. Provide four examples of external secondary data sources.
8. Which is the most commonly used research design?
9. Distinguish between a factual survey and an opinion survey.
10. How does the observation method differ from the experiment method?
11. What is the most common instrument used in collecting primary data?

12. In questionnaires, distinguish between open-ended, multiple choice, and dichotomous questions.
13. Provide examples of a Likert scale and a semantic differential scale used to measure attitudes.
14. What is a sample?
15. What questions must be determined in developing an appropriate sample?
16. Differentiate a simple random sample and a stratified random sample.
17. Describe three methods of collecting primary data.
18. Differentiate probability samples and nonprobability samples and give an example of each.

Scenarios

1. As the new marketing manager of a full-service FBO, you have been asked to conduct some market research. First, however, you must get a handle on the uncontrollable variables influencing the rate of student pilot starts at your FBO. What are they?
2. As a summer intern at Exceptional FBO, you have been asked to gather some primary and secondary data regarding the used aircraft sales market. Specifically, you must gather data about industry trends affecting used aircraft sales and the interest in used aircraft among potential buyers. What are some sources of primary and secondary data you could search?
3. As marketing manager at Joe's FBO, you feel that marketing research is needed to enable your FBO to be successful in the challenging times ahead. Specifically, you are interested in the perceptions of based pilots about your FBO's fuel prices, rates for T-hangars, and line service. As you begin your market research process, you must decide whether to utilize survey, observation, or experiment methods. Which one do you choose, and why?
4. Based on your response to scenario 3, how will you conduct research to determine perceptions on each of the three areas of interest? What type of research instrument(s) will you utilize? What questions, items, or experiments will guide your research effort? Who will you include in your sample? How will you collect data?
5. You have collected a great deal of data regarding the perceptions of based pilots about your FBO's fuel prices, rates for T-hangars, and line service. In general terms, these pilots are quite pleased with your low fuel prices, feel that rates for T-hangars could be lower, and would like to see more experienced and knowledgeable line service personnel. How would you prepare a presentation of these findings to senior management? What would the presentation look like? They have asked you not to whitewash the findings but rather to present the good and bad of your findings. Additionally, what can you recommend to senior management to improve in these areas?

Bibliography

Prather, C. Daniel. 2009. *General Aviation Marketing and Management: Operating, Marketing, and Managing an FBO*. 3rd ed. Malabar, FL: Krieger Publishing Company.

Young-Brown, Fiona. 2022. "New Business Jet Sales Forecasts: The 2022 Report." SherpaReport. November 28, 2022. https://www.sherpareport.com/aircraft/business-jet-sales-forecasts-2022.html.

10

Transportation Needs Assessment

In Chapter 10

Objectives

At the end of this chapter, you should be able to:

1. Explain the business-to-business market and give several examples.
2. Describe the following demand patterns in the organizational market: direct channels, derived demand, and inelastic demand.
3. Name and explain the three types of organizational purchase decisions.
4. Describe the buying center concept and identify and explain the traditional five roles of the members.
5. Describe the four major areas of investigation in a business aircraft travel analysis.
6. Distinguish between geographic, volume, and time dispersion.
7. Identify the three levels of airline service and how each relates to business aircraft use.
8. Describe five types of business aircraft use.
9. Highlight the five principal factors to consider in the equipment selection process.

10. Summarize the major considerations in the cost of owning an aircraft.
11. List the principal expenses under fixed and direct operating (variable) costs of use for an aircraft.
12. Explain the significance of a cash flow analysis.
13. Determine principal and interest payments using a loan amortization schedule.
14. Describe the use of net present value in aircraft purchase decisions.
15. Explain break-even analysis as a sales tool for business aircraft.

Business-to-Business Marketing

The focus of this chapter is the travel analysis, which serves as a powerful marketing tool used to assist non-users of business aircraft in working through an in-depth transportation needs assessment. The fictional prospect for the study used in this chapter is Champions Stores, Inc., a large sporting goods retailer, with its home office located in Montgomery, Alabama. To be effective in selling business aircraft, marketers must understand the nature of organizational markets, their unique demand, and their purchasing characteristics.

NATURE OF ORGANIZATIONAL CUSTOMERS

Business-to-business marketing is a term that pertains to buying and selling goods and services between businesses. The products purchased are either for resale or for use by the purchasers in their day-to-day business operations. This type of marketing is far different from marketing products to household consumers. The term customer is used to describe business purchasers, whereas consumer commonly refers to purchases by individuals for personal needs. Business-to-business marketing is occurring when Cessna sells an aircraft to one of its dealers, and it also occurs when the dealer in turn sells the airplane to Southern Equipment & Supply Corporation for executive travel. When Office Depot sells office supplies to the local FBO, it is engaging in business-to-business marketing.

UNIQUE CHARACTERISTICS OF ORGANIZATIONAL MARKETS

When formulating strategies and developing marketing mixes, marketers will find that characteristics and demand patterns of the organizational market are different from the consumer market. Organizational markets tend to be more geographically concentrated than consumer markets. Many industries are located in specific areas of the country. Most aircraft manufacturers are located in Wichita, Kansas, and California's Silicon Valley is the home of the computer chip industry. This concentration of customers does offer efficiency opportunities for marketers, especially in promotion and distribution.

The potential number of customers in the organizational market is considerably less than in most consumer markets. Gulfstream Aerospace Corporation, a wholly owned subsidiary of General Dynamics, may sell its Gulfstream G800 to fewer than 1,500 organizations throughout the world. When segmenting this market, marketers must evaluate carefully whether there is a sufficient number of homogeneous businesses to make the target market a legitimate business opportunity. The small number of potential customers also stresses the need to develop strong customer relationships to ensure repeat business.

Demand patterns in the consumer market differ from demand patterns in the organizational market in the following areas:

1. *Direct channels.* Business buyers traditionally purchase directly from the manufacturer rather than from a middleman as consumers do. This is especially true for products that are complex and expensive. Manufacturers will often use industrial distributors to sell and distribute products that are inexpensive and frequently purchased as accessories and supplies.
2. *Derived demand.* Manufacturers buy products to be used in the production of business-to-business goods and consumer goods. Thus, as the demand for these finished goods increases, the demand for components will also increase. For example, the need to purchase passenger seats by Beechcraft is driven by the demand for its airplanes.
3. *Inelastic demand.* The demand for business goods tends to be inelastic, which means that the demand for a good or service is not sensitive to changes in price. This is opposite to elastic demand, where there are significant changes in quantity demanded as a result of a meaningful change in price. This inelastic demand characteristic occurs because the organizational product is often only a fraction of the total price of the final product of which it is part and will have little effect on the product's total price. Demand will not change with a change in price in the short run because it is difficult for manufacturers to modify production equipment that has been designed to handle specific component parts. The demand for corporate aircraft tends to be inelastic because the importance of purchase price is mitigated by the potential purchaser's need for speed, cabin configurations, capacity, avionics, and cost of use.

BUYING PROCESS

As businesses today strive for increasing productivity, the buying function in organizations has taken on added importance as a profit center. It is now viewed that investment in goods and services can be strategically managed and controlled to improve profitability and help maintain a competitive advantage. This changed perception of accountability of the purchasing function can spell opportunity for aircraft marketers who understand the change and are able to develop presentations to fit this new emphasis.

Organizational buying decisions are highly variable—ranging from routine decisions, which require little time and effort, to complex decisions entailing in-depth negotiations between the salesperson and the company. Organizational purchase decisions can be categorized into three types: straight rebuy, modified rebuy, and new buys. **Straight rebuys** are simply reorders. The products ordered are usually standard products that are routinely used and maintained in inventory. Straight rebuys would be similar to your purchasing bread and milk at the convenience store on your way home from school or work. **Modified rebuy** situations are essentially straight rebuy situations that require some additional information due to a change in price or specifications, or dissatisfaction with the present supplier. **New buys** involve products or services never considered before by the company. There is a high degree of risk and cost associated with this category of purchase decision. The investigation into the purchase of a business aircraft by Champions Stores fits into this category.

The increasing accountability and complexity of the purchasing function has led to the development of the buying center concept that pulls together key individuals who provide different expertise needed to make quality major purchases. The size of the group will vary from company to company, and the membership will also change depending upon the product being purchased. In the business aircraft purchase decision, one of the members will certainly be the chief pilot. Different members in the buying center have different roles in the decision. The five traditional roles in the buying center are users, gatekeepers, influencers, deciders, and buyers. **Users** initiate the process by identifying the need, based on their intended use of the product or service. **Gatekeepers** have the responsibility and authority to control information. This role is often played by the purchasing manager. Gatekeepers can determine which suppliers have access to the organization and its decision makers. **Influencers** are usually technical employees who have defined the criteria the purchase must meet. Sometimes the influencer is an outside consultant with expertise in the specific area under investigation. The **decider** is the executive who has the authority to select which product to purchase. Sometimes, the decision to purchase is not made by one individual but by a group of individuals selected to participate as an executive committee. The **buyer** is the employee who actually has the authority to place the order with the selected vendor. It is usually an executive in the purchasing department. To be successful in selling to businesses, salespeople must be able to identify the various members of the buying center and understand their roles. This is oftentimes a challenge. The buying center concept emphasizes the importance of comprehending the corporate culture in marketing to organizational buyers.

Clearly, business-to-business marketing is unique. However, armed with the knowledge of this important aspect of marketing, the aircraft salesperson approaching a business such as Champions Stores will understand and appreciate the uniqueness of the market and the marketing strategies required to be successful.

Travel Analysis

The potential use of a business aircraft is based on its ability to make travel more efficient by either reducing travel time or increasing productivity for a given amount of time. **Travel analysis** is an evaluation of a firm's current travel modes and the amount and nature of travel it presently undertakes. There are four major areas of investigation that guide an aircraft sales representative in attempting to determine if a business could use a company airplane. They are (1) amount and nature of travel; (2) travel dispersion; (3) type and frequency of airline service; and (4) potential aircraft utilization.

It's necessary to know the amount and nature of travel to determine whether there is enough travel to make a business aircraft feasible and if it is the kind of travel for which a private aircraft is suited. Travel dispersion categorizes the trips in terms of distance, frequency, and volume of passengers. This information is useful in further defining a firm's travel patterns and determining whether these patterns are suitable for business aircraft use. The type and frequency of airline service is studied to determine the amount of time being spent traveling and whether a business airplane could reduce that time. The culmination of this study is to estimate the total annual utilization of a business aircraft for the firm.

AMOUNT AND NATURE OF TRAVEL

Evaluating the possible uses of a business aircraft begins with estimates about the overall amount of travel within the organization and the potential growth of such travel. However, this kind of evaluation can be more of a limiting factor than a justifying one. In other words, just proving the existence of a large quantity of travel is not necessarily sufficient evidence that the company could use an aircraft economically, as some trips may not be suited to business aircraft use.

The amount and nature of travel are determined by reviewing a prospective customer's past travel records. Depending upon the size of the firm and amount of travel, an average month or quarter is generally selected for analysis.

In analyzing Champions Stores, Inc., based in Montgomery, Alabama, one would look at the firm's travel record for one month. Assuming that the month selected is representative of travel throughout the year, the data can therefore be used to make annual projections.

An analysis of the travel within this sample period by a sales representative indicated that 19 individual round trips were made to 14 separate destinations (see Table 10-1). The trips were made by 16 employees including 4 executive officers, 3 department managers, 6 buyers, and 3 other administrative personnel. The information covers travel primarily by employees based at the company's home office in Montgomery.

Table 10-1. Potential Aircraft Utilization—Champions Stores, Inc.

From Montgomery, AL, to:	Avg # passengers	Total round trips per month	Total annual round trips	Number of one-way miles	Total miles
1. Atlanta, GA	2	2	24	160	7,680
2. New Orleans, LA	2	2	24	275	13,200
3. Greenville, SC	2	1	12	280	6,720
4. Charlotte, NC	4	1	12	330	7,920
5. Greensboro, NC	3	1	12	480	11,520
6. Mexia, TX	3	1	12	610	14,640
7. Fitzgerald, GA	3	1	12	180	4,320
8. Dallas, TX	2	1	12	600	14,400
9. London, KY	1	1	12	400	9,600
10. El Paso, TX	2	1	12	1,200	28,800
11. Jacksonville, FL	2	2	24	325	15,600
12. Blount, TN	2	1	12	275	6,600
From New Orleans, LA, to:					
13. Sherman, TX	2	1	12	475	11,400
14. Jackson, MS	2	2	24	180	8,640
15. Dallas, TX	2	1	12	450	10,800
		19	**228**[1]		**171,840**[1]

[1] Since the potential total annual miles is likely to exceed any one aircraft's capabilities, for the purposes of this travel analysis, this amount is reduced by 25 percent to reflect trips which will probably be made by other travel modes due to scheduling conflicts, maintenance requirements, etc. This reduction results in a potential 171 round trips and 128,880 miles, or 475 to 7,900 hours of flying time, depending on the aircraft selected.

Records indicate that the company's primary modes of travel are by automobile and scheduled airline. Costs of transportation were not provided. In addition, charter service has been utilized in the past. Poor airline service to company destinations and the emergency need to travel were listed as reasons for using charter service. The number of passengers on these charter flights was two to three people.

Approximately 50 percent of the Champions Stores' travel is scheduled (20 percent scheduled one to two weeks in advance and 30 percent scheduled two to five days in advance). Scheduled trips lend themselves to business aircraft usage due to the flexibility of scheduling, thereby accommodating many more trips on the aircraft. The remaining 50 percent of travel, however, was listed as on-demand. For on-demand or emergency-type trips, the availability of an immediate, fast transportation mode is an obvious necessity.

TRAVEL DISPERSION

An analysis of an organization's geographic, time, and volume dispersions of business travel is very important to a salesperson in determining the need for a corporate aircraft. The object of this analysis of **travel dispersion** is to examine the environment within which a company aircraft would operate, including the cities served, distances, and schedules to be maintained. Such an examination reveals valuable information regarding the efficiency of past travel and the probability of improving the efficiency.

Geographic dispersion of business destinations partially indicates whether or not a company aircraft can be effectively substituted for present travel (i.e., if present travel is primarily between large metropolitan cities with frequent and direct airline service, chances for substantial savings in employee time may be minimal). Volume dispersion is the number of people traveling and indicates the relative importance of each destination. Time dispersion is the interval between trips taken by various individuals to the same or proximate destinations. This information helps determine the potential for combining company trips with the aircraft, which enables the aircraft to be used more efficiently. From this investigation of travel dispersion comes a clear picture of existing travel patterns, how a business aircraft could fit into these patterns, and how a company would benefit from using a company plane.

Champions Stores' travel destinations are located, for the most part, in the southeastern part of the United States, within the states of Texas, Georgia, Florida, Louisiana, Kentucky, North Carolina, South Carolina, Tennessee, Alabama, and Mississippi. The most distant destination within the company's primary marketing area is about 610 miles. Airline trip data shows the longest trip undertaken to be approximately 1,200 miles to EI Paso, Texas.

Trips during only certain times of the year may reduce the need for a business aircraft. Fortunately, an examination of the company's past business travel indicates that it is not seasonal. Assume, for the example, that travel will occur with equal frequency throughout the year. Checking the trips made by Champions Stores shows that the most frequently visited cities were Atlanta, Georgia; New Orleans, Louisiana; Jacksonville, Florida; and Jackson, Mississippi. The frequency of air travel to other destinations will undoubtedly increase with the availability of a company aircraft. Most companies find that passenger load factors tend to grow as executives learn how to use the aircraft to their advantage.

TYPE AND FREQUENCY OF AIRLINE SERVICE

Airline services provide a valuable business tool. However, these services have undergone considerable changes since deregulation in 1978. The trend has been for certified carriers to concentrate more on service to large hub cities and less to smaller cities. Conversely, business continues to expand from large metropolitan areas to smaller cities. When the present mode of travel is primarily scheduled airlines, the kind of airline service available to destinations determines the practicality of a business aircraft.

Three distinct classes of airline service exist: direct, indirect via connections, or none. The frequency of service will further modify the direct and indirect levels. If there are both frequent and direct airline flights to a company destination, a business aircraft's only measurable advantage may be its ability to transport company travelers at a savings in total direct costs. If service is infrequent and/or indirect, a company aircraft can significantly reduce travel time, airport layovers, and overnight stays, as well as take advantage of direct cost savings through group travel. If no airline service is available to a company destination, the alternative is usually either automobile travel or a combination of airline and rental car. An aircraft can generate substantial savings depending upon the proximity of the destination to one of the 6,000 public airports not served by scheduled airlines.

An examination of Champions Stores' travel indicates that the majority of the travel is to cities with airline service. However, a significant portion of these cities (50 percent) require making connections due to lack of direct flights. The breakdown of the company's travel can be divided into the following classes of airline service:

1. Frequent direct: 6 percent
2. Frequent indirect: 25 percent
3. Infrequent direct: 13 percent
4. Infrequent indirect: 25 percent
5. No airline service: 31 percent

POTENTIAL AIRCRAFT UTILIZATION

The projected use of a company airplane is an integrated function of all the elements discussed thus far. It is relevant to address both the amount of use the aircraft would receive and the ways in which it would be employed.

Measuring the potential for a company-owned aircraft requires some subjective analysis since the dates of individual trips are not known and the potential grouping of such trips involves an approximation of an average passenger load. Based on the data in the example, this average passenger load is estimated to be two to three people. In all probability, the passenger load will increase as the company finds new ways of using the aircraft to its advantage. Table 10-1 outlines the potential utilization for a company aircraft over a one-year period. As shown in this table, a conservative estimate indicates potential for 228 round trips covering approximately 171,840 miles. Although the aircraft will be based at the company headquarters in Montgomery, it would be used for several trips originating from the company's distribution warehouse in New Orleans. These figures have been included in the potential.

The amount of utilization indicated above is likely to be in excess of any single aircraft's capabilities. This is because of the large number of potential flying hours and round trips. With this type of utilization, conflicts are likely to occur regarding the availability of the aircraft for other business trips and necessary maintenance. For these reasons, Champions Stores may wish to consider a second aircraft at some time in the future after initial acquisition.

For this analysis, the annual potential has been reduced by 25 percent to more accurately reflect realistic figures for one aircraft. This reduction allows for such issues as occasional maintenance and scheduling conflicts. The 25 percent reduction results in a more conservative potential for 171 round trips covering approximately 128,880 miles annually. Annual hours of utilization are determined by the following formula:

$$\frac{\textit{Annual statute miles traveled}}{\textit{Cruise speed in miles per hour}}$$

For a used twin-engine turboprop aircraft being considered by the management of Champions Stores, the annual hours of utilization would be 128,880 ÷ 283 = 455 hours over approximately 200 flight days.

Types of Business-Use Aircraft

"Let the model fit the mission" is the rule in selecting a business airplane. Recognizing this, manufacturers offer numerous models—including fixed-wing or rotary-wing (helicopter), single-engine or multi-engine, piston or pure jet—and each can be tailored to meet the specific requirements of a firm. "Tailored" is an appropriate word for the business airplane. Just as there are wardrobes for different occasions, there are airplanes for different uses. Like a wardrobe, once the proper airplane is selected, it can be altered to fit specific uses with the selection of avionics equipment, seating arrangements, wheels or floats (or both), and cargo or passenger configurations (or both).

The purpose of this section is to briefly review the categories of aircraft that a firm may consider. The next section will focus on the equipment selection process and how it relates to the hypothetical example of Champions Stores, Inc.

SINGLE-ENGINE AIRCRAFT

Most small businesses start with a single-engine airplane. This beginning is commonly because of an employee who uses an airplane the way other employees use their automobiles. From this use comes recognition of the benefits that can be translated to other employees in similar situations.

The small business owner, the professional, or one of the key employees of a relatively small business usually flies an aircraft in this category personally as the pilot. A single-engine airplane's range is best utilized in frequent trips of 1,000 to 1,200 miles or less, although it is capable of extended flight. A long flight requiring frequent business stops en route also can be handled well by the single-engine model. It has the capability to fly into and out of most airports, including grass strips. Since the traveler usually flies it, the cost of a professional pilot is saved.

Despite their relatively small size and low price tag, these aircraft are capable of carrying the most sophisticated instruments and communications equipment available, such as satellite-based Global Positioning Systems (GPS) and a variety of all-weather flight control and guidance equipment.

Since most of the flights are usually over short-stage lengths, the speed of one model over another often is not the most important consideration. Over a 300-mile distance, for instance, an airplane traveling at 150 miles an hour will take two hours to complete the trip, while one traveling at 180 miles an hour will do it just 20 minutes faster.

Turbocharging in engines raises both the speed of the airplane and its ability to operate at higher altitudes. This makes possible some "over-the-weather" flying and permits taking advantage of more favorable winds. These factors make longer distance travel more practical and begin to place a premium on speed when greater distances are a consideration. Convertibility of most single-engine models to a cargo configuration enables carrying displays, samples, and similar equipment.

There are many modern piston-engine aircraft available to serve this entry-level business market. Cirrus Aircraft, Diamond Aircraft Industries, Piper Aircraft, Inc., and Textron Aviation all offer a number of different and well-proven single-engine aircraft for business use. Cirrus offers the SR20 and SR22. Diamond Aircraft offers the DA 20, DA40, DA50, and twin-engine DA42 and DA62. Piper Aircraft offers the Archer, Seneca, M350, M500, and M600. Textron Aviation offers the Cessna Skyhawk, Skylane, and Turbo Stationair. Although single-engine aircraft allow the most economical entry into business aviation, businesses will still have to consider whether the benefits justify the costs. A new single-engine piston aircraft will have a price tag of $160,000 to $850,000 or more, depending on the engine and avionics selected. Used aircraft may be more economical and can be acquired for less (in some cases, a great deal less) than the price of new models.

LIGHT TWIN AIRCRAFT

More than just an additional powerplant is gained with a twin-engine aircraft. Utility increases many times over. In the twin field, night and weather travel takes on added meaning. While seating capacity and payload of the light twin does not vary much from the high-performance single-engine models, the added powerplant expands the use during darkness and adverse weather. Deicing equipment may be added for convenience and safety.

Seating capacity ranges from four to six. The light twin sometimes is flown by a professional pilot and sometimes by the individual businessperson who is making the trip. Since a long-distance flight is more likely to encounter varying weather conditions, the twin increases mobility for the company whose travel profile includes trips to different parts of the country.

Prices for light twin-engine piston aircraft can range from about $450,000 to more than $850,000, depending on the equipment installed. Piper's Seminole and Seneca V models and the popular Beech Baron 58 are excellent choices for economical acquisition and operating costs as compared to turbine aircraft.

MEDIUM TWIN PISTON AIRCRAFT

When a company has a number of people traveling over the same routes, when inflight conferences are required, or when all-weather operations are a routine matter, a medium twin is appropriate.

Customizing interiors to fit the specific needs and desires of the company begins in this range. High-density seating in some models provides airline comfort for up to 10 or 12 passengers. Foldout tables, side-facing seats, or swivel seats make a mobile conference room. A bedroom will allow an executive to arrive at the destination thoroughly refreshed. A professional crew usually flies the medium twins. Their all-weather capability, range, and speed provide great flexibility for short and long-distance flights.

TURBOPROPS

A turboprop provides the best of two worlds—the lower costs of propeller-driven aircraft with some advantages of the jet. Falling into the medium twin category, the turboprop usually is professionally flown. Its jet power and pressurization makes it well-suited for medium and long trips at average speeds over 300 miles per hour, yet it operates efficiently on short runs. This versatility is demonstrated by the Pilatus PC-12. With a 330 cubic foot pressurized cabin volume, the PC-12 can carry nine passengers over 1,600 nautical miles with VFR reserves and 1,400 nautical miles with IFR reserves.

Turboprops have higher operating costs than piston aircraft, partially because they consume more fuel per hour of flying. At that same time, the range is greater, allowing greater distances to be covered. The initial purchase price is higher than for piston-powered twins, but it is still under the cost of most pure jets (some VLJs being the exception). The turboprop can fly into and out of smaller airports than the pure jet. As U.S. industry moves away from larger cities, the need to use smaller airports can be an important consideration. This is a major consideration for a company like Champions Stores.

A number of foreign and domestic manufacturers offer turboprops designed for the business market. The leading twin-engine turboprop aircraft is the Beechcraft King Air series with five different versions and the King Air's larger cousin, the 1900 Airliner.

PURE JETS

At the top of the business fleet is the pure jet. With speeds well over 500 miles per hour, it rivals the best of the airliners, and in flexibility, the best of the piston-powered aircraft. The mission of the business jet is to compress great distances into short expanses of time. Almost invariably professionally flown, the pure jet moves corporate executives to widely scattered points and returns them in a matter of hours. The environment of the jet is high altitude. For this reason, it is most efficient for medium and long-distance travel. Because of its speed, the jet, probably more than any other business airplane, is used most frequently to drop off and pick up individuals over wide distances.

Business jets have been designed in a variety of sizes and capabilities to meet the needs of various target markets. The smallest, known as a very light jet (VLJ), are able to carry from four to eight passengers and are certificated for single-pilot operation. These smaller jets can be purchased for between $1 million and $5 million, depending on the avionics and options selected. The Cirrus Vision Jet, for example, costs $2 million and can carry 6 passengers at 345 miles per hour. The HondaJet is priced at $4.9 million and can carry 6 passengers at 423 miles per hour. The Cessna Citation Jet M2 is priced at $4.6 million and can carry 6 passengers at 465 miles per hour.

The majority of business jets in operation today, however, seat eight to ten passengers in a typical business configuration and operate efficiently over transcontinental or transatlantic distances. Gulfstream and Bombardier together account for 68 percent of the market. The G280, G500, G550, G600, G650, and G700 dominate the Gulfstream product line. The G700 has, according to Gulfstream, the most spacious cabin in the industry, with a 7,500 NM range and speed of Mach 0.92. Bombardier offers the Learjet 75 Liberty, Challenger 350, Challenger 650, Global 5500, Global 6500, Global 7500, and Global 8000. The Global 8000, according to Bombardier, can carry 17 passengers a distance of 7900 NM at speed of Mach 0.925.

As more and more larger corporations turn to business aviation as a tool to increase productivity, a new class of business jet—the super midsize aircraft—is beginning to emerge. These aircraft are larger, but not as large as the so-called large class of jet. Their attractiveness is that they allow large teams of employees to be transported economically over longer ranges than standard midsize jets.

The IAI Galaxy, Raytheon Hawker Horizon, Cessna Citation X and the Dassault Falcon 2000 and Falcon 50EX are examples of this new class of jets. The Galaxy, for example, has a cabin that is 6 feet 3 inches high and 7 feet 2 inches wide. Powered by two Pratt & Whitney Canada PW306A engines, it has a range of 3,602 nautical miles at a Mach 0.82 cruise speed. The Falcon 2000 is powered by two CFM International CFE738-1-1B turbofans that each produce 5,918 pounds of thrust. The cabin is 26 feet 3 inches long, 6 feet 2 inches high, and 7 feet 8 inches wide.

Large business jets are gaining popularity with global corporations that need intercontinental travel. Nonstop flights such as Chicago–Tokyo, New York–Abu Dhabi, and London–Honolulu are now well within the capability of aircraft such as the Boeing Business Jet (BBJ), the Gulfstream G650 and G700, and the Bombardier Global 6500, Global 7500, and Global 8000. Each of these aircraft has a range of 6,500 NM or more and can cruise at speeds approaching Mach 1.0.

HELICOPTERS

Corporate use of helicopters is not new. The first civil helicopters were placed into use right after World War II. Corporate reliance on helicopters has expanded dramatically, growing with the machine itself. Today, Robinson, Bell, Sikorsky, Schweizer, Leonardo, and MD Helicopters produce highly efficient business helicopters.

The business applications of helicopters are almost endless, including herding livestock; moving bank papers and checks; harvesting seed cones from the tops of coniferous trees for propagation of the best species without damage to the trees; timely movement of work crews and material for construction projects; and aerial surveying/photography, to name just a few.

However, the most visible business application of helicopters is for the reliable, rapid transport of corporate executives. Many CEOs who regularly fly in helicopters refer to them as "time machines" because of the great savings in executive time made possible by the helicopters. The concept of portal-to-portal travel really pays off in convenience and time when one is able to eliminate ground travel by limo or taxi to and from the airport. Many firms have corporate helipads adjacent to their headquarters. The passengers walk to the helicopter and, ideally, fly directly to a heliport within walking distance of their destination.

When it is not practical to make the entire trip by helicopter, there is still a considerable advantage in using a corporate helicopter to shuttle passengers between the airport and their destination. There really aren't any typical business helicopters. They range from the compact but practical Robinson R-22, which is the world's smallest commercial helicopter, to the 44-passenger Boeing Chinook. Some of the purely corporate machines are specially outfitted with plush upholstery, swivel chairs, and environmental control systems and are flown by a two-pilot crew. Others are much more austere, and some are flown by the CEO. However, the helicopters in use today are third-generation helicopters, which incorporate design features that have been proven safe, reliable, and practical during many millions of hours of helicopter flight.

Equipment Selection Process

The choice of a business aircraft must follow a detailed and comprehensive evaluation of a company's travel requirements, its current financial position, and intangible benefits that accrue through aircraft ownership. An aircraft's capability compared to the company's need must also be evaluated. The rule of thumb most commonly used is that the aircraft should be no more than is needed to satisfy most of the company's requirements. An aircraft with substantially greater capabilities than the company needs may have an adverse impact on long-term ownership.

As with any management decision, selecting suitable equipment is a matter of determining the relative importance of each of several factors, and then making a choice which best fits the resulting profile. There are normally five principal rational factors upon which to base an aircraft and equipment selection analysis. While all of these factors are important, the degree of importance of each factor rests with specific travel requirements.

1. *Trip distances and number of passengers.* This information will help decide the size, range, and payload requirements that must be met. This factor is also important in selecting necessary or desirable equipment.
2. *Use and users of the aircraft.* Expected users of the aircraft will affect the type of aircraft, seating arrangements, performance requirements, and interior appointments. Special uses, such as cargo needs, will also affect the selection.
3. *Environmental aspects of route and destinations.* The need for special systems (such as pressurization and turbocharging), runway performance requirements, and navigational packages are often predicted by these factors.
4. *Frequency of trips.* This information helps qualify the relative importance of other factors. In addition, trip frequency requirements aid in equipment decisions, such as avionics and convenience options.
5. *Financial and performance considerations.* In any equipment selection decision, this information provides a rationale by properly balancing needs against costs.

The selection process is still subjective to a certain degree. Equipment such as cabin stereo systems, interior appointments, and convenience accessories remain largely a matter of personal taste.

TRIP DISTANCES AND NUMBER OF PASSENGERS

An examination of all potential trips likely to be undertaken by Champions Stores' aircraft indicates that the one-way distances range from approximately 160 to 1,200 miles. Table 10-2 is a frequency distribution of these one-way distances. As shown by this distribution, an aircraft capable of traveling 1,200 miles nonstop could meet 100 percent of the trip legs. However, 94.7 percent of all trip legs fell within the 101 to 700 mile range. Therefore, it would appear more realistic to give primary consideration to those trips falling within the 101 to 700 mile range. The company aircraft should have a nonstop range of at least 700 miles.

Table 10-2. Frequency Distribution of Trip Distances

	Number of trips (legs[1])			
Distance (miles)	**100%**	**75%**	**Percent of total trips**	**Cumulative percent**
0–100	0	0	0	0
101–200	120	90	26	26
201–300	96	72	21	47
301–400	96	72	21	68
401–500	72	54	16	84
501–600	24	18	5.3	89.3
601–700	24	18	5.3	94.7
701–800	0	0	0	94.7
801–900	0	0	0	94.7
901–1,000	0	0	0	94.7
1,001–1,100	0	0	0	94.7
1,101–1,200	24	18	5.3	100
	456[2]	**342**[2]	**100**	

[1] Leg = Point A to Point B.
[2] The 342 annualized trip legs were determined by reducing the original 456 annualized total by 25 percent. (228 round trips × 2 = 456 trip legs × 75% = 342 trip legs.) The 342 legs would translate into 171 round trips.

Based on examination of Champions Stores' travel data, an average passenger load is two to three passengers. However, it is still necessary to establish what the maximum passenger density might be for the company. For example, assume that the salesperson in the interview with company personnel learned that the maximum number of people who have traveled together on past business trips was six. The company does not anticipate the maximum passenger requirement to increase with use of a business airplane. In aircraft selection, primary consideration should be given to aircraft with a maximum of eight seats (six passengers plus two pilots).

USE AND USERS

Champions Stores' aircraft will be used primarily for transporting company executives and other personnel to various business destinations, including company-owned stores and warehouses, as well as to major cities such as Jacksonville, Dallas, New Orleans, and Atlanta where buyers make substantial purchases. The possibility of flying manufacturers' representatives in for meetings with company personnel also exists. Based on the number of potential hours of utilization and safety of corporate executives, the services of a qualified, full-time pilot and copilot will be used in this case.

ENVIRONMENTAL ASPECTS OF ROUTES AND DESTINATIONS

A review of the flight routes that will be flown by the company indicates the enroute terrain, for the most part, is not mountainous. A flight altitude of 5,000 feet above mean sea level would be adequate to meet the minimum enroute IFR (instrument flight rules) requirements for this area of the country.

Other types of terrain that will be encountered involve rough, densely wooded areas (North and South Carolina) and swampy areas (Florida and Louisiana). Additional flights over water may occur in the Gulf Coast area. With the amount of travel that Champions Stores will be doing, the aircraft may occasionally encounter low ceilings and fog as well as icing conditions. The information obtained indicated that a significant portion (50 percent) of the company's travel is of an on-demand or emergency nature. This type of travel would probably require some night flying. In addition, speed in reaching the destination may be important.

Since an analysis of environmental conditions and seating requirements indicate the need for a twin-engine aircraft, for this example, only a twin-engine aircraft will be recommended. High altitudes en route on longer legs are anticipated, so a pressurized aircraft will be needed. Similarly, if high altitudes en route or landing at high elevation airports were anticipated, the airplane would need to have the additional power to operate in the rarefied air at high altitudes.

FREQUENCY OF TRIPS

For this example, a potential for 171 round trips was demonstrated, accounting for approximately 455 hours of utilization annually. Since this indicates an above-average utilization rate, the recommendation will be to select an aircraft that has IFR capability, full deicing equipment for all-weather capability, dual communications, navigational equipment (including a co-pilot instrument panel), and autopilot. The prevailing weather experienced in this part of the country would add validity to this recommendation.

Performance and Financial Considerations

To complete the equipment selection process, the performance characteristics of various aircraft under consideration must be examined in relation to costs. Within the criteria thus far established, a salesperson might now select three or four models that appear to meet the company's needs.

PERFORMANCE ANALYSIS

The technical performance capabilities of the aircraft under consideration must be fully evaluated. These include such factors as short runway performance, high temperature operating characteristics, payload-range capability, speed, and operational reliability.

Every aircraft has a given ability to land and take off on runways of varying lengths. This capability is certificated by the FAA and is shown in the flight manual for the aircraft. Normally, the shorter the runway, the smaller the load the aircraft can carry (of passengers, baggage, and fuel). On extremely short runways, the load restriction may be so great as to not permit landing or takeoff at all. For example, small twin-engine propeller aircraft can operate on runways of 2,000 to 3,000 feet in length, whereas bigger and faster turbine (turboprop and jet) aircraft may require 5,000 to 7,000 feet, especially at higher temperatures. VLJs, although at the small end of the jet market, are able to operate with 2,500 to 3,500 feet available for takeoff and landing.

An aircraft performance analysis must therefore take into consideration the length of runways offered at all airports that the company might wish to use. Those lengths must then be compared to the performance capabilities of the aircraft under consideration. This comparison would indicate what restrictions, if any, might affect the company's operations at particular airports.

Air temperature and airport altitude can also affect an aircraft's performance. The higher the temperature and the higher the altitude, the greater the runway length that is needed under specific payload (fuel and passenger) conditions. Conversely, with a constant runway length, higher temperatures or altitudes will tend to restrict the load an aircraft can carry. When an aircraft carries more fuel to travel longer distances, it invariably needs more runway length in which to take off.

Another performance consideration is the payload range capability of the aircraft. Each aircraft has, according to its particular weight, fuel capacity, engine type, and performance characteristics, a capability to carry a certain payload over a certain distance. A typical payload range diagram is shown in Figure 10-1. For all aircraft, there is a tradeoff between payload and range. All else being equal, aircraft with heavier payloads are unable to fly as far as those with lighter payloads. Some variation to this performance data would result from differing cruise speeds; an aircraft is normally able to fly farther if it travels at slower speeds.

The aircraft is able to carry a maximum payload over a specified range, indicated by points A and B in Figure 10-1. Extending the range of the aircraft is possible with reduced payload, as indicated by points B to C. This tradeoff is a range, represented by the sloping line. Range can be further extended if the operator is willing to further reduce payload by reducing the amount of fuel carried, as indicated by points C and D.

When the payload-range capabilities of the different aircraft under consideration are known, the company is in a position to determine which aircraft will meet its previously considered requirements—namely, the amount of fuel and the number of passengers to be carried.

The payload-range capabilities must also be compared to the runway lengths the company plans to use to determine what actual limitations may exist—either runway length restrictions or payload-range restrictions.

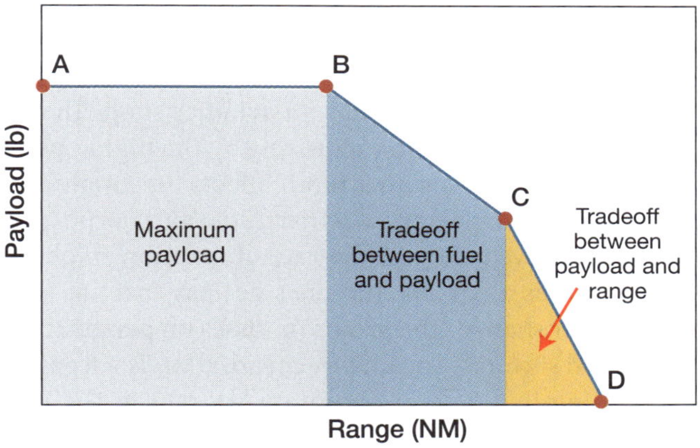

Figure 10-1. Payload range chart.

FINANCIAL ANALYSIS

The final factor in the equipment selection process is the cost of the various aircraft under consideration. Normally, the costs arising from ownership of an aircraft are considered separately from those costs associated with its operation.

Cost of Ownership

Three principal items determine the purchase price of an aircraft: (a) the base price, (b) the price of a customized interior, and (c) the avionics equipment (radios, navigational instruments, radar, and similar items). The costs associated with avionics equipment and customized interiors can add 30 percent or more to the base price of an aircraft. The prospective company may consider an outright purchase, a financial purchase, or lease arrangement. These various options will be considered further in Chapter 11.

Used aircraft may also be considered, often at prices substantially lower than the cost of a new aircraft. Of course, with a used aircraft, it is important to analyze the maintenance records of the aircraft and its engines. Total hours on the engines is also a major consideration if the number of hours is high. However, a good used aircraft may be bought at a considerable price reduction over a new model without a substantial difference in performance or passenger convenience.

The status of production must be examined relative to cost. Each aircraft undergoes a significant evolutionary development after its initial design has been adopted. Thus, improvements to most operating criteria are made through increased engine power, increased weights, longer cabins, and increased speed and range. Prior improvements and the potential for additional improvements must be considered, recognizing that some of the future improvements may or may not be readily incorporated into an earlier model.

A forecast of the future disposal or trade-in value of the aircraft must be made to determine the net aircraft cost to the company (purchase price less disposal value). Although aircraft values vary, a five-year-old, high-performance, single-engine aircraft may have a disposal value of 90 percent; a five-year-old light twin a disposal value of 86 percent; and a turboprop a disposal value of 73 percent. Reliability and maintainability must be investigated with regard to cost. The broad spectrum of business aircraft includes a wide variety of technical and mechanical complexity in engines, avionics, and aircraft systems. Each step in overall complexity causes incremental changes in (1) the amount of spare parts required, (2) technical proficiency of maintenance personnel, (3) cost of maintenance, (4) sophistication of test and maintenance equipment, and (5) overall thoroughness of the maintenance program.

Thus, maintainability is tied directly to the cost of ownership—what the company can support. A more sophisticated aircraft may require more attention for equal reliability. The local resources (either within the company or available at the airport) must be surveyed to determine if reliability might be compromised because of local inadequacies.

For a smaller aircraft operation, maintenance can be accomplished almost entirely by a qualified maintenance repair station, and there would be little or no requirement for the company to keep facilities for its own mechanics. A larger and more sophisticated flight operation usually requires substantial maintenance manpower, many spare parts with room to store them, a machine shop, testing facilities, and perhaps an avionics shop. There would also normally be major hangar facilities, often a hangar used exclusively by the flight operation.

The cost of owning an aircraft affects the amount of income taxes paid. Aircraft are sold to individuals, sole proprietors, partnerships, and corporations. Tax considerations exist for all business enterprises, even though the rate of taxation might differ. A business organized as a sole proprietorship or as a partnership does not pay taxes as such, but the individual proprietors or partners reflect their share of the profits or losses on personal income tax returns. Rates vary according to the individual's taxable income. A corporation is a legal entity that pays its own income taxes.

The nominal federal corporate tax rate in the United States is a flat 21 percent following the passage of the Tax Cuts and Jobs Act of 2017. Forty-four states levy a corporate income tax. Rates range from 2.5 percent in North Carolina to 11.5 percent in New Jersey. Alabama has a 6.5 percent corporate income tax rate. To reflect these combined rates, all financial calculations and analysis involved with the proposal for the purchase of a business aircraft by Champions Stores will use a combined federal and state income tax of 27.5 percent. Tax rates are an incentive for companies to purchase and operate aircraft. For example, each dollar of deductible expense by Champions Stores will actually cost the corporation about 72.5 cents.

The Tax Cuts and Jobs Act of 2017 provides for immediate expensing of capital investments, repeals like-kind exchanges, and makes a host of other changes that impact business aviation. The Tax Cuts and Jobs Act also provides 100-percent expensing, which allows taxpayers to immediately write off the cost of aircraft acquired and placed in service after September 27, 2017, and before January 1, 2023 (January 1, 2024, for longer production period property/certain aircraft). The 100-percent expensing applies to both factory-new and pre-owned aircraft as long as it is the taxpayer's first use of the aircraft. The 100-percent expense deduction phases out starting in 2023, reducing by 20 percent annually through 2026.

At the time of resale, the gain realized between the aircraft sales price and the current book value (called depreciation recapture) is treated as ordinary income. The tax benefits of ownership directly reduce the actual cost of the aircraft. The ownership analysis in Figure 10-2 illustrates how much capital Champions Stores will recover through tax savings and disposition of the aircraft after six years. The monthly net cost of ownership is only $17,042 over the 72-month period.

Twin-Engine Turboprop Aircraft—Six Year Analysis		
Aircraft Acquisition Cost		
Purchase Price		$2,230,000
State Sales Tax (6.5%)		$144,950
Total		$2,374,950
Depreciation Expense		$2,230,000
Resale Value (71%)		$1,583,300
Six Year Ownership Analysis		
Tax savings (27.5% combined state and federal corporate tax rate)		
100% Bonus Depreciation	$2,230,000	
Total Tax Savings		$2,230,000
Disposal of Aircraft*		
Resale Value	$1,583,300	
Less Taxes on Sale	$435,408	
Net Proceeds from Sale		$1,147,892
Net Cost of Ownership—6 years		$1,227,058
Per Year		$204,509
Per Month		$17,042

* If the aircraft is traded in rather than sold outright, the taxes due at sale will be deferred. The depreciation basis on the new aircraft will be decreased by the trade-in value since the book value is zero.

Figure 10-2. Ownership analysis.

Cost of Use

The cost of use includes two types of expenses: fixed costs and direct operating expenses (variable costs). **Fixed costs** include those expense items which are incurred regardless of the amount of flying performed. Examples include crew salaries, recurrent training, insurance, and hangar rental or tie-down expense. Direct operating expenses or **variable costs** are the actual expenses for fuel, maintenance, and miscellaneous expenses that occur as a direct result of hours flown. Some aircraft components have predetermined or expected normal service lives that can be used to calculate an hourly cost of operation. For example, aircraft engines must be completely overhauled after 2,100 to 3,600 hours depending on the engine. Other components such as the airframe, propellers, and avionics are accounted for by conservative estimates of their maintenance requirements.

Figures 10-3 and 10-4 present the major items included under fixed and direct operating expenses for a twin-engine turboprop aircraft under consideration by Champions Stores. The figures are only illustrative. The actual costs would vary due to differences in accounting methods as well as differences in the cost of such items as fuel, labor services, engine overhaul, remanufactured engines, and avionics. In addition, the manner in which the aircraft is flown and used (number of hours flown annually, power settings used, types of airports encountered, environmental conditions, experience of the pilot, etc.) will have a direct effect on the actual hourly cost of use.

Expense Category	Estimated Cost Per Year
Crew Salaries	
Captain	$100,000
Co-Pilot	$85,000
Benefits	$60,150
Hangar Rental	$24,147
Insurance[1]	
Hull (Physical Damage Coverage)	$10,920
Single Limit Liability ($25 million per occurrence)	$8,500
Guest Voluntary Settlement Coverage	$1,000
Recurrent Training	$15,600
Computerized Maintenance Program	$1,850
Aircraft Modernization	8,920
Refurbishing	$8,280
Weather Service	$3,235
Total Annual Fixed Costs	$327,602

[1]$500,000 GVS coverage.
$5,000 medical payments coverage at no charge.

Figure 10-3. Fixed costs for a twin-engine turboprop business aircraft.

Expense Category	Estimated Cost Per Hour
Fuel (1)	$597.77
Maintenance Labor (2)	$104.00
Parts—Airframe, Engine, Avionics (3)	$115.00
Engine Restoration (4)	$127.00
Propeller Overhaul	$6.00
Miscellaneous Expenses	
Crew Expenses	$135.00
Landing/Parking Fees	$6.00
Supplies/Catering	$32.00
Total Direct Operating Costs Per Hour	$1,122.77

(1) Fuel costs .... $5.29 per gallon
Gallons per hour 113
(2) Maintenance labor costs per hour $69
Maintenance hours per flight hour 1.5
(3) Engine Model PT6A-42
(4) 3,600 hours

Figure 10-4. Direct operating expenses (variable costs) for a twin-engine turboprop business aircraft.

Cash Flow Analysis

One the most frequently misunderstood and misused business terms is cash flow. It is often mistaken for operating income, revenue, or profit. A profitable FBO will need substantial inflows of cash from outside sources to ensure that profit objectives are met. You can't spend profit; you only spend cash. Accurate cash management is as critical to a successful long-term business venture as accurate fuel management is for a long-distance flight. A **cash flow analysis** completed by aircraft salespeople is essential not only for selling aircraft to corporations with in-house flight departments but also for all types of business aircraft acquisition. This includes company-owned aircraft with operations contracted to another company, wet or dry lease, and fractional ownership. These variations will be discussed in detail in Chapter 11. Every prospect must understand thoroughly the impact the airplane will have on cash flows each year it is used.

When a company like Champions Stores is considering the purchase of a business aircraft, it is concerned with more than the initial purchase price and the down payment amount. The net, after-tax cost of operating the aircraft projected on a year-to-year basis for the entire period of ownership is of vital importance. This may turn out to be the key factor in the decision to buy or not to buy. Keep in mind that a business can deduct expenses associated with private aircraft ownership, such as fuel, maintenance, and management costs if the aircraft is used for business purposes 50 percent of the time. It is important to note that there are specific qualifications that must be met to receive these benefits. The cash flow analysis example in Figure 10-5 on the next page demonstrates this net after-tax cost for Champions Stores.

Experience has demonstrated that the cash flow statement can accomplish the following benefits for the salesperson:

1. It adds a professional touch to the sales presentation.
2. It assists the salesperson in dealing with the company's financial concerns.
3. It satisfies the prospect's need for detailed cost information and net present value analysis.
4. It helps move the sales process toward a favorable conclusion.

The significance of a cash flow analysis is that it shows the potential user an accurate estimate of the total after-tax cost of owning a business aircraft and projects the changes in the company's cash flow year by year. The following definitions are relevant:

1. *Fixed Cost* (Figure 10-3). Annual fixed costs have been increased by an inflation factor of 3 percent.
2. *Loan Balance Payoff* = $651,468 because there are two years remaining on the loan contract.
3. *Taxes Due at Sale* are $48,536.88. This represents a corporate tax rate of 21 percent multiplied by the selling price ($1,583,300) in excess of book value ($1,352,172.).
4. *Depreciation* method is double-declining balance. A 25-year life with $100,000 was used. Cumulative depreciation at the end of six years is $877,828.
5. *Operating Expenses* (Figure 10-4). Annual direct operating costs have been increased by an inflation factor of 3 percent.
6. *Disposal of Aircraft* is based on the present resale value of a similar six-year-old aircraft in relation to its original retail price (71 percent).
7. *Total Cash Flow* indicates the total after-tax cost of ownership over the six-year period.
8. *Cost Per Hour* is the average annual after-tax cost per hour of owning and operating the twin-engine turboprop aircraft ($1,545,659 ÷ 2,730 hours).
9. *Net Present Value Cost* is derived from the money value rate of 18 percent. It represents the actual amount the aircraft will cost, based on borrowing money and keeping the company's funds free for reinvestment in the company at its average return on investment rate.

Input Data

Aircraft Cost: $2,230,000
State Sales Tax (6.50%): $144,950
Total Acquisition Cost: $2,374,950

Federal Income Tax Rate: 21%
Finance Rate: 9.25% APR, 8 years
Money Value: 18%

Monthly Payment: $29,836.93
Inflation Rate: 3%
Annual Hrs of Utilization: 455

Expenditures	Year 0	Year 1	Year 2	Year 3	Year 4	Year 5	Year 6
Fixed Cost		$327,602	$337,430	$347,553	$357,980	$368,719	$379,780
Down Payment (15%)	$356,243						
Balance of Purchase	$2,018,707						
Principal Payment		$178,766	$196,021	$214,942	$235,689	$258,438	$283,384
Interest Payment		$179,278	$162,022	$143,102	$122,355	$99,605	$74,659
Loan Balance Payoff							$651,468
Taxes Due at Sale							$48,537
Operating Expenses		$510,860	$526,186	$541,971	$558,230	$574,978	$592,227
TOTAL EXPENDITURES		$1,196,506	$1,221,659	$1,247,568	$1,274,254	$1,301,740	$2,030,056
Aircraft Loan	$2,018,707						
Disposal of Aircraft (71%)							$1,583,300
TOTAL CHANGE (before taxes)		($1,196,506)	($1,221,659)	($1,247,568)	($1,274,254)	($1,301,740)	($446,756)
TAX REDUCTIONS							
Fixed Cost		$327,602	$337,430	$347,553	$357,980	$368,719	$379,780
Depreciation		$178,400	$164,128	$150,998	$138,918	$127,804	$117,580
Interest		$179,278	$162,022	$143,102	$122,355	$99,605	$74,659
Operating Expenses		$510,860	$526,186	$541,971	$558,230	$574,978	$592,227
TOTAL TAX REDUCTION		$1,196,140	$1,189,767	$1,183,624	$1,177,483	$1,171,106	$1,164,247
CHANGE IN CASH FLOW	($356,243)	($366)	($31,893)	($63,944)	($96,771)	($130,634)	($865,809)

TOTAL CASH FLOW ($1,545,659)
Cost per Hour ($566)
Net Present Value Cost ($845,763)

$$\text{Cost per Mile} = \frac{\text{(Average Annual Cost)}}{\text{(Cruise Speed} \times \text{Annual Hrs)}} = \frac{\$845,763}{238 \times 455} = \$7.81$$

$$\text{Cost/Seat Mile} = \frac{\text{(Cost per Mile)}}{\text{(Passenger Seats)}} = \frac{\$7.81}{6} = \$1.30$$

Note: Bonus depreciation was not used in this example. Consult a tax advisor for specifics.

Figure 10-5. Twin-engine business aircraft purchase cash flow analysis.

Financing Aircraft

Attractive low-rate, long-term financing on up to 100 percent of the aircraft purchase price is essential in marketing aircraft. Some lending institutions have eliminated the down payment requirement, offer variable interest rates based on one or two percentage points over prime, and offer terms of 12 years or more. AOPA Finance advertises comprehensive and competitive loan structures which include fixed or adjustable rates and 5–20 year terms. They have access to more than a dozen aircraft lenders with the ability to finance everything from piston singles to light jets. Their streamlined application process can produce financing decisions in 1–2 business days.

Table 10-3 presents how a $100 loan at 9.25% interest is paid off over an eight-year period by a level monthly payment. The table also presents the total annual interest and principal payments and the year-end balance of each year of the loan.

Table 10-3. Sample Loan Amortization Schedule, 9.25% Monthly Fixed Rate

Year	Annual interest	Annual principal	Year ending balance
1	8.880811	8.855453	91.144547
2	8.026046	9.710218	81.434329
3	7.088775	10.647489	70.786840
4	6.061036	11.675229	59.111611
5	4.934094	12.802170	46.309441
6	3.698376	14.037889	32.271553
7	2.343380	15.392884	16.878669
8	0.857595	16.878669	0

The twin-engine turboprop aircraft being proposed to the management of Champions Stores is being financed over an eight-year period at 9.25 percent annual percentage rate (APR). After making a 15 percent down payment of $356,243, a fixed-rate loan for 8 years of $2,018,707 was arranged using Table 10-3. The following finance data for the cash flow analysis can be determined:

Monthly Payment	1.478022 × $20,187.07 = $29,836.93
1st Year Annual Interest	8.880811 × $20,187.07 = $179,277.55
1st Year Principal	8.855453 × $20,187.07 = $178,765.65
Loan Balance Payoff (end of year 6)	32.27155 × $20,187.07 = $651,468.10

Net Present Value

The concept of **net present value (NPV)** is widely used by companies as they approach investment decisions. NPV helps determine the profitability of an investment. Financial comparisons among types of aircraft cannot be made accurately without NPV because this technique will tell the purchaser how much the aircraft will really cost over a predetermined period. Note that discount rate is the interest rate used to calculate net present value (NPV).

Table 10-4. Net Present Value Table.

	Interest rate					
Period	**10%**	**12%**	**14%**	**15%**	**16%**	**18%**
1	0.909	0.893	0.877	0.870	0.862	0.847
2	0.826	0.797	0.769	0.756	0.743	0.718
3	0.751	0.712	0.675	0.658	0.641	0.609
4	0.683	0.636	0.592	0.572	0.552	0.516
5	0.621	0.567	0.519	0.497	0.476	0.437
6	0.564	0.507	0.456	0.432	0.410	0.370
7	0.513	0.452	0.400	0.376	0.354	0.314
8	0.467	0.404	0.351	0.327	0.305	0.266
9	0.424	0.361	0.308	0.284	0.263	0.225
10	0.386	0.322	0.270	0.247	0.227	0.191

Money that will be received in the future is presently worth considerably less than its stated value. The promise of $10,000 twenty-five years from now sounds good, but if 10 percent per annum could be earned on the investment, then this promise is now worth less than $1,000. The present value of future payments is the reciprocal of compound interest.

This reciprocity of compound interest and present value is illustrated by the following example:

Today		**5 years later**
$1,000 Compounded at 9%	=	$1,538,62

$1,538.62 is the present value of $1,000 in five years

The present value of money due in the future will differ from company to company. It depends upon the rate of return (money value or discount rate) that is either available to the company or that the company has the ability to earn internally. This explains why a company can borrow for use in its business and still make money. The loan from the financial institution requires a lower rate of interest than can be achieved by the borrower.

Net present value is used as the final step in the cash flow statement. This statement illustrates the net cash flow for each year Champions Stores owns and operates its aircraft. The present value of each of these net cash flows is determined and summarized; the resulting figure is the net present value (Table 10-5). This dollar figure tells the company how much money must be invested now at the company's stated money value to earn enough cash to meet all of the aircraft expenses as they come due each year. The net present value figure also brings six years of expenses to a single figure. Prospective aircraft purchasers can use net present value during the evaluation stage to compare the total expense of owning and operating comparable aircraft.

Table 10-5. Net Present Value of Cash Flow, Twin-Engine Turboprop Aircraft (Money Value Rate 18%).

Year	Actual cash flow	Interest rate	Present value
0	($356,243)	× 1.00	($356,243)
1	($366)	× 0.847	($310)
2	($31,893)	× 0.718	($22,899)
3	($63,944)	× 0.609	($38,942)
4	($96,771)	× 0.516	($49,934)
5	($130,634)	× 0.437	($57,087)
6	($865,809)	× 0.370	($320,349)
Total Cash Flow	($1,545,659)		($845,763)

Sales Application/Break-Even Analysis

The travel analysis is a powerful means of assisting a firm in analyzing the feasibility of purchasing an airplane for employee travel. In situations where the prospective firm is going to use the airplane to generate revenue, the break-even analysis is more appropriate. The aircraft salesperson will find it useful to calculate the prospective buyer's break-even point—that point at which the cost of operating the aircraft exactly matches the revenues generated through such activities as flight instruction or charter. Since business firms must do better than just break even, this analysis will help determine revenue levels sufficient to generate a predetermined profit objective.

To apply **break-even analysis**, two types of costs must be determined. Fixed costs are those whose level remains unchanged when hourly usage changes (e.g., monthly interest on aircraft loans, insurance, crew salaries, general overhead allocation). Direct operating expenses are those that do change in proportion to changes in aircraft use, and include gas, maintenance, and hourly charges for maintenance reserves. To illustrate break-even analysis, a sales proposal based on a twin-engine aircraft used for charter purposes by a hypothetical company, Seacoast Charter, Inc., would be based on the following data:

Annual total fixed cost = $203,244
Charter revenue per hour = $1,200
Direct operating expense per hour = $781

Break-even hours is the point where total fixed and direct operating expenses equal total charter sales revenue. It can be determined by using the following formula:

$$BE\ (hrs) = \frac{\text{Total Fixed Costs}}{\text{Charter Revenue per Hour} - \text{Direct Operating Expense per Hour}}$$

$$= \frac{\$203{,}244}{\$1{,}200 - \$781}$$

$$= 485 \text{ hours}$$

Either raising or lowering the hourly charter rate can change the break-even hours. If the competitive environment would allow an increase of $50 per hour to $1,250, the new break-even hours would be reduced by 52 hours to 433 hours.

The president of Seacoast Charter would also like to know how many charter hours the firm must sell to make $24,998 in the next 12 months. Using the following formula, the aircraft salesperson would be able to provide the president with the answer.

$$\text{Hours Required} = \frac{\text{Total Fixed Costs + Profit}}{\text{Charter Revenue per Hour} - \text{Direct Operating Expense per Hour}}$$

$$= \frac{\$203{,}244 + \$24{,}998}{\$1{,}200 - \$781}$$

$$= 545 \text{ hours}$$

To further assist Seacoast Charter in planning, the break-even concept can be used to determine the number of charter customers required over the next 12 months to meet the $24,998 profit objective. A review of past sales records indicates that the typical charter flight lasted 7.5 hours. Since 545 total hours are required, and the average hourly usage per charter flight was 7.5 hours, then approximately 73 customers (545 hours ÷ 7.5 hours) must be sold during the next year.

In spite of some limitations, break-even analysis can be a powerful tool for aircraft salespeople to use in marketing business aircraft to corporations that will use the aircraft commercially to generate profits.

Summary

By conducting a transportation needs assessment, an FBO in the business of selling aircraft can generate aircraft sales while also introducing a company to the world of business aviation. Travel challenges can be solved, time in transit can be reduced, and efficiency can be enhanced for the company that begins using business aircraft. The transportation needs assessment is an important productivity tool for an FBO that can be useful in business-to-business marketing and sales.

Key Terms

break-even analysis. An analysis of the number of units of product or the sales of services that must be sold to cover the fixed and variable costs of production.

business-to-business marketing. The marketing of products or services to other businesses and organizations rather than to traditional individual customers.

buyer. The employee who has the authority to place the order with the selected vendor. It is usually an executive in the purchasing department.

cash-flow analysis. An analysis that determines a company's working capital, which is the amount of money available to run business operations.

decider. The executive who has the authority to select which product to purchase.

fixed costs. A cost that does not change with an increase or decrease in the amount of goods or services produced or sold. Fixed costs can be direct or indirect.

gatekeepers. Individuals involved in the buying process who have the responsibility and authority to control information. This role is often played by the purchasing manager.

influencers. Usually technical employees who have defined the criteria that a purchase must meet. Sometimes the influencer is an outside consultant with expertise in the specific area under investigation.

modified rebuy. Straight rebuy situations that require some additional information due to a change in price or specifications or due to dissatisfaction with the present supplier.

net present value (NPV). The difference between the present value of cash inflows and the present value of cash outflows over a period of time. NPV is used in capital budgeting to analyze the profitability of a projected investment or project.

new buys. Purchases involving products or services never considered before by the company. There is a high degree of risk and cost associated with this category of purchase decision.

straight rebuys. Reorders. The products ordered are usually standard products that are routinely used and maintained in inventory.

travel analysis. An evaluation of a firm's current travel modes and the amount and nature of travel presently undertaken. An FBO can undertake a travel analysis for a company, possibly resulting in an aircraft sale or charter activity.

travel dispersion. As part of a travel analysis, an examination that categorizes an organization's trips in terms of distance, frequency, and volume of passengers. This information is useful in further defining a firm's travel patterns and determining whether these patterns are suitable for business aircraft use.

users. Individuals involved in buying who initiate the process by identifying the need for a product (aircraft) based on their intended use of the product or service.

variable costs. Costs (expenses) that change in proportion to how much a company produces or sells.

Review Questions

1. Describe business-to-business marketing.
2. Identify and explain three business market characteristics and demand patterns that are different from the consumer market.
3. Differentiate the three types of buying decisions made by organizations and explain the buying center concept.
4. What is the purpose of a travel analysis?
5. How can the amount and nature of a firm's travel be determined?
6. What is the object of the travel dispersion analysis?
7. Distinguish between geographic, volume, and time dispersion.
8. Describe the general trend of airline services since deregulation.
9. What are the three levels of airline service and how do they relate to business aircraft use?
10. What is meant by the statement, "Let the model fit the mission?"
11. Distinguish between the single-engine and light twin-engine aircraft in terms of performance.
12. What are the major criteria for stepping up to a medium twin?
13. When would the use of a corporate helicopter be prudent?
14. What is the significance of determining the use and users of the aircraft?
15. Describe what is meant by the environmental aspects of routes and destinations?
16. Why is it important to determine the frequency of trips?
17. What are the major factors to consider in a performance analysis?
18. What is a payload range chart?
19. Discuss the importance of status of production, trade-in value, and reliability and maintainability in selecting an aircraft.
20. Describe the significance of depreciation expense to a corporation.
21. Distinguish between cost of ownership and cost of use.
22. Provide some examples of fixed costs of use and direct operating costs.
23. Determine the cost per mile for an aircraft that has an estimated annual cost of $50,000; cruise speed of 200 miles per hour; and 500 estimated annual flying hours. If this aircraft has five passenger seats, what is the cost per seat mile?
24. Identify three benefits of a cash flow analysis to the sales process.
25. Use the sample loan amortization schedule to determine the monthly interest on an eight-year, 9.25 percent loan for $450,000.
26. Compound interest is the reciprocal of present value. Explain how prospective aircraft purchasers use net present value analysis in their decision-making process.
27. Describe how break-even analysis can be used as a sales tool.

Scenarios

1. As an intern in the aircraft sales division of Executive Flight Management, you have been tasked with studying the buying center concept and determining the key individuals in each of the five roles in the buying center at Wayne's Widgets, Inc. What are these roles, and how would you figure out the individual in each of these roles within that company?
2. As a new aircraft sales associate with Executive Aircraft Sales, you have been asked to perform a travel analysis of Jeff's Airport Consulting. The only information given to you appears in the following table. Complete the table (similar to Table 10-1) and conduct a full travel analysis for this company.

From Tampa, FL, to destination	Average number of passengers	Total round trips per month	Total annual round trips	Number of one-way miles	Total miles
Lakeland, FL	3	2	24		
Tallahassee, FL	3	3	36		
Miami, FL	3	3	36		
Orlando, FL	2	1	12		
Atlanta, GA	2	1	12		
Nashville, TN	4	1	12		

3. In the beginning phases of conducting a travel analysis for a corporate executive, you realize he is very interested in aviation and he asks you for an explanation of the different types of aircraft that are available and the preferred uses of each type. What do you tell this executive?
4. Using the information gathered in scenario 2, perform an equipment selection process to arrive at three or four aircraft that would appear to meet the needs of Jeff's Airport Consulting.
5. Your manager has asked you to conduct a break-even analysis for a company, East Coast Charter. Determine the total revenue hours required to break even by using the following data.

   Annual total fixed cost = $189,307
   Charter revenue per hour = $1,150
   Direct operating expenses per hour = $708

Bibliography

Prather, C. Daniel. 2009. *General Aviation Marketing and Management: Operating, Marketing, and Managing an FBO.* 3rd ed. Malabar, FL: Krieger Publishing Company.

11

Methods of Acquiring a Business Aircraft

In Chapter 11

Objectives

At the end of this chapter, you should be able to:

1. Compare and contrast the purchase of new versus used aircraft.
2. Give several reasons for the company-owned, management company-operated method of acquiring a business aircraft.
3. List the primary factors on which finance charges on an aircraft loan are based.
4. Describe the four methods available to owners desiring to sell their aircraft.
5. Discuss some of the factors to consider in purchasing a used aircraft.
6. List several of the major points included in an aircraft sales contract.
7. Distinguish between simple interest and add-on interest.
8. Describe floor planning as a financial technique.
9. Determine the retail price of an aircraft using the markup formula.
10. Discuss the advantages and disadvantages of leasing.
11. Compare the capital lease with the operating lease.

12. Discuss the major elements in fractional ownership programs.
13. Identify some of the advantages of fractional ownership.
14. Explain how a firm might use charter aircraft for business purposes.
15. Distinguish between chartering and contract flight service.
16. Summarize the four major methods of acquiring business aircraft.

Introduction

The decision to acquire a business aircraft is a major step for any business. A company that has never owned or operated an aircraft must first determine that an aircraft is a worthwhile acquisition. Companies that already operate aircraft and want to expand or upgrade their fleets possess the aviation experience to guide them in evaluating new equipment. Once there is agreement that an aircraft is desirable, management can select a properly equipped make and model to meet the company's needs.

As previously discussed, need and cost are the basic considerations, but potential users of business aircraft also must weigh many other factors to determine whether an aircraft has a valid place in their organizations. Many companies seek outside advice in making their business aviation decisions. Sales representatives from the aircraft dealers and distributors, as well as specialized aviation consulting firms, offer advice and counsel. Assistance is often available from other companies, including members of NBAA who operate aircraft.

Chapter 10 demonstrated that weighing the potential need for an aircraft usually involves detailed examination of company travel records covering a representative time period to measure total volume and to identify travel patterns. This examination should reveal how many employees travel regularly, which ones do the most traveling, where they go, at what times of the day or week, the typical length of trips, the extent of group travel, and the proximity of frequently visited destinations to airports. The total annual cost of travel and the value per man-hour (VMH) of those traveling are usually considered in comparing airline and automobile travel with a business aircraft.

Because of the wide range of aircraft available, it is important to identify company travel characteristics and requirements as clearly as possible in order to match them with aircraft capabilities. Some companies that have experience with business aircraft have developed internal checklists to help management evaluate and select aircraft.

A great majority of aircraft operated by business firms are owned or leased by the companies that use them, but a growing number of users are choosing fractional ownership. The point is that a company seeking private air transportation can obtain it in a variety of different ways. Although there are many variations and combinations among the methods of acquiring use of a business aircraft, they can be reduced to four basic methods:

1. Company-owned—new or used
   a. Company-owned aircraft—in-house flight department
   b. Company-owned aircraft—management company operated
   c. Joint ownership—in-house flight department
   d. Co-ownership—management company operated
2. Leasing—wet or dry
   a. Capital lease
   b. Operating lease
3. Fractional ownership
4. Charter—individual or contract

What might be an appropriate method for one company may be completely inappropriate for another. Like a suit of clothes, the method has to fit the company's needs to wear well. This chapter will discuss the four basic methods, along with slight variations.

Company-Owned Aircraft

The principal advantages of a company-owned aircraft are optimum utility, convenience, and safety. Consequently, business aviation departments get maximum use from their aircraft. All business owners conduct flight operations in accordance with FAA regulations, typically 14 CFR Part 91, but operations may be conducted under Part 125 or Part 135.

Usually, one company-owned aircraft, efficiently used, can satisfy 75 percent of the air transportation needs of the people it is intended to serve. Anything over 75 percent will usually necessitate special charter or lease arrangements. Many companies have different types of aircraft in their fleets to meet various needs.

A whole aircraft in-house flight department affords the highest possible levels of control, service, and security/confidentiality. If there are no intercompany scheduling conflicts or maintenance downtime, the aircraft will always be available. If the aircraft is not available, the owner can use charter, airlines, timeshare, or interchange to meet flight demands.

A **time-sharing agreement** involves the lease of an aircraft with flight crew to another party, and no charge is made for the flights conducted under that arrangement other than the following:

1. Fuel, oil, lubricants, and other additives
2. Travel expenses of the crew, including food, lodging, and ground transportation
3. Hangar and tie-down costs away from the aircraft's base of operations
4. Insurance obtained for the specific flight
5. Landing fees, airport taxes, and similar assessments
6. Customs, foreign permits, and similar fees directly related to the flight
7. In-flight food and beverages
8. Passenger ground transportation
9. Flight planning and weather contract services
10. An additional charge equal to 100 percent of the expenses listed under number 1

Under an **interchange agreement**, a person or company leases its aircraft to another company in exchange for equal time, when needed, on the other company's aircraft, and no charge, assessment, or fee is made, except that a charge may be made not to exceed the difference between the cost of owning, operating, and maintaining the two aircraft.

A company-owned aircraft is the most flexible method of business flying. As owner, the company is not subject to restrictions imposed by charterers or lessors with regard to insurance requirements, operating restrictions, and other contractual provisions. On the other hand, having an owned aircraft can be inflexible if the company is not getting the hourly utilization expected, or if it has purchased the wrong aircraft and must dispose of it.

The owner maintains total control over and manages aircraft operations. As such, the owner is completely liable for all operations. All flight department personnel are on the owner's payroll, and the owner must deal with in-house personnel issues. Crew quality is consistent and owner-controlled, and the owner is directly in charge of training crew and maintenance personnel.

The cost per hour flown is the lowest of any of the methods of operation as long as the annual hourly utilization is achieved. Ideally, a company should use its own aircraft as extensively as possible to derive the greatest productivity from business flying.

Operating costs vary depending on aircraft use, and the lowest cost of operations is realized at reasonable utilization levels (more than 400 flight hours per year), although deadheading or positioning costs can play a factor. To help offset costs, a flight department can opt to charter out its aircraft, but only after receiving Part 135 approval to do so.

Since the department operates under 14 CFR Part 91, the federal excise tax (FET) does not apply; instead, the noncommercial fuel tax is applied. The aircraft may be fully depreciated over a six-year period, realizing the maximum tax benefit for the company. However, state sales tax must be paid on the acquisition cost. This option requires a higher capital investment of the negotiated acquisition cost, but the owner has the freedom to purchase any aircraft at any price. The owner also has complete control over how the aircraft is outfitted. In addition, the aircraft can be sold, upgraded, or downgraded at any time.

COMPANY OWNED, MANAGEMENT COMPANY OPERATED

A **company-owned, management company-operated** aircraft is attractive to firms not wanting to take on the responsibility of operating their own aircraft. Under contract, the management company provides crew, maintenance, and all administrative responsibilities. Because of this arrangement, the owner shares liability with the management company. Flight department personnel are not on the owner's payroll.

This method can provide excellent, customized service. Like a company-owned, in-house flight department, the aircraft is nearly always available. If the aircraft is not available due to maintenance or scheduling conflicts, the owner can use charter, airlines, timeshare, or interchange to meet flight demands.

The level of safety can vary widely, depending on the competence and operating philosophy of the particular management company. Nearly all management companies that offer this type of service operate under Part 135 of the Federal Aviation Regulations, which is designed for commercial operators and requires higher minimum safety standards than Part 91 (which is the FAR most company-owned and operated aircraft are operated under). However, these are minimum regulations and not closely scrutinized by the FAA. As a result, there is considerable variance in the safety standards adhered to by individual management companies.

As a rule, the company-owned, management company-operated method is expensive simply because the company has to pay for the services provided. One of the major selling points for using management company services is that the company owning the aircraft will be able to save some fixed costs by selling time on the aircraft when the owning company is not using it. In some cases, selling time is valid and workable. Operating costs vary depending on aircraft use, and the lowest cost of operation is realized at reasonable utilization levels, but deadheading or positioning costs can increase these costs.

Simply stated, aircraft management firms offer companies operating one or two aircraft with the economies of scale generally available only to large fleet operators. The scope of services differs widely among the many aircraft management firms. Most of the larger firms provide flight planning, 24-hour central dispatch and flight following, storage, insurance, training, backup pilots, and most maintenance. Some firms have agreements with their customers whereby each customer has an entire fleet of aircraft at its call, if necessary. For example, if a company owns one aircraft but needs four others for some special purpose one day, it can borrow time, in effect, on these other aircraft, with the stipulation that it will repay this borrowed time by permitting other companies to use its aircraft.

In addition to time-sharing agreements, virtually all aircraft management firms can charter a customer's aircraft under a commercial certificate, which also improves utilization while helping to offset some of the client's operating costs. The owners pay the noncommercial fuel tax as long as they maintain possession of and control over the aircraft. The aircraft may be fully depreciated over a six-year period, realizing the maximum tax benefit for the company. However, state sales tax must be paid on the acquisition cost.

This option requires higher capital investment of the negotiated acquisition cost, but the owner has the freedom to purchase any aircraft at any price. The owner also has complete control of aircraft options. The aircraft can be sold, upgraded, or downgraded at any time.

In summary, there are five distinct advantages of using a management company for aircraft operations:

1. It maintains an arm's-length arrangement with the owner in which all the aircraft-related administrative functions are performed outside the owner's company, thus relieving the need to commit internal resources.
2. It can deliver Part 135 charter revenues back to the owner to help defray costs.
3. It removes from the company any political or employee-sensitive, aircraft-related cost accounting.
4. It provides anonymity and security because an owner's aircraft becomes part of a fleet of many owners, and those who might be trying to use internet tracking programs or the FAA website to identify a particular aircraft user find it extremely difficult.
5. It maintains a pragmatic perspective toward the owner's aircraft. The aircraft is looked upon as a business asset detached from personal involvement, perhaps unlike an aircraft operated by an in-house flight department.

JOINT OWNERSHIP, IN-HOUSE FLIGHT DEPARTMENT

The **joint ownership, in-house flight department** arrangement is defined in 14 CFR §91.501(c)(1) as an "arrangement whereby one of the registered joint owners of an airplane employs and furnishes the flight crew for that airplane and each of the registered joint owners pays a share of the charge specified in the agreement." Under this agreement, one registered owner may provide the flight crew and the other registered joint owner(s) may pay a share of the fixed ownership costs as specified in the agreement. Each joint owner is responsible for individually covering their own direct operating costs. All joint owners must be named on the registration certificate of the aircraft.

A joint-ownership, in-house flight department arrangement can also provide excellent and customized service. However, aircraft availability requires coordination between the joint owners and advance planning. If the aircraft is not available, either owner can use charter, airlines, timeshare, or interchange to meet flight demands.

Owners maintain control over and manage aircraft operations, and the liability for these operations is shared by both owners. Operating costs vary, depending on aircraft use (again, the lowest cost of operations is realized at reasonable utilization levels), and deadheading or positioning costs increase these costs. To help offset operating costs, the owners can opt to charter out their aircraft, but this may put more of a squeeze on aircraft availability.

Owners pay the noncommercial fuel tax since they operate the aircraft under Part 91. However, FET charges could apply if an owner's aircraft share does not closely match the percentage of use. For example, Company A owns 90 percent of an aircraft, while Company B owns 10 percent, but each uses the aircraft equally. Because Company B's share is not proportional to its aircraft use, the IRS deems this to be a commercial operation (and FET applies), even though operations are conducted under Part 91. Aircraft depreciation is shared by the owners and they must pay state sales tax on their share of the aircraft acquisition fee.

This option requires a higher capital investment for the negotiated acquisition cost on the part of the owners. They must also agree on what aircraft to purchase and how to outfit it. Either owner can sell its share in the aircraft at any time, and the aircraft can be sold, upgraded, or downgraded as needed.

CO-OWNERSHIP, MANAGEMENT COMPANY OPERATED

A **co-ownership, management company operated** arrangement also provides customizable service, but aircraft availability requires coordination and planning. If the aircraft is not available, either owner can use charter, airlines, timeshare, or interchange to meet flight demands.

Owners maintain control over, but delegate the management of, aircraft operations. Liability for these operations is shared by the owners and the management company. Flight department personnel are not on the owners' payroll, and crew quality is consistent. The owners also delegate control of crew and maintenance personnel training to the management company.

Operating costs are inversely proportional to aircraft use, and deadheading or positioning costs will increase these costs. Annual operating costs may be higher than joint ownership due to management fees. To help offset operating costs, the owners can opt to charter out the aircraft, but this could adversely affect availability.

Owners pay the noncommercial fuel tax as long as they maintain possession of and control over the aircraft. However, the aforementioned share/use percentage rule applies, as well. Aircraft depreciation is shared by the owners, and they must pay state sales tax on their share of the aircraft acquisition price.

This option requires the owners to ante up a high capital investment of the negotiated acquisition cost. They must also agree on what aircraft to purchase and how to outfit it. Either owner can sell its share in the aircraft at any time, and the aircraft can be sold, upgraded, or downgraded as needed.

NEW VERSUS USED AIRCRAFT

The demand for new and used business aircraft has been strong since the mid-1990s. Although many companies have considered fractional ownership or charter, others have realized that a company-owned aircraft is an excellent choice. It will remain the prime source of large and small business aircraft. Used aircraft are generally less expensive to purchase; however, prices have drifted upward in recent years, reflecting scarcity of certain models, particularly trainers. However, an intelligent decision about buying new or used should draw on all aspects of expense, not simply the purchasing price.

Many new aircraft dealers and distributors are active in the used aircraft market because they frequently take older aircraft in trade against the sale of new aircraft. Also, some firms specialize in handling used aircraft. These firms, operating similarly to used automobile wholesalers, usually sell in large numbers, often to dealers and distributors overseas; they are also active in the reconditioning of individual aircraft for sale at retail. There are also brokers for the sale of used aircraft.

Although the used aircraft market can be compared to the used automobile market in some respects, it is very different in at least one critical aspect. While the buyer of a used automobile might buy a "lemon," this is definitely not the case with used aircraft. Aircraft must be licensed by the FAA when initially put into service and then must be relicensed annually thereafter. The licensing procedure requires the aircraft to be subjected to periodic inspections to ensure that it is being maintained in airworthy condition. Records of inspection, along with records of maintenance and repair activities, are a permanent part of each aircraft's records and are passed along from one owner to another. Thus, it is possible to get a good picture of a used aircraft's current condition by studying the records of its usage, maintenance, and repair. This requirement for regular inspections of aircraft and written records of repairs and overhauls may also partially explain why an active used aircraft market exists today and why there is ready acceptance of well-maintained, used aircraft by buyers. In addition, many used aircraft have enjoyed stable market values at a high percentage of their original purchase prices. The AOPA provides prospective aircraft buyers with tips, including a checklist of special precautions for prospective used aircraft purchasers, on its website (AOPA, n.d.).

Good pre-owned aircraft represent substantial value. Eighty-five percent of all corporate aircraft sold in the United States are pre-owned (Young-Brown 2021). A company can buy a five-year-old aircraft, reconfigure the interior to its specific requirements, upgrade the avionics with the latest safety enhancements, and have the equivalent of a brand-new aircraft at a fraction of the cost. The company's financial exposure is minimal, because, historically, used aircraft hold their values over time. They are very liquid assets. A five-year-old aircraft can retain 80 to 90 percent of its original value, and many aircraft, such as King Airs, have actually appreciated beyond their original cost.

Despite the active sales in used aircraft in recent years, new aircraft still offer some very sound advantages. First, financing is apt to be more liberal on a new aircraft, with lower interest rates and longer repayment terms. Lending institutions tend to feel that their investments are better secured with new rather than used equipment and will make some financial concessions to encourage new purchases.

Similarly, insurance companies are generally more eager to insure new rather than used aircraft, and their rates reflect that attitude. A new aircraft has no wear on the components, so there is a greater statistical probability that everything will function normally for a longer period of time than on a used aircraft.

A new aircraft warranty can also be an advantage, particularly if a firm is considering buying a sophisticated single-engine or twin-engine aircraft with complex systems. Though most modern aircraft are reasonably trouble-free, there is definitely a correlation between maintenance cost and systems complexity; the more complex an aircraft, the more it will cost to maintain.

Another consideration is the fact that a new aircraft has no maintenance or operation history. The first buyer has the opportunity to control the break-in and day-to-day flight record of the aircraft. A firm can strictly regulate operating practices and make certain the aircraft is properly treated to maximize utility and efficiency. Though logbooks can give some indications of how well or poorly a used aircraft was treated, there is no way to know for sure.

High among the benefits of buying a new aircraft are the advantages that go with better performance, greater comfort, improved efficiency, and personalized appearance. Innovations in aerodynamics and powerplants often allow new aircraft to realize better speed and efficiency than older models. State-of-the-art avionics are part of the newer equipment. While it is true that new communication radios and navigation equipment may be fitted to older aircraft, avionics installations typically will be simpler and cleaner if done at the factory when the aircraft is built. Also, a buyer may realize a lower price purchasing new radios with the aircraft, because the manufacturer can benefit from volume discounts not always available to outside vendors.

Cabin comfort is a subjective judgment, but there is little doubt that interior appointments and even cabin size improves with newer models. Today's aircraft commonly offer more luxurious and durable fabrics and leathers than older models. Buying new also offers a firm the option of personalizing the paint and interior to its individual taste. How important these latter items are to a firm in evaluating a new versus used aircraft is really a management decision.

MAINTENANCE

Whether purchasing a new or used aircraft, maintenance is a major factor that prospective owners need to study carefully. Aircraft must be maintained according to strict FAA rules and regulations. Good maintenance can be costly, but it is infinitely less expensive than having an engine quit somewhere between airports. Also, a well-maintained aircraft will bring a higher price when it is time to trade it in.

There are hundreds of FBOs located on virtually every sizable airport in the country, as well as around the world, that provide maintenance. These businesses must meet stringent FAA requirements. Many FBOs are also the authorized service centers for the major airframe and engine manufacturers.

Larger corporate operators of business aircraft have their own in-house maintenance organization, or possibly they share a maintenance operation with two or three partners. This concept is generally only viable with companies operating a fleet of aircraft.

FINANCING THE AIRCRAFT PURCHASE

Most companies have lines of credit available through their banks. However, it is often preferable to keep this credit available for other needs, such as short-term borrowing, working capital requirements, or capital improvements. There are a number of aircraft financing specialists, including banks, finance companies, and the manufacturer's finance organizations. The majority of these institutions finance nationwide and are able to handle most transactions through their website or banking app. Although phone calls are still common, more information is submitted via the company's website with email interaction to create the most convenience for customers. With the initial interaction, preliminary financial information is provided along with a complete description of the aircraft. Scanned or downloaded financial statements will need to be uploaded for the company's review. A credit investigation and credit report are handled entirely online. In many instances, a decision is made on the loan within hours of receipt of the financial statements.

Most finance charges on aircraft loans are based primarily on four factors:

1. *Amount of the loan*—A larger loan may warrant a lower rate than a small loan.
2. *Amount of the down payment*—Greater equity in the aircraft results in less risk, thus a lower rate.
3. *Terms of the loan*—Lenders tend to look for a higher rate over a long term as a hedge against inflation.
4. *Credit strength of the borrower*—The most credit-worthy customers will enjoy the best rates.

Most financial institutions will require a down payment of 20 percent on a used aircraft and 25 percent on a new aircraft. The additional amount for new aircraft is because of increased depreciation that occurs during the first year. Lenders experienced in aircraft finance keep abreast of the total aircraft market and consider this in setting down payment rules on specific aircraft. If a company can purchase an aircraft at an exceptionally good price, a smaller down payment would be requested. Once again, terms of the loan and credit of the borrower are factors in determining the necessary amount of cash required on the purchase.

The majority of aircraft loans are repaid in monthly installments. Aircraft loan specialists know that some borrowers have specific needs. Repayment plans have been set up on quarterly, semiannual, or annual schedules. Occasionally, fixed-principal payments plus interest are arranged. Under this plan, each payment is smaller than the one before it since interest is less as the principal balance declines. Occasionally, a company may desire smaller monthly payments than would normally be necessary to repay the loan. The lender may be able to arrange such a loan with a balloon payment at the end, which would be paid in a lump sum or would be refinanced. These basic plans vary among aircraft lending institutions.

Lending institutions specializing in aircraft financing are equipped to handle the paperwork involved with aircraft purchase and financing in an orderly and rapid manner. They have direct connections with the FAA in Oklahoma City and can obtain a title search on an aircraft in a matter of hours. There are often documents pertaining to the aircraft that may cloud the title, such as forms unrecorded for some reason or old liens which have not been released. The lender can usually clear up these problems in a short time. The registration of an aircraft is also handled by the lender. This is an area where the financial institution can be of considerable assistance to the borrower.

Strong economic growth in recent years and unprecedented demand for business aircraft have created a favorable climate for financing aircraft. First, banks and financial institutions that have not previously been willing to fund business aircraft purchases have overcome their preconceptions about the market in a bid to share in this period of strong demand. Second, relatively low interest rates and abundant capital markets have combined to make borrowing an attractive and feasible proposition. That being said, rates are variable and by late 2022 had increased significantly.

With new sources of capital in the business aviation loan market, there have been greater financing choices and more competitive deals. The residual values of business aircraft have proven themselves to be stronger than those of commercial aircraft, which has motivated additional sources of capital.

Internet and app-based finance tools have further expanded the options available to business aircraft purchasers. Following the trend in retail banking, there is now a competitive marketplace with multiple firms offering highly competitive interest rates. This has been possible due to the reduced overhead and greater efficiency made possible by technology. At the same time, however, a degree of knowledge related to aircraft financing and acquisition options goes a long way to making sense of the marketplace.

Aircraft manufacturers also play a vital role in securing funding for sales of both new and used aircraft in their broad portfolio of products. However, manufacturers generally prioritize their own financing options. A savvy buyer must be aware of this and shop around for the best rates. After all, interest costs can greatly impact total out-of-pocket costs.

Buying and Selling Used Aircraft

THE MARKET

The sources of used aircraft are numerous. Aircraft manufacturers estimate that one out of every four new aircraft go to first-time owners, while three out of four new aircraft go to individuals and businesses trading in an older aircraft. This chain reaction provides a constant supply of pre-owned aircraft and puts the FBO actively in the used aircraft business. Often the profit on the transaction is not fully realized until the trade-in aircraft is successfully sold. Other major sources for used aircraft are (1) businesses in distressed industries; (2) individual owners; (3) repossessions from banks, leasing companies, and finance companies; (4) foreign sellers; and (5) corporate owners who desire to replace their aircraft.

Owners desiring to sell their aircraft can approach the sale in one of four ways. The best approach will depend upon the owner's desire to receive top dollar for their aircraft, the owner's know-how in handling the details of the transfers, and their ability to expose the aircraft to a sufficient number of qualified prospects. Following are the four approaches and the advantages and disadvantages of each:

1. *Sale by owner.* If a buyer can be found quickly, this approach has the potential to generate the highest profit. However, the owner must have tracked the market well enough to know precisely what the aircraft is worth. Further, owners may have difficulty in generating adequate exposure for their aircraft. That being said, the internet has definitely made this process easier, as websites such as Trade-A-Plane can be very useful. Finally, the owner likely lacks the expertise required to handle the many details of the exchange.
2. *Sale by a broker.* A broker acts as an agent to bring a buyer and a seller together. This method involves listing the aircraft with an established broker who will then represent the owner in the sale of the aircraft. When the sale has been completed, the broker will deduct a specific percentage of the selling price for their services. A 5 percent commission, for example, reimburses the broker for the exposure, know-how, and prompt action. The broker will handle all details in the transfer, saving the owner considerable time.
3. *Sale to a dealer.* From an economic standpoint, selling or trading an aircraft to a dealer is like selling it wholesale. The dealer must buy the aircraft at a price which allows a markup sufficient to cover expenses on the transaction and generate an appropriate profit. A dealer takes physical possession of the aircraft for resale, often upgrading the interior or avionics before it goes on the market. This method is the quickest and simplest of the approaches, but with an obvious cost.
4. *Sale to an original equipment manufacturer (OEM).* An OEM's resale group normally offers good after-sales support, pilot training, and referrals to insurance agencies, FBOs, and maintenance shops that have experience with the particular aircraft. At the same time, OEMs usually carry out an extensive inspection of any trade-in or resale aircraft in their own shops before it goes on the market. This can mitigate a substantial amount of risk to the pre-owned aircraft customer, but also adds to the cost.

Currently, about 80 percent of used business aircraft transactions worldwide are completed through independent dealers and brokers. The choice between a dealer, broker, or OEM is often not clear-cut, since each sector has its advantages. OEMs are a particularly good source for higher-valued business aircraft because of their quality business practices. By the same token, there are many ethical brokers and dealers that present a good option.

Although many late-model aircraft changing hands are normally still under a manufacturer's warranty, which will transfer to the new owner, most dealers and brokers sell older aircraft on an as-is basis without warranties. For this reason, buying an aircraft from a dealer with an extensive maintenance capability is often advisable, especially if that dealer is situated near where the individual or company plans to base the aircraft. However, this may not be feasible.

While most independent dealers do not offer warranties on used aircraft, those with in-house maintenance capability are more receptive to negotiating special after-sale customer-support programs. But even without on-site maintenance, independent dealers offer some advantages not always available from manufacturers that sell the aircraft they have taken in trade for new equipment. The dealers tend to be smaller and more streamlined and, for this reason, decisions as to what will be included in the price of an aircraft can be done more rapidly because there is no large bureaucracy to deal with. Arrangements include upgrades, modifications, and maintenance that needs to be done on the aircraft before it is delivered to the buyer. Importantly, a reputable dealer is always trying to build a special relationship with customers to generate return customers and additional sales.

Although dealers and OEMs should be focused on providing an aircraft to meet customer needs, they may be more concerned about selling aircraft in current inventory, regardless of customer desires. Thus, it is important for prospective buyers to be firm as to their specific needs, rather than purchasing an aircraft that provides subpar performance for their situation.

Prices for a quality used aircraft depend on recent market trends for the specific model being considered. The best benchmark for appraisal is what the prices have been for the past six months. This information can be obtained from dealers or brokers, who can research this through the four recognized database sources: the Aircraft Bluebook, VREF, JETNET, and AMSTAT.

Although prices of late-model used aircraft tend to be high, some buyers are willing to spend the money, since waiting for the delivery of a new aircraft can average one to two years from the time they are ordered. Although a used aircraft may cost less, many older aircraft require significant upgrades or refurbishment that can be time consuming, particularly in a tight market.

PURCHASING USED AIRCRAFT

It is important to examine the history of the aircraft, regardless of its age, by making a comprehensive inspection of all records pertaining to the aircraft's operation and maintenance. Buyers are encouraged to have the aircraft inspected by a qualified mechanic (and a pilot, in the case of higher-valued business aircraft). If incomplete maintenance logbooks are discovered, the buyer should initiate an in-depth research effort to fill in any gaps in the aircraft's maintenance history.

Some manufacturers who accept trade-in aircraft actually interview past owners and speak with the managers of facilities that have maintained the aircraft. The company will also contact the FAA to find out if any Form 337s have been filed for the aircraft. An FAA Form 337 must be completed in the event of a major alteration or repair to an aircraft. Form 337s are examined because the information they provide may have a bearing on any work that the buyer might want to perform on the aircraft. If the buyer is considering a significant upgrade to the avionics or a completely new interior, the Form 337 will indicate what weight-and-balance changes have been made as a result of the alterations.

In addition to the maintenance log, the prospective buyer should review the airframe log, which indicates hours flown and cycles, as well as incidents and accidents. A complete airframe log should also indicate compliance with past airworthiness directives (ADs) as well as the manufacturer's recommended inspection schedules. Airworthiness directives are used to notify aircraft owners of unsafe conditions about their aircraft and to prescribe the conditions under which the aircraft may continue to be flown. The FAA maintains a database of ADs on its website. ADs should be searched by make/model of aircraft to verify which ADs have applied to the aircraft in question (and determine if they were addressed appropriately).

Airworthiness certificates are issued by a representative of the FAA after the aircraft has been inspected, is found to meet the requirements of the Federal Aviation Regulations (FARs), and is in a condition for safe operation. This certificate is displayed in the aircraft and is transferred when the aircraft is sold. It is important to note that the standard airworthiness certificate remains in effect as long as the aircraft receives the required maintenance and is properly registered in the United States. It does not assure that the aircraft is currently in a safe operating condition. A general guideline when looking at logbooks is to note the ratio of flight hours to cycles. Fewer cycles (takeoffs and landings) normally means that less stress has been put on the airframe. As a rule of thumb, buyers should not consider an aircraft that has fewer than two flight hours per cycle, because the aircraft will probably require some near-term heavy maintenance. Pressurized aircraft can become fatigued over time with excessive pressurization/de-pressurization cycles.

Once the logbooks have been inspected, a demonstration flight that allows the buyer to make a trial run may be in order. Most OEMs and dealers will permit this. However, unlike a short flight in the vicinity of the airport in a small aircraft in which the seller usually bears the cost, the buyer will have to pay the seller for any expenses incurred on a long demonstration flight.

For most heavy turboprop and jet equipment, a demonstration flight over a planned route is very desirable. If there is going to be a problem with the pressurization system, it will likely occur when the aircraft reaches flight altitude. For those companies that do not want to make a demonstration flight in the form of an actual point-to-point trip, a test flight of at least one hour at different altitudes is recommended.

In addition, any squawks revealed in the demonstration or short test flight allow the buyer to go into the all-important pre-purchase inspection with at least some knowledge of what should be looked at more closely. The former owner's maintenance facility is likely to be aware of something that perhaps was not entered into the logbook by a previous owner, since the authorized service center or OEM may have done the repairs. This is especially true if the aircraft has been maintained under some type of factory maintenance plan, which is always a good reference when considering a pre-owned aircraft.

Additionally, the buyer should ask if the engines are on a recognized engine management program, because those that are will have a complete set of maintenance records. Diligence at this point can avoid costly repairs later.

PRE-PURCHASE INSPECTION

The aircraft buyer should approach a **pre-purchase inspection** in a proactive fashion. The first thing to examine is any sign of corrosion and cracking. Corrosion is irreversible in its deteriorating effects on the airframe, and it is important to know whether damage has been done to the aircraft. It is also important to know if maintenance squawks have been addressed to ensure that there are absolutely no hidden problems waiting to appear.

Technicians should perform a thorough engine inspection. They should check compression, examine inside with a borescope, and perform an oil analysis. If there is a problem with the engine, that should be factored into the purchase price. Technicians should check the mechanical components, pulleys, linkages, and other mechanical parts. These are readily replaced, if necessary, but needed repairs should be identified prior to the purchase, not after. It is important for the buyer to look for functional avionics. If the airframe and engine are acceptable but avionics equipment needs upgrading, it should be installed at the time of purchase so that it can be included in the financing package and possible dealer discounts on avionics at time of purchase can be used. This is also the time to upgrade the interior if it needs work.

A complete pre-purchase inspection can take from several hours for a light single-engine aircraft to seven or eight days for a typical business jet. With the advice of the person who has reviewed the logbooks, the buyer should go to the shop with a complete written description of the specific items the pre-purchase inspection is to cover. This is important because the OEMs and most service centers will offer a pre-packaged type of pre-purchase inspection. It is important to make sure that the inspection covers anything not included in the package that the adviser recommends.

If the aircraft under consideration is almost due for a major inspection, the buyer may want to use that event as the basis for any pre-purchase inspection. The major inspection that would have to be done anyway could be the foundation for the inspection.

Pre-purchase inspections are not free. Sellers are not obligated to cover the pre-purchase inspection costs. An inspection on a light single-engine aircraft can cost several hundred dollars, while one on a turbojet-powered business aircraft may cost $8,000–30,000, depending on its size and complexity.

Although the buyer normally pays for the inspection, the buyer can negotiate with the seller to pay for repairs that might be needed based on what is discovered. Most reputable sellers will agree to do that, even though the exact repairs and their dollar value will be negotiated.

In summary, the goal of every pre-purchase inspection is to find what needs to be corrected so the aircraft will be airworthy and ready to fly upon acceptance. The buyer may have decided beforehand that the aircraft needs repainting, the avionics suite upgraded, or a new interior installed. Even if the buyer plans to pay for these upgrades, it may be beneficial to discuss with the seller to ensure that the desired upgrades are appropriate for the aircraft. The important thing is that the aircraft is flyable with no problems upon acceptance.

The following list includes the major items to be considered in evaluating a used aircraft:

1. General:
   a. What are the total hours on the airframe?
   b. How many hours were flown while seller had it?
   c. What is the date of latest annual inspection?
   d. When was the latest 100-hour inspection?
   e. How many hours since the latest annual or 100-hour inspection?
   f. Have you checked carefully for metal corrosion inside wings and tail?
   g. Are there any signs of touch-up painting? Has the aircraft been in any accidents?
   h. Are all parts readily available?
   i. How many gallons of fuel does it use per hour?
   j. How many quarts of oil are required?
   k. Does the aircraft look clean and well-cared for?
2. Engine:
   a. What is the total time? Has the engine ever been overhauled?
   b. Has it had a top or major overhaul? When?
   c. What is the total time since overhaul?
   d. Is the engine clean and free of rust and corrosion?
   e. Is there evidence of oil leaks?
   f. Is there evidence of chafing of hoses?
   g. Are there metal particles in the oil screen?
   h. Does the engine turn up to maximum-rated RPM on the ground?
   i. Have you checked the cylinders for compression?
   j. How much will a new or exchange engine cost?
3. Propeller:
   a. Is the finish in good condition?
   b. Is there any looseness in the propeller?
   c. Have all propeller bulletins been complied with?
   d. Is there any evidence of oil leaks?
   e. Is the spinner in good condition and secure?
4. Wings:
   a. Are there cuts in the leading edges?
   b. Are there dents?

5. Controls:
   a. Do all surfaces move freely and evenly?
   b. Are hinges in good shape?
   c. Do control cables have proper tension? Are they securely attached?
   d. Are cables rusty or worn looking?
   e. Is everything properly secured?
6. Landing gear:
   a. Are tires worn or cracked?
7. Doors and windows:
   a. Do they open easily?
   b. Are hinges loose or twisted?
8. Cabin interior:
   a. Is upholstery clean?
   b. Is the windshield in good condition?
   c. Do the seats move easily and lock securely?
   d. Does the heater work?
9. Radios and instruments:
   a. Have you checked all radios and instruments?
   b. Are all installations neat?
   c. Does VOR equipment meet accuracy tolerances?
   d. Is there a record of VOR equipment checks for IFR operation?
   e. Are transmitters FCC type-accepted?
   f. Are they listed on the FCC license?
   g. Are all instruments properly calibrated?
   h. Do gyros precess excessively?
   i. Was an altimeter/static system inspection for IFR completed within the last 24 months?

NEGOTIATING THE PURCHASE

When all inspections and evaluations are satisfactory, it is time to make the owner an offer. The offer should allow for an adequate markup. This format will allow the dealer to put money into the aircraft to make it attractive to a prospective buyer. A dealer attempting to build a sound aircraft sales business will not follow the principal of "Buy the aircraft for as little as possible, put as little money as possible in the clean-up phase, and then sell the aircraft at the highest price possible."

When the offer has been accepted, a binder is given along with the signing of a simple sales agreement. The sales agreement identifies the parties, the specific aircraft by N-number, price, date of closing, and any other terms or conditions of the sale.

This is the definitive purchase agreement spelling out all of the criteria that must be met before the aircraft is accepted. For example, sales contracts generally state that the aircraft will be delivered to the buyer in airworthy condition as a baseline, but they can also include all of the conditions agreed to. They could include repairs, refurbishment, the completion of a successful test flight, and/or the delivery time and date. If a certain component the buyer wants installed is not available by the time the aircraft is scheduled for delivery, it is important that the buyer and seller have an understanding that the component will be installed by a specific date.

With all the points to be covered in buying a used aircraft, the final responsibility for what is ultimately delivered rests with the buyer. The buyer must beware.

The sample sales contract shown in Figure 11-1 covers many points aimed at protecting the interests of the buyer and seller. Obviously, the particular points in an agreement of this type are open to negotiations originating from either side.

(Buyer's name) ("Buyer") hereby formally offers to purchase one *(manufacturer) (model)* bearing *(manufacturer's Serial No.)* and *(FAA Registration No.)* ("Aircraft") from *(Seller's name)* ("Seller") for an agreed-upon price of $_______USD subject to the following terms and conditions:

1. Receipt by Seller within _____hours of a deposit in the amount of $_________USD from Buyer, which shall be refundable to Buyer in whole or in part as specified herein.
2. Seller has made representations to Buyer that the subject Aircraft, with the specifications as presented to Buyer on __________*(date)*, is in good working order and properly maintained, that the paint and interior as ____________*(representative condition)*, and that it will be delivered to Buyer in an airworthy condition with no fuel, oil, or hydraulic leaks, and with all integral components and systems in normal operating order.
3. Seller represents that it is the legal owner of the Aircraft, holding good and beneficial title thereof, and at the time of delivery will be able to transfer free and clear title to the Aircraft to Buyer on or before __________*(date)*.
4. Seller shall make the Aircraft available to Buyer at ____________*(location)* no later than __________*(date)* to allow Buyer to perform a pre-purchase inspection, which inspection shall be completed no later than __________*(date)*, for purposes of verification of specifications and representations as to appearance and condition. The cost of performing this inspection shall be borne by Buyer; the cost of positioning the Aircraft shall be borne by Seller.
5. Upon completion of the above inspection, Buyer may, at its sole and absolute discretion, elect not to proceed with the purchase, such decision to be made within _____hours of completion of the inspection. In that event, Seller shall immediately refund to Buyer the deposit monies previously tendered, less Seller's direct expenses for moving the Aircraft to and from ___________*(location of inspection)*. However, if the inspection reveals the representations of the condition of the Aircraft were knowingly or significantly inaccurate, and Buyer's election not to purchase is based on these revelations, then the deposit monies held by Seller shall be immediately returned to Buyer in full, and Buyer shall not be liable or responsible to Seller for any costs incurred by Seller whatsoever.
6. If, after completion of the inspection, Buyer wishes to proceed with the purchase, Buyer will notify Seller within _____hours of such intent, and Seller hereby agrees to rectify, at Seller's expense, any discrepancies revealed by the inspection.
7. Upon such notification to proceed, Buyer's deposit shall become binding and nonrefundable pending structure and execution of a contract of sale to be finalized within ____days, and delivery of the Aircraft on or before __________*(date)*. Both parties agree to exercise their respective best efforts to formulate and finalize this contract.
8. Seller, upon receipt of this offer to purchase, will immediately notify Buyer in writing by letter, e-mail, or fax of Seller's understanding, acceptance, and agreement with the terms and conditions herein.

This sample is for informational purposes only and is not intended to be used as a legal contract. Consult a qualified attorney for legal advice.

Figure 11-1. Sample sales contract.

Before the closing date, the buyer should initiate a search of the records and encumbrances affecting ownership of the aircraft with the FAA. Copies of aircraft records can be requested via the FAA website at registry.faa.gov. A title search company may also be used to perform this search. When the title search is received, it will show the present owner, the lien-holder if any, and the dollar amount of the lien.

AIRCRAFT REGISTRATION

After purchasing the used aircraft, a **certificate of aircraft registration** must be secured from the FAA Aircraft Registry. An aircraft is eligible for registration only if it is owned by a citizen of the United States or a governmental unit and is not registered under the laws of any foreign country. An Aircraft Registration Application, AC Form 8050-1, must be completed and submitted to the FAA.

When applying for a certificate of aircraft registration, an Aircraft Bill of Sale, AC Form 8050-2, must also be submitted. Until the permanent certificate of aircraft registration is received, the pink copy of the application serves as a temporary certificate for 90 days and must be carried in the aircraft.

Financing

Financing the acquisition of an aircraft, while possibly expensive, can be facilitated using any of three basic financing alternatives: cash, installment loans, and floor planning contracts.

Paying cash for expensive inventory, like aircraft, is generally considered unwise. Most managers of FBOs need capital for operating expenses and therefore must look to outside sources for funds to purchase used aircraft. Paying cash is the simplest of the three methods, but usually not practical.

To build adequate levels of inventory, newer aircraft dealers will turn to installment loans for their source of funds. These types of loans are available from banks and finance companies like Textron Financial Corporation and CIT Corporation. Financing aircraft inventory by this method requires equal monthly payments over a period of six months or more. The payments include an interest charge and a partial principal payment. Financial institutions offer loans on either a simple interest basis or on an add-on interest basis.

Simple interest is charged only on the outstanding balance of the loan. The required monthly payment can be determined from financial tables or by multiplying the stated interest rate by the outstanding balance at the end of each month. A $50,000 one-year loan at 12 percent APR (annual percentage rate) would require monthly payments of $4,442.50. Since the interest is charged only on the outstanding balance of the loan, the annual percentage rate under this method of financing equals the stated rate.

The add-on interest method of determining monthly payments is commonly used in aircraft financing and results in a much higher APR than does the simple interest method. The one-year $50,000 loan with a stated interest rate of 12 percent used in the above example would require monthly payments of $4,666.50 with the add-on method. Aircraft dealers need to understand the difference between simple and add-on interest methods of computing finance changes to efficiently finance their aircraft inventory.

Established aircraft dealers will employ the use of **floor planning** contracts to assist them in maintaining a good selection of aircraft. Floor planning is a financial arrangement whereby the bank, or other financial institution, will provide the dealer with short-term financing at moderate interest rates. With a floor plan, the initial investment needed to buy aircraft is a fraction of the aircraft's price. As soon as the aircraft sells, the dealer immediately realizes profits from the sale and can pay back the financial institution the initial value of the loan plus interest.

Floor plan programs vary depending on competition, economic conditions, and geographical location. A typical program will charge the dealer one percent per month on the wholesale value of the aircraft. The bank will either take title to the aircraft or place a lien on the title as its protection in the event of default by the dealer. The dealer will have from four to six months to sell the aircraft. If the aircraft is still in inventory at the end of this time, the aircraft will be placed on an installment loan basis, and the dealer will be required to make monthly principal and interest payments.

Floor planning is the preferred method of financing inventory. It allows the dealer to carry an adequate inventory of used aircraft while conserving capital. Since only interest is being paid on the wholesale value of inventory, the monthly cost is much less than the installment loan method where both principal and interest must be paid. The major disadvantage of floor planning is the tendency to carry too many or too expensive aircraft in inventory because of the minimum cost associated with this method.

Retailing Aircraft

Since the objective of pricing is both sales and profit, the dealer must be very careful to select the right aircraft sales price. In pricing, a number of issues must be considered. Some of the more important ones are the following:

1. *Price competition from competitors.*
2. *Effects on exchange.* Price is simply value expressed in terms of dollars. Potential buyers will equate the price of the aircraft with the perceived quality.
3. *Influence on profits.* The selling price must generate sufficient revenue to cover expenses and to provide an acceptable profit.

The pricing technique traditionally used in aircraft sales is markup pricing. Markup is the dollar amount added to the cost of the aircraft to determine the selling price. The size of the markup is the result of two factors:

1. Expenses to prepare the aircraft for resale, marketing, financing, general overhead allocation, and a target profit.
2. Inventory turnover rate—Usually, the greater the turnover rate, the smaller the markup required to accomplish the FBO's objective.

Markup is expressed as a percentage of selling price, and the formula used to determine the retail selling price of the aircraft is:

$$\textit{Selling Price} = \frac{\textit{Cost}}{\textit{100\% – Markup \%}}$$

The following example illustrates how Ace Aviation, Inc., determined the retail price for a used aircraft that cost $90,000, and the profit on the completed transaction that took three months to close.

Retail Price [$90,000 ÷ (100%–38% markup)]	$145,161
Purchase Price	*$90,000*
Gross margin or gross profit (38%)	$55,161
Expenses	
Floor plan—1% ($90,000 × 0.01 × 3 months)	$2,700
Insurance	
Hull coverage—$1.00 per $100 of aircraft value ($900 × $1.00 ÷ 4)	$225
Liability—$1,000,000 single limit, $800 per year ($800 ÷ 4)	$200
Minor repairs and aircraft detailing	$1,450
Selling costs	
Advertising	$1,350
Sales commission—10% of gross profit (0.10 × $55,161)	$5,516
General overhead	*$2,500*
Total expenses	*$13,941*
Net profit before taxes	$41,220

Leasing

Leasing is another way of acquiring the use of a business aircraft. Although there are various types of leases, generally, a lease is a transfer of an asset (aircraft) without transfer of title. Ownership remains with the owner (**lessor**), while use of the asset is transferred to the **lessee** (renter/operator).

Business aircraft can be leased from professional leasing companies; some banks; aircraft manufacturers, either directly or through their finance subsidiaries; and even through some larger aircraft dealers, distributors, and fixed-base operators.

Leasing is typically preferred for a first aircraft or if the company has been downsizing, because then it will only show up on the books as an operating expense. Leasing is not as common today in business aviation as it once was. Aircraft were commonly leased in years past because of concerns that the aircraft would become obsolete over time. However, history has shown that some used aircraft types have become more valuable than when new. Although interest rates were low during the 2020–2021 period, rates had increased significantly by late 2022. When rates are lower, it may be easier to offset the expense through financing rather than a lease.

Other financiers take the view that leases are still in vogue in the right circumstances, such as for customers who want lower debt loads and a higher return on the asset base of the company. Apart from keeping the aircraft off the balance sheet, other features include a lower annual cash outflow and a slower amortization of the cost, which is more evenly spread and never taken down to zero. In these days of long production backlogs for new business jets, for example, leases also allow companies to take advantage of an interim aircraft while waiting for their new model to be delivered.

Essentially, the lease versus loan equation comes down to an individual customer's propensity for risk—the customer's experience as an aircraft operator and level of confidence about reselling the asset. With a lease, a customer is taking no risk on how the aircraft will hold its value, since the asset is entirely owned by the lessor. The client basically forfeits the tax benefits associated with aircraft ownership in favor of a reduced rental rate, with the lessor taking the fiscal breaks.

Similar to automobile leases, aircraft leases will routinely specify detailed maintenance requirements for the aircraft and specifications for the condition in which it must be returned at the end of the lease term. The assumption is generally made that all parts will be in their mid-time-between-overhaul condition, and it will normally be a requirement that the next major checks have been completed. Insurance also has to be maintained, with specified coverage. Some manufacturers of large corporate aircraft are willing to tie guaranteed maintenance costs per flight hour programs to a lease.

A lease may be either short-term—a few months or a few years—or long-term, as many as 15 or 20 years. The maximum length of the lease is determined mostly by the type of aircraft. Average lease terms are 8 to 10 years, but it is common for these to be terminated early as the customer's needs change. It is not uncommon in the United States for operators to break their original leases before the 5-year mark. This trend has underscored the importance of ensuring that sufficiently flexible cancellation terms are written into a lease.

There are two basic methods of leasing an aircraft—wet or dry. A **wet lease** is a contract whereby the owner of the aircraft (the lessor) makes an aircraft available for the user (the lessee) and also provides everything needed to operate the aircraft: at least one crewmember, fuel and oil, maintenance, insurance, and storage. Additional flight crew members may also be provided. The lessee's rental payment includes a fee that usually covers the cost of ownership, fixed and variable operating costs, and reserves, plus a profit to the lessor. In many ways, the wet lease is similar to a charter except that the wet lease is usually made for a longer period of time. Depending on whether the lessor can provide these services more efficiently than the lessee, the rental payment for a wet lease may or may not be less expensive for a company. A **dry lease** or net lease is the more common type of lease arrangement. In this case, the lessor supplies only the aircraft for a fee, and the lessee is obligated for all fixed and variable operating expenses, including fuel, crew, etc.

ADVANTAGES AND DISADVANTAGES OF LEASING

Some of the advantages of leasing are summarized below:

- *Conservation of capital.* One of the major advantages of leasing is that it conserves working capital. Generally, firms engaged in leasing do not require a substantial down payment at the beginning of the lease. Depending on the creditworthiness of the lessee, only one or two months' advance payment may be required, whereas the down payment required on the purchase of an aircraft using loan financing can be 15 percent of the purchase price or more. This savings can be substantial, assuming the lessee earns more on its working capital than the effective interest rate of the lease.
- *Tax savings.* There are two ways a company can benefit from the tax savings of leasing. First, the full amount of each monthly lease payment of a properly structured lease is a deductible business expense for federal income tax purposes. Under the purchase scenario, a company is entitled to depreciation deductions, but only the interest portion of their loan payment is deductible. Second, if a company cannot take full advantage of its depreciation deductions, a leasing company can generally take full advantage of the tax benefits of depreciation and pass the benefit of these deductions to the lessee in the form of a lower monthly lease payment.
- *Preservation of credit lines.* A lease is generally not considered debt and, in most instances, does not restrict a company's borrowing capacity or reduce the amount of funds available under existing credit lines.
- *Flexibility.* No assets are required to refinance or to liquidate before upgrading equipment. Leasing makes it easier to upgrade and time acquisitions with changing market conditions and company growth.
- *Extends length of financing.* This is an important subcategory of the preceding benefit. In contrast to typical loans, leases may be obtained for nearly the entire length of the economic life of the aircraft.
- *Reduces the risk of technological and physical obsolescence.* The risk associated with the expected value of an aircraft at the end of the lease term is placed on the lessor. In contrast, if the company purchased the aircraft, and the expected value of the aircraft declines, the overall cost of ownership to the company would increase.

There are several disadvantages of leasing. During the lease term, the lessee usually cannot own the aircraft or have an equity interest in it. Should the aircraft have a residual value higher than the amount used to determine the lease rental payments, the lessor would receive this gain as owner, not the lessee. An improperly structured lease could be determined to be a purchase agreement or fail to meet the Internal Revenue Service (IRS) guidelines for a lease and the lessee would lose the tax and accounting benefits of leasing. Depending on the specific terms and conditions, a lease may cost the lessee more than a purchase. For instance, if the lessor requires additional insurance coverage or maintenance to be performed by the lessee, this can result in higher costs than if the aircraft had been purchased.

TYPES OF LEASES

Leasing companies offer many different types of leases with different term lengths and various options. Within the leasing industry, the accounting profession, and under the Internal Revenue Code, there are numerous names or titles for leases. As a consequence, sometimes there is a great deal of overlap and confusion, since the same type of lease may be known to the lessee, lessor, tax accountant, and financial analyst by a different name. However, from a lessee perspective, there are two basic types of leases: a capital lease, and an operating lease.

A **capital lease** resembles the acquisition of a business aircraft with the use of debt financing, and for income tax and financial accounting it is treated exactly like a loan. The aircraft is included as an asset, and the lease obligation (payments) is recorded as a liability on the lessee's balance sheet. The lessee is allowed to include only the imputed interest portion of the lease payment and the applicable depreciation amounts for the period as expenses and as a tax deduction. Under this form of lease, the company's monthly rental payment will amortize the entire cost of the aircraft plus a fair return (interest) for the lessor. At the termination of the lease term, the lessee has the option to purchase the aircraft for $1.00 or some other nominal amount.

The lessor may offer various options, such as an early termination based on a formula similar to paying off a loan early. For example, assume that a company has a seven-year capital lease for a $100,000 aircraft with the option to terminate the lease and purchase the aircraft at the end of five years. The lease contract calls for monthly payments of $1,634.40 for a total of $137,289.60 plus a $1.00 purchase option. At the conclusion of the 84-month period, the lessee would have paid the entire cost of the aircraft plus an effective rate of interest of 9.5 percent per year over the term and can acquire the aircraft for $1.00. If the lessee wishes to terminate the lease early, the payoff or purchase price to the lessee would be $35,596.56 plus the $1.00 purchase option. This amount is equal to the amount necessary to pay off a 9.5 percent $100,000 loan at the end of five years. An amortization table can be used to determine the balance remaining for any given number of months.

A **synthetic lease** can be complicated, commonly involving a special-purpose entity. For accounting purposes, the lessee does not show the aircraft as an asset or the lease as a liability. Rather, the lease is shown as an expense on the income statement. For tax purposes, the lessee is recognized as having sufficient benefits and obligations of ownership to be considered the owner of the aircraft. In this case, the lease is treated as a loan. In this way, the aircraft can be owned and leased at the same time, depending on the interpretation.

The more traditional **operating lease**, which has become a standard feature of the commercial airline finance market, is suitable for those who cannot enjoy further tax benefits and who want to get their aircraft completely off the books. An operating lease, which is known as a "true lease" according to IRS regulations, provides the lessee with the use of the aircraft for a fixed period of time in exchange for rental payments. At the conclusion of the lease term, the lessee returns the aircraft to the lessor. Alternatively, the lessor may offer a purchase option, but the amount of this purchase option must be for the fair market value of the aircraft. Usually, this type of lease is recognized by the accounting profession in accordance with Generally Accepted Accounting Principles (GAAP) and by the IRS as a lease and not a purchase, and the company receives the accounting and tax benefits of leasing. Neither the aircraft nor the lease obligation is recorded on the company's balance sheet, and the rental payments are fully deductible for federal income tax purposes.

The guidelines established by the IRS and GAAP specify the accounting and tax treatment of leases based on the specifics of the lease agreement. These guidelines should be consulted to be sure the lease agreement being proposed will be treated as a lease.

The structuring of operating lease payments is one of the more complicated aspects of leasing. Payments can be structured using either pre-tax, after-tax, return on investment (ROI), or return on equity (ROE) structuring methodologies. Ordinarily, a lessor estimates the residual value of the aircraft at the termination of the lease contract. It then calculates the rental amount required to achieve its required rate of return, taking into consideration the tax benefits (e.g., depreciation deductions) available to it as the owner of the aircraft.

Fractional Ownership

The concept of **fractional ownership** was started by Executive Jets' NetJets program with four fractional jet owners in 1986. It evolved from a program that began in 1964 when the Pennsylvania Railroad provided the start-up capital for Executive Jet Airways. The new company ordered ten of the then brand-new Learjet 23s, and the mission was to provide a service where people would buy blocks of usage, and jets would be dispatched with efficiency to take customers wherever they wanted to go. The company went international in 1965 and changed its name to Executive Jet Aviation. By

1974, Executive Jet (or EJA as it was widely known) had expanded its fleet to include aircraft other than Learjets, up to and including a Boeing 707, until it was bought in 1986 by RTS Capital Services, a New York firm engaged in equipment financing through leveraged leasing. This gave EJA additional capital and aircraft for its charter fleet and provided RTS with operational and technical support for its fleet of leased aircraft.

The name was changed to Executive Jet, Incorporated, which became the parent company of the NetJets' fractional ownership program.

The basis of the fractional ownership concept was to combine the flexibility of chartering with the advantages of ownership. This concept is not new, however. The genius of fractional ownership came in the form of a core fleet of aircraft. The core fleet is a group of aircraft owned by the fractional ownership provided directly and not resold to users. This fleet is used to supply transportation to shareowners when the inevitable scheduling conflicts occur. The application of the core fleet concept has proven to be the basis of fractional ownership success.

Figure 11-2. Entrance sign to the NetJets terminal and hub at Columbus International Airport. *(Judeburnside, commons.wikimedia.org/wiki/File:NetJets_HQ_Sign.jpg, CC BY-SA 4.0, creativecommons.org/licenses/by-sa/4.0/)*

FRACTIONAL OWNERSHIP PROGRAMS

Fractional ownership programs are multi-year programs covering a pool of aircraft, each of which is owned by more than one party and all of which are placed in a dry lease exchange pool to be available to any program participant when the aircraft in which such participant owns an interest is not available. As an integral part of these multi-year programs, a single company provides the management services to support the operation of the aircraft by the owners and administers the aircraft exchange program on behalf of all participants. By purchasing an interest (share) in an aircraft that is part of the program, an owner gains round-the-clock access to a private jet at a fraction of the cost. In addition to access to the aircraft in which it owns an interest, it also has access to all other aircraft in the program, as well as the support of a management company that will handle all arrangements relating to maintenance, crew, hiring, and all administrative details relating to the operation of a private aircraft.

Share size determines the amount of the down payment, the monthly management fee, and the annual flight hour allocation. For example, a one-quarter share will require a down payment equal to one-quarter of the manufacturer's suggested retail price. The down payment secures the one-quarter share access to the aircraft, or through the interchange agreement, another aircraft in the program, 24 hours a day, 7 days a week, for up to 200 hours of occupied flight time per year. The monthly management fee is also related to the share size and covers all operational costs of the aircraft. This fee takes care of pilots, maintenance, catering, and all other operational aspects of owning a private jet. Therefore, in total, fractional owners pay a proportionate part of the list price for an aircraft, typically one quarter share, and then pay the fractional ownership company a fee for each occupied flight hour and an overall fixed management fee that covers deadhead, maintenance, and administration of the program.

Share sizes are typically available incrementally from one-sixteenth or 50 flight hours per year; one-eighth or 100 flight hours per year; one-quarter or 200 flight hours per year; to one-half or 400 flight hours per year. Share owners may upgrade to a larger aircraft or downgrade to a smaller aircraft, trading flight hours based upon a predetermined exchange rate. Share size also determines simultaneous availability of multiple aircraft; the larger the share, the more likely multiple aircraft are available. There is also a fee charged for occupied hours flown. Owners share tax liabilities and benefits as a percentage of the share owned. See Table 11-1 for a quick look at the quarter share cost, fixed annual management fee, and hourly operating costs of five typical models.

Table 11-1. Typical Costs of Fractional Ownership

Model	Quarter share purchase cost	Fixed annual management fee	Hourly operating cost
Cirrus Vision	$521,244	$47,988	$1,059
Hawker 800XP	$3,090,000	$244,698	$1,807
Citation Ultra	$1,670,000	$182,580	$1,341
Beechjet 400A	$1,607,000	$179,880	$1,355
Gulfstream IV SP	$7,400,000	$468,000	$3,051

Effective February 2005, fractional aircraft operations were required to fly under either 14 CFR Part 91 Subpart K or 14 CFR Part 135. Subpart K addresses the issues of safety of flight; regulatory compliance; pilot qualifications; aircraft maintenance and technician training requirements; aircraft weight, size, and runway landing requirements; and the installation of advanced safety equipment on aircraft. Under Subpart K, passengers would see little difference, except the requirement for the lead passenger to show a photo ID to the flight crew and provide verbal acknowledgment for all other passengers. Part 135 flights are subject to Transportation Security Administration (TSA) regulations which require each and every passenger to present a valid, government-issued photo ID to the flight crew for positive identification.

A lower capital outlay equal to the share bought must be paid up front, and this acquisition cost may or may not be negotiable depending on the provider. Owners can lease or purchase their shares, but they are limited to selecting an aircraft available via the provider. Fractional aircraft of a given program generally have standard interiors and exteriors, and the share owners usually have no say in how the aircraft are outfitted.

Owners can upgrade or downgrade their aircraft at any time (hourly rates for upgrades/ downgrades are charged via a predetermined sliding scale). In addition, owners may liquidate their shares after meeting a minimum time requirement or paying an early withdrawal penalty. In any case, share sellers must pay a remarketing fee to the fractional provider, which ranges anywhere from four to ten percent of the aircraft's selling price. Furthermore, the aircraft's residual value may be lower due to higher cycles and airframe hours (fractional aircraft each average more than 1,100 flight hours per year).

In 1986, when NetJets began, there were four fractional jet owners; by 1993, there were 89 and the number was growing fast. NetJets aircraft range from light jets like the Cessna Citation SII, Citation V-Ultra, and Citation Excel to the midsize Citation VII, Hawker 800XP, and Hawker 1000, and the super-midsize Dassault Falcon 2000, the Citation X, which is the world's fastest business jet, and the Boeing Business jet. By late 2022, NetJets announced plans to add up to 175 super-midsize Citation Longitude aircraft and up to 150 of the new large cabin Citation Hemisphere aircraft. The company also had plans to add the Bombardier Global 7500.

In 1998, Berkshire Hathaway, Inc., acquired NetJets, adding strong confirmation to the considerable value in fractional ownership. The Berkshire Hathaway acquisition also added financial resources and strength, ensuring NetJets' continued growth around the world.

Bombardier entered the fractional ownership market in May 1995 with its Dallas-based Flexjet program. The Flexjet program began with 22 owners and today has 10,000 owners and a fleet of more than 250 aircraft and helicopters. At a portion of the full-ownership cost, a company or high-net-worth individual can purchase shares in a Phenom 300; Challenger 350; Gulfstream 450, 500, 650, or 700; and a Sikorsky S-76.

Additional fractional ownership companies include PlaneSense, Airshare, AirSprint, Nicholas Air, Northern Jet Management, and West Coast Aviation Services. According to information produced by ARGUS, the fractional aircraft companies in North America flew over 760,000 hours in 2021 (see Table 11-2). This was an increase of more than 50% compared to 2020, and up over 20% compared to pre-pandemic levels in 2019 (Copley 2022).

Table 11-2. Largest Fractional Ownership Companies in North America, 2021

Operator	Hours flown in 2021
NetJets	478,444
Flexjet	178,053
PlaneSense	42,907
Airshare	20,955
Airsprint	19,032
Nicholas Air	18,023
West Coast Aviation Services	4,592
Northern Jet Management	3,396

Source: Copley 2022.

ADVANTAGES OF FRACTIONAL OWNERSHIP

Fractional ownership offers many unique advantages over full ownership. Aircraft availability is guaranteed at any time with as little as four hours' notice, and all aspects of the aircraft's operation are managed by a provider. All of the leading providers, and most of the new entrants, do not charge for deadhead flight segments. A deadhead leg is one in which the aircraft is positioned without passengers for subsequent use. In a fractional ownership, deadhead legs are required to position the aircraft for a shareowner's use, position the aircraft for use by one of the other aircraft shareowners, or return the aircraft to its base of operations. If a fractional owner operates to and from the same point of origin, the benefits of a fractional share can be substantially diminished. However, positioning flights are common, and more frequent deadhead legs further justify fractional ownership.

It has been estimated that roughly 80 percent of fractional owners are new to business aviation, and many of the other 20 percent use fractional participation to supplement their own in-house business flight capability. The advantages of fractional ownership regarding the deadhead segments and the availability of multiple aircraft have enabled traditional flight departments to become more efficient through the use of supplemental lift. The term supplemental lift describes the use of a fractional share to supplement an existing corporate fleet. Supplemental lift is used to reduce the costs of deadheading, to facilitate maintenance schedules, and as a fleet multiplier when the demand for aircraft exceeds the flight department's existing fleet. This provides a flight department additional aircraft types. For example, a Challenger 604 or Global Express may be a perfect fleet complement for an intercontinental flight with 10 passengers aboard, while an economical Eclipse 500 may be just right when two passengers are flying a short distance.

Aircraft availability is essential to the success of a fractional ownership program. Aircraft availability is enabled by the core fleet by limiting the number of shares sold per aircraft and by drawing upon charter aircraft. The core fleet, as previously mentioned, is a number of aircraft that are held in reserve and in which shares are not sold.

Fractional ownership offers all the usual financial advantages of owning capital equipment, plus the unique advantage in that the terms of the fractional agreement typically guarantee the liquidity of the investment. A fractional share offers an effective means of air transportation, with costs directly proportionate to utilization.

Even with these many advantages, it pays to consider the following four general categories of aircraft ownership and operating costs and make an informed decision of the benefits of fractional ownership versus purchasing:

1. Acquisition and capital costs;
2. Direct operating costs, which includes items such as fuel and maintenance;
3. Indirect operating costs, which include insurance, hangar rent, pilot salaries and benefits, and recurrent training; and
4. Other deductible expenses, such as interest expense and aircraft depreciation for tax purposes, which can be deducted from a company's income tax burden and hence help to offset the cost of ownership of the aircraft.

Experts explain that fractional ownership may not make economic sense for the typical corporate flight operation. However, it is a good option for users with extremely low flight time requirements. The break-even point between the costs of full ownership and fractional ownership occurs somewhere between 100 and 200 flight hours per year. If flying more than this, full aircraft ownership is less expensive. Additionally, charter offers a viable alternative to fractional ownership in these hour ranges, and any company considering buying a fractional ownership aircraft for flight times less than 200 hours per year should investigate the charter option, as well.

SUBSCRIPTION MODEL

Just as subscription-based media (i.e., Netflix, Amazon Prime Video, Spotify, etc.) has become mainstream, subscription-based aviation is now available. For example, Wheels Up is based on this popular **subscription model**. Wheels Up owns its own fleet of aircraft that customers are able to reserve via their app. In contrast to fractional ownership, the subscription model does not require a significant up-front investment or long-term commitment. Members pay an initiation fee and annual dues, which guarantees hourly pricing on a pay-as-you-fly basis.

Charter

Charter service companies provide aircraft and crew to the general public for on-demand, unscheduled transportation under a Part 135 certificate. Charter offers the ultimate flexibility in air travel. Chartering an aircraft is similar to hiring a taxi for a single trip. The charter company provides the aircraft, flight crew, fuel, and all other services for each trip. The client pays a fee, usually based on mileage or time, plus extras such as waiting time and crew expenses. Chartering aircraft is particularly attractive for a firm that does not frequently require an aircraft or does not often need a supplement to its aircraft.

Chartering can also be cost effective for a group of executives traveling together or for an emergency. When an individual businessperson is traveling alone, the airlines, including regional carriers, would be more cost efficient, especially if the trip is between two cities well served by scheduled carriers.

In the past, chartering a Learjet or Gulfstream to Las Vegas evoked a certain glamorous image. Today, chartering is a working tool for business. Indeed, although charter travel is expensive, it provides greater value due to on-demand scheduling flexibility, closer proximity to business sectors, increased productivity, greater security, and overall time savings.

Charter costs can range from $2,600 per hour for a four-seat aircraft to $14,000 per hour for an ultra-long-range 19-seat aircraft (see Table 11-3). In addition, there may be extra fees for position, waiting, catering, airport use, crew overnights, and so forth. Charges vary from region to region, with the highest rates being levied in the northeastern United States and southern California.

Table 11-3. Average Hourly Charter Rates

Aircraft type	Passenger capacity	Range (NM)	Hourly rate
Light	4–8	2,100–2,300	$2,600–$3,500
Midsize	6–8	2,200–3,500	$4,200–$5,100
Super midsize	8–10	3,000–4,200	$5,200–$6,100
Large	9–19	3,500–7,800	$6,600–$7,500
Ultra long range	10–19	3,500–7,800	$8,500–$14,000

Source: Clay Lacey Aviation, n.d.

One of the most comprehensive resources available for charter customers is the Air Charter Guide, a database of more than 3,000 charter operators worldwide, including 1,800 in the United States. It is available at aircharterguide.com.

Most of the revenue gained from a charter flight goes to the aircraft owner (charter companies seldom own more than a couple of aircraft—most of their fleets are on leaseback or other agreements with the actual owners or lessors) with the charter operator receiving a commission, usually between 10 and 15 percent of the cost of the entire trip. The charter rate can be *wet*, meaning the costs for fuel, onboard catering, landing and positioning fees, crew expenses, and other charges are included in the cost. A *dry rate* means that these and other charges are added onto the hourly rate. Most charter firms also charge a two-hour-per-day minimum rate on their jet-powered aircraft and a one-hour minimum on their turboprops.

The weak economy during the early 1990s, the early-2000s recession, and the 2007–2008 great recession along with a rash of company acquisitions have forced a number of companies to reduce the size of their fleets or eliminate them entirely. Many of these companies turned to chartering aircraft as an alternative. Some corporations opted for the least costly havens of aircraft management firms, while others simply appended their aircraft onto a convenient Part 135 charter certificate to defray the costs of ownership.

Since the growth of fractional ownership, many of the better charter operators are busy supporting the fractional companies. Backup lift provided to fractional ownership companies provides the nation's charter services with substantial revenue. Backup lift support is not the only form of flight services that charter operators offer to fractional providers. When faced with the inevitable grounded aircraft, a fractional provider must respond quickly. Response to a grounded aircraft is frequently more readily facilitated by a charter organization. Getting flight crews, technicians, tools, and parts to the disabled aircraft as quickly as possible is essential to the fractional provider. Consequently, fractional ownership has stimulated significant air charter business in recent years.

Many corporate aircraft operators charter aircraft for the following reasons:

1. *To keep flying when its own aircraft are down.* When company aircraft are in for maintenance, repair, outfitting, or refurbishment, chartering allows employees to continue to fly as usual.
2. *Supplement its airlift capability.* A flight department can offer broader services by chartering aircraft of similar capacity to their own or aircraft with different mission capabilities (helicopters or corporate aircraft, for example).
3. *Avoid over-equipping.* Generally, it is more cost efficient to charter occasionally than it is to underutilize a larger aircraft.
4. *Have a less expensive alternative to airline travel.* If a company needs to transport a large number of people to a single location at one time, it may be less expensive and more convenient to charter a large aircraft than it would be to send the group on the airlines.

5. *Test the business aviation waters.* Chartering may be the safe method for a company to become involved with business aviation. The classic way in which companies get their own aircraft is through an evolutionary process that begins with spot chartering and leads to contract chartering, leasing, participation in an aircraft management program, and finally, establishment of a corporate flight department.
6. *Re-enter the field of business aviation.* Many companies gave up their aircraft during the last recession and have now found that chartering is a good way to once again enjoy the benefits of business aviation without making a capital commitment.
7. *Fly before buying.* For those companies that are contemplating upgrading to a new class of aircraft or adding equipment, chartering is a good way to conduct an in-depth operational evaluation of additional capability.

As commercial operators, charter firms must conform to more stringent operating and maintenance requirements called for in 14 CFR Part 135. In addition, each charter operator, regardless of the types of aircraft used, must have an air taxi certificate on file with the FAA. This certificate is issued by the FAA after proper application and local inspection. It also evidences minimum insurance coverages and limits.

The following checklist includes the major factors to be considered in evaluating a charter operator's performance. Many companies also use the services of a consultant to perform an impartial safety audit of charter operators or contract flight departments that have used specific operators in the past.

1. Operations:
    a. Pilot qualifications and records: total hours, time in type, and ratings.
    b. Pilot training: source, flight training, ground school, and continuing proficiency training.
    c. Pilot turnover: average length of employment.
    d. Flight crew knowledge of the operations manual.
    e. Schedule, average weekly flight time, and working conditions.
2. Maintenance:
    a. Number of personnel, regular and temporary.
    b. Staff qualifications: records and experience, school training, and average number of years' experience.
    c. Staff turnover: average length of employment.
    d. Supervision and sign-off authority.
    e. List of factory approvals for service work, including rebuilding.
    f. Equipment and shop facilities: airframe, powerplant, and avionics.
    g. Recordkeeping: computer, staff, and facilities.
    h. Company maintenance manual evaluation.
    i. Program for timed removal of key aircraft components.
    j. Airworthiness directives (AD) compliance.
    k. Ground safety, including fueling, servicing, and fire and crash facilities, if any.
    l. FAA repair station approval?
    m. Are engine overhauls completed in house? If not, where?
    n. Premature failures of engines and major components.
    o. Spare parts stock.

3. Fleet Equipment:
   a. Type and number of aircraft, including year of manufacture.
   b. General condition of aircraft.
   c. Survival equipment, including over-water flights.
   d. Weight and balance records, including staff responsibility.
   e. Instruments: avionics for IFR flights and for international flights over water.
   f. Cabin equipment: catering service, phones, seating, lighting, and air conditioning.
4. Fitness:
   a. Financial condition and credit rating.
   b. Insurance coverage, including copy of certificate.
   c. Owner and length of time in business.
5. Safety:
   a. Total hours flown during the past five years.
   b. Number and type of incidents.
   c. Accidents: minor, major, and fatal.
   d. Ratio of hours flown to accidents.
6. Morale:
   a. Responsiveness of staff.
   b. Flight crew professionalism, general appearance, and courtesy.
   c. Evaluation of management.

Service can vary widely among charter companies, ranging anywhere from poor to excellent. Aircraft availability depends on market demand, and there is no guarantee of aircraft availability from any one charter operator. If a particular charter aircraft is not available, another vendor or the airlines must be used to meet travel demands.

Crew and mechanics are employed by the charter provider, which also controls personnel training. Crew changes are likely as they rotate from a pool. The charter firm is fully liable for the flight.

The charter option typically provides the lowest cost at lower usage levels, and reduced hourly charges may be negotiated at higher utilization rates (commonly referred to as block charter). Charter customers must pay for all ancillary charges, including deadheading and positioning costs, catering bills, landing fees, taxes (FET applies), and so on. No depreciation tax benefits are available to charter customers, but they may write off charter costs as a business expense.

CONTRACT FLIGHT SERVICE

Contract flight service is the same as chartering an aircraft, except that the customer buys a block of aircraft time, mileage, or trips, usually over a certain period. Contract flight service is particularly suited to a company that has frequent and predictable need for business aircraft but at a level that is not enough to justify owning or leasing an aircraft. This method also is used by companies who operate aircraft but need to supplement their own service.

Contract flight service can be very effective for a company that requires frequent travel that can be planned well in advance and for companies scheduling many simultaneous trips in different directions.

Almost all charter operators will negotiate flight service contracts over a specified time period based on aircraft miles, hours, or trips. In terms of cost, this arrangement can be more attractive than individual charter flights. However, similar to charter flights, beyond 200 hours of annual use, the company will probably find it less costly to consider leasing or owning.

Comparison of Methods

As a general guideline, charter service is best when annual utilization is less than 100 hours. Fractional ownership is the preferred approach when utilization is between 100 and 400 hours per year, and total ownership is best when annual utilization is above 400 hours.

Any one of these estimates is not a precise indictor of which type of service is best in all cases. The choice is not based solely upon annual utilization rates. The best method is affected by a number of factors, which include the following:

- Route structure
- Daily round trips
- Extended-stay, one-way trips
- Fixed or variable passenger capacity
- Demand for multiple aircraft
- Preference for new or used aircraft
- Positioning or deadhead legs
- Owner status (no flight department or an existing flight department)
- Service quality
- Cost
- Liability
- Capital commitment
- Tax consequences

Another underlying factor is the level of control. A business must consider who they want to control such factors as aircraft availability, type, and quality as well as liability and crew qualifications and training.

The dilemma is that in business aviation, one size does not fit all. What may work for one company is not necessarily the right move for another, and a choice made today may not meet next year's travel needs. The stakes are quite high. Business aviation is a complex field where the wrong choice can cost a lot of money.

To justify establishing a new flight department to support a corporate aircraft, the annual utilization rate should be forecast between 350 and 400 hours at a minimum. An existing flight department, one with operational and support resources already established, should have a forecast annual utilization rate of at least 250 hours. In either case, however, purchase of a used aircraft instead of a new aircraft can reduce the annual utilization rate estimate by as much as 100 hours.

The used aircraft purchase evaluation must also take into consideration the costs associated with maintaining aging airframes, powerplants, associated systems, and noise abatement.

One reason for the interest in fractional ownership in recent years is the increased residual value of business aircraft, particularly business jets.

Leasing aircraft reached its peak during the mid-1990s. It kept aircraft off of companies' balance sheets. This changed during the late-1990s when a company could buy an aircraft, operate it for two or three years, and sell it at well above what it cost. Consequently, leasing has lost its popularity.

Whether buying, leasing, fractional ownership, or charter, the same rule still applies. The company must know what its travel requirements are before utilizing business aviation. Its needs must be determined, not its wants.

Table 11-4 can be used to compare and contrast various types of aircraft acquisition and management methods. By considering variables such as service quality, aircraft administration, crew quality, operating costs, cost offsets, liability, tax consequences, capital commitment, and aircraft acquisition and disposition, a thorough analysis can be made resulting in an informed choice of the most appropriate method.

Table 11-4. Comparison of Aircraft Acquisition and Management Methods

		Company owned In-house flight dept.	Company owned Management co.	Joint ownership In-house flight dept.	Co-ownership Management co.	Fractional ownership	Charter
Service	Highest level of control/service	X					
	Potentially excellent; customizable		X	X	X		
	Potentially excellent; less customizable					X	X
	Possible inconsistent service among vendors						X
	Best possible confidentiality/security	X					
	Maximum control over safety options	X					
Availability	Immediate availability likely	X	X				
	Requires coordination & planning			X	X		
	Guaranteed; requires 4–8 hr. advance notice					X	
	Not guaranteed; depends on vendor/ demand						X
	If aircraft unavailable, must use charter or airlines	X	X	X	X		X
	More than 1 aircraft may be available at same time					X	O
Aircraft administration	Owner(s)/lessee maintains total control over and manages aircraft operations	X		X			
	Owner(s)/lessee maintains control over but delegates management of aircraft operations to management company		X		X		
	Owners maintain control over but delegate management of aircraft operations to fractional provider					X	
	Personnel on owner's payroll; must deal with in-house personnel issues	X		X			
	Personnel not on owner's payroll		X		X	X	X
Crew quality and control	Consistent; owner-controlled	X		X			
	Consistent; owner input allowed; crews assignable		X		X		
	Crew changes likely; rotating from pool					X	X
	May be able to request specific crew or use own crew					X	
	Owner(s) controls training of crew and maintenance personnel	X		X			
	Owner(s) delegates control of pilot and mechanic training		X		X	X	
	No control of pilot or mechanic training						X

		Company owned In-house flight dept.	Company owned Management co.	Joint ownership In-house flight dept.	Co-ownership Management co.	Fractional ownership	Charter
Operating costs	Variable; dependent on utilization	X	X	X	X		O
	Fixed on per-hour basis (flight time + set ground time per operation); high cost for hours exceeding contract					X	
	Subject to deadhead/positioning expense	X	X	X	X		X
	Subject to ancillary charges (catering, landing, etc.)						X
	All fees (e.g., deadhead/positioning) included, except for intl. handling/customs					X	
	Potential higher annual costs due to management fee		X		X		
	Lowest cost of operations at reasonable utilization levels	X					
	Higher costs at high utilization levels (compared to other forms of ownership)					X	
	Lowest overall cost at minimum utilization levels						X
Cost offsets	A charter option may be available to help offset costs	X	X	X	X		
	Fleet discounts may be available for fuel, insurance, crew training		X		X		
Liability	Completely liable	X		X			
	Shared liability with management company		X		X		
	Shared liability with fractional provider					X	
	Passenger(s) may not be immune from liability						X
Taxes[1]	No commercial federal excise tax	X	O		X		
	Commercial federal excise tax applies (or may apply in certain situations)			X		X	X
	Noncommercial fuel tax applies	X	O	X	X		
	Owners share tax liabilities and benefits			X	X	X	
	Maximum depreciation benefit	X	X				
	Owners share depreciation benefit			X			
	Owners share depreciation benefit proportional to the share owned				X	X	
	No depreciation benefit available (as no aircraft owned)						X

Table -11-4. (continued)

		Company owned In-house flight dept.	Company owned Management co.	Joint ownership In-house flight dept.	Co-ownership Management co.	Fractional ownership	Charter
Capital Commitment	Higher capital investment of negotiated acquisition cost	X	X				
	Owners share capital investment of negotiated acquisition cost			X	X		
	Lower capital outlay equal to a percentage of aircraft share					X	
	No capital commitment						X
Aircraft Acquisition and Disposition	Can purchase or lease any aircraft at any price, selecting desired make/model, interior, and exterior	X	X				
	Can jointly purchase or lease any aircraft at any price, selecting desired make/model, interior, and exterior			X	X		
	Can purchase or lease, limited to aircraft available from provider; no aircraft customization; aircraft flown may be different than owned aircraft					X	
	Can choose when to upgrade, downgrade, or sell	X	X				
	Can jointly choose when to upgrade, downgrade, or sell			X	X		
	Can upgrade at any time; can downgrade/sell (subject to minimum time requirements, early withdrawal penalty, and/or remarketing fee).					X	
	Not applicable (no ownership)						X

X = Applies
O = May apply, depending on the particular situation/arrangement.
Adapted from NBAA material (NBAA 2016).
[1]Meant as a general guide and overview; please contact your tax advisor.

Summary

Although many companies have acquired the use of business aircraft through various methods, few companies suddenly have purchased or leased their own aircraft without having some previous experience that helped identify their needs. The normal introduction into business aviation is through a process that allows adjustment to one level before ascending further. Sales representatives use their own aircraft or rent them for business purposes or may begin by chartering. If the demand is great enough, contracting for a block of time is the next logical step. If the amount of chartering indicates that a firm would be better off with an aircraft of its own, wet leasing might be considered. While wet leasing, the company has the opportunity to evaluate whether or not it should progress up the ladder to dry leasing. Here a company might want to enter first into a short-term dry lease as a trial. After this, the company should have enough experience in business aviation and sufficient knowledge of its needs to determine whether or not to enter a fractional ownership program or to purchase an aircraft outright, enter into a long-term dry lease, or step back to one of the previous rungs on the ladder more appropriate to its requirements.

Key Terms

capital lease. A lease in which the lessor only finances the leased asset, and all other rights of ownership transfer to the lessee. It is considered a purchase of an asset for accounting purposes, requiring the lessee to book assets and liabilities associated with the lease.

certificate of aircraft registration. One of the FAA-required documents that are maintained on board an aircraft, this certificate validates the aircraft's registration with the FAA and indicates the legal owner.

charter. Provides aircraft and crew to the general public for hire under a Part 135 certificate. The charter company provides the aircraft, flight crew, fuel, and all other services for each trip. The client pays a fee, usually based on mileage or time, plus extras such as waiting time and crew expenses.

company-owned aircraft. An arrangement where a company owns one or more aircraft and operates these aircraft with in-house personnel. The principal advantages of a company-owned aircraft are optimum utility, convenience, and safety.

company-owned, management company operated. An arrangement where a company owns one or more aircraft, but rather than employing in-house personnel, the company utilizes a management company for the operation of the aircraft.

contract flight service. The same as chartering an aircraft, except that the customer buys a block of aircraft time, mileage, or trips, usually over a certain period. Contract flight service is particularly suited to a company that has frequent and predictable need for business aircraft, but not enough to justify owning or leasing an aircraft.

co-ownership, management company operated. In this arrangement, two co-owners of an aircraft utilize a management company for operation of the aircraft. Due to multiple owners, this arrangement requires coordination for aircraft use. Owners maintain control over, but delegate the management of, aircraft operations.

dry lease. The lessor supplies only the aircraft for a fee, and the lessee is obligated for all fixed and variable operating expenses, including crew, fuel, etc.

floor planning. A financial arrangement with a bank or other financial institution that provides a loan to the dealer (FBO) for the initial investment needed to buy aircraft, which is a fraction of the aircraft's price. As soon as the aircraft sells, the dealer immediately realizes profits from the sale and can pay back the financial institution the initial value of the loan plus interest.

fractional ownership. An expanded form of co-ownership in which owners purchase a share (fractional amount) of an aircraft. The share allows a certain number of flight hours per year in proportion to the size of share purchased. For example, if a full share of an aircraft allows for 1,200 flight hours, a one-sixteenth share would allow for 75 hours annually.

interchange agreement. An arrangement whereby a person or company leases his aircraft to another person in exchange for equal time, when needed, on the other person's aircraft, and no charge is made, except that a charge may be made not to exceed the difference between the cost of owning, operating, and maintaining the two aircraft.

joint ownership, in-house flight department. An arrangement in which one of the registered joint owners of an aircraft employs and furnishes the flight crew for that aircraft, while each of the registered joint owners pays a share of the charges specified in the agreement.

leasing. An arrangement whereby there is transfer of an asset (aircraft) without transfer of title.

lessee. The person who holds the lease (and use) of an asset (aircraft) from the owner, the lessor.

lessor. The owner who leases an asset (aircraft) to another, the lessee.

operating lease. A short-term lease for the use and possession of an aircraft by the lessee for a specified amount of time. The lessor maintains ownership of the aircraft.

pre-purchase inspection. Physical inspection of an aircraft prior to purchase. Performed by an A&P mechanic, the purpose is to uncover any issues with the aircraft and determine its airworthiness prior to purchase. This can involve a test flight.

subscription model. A model in which members pay an initiation fee and annual dues, which guarantees hourly pricing on a pay-as-you fly basis. This does not require a significant up-front investment or long-term commitment.

synthetic lease. Often complicated leases traditionally involving a special-purpose entity. For accounting purposes, the lessee does not show the aircraft as an asset or the lease as a liability, but the lease is shown as an expense on the income statement. For tax purposes, the lessee is recognized as having sufficient benefits and obligations of ownership to be considered the aircraft owner. In this case, the lease is treated as a loan. In this way, the aircraft can be owned and leased at the same time, depending on the interpretation.

time-sharing agreement. An arrangement whereby a person leases his or her aircraft with flight crew to another person, and no charge is made for the flights conducted under that arrangement other than out-of-pocket expenses (e.g., crew travel expenses, landing fees, catering costs), including an amount equal to twice the cost of fuel used on the flight.

wet lease. Contract whereby the lessor makes an aircraft available to the lessee and also provides everything needed to operate the aircraft: at least one crewmember, fuel and oil, maintenance, insurance, and storage.

Review Questions

1. Why is a company-owned aircraft the most flexible method of business aviation?
2. What are time-sharing and interchange agreements?
3. List some of the advantages of company-owned aircraft operated by a management company.
4. What are some of the pros and cons of joint ownership?
5. Finance charges on aircraft loans are primarily based on four factors. What are they?
6. What is the reason for the strong competition in the field of aircraft finance in recent years?
7. Describe four methods owners may use in selling their aircraft.
8. What are some of the areas to be considered in evaluating the purchase of a used aircraft?
9. Define the following: FAA Form 337; airworthiness directives; and airworthiness certificates.
10. What are the major points covered in an aircraft sales contract?
11. Distinguish between simple interest and add-on interest.
12. What is a floor planning contract?
13. Give an example of the retail price of an aircraft, including all of the items in the markup formula.

14. Distinguish between a dry lease and a wet lease.
15. List four distinct advantages of leasing an aircraft.
16. What is the primary disadvantage of leasing?
17. What is a capital lease and how does this differ from an operating lease?
18. What are synthetic leases?
19. How was the concept of fractional ownership started?
20. What are fractional ownership programs?
21. Who are the major fractional providers?
22. What is the function of 14 CFR Part 91, Subpart K?
23. What is meant by the term "supplemental lift"?
24. When might chartering an aircraft be considered the most effective method of acquiring the use of a business aircraft?
25. List some of the reasons why corporate aircraft operators may charter aircraft.
26. What are the major factors to be considered in evaluating a charter operator's performance?
27. How does a straight charter differ from contract flight service?
28. What are the general guidelines, in terms of annual hourly utilization, when considering charter, fractional ownership, company ownership, or leasing?
29. Compare and contrast fractional ownership with a company-owned aircraft in terms of service quality, aircraft administration, crew quality, operating costs, liability, tax consequences, capital commitment, and aircraft acquisition and disposition.

Scenarios

1. You were recently able to convince a company, Media Consultants International, of its need for a corporate aircraft, and it has decided on a HondaJet. The company would like to own the aircraft, but it does not want the hassle associated with an in-house corporate flight department. So, you suggest a company-owned, management company-operated option. It asked you to fully explain this option, including the pros and cons. What do you say?
2. You work in the aircraft sales division of Corporate Jet Transport. A client has decided to purchase an aircraft but does not have the $850,000 necessary to complete the sale. Rather than lose the sale, you need to assist this client with financing. What are this client's options?
3. In preparing a used but very clean Cessna 172 for sale, you need to determine the selling price. The aircraft was purchased by your FBO for $92,000, but it has since had a new paint job, new avionics installed, etc. These and other expenses, plus profit, total 35 percent markup. Based on the formula in this chapter, what would the selling price need to be to allow recovery of the cost plus markup?

4. A prospective client was considering purchasing an aircraft from you. However, this person is now leaning toward fractional ownership. As a matter of fact, many of your prospective clients are leaning toward fractional ownership. The FBO for which you work currently sells only used aircraft. Should your FBO consider getting involved in the fractional ownership market? If so, how would your FBO do that?
5. As a new sales associate with Executive Aircraft, you have been tasked with fully researching methods that may be used by a company to acquire a business aircraft. This presentation will be part of every sales presentation, allowing clients to see all available options for acquiring a business aircraft. What do you include in this presentation? Can you explain?

Bibliography

AOPA (Aircraft Owners and Pilots Association). n.d. "Tips on Buying Used Aircraft." Accessed January 25, 2023. https://www.aopa.org/go-fly/aircraft-and-ownership/buying-an-aircraft/tips-on-buying-used-aircraft.

Clay Lacey Aviation. n.d. "Private Jet Charter Cost Estimator & Rental: Private Jet Prices." Accessed December 24, 2022. https://www.claylacy.com/jet-charters/charter-costs/.

Copley, Nick. 2022. "Largest Fractional Aircraft Ownership Companies in 2021." SherpaReport. February 16, 2022. https://www.sherpareport.com/aircraft/largest-fractional-2021.html.

NBAA (National Business Aviation Association). 2016. *NBAA Management Guide.*

Prather, C. Daniel. 2009. *General Aviation Marketing and Management: Operating, Marketing, and Managing an FBO.* 3rd ed. Malabar, FL: Krieger Publishing Company.

Young-Brown, Fiona. 2021. "Used Business Jet Sales are Surging." SherpaReport. August 9, 2021. https://www.sherpareport.com/aircraft/used-jet-sales-surging.html.

12

Management Functions and Organization

In Chapter 12

Objectives

At the end of this chapter, you should be able to:

1. Summarize the characteristics of well-managed FBOs.
2. Discuss the importance of planning.
3. Describe the step-by-step approach to planning.
4. Distinguish between line and staff personnel.
5. Define unity of command and span of control.
6. Explain the purpose of an operations manual.
7. Discuss the role of leadership in developing and directing various types of business plans, including strategic plans and operational plans.
8. Define personality and motives as they relate to understanding employees.
9. Compare and contrast Maslow's theory of human wants and needs with Herzberg's motivators and hygiene factors.
10. Describe the decision-making process.
11. Explain the purpose and benefits of employee empowerment.
12. Discuss the purpose of the controlling process.

Managing a Fixed-Base Operation

Today's FBOs operate in a complex environment, rich with competitive market forces. Innovation is key to success. Those businesses that intend to survive must learn to love change—much of which cannot be controlled. Firms can only expect to successfully compete in this marketplace if they are willing to quickly adapt to changing customer preferences, pursue fast-paced innovation, and achieve flexibility by empowering employees to reach their full potential. Rather than avoiding challenges as they arise, the wise FBO manager embraces these challenges as an opportunity for continued improvement. Leading well through the changes allows the FBO to stay ahead of competitive forces and even create a competitive advantage.

Even in this complex environment, FBO owners and managers have tremendous opportunities to influence (and even control) the future profit performance of their businesses. However, in order to do so, they need to objectively assess where the business is now and how the management team must evolve in terms of management expertise to continuously improve.

Well-managed and successful FBOs have been astute at developing strong organizational cultures that reflect the values and practices of their owners and managers. In fact, one of the primary roles of management is to shape and manage the values of the company. The outstanding FBOs have certain core values that are considered almost sacred throughout their organizations. Employees have a sense of ownership. This leads to high morale and a can-do attitude shared by all employees. Firms with distinctive cultures provide meaning for their employees. This provides a purpose in life that all humans are searching for, and as a result, employee happiness and productivity are generally higher. In short, a strong culture is the binding agent that holds everything together.

Change requires the FBO to respond swiftly. Well-managed FBOs get quick action because they maintain organizational fluidity. For example, they have developed successful techniques for informal communication. They use special methods and unorthodox approaches to attack difficult problems or effect sudden change. In short, they are not bureaucratic and inflexible. They have been successful in promoting the spirit of entrepreneurship and capitalism throughout the organization. In fact, it is part of their culture. Employees feel and act like co-owners of the FBO. All employees should understand the concept of risk and return and the link between productivity and profitability. FBOs that leverage the entrepreneurial spirit of employees are likely to be the most profitable in the future.

Certainly, getting the job done on schedule and at a reasonable price is an FBO's continuing challenge. However, companies cannot become so production-oriented that employees are treated like objects. This approach can work in the short term, provided the company has enough supervisors to watch employees every minute of the day. But obviously this approach is not conducive to long-term productivity. Well-managed FBOs successfully balance the concern for people and production. They understand and practice the philosophy that people are their most important assets. There is genuine respect for the individual and an abiding faith that the source of productivity gain is through people.

Figure 12-1. Happy FBO employee. *(Olena Yakobchuk/Shutterstock.com)*

Well-managed FBOs use positive reinforcement. It is specific and immediate. Their programs are commonly designed to enhance the employee's self-image. Employees are encouraged to achieve their full potential. Well-managed FBOs do not expect employees to be motivated in a vacuum. They promote an environment of achievement and teamwork. It becomes part of their culture. They expect extraordinary results from ordinary people and get it through positive reinforcement.

Quality conscientiousness is another important trait of well-managed FBOs. With some, it is almost an obsession. Therefore, they encourage the attitude, and reward the behavior, of making quality a priority. Excellence is a motivating factor. The result is more competitive pricing, a satisfied customer, and higher profits.

Well-managed FBOs strive to maintain an awareness of the industry's technological advancements, trends, and concepts. They are not timid about applying new technology, such as the integration of simulators into flight training and computerized management information systems in recordkeeping, financial planning, and management. They attend trade shows and seminars to discover new approaches and methodology. They understand that such expenditures are an investment in the future. The end result is greater efficiency, which leads to a competitive advantage and higher long-term profits.

Well-managed FBOs are marketing-oriented. They have a complete understanding of their markets and know their niche in those markets. They know their strengths and weaknesses and those of the competition, and they have been successful in differentiating themselves from their competitors. Well-managed FBOs stress their technological and/or service orientation, focusing on quick turnaround time, quality, and reliability. In short, they compete as much as possible on anything other than price.

The well-managed FBOs have paid their dues in the community, to trade associations, and to customers. They listen and learn and use that valuable knowledge to prepare strategic and tactical plans. They are proactive, rather than reactive, in their marketing efforts.

Marketing efforts will be ineffective if deception is used. Thus, an important corollary to the marketing orientation is honesty in dealing with people. Customers, suppliers, and even employees have respect for an FBO's integrity. Often, business deals begin (and possibly end) on a handshake and an honest word. One's word becomes one's contract, and relationships are built on trust rather than suspicion. This philosophy builds long-term relationships that are extremely beneficial, particularly during tough times.

Finally, well-managed FBOs use metrics and performance standards to evaluate their success. Making data-based decisions is only possibly with a robust management information system that provides timely and accurate reporting by profit and cost centers. Administration is viewed as a support function, rather than a stand-alone functional area. Those in administration should understand their service role, providing insight into business performance to benefit those in operational positions. Reports are formatted in a manner that operations personnel can easily understand and use to better manage the business.

In short, whether it is job or equipment costing, purchasing and inventory control, or financial management, the system works and employees know how to use the information provided. Moreover, direct costs and overhead expenses are budgeted and then compared to actuals, and corrective strategies are taken when appropriate. Well-managed FBOs know how to evaluate their cost and capital structures, yielding information that results in better pricing strategies. This provides valuable information on how to be competitive and profitable.

Although these concepts seem simple, they are not necessarily easy to achieve in practice. However, considered in total, they do provide a framework for a well-managed FBO. Excellence is, in fact, achievable, but only in degrees. Few FBOs have completely mastered all of these attributes, which should not be surprising. Excellence is a journey, not a destination. These principles imply degrees of achievement and the need for continuous improvement. Thus, higher levels of success may be reached.

Planning

Effective management begins with planning, which in turn implies setting goals. **Planning** is the most important function in establishing and maintaining a business. In essence, planning is problem solving and decision-making wrapped up as one. This includes speculating on the future (both near and far), setting objectives (short and long term), considering alternatives, and making choices.

Planning for the future necessitates flexibility to cope with the unexpected, setting timetables, establishing priorities, and deciding on the methods to be used and the employees who will be involved. A manager must analyze the existing situation, formulate targets, and apply both logic and creativity to all the details in between.

Owners and managers of small FBOs typically are so busy running their operations that they often defer planning as a lower priority. Yet, its importance cannot be overemphasized. As the manager of a small FBO, planning takes on added significance because, unlike larger organizations with ample financial resources, no or minimal planning can put a smaller firm out of business.

Small FBOs may avoid planning because most owners and managers would prefer to be doing something physical like flying or overhauling an engine. Some employees may be suspicious of planning because they realize it has to do with the future, not the present, and the future is really unpredictable. Furthermore, many people have never been taught how to plan and do not have any idea how to proceed. Maybe they resist the need for imposing self-discipline or do not have enough confidence in themselves. Perhaps they are reluctant to think on a conceptual level. Perhaps they have never mastered the art of establishing priorities.

Whatever the reasons, deferred or a lack of planning can have significant consequences. Planning gives purpose and direction to daily business activities. Without it, such activities are aimless and uncoordinated.

TYPES OF PLANS

Strategic plans, or long-term plans, are established by top management to provide overall direction to company efforts. The strategic plan presents the company's big picture of the future. It ensures that company goals, if achieved, will contribute toward the company's vision, mission, and values. Strategic plans are needed to cope with an ever-changing environment and establish the path toward continued future success.

Tactical plans are generally shorter-term plans that address how the company will implement the strategic plan. Tactically, how does a company implement its strategy? Think of all the resources needed to execute on strategy. Examples of FBO tactical plans include an aircraft fleet plan, hangar expansion plan, succession plan, etc.

Operational plans are very short-term plans, even daily plans, that address what needs to happen on a daily basis to execute tactical plans. Operational plans address day-to-day work details and are designed to standardize employee behavior. Examples of FBO operational plans include the performance appraisal plan, aircraft scheduling plan, crew duty plan, etc. It is quite common for operational plans to be in the form of standard operating procedures or operating directives, or service policies, such as:

- We will inventory only those aircraft parts with a high turnover rate.
- We intend to add to the product line of our counter sale of up to three new items each year.
- We will always have one single-engine aircraft available for short-notice charter flights.

Contingency plans, also known as **business continuity plans**, are designed to prepare for various events that may disrupt business activity. By considering how a company can continue operating, even returning to normal operations in the midst of a crisis, these plans are proactive and forward-thinking. These plans are designed to minimize operational impacts regardless of the scenario.

Development of a business continuity plan consists of four steps: (1) conduct a business impact analysis; (2) identify and document sources of data and procedures to recover critical business functions and processes; (3) organize a business continuity team and compile a business continuity plan; and (4) conduct training for the business continuity team and exercise the plan. It is important to include perspectives from the various FBO departments (such as maintenance, customer service, and finance) to ensure that vulnerabilities are considered and specific recovery plans are developed.

Single-use plans are formulated for specific situations, including special events. Generally, a single-use plan would be developed for a fly-in, presidential visit, or airshow. Such a plan would consider personnel, safety, security, parking for additional aircraft, costs, etc.

Budgets are plans that have been translated into dollars-and-cents projections, which are the culmination of a great deal of careful analysis. In effect, they are both guides to follow and targets to shoot for. Materials budgets, sales budgets, labor budgets, and budgets for capital expenditures all become standards for management action. Good budgeting is needed to direct internal activity and to assign responsibility.

STEP-BY-STEP APPROACH TO PLANNING

The following outline will help to internalize the process of planning. Practice makes perfect, and it is often helpful to plan for something concrete the first time around, such as an open house in conjunction with the annual air show.

1. Assess the present state of affairs—external (the economy, competition, etc.) as well as internal.
2. Set a target date for the activation of the plan.
3. Make a forecast of the future state of affairs (at the target date and, thereafter, for the duration of the proposed plan).
4. List specific objectives that are both reasonable and attainable.
5. Develop methods for reaching the objectives.
6. Work out the details by using the Five Ws (Who? What? Where? When? Why?) and How?
7. Determine the resources available and the structure of the plan with a time schedule.
8. Document all of the details.
9. Set up a control system to monitor the plan's operation and to make adjustments for deviations from planned outcomes.
10. As the plan unfolds, make the necessary changes to compensate for such deviations.

Planning is disciplined thinking that is based on the present and oriented to the future. Plans begin with an analysis of the way things are and a forecast of the way things will (or should) be. Of course, predicting future events based on an extrapolation of current—and incomplete—information can never by entirely accurate. Yet failing to plan is planning to fail.

Organization

As a business grows and sales increase, additional duties and responsibilities are assumed. Additional personnel are required, and the need for specialization and division of work becomes apparent. Each new employee must be placed in an appropriate niche and assigned specific duties. It is up to management to define those niches and then hire or appoint the right people to fill them.

Over time, a company's management is increasingly challenged by the task of coordinating the activities of daily operations. Each business depends on the people who, interlocked and strategically deployed in some structural arrangement, perform all the functions necessary for the total system to accomplish its objectives. This framework or structure, called organization, represents the overall strategic design for operating the business.

Figure 12-2 depicts a sample organizational structure for a small FBO.

ORGANIZATIONAL THEORY

All organizations have managers and employees, but the exact makeup of the organization, including reporting relationships, number of managers, degree of specialization, etc., varies. There are numerous theories that have been advanced over the years in an effort to make sense of organizational dynamics. **Organizational theory** is the study of these various concepts.

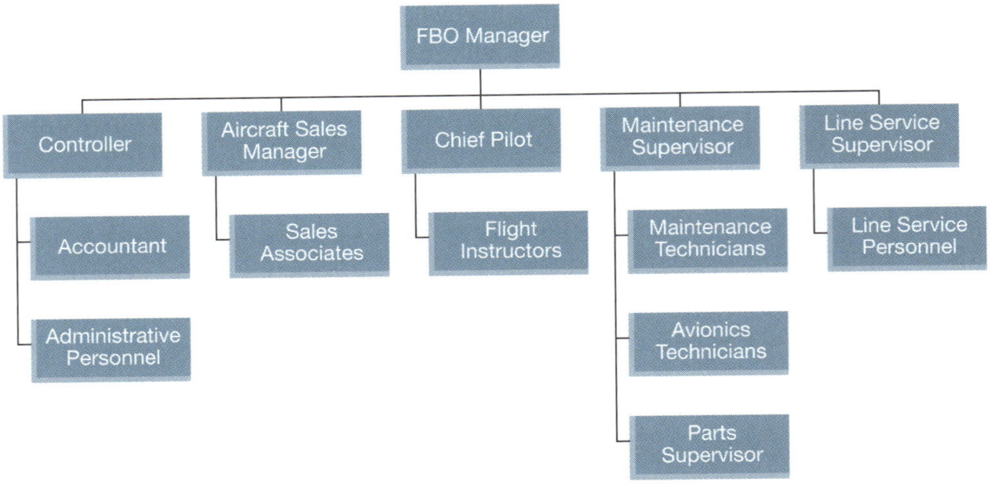

Figure 12-2. Small FBO organizational structure.

Theories of organization cannot specify wholly "right" answers. Nevertheless, the small FBO manager should be familiar with the dimensions that are most frequently discussed by organizational theorists. Some examples are conflicts between individual and organizational goals, departmentalization, line and staff positions, flat versus tall organizations, and unity of command.

Employee Goals and Company Goals

It should be recognized that the employees working in an organization are there primarily to satisfy their own needs. Perhaps they want security, financial income, a sense of belonging as part of a group, or a prestigious title. Although they will work willingly toward the firm's objectives, this occurs only if their personal goals can be achieved alongside organizational goals. If an employee perceives organizational goals to be in conflict with their personal goals, an inner struggle begins, often resulting in lower morale and declining productivity. Generally, an employee will choose to pursue personal goals first. For the sake of internal harmony, a manager must concentrate on reconciling any differences that arise.

To be effective, all goals, whether personal or company, should be SMART:

- **S**pecific—Each goal should be simple, sensible, and significant.
- **M**easurable—Each goal should be measurable with an associated metric.
- **A**chievable—Each goal should be attainable.
- **R**elevant—Each goal should be reasonable, realistic, and results-based.
- **T**imely or time-bound—Each goal should be time-based or time-sensitive.

When developed using the SMART protocol, goals are more likely to be achieved. Once developed, evaluating progress toward goal attainment and reviewing goals, to include development of new goals, will bring the goal-setting and goal-achieving process full circle.

Figure 12-3. SMART goals. *(marekuliasz/Shutterstock.com)*

Departmentalization

As anyone in business knows, a wealth of activities must be performed by employees in numerous skill areas. Handling these myriad tasks is made easier by classifying the many work details into departments. **Departmentalization** refers to the process in which segments of the business that have interrelated work functions are grouped together (in departments) under the supervision of a single specialist. In addition to line service, flight instruction, and maintenance departments, other departments commonly found at FBOs include aircraft sales, charter and rental, and corporate flight service.

Line and Staff Personnel

Most organizations have been arranged according to the line-and-staff concept. **Line personnel** are directly involved in the operation of the business, giving and receiving orders along the chain of command from the head of the company down to the lowest-level worker. Examples of line personnel at an FBO include flight instructors, pilots, line service employees, customer service representatives, etc. **Staff personnel**, on the other hand, are outside this direct chain of command. They are present to aid and support the line personnel. Examples of these staffers include administrative assistants, legal advisors, accountants, human resource specialists, and other supportive service workers. These individuals possess a much more limited kind of authority. Within their own specialized areas of responsibility, of course, they direct their own department personnel.

Organizational Structure

As a business grows, the **organizational structure** develops layers of authority: top, middle, and lower (supervisory) management. Communication barriers tend to form between the layers. Those at the top of the hierarchy usually have little contact with those at the bottom. In the traditional tall organizational structure, employees become relatively confined within their own specialized positions, and dissatisfaction begins to emerge from people in middle and lower positions. Broadly interpreted, they feel that they are not really making a significant contribution to the business. This attitude spreads or deepens, and decisions are increasingly likely to be made at the top and filtered down to the bottom levels.

Furthermore, management positions multiply. The organization can gradually become top-heavy, with many high-paying positions at the executive level. In this case, rigidity sets in, which can hamper creative problem solving, resulting in an overabundance of red tape.

In organizations with a flat structure, on the other hand, there are only one or two levels of management. The supervisory leadership exercised by the executives is of a more personal nature, with more face-to-face contact. Employees in lower management niches take on more responsibility for their efforts and make more decisions. The fact that these individuals are closer to the action than higher-level management and are permitted to make decisions on the spot makes for increased initiative and higher morale.

Unity of Command

The **unity of command** principle is one policy that should seldom be violated. Most workers would agree that no employee should have to answer to more than one supervisor. Having more than one supervisor can cause confusion—for example, as when an employee working under a partnership arrangement is given two opposing directives by the partners. Thus, it is important to have clear unity of command so employees know to which one supervisor they report. The basic principle of unity of command states that an employee should be responsible to only a single supervisor, and that supervisor should be responsible to only a single supervisor, and so on. A clear organizational chart with reporting lines can help employees visualize the unity of command principle.

Span of Control

The **span of control** (or span of management) is another important concept. The average manager finds it relatively easy to oversee one to several employees: to watch over them, train them, direct them, and guide them. As the number of subordinates increases, it becomes more and more difficult for the supervisor to devote enough attention to each person. At some point, the manager (or possibly the employees) will likely reach a breaking point.

How many employees a supervisor can oversee depends on several factors: the supervisor's capabilities, the abilities and characteristics of the subordinates, and the nature of the work being performed. The greater the span of management (that is, the number of individuals under one supervisor), the fewer the number of supervisors and departments are necessary. A narrow span, however, enables supervisors to work more closely with their employees. This balance must be achieved in the best interest of the company.

The owner of the average small FBO can often manage up to six or eight subordinates before things become too unwieldy. This often results in several shift supervisors who oversee six or eight employees on a given shift, with a department director or manager who then oversees the shift supervisors.

Decentralization

As a business grows, the mass of work details increases. Yet it is hard for the entrepreneurial, Type-A personality to delegate responsibilities to employees who may be less skilled and less motivated. Indeed, some managers keep a firm grasp on everything. They maintain control where power, authority, and tight supervisory controls are centralized. At the other extreme is **decentralization**, possibly to a point where a capable group, to a large degree autonomous, manages each major division of the business. This concept of decentralization—organizing a firm around self-governing profit centers banded together in a functional team—maximizes individual initiative, ensures localized decision-making, and facilitates responsibility.

DEVELOPING AN OPERATIONS MANUAL

Operating a company without a formal set of operating procedures can be detrimental. Commonly, standard operating procedures are incorporated into an operations manual. Rarely can objectives be reached without such a manual. There are at least eight ways an operations manual can benefit a company:

1. It establishes a comprehensive source of company policies and procedures.
2. It facilitates even-handed, consistent administration of personnel policies.
3. It promotes continuity in management style throughout the organization.
4. It helps identify problems before they arise, minimizing crisis management.
5. It reduces the number of emotional decisions, encouraging a pro-business climate of objectivity.
6. It defines authority clearly and distributes responsibility.
7. It becomes a training tool for employees.
8. It offers examples of standard forms, reducing the number and variety of forms used.

In any small FBO, there may be little time to devote to the development of an operations manual. FBO management must personally endorse the project and provide leadership to keep it moving, establish deadlines, and appoint a champion in the company to get the job done.

The manager must gather all existing procedures, systems, and forms. Ideas from all levels of management and staff must incorporated. The manual must be discussed with all operations personnel to ensure that all actual day-to-day working needs are addressed. Concurrently, a checklist of points covered in the company's operations manual should be prepared. These 10 basic sections should be included:

1. *Introduction*—Purpose of the manual; how the company started; business objectives and philosophy; description of products and services; economics of the business.
2. *Organization chart*—Who reports to whom; job descriptions; addresses of company's facilities; importance of each department and division.
3. *General employee information*—Attitude toward and expected standards for interactions with customers, suppliers, and other employees; statement on how to handle telephone callers and visitors; housekeeping policies.
4. *Personnel administration*—Hiring practices; employment forms; when and how workers are paid; outside employment; reprimands; hours of operation; coffee breaks and lunch hours; dress code; personal behavior; frequency of salary reviews; advancement opportunities; benefits paid by the company; contributory benefits; explanation of payroll deductions; labor laws; use of time cards; scheduling; overtime; vacation entitlement and holidays.
5. *Products and services*—Customer relations; supplier relations; sales procedures; taking pride in what the company does.
6. *Paperwork*—Administrative procedures; ensuring accountability; billings; sample of each form; purpose of each document; routing flow chart for paperwork; summary of deadlines and due dates.
7. *Safety and security*—Protection of physical premises; personal security; statement about protection of company assets; importance of safety to the employee and the company; handling of confidential information.
8. *Emergencies*—How to handle accidents; what to do in case of fire; emergency telephone numbers; power failures; robberies and thefts.
9. *Maintenance and repair*—Telephones; service personnel; repairs; who should authorize; trash removal; key control; handling of equipment; property damage or loss.
10. *Legal*—Compliance with local, state, and federal laws; handling of regulatory agencies; inspections; recordkeeping requirements; maintaining ethical standards.

The instructions should be presented in a logical order and be specific. Exceptions should be stated if those exceptions have occurred frequently in the past. Language and examples should be common to the company's employees. Finally, a qualified outsider (preferably an educator or a professional editor) should perform thorough proofreading and editing.

A digital PDF file accessible on a shared server or cloud-based platform permits great flexibility in using, reviewing, and updating material. The sections should be divided based on the major categories of topics covered. Within each section, the material should be in outline form. Generally, a "Miscellaneous" section should be avoided, to minimize the chance of poor categorization.

Each page should contain the section title, the date the page was issued, and a page number. This simplifies both the task of keeping the manual updated and the distribution of new or revised material. The completed manual should include a thoroughly cross-referenced index to the topics covered.

A chain of command should be established to make revisions, with upper management approving all proposals for change. Otherwise, duplication and overlap will create confusion. Finally, the operations manual should be reviewed at least once annually, because a growing company is always changing.

Directing

Once the plan has been prepared and the firm has been organized and staffed to carry out its objectives, the next step is putting the plan into action and **directing** it. Up to this point, most of the activity has been in the mind of the planner(s). Now the game really begins. Organizational employees must be motivated, persuaded, led, coordinated, and encouraged. This requires active management, with a focus on teamwork, supervision, and productivity.

LEADERSHIP

Leadership involves interaction. It is a way of behaving—of persuading and inducing, and of guiding and motivating. A totally rounded leadership form calls for a mastery of certain skill areas, the creation of the right climate within which the work group can function properly, and the direction and control of group activities.

Leadership style is often a reflection of personality; however, a single, consistent type of behavior may not always be applicable or desired. What works well with one person (or group) may not necessarily work at all with the next. Individuals, as well as groups, are extremely varied. Consequently, effective leadership requires an eclectic approach, taking into account the three-way match among the leader, group members, and situation at hand. Most people, over the long term, tend to rely on the style that yields the best results.

Many of us are guilty of holding stereotypical notions about leaders. We tend to believe that a good leader is one who commands respect; who electrifies the atmosphere when entering a room; and who is, without a doubt, aggressive, domineering, capable of manipulation, a skilled communicator, and an extrovert. Our concepts even go beyond personality to physical attributes. We may think that a good leader is usually taller and heavier (and more attractive) than others.

Oddly enough, some of the greatest leaders in world history, and many capable managers of major corporations, have been quiet, unassuming, introspective, short, and thin. Management experts have often theorized about the kinds of personal traits necessary for effective performance in the role of leader. Studies have compared the qualities of top executives with the qualities of unsuccessful leaders in order to uncover the characteristics that differentiate them. Several distinguishing attributes keep appearing; however, it is important to keep in mind that leadership has three dimensions: the leader, those who are led, and the individual situation. Consequently, whether one rates high or low in these attributes does not necessarily make an individual a good or bad leader.

A review of the following list of personal traits can be valuable in dealing with others:

- Adaptability
- Alertness
- Communication skills
- Confidence
- Creativity
- Curiosity
- Dependability
- Drive
- Enthusiasm
- Evaluation skills
- Flexibility
- Human relations skills
- Maturity
- Open-mindedness
- Optimism
- Patience
- Persuasive powers
- Poise
- Resourcefulness
- Sensitivity to others
- Supportiveness
- Teaching ability
- Tolerance
- Warmth
- Willingness to listen
- Willingness to take chances

In addition to specific personal traits, the effective leader needs to possess certain skills, which include the following:

- The ability to establish priorities
- A capacity for giving credit when due
- Planning and scheduling skills
- Proficiency in problem solving
- A willingness to delegate responsibility to others

True leaders invest in their employees and refer to them as teammates rather than subordinates. As John Maxwell has said, "Everything rises and falls on leadership" (Bowie 2015). Thus, effective leadership is integral to the success of an organization and can impact employee morale, retention, productivity, company culture, and much more.

UNDERSTANDING EMPLOYEES

Each individual within an organization is a complex, multifaceted person. Among his or her many sides are the intellectual, physical, and emotional as well as the economic, social, political, and moral. It is not surprising, then, that people's behavior can be as complex and as difficult to interpret as people are themselves.

An individual's personality is composed of the following:

1. *Values.* Values are concepts we come to accept over the years as we interact with others and with our environment.
2. *Attitudes.* Attitudes serve as vehicles for organizing knowledge, for adjusting to the world around us, for shielding us from confusion and pain, and for orienting us toward things that are pleasurable.
3. *Response traits.* We have habitual ways of responding to and dealing with others.

A review of any basic psychology text can provide many insights into human behavior. In turn, psychological understanding can enhance a manager's capability in motivating and directing employees.

Motives are the energizing forces that drive all of us and are behind most behavior. Many of our actions result from the interplay of several motives. Some motives are largely rational and based on logic; for example, filing an IFR flight plan under marginal weather conditions. In this instance, the motives are quite clear and logical. Using this example, the pilot desires to avoid an accident that could occur and endanger life and property and also avoid a violation of FAA regulations.

On the other hand, many motives are of an emotional (or non-rational) nature. The line of demarcation between rational and emotional motives is rather hazy. Not filing an IFR flight plan may be based on the emotional motive: fear of being cited by the FAA.

Furthermore, what motivates one person does not necessarily motivate the next. The same motive can lead to varied behaviors in different individuals. The same behavior in different individuals can result from different motives.

All of us are driven by many motives: economic, safety, and social motives as well as physiological ones like hunger, thirst, the need for sleep, and sex. The majority of our motives, however, are learned—those that we develop as we interact with our environment. One way to better understand the subject of human needs and wants is to review a notable theory proposed many years ago by the eminent psychologist Abraham Maslow. The well-known **Maslow's hierarchy of needs** organizes human needs on different levels according to their potency for influencing behavior (Figure 12-4). Maslow reasoned that all of us are constantly struggling upwards to attain higher steps on this pyramid of needs until we reach its pinnacle. From time to time, most employees are restrained from proceeding up the hierarchy or may be knocked down to lower levels by outside conditions (or, perhaps, by inner forces).

Translating Maslow's concepts into modern human resources thinking, we can expect employees to seek such things as:

1. *Physiological Needs (Level 1)*—A salary competitive with other firms with similar positions, adequate to provide the necessities of life.

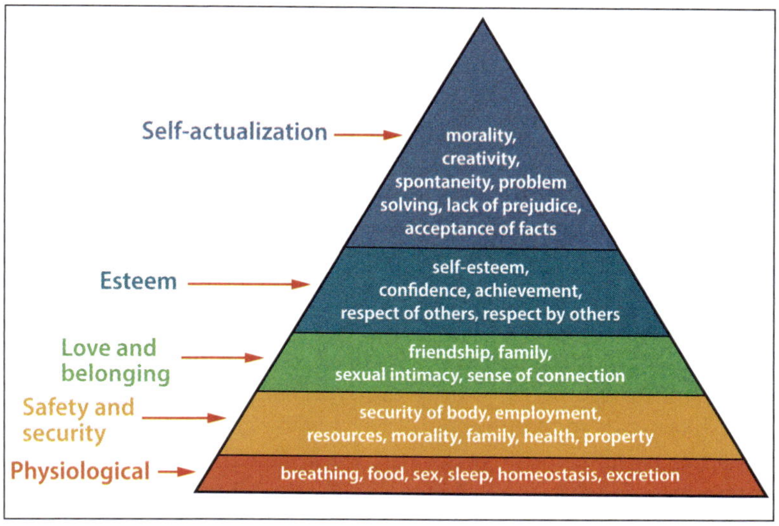

Figure 12-4. Maslow's hierarchy of needs.

2. *Safety Needs (Level 2)*—Job security and safe working conditions. This need may lead to health and life-insurance coverage for the employee's spouse and children and a 401K program.
3. *Love and Belongingness Needs (Level 3)*—The feeling of being part of an organization and having a place in the group; acceptance by coworkers and employer; and a friendly environment.
4. *Esteem Needs (Level 4)*—Ego satisfaction, recognition (an occasional pat on the back), authority, and status within the group; the belief that the person's work is both responsible and respected.
5. *Need for Self-Actualization (Level 5)*—A chance for growth and the opportunity to demonstrate initiative; encouragement for the individual to participate and contribute to the fullest.

Several other well-known management theories have also had significant impacts on human resource management. These theories, discussed below, are important for managers to consider.

Theory X and Y

More than 50 years ago, management theorist Douglas McGregor investigated the attitudes of supervisors toward their employees, resulting in **McGregor's Theory X and Theory Y**. Those who subscribe to what McGregor termed the Theory X approach are convinced that the average person doesn't like to work, has little if any ambition, and tries to avoid responsibility. Consequently, these supervisors feel that they need to watch workers closely (micromanagement) and depend on the strategic application of both rewards and punishment in order to obtain satisfactory performance.

Other supervisors follow a different philosophy, the more positive Theory Y approach. They believe employees consider work to be as natural as play and rest, and that once committed to specific objectives, they will not only put out effort willingly but will also seek responsibility. Theory Y managers more readily believe in employee empowerment and avoid micromanaging employees.

Experience has shown that a Theory Y manager will create higher employee morale and greater employee productivity than a Theory X manager. Employees often live up to their manager's expectations and are greatly impacted by employee–management relations.

Theory Z

Created by Dr. William Ouchi and founded on Japanese management techniques, **Theory Z** takes McGregor's Theory Y one step further. Theory Z includes a substantial delegation of responsibility, trust in each individual, and decision by group consensus. Employee loyalty to the company can be enhanced by providing a job with strong focus on the well-being of the employee, both on and off the job. These concepts are characteristically seen in Japanese companies. Of course, some of their attributes (such as lifetime employment) cannot be incorporated easily into our own economy. Still, owners of small FBOs might well profit by modifying and applying other attributes to their own enterprises; for example, the participative approach to decision-making and a genuine concern for one's employees.

Job Motivators and Hygiene Factors

In the 1960s, management theorist Frederick Herzberg researched the workplace to uncover those factors that appeared to exert some influence on the job satisfaction or motivation of employees. **Herzberg's two-factor theory** presents distinct sets of such factors: motivators (or satisfiers) and hygiene factors (dissatisfiers). Herzberg maintained that motivators appeal to higher level human needs and, therefore, not only motivate employees but can also increase the level of job satisfaction. Examples include recognition, responsibility, advancement, growth, and the work itself. On the other hand, some factors in the workplace that cater to individuals' lower needs (hygiene factors) apparently do little to encourage worker motivation. Nevertheless, they can, of course, contribute to employee dissatisfaction. Salary, working conditions, company policies, and relations with one's supervisor are hygiene factors. In essence, the presence of these hygiene factors don't necessarily have great impact, but their absence can significantly impact employee behavior and productivity.

Obviously then, owners and managers of FBOs might do well to review Herzberg's findings. More highly motivated and satisfied employees might be developed through effective management policies that create:

- High-quality working conditions
- Employee security
- More responsibility delegated to employees
- Productive teams with common goals and decision-making
- Flexible schedules
- Enhanced or redesigned jobs
- Opportunity for promotion
- Rewards for exceptional contributions

Clearly, management should be focused on motivating employees; even so, discipline may occasionally be required. The purpose in discipline is to change negative behaviors. If these behaviors can be changed using positive reinforcement, that should be attempted first. When necessary, discipline (or negative reinforcement) should be conducted in private. The goal is not to humiliate the employee. Rather, the goal is to get the employee's attention and correct negative behavior.

EMPOWERING EMPLOYEES

Employees are responsible for making themselves perform well, but managers are responsible for creating an environment where that seems possible. As discussed in chapter six, **employee empowerment** means releasing an individual's power to succeed by removing the barriers that prevent it, such as lack of skills, not enough direction, or too little responsibility and authority. In order to empower an employee, managers must create small successes and recognize the employee for the success. To stimulate these small successes, managers must establish an environment where employees feel they can succeed. This means encouraging creativity, setting goals, giving feedback, and recognizing performance.

Effective feedback needs to be timely, specific, and should focus on the behavior, not the individual. Positive feedback should be offered, and alternatives should be provided so employees can set measurable performance goals. Negative feedback should be depersonalized, while managers should personalize the positive.

Coaching is one method managers can use to give feedback. But it can also be used to teach, motivate, or challenge employees. There are seven basic steps in the coaching process:

1. Observe performance and record observations.
2. Analyze performance so it can be linked to behaviors.
3. Provide feedback that is timely and specific.
4. Interview by asking open- and closed-ended questions.
5. Set goals and action plans for higher performance.
6. Follow up on action plans to fine-tune performance.
7. Reinforce effective behaviors by complimenting efforts and results.

Although informal feedback is important, the need for a formal performance appraisal is necessary. It is important that managers and supervisors clearly outline expectations, observations, and evaluations in writing. Frequent and comprehensive work sampling and written open-ended appraisals are necessary. If employees are surprised by information in their annual appraisals, they are not receiving enough informal feedback.

The **360-degree feedback** or performance appraisal includes feedback from coworkers, subordinates, supervisors, managers, and the employee. This anonymous feedback from subordinates, peers, and supervisors is especially useful for those not in a managerial role. It is much more enlightening than feedback only from a manager, which has traditionally been the extent of performance appraisals.

DECISION-MAKING

In business, most management decisions are made by intuition. Although data-based decision-making is much preferred, owners of small FBOs in particular may tend to rely on intuition.

Intuitive decision-making stems partially from a lack of familiarity with problem-solving techniques and partially from the realization that extensive resources—time, energy, and funds—should only be diverted to the most serious and complex problems. Happily, these major problems do not occur very often. When they do (for example, when contemplating a major building expansion or marketing campaign), the manager may benefit from the assistance of an experienced consultant.

Fortunately, most problems in business repeat themselves, so once a satisfactory solution has been worked out (or accidentally hit upon), the entrepreneur knows how to solve the problem the next time it arises. Only the new, infrequent, unique problems present a strong challenge.

Decision-making is but one step in the problem-solving process. It is the last step in which the manager chooses the one alternative that seems best. The whole decision-making process is as follows:

1. *Diagnose the problem.* On a sheet of paper, the manager writes a clear statement of the problem's essence. This will help to clearly identify the problem as the manager works towards a solution. Many problems are quite complex. Often there is a need to go further and break down the original problem statement into its major parts. Each part should then be summarized and written down as a sub-problem statement. Another useful trick is to draw a simple diagram of the problem situation, making certain to put in all the elements involved.
2. *Gather information.* Hunt for pertinent information to help solve the problem. Facts are not only available from internal records, external sources of data, and primary research but they are also readily obtained from personnel.
3. *Generate alternative solutions.* Develop a number of alternative solutions to the problem. Creative thinking can lead to robust alternatives.
4. *Evaluate the alternatives.* Rate the alternatives according to each of several criteria; for example, cost, time, judged effectiveness or payoff, effect on management, and so on. Use a simple numerical rating scale, such as 0 = Poor, 1 = Fair, 2 = Good, 3 = Very Good, and 4 = Excellent. If some criteria are more important to the firm than others, then assign more weight to those in the analysis.
5. *Select the best alternative(s).* At this point, the manager makes the best decision based on data available and analysis performed.
6. *Translate the decision into action.*

Of course, many more sophisticated techniques may be used for solving business problems. For the most part, these approaches are used by larger companies and not by small firms. Examples of these methods are those that take into account chance or probability, use mathematics and statistics, require computer programming, or are based on simulation. These include game theory, decision theory, queuing theory, decision matrices, simulation, and linear programming. All of these more advanced methods are too complex for this chapter. A number of good texts are available on the topic of decision-making in business and industry.

Controlling

It is important to measure the results of the organizational plan while it is unfolding, as well as make adjustments where and when needed. Logically, the control function cannot be separated from the planning function; they are interdependent, much like the two sides of the same coin.

Controlling is a process that includes analysis, setting standards, monitoring, securing feedback, and taking corrective action.

1. *Analysis*—Study and compare, for quantity and quality, the output of people and machines, the services provided, and the systems employed. Examine everything with a careful eye to standards and decision-making.
2. *Setting Standards*—As a result of analysis, establish acceptable standards of performance in all areas. In turn, these standards become control valves, quantitative and qualitative measurements for future performance, and guidelines for projecting cost, time, and sales.
3. *Monitoring*—The need for regular inspection and performance checks to note exceptions to the standards that have been set and possible reasons for the deviations.
4. *Securing Feedback*—A foolproof system for reporting deviations from standards must be established so that the proper people are notified regularly and promptly.
5. *Corrective Action*—Finally, all exceptions to the established standards must be acted on. Adjustments need to be made promptly so that contingent outcomes are brought back on target.

All areas of the business must be subject to this control function. Generally, managers readily think of inventory control, order processing, quality control, and production control. Yet controls are just as necessary in the personnel area (for example, in performance evaluations); in the financial area (where ratios can be used to investigate a variety of problems); and in the long-term planning of projects (where capital plans can be projected years in the future). For control is, in essence, self-discipline.

COMMUNICATION

Service organizations such as FBOs run on **communication**. Prospective customers are located, contacted, and persuaded to buy products and services through communication. Similarly, employees are recruited, hired, trained, and directed; departments are managed; and machines are operated. Communication is the oil that lubricates the various gears and cogs in the free-enterprise system.

In the process of communication in business, a number of components are involved. Indeed, communication in business appears to be a closed system with all parts interacting in synergistic fashion. The major elements that simplify a company's external communications with its customers are:

1. *Source*—The sender or originator of the messages.
2. *Messages*—Information emitted by the source and directed to the receivers.
3. *Media*—The various carriers or transmitters of the messages (such as voice, written, radio, newspapers, billboards, internet, and social platforms).
4. *Receivers*—Those for whom the messages are intended.

Figure 12-5. Communication methods. *(Artistdesign29/Shutterstock.com)*

5. *Feedback*—Customer reactions, demographic information, and other facts returned by or received from customers to assist management in its decision-making.

Improvements within any of these areas—for example, in the quality of messages sent or the refinement or elaboration of the feedback process—improve the productivity of the entire communication system.

Applied to a firm's internal organization, communication starts with verbal or written messages (orders, instructions, and the like) passed down from the top to lower levels. Feedback moves upward, completing the system. Of course, the effectiveness of this internal system also depends on unimpeded horizontal communication on each individual level. Unfortunately, poor communication is commonly observed within organizations, perhaps due to the pressures of day-to-day details, which often make communicating on a face-to-face basis nearly impossible.

All messages to employees should be transmitted in terms that can be clearly understood and that convey the manager's exact meaning. To accomplish this objective, employers must understand the employees' point of view. Good listening skills constitute an important asset in communication; half-hearted listening interferes considerably with effective management. Encourage employees to listen, too. Employees should understand instructions and be encouraged to ask questions. As a final point, all supervisory personnel should be effective communicators.

Summary

The effective management of an FBO requires attention to planning, organizing, directing, and controlling. Traditionally, management texts have focused on these four functions of a manager. But, to be a true leader, one must reach the heart of employees by investing in their lives, mentoring them, proving opportunities for them, growing them. After all, managing well also requires leading well.

Key Terms

360-degree feedback. A performance appraisal process in which each employee receives confidential, anonymous feedback from the people who work around them. This wholistic feedback is more comprehensive than feedback only from a single manager.

budget. A forecast of revenue and expenses over a specific future time period. A budget serves as a plan of action for management and is also used to compare against actuals at the end of an accounting period.

business continuity plan. A plan that outlines how a business will continue operating during an unplanned disruption. The focus is on maintaining operations during the event and returning to normal operations after the event.

coaching. A method managers can use that incorporates mentoring and performance feedback to guide and grow employees.

communication. Using written and verbal means to convey information both to and from employees. Effective communication is a characteristic of a high-performing organization.

contingency plan. Also known as a business continuity plan, this plan prepares for various unplanned future events that may impact the business.

controlling. A managerial function that includes analysis, setting standards, monitoring, securing feedback, and taking corrective action.

decentralization. Organizing a firm around self-governing profit centers banded together in a functional team, which maximizes individual initiative, ensures localized decision-making, and facilitates responsibility.

departmentalization. The process in which segments of the business that have interrelated work functions are grouped together (in departments) under the supervision of a single specialist. Examples of FBO departments include flight operations, aircraft sales, finance, and marketing.

directing. The process of motivating, persuading, leading, coordinating, and encouraging employees. This requires active management, with a focus on teamwork, supervision, and productivity.

employee empowerment. Releasing an individual's power to succeed by removing the barriers that prevent it, such as lack of skills, not enough direction, or too little responsibility and authority. Allowing employees to make decisions to resolve customer complaints is an indication of empowerment.

Herzberg's two-factor theory. A workplace management theory that identifies factors affecting job satisfaction: Motivators (or satisfiers) appeal to higher level human needs; they not only motivate employees but can also increase the level of job satisfaction. Hygiene factors (dissatisfiers) cater to individual's lower needs; they do little to encourage worker motivation but can contribute to employee dissatisfaction.

intuitive decision-making. The process by which information acquired through life experience is relied upon to form a decision. Decision by intuition.

leadership. The ability to influence and guide followers to effect positive results in the organization. Leadership differs from management in that it is more focused on each employee and adds value to employees so they, in turn, add value to customers and the organization.

line personnel. Personnel directly involved in the operation of the business. Line functions include flight instructor, pilot, line service, customer service representative, dispatcher, etc.

Maslow's hierarchy of needs. A theory of human motivation based on a hierarchy of needs, the lowest of which must be satisfied before an individual moves up to the next level. Levels include (in order from lowest to highest) physiological, safety, belongingness and love, esteem, and self-actualization.

McGregor's Theory X and Theory Y. Two opposing managerial views of employees. A Theory X manager views employees as disliking work, which requires the manager to persuade, compel, and warn employees with punishment. A Theory Y manager assumes employees enjoy their jobs, which results in a manager who empowers employees and provides opportunities for responsibility, teamwork, and self-direction.

operational plan. A very short-term plan that addresses what needs to happen on a daily basis to execute tactical plans. Operational plans address day-to-day work details and are designed to standardize employee behavior.

organizational structure. The makeup of an organization, often visualized in an organization chart. It defines reporting relationships and indicates how activities are directed toward the achievement of organizational goals.

organizational theory. The study of the group of concepts and theories that explain how individuals behave in organizations.

planning. The process of preparing for the future in an organization. For instance, by assessing an organization's goals and creating a realistic, detailed plan of action, the manager can better ensure the company remains competitive.

single-use plan. A plan formulated for a specific situation or event, such as special events like airshows or fly-ins.

span of control. The number of subordinates or direct reports a supervisor is responsible for.

staff personnel. Personnel not directly involved in the operation of the business. These personnel serve in support roles and facilitate the activities of line personnel. Staff functions include accountant, human resource manager, attorney, etc.

strategic plan. A plan that defines the organization's future direction with a long-term perspective.

tactical plan. A shorter-term plan that outlines the necessary steps to take to achieve a goal or address a problem. A tactical plan supports goal achievement toward fulfillment of the strategic plan.

Theory Z. Ouchi's Japanese management theory that includes a substantial delegation of responsibility, trust in each individual, and decision by group consensus. Employee loyalty to the company can be enhanced by providing a job with strong focus on the well-being of the employee, both on and off the job.

unity of command. The principle that each employee should only report to one supervisor.

Review Questions

1. Identify and briefly describe the characteristics of well-managed FBOs.
2. Why is planning considered to be the most important management function?
3. Provide examples of plans an FBO may develop.
4. List the step-by-step approach to planning.
5. How can employee goals be at odds with company goals?
6. What is the purpose of departmentalization?
7. Describe the line-and-staff concept.
8. What are some problems associated with flat and tall organizational structures?
9. Explain the organizational principles of unity of command and span of control.
10. What is the purpose of an operations manual?
11. Why is effective leadership so important in directing a company?
12. Identify ten personality traits that can be helpful in dealing with others.
13. Define personality and motives.
14. Discuss Maslow's levels of human needs and wants.
15. Discuss McGregor's Theory X and Theory Y approaches.
16. What are the motivators and hygiene factors described by Herzberg?
17. What is meant by empowering employees?
18. Describe the six steps in the decision-making process.
19. Provide several examples of the control function in such areas as marketing, line service, and parts inventory.
20. Why is communication the "oil that lubricates the various gears and cogs in the free-enterprise system"?
21. Describe how communication is applied to a firm's internal organization.

Scenarios

1. Two months ago, you resigned your position as FBO manager at a small hub airport to manage an FBO at a medium hub airport. Now, two months into your new position, you have learned that the current director of line service has an extremely poor work ethic. He rarely attends required meetings and seemingly offers little input into the operation of the organization. In fact, other employees have mentioned how this employee has never given 100 percent to his job since he was hired five years ago. As a result, the success of his department (and the FBO) is suffering. This individual is the son of the FBO owner, the same owner who hired you. What options do you have and which will you pursue?
2. One year into your new position as manager of an FBO with 25 employees, you are feeling as if most employees don't respect you and don't enjoy coming to work. Employees rarely participate in company meetings, and customer service seems to be nonexistent at times. Some aircraft owners have even moved their aircraft to another FBO located on the field. As you look out your office window, business seems to be booming at the FBO located across the field. You then glance at your FBO's year-in-review numbers and can't avoid seeing the declining sales and reduced net profit. Just then, your phone rings. The owner of the FBO is calling you after looking at the year-in-review numbers, and the owner strongly urges you to fix the problem. As you begin this new year, what approach should you take?
3. You just graduated from college this past spring with a degree in aviation management. After searching for jobs in the aviation industry all summer, you finally discovered an opening for FBO manager at a nearby FBO with ten employees. To your delight, you were interviewed and offered the position. You readily accepted. It is Sunday afternoon, and you anxiously await your first day on the job tomorrow. You've read a great deal in college about various leadership styles, management principles, etc. However, you have never actually supervised employees before. What philosophy/management style will you adopt as you manage this organization and these ten employees?
4. As the new manager of a small FBO with eighteen employees (not including yourself), you have decided a new organizational chart is needed. The FBO currently has administration (three employees), line service (eight employees), flight instruction (three employees), and a small charter operation (four employees). Each department has a manager. Draw an organizational chart for this organization.
5. A recent employee survey shows that employees are dissatisfied with the level of communication by management throughout the organization. Many employees feel as if they are in the dark regarding major management decisions and future plans for the FBO. How do you, as manager of the FBO, correct this? What are your ideas to improve the flow of communication throughout the organization?

Bibliography

Bowie, Deborah. 2015. "Everything Rises and Falls on Leadership." *Business in Greater Gainesville* (August 2015). https://businessmagazinegainesville.com/everything-rises-falls-leadership/.

Maslow, Abraham. 1970. *Motivation and Personality*, 2nd ed. New York: Harper & Row.

Prather, C. Daniel. 2009. *General Aviation Marketing and Management: Operating, Marketing, and Managing an FBO*. 3rd ed. Malabar, FL: Krieger Publishing Company.

13

Risk Management

In Chapter 13

Objectives

At the end of this chapter, you should be able to:

1. Discuss the role of risk mitigation in FBO management.
2. Explain the different types of risks an FBO may face on a daily basis and how these risks may be mitigated.
3. Discuss the various types of insurance policies an FBO would be expected to have in effect.
4. Discuss the importance of COVID-19 mitigation.
5. Discuss how COVID-19 mitigation can be enhanced for an FBO.
6. Discuss the importance of safety for an FBO.
7. Explain how safety can be enhanced at an FBO.
8. Discuss the role of security at an FBO.
9. Explain how security can be enhanced at an FBO.

Introduction

This chapter discusses four important considerations in managing risk for an FBO: insurance, COVID-19 mitigation, safety, and security. Regardless of its skill at serving customers, an FBO that neglects any of these four areas will incur additional expenses, a poor reputation, and possibly legal action, which could result in the eventual bankruptcy of the business. Thus, it is imperative for FBO managers to be proactive in these areas by actively minimizing liability.

Insurance

An FBO will be exposed to a number of different risks on a daily basis. These risks, although they can be mitigated, can never be completely eliminated. Thus, FBOs purchase insurance policies, educate employees, and develop plans and procedures to mitigate these known risks. Many FBO lease agreements actually require FBOs to purchase insurance policies proving specific coverages and in certain amounts to protect both the FBO and the airport from any possible claims. Typical insurance policies for an FBO would provide coverage for:

- Workers' compensation
- Aircraft liability (damage to company-owned and non-owned aircraft)
- Airport liability
- Hangarkeeper's liability
- In-flight hangarkeeper's liability
- Business auto liability
- Environmental impairment (pollution) insurance
- Property insurance
- Commercial liability

WORKERS' COMPENSATION

All businesses, including FBOs, have a legal responsibility to their employees to make the workplace safe. To protect employers from lawsuits resulting from workplace accidents and to provide medical care and compensation for lost income to employees hurt in workplace accidents, businesses are required to buy **workers' compensation insurance**. Workers' compensation insurance covers workers injured on the job, whether they are hurt on the workplace premises or elsewhere, or in auto accidents while on business. It also covers work-related illnesses. Workers' compensation provides payments to injured workers, without regard to who was at fault in the accident, for time lost from work and for medical and rehabilitation services. It also provides death benefits to surviving spouses and dependents. Typical workers' compensation limits for FBOs are $1,000,000 bodily injury by accident, $1,000,000 bodily injury by disease policy limit, and $1,000,000 bodily injury by disease each employee.

AIRCRAFT LIABILITY

Aircraft liability insurance covers the FBO for liability, including liability to passengers or resulting from the ownership, operation, maintenance, or use of all owned, non-owned, leased, or hired aircraft on, or in connection with, any premises. To mitigate these risks, FBOs purchase aircraft liability insurance. Insurance alone, however, is not enough. FBOs require check-out of aircraft for new pilots, which includes some flight time with an instructor to be certain of the pilot's capabilities before renting the aircraft. FBOs also hire qualified and competent flight instructors to adequately train flight students. The typical minimum limit for a policy of this sort would be $1,000,000 each occurrence.

AIRPORT LIABILITY

Similar to a mortgage company requiring the homeowner to maintain property insurance naming the mortgage company as insured, airports must also protect their interests by requiring FBOs to maintain appropriate **airport liability insurance**. This coverage provides for the liability resulting out of, or in connection with, ongoing operations performed by, or on behalf of, the FBO under the FBO lease agreement or the use or occupancy of airport premises by, or on behalf of, the FBO. Typical policy limits would be $1,000,000.

HANGARKEEPER'S LIABILITY

This risk is specific to storing aircraft in a hangar and the liability that results from storing assets belonging to others, requiring FBOs to obtain **hangarkeeper's liability insurance**. If the hangar catches fire, the FBO would not only need insurance to cover the damage to the hangar but also insurance to cover the damage to aircraft and equipment stored inside the hangar. In essence, FBOs are required to maintain this insurance for aircraft in their care, custody, or control. Typical limits would be $1,000,000 each aircraft and $2,000,000 each occurrence (all aircraft).

Figure 13-1. Aircraft in storage. *(iurii/Shutterstock.com)*

IN-FLIGHT HANGARKEEPER'S LIABILITY

In-flight hangarkeeper's liability insurance policies are designed to cover liability resulting from the pickup and redelivery of aircraft, test flights, instruction, and charter flights. This policy differs from an aircraft liability policy in that in-flight hangarkeeper's policies cover damage to aircraft in flight, whereas aircraft liability policies cover liability to passengers and aircraft that are not in flight. Typical limits would be $1,000,000 each aircraft and $1,000,000 aggregate.

BUSINESS AUTO LIABILITY

In addition to the use of aircraft, FBOs utilize automobiles to a large degree in connection with their business. Flight crews may use an FBO-owned courtesy car. Customer service personnel might park a private auto for a client. The FBO might provide limousine service. Each of these occurrences simply increases risk to the FBO. Thus, **business auto liability insurance** becomes necessary. This policy will cover all owned, hired, and non-owned vehicles and will typically have a $1,000,000 policy limit for each occurrence (bodily injury and property damage combined).

ENVIRONMENTAL IMPAIRMENT (POLLUTION) INSURANCE

FBOs are at great risk for causing environmental pollution. They maintain fuel farms, store moderate amounts of hazardous chemicals, and generate hazardous waste in the form of used oil, for example. If these are not stored and disposed of properly, the FBO can face serious consequences. Although proper procedures are most effective at preventing environmental problems, FBOs may be required to maintain **environmental impairment (pollution) insurance**. This insurance will cover the FBO from liability resulting from pollution or other environmental impairment arising out of, or in connection with, work performed under the lease agreement, or which arises out of, or in connection with, the use or occupancy of airport premises in connection with the lease agreement. The typical policy limits are $1,000,000 each claim and $2,000,000 annual aggregate.

PROPERTY INSURANCE

FBOs have extensive property that is at risk for fire, vandalism, and theft. The potential for fire at an FBO is very high, mainly due to the large volumes of aviation fuel being stored and moved. The wise FBO manager will practice proper fire fuel safety as detailed in Chapter 4. Additionally, FBOs use fire resistant materials, automatic fire sprinkler systems, and fire extinguishers. Personnel should also be trained in proper housekeeping practices, fire prevention, and firefighting. Although rare, vandalism is always a possibility. This can be prevented by proper security equipment and procedures (discussed later in this chapter). Likewise, theft is an ever-present risk at FBOs. This may include theft of pilot supplies, cash, aircraft parts, or the aircraft themselves. This may be perpetrated by employees or external customers. In any event, this risk can be minimized by security equipment and procedures as well as by having proper checks and balances and hiring only employees that have successfully completing background checks.

In addition to procedures to mitigate these risks, FBOs will carry **property insurance** policies to minimize any financial loss associated with this. This policy will have the airport as an added insured. This insurance will cover any existing or constructed buildings, structures, or any other improvements to real property located on the property leased by the FBO. Typical policy limits for property insurance are $1,000,000.

COMMERCIAL LIABILITY

Similar to all businesses, FBOs should also have a general commercial liability policy in place. This policy will protect the business from financial loss if the business is found liable for personal or advertising injury cause by the business. Commonly, the FBO is protecting itself against lawsuits from individuals injured on FBO property. This includes an individual being injured by a tug, falling while entering the FBO terminal building, etc.

COVID-19 Mitigation

The **coronavirus disease (COVID-19)** global pandemic caused by the virus severe acute respiratory syndrome coronavirus 2 (SARS-CoV-2), which was first identified in Wuhan, Hubei, China in December 2019, has wreaked havoc on the global aviation industry. Due to federal guidance and state stay-at-home orders in 2020, the vast majority of the U.S. population was essentially sheltering in place rather than travelling by air. Across the country, conferences and conventions were canceled, sporting events were canceled, schools moved to online instruction, and restaurants and shopping malls closed. Even as recently as summer 2021, some states continued to have numerous restrictions in place on the movement of individuals. In many areas, restaurants were only open for take-out or curbside delivery, large gatherings of individuals were prohibited, schools and universities were virtual, and vacation plans were canceled. For example, passengers on scheduled airlines were required to wear face coverings during summer 2021 through spring 2022. Things have improved, but we expect these restrictions to ebb and flow as new variants of the virus are identified and hot spots are addressed by state and federal health officials.

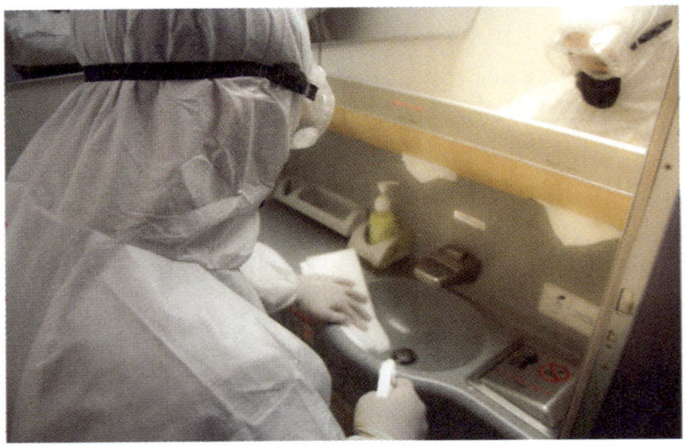

Figure 13-2. Aircraft lavatory COVID cleaning.
(Pojana Jermsawat/Shutterstock.com)

These actions, while intended to constrain the spread of COVID-19, have significantly impacted the global economy, including businesses both large and small, in the United States and around the world. Not only has the aviation industry not been immune to these effects, it has been disproportionally impacted. Experiencing aviation requires in-person interaction, rather than, for example, an e-commerce business such as Amazon, where customers can experience the benefits of Amazon at a distance. Airports are constrained in generating revenues without aircraft operations, food and beverage sales, and automobile parking revenues, for example. Fixed-base operators cannot sell fuel to idle aircraft. Aircraft manufacturers don't sell aircraft to airlines that now have excess capacity. The impacts on the aviation industry are extensive and examples are numerous.

As an indicator of COVID impacts on aviation, the U.S. Transportation Security Administration (TSA) has been reporting the number of U.S. daily passenger screenings. The worst reported day during the first five months of 2020 occurred on April 14, 2020, when the number of passenger screenings were only 4 percent of that same day a year prior (87,534 versus 2,208,688). Fortunately, by summer 2021, passenger screenings had increased to approximately 2 million daily, approximately

80 percent of the same day a year prior (2 million versus 2.5 million). By late 2022, the number of daily passenger screenings were just slightly below pre-COVID numbers (TSA 2022).

By summer 2021, domestic system-wide airline load factors were almost equal to pre-COVID 2019 load factors. Although load factors dipped to below 10 percent in April 2020, by summer 2021, load factors averaged 89.2 percent, which is almost equal to 90.2 percent load factors for summer 2019 (pre-COVID). By late 2022, system-wide load factors exceeded pre-pandemic load factors. This indicates a faster-than-expected recovery (A4A 2021).

The effects of the COVID-19 pandemic were too great for some airlines, with airlines such as Compass Airlines, ExpressJet Airlines, Miami Air International, RavnAir Group, and Trans State Airlines ceasing operations. Airlines have been drastically reducing capacity by parking idle aircraft. At the height of the pandemic (mid-May 2020), U.S. passenger airlines had parked 3,204 idle aircraft, which represented 52 percent of the active airline fleet. Fortunately, by September 2020, the number of idle aircraft had been reduced to 1,779, representing 29 percent of the active fleet. By June 30, 2021, U.S. passenger airlines had 5,242 active aircraft (A4A 2021). By late 2022, U.S. passenger airlines had 5,537 active aircraft (A4A 2022).

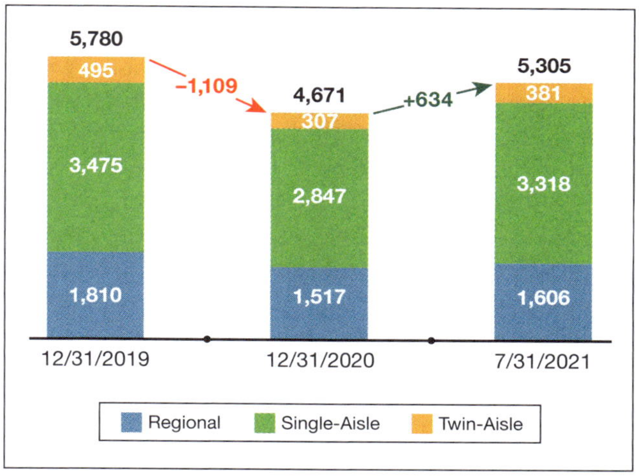

Figure 13-3. Active U.S. aircraft. *(A4A 2021)*

Airlines took numerous measures to minimize the impacts of the COVID-19 pandemic on operations, including the following:

- Reducing capacity, and parking and/or retiring older aircraft.
- Converting passenger aircraft to partially or fully cargo aircraft.
- Reducing compensation for executives and implementing voluntary leave and early retirement programs.
- Freezing hiring and non-essential spending.
- Consolidating airport facilities and halting expansion projects.
- Simplifying onboard offerings.
- Negotiating more favorable terms with airports, regional airlines, caterers, fuelers, and other vendors.
- Deferring deliveries of new aircraft and reducing non-aircraft capital expenditures.
- Securing additional funding by borrowing, selling stock, and/or federal support.
- Selling or mortgaging capital assets.
- Suspending share repurchases and the payment of future dividends. (A4A 2021)

Although passenger enplanements greatly suffered during the pandemic, air cargo was not as negatively impacted. Air cargo volumes were generally about 10–30 percent less than pre-COVID. However, air cargo found a way to fill a niche during the pandemic. The air cargo industry has played a critical role in keeping global supply chains moving. For example, aircraft have enabled the rapid movement of personal protective equipment (PPE), CT scanners, MRI equipment, and ventilators to COVID-19 hotspots around the world. Some airlines, such as Air Canada and China Eastern, have either partially or fully converted passenger aircraft to carry additional cargo by removing seats (Horton 2020).

In addition to airline impacts, airports have also been impacted. Airport revenues are closely linked to passenger enplanements, impacting passenger facility charge (PFC) collections, parking revenues, landing fee revenues, and food and beverage concessions revenues. In addition to revenue impacts directly correlated to lower passenger enplanements, airports also waived fees and rents for airlines, concessionaires, rental car companies, and fixed-base operators (Villard 2020).

Fortunately, the U.S. Congress passed legislation designed to financially strengthen the U.S. economy through the COVID-19 pandemic. Specifically, the **Coronavirus Aid, Relief, and Economic Security (CARES) Act**, signed by President Donald Trump on March 27, 2020, provided funds for airlines, airports, and the business aviation community. Passenger airlines are eligible to receive $25 billion in loans and loan guarantees, while cargo carriers are eligible for an additional $4 billion. The loans were conditional on job protection, preventing a recipient airline from laying off or furloughing employees until September 30, 2020. Restrictions include a prohibition on buying back shares of their own stock for a year after the loan is fully paid off, prohibition of issuing dividends to shareholders while receiving aid, and capping executive compensation at 2019 levels. This legislation included $10 billion in funds to be awarded as economic relief to eligible U.S. airports affected by the COVID-19 pandemic. Additionally, it provides funds to increase the federal share to 100 percent for Airport Improvement Program (AIP) and supplemental discretionary grants planned for the 2020 fiscal year (Slotnick 2020; FAA 2022).

Companies with business aircraft that had their operations suspended or have suffered more than a 50 percent decline in business due to the COVID-19 pandemic were eligible for a 50 percent credit on qualified wages against their employment tax obligations. A deferment of the employer share of Social Security taxes was permitted through December 31, 2020, with deferred taxes paid over a two-year period. A separate $17 billion in loans is specified for companies critical to maintaining national security. This might include companies such as Boeing, Northrop Grumman, and Lockheed Martin (FAA 2020; NBAA 2020).

Starting January 26, 2021, all air passengers traveling into the United States, including by private flights, air charter, and general aviation aircraft, were required to show proof of a negative COVID-19 test result or documentation of having recovered from COVID-19, regardless of vaccination status. All passengers were required to complete an attestation affirming their compliance with the CDC requirements and provide it to their aircraft operator (NATA 2021). As of early 2023, the testing requirement for air travelers has eased and testing is required only for passengers arriving from certain countries; however, non-U.S. citizens must show proof of being fully vaccinated with the primary series of the COVID-19 vaccine before boarding a flight to the U.S. These guidelines continue to evolve, so it is best to verify current guidance with the Centers for Disease Control and Prevention (CDC).

FBOs have had to adopt new protocols to operate during the COVID era, especially those addressing cleaning, disinfecting, and employee, crew, and passenger health. *Aviation International News*, in its 2021 FBO Survey, gathered the following insights from several FBOs regarding their management of COVID (AIN 2021):

> We stayed up-to-date on changing local and federal guidelines daily. We created [branded]...face masks, which were given to all employees as well as offered to customers who were in need. In addition, we made conscious efforts to minimize points of contact, such as providing snacks that were individually wrapped, removing all lobby magazines, and placing a buffer at our front desk to respect the six-feet social distancing. We also provided ample hand sanitizer stations and increased our daily cleanings of all lobby areas and touch points. One tool that was very instrumental in our cleaning was the electrostatic sprayer that allowed us to spray down all our lobby furniture to ensure the safety of our guests.
>
> —Wilson Air Center Memphis

> All employees are required to take their temperatures before the start of their shift and must wear a mask before entering the terminal building. We bought two UV lights that we rotate through our facilities and invested in an ionizing sprayer. There are hand sanitizing stations throughout the lobby and signs promoting social distancing. Line crew ask if assistance is needed with luggage and if it is okay to handle it. They sanitize the equipment and their workspace regularly. In our crew suite, we created a process that allows visitors to use [snooze] rooms and still keep the areas sanitized. After the rooms are used, a [CSR] will disinfect the area.
>
> —Sugar Land Regional Airport

> Hours and staffing were adjusted to accommodate increased demand while maintaining a safe environment for customers and employees. We stayed on top of changing CDC advisories and implemented new internal protocols as warranted, achieving NATA Safety 1st Clean certification early on. Gloves and masks are worn when staff deliver luggage, vehicles, or other items to customers. We added a full-time custodian and brought back amenities such as fruit, popcorn, and cookies, freshly prepared and wrapped with care.
>
> —Base Operations, Paige Field

> We were early adopters of CDC recommendations and NATA's Safety 1st Clean program, [which] is regularly audited, and all employees are held accountable for adherence and administration. Most notably, last summer we began an in-house Covid testing program administered by a medical doctor who now leases an office space at the FBO. This allows us to test employees, their families, select vendors, customers, and customers' pilots as needed.
>
> —Million Air Dallas

> Protective barriers were installed at the front desk and masks are mandated. We also stepped up our cleaning for the gym, crew cars, and snooze rooms [and] once used, it must be thoroughly cleaned and disinfected before it is returned to service. Social distancing has been a challenge for our employees, but we have spread out workstations. If an employee does call out of work, their direct supervisor fills out a COVID questionnaire that describes symptoms and any close contact that employee may have had in the last 48 hours.
>
> —Heritage Aviation

Although protocols may vary among FBOs, active COVID mitigation and management was necessary during this time, and it will likely continue to be necessary to some degree in the future.

Safety

Safety begins on the ramp and continues throughout the hangar and into the terminal building. As discussed in Chapter 4, line service has inherent dangers (such as spinning propellers, jet blast, high noise levels, moving aircraft and vehicles, and fuel). Wise FBO managers begin training new line service personnel on the importance of safety on day one. The National Air Transportation Association (NATA) created a Safety 1st line service training program specifically to assist FBOs with educating line service personnel about the importance of safety on the ramp. This program has been used by FBOs nationwide to educate line service specialists about proper towing techniques, fire safety, proper marshalling, etc. Other FBOs have created their own form of safety training, which may include daily safety briefings, monthly safety meetings, and employee of the year award.

Figure 13-4. OSHA inspector. *(Billion Photos/Shutterstock.com)*

In addition to safety on the ramp, the **Occupational Safety and Health Administration (OSHA)** demands safety throughout the workplace. Specifically, FBOs must furnish for employees a workplace free from recognized hazards. FBOs must comply with all occupational safety and health standards issued under the **Occupational Safety and Health Act.** Furthermore, employees have the right to request an inspection by OSHA if they sense an unsafe work environment, requiring the employer to correct workplace hazards if a citation is issued. In any event, FBOs have a vested interest in maintaining a safe working environment for all employees and should attempt to enhance workplace safety in all areas.

The FAA, in harmony with the International Civil Aviation Organization (ICAO), has issued guidance to airports in creating safety management systems (SMS). SMS consists of four main elements: (1) safety policy and objectives, (2) safety risk management, (3) safety assurance, and (4) safety promotion. The application of a systematic, proactive, and well-defined safety program (as is inherent in a SMS) allows an organization producing a product or service to strike a realistic and efficient balance between safety and production. Principal to implementing an SMS is conducting a safety risk assessment and proactively creating a safety culture. FBOs should strive toward SMS development and implementation, possibly even considering various stages of IS-BAO (International Standard for Business Aircraft Operations) certification to validate the safety posture. It is imperative that all FBO employees have a high level of safety awareness.

Security

September 11, 2001, was a terrible day on which aviation was used to attack the United States. The world changed on this day, and general aviation was not immune from this change. In fact, GA became the target of lawmakers and others concerned about the security of our nation. GA was seen as a weak link in the national security chain and the target of criticism. Many agree that GA aviation facilities are potentially high-profile targets with large congregations of people, extensive structures, storage of large volumes of fuel and chemicals, and access to sophisticated aircraft. Today, however, GA has righted itself and is once again seen as a safe and vital link in the nation's air transportation system. However, this was not accomplished overnight, and the risk to losing this trust is great. Thus, FBO managers must take active measures to maintain and enhance security at their facilities.

Figure 13-5. Pentagon on September 11, 2001. *(Everett Collection/Shutterstock.com)*

In response to the concern about the lack of security at GA airports, the newly created Transportation Security Administration (TSA) in May 2004 created *Security Guidelines for General Aviation Airports,* also referred to as Information Publication A-001. Version 2 of A-001, *Security Guidelines for General Aviation Airport Operators and Users,* was published in 2017 (TSA 2017). These guidelines provide specific guidance to GA airport managers and FBO managers in how to enhance security at their facilities. Truly, security needs to be a cooperative effort by both airport management and FBO management (as well as all other businesses located on airport).

As an information publication, the aim is to provide a set of federally endorsed security enhancements and methods for determining when and where these enhancements may be appropriate. It only applies to smaller airports that are not required to comply with 49 CFR Part 1542. In developing the guidelines, the TSA understood that a one-size security approach would not fit the entire spectrum of GA airports. The document provides options, ideas, and suggestions for the airport operator, tenants, and users to enhance security of the airport. The guide covers the following sections:

- ***Gathering Intelligence.*** By relying on information provided by TSA; various federal, state, or local resources; and knowledge of customers and the industry, FBOs and airports can make risk-based decisions.
  - › Identifying the threat
  - › Eight signs of terrorism
    - – Surveillance
    - – Elicitation
    - – Tests of security
    - – Funding
    - – Supplies
    - – Suspicious people
    - – Rehearsal
    - – Deployment
  - › People
  - › Aircraft
  - › Infrastructure
- ***People.*** GA operators are in a unique position to see and meet pilots and passengers. Suspicious activities, such as inappropriate questions and odd forms of payment, can be more quickly noted and authorities could be alerted.
  - › Passengers and visitors
    - – GA passengers are generally better known than the typical airline passengers.
    - – Visitor escorts into movement area.
    - – Suspicious activities, such as cash for flights or probing and inappropriate questions.
    - – PIC should verify identify of passengers, baggage, and cargo.
  - › Flight schools and student pilots
    - – Require flight students to use proper entrances/exits.
    - – Establish positive ID.
    - – Control aircraft ignition keys.
    - – Consider having student pilots check in before being allowed access to aircraft.
    - – No keys to students without instructor or management approval.
    - – Different ignition and door lock keys.
  - › Aircraft renters
    - – Regular renters are well known, and new renters are required by insurance companies to complete a flight check.
    - – ID should be identified.
    - – First-time renters should be familiarized with local airport operations.
    - – Operators providing rental aircraft should be vigilant for suspicious activities.
  - › Transient pilots
    - – ID non-based pilots and aircraft using the facilities (sign-in, sign-out, and assigned parking spots).

- ***Aircraft.*** The primary goal of GA security is to prevent the intentional misuse of GA aircraft. Securing aircraft is the most effective means to accomplish this goal.
  - Ensuring that door locks are consistently used to prevent unauthorized access or tampering with the aircraft.
  - Using keyed ignitions where appropriate.
  - Controlling access to the keys.
  - Storing the aircraft in a hangar, if available, and locking hangar doors.
  - Using an auxiliary lock to further protect aircraft from unauthorized use.
  - Using commercially available options, such as locks for propellers, throttle, and tiedowns.
  - Ensuring that aircraft ignition keys are not stored inside the aircraft.
  - Discussing transfer of control for before and after maintenance procedures to avoid leaving aircraft open with keys in between the hand-off.
  - Using heat shields and aircraft covers to block the window to prevent easy visibility of the aircraft's contents.
- ***Infrastructure.*** Airport infrastructure, including hangars, must be secured properly to prevent entry by unauthorized personnel.
  - Hangars
    - One of the most effective ways to secure GA aircraft.
    - Hangar locks, proper lighting, alarms.
  - Locks
    - Simply a delaying device, not a complete bar to entry.
    - Includes combination locks, cipher locks, key locks, and advanced electronic key technologies.
  - Key control
  - Perimeter security
    - Walls, fencing, natural barriers, electronic barriers.
    - Expending resources on unnecessary security enhancements (complete perimeter fencing) instead of more facility-specific and effective methods (tiedown chains with locks) may be detrimental to airport's security posture.
  - Closed-circuit television (CCTV)
  - Intrusion detection systems (IDS)
  - Fencing
  - Access points
  - Gates
    - Vehicle gates.
    - Pedestrian gates.
  - Lighting
    - Prevents theft, vandalism, or other illegal activity at night.
    - Connected to emergency power source, if possible.
    - Ensure lighting does not interfere with aircraft operations.
  - Signage
    - Provides a deterrent by warning of facility boundaries and consequences of violation.
    - Warnings against trespassing, unauthorized use of aircraft, and tampering with aircraft, and reporting of suspicious activity.
    - Should include phone number of local law enforcement, 911, or 1-866-GA-SECUR.

- › Identification system
  - – Method of identifying airport employees.
  - – Range from simple laminated ID card with photo to swipe card with biometric data.
- › Airport planning
  - – Planning of security should be an integral part of any project undertaken.
  - – Prevent unauthorized access, security of construction staging areas, and prevent inadvertent movement area entry.

- ***Other Facilities.*** For GA airports without a perimeter fence, tenant facilities (including FBOs) may have access to the aircraft parking, movement, and public areas of the airport.
  - › Airport tenant facilities
  - › Aircraft and vehicle fueling facilities
  - › Fuel storage equipment and facilities
  - › Military facilities
  - › Fixed-base and corporate-based operators
- ***Airport Watch Programs.*** Airport users can be the eyes and ears needed to thwart criminal activities. Programs include the Aircraft Owners and Pilots Association's (AOPA) Airport Watch, the DHS "If You See Something, Say Something" campaign, or the TSA "This is My Airport" campaign.
- ***Security Awareness Training.*** Both the TSA and AOPA have developed security awareness training that provides information on suspicious behavior patterns, appropriate responses to such behavior, and GA airport watch programs.
- ***Reporting Procedures.*** Critical and immediate incidents or threats can be reported to 911. Suspicious activity at an airport can also be reported to the TSA via the GA-SECURE hotline. The toll-free number is 866-GA-SECUR (1-866-427-3287), which operates 24 hours per day, 7 days per week.
- ***Security Procedures and Communication.*** Written security procedures can emphasize elements such as awareness, prevention, preparation, response, and recovery.
  - › Local airport security committee
  - › Law enforcement officer (LEO) support
  - › National Terrorism Advisory System (NTAS)
  - › Threat communication system
- ***Specialty Operations***. Ensuring secure agricultural aircraft operations incudes securing aircraft, as well as chemical storage areas.

The two most effective aspects of the guidelines are found in Appendices A and B of the guidelines. Appendix A contains the Airport Security Assessment and Protective Measures Matrix. This tool allows GA airport operators and FBO managers to establish a baseline from which to develop security measures with the intent of preventing the unauthorized use of aircraft; to protect the health and welfare of tenants, users, and employees at the airport; and, as a critical asset to the region, to protect the airport from being degraded. Upon completion of this task, readers can utilize Appendix B—Airport Security Program Template. This template can be used in developing a security program. Overall, the TSA security guidelines are an excellent reference for airport operators and FBO managers to more effectively adopt an overall security posture and strengthen the security of these important GA airports.

An important component of any security program is the concept of challenge procedures. Required at all TSA Part 1542 airports (air carriers), this involves challenging individuals in the sterile area (or air operations area [AOA]) with no ID badge visible on their person. This is most effective on the ramp or flight line. However, it becomes difficult at GA facilities because there are typically a large number of flight crew and passengers on the ramp with no ID badge. These individuals don't work at the airport and may be transient; thus, they would not have an airport-issued ID badge. Common sense and a sense of vigilance are required to recognize suspicious behavior and effectively apply the challenge procedure at GA airports.

Finally, a security threat may be received via the telephone. This may include a bomb threat or other threat against the business or GA aircraft operations. The key is to listen closely to the caller's voice (accent, roughness, gender) and discern as much information as possible so that an assessment of the threat may be made. If possible, it is best to alert someone to the call while the caller is still on the line. Typically, threat assessment will be made after the call has ended in consultation with local law enforcement and local management (airport and FBO).

Summary

Effectively managing risks to FBOs requires a multifaceted approach. Carrying appropriate insurance, implementing robust COVID protocols, developing a safety management system (SMS), and properly securing the FBO and all related assets will contribute to this multifaceted approach. The wise FBO manager effectively mitigates risk in a comprehensive fashion, with employees endeavoring to conduct safe and secure operations.

Key Terms

aircraft liability insurance. Insurance that covers the FBO for liability, including liability to passengers or resulting from the ownership, operation, maintenance, or use of all owned, non-owned, leased, or hired aircraft on, or in connection with, any premises.

airport liability insurance. Insurance that provides for the liability resulting out of, or in connection with, ongoing operations performed by, or on behalf of, the FBO under the FBO lease agreement or the use or occupancy of airport premises by, or on behalf of, the FBO.

business auto liability insurance. Insurance that covers all owned, hired, and non-owned vehicles for bodily injury and property damage.

Coronavirus Aid, Relief, and Economic Security (CARES) Act. Legislation that became law in March 2020 in response to the economic impacts of the COVID-19 pandemic. It provided funds for airlines, airports, and the business aviation community.

coronavirus disease 2019 (COVID-19). A disease caused by the SARS-CoV-2 virus. This virus spreads in three main ways: (a) breathing in air when close to an infected person; (b) having small exhaled droplets from an infected person land on the eyes, nose, or mouth of the uninfected person; and (c) touching of eyes, nose, or mouth with hands infected with the virus.

environmental impairment (pollution) insurance. Insurance that covers the FBO from liability resulting from pollution or other environmental impairment arising out of, or in connection with, work performed under the lease agreement, or which arises out of, or in connection with, the use or occupancy of airport premises in connection with the lease agreement.

hangarkeeper's liability insurance. Insurance specific to storing aircraft in a hangar and the liability that results from storing assets belonging to others.

in-flight hangarkeeper's liability insurance. Insurance designed to cover liability resulting from the pickup and redelivery of aircraft, test flights, instruction, and charter flights.

Occupational Safety and Health Act. Signed into law in 1970, this federal law governs occupational health and safety in the private sector and federal government. It created the Occupational Safety and Health Administration (OSHA) and the National Institute for Occupational Safety and Health (NIOSH).

Occupational Safety and Health Administration (OSHA). A federal agency within the U.S. Department of Labor that is designed to ensure safe and healthy working conditions by setting and enforcing standards and providing training, outreach, education, and assistance.

property insurance. Insurance that covers property, such as tools and machinery. This type of policy does not cover aircraft or vehicles stored in a hangar.

workers' compensation insurance. Insurance designed to replace wages and provide medical benefits to employees injured on the job. It also covers work-related illnesses.

Review Questions

1. What types of risks are FBOs exposed to? Why is it important to mitigate these risks?
2. Why is safety important to an FBO?
3. Explain the different types of insurance an FBO may need.
4. What areas are addressed by the TSA publication *Security Guidelines for General Aviation Airport Operators and Users?*
5. What role does the AOPA Airport Watch Program play in FBO security?
6. What are challenge procedures?
7. What should be remembered when answering a telephone threat?

Scenarios

1. During the past few years, insurance rates have been increasing dramatically. You are an FBO manager confronted with higher rates in workers' compensation, hangarkeeper's liability, business auto liability, environmental pollution insurance, aircraft liability insurance, property insurance, and employee medical insurance. Obviously, it may be more expensive *not* to be insured. However, what can you do to minimize the financial impact of these increasing insurance premiums?
2. You have been recently hired as the manager of risk management at a full-service FBO. The FBO manager has asked you to conduct a comprehensive risk assessment for the FBO, including the risks associated with fire, crime/theft, aircraft, business auto, environmental, and hangarkeeper's. Specifically, what are your ideas to reduce risk in these areas?
3. As manager of an FBO at a GA facility, you have grown more concerned about security since the events of 9/11. What are some areas you should be considering when ensuring the security of your facility as well as the GA airport? What ideas do you have to ensure a secure GA airport?
4. Safety is definitely a concern in the operation of an FBO. Just last week, you had an employee hit by a tug, another badly burned in a fueling incident, and yet another employee injured in the maintenance shop. What are some considerations for your FBO in attempting to ensure a safe working environment for your employees? Specifically, how do you prevent such incidents from occurring in the future?

5. Your goal as FBO manager is to run a safe, secure airport operation with adequately trained staff. You realize you cannot eliminate all risk. However, your goal is to reduce your business's exposure to risk as much as possible. Obviously, insurance is one way to reduce your financial risk from aircraft accidents, fire, liability, etc. However, insurance by itself is not enough. What else can you do as FBO manager to reduce the risks associated with operating an FBO?

Bibliography

A4A (Airlines for America). 2021. *Impact of COVID-19: Data Updates.* https://www.airlines.org/dataset/impact-of-covid19-data-updates/.

A4A (Airlines for America). 2022. Emerging from the Pandemic. November 26, 2022. https://www.airlines.org/wp-content/uploads/2022/11/A4A-COVID-Impact-Updates-27.pdf.

ACI (Airports Council International). 2022. "The Impact of COVID-19 on Airports—and the Path to Recovery." October 6, 2022. https://aci.aero/2022/10/06/the-impact-of-covid-19-on-airports-and-the-path-to-recovery/.

AIN (Aviation International News). 2021. *FBO Survey 2021: The Americas.* https://www.ainonline.com/sites/ainonline.com/files/pdf/fbo_survey_2021_the_americas_.pdf.

FAA (Federal Aviation Administration). 2020. "Novel Coronavirus (COVID-19) Update." https://www.faa.gov/newsroom/novel-coronavirus-covid-19-update-0.

FAA (Federal Aviation Administration). 2022. "2020 CARES Act Grants." Last modified August 25, 2022 .https://www.faa.gov/airports/cares_act.

Horton, Will. 2020. "These Airlines Will Next Remove Seats to Carry Cargo and Medical Supplies on Passenger Aircraft Turned into Freighters." *Forbes*, April 13, 2020. https://www.forbes.com/sites/willhorton1/2020/04/13/these-airlines-will-next-remove-seats-to-carry-cargo-and-medical-supplies-on-passenger-aircraft-turned-into-freighters/.

NATA (National Air Transportation Association). 2021. "CDC Order Imposes COVID-19 Entry Testing Requirements for All Arriving Air Travelers." January 13, 2021. https://www.nata.aero/pressrelease/cdc-order-imposes-covid-19-entry-testing-requirements-for-all-arriving-air-travelers.

NBAA (National Business Aviation Association). 2020. "Key Provisions for General Aviation Businesses in the CARES Act." May 11, 2020. https://nbaa.org/aircraft-operations/safety/coronavirus/key-provisions-for-general-aviation-businesses-in-the-cares-act/.

Prather, C. Daniel. 2009. *General Aviation Marketing and Management: Operating, Marketing, and Managing an FBO.* 3rd ed. Malabar, FL: Krieger Publishing Company.

Slotnick, David. 2020. "Airlines Will Get the $60 Billion Bailout They Asked For in the $2 Trillion Coronavirus Stimulus Bill That Trump Signed into Law. It Also Prohibits Layoffs, Stock Buybacks, and Dividends." *Insider.* March 27, 2020. https://www.businessinsider.com/airlines-coronavirus-bailout-senate-stock-buybacks-2020-3.

TSA (Transportation Security Administration). 2017. *Security Guidelines for General Aviation Airport Operators and Users.* Information Publication A-001, Version 2. July 2017. https://www.tsa.gov/sites/default/files/2017_ga_security_guidelines.pdf.

TSA (Transportation Security Administration). 2022. "TSA Checkpoint Travel Numbers." Accessed January 31, 2023. https://www.tsa.gov/coronavirus/passenger-throughput.

Villard, Philippe. 2020. "COVID-19: Waiving Airport Concession Fees to Relieve Airports' Financial Stress in a Time of Crisis." Airports Council International. March 26, 2020. https://blog.aci.aero/covid-19-waiving-airport-concession-fees-to-relieve-airports-financial-stress-in-a-time-of-crisis/.

14

Financial Planning and Control

In Chapter 14

Objectives

At the end of this chapter, you should be able to:

1. Describe the purpose and major categories of the balance sheet and income statement.
2. Distinguish between balance sheet, income statement, and management ratio analysis and give examples of each.
3. Explain the purpose and factors affecting pro forma statements.
4. List the steps in preparing a pro forma statement.
5. Define break-even analysis and summarize the steps in calculating the break-even point.
6. Discuss the importance of cash flow budgets and give several examples of typical budget reports.

7. Distinguish between working capital, equity capital, and debt capital and identity the major sources of loans for each.
8. Discuss the importance and process of short-term and long-term financing.
9. Compare and contrast EBITDA analysis and discounted cash flow analysis in determining the value of an aviation business.

Introduction

Financial planning affects how and on what terms an FBO will be able to attract the funding required to establish, maintain, and expand the business. Financial planning determines the number and type of aircraft an FBO can afford to buy, the services provided, and whether or not the FBO will be able to market them efficiently. It affects the human and physical resources the FBO will be able to acquire to run the business. In short, it will be a major factor in determining the profitability of the business. This chapter provides an overview of the essential components of financial planning and management.

Financial Management

Financial management is the use of financial statements that reflect the financial condition of a business to identify its relative strengths and weaknesses. It enables the firm to plan, using projections, the future financial performance for capital, asset, and personnel requirements to maximize the return on the shareholders' (owners') investment.

Specifically, a financial management system enables the firm to:

1. Interpret past performance.
2. Measure present progress.
3. Anticipate and plan for the future.
4. Control operations.
5. Uncover significant trends.
6. Compare results with similar firms within the particular industry.
7. Make financial decisions.
8. Comply with government regulations.

GAAP

The categories and format of financial statements are established by a system known as **Generally Accepted Accounting Principles (GAAP)**. These standardized set of accounting principles are issued by the **Financial Accounting Standards Board (FASB),** a not-for-profit organization. GAAP is designed to improve the clarity, consistency, and comparability of financial information. GAAP applies to all publicly traded companies. GAAP greatly aids in standardizing financial reporting, making financial statements easily interpreted across industries and companies.

BALANCE SHEET

The **balance sheet** provides a picture of the financial health of a business at a given moment, usually at the close of an accounting period. It lists in detail those material and intangible items the business owns (known as its assets) and what money the business owes, either to its creditors (liabilities) or to its owners (shareholders' equity or net worth of the business).

Assets include not only cash, merchandise inventory, land, buildings, equipment, machinery, furniture, patents, and trademarks but also money due from individuals or other businesses (known as accounts receivable or notes receivable).

Liabilities are funds acquired for a business through loans, or the sale of property or services to the business on credit. Creditors do not acquire business ownership but rather promissory notes to be paid at a designated future date.

Owner's equity (or net worth or capital) is money put into a business by its owners for use by the business in acquiring assets.

At any given time, a business's assets equal the total contributions by the creditors and owners, as illustrated by the following formula for the balance svheet:

Assets = Liabilities + Owner's Equity

This formula is a basic premise of accounting. If a business owes more money to creditors than it possesses in value of assets owned, the net worth or owner's equity of the business will be a negative number.

The balance sheet is designed to show how the assets, liabilities, and net worth of a business are distributed at any given time. It is considered a snapshot in time, and it is only accurate on the day it is prepared. It is usually prepared at regular intervals—for example, at each month's end, but especially at the end of each fiscal (accounting) year.

By regularly preparing this summary of what the business owns and owes (the balance sheet), the business owner/manager can identify and analyze trends in the financial strength of the business. It permits timely modifications, such as gradually decreasing the amount of money the business owes to creditors and increasing the amount the business owes its owners.

All balance sheets contain the same categories of assets, liabilities, and owner's equity. Assets are arranged in decreasing order of how quickly they can be turned into cash (liquidity). Liabilities are listed in order of how soon they must be repaid, followed by retained earnings (net worth or owner's equity), as shown in Figure 14-1, the sample balance sheet of XYZ Aviation Company (see next page).

Balance Sheet Categories

Assets are anything the business owns that has monetary value.

- *Current assets* include cash, government securities, marketable securities, accounts receivable, notes receivable (other than from officers or employees), inventories, prepaid expenses, and any other items that could be converted into cash within one year in the normal course of business.
- *Fixed assets* are those acquired for long-term use in a business and include such items as land, facilities, equipment, machinery, leasehold improvements, furniture, fixtures, and any other items with an expected useful business life measured in years (as opposed to items that will wear out or be used up in less than one year and are usually expensed when they are purchased). These assets are typically not for resale and are recorded in the balance sheet at their net cost less accumulated depreciation.
- *Other assets* include intangible assets, such as patents, royalty arrangements, copyrights, exclusive-use contracts, and notes receivable from officers and employees.

Liabilities are the claims of creditors against the assets of the business (debts owed by the business). **Debt** is an obligation that requires one party, the debtor, to pay money or other agreed-upon value to another party, the creditor.

- *Current liabilities* are accounts payable, notes payable to banks, accrued expenses (wages, salaries), taxes payable, the current portion (due within one year) of long-term debt, and other obligations to creditors due within one year.
- *Long-term liabilities* are mortgages, intermediate and long-term bank loans, equipment loans, and any other obligations from money due to a creditor with a maturity longer than one year.

Owner's equity is the equity attributed to owners or shareholders. Owner's equity, or net worth, equals the assets of the business minus its liabilities. Net worth equals the owner's equity. This equity is the investment by the owner plus any profits or minus any losses that have accumulated in the business.

XYZ Aviation Company
Balance Sheet
December 31, 20__

ASSETS	
Current Assets:	
Cash	$52,500
Accounts receivable	40,000
Prepaid expenses; including insurance premiums	10,000
Inventory of aircraft	284,650
Parts	23,000
Total Current Assets	$410,150
Fixed Assets:	
Shop equipment	$21,500
Office equipment	7,000
Parts room	5,000
Improvements to leased facilities	100,000
Less depreciation and obsolescence	($17,500)
Total fixed assets	$116,000
Total Assets	$526,150
LIABILITIES AND OWNER'S EQUITY	
Liabilities:	
Trade accounts payable	$21,700
Notes payable (aircraft)	220,500
Other payables	17,000
Accruals	10,000
Total Liabilities	$269,200
Owner's Equity:	
Investors' contribution (capital stock or capital loans)	$200,000
Add Surplus	56,950
Total Owner's Equity	$256,950
Total Liabilities and Owner's Equity	$526,150

Figure 14-1. Balance sheet for XYZ Aviation Company.

INCOME STATEMENT

The second primary report included in a business's financial management picture is the **income statement** (or statement of income). The income statement is a measure of a company's sales and expenses over a specific period of time. It is also prepared at regular intervals (again, each month and fiscal year end) to show the results of operating during those accounting periods. It too follows Generally Accepted Accounting Principles (GAAP) and contains specific revenue and expense categories regardless of the nature of the business. Refer to the sample income statement for XYZ Aviation Company shown in Figure 14-2.

XYZ Aviation Company
Income Statement
December 31, 20__

Income:	
Sales of aircraft	$130,000
Gross receipts from flight training, charter, and other flights	28,800
Receipts from sale of parts and accessories	48,000
Gross receipts for maintenance and repair of customers' aircraft	30,000
Gross receipts from line service (sale of fuel, cleaning, washing, and other services to customers' aircraft)	164,000
Payments received for storage of customers' aircraft	14,000
Gross Income	$414,800
Cost of Goods:	
Cost of aircraft sold	$102,000
Cost of fuel, spare parts, and other costs charged directly against receipts from flights and charters listed above (not including labor)	14,000
Cost of parts and accessories sold to customers	38,000
Cost of parts and accessories charged against receipts for maintenance and repair of customers' aircraft	10,000
Cost of line services to customers' aircraft (including cost of fuel sold, but not including labor	89,000
Total direct costs (excluding labor)	$253,000
Gross Profit (on sales)	$161,800
Operating Expenses:	
Salaries	$70,000
Rent, heat, utilities	15,000
Insurance (on aircraft, structures, equipment, liability, and other insurance)	20,000
Advertising and sales promotion	2,000
Interest (on money borrowed to purchase aircraft and other equipment)	5,000
Office supplies	3,000
Bad debts allowances	1,500
Travel and entertainment	500
Dues and subscriptions	200
Depreciation (on buildings, equipment, and other fixed assets which are owned)	20,000
Miscellaneous expenses	5,000
Total Operating Expenses	$142,200
Operating Profit	$19,600
Other Income:	
Dividends	$700
Interest on bank accounts	400
Total Other Income	$1,100
Total Income before taxes	$20,700
Other Expenses:	
Interest expenses	$1,200
Net Income (or Loss) before taxes	19,500
Less provision for income taxes	1,600
Net Income (or Loss) after taxes	$17,900

Figure 14-2. Income statement for XYZ Aviation Company.

Income Statement Categories

The income statement categories can be summarized as follows:

- **Income** (gross sales less returns and allowances)
- Less **cost of goods** or **cost of sales** (costs charged directly against gross sales)
- Equals **gross profit** (gross income, minus direct costs before operating expenses)
- Less **operating expenses** (salaries, rent, heat, utilities, insurance, advertising and sales promotion, interest, office supplies, bad debt allowances, travel and entertainment, dues and subscriptions, depreciation, and miscellaneous expenses such as automobile expenses, legal fees, and so forth)
- Equals **operating profit** (profit before other nonoperating income or expense)
- Plus **other income** (income from dividends on investments, interest on bank accounts, customer charge accounts, and so forth)
- Less **other expenses** (interest expense)
- Equals **net income (or loss) *before* taxes** (the figure on which taxes are calculated)
- Less **income taxes** (if any are due)
- Equals **net income (or loss) *after* taxes**

Calculation of the *cost of goods sold* or *cost of sales* category in the statement of income (or profit and loss statement as it is sometimes called) varies depending on whether the business is primarily a service organization like an FBO or a manufacturer of aircraft components. The cost of goods sold for an aircraft manufacturer reflects the operational costs that go into producing the aircraft. In manufacturing or a completion workshop (aircraft interior work), it involves not only finished-goods inventories but also raw materials inventories, goods-in-process inventories, direct labor, and direct manufacturing overhead costs. The cost of sales for an FBO reflects the operational costs that go into providing services, including fueling. The online Business Guide produced by the U.S. Small Business Administration provides excellent illustrations of the different methods of calculation for the cost of goods sold and cost of sales for various business types.

Financial Ratio Analysis

The two major accounting statements (balance sheet and income statement) contain a great deal of information about the results of company operations and the current state of the firm's finances. Company management can manipulate this information in ways that yield meaningful insights for decision-making. Specifically, data-based decision-making is supported by **ratio analysis**. The analysis of various financial ratios enables management to spot trends in a business and to compare its performance and condition with the average performance of similar businesses in the aircraft service industry. An FBO can make comparisons of its ratios with other similar FBOs as well as its own ratios for several successive years. Unfavorable trends can be detected. Ratio analysis may provide the all-important early warning indications that allow a firm to solve business problems before they lead to financial collapse.

BALANCE SHEET RATIO ANALYSIS

Important balance sheet ratios measure liquidity and solvency (a business's ability to pay its bills as they come due) and leverage (the extent to which the business is dependent on creditors' funding). Liquidity ratios indicate the ease of turning assets into cash. They include the current ratio, quick ratio, debt-equity ratio, and working capital.

Current Ratio

The **current ratio** is a liquidity ratio that measures a company's ability to pay short-term obligations, or those due within one year. It is one of the best-known measures of financial strength. It is figured as shown below:

$$\textit{Current Ratio} = \frac{\textit{Total Current Assets}}{\textit{Total Current Liabilities}}$$

This ratio reveals if the business has enough current assets to meet the payment schedule of its current debts with a margin of safety for possible losses in current assets, such as inventory shrinkage or collectable accounts. It is current because it includes all current assets and current liabilities. A generally acceptable current ratio is 2 to 1, also presented as 2.00. The minimum acceptable current ratio is obviously 1:1 (or 1.00), but that relationship is usually too close for comfort. A current ratio of less than 1.00 indicates that the company does not have the capital on hand to meet its short-term obligations, such as salaries and the electric bill.

If the business's current ratio is too low, the firm may be able to raise it by the following means:

1. Paying some debts.
2. Increasing the current assets from loans or other borrowings with a maturity of more than one year.
3. Converting noncurrent assets into current assets.
4. Increasing the current assets from new equity contributions.
5. Putting profits back into the business.

Quick Ratio

The **quick ratio**, sometimes called the acid-test ratio, is one of the best measures of liquidity. It is figured as shown below:

$$\textit{Quick Ratio} = \frac{\textit{Cash} + \textit{Government Securities} + \textit{Receivables}}{\textit{Total Current Liabilities}}$$

The quick ratio is a much more exacting measure than the current ratio. By excluding inventories, it concentrates on the liquid assets, with value that is fairly certain. The quick ratio reveals if the business could meet current obligations with "quick" funds on hand, if for example, sales revenues drastically drop.

An acid test of 1:1 (or 1.00) is considered satisfactory unless the majority of the quick assets are in accounts receivable, and the pattern of accounts receivable collection lags behind the schedule for paying current liabilities. The higher the ratio, the better a company's liquidity and financial health. For instance, a quick ratio of 1.5 indicates a company has $1.50 of liquid assets available to cover each $1.00 of current liabilities.

Debt-Equity Ratio

The **debt-equity ratio** is a leverage ratio that indicates the extent to which the firm is dependent upon **debt financing** (borrowed money versus owner's equity):

$$\textit{Debt-Equity Ratio} = \frac{\textit{Total Liabilities}}{\textit{Net Worth}}$$

A high debt-equity ratio indicates a company that has been aggressive in financing its growth with debt. Usually, the higher this ratio, the riskier a creditor will perceive its exposure in the business, making it correspondingly harder for the business to obtain credit.

Working Capital

Working capital is more a measure of cash flow than an actual ratio. The result of this calculation must be a positive number. It is calculated as shown below:

$$\textit{Working Capital} = \textit{Total Current Assets} - \textit{Total Current Liabilities}$$

Bankers look at net working capital over time to determine a company's ability to survive financial crises. Loans are often tied to minimum working capital requirements.

With the exception of the debt-equity ratio, the higher these ratios are, the better, especially if the firm is relying to any significant extent on creditor money to finance assets. That being said, the manager should consider these ratio calculations only as part of the overall financial picture of the FBO.

INCOME STATEMENT RATIO ANALYSIS

Financial ratios can also be calculated for the income statement. These ratios measure a firm's profitability. Profitability ratios simply measure the profitability or unprofitability of a firm. Profits may be measured against a variety of data, such as sales, net worth, assets, etc. Generally, profitability ratios are expressed as percentages rather than proportions or fractions. They include the gross margin ratio, net profit margin ratio, return on assets ratio, and return on investment ratio.

Gross Margin Ratio

The **gross margin ratio** is the percentage of sales dollars left after subtracting the cost of goods sold from income. It measures the percentage of sales dollars remaining (after obtaining or manufacturing the goods sold) available to pay the overhead expenses of the company. Gross profit is income after cost of goods sold. It is preferrable for this ratio to be higher. The gross margin ratio is calculated as follows:

$$\textit{Gross Margin Ratio} = \frac{\textit{Gross Profit}}{\textit{Income}}$$

Net Profit Margin Ratio

The **net profit margin ratio** is the percentage of sales dollars (gross income) left after subtracting the cost of goods sold and all expenses, except income taxes. It provides a good opportunity to compare the company's "return on sales" with the performance of other companies in the industry. It is calculated before income tax because tax rates and tax liabilities vary from company to company for a wide variety of reasons, making comparisons after taxes much more difficult. It is preferable for this ratio to be higher. The net profit margin ratio is calculated as follows:

$$\textit{Net Profit Margin Ratio} = \frac{\textit{Net Profit Before Tax}}{\textit{Gross Income}}$$

The following two additional management ratios derived from the balance sheet and statement of income are important for small businesses such as FBOs.

Return on Assets Ratio

The **return on assets ratio** measures how efficiently profits are being generated from the assets employed in the business when compared with the ratios of firms in a similar business. A low ratio in comparison with industry averages indicates an inefficient use of business assets. The return on assets ratio is calculated as follows:

$$\textit{Return on Assets} = \frac{\textit{Net Profit Before Tax}}{\textit{Total Assets}}$$

Return on Investment (ROI) Ratio

The **return on investment (ROI) ratio** is perhaps the most important ratio of all. It is the percentage of return on funds invested in the business by its owners. In short, this ratio indicates whether the effort put into the business has been worthwhile. If the ROI is less than the rate of return on an alternative, risk-free investment such as a bank savings account or certificate of deposit, the owner may be wiser to sell the company, put the money in such a savings instrument, and avoid the daily struggles of running a small FBO. The stock market has returned 10 percent annually on average. If the FBO's ROI is below 10 percent, greater return on the owner's investment could be generated in the stock market. Of course, it wouldn't be as fun as managing an FBO! The ROI is calculated as follows:

$$\textit{Return on Investment} = \frac{\textit{Net Profit Before Tax}}{\textit{Net Worth}}$$

These liquidity, leverage, profitability, and management ratios allow the business owner to identify trends in a business and to compare its progress with the performance of others through data published by various sources. Benchmarking allows a comparison to an established industry benchmark to determine how the FBO measures up. The owner may thus determine the business's relative strengths and weaknesses.

Forecasting Profits

Financial forecasting, particularly on a short-term basis (one to three years), is essential to planning for business success. This process, estimating future business performance based on the actual results from prior periods, enables the FBO owner/manager to modify the operation of the business on a timely basis. This allows the business to avoid losses or major financial problems should some future results from operations not conform with reasonable expectations. As a business expands, there will inevitably be a need for more money than can be internally generated from profits. Forecasts—or pro forma income statements as they are usually called—provide the most persuasive management tools to apply for loans or attract investor money.

FACTORS AFFECTING PRO FORMA STATEMENTS

Preparation of forecasts (**pro forma statements**) requires assembling a wide array of pertinent, verifiable facts affecting the business and its past performance. These include the following:

1. Data from prior financial statements, particularly:
    a. Previous sales levels and trends
    b. Past gross percentages
    c. Average past general, administrative, and selling expenses necessary to generate former sales volumes
    d. Trends in the company's need to borrow (supplier, trade credit, and bank credit) to support various levels of inventory
    e. Trends in accounts receivable required to achieve previous sales volumes
2. Unique company data, particularly:
    a. Facility capacity
    b. Competition
    c. Financial constraints
    d. Personnel availability

3. Industry-wide factors, including:
    a. Overall state of the economy
    b. Economic status of the FBO industry within the economy
    c. Population growth
    d. Elasticity of demand (responsiveness of customers to price changes) for the products or services the business provides
    e. Availability of aircraft

Once these factors are identified, they may be used in pro formas, which estimate the level of sales, expense, and profitability that seem possible in a future period of operations.

THE PRO FORMA INCOME STATEMENT

In preparing the **pro forma income statement**, the estimate of total sales during a selected period is the most critical forecast. The owner/manager must employ business experience from past financial statements.

If, for example, a 10 percent increase in sales volume is a realistic and attainable goal, the first step is to multiply last year's gross income by 1.10 to get this year's estimate of total gross income. Next, this total must be broken down by month by looking at the historical monthly sales volume. From this one can determine the percentage of total annual sales averaged for each month over a minimum of the past three years. It might be determined that 75 percent of total annual sales volume was realized during the six months from July through December in each of those years and that the remaining 25 percent of sales was spread fairly evenly over the first six months of the year.

Next, an estimate of the cost of goods sold must be made by analyzing operating data to determine on a monthly basis what percentage of sales has gone into cost of goods sold in the past. This percentage can then be adjusted for expected variations in costs, price trends, and efficiency of operations.

Operating expenses (sales, general and administrative expenses, depreciation, and interest), other expenses, other income, and taxes can then be estimated through detailed analysis and adjustment of what they were in the past and what they are expected to be in the future. Putting together this information month by month for a year into the future will result in the firm's pro forma income statement.

A sample pro forma income statement for XYZ Aviation Company is shown in Figure 14-3, and preparation of the information is summarized below.

1. *Income (sales)*—List the departments in the firm. Reasonable projections of the monthly sales for each department are entered in the estimate column ("Est."). The actual sales are entered in the actual column ("Act.") for the month as they become available. Any revenue not strictly related to the business is excluded from the income (sales) column.
2. *Cost of sales*—The cost of sales estimated for each month for each department is entered in the estimate column. For product inventory, the cost of the goods sold for each department is calculated by subtracting the current inventory from beginning inventory plus purchases and transportation costs during the month. The actual costs are entered each month as they accrue.
3. *Gross profit*—Total cost of sales is subtracted from total sales.
4. *Expenses*—There are two main categories of business expenses—overhead (indirect) and operating (direct) expenses. Overhead expenses are what it costs to run the business, such as rent, insurance, and utilities. Operating expenses, on the other hand, are the result of normal business operations, such as materials, labor, and machinery used in production.

    Total direct and indirect expenses for each department are entered in the estimate columns. The actual expenses are entered each month as they accrue. The advantage of departmentalizing expenses is that each segment of the business is held directly accountable. This often proves valuable when analyzing where cutbacks, expansion, or other actions might take place, and time is saved when reviewing specific numbers for segments of the operation. This system can also be useful for monitoring the performance of department managers.

XYZ Aviation Company
Pro Forma Statement of Income
December 31, 20__

Departments	Sales		Cost of Sales		Gross Profit		Expenses						Net Profit	
							Direct				Overhead Indirect			
							Fixed		Variable					
	Est.	Act.	Est.	Act.	Est.	Act.	Act.	Est.	Act.	Est.	Act.	Est.	Est.	Act.
Fueling														
Used Aircraft														
New Aircraft														
Charter/Air Taxi														
Rental														
Flight Training														
Hanger Mgmt.														
Aircraft Mgmt.														
Maintenance														
Parts														
Avionics Sales														
Paint Operations														
Display Case Sales														
Totals														

Figure 14-3. Pro forma statement of income for XYZ Aviation Company.

Expenses may be either fixed or variable in nature. **Fixed expenses**, or fixed costs, are those costs that remain fairly constant, regardless of business volume. For example, if a charter department is established as a profit center, pilot salaries and aircraft lease payments are examples of direct fixed expenses. **Variable expenses**, or variable costs, on the other hand, vary directly with business volume. If using aircraft flight hours as the volume, then fuel and maintenance costs would be examples of direct variable costs. The more flying, the higher the expenses.

Overhead (indirect) expenses are typically fixed and not necessarily aviation-specific. Generally, they cannot be attributed to one particular department. Costs that may fit this description are administrative salaries, telephone, utilities, taxes, rent, advertising/promotion, office supplies, insurance, professional services, and interest. These indirect expenses must be allocated in an equitable, justifiable method to each department or profit center.

One accepted method is to allocate indirect expenses on a square footage basis. If the charter department occupies 20 percent of the total square footage of the facility, then 20 percent of the rent, utilities, administrative, and other indirect costs can be allocated to that profit center. Another common allocation method that works in some situations is to allocate indirect costs as a percentage of sales for that profit center. If the profit center generates 15 percent of the firm's revenues, then 15 percent of the indirect costs are allocated to that profit center.

5. *Net profit*—Total expenses are subtracted from gross profit to determine net profit. Because the individual departments have been divided into individual profit centers, management is now provided with a powerful financial decision-making tool. No longer will unprofitable or marginally profitable departments be hidden.

The pro forma income statement, prepared on a monthly basis and culminating in an annual projection for the next business fiscal year, should be revised not less than quarterly. It must reflect the actual performance achieved in the immediately preceding three months to ensure its continuing usefulness as one of the two most valuable planning tools available to management.

Should the pro forma reveal that the business will likely not generate a profit from operations, plans must immediately be developed to identify what is necessary to at least break even—for example, increase volume, decrease expenses, or put more owner capital in to pay some debts and reduce interest expenses.

BREAK-EVEN ANALYSIS

The break-even point means a level of operations at which a business neither makes a profit nor sustains a loss. At this point, revenue is just enough to cover expenses. **Break-even analysis** enables the firm to study the relationship of volume, costs, and revenue to determine this point.

Break-even analysis requires the FBO owner/manager to define a sales level, in terms of revenue dollars to be earned within a given accounting period, at which the business would earn a before-tax profit of zero. This may be done by employing one of various formula calculations to the business estimated sales volume, estimated fixed costs, and estimated variable costs.

Ordinarily, the volume and cost estimates assume the following conditions:

1. A change in sales volume will have no effect on selling prices.
2. Fixed expenses will remain the same at all volume levels.
3. Variable expenses will increase or decrease in direct proportion to any increase or decrease in sales volume.

The steps for calculating the break-even point are as follows:

1. Obtain a list of expenses incurred by the company during its past fiscal year.
2. Separate the expenses into either a variable or a fixed expense classification.
3. Express the variable expenses as a percentage of sales. For example, let's assume gross income (sales) was $1,200,000; fixed expenses, $400,000; variable expenses, $720,000; and net income, $80,000. Variable expenses are 60 percent of sales ($720,000 ÷ $1,200,000). This would mean that 60 cents of every sales dollar is required to cover variable expenses. Only the remainder, 40 cents of every dollar, is available for fixed expenses and profit.
4. Substitute the information gathered in the preceding steps in the following basic break-even formula to calculate the break-even point.

   $$S = F + V$$

   Where:
   S = Sales at the break-even point
   F = Fixed expenses
   V = Variable expenses expressed as a percentage of sales

This formula means that when sales revenues equal the fixed expenses and variable expenses incurred in producing the sales revenues, there will be no profit or loss. At this point, revenue from sales is just sufficient to cover the fixed and variable expenses. In this formula, S is the break-even point.

Using the numbers in step 3, the break-even point may be calculated as follows:

$$S = F + V$$
$$S = \$400{,}000 + 0.60S$$
$$1.00S - 0.60S = \$400{,}000$$
$$0.40S = \$400{,}000$$
$$S = \$1{,}000{,}000$$

The break-even formula can be modified to show the dollar sales required to obtain a certain amount of desired net income (or loss). To do this, let S equal the sales required to obtain a certain amount of net income (or loss), for example, $80,000. The formula then reads:

$S = F + V + \textit{Desired Net Income}$
$S = \$400{,}000 + 0.60S + \$80{,}000$
$1.00S - 0.60S = \$480{,}000$
$0.40S = \$480{,}000$
$S = \$1{,}200{,}000$

$S = F + V - \textit{Desired Net Loss}$
$S = \$400{,}000 + 0.60S - \$80{,}000$
$1.00S - 0.60S = 400{,}000 - 80{,}000$
$0.40S = \$320{,}000$
$S = \$800{,}000$

Break-even analysis may also be represented graphically by charting the sales dollars required to break even as shown in Figure 14-4.

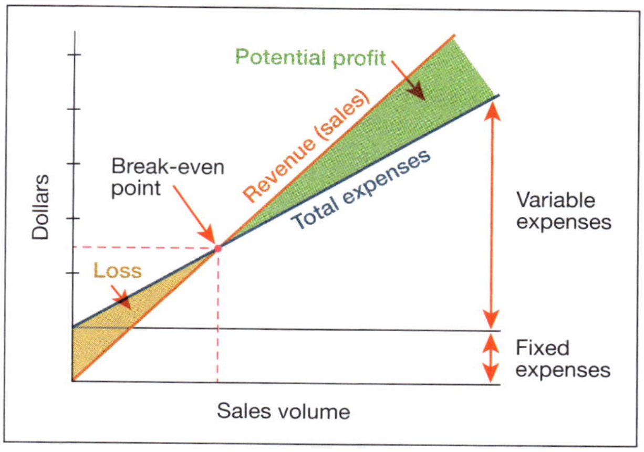

Figure 14-4. Break-even chart.

Budgeting and Cost Control

Budgets are detailed plans that represent set objectives against which to measure results. They are valuable management tools. In effect, they are blueprints that enable the firm to anticipate what will be, in other words, a future state that is yet to be realized, establish specific objectives, and chart the right course to assist the business in attaining those objectives.

Additionally, by monitoring what happens as the firm passes through the budget period, management will be in a position to make necessary adjustments to keep the plan on target.

Cash flow budgets identify when cash is expected to be received and when it must be spent to pay bills and debts. It shows how much cash will be needed to pay expenses and when it will be needed. It also allows the manager to identify where the necessary cash will come from. For example, will it be internally generated from sales and the collection of accounts receivable—or must it be borrowed? The cash flow budget deals only with actual cash transactions; noncash expense items, such as depreciation and amortization of goodwill, are not considered.

The cash flow budget, based on management estimates of sales and obligations, identifies when money will be flowing into and out of the business. It enables management to plan for shortfalls in cash resources so short-term working capital loans may be arranged in advance. It allows management to schedule purchases and payments in a way that enables the business to borrow as little as possible. Because all sales are not cash sales, management must be able to forecast when accounts receivable will become cash in the bank and when expenses—whether regular or seasonal—must be paid so cash shortfalls will not interrupt normal business operations. The cash flow budget enhances control by allowing management to continually compare actual receipts and disbursements against forecast amounts. This comparison helps management to identify areas for timely improvement in financial management.

By closely watching the timing of cash receipts and disbursements, cash balance on hand, and loan balances, management can readily identify such issues as deficiencies in collecting receivables and unrealistic trade credit or loan repayment schedules. Surplus cash that may be invested on a short-term basis or used to reduce debt and interest expenses temporarily can be recognized. In short, it is the most valuable tool management has at its disposal to refine the day-to-day operation of a business. Additionally, it is an important financial tool bank lenders evaluate when a business needs a loan, as it demonstrates not only how large a loan is required but also when and how it can be repaid.

The cash flow budget can be prepared for any period of time. However, a one-year budget matching the fiscal year of the business is generally recommended. As in the preparation and use of the pro forma income statement, the cash flow budget should be prepared on a monthly basis for the next year. It should be revised not less than quarterly to reflect actual performance in the preceding three months of operations to check its projections.

In order to make the most effective use of cash flow budgets to plan profits, reporting devices have to be established. These reports and reviews enable management to compare actual performance with budgeted projections and maintain control of the operations.

Cash flow budgets can be established for sales, cost of goods sold, selling expenses, administrative expenses, direct labor, and other areas. The formats for two typical budget reports are shown in Figure 14-5 (fuel sales budget) and figure 14-6 (administrative expenses budget).

Report of Actual and Budgeted Fuel Sales
for the Year Ending December 31, 20__

Actual	Fuel Sales ($) Budgeted	Quarterly	Variations from Budget (Under) Cumulative
1st Quarter			
2nd Quarter			
3rd Quarter			
4th Quarter			

Figure 14-5. Fuel sales budget.

Budgeted Report on Administrative Expenses
for the Year Ending December 31, 20__

Month of			Year to Date			
Budget	**Actual**	**Variation**	**Budget**	**Actual**	**Variation**	**Remarks**

Figure 14-6. Administrative expenses budget.

Cash flow budgets allow the owner/manager to anticipate problems rather than react to them after they occur. It permits comparison of actual receipts and disbursements against projections to identify errors in the forecast. If cash flow is analyzed monthly, the manager can correct the cause of the error before it harms profitability.

Types, Uses, and Sources of Capital

Capital is critical for both running a business and financing its future growth. The capital to finance a business is of three main types: debt capital, equity capital, and working capital. Every growing business needs all three types of capital. The capital structure of a company will determine the mix of these three types. Capital is typically in the form of cash or liquid assets that can easily be converted to cash. Used by companies to pay for the ongoing production of goods and services to create a profit, companies use capital to invest in such things as labor and building expansion, for example, to create value.

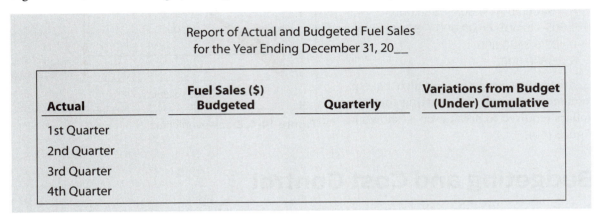

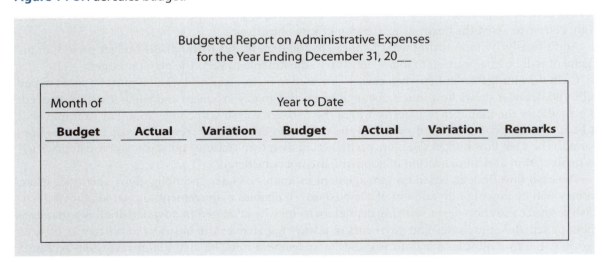

Debt capital is acquired through borrowing. It can be obtained through private or government sources. For established companies, banks and bond issuance are often the most common sources of debt capital. For new companies, friends and family, credit cards, and online lenders may be common sources of debt capital.

Debt capital requires regular payments with interest, as all debt must be repaid. Although companies want to avoid being too highly leveraged—i.e., taking on too much debt—in reality, debt capital allows a business to expand and grow without making huge lump sum payments for expanded facilities or other investments.

Equity capital, or **equity financing,** can be in the form of private equity, public equity, or real estate equity. Both private and public equity are generated through issuance of company stock. Private equity is raised among a closed group of investors. Public equity is raised by an **initial public offering (IPO)** on a stock exchange. Stockholders are offered equity (part ownership) in the company in exchange for their investment in stock. Stockholders earn money on their investment either via share price appreciation or **dividends**, or both.

A company's **working capital** is in the form of liquid assets that are used for fulfilling daily obligations. Working capital represents a company's ability to cover its debts, accounts payable, and other obligations that are due within one year. Working capital can be calculated two ways:

Current Assets – Current Liabilities

Accounts Receivable + Inventory – Accounts Payable

Keep in mind that a company that has more liabilities than assets could soon run out of working capital.

As lenders and investors analyze the requirements of the business, they will distinguish between the three types of capital in the following ways: (a) fluctuating needs (working capital); (b) permanent needs (equity capital), and (c) needs to be repaid with profits over a period of a few years (debt capital).

If a firm is asking for a working capital loan, management will be expected to show how the loan can be repaid through cash (liquidity) during the firm's next full operating cycle, usually a one-year cycle. If the firm is seeking equity capital, it must be raised from investors who will take the risk for dividend returns or capital gains, or a specific share of the business. If the firm is seeking debt capital, management will be expected to show how the capital will be used to increase the business enough to be able to repay the debt within several years (usually not more than seven years).

BORROWING WORKING CAPITAL

Commercial banks are the largest source of working capital loans. These loans have the following characteristics:

1. The loans are short term but renewable.
2. They may fluctuate according to seasonal needs or follow a fixed schedule of repayment (amortization).
3. They require periodic full repayment.
4. They are granted primarily only when the ratio of net current assets comfortably exceeds net current liabilities.
5. They are sometimes unsecured but more often secured by current assets (e.g., accounts receivable and inventory). Advances can usually be obtained for as much as 70 to 80 percent of quality (likely to be paid) receivables and 40 to 50 percent of inventory. Banks grant unsecured credit only when they feel the general liquidity and overall financial strength of a business provide assurance for repayment of the loan.

The firm may be able to predict a specific interval, say three to five months, for which it needs financing. A bank may then agree to issue credit for a specific term. Most likely, management will need working capital to finance outflow peaks in the business cycle. Working capital then supplements equity. Most working capital credits are established on a one-year basis.

Although most unsecured loans fall into the category of a one-year line of credit, another frequently used type, the amortizing loan, calls for a fixed program of reduction, usually on a monthly or quarterly basis. For such loans, the bank is likely to agree to terms longer than one year, as long as the firm continues to meet the principal reduction schedule. It is important to note that while a loan from a bank for working capital can be negotiated only for a relatively short term, satisfactory performance can allow the arrangement to be continued indefinitely.

Most banks will expect the firm to pay off loans once a year (particularly if they are unsecured) in perhaps 30 or 60 days. This is known as the *annual clean up*, and it should occur when the business has the greatest liquidity. This debt reduction normally follows a seasonal sales peak, such as the summer or fall when flying weather is best and most receivables have been collected.

Sometimes a firm finds that it is progressively more difficult to repay or "clean up" within the specified time. This difficulty usually occurs because (a) the business is growing and its current activity represents a considerable increase over the corresponding period of the previous year; (b) the firm has increased its short-term capital requirement because of new promotional programs or additional operations; or (c) the firm is experiencing a temporary reduction in profitability and cash flow.

Frequently, such a condition justifies obtaining both working capital and amortizing loans. For example, management might try to arrange a combination of a $15,000 open line of credit to handle peak financial requirements during the business cycle and $20,000 in amortizing loans to be repaid at a certain amount (e.g., $4,000) per quarter. In appraising such a request, a commercial bank will insist on justification based on past experience and future projections. The bank will want to know how the $15,000 line of credit will be self-liquidating during the year (with ample room for the annual clean up) and how the business will produce increased profits and resulting cash flow to meet the schedule of amortization on the $20,000 portion, in spite of increasing the firm's interest expense.

BORROWING DEBT CAPITAL

Debt capital is usually scheduled to be repaid over longer periods with profits from business activities extending several years into the future. Debt capital loans are, therefore, secured by collateral such as aircraft and other equipment—fixed assets which guarantee that lenders will recover their money should the business be unable to make repayment.

For a debt capital loan, management will need to demonstrate that the debt capital will be used to increase cash flow through increased sales, cost savings, and/or more productivity. Although the building, equipment, or aircraft will probably be used as collateral for debt capital funds, management will also be able to use them for general business purposes. Even if the firm borrows only to acquire a new aircraft, the lender is likely to insist that all aircraft and equipment be pledged.

Instead of bank financing for a particular aircraft, it may be possible to arrange a lease, as discussed in Chapter 11. The firm will not actually own the aircraft, but it will have exclusive use of it over a specified period. Such an arrangement usually has tax advantages. It lets the firm use funds that would have been tied up in the aircraft had the firm purchased it. It also affords the opportunity to make sure the aircraft meets the FBO's needs before it is purchased.

Major equipment may also be purchased on a time payment plan, sometimes called a **conditional sales purchase**. Ownership of the property is retained by the seller until the buyer has made all the payments required by the contract. Remember, however, that time payment purchases usually require substantial down payments, with leases even requiring cash advances for several months of lease payments.

Long-term debt capital loans for more than five but less than fifteen years are also obtainable. Real estate financing with repayment over many years on an established schedule is the best example. The loan is secured by the land and/or buildings the money was used to buy. Most businesses are best financed by a combination of these various credit arrangements.

When an FBO goes to a bank to request a loan, it must be prepared to present the company's case persuasively. Management should bring its financial plan consisting of a cash flow budget for the next twelve months, pro forma balance sheets, and income statements for the next three to five years. Management should be able to explain and amplify these statements and the underlying assumptions on which the figures are based. Obviously, the assumptions must be convincing and the projections supportable. Finally, many banks prefer statements audited by an outside accountant with the accountant's signed opinion that the statements were prepared in accordance with Generally Accepted Accounting Principles (GAAP) and that they fairly present the financial condition of the business.

BORROWING EQUITY CAPITAL

Equity capital sometimes comes from sources other than the business owner or stockholders. Venture capital is one such source. Difficult to define, it is high-risk capital offered with the principal objective of earning capital gains for the investor. While venture capitalists are usually prepared to wait longer than the average investor for a profitable return, they usually expect in excess of 15 percent return on their investment. Often, they expect to take an active part in determining the objectives of the business. These investors may also assist the FBO owner/manager by providing experienced guidance in marketing, product ideas, and additional financing alternatives as the business develops. Even though turning to venture capital may create more bosses, their advice can be as valuable as the money they lend. However, venture capitalists are looking for businesses with real potential for growth and for future sales in the millions of dollars. The show *Shark Tank* is an example of venture capital investors.

Financial Planning

Studies overwhelmingly identify ineffective management as the leading cause of business failure. Ineffective management typically results in poor **financial planning** by management. All too often, the owner/manager of an FBO is so caught up in the day-to-day tasks of managing the operation, seeing that aircraft are maintained, and struggling to collect receivables to meet the payroll that planning is an afterthought. There never seems to be enough time to prepare pro formas or budgets. Often, FBO managers understand their business but not the financial statements or the records, which they feel are for the benefit of the IRS or the bank. Such overburdened owner/managers can scarcely identify what will affect their businesses next week, let alone over the coming months and years.

Success may be ensured only by focusing on all factors affecting a business's performance. Focusing on planning is essential to survival. Short-term financial planning is generally concerned with profit planning or budgeting—tactical, in other words. Long-term financial planning is generally strategic, setting goals for sales growth and profitability over a minimum of three to five years.

LONG-TERM PLANNING

The long-term or strategic plan focuses on pro forma income statements prepared for annual periods of three to five years into the future. It is difficult to imagine all the variables that will affect a business in one year, and projections for three to five years are even more difficult. However, the key is control—i.e., controlling the firm's future course of expansion through the use of the financial tools discussed earlier in this chapter.

The first step is to determine a rate of growth that is desirable and reasonable. Using pro forma statements and cash flow budgets, the next step is to calculate the capital required to finance the inventory, aircraft, equipment, and personnel needs necessary to attain that growth in sales volume. The FBO owner/manager must anticipate capital needs in time to make satisfactory arrangements for outside funds if internally generated funds from retained earnings are insufficient.

Growth can be funded in only two ways: with profits or by borrowing. If expansion outstrips the capital available to support higher levels of accounts receivable, inventory, fixed assets, and operating expenses, a business's development will be slowed or stopped entirely by its failure to meet debts as they become payable. Such insolvency will result in the business's assets being liquidated to meet the demands of the creditors. The only way to avoid this out-stripping of capital is by planning to control growth. Growth must be understood to be controlled. This understanding requires knowledge of past financial performance and of the future requirements of the business.

These needs must be forecast in writing—using the pro forma income statement in particular—for three to five years in the future. After projecting reasonable sales volumes and profitability, the cash flow budget must be used to determine (on a quarterly basis for the next three to five years) how these projected sales volumes translate into the flow of cash in and out of the business during normal operations. Where additional inventory, equipment, or other physical assets are necessary to support the sales forecast, management must determine whether or not the business will generate sufficient profits to sustain the growth forecast.

Often, businesses simply grow too rapidly for internally generated cash to sufficiently support the growth. If profits are inadequate to carry the growth forecast, the owner/manager must either make arrangements to borrow working capital or slow the pace of growth to allow internal cash to catch up and keep pace with the expansion. Because arranging financing and obtaining additional equity capital takes time, this need must be anticipated well in advance to avoid business interruption. Planning is a perpetual process. It is the key to prosperity for any company.

Determining the Value of an FBO

With an increasing number of ownership changes and mergers taking place in the industry, determining the value of FBOs is on the rise. The concept of value is viewed in a variety of ways. Market value is generally defined as the most probable selling price of a property—assuming a willing and informed buyer and seller.

Although this may appear to be a simple concept, "willing and informed" are not always appropriate terms in the sale of a fixed-base operation or other aviation business. Frequently, the owner/operator has reached a value conclusion based on various personal issues associated with the operation (time and money invested, years and effort devoted toward the business, loyalty to employees, retirement needs, etc.) while ignoring the actual foundations that create or diminish the value of the business.

The process of determining the value of a current business must be based upon a more objective and substantial financial analysis. **Business valuation** is always a difficult task, but appraising an FBO is typically even more complex. FBOs as ongoing business enterprises are typically valued by two methods:

- Multiples of earnings before interest, taxes, depreciation, and amortization (EBITDA)
- Discounted cash flow (DCF) analysis

Even though the multiple of EBITDA analysis is the most common in the aviation industry, the discounted cash flow (DCF) analysis is often more appropriate in situations where an unstable market exists. An EBITDA analysis represents the conversion of one year's income into a value, while a DCF projects and evaluates an income stream over time. Both are appropriate means of valuation and use net income after the exclusion of certain non-cash flow items.

EBITDA ANALYSIS

The **multiples of earnings before interest, taxes, depreciation, and amortization (EBITDA)** is best suited for a stable operation that has experienced consistent revenue and expense trends historically, with similar trends expected over the next few years. This does not require a stagnant business, but rather one that has not shown significant fluctuations in either revenue sources or volumes in recent years.

This method analyzes one year's net income, converting it into a value estimate, using a multiple based upon the expected future stability of the business, overall economic climate, and financial risks associated with the business. The ability to project stabilized earnings is critical. An erratic revenue or expense history makes projecting future trends very difficult, which in turn reduces the reliability of the analysis.

Another difficult task in the EBITDA analysis is determining the appropriate multiple. Multiples represent the relationship between the selling price of an FBO or other aviation business, and its net earnings at the time of sale, or its pro forma earnings. The multiple is typically derived from sales of other FBOs or aviation businesses and, therefore, is only as good as the information that is available from either the buyer or the seller. Multiples are "all inclusive" of the buyer's perception of the stability of the business, anticipated growth trends, return on equity requirements, motivation of buyer and seller, and terms of sale. Without obtaining all of the details surrounding the transaction, multiples of EBITDA can be deceiving figures.

DISCOUNTED CASH FLOW ANALYSIS

The **discounted cash flow (DCF) analysis** is typically more appropriate in an unstable market, which probably describes most FBOs and specialized aviation businesses. An unstable market may be a situation where an operator is experiencing significant growth trends or is acquiring a competitor on the field whereby market share and margins are expected to change dramatically, or it might be a scenario where a market is declining as the result of outside (or even internal) influences. In any case, this method works best when changes—either positive or negative—are occurring or are anticipated.

The DCF analysis attempts to determine the value of an investment today, based on expected future cash flows. It projects revenues and expenses into the future based upon historic trends and prospective market and economic conditions. This projection is typically performed on a departmental or classification basis, with each line item addressed individually. This allows for an analysis of specific revenue or expense items that may be expected to grow at a faster rate than others as well as accounts for those items that are fixed or will change as a percentage of another item. The result is a more detailed real-world assessment of an ongoing aviation business. As one might expect, an accurate and supportable projection of revenue and expense trends is the most significant factor in a DCF analysis.

The annual net income stream is converted into a present value by a discounting process. Each year's projected net income is discounted into a present value, using a rate of return consistent with the associated risk (based on the idea that revenues received in the future are worth less than the same revenues received now). Each year's discounted income is added to provide a current value estimate.

In some cases where a significant lease term remains after the selected discounting period (usually five to ten years), a reversionary value is added to reflect the fact that, if there is a continuing lease, the ability to generate income does not stop after the initial discounting period. The discount rate used in a DCF analysis is based upon investor return requirements given the risks associated with the future income stream. Depending upon the physical and economic characteristics of an FBO or aviation business, the existing lease agreement, the competitive environment, and the overall stability of the business, discount rates may vary anywhere from 15 to 30 percent.

The complexity of the EBITDA or the DCF method lies in the evaluation and recasting of financial information presented by the operator, with every operator using their preferred method of bookkeeping. For instance, on the revenue side, many operators do not keep an accurate analysis of historical fuel volumes, types of fuel sales (self-service, full-service, etc.), or the historic margins associated with each. However, such information is critical to the analysis of both past and future fuel revenues, which may significantly impact the profitability (and value) of the business. Expenses are also often inappropriately or incorrectly categorized. A misinterpretation of either revenue or expense items results in a skewing of the EBITDA as well as the corresponding value conclusion.

INTEREST, TAXES, DEPRECIATION, AND AMORTIZATION

Interest, income taxes, depreciation, and amortization are generally excluded from a business valuation. The result is that the firm is valued on a cash basis without consideration to the current owner's equity basis, financing terms, equipment basis, or competency of the accountant. All of the above items (interest, income taxes, depreciation, and amortization) are a direct result of current owner investment and accounting procedures, not day-to-day cash flow, and they differ from operator to operator depending upon the desired taxation and yield results. By excluding these variable items, a business valuation can be done on a similar basis and a true value can be estimated.

REVENUES, COST OF SALES, AND EXPENSES

Revenues generated by an FBO or other aviation business are generally straightforward and typically reflect all income, excluding taxes. However, some forms of revenue—such as aircraft sales—warrant a greater risk than others. Consequently, if significant, these revenues and corresponding expenses are typically extracted from overall revenues and analyzed separately, with alternative multiples or discount rates applied.

Cost of sales has a tendency to become a complex issue when evaluating an operating statement. In general, cost of sales represents the actual cost of the materials associated with the sale of specific items, such as fuel, catering, parts, pilot supplies, etc. In the case of fuel, both taxes and airport flowage fees are typically included, since each is part of the direct selling price and may be reasonably calculated in the wholesale cost of the fuel.

Operating expenses generally create the greatest ambiguity during the valuation process. Every business operator handles the accounting function a little bit differently, with some creative accounting principles applied where appropriate. Although this is fine for the IRS, it is important to assess carefully all categories of expenses to ensure that they are applicable only to the day-to-day operations of the business. A frequent example relates to the owner's compensation package. In some cases, the owner's compensation is well beyond what is normally attributed to the day-to-day management of an operation.

Personal and auto expenses, special management perks, excessive travel budgets, or expenses related to the personal use of company aircraft are not typically included for the valuation process. Likewise, excessive legal or accounting expenses that may occur in a given year would not be included. Typically, more normalized expense allocations are utilized in the valuation.

Another typical error found in many operating statements involves the repair and maintenance expense category. Improvements to facilities or acquisition of equipment are often deemed operating expenses when it is more appropriate to recognize them as one-time capital improvements. Only the routine maintenance associated with the facilities and equipment are pertinent operating expenses. A good rule of thumb is that if it is not a consistent annual expense, then it is probably better categorized as a capital expenditure.

Summary

Successful FBOs not only have a customer-service focus, but they are also managed as a business, with a keen eye on the financial aspects of the business. Financial management, including the ability to produce and interpret various financial statements and ratios, is a skill that if properly developed and addressed will allow the FBO to be profitable and managed well.

The most important factor in determining the value of a current business is simply the level of profitability that is currently presented and that can reasonably be expected to continue over time. Profitability is impacted by several significant components, including:

- Historic operating statistics
- Type and strength of the revenue stream
- Control of material costs
- Expenses associated with the operation of the business

Other significant factors that contribute to value are location (geographic area, size of airport, services offered); length of lease term and/or operating agreements; competition; and the conditions and terms of existing contracts (air carriers, cargo handling, and so forth).

While the influence of the emotional attachment to the business cannot be understated to a seller, the ability to generate a stable, consistent cash flow is the most significant factor in the creation of value for the buyer.

Key Terms

assets. Material and intangible items a business owns, such as cash, merchandise inventory, land, buildings, equipment, machinery, furniture, patents, and trademarks, as well as money due from individuals or other businesses (accounts receivable or notes receivable). Assets are reflected on the balance sheet.

balance sheet. One of three primary financial statements, it provides a picture of the financial health of a business at a given moment, usually at the close of an accounting period. It lists in detail material and intangible items the business owns (assets) and what money the business owes, either to its creditors (liabilities) or to its owners (shareholders' equity or net worth of the business).

break-even analysis. A process for determining the number of units of a product that must be sold to cover the fixed and variable costs of production. It determines how much must be sold for the business to meet expenses and neither lose nor make money (break even).

budget. A detailed financial plan that represents set objectives against which to measure results. It is a blueprint that enables the firm to anticipate what will be, establish specific objectives, and chart the right course to attain those objectives.

business valuation. The process of estimating the economic value of a business.

cash flow budget. A budget that identifies when cash is expected to be received and when it must be spent to pay bills and debts. It shows how much cash will be needed to pay expenses and when it will be needed.

conditional sales purchase. A time payment plan in which a down payment is required and ownership of the property is retained by the seller until the buyer has made all the payments required by the contract.

cost of goods. The direct costs of producing goods sold by the company; similar to cost of sales. This includes the cost of the materials and labor directly used to create the good. It excludes indirect expenses, such as distribution costs and sales force costs. It is often used by manufacturers.

cost of sales. The actual cost of the materials associated with the sale of specific items; often used by retailers. It is also known as cost of revenue and is similar to cost of goods sold.

current ratio. A liquidity ratio that measures a company's ability to pay short-term obligations (those due within one year) from current assets. Current ratio = current assets ÷ current liabilities.

debt. An obligation that requires one party, the debtor, to pay money or other agreed-upon value to another party, the creditor.

debt capital. Capital required when a business is expanding or being altered in some significant and costly way that is expected to result in higher and increased cash flow. Lenders of growth capital frequently depend on anticipated increased profit for repayment over an extended period of time, rather than expecting to be repaid from seasonal increases in liquidity as is the case of working capital lenders.

debt-equity ratio. A leverage ratio that compares total liabilities to total owner's equity. A high debt-equity ratio indicates the company has been aggressive in financing growth with debt capital.

debt financing. Creditor money that comes from trade credit, loans made by financial institutions, leasing companies, and customers who have made prepayments on orders.

discounted cash flow (DCF) analysis. A method of valuing a security, project, company, or asset using the concepts of the time value of money. It attempts to determine the value of an investment today based on projections of how much money it will generate in the future.

dividends. The distribution of some of a company's earnings to shareholders. Dividends, which may be paid in the form of cash or additional stock, are designed to reward investors for investing in the company by purchasing shares of stock.

equity. The investment by the owner plus any profits or minus any losses that have accumulated in the business. This represents the amount of money that would be returned to the owners if all of the assets were liquidated and all of the company's debt was paid off.

equity capital. Capital from private equity, public equity, and real estate equity. For example, stockholders create equity capital from an initial public offering.

equity financing. Money received by a company in exchange for some portion of ownership. An initial public offering of stock is a form of equity financing.

Financial Accounting Standards Board (FASB). The not-for-profit organization that establishes financial accounting and reporting standards for public and private companies and not-for-profit organizations that follow Generally Accepted Accounting Principles (GAAP).

financial forecasting. The process of predicting a business's future financial performance.

financial management. The practice of handling a company's finances in a way that ensures financial success and regulatory compliance.

financial planning. The ongoing process that determines the number and type of human and physical resources a company will need for continued operation. Short-term financial planning is tactical in nature and generally concerned with profit planning or budgeting. Long-term financial planning is generally strategic in nature, setting goals for sales growth and profitability over a minimum of three to five years.

fixed expenses. Expenses or costs that do not change with an increase or decrease in the amount of goods or services produced or sold.

Generally Accepted Accounting Principles (GAAP). A common set of accounting principles, standards, and procedures issued by the Financial Accounting Standards Board (FASB). Public companies (those with outstanding stock) must follow GAAP.

gross margin ratio. The percentage of sales dollars left after subtracting the cost of goods sold from income. It is calculated by dividing gross profit by income.

gross profit. The profit a company makes after deducting the costs associated with making and selling its products, or the costs associated with its services. Gross profit assesses a company's efficiency at using its labor and supplies in producing goods and services.

income. Gross sales less returns and allowances.

income statement. One of three primary financial statements, it summarizes a company's revenues and expenses over a period of time, either quarterly or annually.

initial public offering (IPO). A form of equity capital, an IPO is the process of offering shares of a private corporation to the public in a new stock issuance. Once issued, the private company is referred to as a public company. Stockholder funds used to purchase these initial shares of stock generate equity capital for the business.

interest, income taxes, depreciation, and amortization. Items deducted from earnings in recognition of expenses not necessarily associated with the company's operations.

leverage ratios. A group of financial ratios that examine the ability of a company to meet its financial obligations. These include current ratio, quick ratio, the debt-equity ratio, gross margin ratio, net profit margin ratio, return on assets ratio, and return on investment ratio.

liabilities. An obligation reflected on the balance sheet that has not yet been fulfilled and remains owed by the company. Liabilities are short term (due in 12 months or less) and long term (due in more than 12 months).

multiples of earnings before interest, taxes, depreciation, and amortization (EBITDA). An alternate measure of profitability. By removing the non-cash depreciation and amortization expense, as well as taxes and debt costs, EBITDA attempts to represent cash profit generated by the company's operations.

net profit margin ratio. A measurement of how much net income or profit is generated as a percentage of revenue. It is the ratio of net profits to revenues. This ratio indicates how much of each dollar in revenue translates into profit.

operating expenses. Expenses a business incurs as a result of normal operations, such as materials, labor, and aircraft.

overhead (indirect) expenses. The expenses, or costs, not directly attributed to creating a product or delivering a service. These expenses are ongoing and can be fixed, variable, or both. Examples include rent, insurance, and utilities.

owner's equity. The value of equity in the business attributed to the owners (or shareholders). This is determined by subtracting liabilities from assets, and it is reflected on the balance sheet.

pro forma income statement. A financial statement that predicts future income and expenses based on anticipated sales.

pro forma statements. Statements that present expected company financial results based on past conditions. A budget is a type of pro forma, as it anticipates certain revenues and expenditures for a future period. Pro forma forecasts are hypothetical in nature and can vary significantly from actual results.

quick ratio. An indicator of a company's short-term liquidity that measures a company's ability to meet short-term obligations with current assets. The higher the ratio, the better a company's liquidity and financial health.

ratio analysis. A quantitative method of gaining insight into a company's liquidity, operational efficiency, and profitability by calculating financial ratios from the balance sheet and income statement.

return on assets ratio. A ratio that measures how efficiently profits are being generated from the assets employed in the business when compared with the ratios of firms in a similar business.

return on investment (ROI) ratio. A performance measure used to evaluate the efficiency and profitability of an investment or to compare the efficiency of a number of different investments. It measures the amount of financial return on a particular investment.

revenues. Income received through the selling of goods and services. The main reason a for-profit business exists is to earn revenues for the owners.

variable expenses. Expenses that can change over time, generally in proportion to how much a company produces or sells. Examples include fuel expenses, which vary based on aircraft operational activity and fuel purchases.

working capital. Liquid assets that are used for fulfilling daily obligations. Working capital represents a company's ability to cover its debts, accounts payable, and other obligations that are due within one year.

Review Questions

1. What is the purpose of financial management?
2. Describe the major categories of the balance sheet.
3. Why must the balance sheet balance?
4. Explain the purpose of the income statement.
5. What is the purpose of ratio analysis?
6. Define "working capital."
7. Define the purpose and formula for calculating the current ratio.
8. Define the purpose and formula for calculating the quick ratio.
9. Define the purpose and formula for calculating the debt-equity ratio.
10. Define the purpose and formula for calculating the gross margin ratio.
11. Define the purpose and formula for calculating the net profit margin ratio.
12. Discuss the purpose and formula for calculating the return on assets ratio.
13. Discuss the purpose and formula for calculating the return on investment (ROI) ratio.
14. How does income statement ratio analysis differ from balance sheet ratio analysis?
15. Distinguish between gross margin ratio and net profit margin ratio.
16. Why is the ROI ratio considered one of the most important ratios?
17. What are pro forma income statements?
18. Discuss some of the factors affecting pro forma statements.
19. Describe the steps in preparing a pro forma income statement.
20. Distinguish between direct expenses and overhead expenses.
21. How can overhead expenses be allocated to individual profit centers?
22. What is the purpose of break-even analysis?
23. What are the basic assumptions in preparing a break-even chart?
24. Why are cash flow budgets so important?
25. Provide several examples of typical budget reports.

26. Distinguish between working capital, equity capital, and debt capital.
27. What is the primary source for working capital loans?
28. Why are debt capital loans generally secured by collateral assets?
29. What is the advantage of leasing equipment?
30. What is a conditional sales purchase?
31. How does venture capital differ from other equity finance sources?
32. Distinguish between short-term and long-term planning.
33. Why is long-term planning so difficult for the small FBO?
34. What is the difference between EBITDA analysis and discounted cash flow (DCF) analysis in determining the value of an aviation business?
35. Summarize the important factors in determining the value of an aviation business.

Scenarios

1. You were recently contacted by an old friend who is in the process of establishing an FBO at a busy GA airport. He has asked you to join his management team as chief financial officer. This is an exciting opportunity, and you gratefully accept. During your first meeting with your friend who is now your boss, he asks you to develop a funding plan. In essence, he will need to raise an additional $3 million in start-up funding. What are your thoughts in establishing this plan? What sources of start-up funding are available and how will you recommend which of those to rely on?
2. Upon graduation from college with a degree in aviation management, you and four of your former classmates have decided to start an FBO. A nearby airport has recently issued a request for proposal (RFP) for firms interested in operating a full-service FBO at the field. As you and your partners consider all factors, you determine that you will need additional funds for working capital, equity capital, and debt capital during your first few years of business. What sources are available for these three types of capital? Which options will you most likely pursue, and why?
3. As you finish your first year as owner/manager of a small FBO, you determine your return on investment (ROI) to be 4 percent. Are you satisfied with this performance? If yes, why? If not, what options are available to you at this time?
4. Your group consists of department managers of a large, full-service FBO. The FBO manager has called a meeting of all department managers to report that revenues for all departments have been relatively flat for the past three years. The FBO manager would like to see revenues increase, but feels new ideas are needed. So, she has called each of you into this meeting to brainstorm ways in which to explore new sources of revenue. What does your group come up with?
5. As you and three partners begin planning your new FBO, conversation turns to profit projections. You would like to realize $50,000 in net income in your first year of operation. With projected fixed expenses of $308,000 and variable expenses representing 58 percent of sales, what level of income is required in this first year to reach your desired $50,000 net?

Bibliography

Prather, C. Daniel. 2009. *General Aviation Marketing and Management: Operating, Marketing, and Managing an FBO*. 3rd ed. Malabar, FL: Krieger Publishing Company.

15

Human Resources

In Chapter 15

Objectives

At the end of this chapter, you should be able to:

1. Explain the role of human resources.
2. Describe typical positions at an FBO.
3. Describe the steps in a typical interviewing process.
4. Discuss how prospective FBO employees are recruited.
5. Highlight some issues surrounding the promotion of employees.
6. Describe the importance of employee training.
7. Discuss the importance of and solutions to the turnover problem.
8. Describe the role of human resources in setting salary and benefits.

HR Function

Human resources are the most important resource for FBOs. Without a sufficiently qualified and capable workforce, the FBO would not be able to provide the necessary services to stay in business. For example, consider the importance of line service. Thus, the function of the human resources (HR) department is extremely important for an FBO.

The HR department performs several functions. It assists in recruiting and selecting employees, training and promoting employees, arranging for salary and benefits, and coordinating separation from service. Generally, the HR department acts in a support role to specific departments within an organization (staff function). In this way, department directors and supervisors are able to maintain control of their employees and decide who specifically gets hired, promoted, or fired.

Employment Data and FBO Positions

The aviation industry is a **cyclical industry**. Cycles include periods of strong growth and potentially lack of skilled labor, as well as contraction and an overabundance of skilled labor. At any given time, the industry is either entering, peaking, or leaving one of these two cycles. Prior to the COVID-19 pandemic in 2020–2022, for example, the aviation industry was strong and there was a shortage of skilled labor. During COVID, this issue became more pronounced as the industry experienced a significant contraction due to stay-at-home orders and travel restrictions. Many individuals employed in the industry were furloughed or offered early retirement options to reduce payroll costs during this challenging time. There was, almost at once, an overabundance of skilled labor. However, once the pandemic eased in March 2022, the air travel demand rebounded quickly and the aviation industry was confronted with a great need for additional labor to support this renewed demand. FBOs were not immune to these labor challenges. In fact, all FBO positions were affected, including accountants, avionics technicians, customer service representatives, dispatchers, line service personnel, maintenance technicians, managers, administrators, pilots, and sales personnel.

Figure 15-1. The aviation industry is cyclical. *(PopTika/Shutterstock.com)*

Figure 15-2. FBO staff. *(Tyler Olson/Shutterstock.com)*

Staffing

Employees are the major resource of any firm. The wise FBO manager realizes that the very basis of the human resources function involves people, and hiring the right people is important. Oftentimes, candidates for entry-level FBO positions do not have any aviation experience. Rather than being frustrated by this, the HR department can focus on those individuals with the right attitude and work ethic and then once hired, develop these individuals with adequate training and mentoring. Hiring the right people and training them well can directly affect the profitability of the business. Specific personnel policies should be included in the firm's operations manual. These become useful guides in all areas: recruitment and selection, compensation plan and employee benefits, training, performance appraisals, promotions, and terminations. All HR systems should be carefully designed to both process and retain records related to each employee. This includes application forms, testing and medical records, training records, evaluation forms, changes in status, emergency contact, etc. These records should be readily searchable and maintained in a secure manner.

One practical activity that can be helpful in establishing policy is preparation of **job descriptions** for all positions in the company. Each position should be analyzed, including the specific job title, duties and responsibilities assigned, tasks to be performed, skills required, relationships with other segments of the business, and any other relevant details, such as required levels of education and experience, familiarity with special equipment, and minimum physical requirements. This information will help in advertising job specifications for any opening that arises. It will also protect the FBO from liability, as employees are hired based on their skills, education, and experience as well as their ability to perform the essential functions of the job.

The staffing process includes all activities pertinent to the recruiting, selection, promotion, and training of employees. Outlining the details and correct procedures in advance can prevent errors later on that can create trouble and unnecessary expense.

RECRUITMENT, SELECTION, AND PROMOTION

The most common **recruiting** sources include the following:

- Advertising through general online job platforms, such as Indeed, Monster, Glassdoor, and LinkedIn
- Advertising through aviation-specific online job platforms, such as Avjobs, AviaNation.com, and JSFirm.com
- Advertising in aviation trade publications, such as *Aviation Week*
- Advertising with aviation organizations, such as AOPA or NBAA
- Advertising through posted announcements, window signs, and other point-of-need methods
- Obtaining recommendations (referrals) from colleagues, current employees, and others
- Recruiting through universities, colleges, and other academic venues
- Utilizing employment agencies
- Utilizing temporary agencies
- Accepting applications from drop-in candidates

Hiring is typically a multi-step process. Among the tools available to help in hiring and rejecting applicants are the employment application, the employment interview, the reference check, employment tests, and the probationary period for new employees.

Figure 15-3. Career fair. *(rkl_foto/Shutterstock.com)*

Standard employment application forms are available online. These forms typically require the applicant's name, address, telephone number, work experience, education, health and financial information, and personal data. This form can also be adapted to meet any FBO's particular needs.

The first step in the hiring process requires the company HR department to conduct an initial **applicant screening**. This screening of applications and resumes is for the purpose of developing a list of applicants qualified for the position. Those meeting minimum qualifications for an entry-level position will typically have a certain level of education and some degree of previous work experience (although not necessarily in aviation). Next, the manager of the department in which the applicant may potentially work reviews the list of qualified applicants and either makes a **short list** (reducing the larger list to a smaller, more manageable pool of applicants) or decides to accept the list as-is. If possible, at least three candidates would be interviewed for a position.

The **employment interview** is usually the next step and is one of the major tools in processing job applicants. Essentially, it has two aims: (1) to elicit information to supplement the facts submitted on the application form; and (2) to gain useful insights into the appearance, behavior, and personality of the prospective employee.

Interviewing is often a multi-step process consisting of a number of different interviews for each applicant. Interviews may be with one or several interviewers and may be in-person, via the telephone, or via Zoom, WebEx, Microsoft Teams, or another online platform. There really is no one best way to structure the interview process. It depends on a number of factors, such as organizational resources, number of applicants, level of the position within the organizational structure, and geographic proximity of applicants to the organization.

Although FBOs structure the interview process in different ways, one successful FBO's approach is to invite the applicant to visit the FBO to not only have an interview with the department manager but also tour the FBO and meet other personnel. If pleased with the applicant, the assistant FBO manager invites the applicant back for a second interview. During this interview, there is a focus

Figure 15-4. Employment interview. *(iStock.com/SDI Productions)*

on determining whether the individual truly desires an aviation career or simply seeks a paycheck. If the assistant manager is pleased, the FBO manager invites the applicant back for a third interview.

This process is the same at this FBO whether hiring a line service specialist or a customer service representative. An alternative approach is to have one interview but invite the department manager, the assistant FBO manager, and the FBO manager to participate in this one interview. Telephone interviews or online interviews are typically only used if the applicant is located a long distance away from the organization, or due to COVID requirements. In this situation, conducting at least the initial interview by telephone or online will allow the company to learn more about the applicant without either the organization or applicant having to incur travel expenses.

Because it is comparatively easy for an interviewer to be overly influenced by an outstanding characteristic of an applicant, it is wise to develop and use an **interview rating form** that provides structure to the interview and supports an objective evaluation of each candidate. An example rating form is shown in Figure 15-5. The art of interviewing comes with experience. For those new to conducting interviews, there are numerous resources available online and in the local library that address human resources administration and interviewing techniques.

Generally, it is efficient to conduct **structured interviews**. This requires planning the approach in advance—such as the kinds of questions to be asked, the order in which they will be asked, preferred attributes of a successful candidate, etc. Interviews can also be nondirective and less structured. These interviews are often preferred for upper-level managerial positions. In this case, the interviewer refrains from asking too many questions but instead encourages the candidate to speak in-depth about their qualifications, past experience, goals if hired, etc.

There are certain undesirable characteristics or symptoms that would disqualify an applicant. The following are some that could be considered red flags:

- Evidence of frequent job changes in the past, such as job changes every 6–12 months with no justification (e.g., multiple 12-month internships).
- Excessive indebtedness or poor financial management skills, such as poor credit rating.
- Poor communicative skills, such as avoiding eye contact or mispronunciation of words during the interview.
- Poor emotional control, such as an outburst during the interview.
- Too high a standard of living, such as arriving at the interview in an expensive sports car for an entry-level position.
- Unexplained gaps in the employment record, such as long periods of unemployment for no obvious reason.

As a general rule, it is best for the FBO manager to personally check all references provided by job applicants. A telephone call to each reference with some questions related to that candidate's character, work ethic, personality, strengths, weakness, etc., can be very insightful. Any hesitancy about the candidate can be discerned quite readily on the telephone call and probed diplomatically during the conversation. Alternatively, a simple form letter and questionnaire can be developed to cover the major points of concern.

Typically, most small FBOs do not test job applicants, except when a position requires special skills. Measures of typing speed and accuracy, arithmetic, and spelling tests for clerical employees, flight tests for instructors, and demonstrations of ability to run specialized equipment by line personnel all come under this classification.

Candidate Evaluation Form					
Applicant Name: **Hiring Manager:** **Evaluator(s):**	**Position:** **Department:** **Date:**				
Enter the numeric value corresponding to the applicant's level of qualification and provide relevant comments in the space below.					
Rating Scale: **5 = Exceptional 4 = Exceeds expectations 3 = Meets Expectations 2 = Below expectations 1 = None or N/A**					
	Rating				
	5	**4**	**3**	**2**	**1**
General Background					
Background Candidate's experience and employment history.					
Technical Competency					
Technical Knowledge & Experience Candidate's technical knowledge and past working experiences.					
Accomplishments and Strengths Candidate's achievements and impacts in their work. How do their strengths connect to/match needs of the position?					
Education & Training Breadth and relevance of education and training background.					
People and Leadership Competency					
Presentation/Communication Skills Ability to clearly express ideas and thoughts. Overall presentation.					
Interpersonal and Leadership Skills Relationships with others and ability to work with diverse teams.					
Behaviors and Habits					
Flexibility, Planning, and Organization Responsiveness to change, tolerance, organizational skills.					
Organizational/Cultural Fit Potential to fit into the organization and its culture and expectations.					
Motivation and Initiative Ability to think and act independently and be goal oriented.					
Impression					
Professional Impression and Enthusiasm Self-confidence, maturity, energy level, and passion.					
Totals *(add values in each column)*					
Grand Total *(Sum of column totals above)*					
FINAL SCORE (%) Percentage = (Grand Total ÷ 50) × 100%					
Comments—Summarize your perceptions of the candidate's qualifications and suitability for the position and any other considerations.					

Figure 15-5. Interview rating form.

Some FBOs make use of a variety of tests (whether online or on paper) to aid in their selection processes. These tests may include intelligence tests, personality tests, aviation knowledge tests, tests of selling ability, etc. To avoid **Equal Employment Opportunity Commission (EEOC)** complaints, tests used must be demonstrably both valid and reliable. Further, tests are an added cost to the hiring process and are generally not recommended until a business has grown to a substantial size. Their most valuable contribution is probably in screening out applicants with personality defects or below-average intelligence.

Once the employee is hired, the first few days on the job are crucial for the newly hired person. This onboarding or indoctrination period is the period when a new employee develops expectations, understands responsibilities and job tasks, understands employee benefits and pay schedules, meets coworkers, and considers their long-term role with the company. On-the-job training, especially for entry-level positions such as line service, is important to develop a proficient employee. Some FBOs have experienced success with providing coaching or mentoring for new employees. By assigning an experienced member of the department to coach the new employee, the likelihood of success for the new employee is increased. In this same context, a well-prepared employee handbook can be extremely valuable, including sections such as company history, organizational structure, organizational culture, customer service standards, benefits, work schedules, reporting absences, holidays, etc.

All new-hire employees should be placed in probationary status. Whether lasting a few weeks or a few months, this trial period is a valuable step. It will ensure that the FBO has not made a hiring error. During this time, the new employee should be observed and frequently rated. It is far more difficult to discharge a below-average performer after many months have elapsed, especially if the company is unionized.

Employees who have successfully survived the probationary period are eligible for promotion opportunities within the organization. Many FBOs have positions available from time to time in mid- and top-level management. One option used to fill these positions is to hire individuals outside the organization. This is most appropriate for senior-level management positions that require a great deal of experience. However, for these positions, and many times for lower-level management positions, many FBOs subscribe to a policy of promoting from within. This policy has advantages and disadvantages.

Advantages to promoting from within:

- The FBO knows the employee.
- Recruiting is easier.
- The employee has knowledge of the company.

Disadvantages to promoting from within:

- It limits influx of new ideas.
- It may drive away highly functioning employees.
- It may increase failure rates, as complacency may be higher.

Whether a company decides to promote from within or seek new talent outside the company, promotion is one role of HR that must be handled with tact. New responsibilities may be met by the immature employee with great difficulty. However, a mature employee possessing great leadership skills can propel a company successfully into the future. In any event, FBOs must endeavor to make promotion an attractive option, as they fill open positions and allow employees to seek higher levels of growth and opportunity within the company.

TRAINING

The training function is a vital, ongoing activity that requires the attention of the owner of a small FBO. Employees need and want training not only to perform their jobs satisfactorily and comply with regulatory requirements and/or industry best practices, but also as preparation for eventual promotion. Proper training alleviates many problems in the future.

Following are some of the advantages of well-trained employees:

- Better employee morale
- Increased sales
- Less waste
- Lower turnover rate
- Increased productivity
- Reduced operational costs
- Faster employee development

Figure 15-6. Employee training. *(fizkes/Shutterstock.com)*

Often, a new employee receives adequate initial training but is thereafter expected to "go it alone." In a healthy business operation, training should be continuous. No employee attains 100 percent efficiency or output in their role. There is always room for improvement. Moreover, every worker should have the opportunity to move up the corporate ladder. This implies training for a new and higher position.

In a small enterprise, most training occurs on the job. In essence, the immediate supervisor is held responsible for training the worker. But as a business grows, the need for more thorough and professional training becomes evident. It is never too early to begin making plans for better training in the future, if only to fill additional niches as they open up in the organizational hierarchy.

A careful needs analysis of the organization and all the people in it should be the first step in coordinating training efforts. The following steps are recommended in establishing a training program:

1. Make a needs assessment of the company on a departmental, section, and unit basis.
2. Set the objectives to be accomplished through the training efforts.
3. Determine the curriculum (subject matter). Make certain to include not only product, company, and customer knowledge but also skills development and personal adjustment training.
4. Select the types of training that best serve the purposes of the company.
5. Select the training methods to be used.
6. Set up a timetable and schedule for the program.
7. Select the instructor(s).
8. Control costs.

A wide variety of training methods and techniques are available. Among the more frequently used approaches are lectures, small-group discussions, seminars, conferences, case analyses, programmed instruction, committee work, and role playing. A great deal of training is now available online through a variety of vendors.

For employees being developed for eventual promotion to management levels, there are other useful techniques, including job rotation, special project assignments, management games, sensitivity training, and training at local colleges or by trade associations.

Salary and Benefits

Yet another role of human resources is to coordinate salary and benefits for all employees. Generally, department managers will notify HR of the **salary** for each newly hired employee (within company established salary ranges) so that HR can arrange for employee paychecks (typically electronically via direct deposit). Deductions, in the form of taxes and for items such as health insurance, charitable contributions, and retirement contributions, are also calculated and reflect in the employee's paycheck. In addition to these deductions, the employer is responsible for paying worker's compensation premiums, paying employer taxes, and matching employee retirement contributions per company policy.

Companies can pay employees weekly, biweekly, monthly, or yearly. Typically, weekly or biweekly are most popular. Although it would benefit an employer to only pay employees once per month, many employees (especially in lower-paying positions) cannot afford to wait an entire month for a paycheck. Although this may be due to lack of budgeting on the employee's part, cashflow is important, and only receiving income once per month makes life more difficult.

In addition to salary, many businesses (including many FBOs) include various **benefits** in their employment package. These benefits may include life and medical insurance, contributions to an employee retirement account or defined benefit plan, discount admission to area attractions, employee discounts (such as 20 percent discount on flight instruction), and uniforms. In total, these benefits may add 20 percent (or more) in value above an employee's annual salary. Therefore, salary plus benefits is known as compensation and can be substantially more than an employee's annual salary. This is an important fact to remember as individuals consider the employment packages that may be offered by competing FBOs. FBOs should also promote this in employee recruiting. Salary is important, but benefits are important, as well. Simply ask an employee with no benefits to verify this!

In sum, the HR department plays an important role for an organization by handling salary and benefits. Whether scheduling a speaker to present retirement options to employees, handling paycheck discrepancies, or matching employee retirement contributions, by performing these functions, HR allows line departments the opportunity to focus on their specific areas rather than exerting time and energy on the ever-important responsibility of paying salary and benefits.

The Turnover Problem

One fact of life that is a reality for any small business is employee **turnover**. Every business has it. Some firms lose people at a faster rate than others, but whatever the turnover rate, it always hurts (financially as well as psychologically) to lose a good employee.

There are initial costs involved in locating, interviewing, hiring, and training an employee to the point where he or she reaches full potential. There are also intermediate costs of doing without that person until a replacement is found. Still more expenses are incurred in acquiring the replacement. Clearly, it is in a company's best interest to keep good employees until retirement; however, this is typically not the case.

People leave their jobs for a variety of reasons. Some leave unexpectedly and for unavoidable reasons: medical issues, death, marriage or divorce, relocation, return to school, a better-paying position, and deliberate terminations for cause. However, some losses are avoidable. Employees may leave because of poor supervisory practices on the part of owners or middle managers, internal friction and personality clashes, or management's failure to provide proper incentives or an opportunity to move up the ladder. In these situations, the company is inadvertently losing good employees and then expending more resources in acquiring replacements. Clearly, if a company regularly sees employees resigning, hard questions must be asked.

These hard questions can be asked in an exit interview. Wise FBO managers will make sure that each employee is interviewed in an exit interview upon departing from the company. Is the employee leaving to accept a higher-paying position elsewhere? Were there personal conflicts with management? Were other employees unkind to this employee? What about safety and security? A review of the exit interview findings will be useful to management in taking corrective action to reduce the turnover rate. This step becomes more valuable as the company grows.

In any event, as FBOs hire new employees, they must take care of their existing employees and interview those employees resigning. Only by knowing how employees view the organization and the workplace can a company continue to improve for new and existing employees.

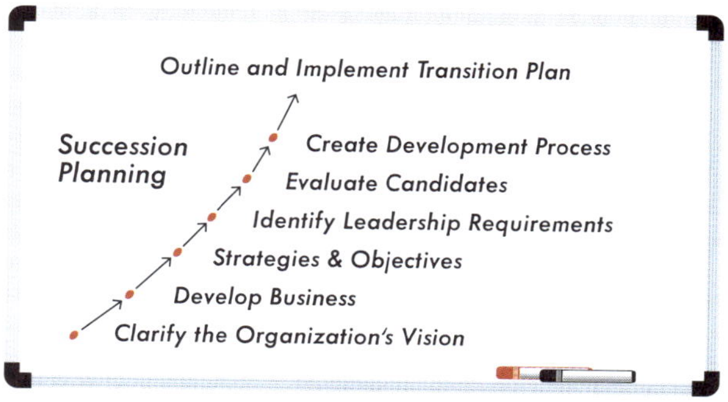

Figure 15-7. Succession planning.

A popular, proactive approach to employee retention and proper management staffing is **succession planning**. This refers to a process of identifying and developing certain high-performing employees for promotion within the company, typically for managerial positions. By considering planned retirements and pending employee departures, management can plan ahead by developing certain employees to move up once a retirement occurs. In this way, there will not be a vacant position, and continuity of the business can be maintained. Some FBOs even allow a promising employee to train alongside a more experienced employee to learn the responsibilities of a position prior to that more experienced employee's retirement.

Summary

The human resources function drives success in all business areas, for without productive and efficient personnel, the business will suffer. Thus, it is of utmost importance for each FBO to make human resources a priority, hire sufficient expertise in this area, and in partnership with HR, develop a plan to adequately staff the FBO, with attention to retention and succession planning.

Key Terms

applicant screening. The process of screening job applications and resumes for the purpose of developing a list of applicants qualified for a vacant position.

benefits. Supplemental to wages/salary, benefits may include life and medical insurance, contributions to an employee retirement account or defined benefit plan, discount admission to area attractions, employee discounts, and uniforms. In total, these benefits may add 20 percent (or more) in value above an employee's annual salary.

cyclical industry. An industry that has cycles including periods of strong growth and potentially lack of skilled labor, as well as contraction and an overabundance of skilled labor. At any given time, the industry is entering, peaking, or leaving one of these two cycles.

employment interview. The opportunity to learn more about a candidate by asking questions, seeking clarification, and presenting scenarios the candidate is required to address.

Equal Employment Opportunity Commission (EEOC). The federal agency responsible for enforcing federal laws that make it illegal to discriminate against a job applicant or employee because of the person's race, color, religion, sex, national origin, age, disability, or genetic information.

hiring. A multi-step process that results in employing someone for wages.

human resources. The department responsible for recruiting and selecting employees, training and promoting employees, arranging for salary and benefits, and coordinating separation from service.

interview rating form. A form that provides structure to the interview and supports an objective evaluation of each candidate by allowing the interviewer to rate each applicant on the same criteria.

job description. A summary of a specific job title, duties and responsibilities assigned, tasks to be performed, skills required, relationships with other segments of the business, and any other relevant details, such as required levels of education and experience, familiarity with special equipment, and minimum physical requirements.

recruiting. The process of advertising positions and seeking applicants for vacant positions.

salary. The wages paid to an employee for work performed, generally stated as an annual salary, and most often associated with professional positions.

short list. The list of the most qualified candidates for a position, having been refined from the entire pool of applicants.

structured interview. A formal type of interview that requires planning the approach in advance, including the kinds of questions to be asked, the order in which they will be asked, preferred attributes of a successful candidate, etc.

succession planning. The process of identifying and developing certain high-performing employees for promotion within the company, typically for managerial positions. By considering planned retirements and pending employee departures, management can plan ahead by developing certain employees to move up once a retirement occurs.

turnover. A reference to the percentage of employees that leave an organization. High turnover is problematic, requiring innovative solutions to minimize turnover (i.e., improve employee retention).

Review Questions

1. Describe the HR function.
2. In what way does HR reduce the workload of other departments within the organization?
3. What types of positions do FBOs typically recruit for?
4. Are there any shortages of skilled people to fill these various positions?
5. List the most common recruiting sources.
6. What is the purpose of interviewing?
7. What are the typical steps in a multi-step interview process?
8. What are some advantages of having well-trained employees?
9. Describe the steps to be taken in establishing a training program.
10. Why can employee turnover be such a problem?
11. What are some methods of promoting employees?
12. Describe the purpose of an exit interview.

Scenarios

1. You are the maintenance manager of a medium-sized FBO. As you arrive into work this morning, your midnight shift maintenance crew reported that two maintenance department employees got into a fistfight during last night's swing shift. At the time, there was no supervisor on duty. Thus, the fistfight was only witnessed by coworkers. Although neither employee was apparently injured, and there were only 2–3 punches thrown, one of those involved in the fight later mentioned to a coworker that he knew how to "finish him off," referring to the employee he had fought with earlier in the evening. Both employees are scheduled to return to work at 2:00 this afternoon. What do you do?
2. As you wrapped up last fiscal year as the manager of a large FBO, an independent auditor's report found substantial loss of inventory. The auditor believes employee theft of company supplies (mainly aircraft parts) is the cause. As you think about this issue, you realize you have no idea which employees could be responsible. What do you do?
3. Your boss, the FBO manager, has asked you to review the applications and resumes recently received for the vacant front desk manager position. As manager of marketing and customer service, you feel qualified to do so. What are some things you are looking for in this position? On what dimensions will you rate applicants in order to short list the few you would like to interview?
4. As manager of human resources for a full-service FBO, you have conducted interviews and performance evaluations, fired employees, and conducted exit interviews. However, you are caught off guard this afternoon as the front desk agent calls to report that her coworker, who just arrived for work, appears drunk. What do you do?
5. You are the manager of human resources at a full-service FBO, and at a recent employee meeting, several employees offered suggestions for how to improve the organization and their quality of work life. Larry, a line service employee, would like flexible work hours. He and his wife recently divorced and he needs to pick up his child from school. He would rather work 5:00 a.m. to 1:00 p.m. rather than his current shift of 7:00 a.m. to 3:00 p.m. Jill, a customer service agent, suggests casual Fridays. She would like employees (including front desk and management) to have the option to wear jeans on Fridays. Lastly, Jacob, a maintenance employee, feels the company needs to adopt an employee suggestion program. He think this program should give cash awards of $100 to employees that submit suggestions that are adopted by the company. At an executive meeting, the FBO manager asks you, as manager of HR, to offer your perspective on each of these suggestions.
6. In the middle of an interview for a vacant manager of human resources at a large, full-service FBO, the interviewer asks you to briefly describe your philosophy regarding managing employees. In particular, the interviewer would like to hear how you plan to recruit employees, motivate employees, and discipline employees.
7. The FBO manager has approached you, as manager of human resources at a large, full-service FBO, to discuss employee wages. The FBO recently completed a study (with your help) on wages at competing FBOs. It appears that wages at your FBO are 5 percent lower than the wages at the two competing FBOs surveyed. This is becoming a problem, as one customer service agent recently departed the company to begin work at a competitor. The FBO manager wants your opinion on how to address this apparent wage disparity. However, he says that unless the FBO can cut expenses in another budget area, the company is currently unable to implement across-the-board wage increase wages of 5 percent.

Bibliography

Prather, C. Daniel. 2009. *General Aviation Marketing and Management: Operating, Marketing, and Managing an FBO*. 3rd ed. Malabar, FL: Krieger Publishing Company.

16

Present and Future Challenges

In Chapter 16

Objectives

At the end of this chapter, you should be able to:

1. Discuss pre-COVID-19 considerations.
2. Discuss the industry outlook for FBOs.
3. Discuss industry trends for FBOs.
4. Explain the challenge of UAS/drones to FBOs.
5. Explain the challenge of VLJs to FBOs.
6. Explain the challenge of fractional ownership to FBOs.
7. Explain the challenges of providing exceptional customer service.
8. Describe how fuel prices create challenging times for FBOs.
9. Explain the challenge of sustainability to FBOs.
10. Consider the security challenges facing FBOs.
11. Explain the challenge of consolidation in the FBO industry.
12. Explain the challenge of revenue diversification to FBOs.
13. Explain the challenge of labor issues to FBOs.

Introduction

As seen throughout the chapters in this text, an FBO business requires attention to many different areas to ensure future success for the FBO. There are many moving parts in the FBO business. Each of these areas is critical to the overall mission of the FBO, and yet they also present unique challenges.

In this chapter, we will examine the outlook for the industry, paying particular attention to various trends impacting FBOs. Next, we'll tackle some serious future challenges facing FBOs and consider how they might respond to these challenges.

Pre-COVID-19

Although industry impacts due to COVID-19 are widespread, as explained in Chapter 13, they are not indicative of the aviation industry that as of late 2019 was very strong, with U.S. airlines earning a record $247 billion in operating revenues in 2019 on greater than 80 percent load factors system-wide. Indeed, in all sectors of the United States economy as of late 2019, business growth was strong and labor was in short supply. There were a record 6.7 million job openings in the United States. From truck drivers to Silicon Valley employees, there appeared to be a skills gap across the economy as full employment became a reality. One main contributor to this labor shortage is the record retirements of the baby boomer generation (born between 1946–1964). The baby boomer generation peaked at 78.8 million and is considered the largest living adult generation. Estimates of the impacts of this generation on the workforce are staggering. Analysts estimate that 4 million baby boomers retire annually—almost 11,000 daily. Although the next generation, Generation X (born 1965–1980), peaked at 65.8 million, it potentially has 13 million fewer workers in the workforce. The next generation, Millennials (born 1981–2000), peaked at 76.2 million, which will eventually outnumber both baby boomers and Generation X in the workplace. (BTS 2020; Cox 2018; Kessler 2014; Working Together 2014)

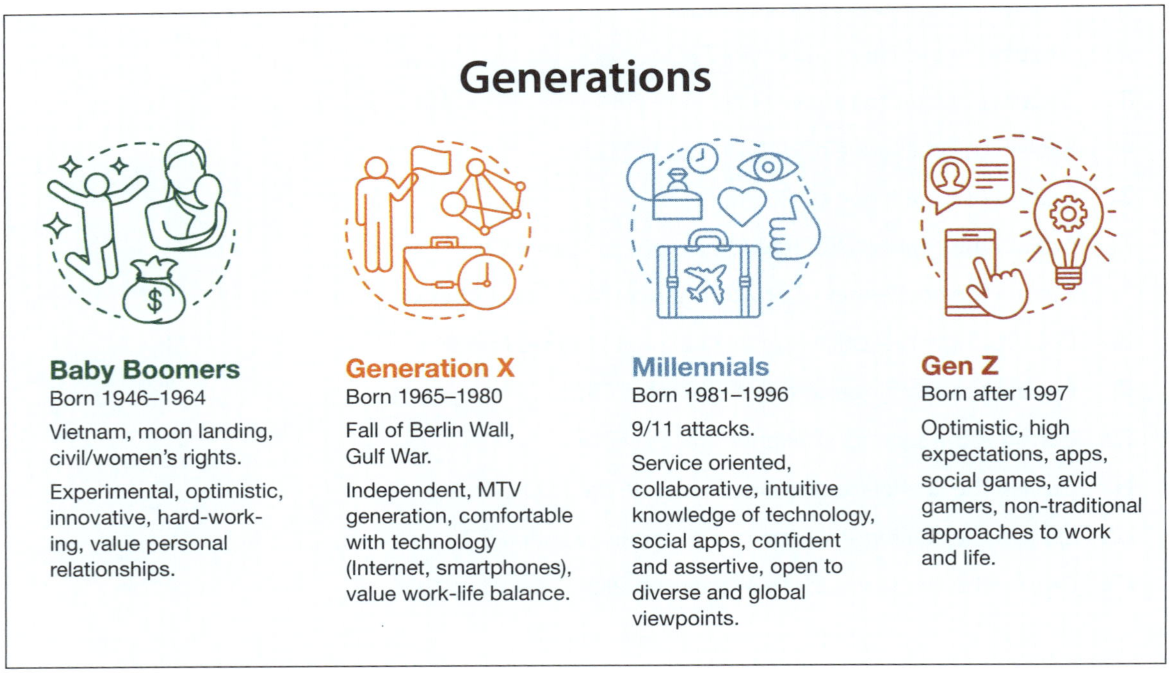

Figure 16-1. The generations. *(Adapted from iStock.com/bsd555)*

The aviation industry generates significant economic impacts. Globally, the aviation industry contributed $2.7 trillion to global GDP in 2017. Further, 34.6 percent of worldwide trade, by value, was carried by air in 2017 (amounting to $6 trillion). Daily around the world, 123 million passengers were flown on 120,000 aircraft flights in 2019. There are 3,384 FBOs in the United States, an increase of 2.5 percent between 1995 and 2015. To enable this level of activity, a significant amount of skilled labor is required. In 2020, the worldwide aviation industry supported 87.7 million jobs and directly employed 11.3 million people. In the United States alone, 10.6 million people work directly in the aviation industry. (FAA 2022b; IATA 2020; NATA 2017)

Outlook/Trends

Trends are those factors that apply to the majority of FBOs in the industry. For example, any factor that stimulates GA aircraft sales, in the long term, will help the FBO industry. An improving U.S. economy and growth in corporate net profits also contribute to an improved outlook. Analysts of the industry see the following trends among FBOs in 2022 and onward:

- *Increase in the number of airport-operated FBOs.* Traditionally, private sector funds represented the majority of funding for FBOs. Although private sector investment still represents funding at 65 percent of FBOs, public sector investment (often municipal) is increasing. The one factor that has impacted this trend is the declining return on investment (value proposition) for private investment at airports, especially airports dependent on piston-powered aircraft operations (NATA 2017).
- *Declining avgas consumption.* Although business jet activity has generally remained robust (with exception due to the COVID pandemic), piston-powered aircraft operations are more elastic, generating fewer flight hours and avgas fuel sales as the price of fuel increases, or the COVID pandemic takes hold, for example. Additionally, as the number of private pilot certificates has dropped 32 percent from 2000 to 2014, fewer flight hours, and gallons of avgas sold, result (NATA 2017).
- *Investment in FBO facilities.* Airports and municipal economic development agencies are considering FBOs as gateways to the local community and region, bringing economic development and jobs to the area. As a result, airports are requiring FBOs to invest in facility upgrades as leases come up for renewal. To counteract these increased operating costs has required many FBOs to begin charging for goods and services that were once free. For example, services such as ground power and potable water, which may have been previously included with the cost of fuel, are now billed as a separate charge (NATA 2017).
- *FBO industry consolidation.* The need for enhanced economies of scale, the pending retirement of an independent FBO owner without a succession plan to ensure business continuity, or the unwillingness or inability to invest in facility improvements required by the airport are all situations that can motivate the owner of an independent FBO to join a chain (or be bought out by the competition). Consolidation does provide some benefits to aircraft owners/operators, such as improved efficiency; better service; additional investment in facilities, training, and equipment; and crucial initiatives to meet user demands, such as self-serve avgas. Even so, past consolidation has not reduced the number of FBO locations. That being said, the U.S. Department of Justice (DOJ) has the authority to review FBO mergers in an effort to ensure that some degree of competition remains to protect consumer rights. It may be that the DOJ stipulates certain requirements of the merger to be approved. For example, consider the merger between Landmark Aviation and Signature Flight Support. The DOJ required the divestiture of locations at airports where the two companies had overlapping locations (NATA 2017).
- *Competition.* The FBO business is very competitive. Competition may exist with another FBO at the same airport or any FBO located at airports along a route of flight. Specific competition

may be known or unknown. It is difficult to ascertain all the FBOs on every route of flight for each aircraft. Keep in mind that pilots have options in deciding where to land, where to purchase fuel, and where to remain overnight based on cost, convenience, reputation, and FBO services. Some charter operators that utilize network pricing may add a customer surcharge to use FBOs out of network (NATA 2017).

- *Comprehensive business centers.* FBOs catering to corporate clients and high-net-worth individuals have created comprehensive business centers to meet the needs of these clients. FBOs seeking to attract more corporate jet traffic should consider how to develop a comprehensive business center, to include conference rooms, catering, video conferencing, high-speed wireless internet, voicemail, and other types of services in demand by these clients. These facility enhancements can support business deals without ever leaving the airport.

Future Challenges

The business of providing services to aircraft and their passengers is an exciting business. At the same time, however, it is a dynamic business. Indeed, just as the GA industry is dynamic, so is the industry of providing aviation services in the form of fixed-base operations. Why is this business so dynamic? It is mainly due to the changing industry and the challenges the industry presents to the fixed-base operator.

BUSINESS CONTINUITY

The COVID pandemic taught companies around the world the importance of planning for the unknown. As strange as that seems, it can be done. **Business continuity** planning refers to the process whereby an entity considers the continued delivery of goods and services during a disruption to normal business processes, whether due to a cyberattack, flood, pandemic, etc. This requires the creation of systems of prevention (to prevent or minimize the likelihood of the disruption) and recovery (to return to normal operations after an event occurs). A prevention and recovery plan (i.e., a business continuity plan) should consider the following:

- Cross-utilization and supplemental personnel
- Redundant systems
- Data backup and restoration
- Customer interaction and relationship management
- Supply chain disruption, including alternate delivery methods
- Ransom payments for cyber attacks

Figure 16-2. Business continuity. *(master_art/Shutterstock.com)*

FBOs are certainly not immune to disruption to business operations. Therefore, a well-managed FBO will have a business continuity plan that considers various types of business disruptions, which include fuel supply issues, such as those created in 2021 when the Colonial Pipeline was affected by a cyberattack, for example.

Specifically related to the return to normal operations post-COVID, the National Air Transportation Association (NATA) distributed guidance in May 2020 on best practices and standardized protocols for COVID-19 management during this transition to normal operations. The guidance addresses screening, communications, staffing, and cleaning and disinfecting. FBOs are encouraged to adopt these standards, as "[s]tandards create consistent handling and habits—they eliminate the need for ad hoc management and heavy 'cognitive' brain engagement to manage each situation as a new one" (NATA 2020, 1).

UNCREWED AIRCRAFT SYSTEMS/DRONES

As **uncrewed aircraft system (UAS)** technology continues to advance, the initiative to fully integrate UAS, including passenger-carrying UAS, in the National Airspace System (NAS) continues in earnest. According to a report by the Association for Unmanned Vehicle Systems International (AUVSI), the cumulative economic impact of UAS integration into NAS is projected to be $82.1 billion during 2015–2025. AUVSI projects 103,776 new jobs will be created and states will collect more than $482 million in tax revenues during that time frame. Based on this, AUVSI states that "Every year that integration is delayed, the United States loses more than $10 billion in potential economic impact" (AUVSI 2013, 2).

FBOs will need to consider the future of UAS, including UTM (unmanned aircraft system traffic management). According to the FAA, "UTM development will ultimately identify services, roles and responsibilities, information architecture, data exchange protocols, software functions, infrastructure, and performance requirements for enabling the management of low-altitude uncontrolled drone operations" (FAA 2022b). UTM will bring eVTOL (electric vertical take-off and landing) UAS to airports, and FBOs should be prepared to accommodate these unmanned aircraft. This will include the development of charging infrastructure as well as consideration for passenger loading and unloading, maintenance, etc.

Figure 16-3. Prototype passenger UAS. *(u3d/Shutterstock.com)*

Figure 16-4. Very light jet (VLJ). *(Ivan Cholakov/Shutterstock.com)*

VERY LIGHT JETS

Although the once-projected demand for **very light jets (VLJs)** didn't materialize as expected, FBOs must still accommodate (and even cater to) these aircraft. Although small jet aircraft are not new to the world of aviation, the VLJ is considered innovative in many ways. Specifically, VLJs are turbine-powered aircraft with a take-off weight of 10,000 pounds or less and certificated for single-pilot operations. VLJs commonly offer four to nine passenger seats, cruise speeds around 400 miles per hour, and an operating range between 1,100 to 2,300 miles. Along with modern turbine engine technologies, these next generation light jet aircraft incorporate highly integrated avionics, along with advanced cockpit automation, refined passenger amenities, and simplified aircraft systems designed to reduce pilot workloads.

VLJs include the Cirrus Vision, HondaJet, One Aviation Eclipse Jet, Embraer Phenom, and Cessna Citation Jet M2 (see Table 16-1).

Table 16-1. VLJ Comparison

VLJ	Speed	Price	Passengers
Cirrus Vision	345 mph	$2 million	6
HondaJet	423 mph	$4.9 million	4–6
One Aviation Eclipse	430 mph	$3 million	4–5
Embraer Phenom	465 mph	$4.5 million	5–7
Cessna Citation M2	465 mph	$4.6 million	6

A significant marketing approach employed by VLJ manufacturers is avoiding the airfield congestion and landside inconveniencies presently experienced by major commercial airports. VLJs allow the traveler to take advantage of smaller GA airports, since less congestion affords flexible arrival and departure times while allowing for shorter, direct flights to similar city pairs. Additionally, these VLJs are able to utilize airports with runways as short as 2,300 to 3,400 feet.

What does this mean for FBOs? First, even FBOs at small GA airports need to prepare for possible VLJ operations. Obviously, these VLJs will need to be serviced, maintained, and accommodated. FBOs will need to offer Jet A fuel services and have the facilities and amenities expected by the owner/operator of these aircraft. For example, consider a point-to-point air taxi operator utilizing VLJs that arrives at an airport and requires service by the local FBO. The aircraft will arrive with fare-paying passengers who will need various services within the airport/FBO terminal building. Beyond the building, these passengers will likely be interested in a rental car, catering, a business center, etc. In essence, the FBO manager must focus not only on the aircraft but on the passengers and flight crew, as well. Maintaining these aircraft will require turbine-engine repair facilities, possible turbine-engine run-up areas, power carts, and possible aircraft deicing. These aircraft will also require tie-down areas, hangars, and security. Much of this is not new to FBOs; however, servicing an increasing number of jet aircraft in the form of VLJs may indeed have an impact on the manner in which an FBO is operated, requiring the FBO manager and staff to focus on attracting and servicing these aircraft.

FRACTIONAL OWNERSHIP

The growth in fractional ownership of aircraft, especially corporate jet aircraft, will also have a disproportionate impact on the FBO business. Why? Companies such as NetJets (which has more than 750 business jets in operation) typically fly their aircraft significantly more than an equal number of airplanes operated by a single corporation. For example, NetJets operates its aircraft on average 1,100 hours annually, whereas a corporation may only operate its aircraft 400–700 hours annually. Thus, each NetJets aircraft is similar to two or three business jets simply because they are so heavily utilized.

Although NetJets currently has a formal relationship with Signature Flight Support, there is not a Signature located at each airport that NetJets visits. Thus, NetJets searches for new FBOs to partner with, placing an emphasis on the following six criteria: safety, quality of service provided to owners and crewmembers, facilities and amenities, partnership development, maintenance capability, and price. NetJets is aware that poor FBO customer service reflects on its operation, as well; thus, if an FBO is interested in attracting companies such as NetJets and riding the wave of fractional ownership, it should focus on these six criteria and endeavor to cater to NetJets clientele. As NetJets explains,

Figure 16-5. Fractional aircraft owner. *(Juice Dash/ Shutterstock.com)*

"NetJets continues to seek out long-term business partnerships with those organizations that share our vision of providing exceptional service in this dynamic industry" (NetJets 2023).

CUSTOMER SERVICE

As discussed in Chapter 6, customer service is an extremely important aspect of operating a successful FBO in today's competitive GA environment. As such, customer service presents a challenge to FBOs. How can an FBO maintain, and even increase, the level of customer service offered to its patrons while at the same time controlling expenses, retaining quality personnel, and staying ahead of the competition? Obviously, there is no simple answer. This is especially true with the diverse customers typical of an FBO. However, the focus on customer service must remain at the forefront of everything an FBO does. In fact, customer service should take the backseat only to safety. Many FBO managers would argue that if safety is made a top priority, customer service will follow. However, why leave that to chance? Yes, it is important to focus on safety, but managers should also make sure that FBO personnel are trained in customer service.

Figure 16-6. Customer service representatives.
(Tyler Olson/Shutterstock.com)

As FBOs throughout the nation begin focusing on customer service, a smile and a handshake will no longer be enough. The successful FBO must be *the most* customer-focused and safest FBO around. In fact, the number one goal of an FBO manager should be to attract customers and based tenants from competing FBOs. One way to do this is to provide superior customer service. This requires empowering employees to satisfy customers regardless of the situation. This also requires staying aware of any customer service initiatives adopted by the competition. Train, educate, and instill the importance of customer service to all employees, including those working the line (who have the first face-to-face contact with customers) as well as the front desk and those in management. Whether an FBO brings in a consultant to conduct customer service training on a regular basis, or simply conducts employee meetings on a regular basis with customer service training videos, the wise FBO manager is aware of the need for continued enhancement of customer service throughout the organization. The challenge, however, will be to maintain this focus, without becoming stagnant, and bettering the competition.

FUEL PRICES

As the price of crude oil surpassed $100 per barrel during 2008 and again during the 2011–2014 time period, the aviation industry gasped. However, although this increase in the price of fuel impacted the bottom line for all airlines (except those with extensive fuel hedging contracts taking advantage of lower prices), people were still flying, and in fact, load factors during 2007–2008 averaged near 85 percent. What about GA activity during times of high fuel prices? Obviously, the impact of rising fuel prices has been greater on GA. Although business aviation remains strong, those flying for recreation may not be flying as much or may be looking at more fuel-efficient aircraft when fuel costs are so high. What does this mean for FBOs? Obviously, FBOs have to be much more cognizant today of the prices charged for fuel. Competition among FBOs based on fuel prices alone has greatly intensified in the recent past. In fact, many GA pilots will travel outside their local area simply to purchase fuel at an FBO offering lower fuel prices. Many pilots stay current on fuel prices by visiting websites such as airnav.com and 100LL.com or by using apps such as AvGas Now, AirNav FBO, or FBO Fuel Prices.

The margins FBOs experience between their fuel price and net profit per gallon are relatively thin. For example, if avgas costs the FBO $3.00 per gallon, and truck cost, insurance, fuel flowage fee, maintenance, and rent amount to $0.92 per gallon, a retail price of $4.63 per gallon equals a net profit of $0.71 per gallon. Thus, as wholesale fuel prices increase, FBOs generally have no option but to increase their retail fuel prices. The key is to be aware of what the competition is charging per gallon and focus on cost control to the extent that fuel prices can remain competitive. An FBO manager may create elaborate spreadsheets showing the FBO's cost for fuel, indirect costs associated with fueling, retail price, and net per gallon on a daily, monthly, and yearly basis.

Figure 16-7. Fueler price sign. *(C. Daniel Prather)*

Just as fuel costs are one of the two largest costs for an airline (the other being labor), fuel is one of the largest sources of revenue for an FBO. Thus, a wise FBO manager will continually analyze fuel costs, prices, and net profit on a regular basis. As with most goods, the supply and demand equation holds true at FBOs. With fuel prices lower than the competition, demand will increase, possibly disproportionately. With disproportionate demand, an FBO may actually increase revenues by lowering fuel prices. For example, it is better to sell 10,000 gallons at $3.00 per gallon ($30,000 gross), than 7,500 gallons at $3.50 per gallon ($26,250). The key for the FBO manager is to find the balance where revenues will increase with lower fuel prices; otherwise, revenues will decrease.

Figure 16-8. Sustainable aviation fuel. *(Scharfsinn/ Shutterstock.com)*

SUSTAINABILITY

As the aviation industry continues to minimize its impact on the environment, operators of aircraft and ground support equipment have explored **sustainability** as a standard of operation. For example, the use of **sustainable aviation fuel (SAF)** has received significant support from organizations such as the National Business Aviation Association (NBAA). As a drop-in fuel, biomass SAF can be safely used in any turbine-powered aircraft. The suppliers of fuel—and dispensers of fuel, such as FBOs—are playing a major role in SAF. For example, in April 2021, Signature Flight Support announced that 1 million gallons of SAF (30/70 blend of renewable feedstock and conventional Jet A) had been supplied through its Signature Renew Program at San Francisco International Airport. This milestone marked the first time in history that a single FBO location had delivered such a substantial and consistent supply of SAF to business aircraft. Operators of aircraft fueled with SAF have experienced a 25 percent reduction in direct carbon output compared to aircraft fueled with traditional jet fuel.

The FAA, Environmental Protection Agency (EPA), and industry partners are committed to developing a replacement for leaded avgas used in piston-powered aircraft. According to the FAA:

> Avgas is the only remaining lead-containing transportation fuel. Lead in avgas prevents damaging engine knock, or detonation, that can result in sudden engine failure. Lead is a toxic substance that can be inhaled or absorbed in the bloodstream (FAA 2020, para. 1).

This is a significant concern, as 167,000 piston-engine aircraft operating in the United States rely on avgas. The FAA Piston Aviation Fuel Initiative (PAFI) is a rigorous testing program to evaluate unleaded fuel alternatives that will be as operationally safe and effective as leaded avgas in piston-engine aircraft. PAFI has four elements: (1) fleet-wide authorization qualification test program, (2) new alternative fuel proposals and certification, (3) establishment of FAA safety standards, and (4) safely deploy and transition to a new fuel (FAA 2022a).

As of 2023, efforts were underway to explore the use of hydrogen as an aircraft fuel source. The FAA is considering: (a) various types of fuel cell devices, (b) hazard analysis and mitigation, (c) rulemaking, (d) cost/benefit analysis, and (e) program management. Specifically for unmanned aircraft, the FAA considers hydrogen a lightweight and flexible fuel cell system with hydrogen and oxygen storage enabling long duration flight.

Electric propulsion of ground support equipment as well as small VTOL aircraft is currently available. Specifically for FBOs, rechargeable battery-powered tugs are commonplace. Electric propulsion is also commonplace for golf carts. Although battery technology continues to evolve, the benefits of adopting this technology has apparently exceeded direct and indirect costs for many FBOs. An FBO intent on practically committing to sustainability will find numerous options on the market.

Each of these developments will require FBOs to consider how to provide alternative fuels for aircraft in the future. This may require separate fuel storage areas as well as the infrastructure needed to deliver these alternative fuels to aircraft.

Similarly, FBO terminal buildings will need to be more environmentally friendly moving forward. Low-flow toilet fixtures, water-wise landscaping, use of reclaimed water for landscape irrigation, LED lighting, and strategic use of natural lighting are examples of how new terminal buildings are meeting more stringent environmental standards. Existing FBO buildings can be retrofitted with a focus on environmental sustainability. Overwhelmingly, customers, investors, and employees appreciate a more sustainable workplace.

SECURITY

As one may gain by reading this chapter, future challenges are not always new challenges. Security, while always a consideration, became the number one priority after the terrorist attacks of September 11, 2001. While GA airports had always had some form of security in place, an active effort at enhancing security at GA airports (as well as commercial-service airports) began after September 11. As discussed in Chapter 13, security is much more of a concern today, and GA airports and FBOs have taken great strides to enhance security. However, future challenges in this area remain. GA and FBOs have been viewed as a weak link in the aviation security chain for quite some time.

Figure 16-9. Reporting a security concern. *(LEDOMSTOCK/Shutterstock.com)*

To prevent continued concern about GA security, FBOs will have to remain vigilant about maintaining and increasing security of personnel, facilities, and equipment. This will remain a challenge because FBOs will always be confronted with the possibility of terrorists using GA to launch attacks on U.S. soil. Indeed, the absence of such attacks spells success for the GA industry and FBOs. Yet, as technology continues to advance, FBO managers must remain vigilant and current both on new technology that may be used to compromise FBO security as well as that to enhance FBO security.

CONSOLIDATION

Consolidation was mentioned as a trend affecting the FBO industry. This trend also presents challenges. The major challenge centers around the consideration of whether to remain independent or become part of a chain. Arguably, consolidation in the FBO industry will continue. The larger FBO chains will continually seek out successfully independent FBOs to acquire. These larger chains experience great economies of scale and may convince many independent owners to become part of a larger organization. At the same time, however, independent FBOs will have to seriously consider the pros and cons of remaining independent versus becoming part of a chain. Truly, each FBO has a unique situation and as such, becoming part of a chain FBO may or may not be appropriate.

Figure 16-10. FBO. *(Jure Porenta/Shutterstock.com)*

Another challenge associated with consolidation is the post-consolidation phase. Just as in airline mergers (when two companies become one), the merging of an independent FBO with a nationwide chain presents challenges. The nationwide chain will promulgate certain directives that will apply to many areas of the business, including training, management information systems, uniforms and logos, and hiring practices. The culture of the FBO will likely change and employees will have to learn how to work in this new environment. Management will also likely have a difficult time during this transition as they may no longer have the complete independence in decision-making that they once had. For these reasons, this phase is challenging, but it is usually eased with the corporate chain's support in these many areas.

Figure 16-11. Diversification into large jet maintenance. *(aappp/Shutterstock.com)*

REVENUE DIVERSIFICATION

FBOs, just like airports, wisely seek additional sources of revenue. If this additional revenue is earned from the same operation or customer base, it is not very diverse. For example, by relying only on fuel sales to cover overhead costs, an FBO would likely suffer financial distress if fuel sales significantly declined. Therefore, to remain successful in the future, FBOs are challenged to seek additional, diverse sources of revenue. This **revenue diversification** can create a more financially stable FBO. For example, an FBO may offer products such as headsets, sectional charts and approach plates, aviation books, and other items useful for flight students and transient pilots. Also, an FBO that does not currently offer maintenance or aircraft sales may consider offering these services to diversify revenues. A comprehensive FBO with numerous products and services is better positioned to weather business downturns than one relying on a single source of revenue.

The management team of one successful FBO considers themselves opportunists. They are always open to new possibilities and act quickly if a promising situation presents itself at the right time. As a result, this company has a connection with a personal shopper for clients, conducts pilot training in Africa, has an extensive aircraft sales and charter division, and is gearing up to offer mentor pilots to VLJ owner/operators. When asked, the management team of this FBO also sees opportunities for revenue diversification in maintaining aircraft, selling fuel, and selling aircraft. Clearly, if one aspect of this business declines dramatically, the company's revenue base is so diverse that this decline would not cripple the company. That will be the key to surviving the challenges that lie ahead.

At the same time, however, pursuing too many things may prove disastrous to an FBO. Although it may be best to do a lot of things at one airport, rather than one thing at many airports, each FBO is in a unique situation and, as such, will have to evaluate opportunities one by one. The management staff of the FBO mentioned previously looks at opportunities and asks this question: "If we fail at this, will it bankrupt the company?" In other words, expanding into innovative areas is fine, as long as you don't bank the entire company on it. That way, risk into these unknown areas is mitigated and success is easier to realize.

LABOR ISSUES

Pre-COVID, there was a shortage of skilled personnel in the aviation industry. Pilots, maintenance technicians, and other skilled aviation personnel were in high demand. Although COVID certainly minimized, or even eliminated, the labor shortages, this is expected to be only a short-term reprieve. Experts are planning for these labor shortages to return as more people resume flying and as retirements continue. Pre-COVID, and as the aviation industry returns to more normal operations, FBOs are challenged in attracting and retaining experienced professionals. Additionally, FBOs hire more entry-level employees each year than any other aviation service business, generally filling line service and customer service roles. As a result, properly staffing an FBO with qualified and knowledgeable employees will continue to remain a challenge. For instance, an FBO may hire a new flight instructor only to see that flight instructor leave after acquiring the minimum number of flight hours needed to be hired by a popular regional air carrier. This will force FBO managers to consider various measures necessary to not only attract but retain qualified employees.

Figure 16-12. Helicopter flight training. *(Tom Buysse/Shutterstock.com)*

What type of measures are appropriate? It depends on how urgent the staffing needs are for an FBO. During a labor shortage, job seekers will have more options and typically numerous job offers with competitive pay rates. Thus, FBOs must use innovative recruiting techniques to attract these in-demand employees. Higher starting pay rates, sign-on bonuses, and attractive benefit packages will likely be necessary to attract qualified candidates in the future. Tuition reimbursement plans, opportunities for advancement, and favorable work hours will likely be necessary to aid in employee retention.

Summary

The FBO business has experienced a number of challenges in the past and will continue to experience challenges in the future. By understanding trends and projected future challenges, FBO managers are better prepared for future uncertainty. Students of the FBO business should remember that avoiding challenges is not the goal. Rather, overcoming these challenges is the objective. By focusing on employees and customers, an FBO can make positive contributions to the aviation industry.

Key Terms

business continuity. The process whereby an entity considers the continued delivery of goods and services during a disruption to normal business processes. This requires the creation of systems of prevention (to prevent or minimize the likelihood of the disruption) and recovery (to return to normal operations after an event occurs).

consolidation. A decrease in the total number of FBOs due to mergers, closures, and becoming affiliated with a chain.

revenue diversification. The generation of additional revenue streams from diverse sources, such as flight instruction, fuel sales, charter, and aircraft sales, which creates a more financially stable FBO.

sustainability. Efforts to minimize environmental impacts by adopting environmentally friendly technologies and initiatives, such as electric tugs, biofuels, low-flow toilets, solar panels, LED lights, etc.

sustainable aviation fuel (SAF). Innovative biomass fuel that can be safely used in any turbine-powered aircraft.

uncrewed aircraft systems (UAS). Aircraft and related systems that operate without a pilot on board. Also referred to as drones.

very light jets (VLJs). Turbine-powered aircraft with a take-off weight of 10,000 pounds or less and certificated for single-pilot operations. VLJs commonly offer four to nine passenger seats, cruise speeds around 400 miles per hour, and an operating range between 1,100 to 2,300 miles.

Review Questions

1. What are some trends affecting the FBO industry?
2. What trend projected to affect the FBO industry should be of greatest concern to an FBO manager?
3. Explain business continuity.
4. How will UAS be a challenge to the FBO industry?
5. Why are very light jets considered a challenge to FBOs?
6. Can fractional ownership benefit FBOs?
7. How should FBOs meet the challenge of customer service?
8. Why should FBOs be concerned with fuel prices?
9. How can an FBO meet the sustainability challenge?
10. How can FBOs meet the security challenge?
11. Why is consolidation considered a challenge to FBOs?
12. How can FBOs meet the revenue diversification challenge?
13. Why should FBOs be concerned about labor issues?

Scenarios

1. As the manager of a small FBO at a small GA airport (as well as the airport manager), you recently had a discussion with the city manager (your boss). He asked you about the new eVTOL aircraft and companies like Uber Elevate. Specifically, he wants you to examine the impact of UAS on the airport and what your FBO needs to do to cater to them. What factors should you consider?
2. You are currently the FBO manager of a full-service FBO at a large commercial-service airport. This airport has a total of three FBOs on the field. A recent customer survey revealed less-than-satisfactory ratings for customer service at your FBO. At the same time, you hear that the two competing FBOs offer excellent customer service. How serious should you consider this to be? What can you do to enhance customer service at your FBO? How will you measure the results of your efforts?
3. Fuel prices are continuing to rise, and you know that many GA pilots will fly to other airports to gas up with lower-priced fuel. As FBO manager of a small FBO, you are faced with the following situation: Your last shipment of fuel cost $3.50 per gallon and your other expenses associated with each gallon total $0.98. You desire at least an $0.80 per gallon net profit. Based on these numbers, your fuel would be priced at $5.28 per gallon. However, you must stay competitive. How would you increase your fuel revenue? Would you charge more or charge less, and why?
4. Your FBO currently sells fuel and offers flight instruction. Your revenues have been relatively flat over the past two years, and you need to increase these numbers. You heard another FBO manager mention revenue diversification, and you feel you need to give this a try. How do you diversify revenue at your FBO?
5. As the newly hired human resource manager, you realize that your FBO is short-staffed. It has also had a retention problem in the past. Develop a plan that addresses attracting quality candidates for vacant positions as well as retaining current employees.
6. As the newly hired director of operations at a large, full-service FBO, you have been tasked with developing a sustainability plan for the FBO. What might you include in this plan? Specifically, how can your FBO be more sustainable?

Bibliography

Airports Council International. 2020. "Predicted Global Impacts of COVID-19 on Airport Industry Escalates." Press release, May 5, 2020. https://aci.aero/2020/05/05/predicted-global-impact-of-covid-19-on-airport-industry-escalates/.

AUVSI (Association for Unmanned Vehicle Systems International). 2013. *The Economic Impact of Unmanned Aircraft Systems Integration in the United States*. Arlington: AUVSI. https://www.auvsi.org/our-impact/economic-report.

Aviation International News. 2007. "FBO Survey 2007." March 28, 2007. https://www.ainonline.com/aviation-news/aviation-international-news/2007-03-28/fbo-survey-2007.

BTS (Bureau of Transportation Statistics). 2020. BTS (website). https://www.bts.gov/.

Cox, Jeff. 2018. "The U.S. labor shortage is reaching a critical point." CNBC, July 5, 2018. https://www.cnbc.com/2018/07/05/the-us-labor-shortage-is-reaching-a-critical-point.html.

Experimental Aircraft Association (EAA). n.d. EAA (website). Accessed January 15, 2023. https://www.eaa.org/.

FAA (Federal Aviation Administration). 2019. *Fair Treatment of Experienced Pilots Act (The Age 65 Law): Information, Questions and Answers.* May 9, 2019. https://www.faa.gov/sites/faa.gov/files/pilots/intl/age65_qa.pdf.

FAA (Federal Aviation Administration). 2020. "Aviation Gasoline: About Aviation Gasoline." Accessed November 19, 2020. https://www.faa.gov/about/initiatives/avgas/.

FAA (Federal Aviation Administration). 2022a. "Piston Engine Aviation Fuels Initiative PAFI: Background and Program Update." Last modified October 28, 2022. https://www.faa.gov/about/initiatives/avgas/piston-engine-aviation-fuels-initiative-pafi-background-and-program-update.

FAA (Federal Aviation Administration). 2022b. "Unmanned Aircraft Systems Traffic Management (UTM)." Last modified August 16, 2022. https://www.faa.gov/uas/research_development/traffic_management/.

IATA (International Air Transport Association). 2020. *Global Fact Sheet: Aviation Benefits Beyond Borders.* September 2020. https://www.iata.org/en/iata-repository/pressroom/fact-sheets/fact-sheet-benefits-aviation-statistics/.

Kessler, Glenn. 2014. "Do 10,000 baby boomers retire every day?" *The Washington Post,* July 24, 2014. https://www.washingtonpost.com/news/fact-checker/wp/2014/07/24/do-10000-baby-boomers-retire-every-day/.

NATA (National Air Transportation Association). 2017. *The State of the FBO Industry.* March 31, 2017. https://www.nata.aero/data/files/gia/nata%20formal%20response%20on%20state%20of%20the%20industry.pdf.

NATA (National Air Transportation Association). 2020. *Transitioning to "Normal" Operations: Joint Guidance for FBOs and Aircraft Operators.* May 20, 2020. https://www.nata.aero/assets/Site_18/files/Coronavirus/NATA_Guidance%20For%20Transitioning%20to%20Normal%20Operations_Current%20Revision.pdf.

NATA (National Air Transportation Association). 2021. "CDC Order Imposes COVID-19 Entry Testing Requirements for All Arriving Air Travelers." Press release, January 13, 2021. https://www.nata.aero/pressrelease/cdc-order-imposes-covid-19-entry-testing-requirements-for-all-arriving-air-travelers.

NBAA (National Business Aviation Association). 2020. "Key Provisions for General Aviation Businesses in the CARES Act." May 11, 2020. https://nbaa.org/aircraft-operations/safety/coronavirus/key-provisions-for-general-aviation-businesses-in-the-cares-act/.

NetJets. 2023. "Welcome to the NetJets Suppliers Website." Accessed February 7, 2023. https://www.netjets.com/en-us/suppliers.

Prather, C. Daniel. 2009. *General Aviation Marketing and Management: Operating, Marketing, and Managing an FBO.* 3rd ed. Malabar, FL: Krieger Publishing Company.

Slotnick, David. 2020. "Airlines Will Get the $60 Billion Bailout They Asked For in the $2 Trillion Coronavirus Stimulus Bill That Trump Signed into Law. It Also Prohibits Layoffs, Stock Buybacks, and Dividends." *Insider,* March 27, 2020. https://www.businessinsider.com/airlines-coronavirus-bailout-senate-stock-buybacks-2020-3.

Transportation Security Administration (TSA). 2021. "TSA Checkpoint Travel Numbers." https://www.tsa.gov/coronavirus/passenger-throughput.

van de Wouw, Niall. 2020. "Air cargo in stable condition following coronavirus crisis." *Air Cargo News,* May 20, 2020. https://www.aircargonews.net/business/supply-chains/air-cargo-in-stable-condition-following-coronavirus-crisis/.

"Working Together." 2014. *GuideStone Magazine* 13: 8–10.

APPENDIX A

SAMPLE FBO LEASE AGREEMENT

Note: This sample is for informational purposes only and is not intended to be used as a legal contract. Consult a qualified attorney for legal advice.

FBO LEASE AGREEMENT

THIS AGREEMENT is made effective and __________ *(date)*, by and between the DEPARTMENT OF TRANSPORTATION, AERONAUTICS DIVISION, hereinafter referred to as "DIVISION" and ______________ *(FBO name)*, with authority to do business in the State of ______________ *(state)*, hereinafter referred to as "FBO."

WITNESSETH:

WHEREAS, DIVISION now owns, controls, and operates the ______________ Airport, hereinafter referred to as "Airport", located in ______________ County, State of ______________;

WHEREAS, Fixed Base Operation (FBO) services are essential to the proper accommodation of general aviation at the airport; and

WHEREAS, DIVISION deems it advantageous to itself and to its operation of the Airport to Lease unto FBO certain premises and to grant unto FBO certain rights, privileges and uses therein, as necessary to conduct its fixed base operation as hereinafter set forth.

NOW THEREFORE, for and in consideration of these premises and the mutual promises and covenants of the parties hereto, it is agreed as follows:

ARTICLE I

TERM

A. The term of this Agreement shall be for a period of one (1) year, commencing on __________ *(date)*, and ending on __________ *(date)*, unless earlier terminated under the provisions of this Agreement. This Lease Agreement will be automatically renewed from year to year in accordance with and acceptance of the terms and conditions herein specified. Such renewal of this Lease Agreement shall be conditional upon the satisfactory performance by it during the term of this Lease Agreement as determined by the DIVISION.

B. Both parties shall have the option to negotiate changes in this lease if FBO exercises its option to renew.

ARTICLE II

LEASED PREMISES

The DIVISION leases to FBO and FBO leases from the DIVISION on a year-round basis, solely for the conduct of FBO's business as a Fixed Base Operator at the Airport the following real property.

A. LEASEHOLD PREMISES: The leasehold premises shall consist of the Fuel and Airport Maintenance Equipment Storage Area which comprises ________square feet, set forth, described and located on Exhibit "A" attached hereto and made a part hereof.

B. PURPOSE: The purpose of the Fuel and Airport Maintenance Equipment Storage Area shall be for the storage of FBO equipment and material related to the legal storage and dispensing of aviation fuels and lubricants. FBO may also store on leasehold premises motorized and non-motorized airport maintenance equipment and material. Further, the Airport Manager is authorized to store NON-DIVISION owned airport maintenance equipment only within leasehold premises.

The DIVISION shall also have the right to store DIVISION owned airport maintenance equipment only without charge by the FBO on leasehold premises for security purposes.

ARTICLE III

RIGHTS AND OBLIGATIONS OF LESSEE

A. REQUIRED SERVICES: FBO is hereby granted the non-exclusive privilege to engage in and FBO agrees to engage in the business of providing the following services:

1. FBO shall maintain vehicle-mounted fuel storage and dispensing tank(s) upon the leased premises, which shall be adequate for the purposes herein described, and in accordance with the approval of DIVISION.

2. FBO shall maintain an adequate supply of aviation fuel and lubricants in the storage tanks located on leasehold premises to meet the reasonable demands for aviation fuels, lubricants.

B. AUTHORIZED SERVICES: In addition to the services required to be provided by FBO as described herein above, FBO is authorized, but not required, to provide the following services and to engage in the following activities:

1. Apron services including loading and unloading of passengers, baggage, mail and freight; and providing of ramp equipment and ramp services such as repositioning of aircraft on the ramp, aircraft cleaning, and other services for commercial operators and other persons or firms.

2. Special flight services, including aerial sightseeing, aerial advertising, and aerial photography.

3. The sale of new and used aircraft.

4. Flight training.

5. Aircraft rental.

6. Aircraft charter operations, conducted by FBO or a subcontractor of FBO in accordance with applicable Federal Aviation Regulations.

C. OPERATING STANDARDS: In providing any of the required and/or authorized services or activities specified in this Agreement, FBO shall operate for the use and benefit of the public and shall meet or exceed the following standards:

1. FBO shall furnish service on a fair, reasonable and non-discriminatory basis to all users of the Airport. FBO shall furnish good, prompt, and efficient service adequate to meet all reasonable demands for its services at the Airport. FBO shall charge fair, reasonable, and non-discriminatory prices for each unit of sale or service provided; however, FBO may be allowed to make reasonable and non-discriminatory discounts, rebates, or other similar types of price reductions to volume purchasers.

2. FBO shall meet all expenses and payments in connection with the use of the premises and the rights and privileges herein granted, including taxes, permit fees, license fees, registrations, and assessments lawfully levied or assessed upon the premises or property at any time situated therein and thereon. FBO may, however, at its sole expense and cost, contest any tax, fee or assessment as provided by__________ *(state)* law.

3. FBO shall comply with all federal, state, and local laws, rules and regulations which may apply for the storage and dispensing of aviation fuels and to the conduct of the businesses contemplated, including rules and regulations promulgated by DIVISION and FBO shall keep in effect and post in a prominent place all necessary and/or required licenses or permits.

4. FBO shall keep and maintain the leased premises in good condition and order, and shall surrender the same upon the expiration of this Agreement, in the condition in which they are required to be kept, reasonable wear and tear and damage by the elements not caused by FBO's negligence excepted.

5. FBO shall maintain and operate all facilities associated with the storage of FBO's petroleum products, chemicals, or other products located only within the Fuel and Airport Maintenance Equipment Storage Area leased premises described by Article II, paragraph A of this agreement, in compliance with all Federal and State laws. Any new fuel tank installations installed on FBO's leased Fuel and Airport Maintenance Equipment Storage Area shall require the permission of the DIVISION and shall be above ground storage tanks and shall comply with Uniform Fire Code provisions as administered by State Fire Marshals Office and all applicable Federal rules.

6. In the event that soils or other materials are found on FBO's leased Fuel and Airport Maintenance Equipment Storage Area as described by Article II, paragraph A, that are "Hazardous or Deleterious Substances" as defined by the State Environmental Cleanup and Responsibility Act, 75-10-701 et seq., State. Code Ann. ("CERCRA"), "Hazardous Substances" as defined by the Comprehensive Environmental Response, Compensation and Liability Act, 42 U.S.C. S9600, et seq., ("CERCLA"), "Hazardous Waste" as defined by the State Hazardous Waste and Underground Storage Tank Act, S75-10-401, et seq., or the Solid Waste Disposal Act, as amended by the Resource Conservation and Recovery Act, 42 U.S.C. S6901 et seq., or which require special remediation or disposal pursuant to any other applicable law, Lessee shall excavate, handle, and dispose of such soils or other materials only in compliance with such statutes and regulations. In the event that the FBO leaves any of the above described materials on the property, the DIVISION may, at its option, have wastes properly disposed of with FBO responsible for the cost of storage, transport, and disposal of wastes.

All Hazardous Materials must be appropriately labeled and stored. In the event that a hazardous material spill occurs on the leased property or on DIVISION owned airport premises, it is the responsibility of the FBO to have the spill cleaned up according to State and Federal Laws and Regulations. FBO is aware that there are significant penalties for improperly disposing of wastes or submitting false information, including the possibility of fine and imprisonment for knowing violations.

D. SIGNS: FBO shall not erect, construct, or place any signs or advertisements pertaining to its business upon any portion of the Airport, other than upon the Fuel and Airport Maintenance Equipment Storage site. Prior to the erection, construction, or placing of any signs or advertising matter upon the leasehold areas, FBO shall submit to the DIVISION for its approval, in writing, such drawings, sketches, designs, dimensions, type, and character of advertising matter and proposed location. Notwithstanding any other provision of this Agreement, said sign(s) shall remain the property of FBO. FBO shall remove, at its expense, all lettering, signs, and placards so erected on the Airport at the expiration of the term of this Agreement.

E. NON EXCLUSIVE RIGHT: It is not the intent of this Agreement to grant to FBO the exclusive right to provide any or all of the services described in this article at any time during the term of this Agreement. DIVISION reserves the right, at its sole discretion, to grant others certain rights and privileges upon the Airport which may be similar in part or in whole to those granted to FBO. However, DIVISION does covenant and agree that:

1. It shall enforce all minimum operating standards or requirements for all aeronautical endeavors and activities conducted at the Airport;

2. Any other operator of aeronautical endeavors or activities will not be permitted to operate on the Airport under rates, terms, or conditions which are more favorable than those set forth in this Agreement;

3. It will not permit the conduct of any aeronautical endeavor or activity at the Airport except under an approved lease and operating agreement.

ARTICLE IV

APPURTENANT PRIVILEGES

A. USE OF AIRPORT FACILITIES: In connection with this Agreement, FBO shall have full access, together with its employees and invitees, its sub-lessees and their employees, without charge, to and from the leased premises, and to and from all public spaces and facilities on the airport including the use of landing areas, runways, taxiways, and aircraft parking areas designated by the DIVISION.

B. NON-COMPETITION: DIVISION shall not engage directly or indirectly in any of the activities described in Paragraphs A & B of ARTICLE III of this Agreement.

ARTICLE V

PAYMENTS

A. RENT & FEES: In consideration of the rights and privileges granted by this Agreement, FBO agrees to pay to DIVISION during the term of this Agreement the following:

1. RENT: The Division agrees to waive customary rental fees charged for leasing unimproved ground for the Fuel and Airport Maintenance Equipment Storage Area in exchange for FBO to perform Airport Management Duties and Responsibilities. These airport management duties are covered by separate written agreement.

2. FEES: FBO shall collect a fuel flowage fee and pay to the DIVISION the amount per gallon set by the DIVISION from time to time for all aviation fuels sold by FBO, including fuels used by FBO in its own operations except any fueling operations conducted __________. Fuel flowage fees shall be collected regardless of when such activity occurred during the calendar year and also with no regard to where the re-fueling operation occurred, for example on airport or off airport premises except at __________.

B. PAYMENTS:

1. The fees specified in ARTICLE V, Paragraph A.2 above shall be paid to the DIVISION on or before the tenth (10th) day of each month following the month in which fees were paid to FBO. FBO shall keep true and accurate records, which shall show the total gallonage of aviation fuels used. With the payment of the charges specified in this paragraph, FBO shall submit a report of gallonage using Exhibit A.

C. RECORDS: In addition to records and reports required by Paragraph B.1 above, FBO shall provide and maintain accurate records of retail fuel sales and adjusted gross receipts derived under this Agreement, for a period of three (3) years from the date the record is made. The DIVISION or its duly authorized representative shall have the right at all reasonable times during business hours to audit the books, records, and receipts of FBO, and to verify FBO's fuel sales and adjusted gross receipts and tie down fees collected.

D. DISPUTES: In the event that any dispute may arise as to fuel sales collected, the amount claimed due by the DIVISION shall be paid forthwith. The dispute shall be submitted to a Certified Public Accountant, agreeable to both parties, who shall determine the rights of the parties hereunder to conformity with generally accepted accounting principles. The fees due said accountant for such service shall be paid by the unsuccessful party, or in the event the determination is partially in favor of each party, the fee shall be borne equally by the parties.

ARTICLE VI

UTILITIES

Except for utilities furnished for Airport security lighting by the DIVISION, FBO shall assume and pay for all costs or charges for utility services furnished to FBO during the term of this Agreement.

ARTICLE VII

INSURANCE

A. REQUIRED INSURANCE: FBO shall obtain and maintain continuously in effect at all times during the term of this Agreement, at FBO's sole expense, Public Liability and Property Damage insurance with limits of not less than _________ Dollars ($_________) for injury to or death of any one person, subject to a limitation of not less than _________ Dollars ($_________) for all persons injured or killed in the same accident and with limits of not less than _________Dollars ($_________) for damage to and destruction of property as the result of any injury or damage caused by FBO's negligence in its operations under this Lease.

B. NOTICE: DIVISION agrees to notify FBO in writing as soon as practicable of any claim, demand, or action arising out of an occurrence covered hereunder of which DIVISION has knowledge, and to cooperate with FBO in the investigation thereof.

ARTICLE VIII

INDEMNIFICATION

FBO will indemnify and hold the DIVISION harmless from any loss, liability, or expense for injury to or death to any person, or loss or destruction of any property caused by FBO's negligent use or occupancy of the Leased Premises, except a loss, liability or expense caused by the sole negligence or sole willful misconduct of the DIVISION, its agents or employees. FBO hereby expressly waives any and all claims against the DIVISION for compensation for any and all losses or damage sustained by reasons of any defect, deficiency, or impairment of any electrical service system, or electrical appliances or wires serving the Leasehold of FBO.

ARTICLE IX

LESSEE AS INDEPENDENT CONTRACTOR

In conducting its business hereunder, FBO acts as an independent contractor and not as an agent of DIVISION. The selection, retention, assignment, direction, and payment of FBO's employees, if any, shall be the sole responsibility of FBO. FBO shall at all times during the term of this Agreement maintain Workers Compensation Insurance on its employees directly related to the operation of the FBO. Copy of Workers Compensation Certificate of Insurance shall be provided to the DIVISION.

ARTICLE X

ASSIGNMENT

FBO shall not, in any manner, directly or indirectly, assign, transfer, or encumber this Lease and concession agreement or any portion thereof, or interest therein, or sublet or sublease the whole or any part of the premises or facilities let to it, nor license the use of same, in whole or in part, by any other person, firm, or corporation, without the written consent of the DIVISION; provided that the foregoing shall not prevent the assignment of this Lease and concession agreement to any corporation with which FBO may merge or consolidate, or which may succeed to the business of FBO, and which resultant or succeeding corporation shall continue the operation of the business authorized under the concession granted herein at the Airport.

This Lease and concession agreement shall be binding upon and shall inure to the benefit of the successors, heirs, and assigns of the parties hereto.

ARTICLE XI

NON-DISCRIMINATION

FBO, its agents and employees shall not discriminate against any person or class of persons by reason of race, color, creed, or national origin in providing any services or in the use of any of its facilities provided for the public, in any manner prohibited by the applicable Federal Aviation Regulations.

ARTICLE XII

DEFAULT AND TERMINATION

A. TERMINATION BY LESSEE: This Agreement shall be subject to termination by FBO in the event of any one or more of the following events:

  1. The abandonment of the Airport as an airport or airfield for any type, class, or category of aircraft.

  2. The default by DIVISION in the performance of any of the terms, covenants, or conditions of this Agreement, and the failure of DIVISION to remedy or undertake to remedy, to FBO's satisfaction, such default within a period of thirty (30) days after receipt of written notice from FBO to remedy same.

  3. Damage to or destruction of all or a material part of the premises or airport facilities necessary to the operation of FBO's business.

  4. The lawful assumption by the United States, or any authorized agency thereof, of the operation, control, or use of the airport, or any substantial parts thereof, in such a manner to restrict FBO from conducting business operations for a period in excess of ninety (90) days.

B. TERMINATION BY LESSOR: This Agreement shall be subject to termination by DIVISION in the event of any one or more of the following events:

  1. The default by FBO in the performance of any of the terms, covenants, or conditions of this Agreement, and the failure of FBO to remedy, or undertake to remedy, to DIVISION's satisfaction, such default within a period of thirty (30) days after receipt of written notice from DIVISION to remedy same.

  2. FBO files a voluntary petition in bankruptcy, including a reorganization plan, makes a general or other assignment for the benefit of creditors, is adjudicated as bankrupt or if a receiver is appointed for the property or affairs of FBO and such receivership is not vacated within thirty (30) days after the appointment of such a receiver.

  3. State legislative of Division action which would cause the DIVISION to abandon, close, return to the Airport Authority, other legal airport sponsor, or otherwise discontinue operating the airport.

C. EXERCISE: Exercise of the rights of termination set forth in Paragraphs A and B above, shall be by notice to the other party within thirty (30) days following the event giving rise to the termination.

D. REMOVAL OF PROPERTY: Upon termination of this Agreement for any reason, FBO, at its sole expense, shall remove from the premises all signs, trade fixtures, furnishings, personal property, equipment, and materials which FBO was permitted to install or maintain under the rights granted herein. If FBO shall fail to do so within thirty (30) days, then DIVISION may effect such removal or restoration at FBO's expense, and FBO agrees to pay DIVISION such expense promptly upon receipt of a proper invoice therefor.

E. CAUSES OF BREACH; WAIVER:

1. Neither party shall be held to be in breach of this Agreement because of any failure to perform any of its obligations hereunder if said failure is due to any cause for which it is not responsible and over which it has no control; provided, however, that the foregoing provision shall not apply to failures by FBO to pay fees, rents, or other charges to DIVISION.

2. The waiver of any breach, violation, or default in or with respect to the performance or observance of the covenants and conditions contained herein shall not be taken to constitute a waiver of any such subsequent breach, violation, or default in or with respect to the same or any other covenant or condition hereof.

ARTICLE XIII

MISCELLANEOUS PROVISIONS

A. ENTIRE AGREEMENT: This Agreement constitutes the entire understanding between the parties, and as of its effective date supersedes all prior or independent agreements between the parties covering the subject matter hereof. Any change or modification hereof must be in writing signed by both parties.

B. SEVERABILITY: If a provision hereof shall be finally declared void or illegal by any court or administrative agency having jurisdiction, the entire Agreement shall not be void, but the remaining provisions shall continue in effect as nearly as possible in accordance with the original intent of the parties.

C. NOTICES: All notices shall be sent to:

____________________ and ____________________, Aeronautics Division,

____________________ *(street address),* ____________________ *(city, state, zip code)*

LESSOR

DEPARTMENT OF TRANSPORTATION

____

BY: Administrator, Aeronautics Division, Date

____

LESSEE Date

____

LEGAL REVIEW Date

EXHIBIT A

______________ AERONAUTICS DIVISION

______________ AIRPORT

For ______________________ *(month, year)*

1. Fuel and Airport Maintenance Equipment Storage Area: Tank farm, ___________ sq. ft. @ $___________ /sq ft/annum, payable July 1 of each contract year $ ___________

2. Fuel Sales:
   100 Octane = ___________ gallons
   Total = gallons x $___________ /gallon = $______________

PAYMENT FOR MONTH: $ ________________

CHECK # ______________________________

By: ___________________________________

Title:__________________________________

APPENDIX B

FAA Advisory Circular 150/5190-7, Minimum Standards for Commercial Aeronautical Activities

U.S. Department of Transportation

Federal Aviation Administration

Advisory Circular

Subject: MINIMUM STANDARDS FOR COMMERCIAL AERONAUTICAL ACTIVITIES

Date: August 28, 2006
Initiated by: ACO-100

AC No: 150/5190-7
Change:

1. PURPOSE. This advisory circular (AC) provides basic information pertaining to the Federal Aviation Administration's (FAA's) recommendations on commercial minimum standards and related policies. Although minimum standards are optional, the FAA highly recommends their use and implementation as a means to minimize the potential for violations of Federal obligations at federally obligated airports.

2. CANCELLATION. AC 150/5190-5, *Exclusive Rights and Minimum Standards for Commercial Aeronautical Activities* (Change 1), dated June 10, 2002, is cancelled.

3. BACKGROUND. In accordance with the Airport and Airway Improvement Act of 1982, 49 United States Code (U.S.C.) § 47101, *et seq.,* and the Airport Improvement Program Sponsor Assurances, the owner or operator of any airport (airport sponsor) that has been developed or improved with Federal grant assistance or conveyances of Federal property assistance is required to operate the airport for the use and benefit of the public and to make it available for all types, kinds, and classes of aeronautical activity.[1] The Surplus Property Act of 1944 (as amended by 49 U.S.C., §§ 47151-47153) contains a parallel obligation under its terms for the conveyance of Federal property for airport purposes. Similar obligations exist for airports that have received nonsurplus government property under 49 U.S.C. § 47125 and previous corresponding statutes.

These Federal obligations involve several distinct requirements. Most important is that the airport and its facilities must be available for public use as an airport. The terms imposed on those who use the airport and its services must be reasonable and applied without unjust discrimination, whether by the airport sponsor or by a contractor or licensee who has been granted a right by the airport sponsor to offer services or commodities normally required to serve aeronautical users of the airport.

[1] The legislative background for the provisions discussed in this AC began as early as 1938 and evolved under the Federal Aid to Airports Program (FAAP), Airport Development Aid Program (ADAP), and Airport Improvement Program (AIP).

Federal law requires that recipients of Federal grants (administered by the FAA) sign a grant agreement or covenant in a conveyance of property that sets out the obligations that an airport sponsor assumes in exchange for Federal assistance. The FAA's policy recommending minimum standards stems from the airport sponsor's grant assurances and similar property conveyance obligations to make the airport available for public use on reasonable conditions and without unjust discrimination.

4. USE OF THIS AC. This AC addresses FAA's policy on minimum standards and provides guidance on developing effective minimum standards. This AC describes the sponsor's prerogative to establish minimum standards for commercial aeronautical service providers at federally obligated airports. Additionally, this AC provides guidance for self-service operations and self-service rules and regulation of other aeronautical activities. It does not address requirements imposed on nonaeronautical entities, which are usually addressed as part of the airport's contracts, leases, rules and regulations, and/or local laws. The FAA does not approve minimum standards. However, the FAA airports district and regional offices will review proposed minimum standards at the request of an airport sponsor. The FAA regional and district offices may advise airport sponsors on the appropriateness of proposed standards to ensure the standards do not place the airport in a position inconsistent with its Federal obligations.

5. RELATED READING MATERIALS.

a. *FAA Airport Compliance Requirements*, Order 5190.6A, dated October 16, 1989.

b. Further information can be obtained at the Airports District Office (ADO) in your area. A listing of ADOs can be found at http://www.faa.gov/airports_airtraffic/airports/regional_guidance/.

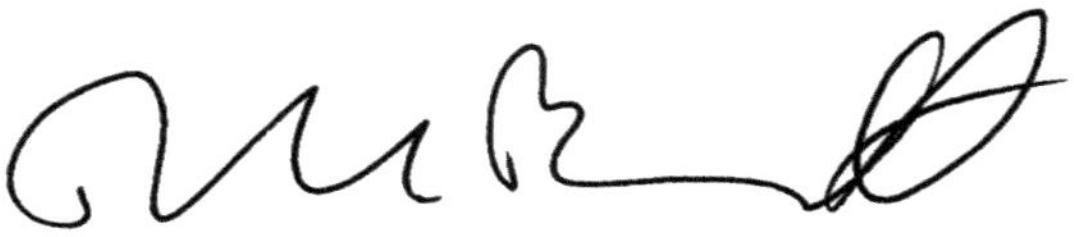

DAVID L. BENNETT
Director, Office of Airport
Safety and Standards

SECTION 1. MINIMUM STANDARDS

1.1. POLICY. The airport sponsor of a federally obligated airport agrees to make available the opportunity to engage in commercial aeronautical activities by persons, firms, or corporations that meet reasonable minimum standards established by the airport sponsor. The airport sponsor's purpose in imposing standards is to ensure a safe, efficient and adequate level of operation and services is offered to the public. Such standards must be reasonable and not unjustly discriminatory. In exchange for the opportunity to engage in a commercial aeronautical activity, an aeronautical service provider engaged in an aeronautical activity agrees to comply with the minimum standards developed by the airport sponsor. Compliance with the airport's minimum standards should be made part of an aeronautical service provider's lease agreement with the airport sponsor.

The FAA suggests that airport sponsors establish reasonable minimum standards that are relevant to the proposed aeronautical activity with the goal of protecting the level and quality of services offered to the public. Once the airport sponsor has established minimum standards, it should apply them objectively and uniformly to all similarly situated on-airport aeronautical service providers. The failure to do so may result in a violation of the prohibition against exclusive rights and/or a finding of unjust economic discrimination for imposing unreasonable terms and conditions for airport use.

1.2. DEVELOPING MINIMUM STANDARDS.

a. Objective. The FAA objective in recommending the development of minimum standards serves to promote safety in all airport activities, protect airport users from unlicensed and unauthorized products and services, maintain and enhance the availability of adequate services for all airport users, promote the orderly development of airport land, and ensure efficiency of operations. Therefore, airport sponsors should strive to develop minimum standards that are fair and reasonable to all on-airport aeronautical service providers and relevant to the aeronautical activity to which it is applied. Any use of minimum standards to protect the interests of an exclusive business operation may be interpreted as the grant of an exclusive right and a potential violation of the airport sponsor's grant assurances and the FAA's policy on exclusive rights.

b. Authority Vested in Airport Sponsors. Grant Assurance 22 *Economic Nondiscrimination* Sections (h) and (i) (see 49 U.S.C. § 47107) provides that the sponsor may establish such reasonable, and not unjustly discriminatory, conditions to be met by all users of the airport as may be necessary for the safe and efficient operation of the airport. The sponsor may prohibit or limit any given type, kind or class of aeronautical use of the airport if such action is necessary for the safe operation of the airport or necessary to serve the civil aviation needs of the public.

Under certain circumstances, an airport sponsor could deny airport users the opportunity to conduct aeronautical activities at the airport for reasons of safety and efficiency.[2] A denial based on safety must be based on evidence demonstrating that safety will be compromised if the applicant is allowed to engage in the proposed aeronautical activity. Airport sponsors should carefully scrutinize the safety reasons for denying an aeronautical service provider the opportunity to engage in an aeronautical activity if the denial has the possible effect of limiting competition.

The FAA is the final authority in determining what, in fact, constitutes a compromise of safety. As such, an airport sponsor that is contemplating the denial of a proposed on-airport aeronautical activity

[2] The word efficiency refers to the efficient use of navigable airspace, which is an Air Traffic Control function. It is not meant to be an interpretation that could be construed as protecting the "efficient'' operation of an existing aeronautical service provider at the airport.

is encouraged to contact the local Airports District Office (ADO) or the Regional Airports Office before taking action. Those offices will then seek assistance from FAA Flight Standards (FS) and Air Traffic (AT) to assess the reasonableness and whether unjust discrimination results from the proposed restrictions on aeronautical activities based on safety and efficiency.

c. Developing Minimum Standards. When developing minimum standards, the most critical consideration is the particular nature of the aeronautical activity and operating environment at the airport. Minimum standards should be tailored to the specific aeronautical activity and the airport to which they are to be applied. For example, it would be unreasonable to apply the minimum standards for a fixed-base operator (FBO) at a medium or large hub airport to a general aviation airport serving primarily piston-powered aircraft. The imposition of unreasonable requirements illustrates why "fill-in-the-blank" minimum standards and the blanket adoption of standards of other airports may not be effective. Instead, in Section 2 of this document, the FAA has provided guidance in the form of questions and examples to illustrate an approach to the development and implementation of minimum standards. It is important that the reader understand that what follows does not constitute a complete model for minimum standards, but rather a source of ideas to which the airport sponsor can turn when developing minimum standards.

d. Sponsor Prerogative to Establish Minimum Standards. When the airport sponsor imposes reasonable and not unjustly discriminatory minimum standards for airport operations through the use of reasonable minimum standards, the FAA generally will not find the airport sponsor in violation of the Federal obligations. Considerations for applying those standards may include, but are not limited to, the following:

(1) Apply standards to all providers of aeronautical services, from full service FBOs to single service providers;

(2) Impose conditions that ensure safe and efficient operation of the airport in accordance with FAA rules, regulations, and guidance;

(3) Ensure standards are reasonable, not unjustly discriminatory, attainable, uniformly applied and reasonably protect the investment of providers of aeronautical services to meet minimum standards from competition not making a similar investment;

(4) Ensure standards are relevant to the activity to which they apply; and

(5) Ensure standards provide the opportunity for newcomers who meet the minimum standards to offer their aeronautical services within the market demand for such services.

Note: There is no requirement for inclusion of nonaeronautical activities (such as a restaurant, parking or car rental concession) in minimum standards since those activities are not covered under the grant assurances or covenants in conveyance of Federal property.

e. Practical Considerations. Many airport sponsors include minimum standards in their lease agreements with aeronautical service providers. While minimum standards implemented in this manner can be effective, they also render the airport sponsor vulnerable to the challenges of prospective aeronautical service providers on the grounds that the minimum standards are not objective. The FAA encourages airport sponsors to publish their minimum standards periodically. Minimum standards can be amended periodically over time; however, a constant juggling of minimum standards is not encouraged. Notifying aeronautical service providers that the changes to minimum standards are to improve the quality of the aeronautical service offered to the public can facilitate earlier acceptance of changes. An airport sponsor can provide for periodic reviews of the minimum standards to ensure that the standards continue to be reasonable. To foster a more receptive environment, the FAA encourages airport sponsors to include aeronautical users in the process leading to changes in minimum standards.

f. Factors to Consider. Numerous factors can and should be considered when developing minimum standards. Airport sponsors may avoid unreasonable standards by selecting factors that accurately reflect the nature of the aeronautical activity under consideration. It is impossible for the FAA to present every possible factor necessary for a task, mostly because of the vast differences that exist between individual airports. Obvious factors one should consider are:

(1) What type of airport is at issue? Is it a large airport or a small rural airport? Will the airport provide service to only small general aviation aircraft or will it serve high performance aircraft and air taxi operators as well?

(2) What types of aeronautical activities will be conducted on the airport?

(3) How much space will be required for each type of aeronautical activity that may prospectively operate at the airport?

(4) What type of documentation will business applicants be required to present as evidence of financial stability and good credit?

(5) To what extent will each type of aeronautical activity be required to demonstrate compliance with sanitation, health, and safety codes?

(6) What requirements will be imposed regarding minimum insurance coverage and indemnity provisions?

(7) Is each minimum standard relevant to the aeronautical activity for which it is to be applied?

g. New Versus Existing Aeronautical Service Providers. Airport sponsors are encouraged to develop minimum standards for new aeronautical business ventures it desires to attract to the airport. Minimum standards may be part of a competitive solicitation to encourage prospective service providers to be more responsive in their proposals. Minimum standards can be modified to reflect the airport's experience and to be watchful for new opportunities (i.e. such as Specialized Aviation Service Operations (SASOs)). Minimum standards should be updated to reflect current conditions that exist at the airport and not those that existed in the past. In any case, once an airport sponsor receives a proposal for a new aeronautical business, it must ascertain whether the existing minimum standards can be used for the new business or new minimum standards should be developed to better fit the new business venture. However, in all cases, the airport sponsor must ensure that in changing minimum standards for whatever reason, it is not applying unreasonable standards or creating a situation that will unjustly discriminate against other similarly situated aeronautical service providers. The FAA stands by the principle that once minimum standards have been established, airport sponsors must uniformly apply them to all similarly situated aeronautical service providers. Some points of consideration are as follows:

(1) Can new minimum standards be designed to address the needs of both existing and future aeronautical business? If not, can a tiered set of minimum standards be developed to address the same type of aeronautical activity but differ significantly in scale and investment (i.e. an FBO building large hangars and serving high performance aircraft and a second FBO building and only T-hangars and serving only smaller general aviation aircraft)?

(2) Was the minimum standard created under a lease agreement (with a specific aeronautical service provider) so the subject standard may not be reasonable if applied to other aeronautical service providers?

(3) Has conformance to the minimum standards been made a part of the contract between the aeronautical service provider and the airport sponsor?

(4) Has the financial performance of the airport improved or declined since the time the minimum standards were implemented?

1.3. MINIMUM STANDARDS APPLY BY ACTIVITY.

Difficulties can arise if the airport sponsor requires that all businesses comply with all provisions of the published minimum standards. An airport sponsor should develop reasonable, relevant, and applicable standards for each type and class of service.

a. Specialized Aviation Service Operations. When specialized aviation service operations (SASOs), sometimes known as single-service providers or special FBOs, apply to do business on an airport, "all" provisions of the published minimum standards may not apply. This is not to say that all SASOs providing the same or similar services should not equally comply with all applicable minimum standards. However, an airport should not, without adequate justification, require that a service provider desiring to provide a single service or less than full service also meet the criteria for a full-service FBO. Examples of these specialized services may include aircraft flying clubs, flight training, aircraft airframe and powerplant repair/maintenance, aircraft charter, air taxi or air ambulance, aircraft sales, avionics, instrument or propeller services, or other specialized commercial flight support businesses. Airport sponsors generally do not allow fuel sales alone as a SASO, but usually require that fuel sales be bundled with other services.

b. Independent Operators. If individual operators are to be allowed to perform a single-service aeronautical activity on the airport (aircraft washing, maintenance, etc.), the airport sponsor should have a licensing or permitting process in place that provides a level of regulation and compensation satisfactory to the airport. Frequently, a yearly fee or percentage of the gross receipts fee is a satisfactory way of monitoring this type of operation.

c. Self-Fueling and Other Self-Service Activities. Since self-service operations performed by the owner or operator of the aircraft using his or her own employees and equipment are not commercial activities, the FAA recommends that airport sponsor requirements concerning those non-commercial activities be separate from the document designed to address commercial activities. Airport rules and regulations or specific language in leases can better address requirements concerning self-service operations and other airport activities.

Self-fueling means the fueling or servicing of an aircraft (i.e. changing the oil, washing) by the owner of the aircraft with his or her own employees and using his or her own equipment. Self-fueling and other self-services cannot be contracted out to another party. Self-fueling implies using fuel obtained by the aircraft owner from the source of his/her preference. As one of many self-service activities that can be conducted by the aircraft owner or operator by his or her own employees using his or her own equipment, self-fueling, differs from using a self-service fueling pump made available by the airport, an FBO or an aeronautical service provider. The use of a self-service fueling pump is a commercial activity and is not considered self-fueling as defined herein.

In addition to self-fueling, other self-service activities that can be performed by the aircraft owner with his or her own employees includes activities such as maintaining, repairing, cleaning, and otherwise providing service to an aircraft, provided the service is performed by the aircraft owner or his/her employees with resources supplied by the aircraft owner. Title 14 Code of Federal Regulations (CFR) Part 43 permits the holder of a pilot certificate to perform specific types of preventative maintenance on any aircraft owned or operated by the pilot.

1.4. THROUGH THE FENCE OPERATOR. The owner of an airport may, at times, enter into an agreement (i.e. access agreement or lease agreement) that permits access to the public landing area by independent operators offering an aeronautical activity or to owners of aircraft based on land adjacent to, but not a part of, the airport property**.** However, a through-the-fence operation could undermine an airport's minimum standards unless the airport sponsor is careful to apply its minimum standards through an airport access agreement, including conditions to protect the airport's ability to meet all of its Federal obligations.

a. No Obligation to Permit Through-the-Fence. The obligation to make an airport available for the use and benefit of the public does not require the airport sponsor to permit ground access by aircraft from adjacent property. Through-the-fence arrangements can place an encumbrance upon the airport property and reduce the airport's ability to meet its Federal obligations. As a general principal the FAA does not support agreements that grant access to the public landing area by aircraft stored and serviced off-site on adjacent property.

In some cases, however, the airport sponsor may opt to grant through-the-fence access, but it should do so on a case-by-case basis and only when the airport retains its ability to meet its Federal obligations. To minimize the possibility of conflict between a through-the-fence agreement and the airports' ability to meet its Federal obligations, the airport sponsor must retain the legal right to require the off-site property owner or party granted access to the airport to conform in all respects to the requirements of any existing or proposed grant agreement or Federal property conveyance obligation. This includes requirements to ensure operating safety and equitable compensation for use of the airport. Special safety and operational requirements should be incorporated into any access agreement to ensure that the through-the-fence access does not complicate the control of vehicular and aircraft traffic or compromise the security of the airfield operations area.

Proposed new agreements granting access to a public landing area from off-site locations should be reported to the FAA Regional Airports Division with a full statement of the circumstances and a copy of the proposed through-the-fence or access agreement so the FAA can review it for consistency with the airport sponsor's Federal obligations and incorporate it into the current Airport Layout Plan (ALP).

b. Access Agreement. Any through-the-fence access should be subject to a written agreement between the airport sponsor and the party granted access. The access agreement should specify what specific rights of access are granted; payment provisions that provide, at a minimum, parity with similarly situated on-airport tenants and equitable compensation for the use of the airport; expiration date; default and termination provisions; insurance and indemnity provisions; and a clear statement that the access agreement is subordinate to the grant assurances and/or Federal property conveyance obligations and that the sponsor shall have the express right to amend or terminate the access agreement to ensure continued compliance with all grant assurances and Federal property conveyance obligations.

The access agreement should have a fixed contract period and the airport sponsor is under no obligation to accept a proposed assignment or sale of the access agreement by one party to another. It is encouraged that airport sponsors expressly prohibit the sale or assignment of its access agreement.

1.5. RESERVED.

SECTION 2. GUIDANCE ON DEVELOPING MINIMUM STANDARDS

2.1. SAMPLE QUESTIONS. As a guide for the airport sponsor, the following series of questions are provided to address some of the various types of specific services or activities frequently offered to the public:

a. Fuel Sales. The on-airport sale of fuel and oil requires numerous considerations that include, but are not limited to, the physical requirements for a safe and environmentally sound operation. Some recommended considerations are listed below:

(1) Where on the airport will the fuel tanks be installed? Who will control access to the fueling site? What parties will be granted access to the site to receive fueling services?

(2) Will fuel tanks be installed above or below ground? Will fuel trucks be utilized to fuel remotely parked aircraft?

(3) Will the fueling operator have sufficient fuel capacity and types of fuel to accommodate the mix of aircraft using the airport?

(4) How many days' supply of fuel will be available on airport? Are provisions to resupply the on-airport fuel tanks sufficient to ensure a continuous fuel supply?

(5) Will the fueling operator have suitable liability insurance and indemnify the airport sponsor for liability for its fueling operation, including fuel spills and environmental contamination?

b. Personnel Requirements. An aeronautical service provider's need for personnel will be dictated by the size of the airport and the public demand for aeronautical services. In all instances, an airport sponsor will be well advised to ensure that aeronautical service providers have sufficient personnel to run their operation safely and meet aeronautical demand for the services in question. Naturally, the personnel requirements will vary with the specific aeronautical service being offered.

(1) How many fully trained and qualified personnel will be available each day and over what hours to provide aeronautical services? Will this reasonably meet the demand by aeronautical users?

(2) Describe the training and qualifications of personnel engaged in the services provided to aeronautical users.

c. Airport and Passenger Services. This is a necessary consideration in those instances where the airport has aeronautical service providers engaged in handling services for air carrier and/or cargo carriers that do not provide their own support personnel on-site:

(1) Provide a list of the equipment and services (both above and below wing) that will be provided by the aeronautical service provider, including ground power units, over night parking areas, towing equipment, starters, remote tie-down areas, jacks, oxygen, compressed air, tire repair, sanitary lavatory service, ticketing and passenger check-in services, office and baggage handling services and storage space.

(2) What provisions have been made regarding passenger conveniences and services?

(a) Access to passenger loading bridges/steps, sanitary rest rooms, boarding hold rooms, telephones, food and beverage service, and other passenger concessions.

(b) Access to concession and ground transportation services for the benefit of passengers and/or crewmembers.

d. Flight Training Activities. On-airport flight training can be provided by the airport sponsor/owner or by a service provider. The minimum standards imposed on flight instruction operations should take the following information into consideration:

(1) What type of flight training will the service provider offer?

(2) What arrangements have been made for the office space the school is required to maintain under 14 CFR 141.25? What is the minimum amount of classroom space that the service provider must obtain?

(3) Will flight training be provided on a full-time or part-time basis?

(4) What type of aircraft and how many will be available for training at the on-airport location?

(5) What provisions have been made for the storage and maintenance of the aircraft?

(6) What provisions will be made for rest rooms, briefing rooms, and food service?

(7) What coordination and contacts exist with the local Flight Standards District Office?

e. Aircraft Engine/Accessory Repair and Maintenance. The applicant for an on-airport repair station is subject to several regulatory requirements under 14 CFR Part 145 *Repair Stations*. Depending on the type and size of the proposed repair station, the following questions may provide helpful guidelines:

(1) What qualifications will be required of the repair station employees? Typically, the holder of a domestic repair station certificate must provide adequate personnel who can perform, supervise, and inspect the work for which the station is rated.

(2) What repair station ratings does the applicant hold?

(3) What types of services will the repair station offer to the public? These services can vary from repair to maintenance of aircraft and include painting, upholstery, etc.

(4) Can the applicant secure sufficient airport space to provide facilities so work being done is protected from weather elements, dust, and heat? The amount of space required will be directly related to the largest item or aircraft to be serviced under the operator's rating.

(5) Will suitable shop space exist to provide a place for machine tools and equipment in sufficient proximity to where the work is performed?

(6) What amount of space will be necessary for the storage of standard parts, spare parts, raw materials, etc.?

(7) What type of lighting and ventilation will the work areas have? Will the ventilation be adequate to protect the health and efficiency of the workers?

(8) If spray painting, cleaning, or machining is performed, has sufficient distance between the operations performed and the testing operations been provided to prevent adverse affects on testing equipment?

f. Skydiving. Skydiving is an aeronautical activity. Any restriction, limitation, or ban on skydiving on the airport must be based on the grant assurance that provides that the airport sponsor may prohibit or limit aeronautical use for the safe operation of the airport (subject to FAA approval). The following questions present reasonable factors the sponsor might contemplate when developing minimum standards that apply to skydiving:

(1) Will this activity present or create a safety hazard to the normal operations of aircraft arriving or departing from the airport? If so, has the local Airports District Office (ADO) or the Regional Airports Office been contacted and have those FAA offices sought the assistance from FAA Flight Standards (FS) and Air Traffic (AT) to assess whether safe airport operations would be jeopardized?

(2) Can skydiving operations be safely accommodated at the airport? Can a drop zone be safely established within the boundaries of the airport? Is guidance in FAA AC-90-66A *Recommended Standards Traffic Patterns and Practices for Aeronautical Operations at Airports Without Operating Control Towers,* 14 CFR Part 105 and United States Parachute Association's (USPA) *Basic Safety Requirements* being followed?

(3) What reasonable time periods can be designated for jumping in a manner consistent with Part 105? What experience requirements are needed for an on-airport drop zone?

(4) What is a reasonable fee that the jumpers and/or their organizations can pay for the privilege of using airport property?

(5) Has the relevant air traffic control facility been advised of the proposed parachute operation? Does the air traffic control facility have concerns about the efficiency and utility of the airport and its related instrument procedures?

(6) Will it be necessary to determine the impact of the proposed activity on the efficiency and utility of the airport, related instrument approaches or nearby Instrument Flight Rules (IFR)? If so, has FAA Air Traffic reviewed the matter and issued a finding?

g. Ultralight Vehicles and Light Sport Aviation. The operation of ultralights and light sport aircraft are aeronautical activities and must, therefore, be generally accommodated on airports that have been developed with Federal airport development assistance. Airport sponsors are encouraged to consider some of the following questions:

(1) Can ultralight aircraft be safely accommodated at the airport? Is guidance in FAA AC-90-66A *Recommended Standards Traffic Patterns and Practices for Aeronautical Operations at Airports Without Operating Control Towers* and 14 CFR Part 103 being followed?

(2) Can all types of Light Sport aircraft be safely accommodated at the airport?

(3) Will this activity present or create a safety hazard to the normal operations of aircraft arriving or departing from the airport? If so, has FAA Flight Standards reviewed the matter and issued a finding?

(4) Will an FAA airspace study be necessary to determine the efficiency and utility of the airport when considering the proposed activity? If so, has FAA Air Traffic reviewed the matter and issued a finding?

h. Fractional Aircraft Ownership. Fractional ownership programs are subject to an FAA oversight program similar to that provided to air carriers, with the exception of en route inspections. The FAA has for a long time and under certain circumstances, interpreted an aircraft owner's right to self-service to include operators. For example, a significant number of aircraft operated by airlines are not owned but leased under terms that give the operator airline owner-like powers. The same is true for other aeronautical operators such as charter companies, flight schools, and flying clubs, which may not hold title to the aircraft, but through leasing arrangements, for example, retain full and exclusive control of the aircraft for long periods of time. The same is true of 14 CFR Part 91 Subpart K. Fractional ownership companies are subject to operational control responsibilities, maintenance requirements, and safety requirements not unlike 14 CFR Part 135 operators. For additional information on fractional ownership, contact your local Flight Standards District Office.

i. Other Requirements. When drafting minimum standards documents, airport sponsors may have to take into account other Federal, state, and local requirements. This includes Federal requirements and guidance by the Transportation Safety Administration (TSA) and the Environmental Protection Agency (EPA), state requirements such as aircraft registration (in some states) and local fire regulations. For guidance on matters such as these, please contact the FAA's Airports District Office (ADO) in your area and/or state aviation agency. A listing of ADOs can be found at http://www.faa.gov/airports_airtraffic/airports/regional_guidance/. Information and contacts regarding state aviation agencies is available at http://www.nasao.org/.

2.2. THROUGH 2.5. RESERVED.

APPENDIX 1. DEFINITIONS

1.1. The following are definitions for the specific purpose of this AC.

a. Aeronautical Activity. Any activity that involves, makes possible, or is required for the operation of aircraft or that contributes to or is required for the safety of such operations. Activities within this definition, commonly conducted on airports, include, but are not limited to, the following: general and corporate aviation, air taxi and charter operations, scheduled and nonscheduled air carrier operations, pilot training, aircraft rental and sightseeing, aerial photography, crop dusting, aerial advertising and surveying, aircraft sales and services, aircraft storage, sale of aviation petroleum products, repair and maintenance of aircraft, sale of aircraft parts, parachute or ultralight activities, and any other activities that, because of their direct relationship to the operation of aircraft, can appropriately be regarded as aeronautical activities. Activities, such as model aircraft and model rocket operations, are not aeronautical activities.

b. Airport. An area of land or water that is used, or intended to be used, for the aircraft takeoff and landing. It includes any appurtenant areas used, or intended to be used, for airport buildings or other airport facilities or rights-of-way, together with all airport buildings and facilities located thereon. It also includes any heliport.

c. Airport District Office (ADO). These FAA offices are outlying units or extensions of regional airport divisions. They advise and assist airport sponsors with funding requests to improve and develop public airports. They also provide advisory services to the owners and operators of both public and private airports in the operation and maintenance of airports. See the FAA Web site for a complete listing of all ADO offices at http://www.faa.gov/airports_airtraffic/airports/regional_guidance/.

d. Airport Sponsor. The airport sponsor is either a public agency or a private owner of a public-use airport that submits to the FAA an application for financial assistance (such as AIP grants) for the airport. In accepting an application for financial assistance, the FAA will ensure that the airport sponsor is legally, financially, and otherwise able to assume and carry out the certifications, representations, warranties, assurances, covenants and other obligations required of sponsors, which are contained in the AIP grant agreement and property conveyances.

e. Commercial Self-Service Fueling. A fueling concept that enables a pilot to fuel an aircraft from a commercial fuel pump installed for that purpose by an FBO or the airport sponsor. The fueling facility may or may not be attended.

f. Exclusive Right. A power, privilege, or other right excluding or debarring another from enjoying or exercising a like power, privilege, or right. An exclusive right can be conferred either by express agreement (i.e. lease agreement), by the imposition of unreasonable standards or requirements, or by any other means. Such a right conferred on one or more parties, but excluding others from enjoying or exercising a similar right or rights, would be an exclusive right.

g. Federal Airport Obligations. All references to a Federal grant program, Federal airport development assistance, or Federal aid contained in this AC are intended to address obligations arising from the conveyance of land or from grant agreements entered under one of the following acts:

> **(1) Surplus Property Act of 1944 (SPA), as amended, 49 U.S.C. §§ 47151-47153.** Surplus property instruments of transfer were issued by the War Assets Administration (WAA) and are now issued by its successor, the General Services Administration (GSA). However, the law imposes upon the FAA (delegated to FAA from The Department of Transportation) the sole responsibility for determining and enforcing compliance with the terms and conditions of

all instruments of transfer by which surplus airport property is or has been conveyed to non-Federal public agencies pursuant to the SPA. 49 U.S.C. § 47151(b).

(2) Federal Aid to Airports Program (FAAP). This grant-in-aid program administered by the agency under the authority of the Federal Airport Act of 1946, as amended, assisted public agencies in the development of a nationwide system of public airports. The Federal Airport Act of 1946 was repealed and superseded by the Airport Development Aid Program (ADAP) of 1970.

(3) Airport Development Aid Program (ADAP). This grant-in-aid program administered by the FAA under the authority of the Airport and Airway Development Act of 1970, as amended, assisted public agencies in the expansion and substantial improvement of the Nation's airport system. The 1970 act was repealed and superseded by the Airport and Airway Improvement Act of 1982 (AAIA).

(4) Airport Improvement Program (AIP). This grant-in-aid program administered by the FAA under the authority of the Airport and Airway Improvement Act of 1982, 49 U.S.C. § 47101, *et seq*., assists in maintaining a safe and efficient nationwide system of public-use airports that meet the present and future needs of civil aeronautics.

h. Federal Grant Assurance. A Federal grant assurance is a provision within a Federal grant agreement to which the recipient of Federal airport development assistance has agreed to comply in consideration of the assistance provided. Grant assurances are required by statute, 49 U.S.C. § 47101.

i. Fixed-Base Operator (FBO). A commercial business granted the right by the airport sponsor to operate on an airport and provide aeronautical services such as fueling, hangaring, tie-down and parking, aircraft rental, aircraft maintenance, flight instruction, etc.

j. Fractional Ownership. Fractional ownership operations are aircraft operations that take place under the auspices of 14 CFR Part 91 Subpart K. This type of operation offers aircraft owners increased flexibility in the ownership and operation of aircraft including shared or joint aircraft ownership. It provides for the management of the aircraft by an aircraft management company. The aircraft owners participating in the program agree not only to share their own aircraft with others having a shared interest in that aircraft, but also to lease their aircraft to other owners in the program (dry lease exchange program).[3] A fractional owner or owner means an individual or entity that possesses a minimum fractional ownership interest in a program aircraft and that has entered into the applicable program agreements. For additional information, please see 14 CFR 91.1001 *Applicability* at http://www.access.gpo.gov/nara/cfr/waisidx_04/14cfr91_04.html and contact your local Flight Standards District Office.

k. Grant Agreement. A Federal grant agreement represents an agreement made between the FAA (on behalf of the United States) and an airport sponsor for the grant of Federal funding.

l. Public Airport. Means an airport open for public use that is publicly owned and controlled by a public agency.

m. Public-Use Airport. Means either a public airport or a privately owned airport open for public use.

[3] A dry lease aircraft exchange means an arrangement, documented by the written program agreements, under which program aircraft are available, on an as needed basis without crew, to each fractional owner.

n. Specialized Aviation Service Operations (SASO). SASOs are sometimes known as single-service providers or special FBOs performing less than full services. These types of companies differ from a full service FBO in that they typically offer only a specialized aeronautical service such as aircraft sales, flight training, aircraft maintenance, or avionics services for example.

o. Self-Fueling and Self-Service. Self-fueling means the fueling or servicing of an aircraft (i.e. changing the oil, washing) by the owner of the aircraft with his or her own employees and using his or her own equipment. Self-fueling and other self-services cannot be contracted out to another party. Self-fueling implies using fuel obtained by the aircraft owner from the source of his/her preference. As one of many self-service activities that can be conducted by the aircraft owner or operator by his or her own employees using his or her own equipment, self-fueling, differs from using a self-service fueling pump made available by the airport, an FBO, or an aeronautical service provider. The use of a self-service fueling pump is a commercial activity and is not considered self-fueling as defined herein. In addition to self-fueling, other self-service activities that can be performed by the aircraft owner with his or her own employees includes activities such as maintaining, repairing, cleaning, and otherwise providing service to an aircraft, provided the service is performed by the aircraft owner or his/her employees with resources supplied by the aircraft owner.

p. Through-the-Fence Operations. Through-the-fence operations are those activities permitted by an airport sponsor through an agreement that permits access to the public landing area by independent entities or operators offering an aeronautical activity or to owners of aircraft based on land adjacent to, but not a part of, the airport property. The obligation to make an airport available for the use and benefit of the public does not impose any requirement for the airport sponsor to permit ground access by aircraft from adjacent property.

Index

C

D

E

F

G

H

I

N

O

P

Q

R

S